# SOVIET MILITARY STRATEGY

Edited by Marshal of the Soviet Union

## V. D. SOKOLOVSKII

Translated and with an Analytical Introduction,
Annotations, and Supplementary Material by

Herbert S. Dinerstein
Leon Gouré
Thomas W. Wolfe

Originally published by the
Military Publishing House of the
Ministry of Defense of the USSR

A RAND CORPORATION Research Study Published by
PRENTICE-HALL, Inc.
Englewood Cliffs, New Jersey

Prentice-Hall International, Inc.
(London • Tokyo • Sydney • Paris)
Prentice-Hall of Canada, Ltd.
Prentice-Hall de Mexico, S. A.

# Preface

This book, issued in the Soviet Union as *Military Strategy,* has been retitled *Soviet Military Strategy* by the U.S. Editors to avoid confusion about the character of the book. This, however, is the greatest liberty that has been taken with the text. The original is presented here *in toto.* Our intent was to render the Russian text precisely, but to avoid the stiffness characteristic of translated works. But when precision and grace of style were in conflict, the former always took precedence.

In view of their special meaning, a few Soviet technical terms have not been put into English and are explained in the glossary at the end of the book.

Where the Soviet authors have quoted foreign sources, the present text supplies the original words rather than a re-translation from the Russian. If, however, the Russian text varies in important ways from the original, the Russian text has been translated back into English and the original text supplied in footnotes. When the U.S. Editors have not been able to locate the original quotation, the reader is so informed.

The Soviet authors' footnotes are indicated by asterisk, dagger, etc., and the U.S. Editors' by Arabic numerals. Square brackets are used to set off words or phrases inserted into the text for purposes of clarification.

In addition to footnotes, the U.S. Editors have supplied longer notes to furnish the reader with other Soviet materials which appeared before and after the publication of the book in the Soviet Union. These notes, designated by Roman capital letters, are inserted after the appropriate sections in the Soviet text. A different

iii

type face has been employed to distinguish them from the Soviet text.

Russian names have been transliterated according to the system of the United States Library of Congress, but, as is usual, geographical place names have followed the standard of the United States Board on Geographic Names.

Soviet works have been cited in the original language, for the convenience of readers of Russian who might want to consult them, and an English translation has been appended for the information of those who do not read Russian. Exceptions are the well-known newspapers *Pravda, Izvestiia,* and *Red Star,* and *Kommunist,* the official journal of the Central Committee of the Communist Party of the Soviet Union.

In the task of finding the proper equivalents for Soviet military and technical terms the U.S. Editors are indebted to Marvin Lavin, Milton Weiner, Col. W. Hastings (USA-Ret.), Brig. Gen. Ralph E. Koon (USAF-Ret.), and Rear Adm. Robert G. Lockhart (USN-Ret.).

Jack I. Gollob of Translavic Associates of Los Angeles collaborated in the preparation of the translation.

This work could not have been prepared for publication so quickly without the devoted efforts of a number of editorial assistants. We are indebted to Becky Goodman, Ian C. C. Graham, Eleanor T. Harris, Dorothy G. Stewart, William Taylor, and Jean Üke. Anita Magnus furnished over-all and invaluable assistance to the U.S. Editors.

Although the book as a whole was the combined responsibility of the U.S. Editors, the Analytical Introduction is largely the work of Thomas W. Wolfe.

The costs of translation were assumed by The RAND Corporation; work of the U.S. Editors on annotations and analysis of the text was undertaken as a part of the Corporation's continuing program of research for United States Air Force Project RAND. The views and conclusions expressed herein by the U.S. Editors do not necessarily reflect the official views or policies of the United States Air Force.

Herbert S. Dinerstein, Leon Gouré, Thomas W. Wolfe
Washington, D. C., and Santa Monica, California
*April, 1963*

# Contents

# U. S. Editors'
# Analytical
# Introduction

In the fall of 1962, the Soviet military newspaper, *Red Star,* published a lengthy review of a new book, *Military Strategy,* bringing the volume to public attention and describing it as the first comprehensive work on the subject to appear in the Soviet Union since 1926. Few Soviet publications in recent years have stirred greater interest abroad in official, scholarly, and public circles than this work, which is now made available in an English translation under the title, *Soviet Military Strategy.*

Contrary to occasional, oversensational commentary on the book in the Western press, it was neither smuggled out of the Soviet Union nor does it reveal secret inside information on Soviet war plans. However, *Soviet Military Strategy* is an important document —certainly the most significant work of its kind to appear in the open literature to date—and it will afford the interested reader many valuable insights into Soviet thinking on strategy and war in the nuclear-missile age.

The new volume—representing the collective work of a group of fifteen Soviet officers headed by Marshal V. D. Sokolovskii,[1]

---

[1] Vasilii Danilovich Sokolovskii (born 1897) holds the rank of Marshal of the Soviet Union and is a Hero of the Soviet Union. At the high point of a distinguished military career he served as First Deputy Minister of Defense (1949–1960) and Chief of the General Staff of the Soviet Army and Navy (1952–1960). He became a member of the CPSU in 1931 and of its Central Committee in 1952, and served as a deputy to the Supreme Soviet (1946, 1950, 1954).

1

former Chief of the General Staff—is of special interest for a number of reasons. In the first place, the unusual accolade accorded the book by hailing it as the first comprehensive Soviet treatment of military strategy since A. Svechin's work 36 years earlier is in itself significant. Svechin, a Tsarist general who transferred his allegiance to the Soviet regime shortly after the 1917 Revolution, was both a leading military theorist of the twenties and the first Chief of the Soviet General Staff.

While his monumental work, *Strategy,* published in 1926, is an acknowledged Soviet classic, it did not give, as the present volume itself observes, "a correct Marxist interpretation of the character and content of strategy, and contained many methodological shortcomings." A good many "Marxist" contributions to strategic thought have, in fact, appeared in Soviet military literature in the three-and-a-half decades between the Svechin work and the present book under Sokolovskii's editorship. Why, then, have the editors of the present work so conspicuously ignored the military literature of the last 36 years?

Part of the object, one may surmise, is to emphasize that the new book is intended to expunge the baneful influence on military strategic thought of Stalin, whose views dominated the scene for most of the period in question and still apparently persist in some corners of Soviet military thought.

A parallel object of the studied omission of Soviet strategic theorists between Svechin's time and the present volume is suggested by the remark in the Introduction to *Soviet Military Strategy* that there are not enough works that take up the many varied problems of strategy in the "open Soviet military literature." This suggests: first, that there may be a more vigorous literature that is closed to many Soviet military readers; second, that there may be important contemporary conceptions that have not been getting through to individuals of many ranks and levels, who are now being put on notice, in effect, not to take their instruction from outmoded strategic mentors; and third, that the present volume may be intended to repair the situation by making widely available materials hitherto held more closely.

Whatever the case may be, it is fairly clear that the present work, although not an "official" treatise in the strict sense of the word, is regarded as an important vehicle of instruction "for a wide circle of Soviet readers and for the military and theoretical training of young officers" (p. 83). Apart from this interest by its Soviet sponsors, there are other substantial reasons, however, for regarding the new collective work as a document of particular significance.

For one thing, its publication comes in the midst of a continuing debate over military doctrine and strategy that has been carried out in the Soviet Union recurrently since Stalin's demise. The impact of modern weaponry on doctrine, strategy, and force structure has fueled this debate, whose most recent phase has unfolded in the wake of Khrushchev's "new strategy" statement of January 1960 and his accompanying program of major military reform. More is to be said later about the relationship of the new book to this debate, but it is immediately evident that great interest attaches to a comprehensive work on strategy prepared at a time when many aspects of military policy appear to be at issue among contending elements of the Soviet bureaucracy.

The book takes on added significance in this connection because it was also written in the context of Khrushchev's unsuccessful attempts to claim Soviet strategic superiority over the West and in the light of a confident American reappraisal of the strategic balance of power. This situation confronts the Soviet leadership with difficult decisions concerning the further development of the Soviet armed forces and the allocation of resources for this purpose. The book, therefore, becomes in a sense a forum for the airing of some of the conflicting concepts of Soviet military requirements, bringing into view, in the process, some of the areas in which future disagreement may arise between Soviet political and military leadership.

Not only does the new volume contribute to understanding Soviet military policy by shedding light on various issues that remain unresolved or on which compromise solutions may have been reached; but equally important, it also reveals broad areas of consensus in Soviet military thought on the effects of nuclear weapons and missiles on Soviet strategy and on the requirements for waging modern warfare. More is to be said later on features of the current Soviet strategic outlook that seem to enjoy general acceptance in the new volume. Perhaps the cardinal point to be mentioned here is that the strategic outlook that emerges from the pages of this work reflects a broad shift from past preoccupation with theater land warfare to a central focus on the problems of global strategic war.

The student of Soviet military thought will recognize this shift in outlook as something that has been taking place gradually for some time under the impact of modern weapons technology and the changing imperatives of world politics, but which now finds expression in greater depth and detail in the new work. At the same time, it is apparent from the book that the new outlook has made rather slow and sometimes grudging headway against the force of tradition and the inertia of established institutions. Certainly, one would hesitate to say that the new outlook now has the field to itself in Soviet military thinking.

The wide range of matters covered in *Soviet Military Strategy,* which will doubtless assure it a solid place in contemporary Soviet military literature, gives further reason for regarding the work with special interest. As a glance at the Contents will show, the subject matter ranges from general strategic concepts and historical development of military doctrines to current problems of developing armed forces and methods of conducting contemporary warfare.

Many questions of prime interest are treated. They include the Soviet conception of a future war and possible ways in which it might be initiated; the role of nuclear weapons and strategic forces; the critical importance of the initial phase of a war; and the combination of factors on which expectation of final victory rests. Without attempting to enumerate them at length, other interesting subjects include the economic implications of military preparedness; problems of air defense and civil defense; targeting concepts; military uses of space; requirements for command and control in modern warfare; and the influence of technology on doctrine and strategy.

In addition to the extensive presentation of Soviet strategic thinking that it affords, one of the more arresting features of the new work is the surprisingly realistic picture it gives of U.S. military power and changes in U.S. and NATO strategy. Although U.S. intentions are distorted in characteristic communist fashion, the image of the United States that emerges from the work suggests a considerable degree of Soviet responsiveness to changes in Western strategic thinking and military posture—a factor of some significance in the long-term strategic dialogue between the United States and the Soviet Union.

While, on the whole, *Soviet Military Strategy* lives up to its description as a comprehensive work on questions of war and strategy in the missile age, it is only fitting to observe that there are notable lacunae in the doctrinal conceptions laid out in the book, and that certain kinds of strategic problems that have been widely discussed in the West are largely ignored, if not altogether missing. Further attention will be given later to these pertinent omissions, but here let it suffice to say that in some cases this may mean simply that there are real gaps in Soviet thinking; in others, that it has been considered best to leave some things unsaid.

For the various reasons briefly outlined above, *Soviet Military Strategy* is a document of great interest to all who would seek a fuller understanding of the factors that determine Soviet strategic thinking and decision making today. Before offering more detailed commentary on the book itself and the background dialogue on doctrine and strategy that preceded its publication, it may facilitate understanding for the casual reader if something is said first about the general relevance of doctrine—both military and political— to the Soviet strategic policy-making process.

## Relevance of Doctrine to Soviet Strategic Policy-making

If this is the reader's first acquaintance with Soviet professional military writing, he is likely to be taken aback by the turgid communist style in which the work is written, by certain obvious distortions of fact concerning the Western world, and by the disconcerting way in which Marxist-Leninist formulas are interwoven with discussion of military theory and requirements. Some readers may even be led to ask whether the present volume, as a representative specimen of the published literature, *really* portrays Soviet military thinking of a serious, professional kind.

This is not surprising. A long-standing task of students of Soviet military thought has been to sift out what may be either political window-dressing or ritual observance of Marxist-Leninist beliefs from professional military doctrine and theory. However, it should not be inferred from this that one can conveniently establish a fixed boundary line between Soviet military and political doctrine

—setting the former apart as authentic for the purpose of understanding what the Soviet military mind considers *really* important, and discarding the latter as irrelevant.

In the Soviet outlook, military doctrine and strategy have no independent life of their own. Both are understood to be permeated by and subordinate to politics—a view that is no less a part of the mental baggage of the Soviet military man than of Soviet political man. It is to be expected, therefore, that a Soviet work on military doctrine and strategy will take its point of departure and seek instruction from political commandments and Marxist-Leninist precepts, even though it may sometimes seem that these are superfluous to consideration of particular military problems under discussion.

The present volume takes its main point of political departure from the XXIInd Congress of the CPSU in October 1961, where a new Party Program was adopted and where important formulations bearing on Soviet military doctrine and strategy were outlined. The book also adverts to the January 1960 session of the Supreme Soviet at which Khrushchev made a major statement signaling a change of direction in defense policy. Implications that relate to tying the book to these particular points of departure, and to the dialogue over military policy that was going on in the year and a half between them, will be discussed later.

While it is clearly evident that the Soviet military theorist takes seriously the injunction that military doctrine and strategy must be integrated at all levels into a larger political design, this does not mean that the process of integration is necessarily smooth, uncomplicated, and always successful. Indeed, it is important to an understanding of the present volume—and of Soviet military literature generally—to distinguish between what might be called the theoretical image of the way doctrine and strategy ought to be formulated, and the way the process appears to work in the real world.

For example, there is abundant evidence of a Soviet belief in the efficacy of theoretical understanding of the laws and nature of war as a basis for the practical decisions that must be taken to build armed forces and prepare them for support of Soviet policy objectives. This has led, among other things, to placing great store on development of a unified body of military theory—based on the laws of war and properly informed, of course, by political doctrine and purposes.

The quest for a unified military doctrine that would reflect the general political line of the Soviet state was, in fact, one of the major questions that first engaged Soviet military theorists in the early twenties. During the long period of Stalin's ascendancy, this question tended to drop out of sight, for the framing of basic military doctrine was largely taken out of the hands of the theoreticians by Stalin himself. However, with the advent of nuclear weapons and Stalin's departure from the scene, the search for a unified military doctrine responsive to the revolution in military technology took on new importance, and again became a dominant object of military-theoretical discussion. A contemporary expression of the great value placed on development of Soviet military doctrine was given recently in the following words by Marshal R. Ia. Malinovskii, the Soviet Minister of Defense:

> Under conditions where the development of weapons goes on at a singularly tempestuous pace, great significance attaches to military-theoretical work . . . in recent years our military-technical thought has made great progress . . . we now have a deep theoretical foundation, which flows from the political nature of our state military doctrine. Soviet military doctrine—based on the policy of our party and resting its leading recommendations on the conclusions of military science—helps us to penetrate deeply into the nature of modern war and its initial period, helps us to determine the most suitable modes of operation in it, and points out the path for development and preparation of our armed forces.[2]

Despite this reverence toward a unified military doctrine and the assumption that it will unlock the mysteries of war and smooth the path of the policy-makers, there also has been abundant evidence that matters have turned out somewhat less satisfactorily than the design would call for.

Several areas of difficulty can be identified. One of these grows out of the quite human circumstance that even in a supposedly monolithic society men sometimes find it difficult to agree with each other. The editor of a Soviet professional military journal

---

[2] Speech by Minister of Defense of the USSR, Marshal of the Soviet Union R. Ia. Malinovskii to the All Army Conference on Ideological Questions, *Red Star*, October 25, 1962.

gave voice to this particular difficulty some time ago in the pages of his publication while making a plea for a unified military doctrine. The editor, Major General P. Zhilin, wrote in 1961 that in view of all the military and political changes taking place in the world, "now, as never before, it is necessary to have a unity of views on all the most important problems of military art and employment of troops." After noting that many discussions of this question had been going on "in the pages of the military press and within the walls of the General Staff academy," General Zhilin added, "unfortunately, in these discussions, no unity of views has been achieved." [3]

Another area of difficulty arises from the perplexing way in which the domain of "military-technical" thought shades into Marxist-Leninist political territory. Because the boundary line is indistinct, it has never proved easy to develop a body of military theory that does not err in the direction of being either too narrow or too diffused to provide appropriate working precepts for military strategy and policy.

The writers of Soviet military texts have customarily sought a middle road between a "narrow technical" approach to military theory, which would be vulnerable to criticism as un-Marxist, and a very broad approach to the study of war as a "social-historical phenomenon," which would, as one group of writers has put it, "dissolve" military science in a sea of social and political considerations and rob it of military specificity. [4]

In a sense, the problem is one of compressing the definition of war so that military-technical aspects of doctrine and strategy can be appropriately dealt with by professional military men and technicians while other aspects are left in political hands. In the view of Major General Zhilin, in the same article mentioned above, it could be said as of May 1961 that "the political side of Soviet military doctrine is laid out with exhaustive clarity in a series of official documents of the Party and Government," but: "in the

---

[3] Major General P. Zhilin, "Discussion about a Unified Military Doctrine," *Voenno-istoricheskii zhurnal* (*Journal of Military History*), No. 5, May 1961, p. 73.

[4] A characteristic discussion of this problem can be found in a text written jointly in 1960 by Major General M. V. Smirnov and several other military theorists. *O sovetskoi voennoi nauke* (*On Soviet Military Science*), Voenizdat Ministerstva Oborony Soiuza SSR, Moscow, 1960, p. 68.

military-technical parts of doctrine . . . there are still not a few disputable and vague propositions." [5] As the reader of the present volume will see for himself, some propositions of a military-technical character still remain in this state.

Another species of problems in the framing of Soviet military doctrine arises in the area where ritual and reality get in each other's way. The difficulties here face both the Soviet military theorist and those who seek instruction from his work. Sometimes it is a question of using old terminology and formulas to ease the transition to new military thought, or sometimes the opposite— giving lip service to new ideas but clinging in substance to old conceptions. In either case, the real message may have to be disentangled from the ritual form in which it is wrapped. There are other aspects of the ritual-reality question that may present more serious and subtle problems of understanding; it is not feasible to explore the range of these problems here, but an example may be worth noting.

It is a preachment of Marxist-Leninist doctrine, for instance, that the morale of capitalist armies is poor and that they have no stomach for fighting to preserve a rotten system in which they feel they have no stake. Is Soviet military theory significantly influenced by this notion in assessing Western military power, or does it merely make a ritual bow in the proper direction and go on to a sober appraisal of the problem in nondoctrinal terms? The answer may never be altogether clear, but as the present book seems to testify, the Soviets presumably have a high respect for Western capabilities and seem prepared to lay aside at least some ritual beliefs when appraising the prospective opponent.

At the same time, one needs to avoid the mistake of confusing ritual beliefs with theoretical tenets that are strongly held by the Soviets, or of supposing that doctrine in general has only a negligible influence on Soviet military thought and behavior. Many doctrinal tenets do, in fact, appear to carry important weight.

One example is the significance attached to correct selection of the "main link," "the main task," or the "main blow." Whether the field of activity be military or political, this notion—an important element in Bolshevik doctrine—has continued to exert

---

[5] Zhilin, *op. cit.,* p. 73.

strong influence on Soviet analysis and behavior. When a particular problem therefore is defined as "the main task," such as the statement in the present volume that "working out methods for reliably repelling a surprise nuclear attack by an aggressor is the main task of Soviet military strategy," the reader is justified in assuming that a high priority lies behind the rhetoric.

Similarly, the idea that correct calculation of the "relation of forces" underlies sound strategic planning and decisionmaking is another doctrinal tenet that operates with special conviction in the Soviet case. Although this idea is hardly a distinctive Soviet discovery, the emphasis given it in Soviet thought suggests that any work outlining a military strategy for the Soviet Union will tend to be particularly sensitive to the relative strength of the major antagonists, as well as to beliefs held in the world about the military power balance.

Another problem area in the search for a unified set of military-theoretical views relates to the inherent difficulty of keeping any body of military doctrine abreast of weaponry in a fast-moving technological age. As the reader will note, the authors of *Soviet Military Strategy* themselves acknowledge quite frankly the difficulties they have faced in connection with the weaponry-doctrine problem. For example, after noting that modern technology has within a very short period of time made available enormously powerful new weapons, they go on to say (p. 331):

> However, the search for new combat methods, new forms of troop organization and new avenues of development of armed forces appropriate for these powerful weapons has proven to be a difficult problem over whose solution theoreticians and practitioners of the military art both here and abroad are laboring persistently.

This problem, indeed, with its far-ranging implications for political and economic decisions as well as military planning, tends to dominate the scene. More than any of the other difficulties mentioned above, it helps to explain why military doctrine, like strategy and policy in general, turns out in Soviet experience to be shaped by pragmatic considerations no less than by theoretical ones.

If one were to attempt to reduce the Soviet strategic policymaking process to a simplified model, drawing on Soviet descriptions of the way it is supposed to work in theory, the result would come out somewhat along the following lines.

In the model image, political commandments flow from the top leadership of Party and government to those who develop Soviet military doctrine. A unified body of military doctrine is generated in turn, bringing together the best conclusions of military-technical thought, integrated with Marxist-Leninist political wisdom. Based on this unified body of military doctrine, appropriate policies and decisions are adopted concerning strategy, force structure, training, and the like. In the process of settling on the most suitable military strategy and policies, the parameters set by economic, technical, political-morale, and other factors come into play. Finally, the circle is closed, as a military posture responsive to the political commandments of the top leadership emerges for support of over-all state policy in peace or war.

This image of the strategic policy process implies a more or less monolithic bureaucratic apparatus, permitting some measure of internal debate on doctrinal and policy issues, but so endowed that when a decision is made, all elements of the bureaucracy fall into line and any policy opposition ceases. In theory, therefore, the strategic policy process unfolds in a purposeful, planned way— yielding a military strategy, posture, and force structure meshed neatly with and answering closely to aims set by the top political leadership.

In practice, however, a somewhat different picture appears to prevail. The bureaucratic decisionmaking process is by no means so smoothly monolithic, but is rather exposed to the play of competing interests among various segments of Party, government, and military bureaucracies. In this more complicated world, the theoretical image of the strategic policy process begins to break down. Doctrine, strategy, forces, technical and economic realities react on each other, and various pragmatic considerations intrude. The result more often than not seems to be the less-than-perfect answer, the necessity to live with a series of adjustments and compromise solutions.

*Soviet Military Strategy* obviously belongs to this latter imperfect but more plausible world, as part of the unfinished dialogue on military doctrine and strategy that has been carried out in the Soviet military press and in various elite statements for the past few years. Before going on to discuss the relationship of the present volume to this debate—behind which has lain a shifting controversy within the Soviet bureaucracy over various practical issues of state and military policy—it may be useful to review for the reader the general character of the debate itself.

## Character of the Soviet Strategic Debate

During the decade since Stalin's death, Soviet military doctrine and strategy have been subjected more or less continuously to debate and modification. One can distinguish at least three perceptible phases in this process. The first phase may be said to have run from about 1953 to 1957, coinciding roughly with the period of Khrushchev's rise to undisputed power. During these years, Soviet military thinking—freed from the restrictive hold of "Stalinist" military science—underwent a series of adjustments to the revolution in military affairs brought about by the nuclear weapon and the jet aircraft. The strategic issues of this period, closely interwoven with foreign policy and internal political-economic considerations, have been examined in detail elsewhere and need not be reviewed here.[6] It was only toward the end of this period that the Soviet Union acquired advanced weapons in sufficient numbers to make the development of a doctrine for their employment an urgent question. At first, therefore, the main emphasis of debate was on how to adapt the new weapons to traditional Soviet concepts, and only later did it become necessary to recast Soviet doctrine.

The second phase of the strategic dialogue opened after the influence of ballistic missile technology had begun to make itself felt about the end of 1957, and at a time when Khrushchev found himself fully in political command. The process of digesting the weapons' revolution of the nuclear-missile age grew increasingly painful in this period for at least the traditionally oriented elements of the Soviet military bureaucracy, now faced with Khrushchev's apparent conviction that the new missile technology offered a way to buttress Soviet security while, at the same time, paring down the oversized conventional portion of the military establishment. One can regard this phase as coming to a close in January 1960 with

---

[6] The reader will find an extensive analysis of the post-Stalin military debate of this period in Herbert S. Dinerstein, *War and the Soviet Union,* Frederick A. Praeger, Inc., New York, 1959. Another account covering the same period may be found in Raymond L. Garthoff, *Soviet Strategy in the Nuclear Age,* Frederick A. Praeger, Inc., New York, 1958. See also J. M. MacMintosh, *Strategy and Tactics of Soviet Foreign Policy,* The Macmillan Co., London, 1962, particularly pp. 88–105.

Khrushchev's "new strategy" speech, which may have been intended as *the* definitive revision of Soviet strategic concepts and force structure in keeping with the requirements of the nuclear-missile age—as Khrushchev saw the situation.

As matters turned out, however, the strategic dialogue did not subside with Khrushchev's new strategy presentation, which, on the contrary, only served to open a new phase in the continuing debate. It is this latter phase, to which publication of the present volume in the Soviet Union in 1962 is immediately related, upon which attention will be focused here. Broadly speaking, the strategic dialogue of these past three years seems to have followed three separate but interrelated tracks:

1. A continuing polemic between Khrushchev and the professional military as a whole.

2. A subsidiary debate between what might be called "radical" and "traditionalist" outlooks within the Soviet military itself.

3. An external dialogue over the strategic power balance in which Soviet and U.S. leadership spokesmen have been the prime participants.

It would be wrong to give the impression that the internal aspects of the continuing Soviet debate on military policy and strategy reveal nothing but contention. There is also a broad consensus on many matters. One should also bear in mind that policy discussion and debate have become somewhat more common in Soviet public life in the past few years than was formerly the case. This applies not only to military policy, but also to other policy areas. Hence, the airing of differences does not necessarily indicate an internal struggle of the kind that can end only with one faction or another losing power.

With regard to the dialogue over military questions, lines in the debate have not by any means always been sharply drawn. On some issues, participants have shifted ground, and proponents of a particular school of thought at one stage of the debate may sometimes be found siding with a contending school at a later stage.[7] To some

---

[7] This is particularly true with regard to military men who first took up the military doctrinal discussion in the period shortly after Stalin's death. Some of those who were standard bearers of a progressive approach at the time of breaking away from Stalinist military doctrine, such as Marshal Rotmistrov and Lieutenant General Krasil'nikov, later have come to find themselves in traditionalist company, in the context of the dialogue of the early sixties. In a way, this may reflect a shift in the grounds of the dialogue itself as much as a change in the views of the participants.

extent, particularly in such publicly available professional military journals as *Communist of the Armed Forces* and the *Journal of Military History,* there seems to have been a definite attempt to encourage discussion of various controversial doctrinal questions.[8]

Nevertheless, after allowance is made for a certain amount of officially sanctioned debate and competition of views within the context of professional military inquiry, it is fairly clear that the strategic dialogue has spilled over into areas of basic disagreement, with practical implications for defense policy and strategy. The polemic involving Khrushchev and the military following his January 1960 speech to the Supreme Soviet is a case in point.

*Dialogue between Khrushchev and the Military.* Khrushchev's January 1960 report to the Supreme Soviet dealt both with Soviet disarmament proposals and with a new military policy.[9] The report apparently was drawn up after consideration of these questions in the Central Committee in December 1959. In this speech, Khrushchev stressed the notion that missiles, for which he claimed a Soviet lead, would be the dominant element in any future war and that conventional armaments, including surface navies and air forces along with large standing armies, were rapidly becoming obsolete. Although maintaining that strategic nuclear blows at the outset of a war would bring unprecedented destruction and might tempt the capitalist adversary to toy with the idea of a surprise attack, Khrushchev argued at the same time that surprise attack was not a feasible policy because any "sufficiently large" state (by which he clearly had in mind the Soviet Union) would always retain enough residual strategic capability to strike back. On these grounds he also maintained that Soviet retaliatory capability deterred the West from starting a war, except possibly in the case of a "madman." Furthermore, Khrushchev took this occasion to boast that

---

[8] The editors of these journals have, for example, invited presentation of various viewpoints on such questions as the importance of the initial period of a war, the relative influence of "subjective" leadership judgments and "objective" strength factors on success in war, the adequacy of Soviet military doctrine, and so on. In general, there has been a tendency for each of these professional journals to favor a particular school of thought; thus, the traditionalist outlook is reflected most often by the *Voenno-istoricheskii zhurnal* (*Journal of Military History*), while the modernist or radical outlook is more likely to appear in *Kommunist vooruzhennykh sil* (*Communist of the Armed Forces*).

[9] "Disarmament: The Way To Strengthen Peace and Assure Friendship among People," Report by Comrade N. S. Khrushchev to a Session of the Supreme Soviet of the USSR, *Pravda,* January 15, 1960.

not only did the Soviet Union now possess "formidable" weapons, but that "those which are, so to speak, about to appear, are even more perfected, even more formidable."

This generally reassuring picture of the Soviet military posture was accompanied by the announced intention to reduce Soviet manpower under arms by one-third—an economically attractive move warranted, according to Khrushchev, by the increased firepower that nuclear weapons now gave the Soviet armed forces.[10] "In our time," Khrushchev said:

> . . . the defense potential of the country is not determined by the number of our soldiers under arms, by the number of persons in uniform . . . the defense capability of the country depends, to a decisive extent, on the total firepower and the means of delivery available. . . . The proposed reduction will in no way weaken the firepower of our armed forces, and this is the main point.

In the months following this Supreme Soviet speech, it became apparent that there was considerable resistance among the Soviet military to Khrushchev's thinking and its practical implications for security policy.[11] Without daring to oppose Khrushchev openly, various military spokesmen began to back and fill in an apparent effort to protect vested military interests and to modify portions of the Khrushchev doctrine at variance with their professional notions of sound military strategy, suitable force structure, and so on.

The bulk of Soviet comment on Khrushchev's January statement naturally applauded it as a significant contribution to Soviet military science and occasionally his position received specific intellectual support in the military press, such as an endorsement of the troop reduction program by Major General G. Pokrovskii, a prominent Soviet military theoretician, who argued that the doctrine of substituting firepower for large numbers of troops was consistent

---

[10] Khrushchev announced a reduction of 1,200,000 from a total of 3,623,000 men in the Soviet armed forces. It should be noted that in this speech Khrushchev's position on manpower reduction was partly qualified by the admission that in the event of imminent war a significant increase in the armed forces might be appropriate.

[11] In fact, the first hint of some divergence of views came immediately after Khrushchev's report. In a speech following the report, Marshal Malinovskii supported Khrushchev's position, including the proposed troop cut, but at the same time he cautioned against over-reliance on missile forces and voiced a reminder that military success would depend on combined use of all types of forces. *Pravda,* January 15, 1960.

with the general trend of modern warfare.[12] However, reservations toward Khrushchev's thinking from the military side of the house became increasingly evident in 1960 and early 1961.[13] In retrospect, these reservations were brought most clearly into focus in an important speech by Marshal R. Ia. Malinovskii, the Soviet Defense Minister, at the XXIInd Party Congress in October 1961.[14] Although the context of the situation in which Malinovskii spoke had been altered by the passage of events, as will be pointed out presently, his speech nevertheless serves as one of the major landmarks in the dialogue between Khrushchev and the military.

In his speech at the Party Congress, Malinovskii took pains not to set his views off in open opposition to Khrushchev, to whom he even applied the seldom-used but flattering term, "our Supreme High Commander." At the same time, the Soviet Defense Minister advanced a set of "theses" of "Soviet military doctrine" that did in fact differ in a number of notable respects from Khrushchev's formulation of January 1960.

To begin with, Malinovskii's statement gave a considerably less optimistic picture of the Soviet defense outlook than that projected earlier by Khrushchev. For example, Khrushchev had deprecated the feasibility of surprise attack on the Soviet Union and expressed full confidence in the credibility of the Soviet deterrent. Whereas Khrushchev suggested that the West would not dare to attack the Soviet Union, except as the irrational act of a Western "madman," Malinovskii now stressed that "in realistically appraising the situation," one must hold that the West was making serious preparations for a surprise nuclear attack. By emphasizing that the most important task of the Soviet armed forces was to be "in constant readiness to repel reliably a surprise attack by the enemy," Malinovskii seemed to be advancing a view at variance with Khrushchev's

---

[12] G. Pokrovskii, "Firepower of the Armed Forces and a Country's Defense Capability," *Sovetskii flot (Soviet Fleet),* March 9, 1960.

[13] An example was a special article in *Red Star,* April 5, 1961, under the heading "New Technology and Mass Armies." The editors' foreword used the familiar device of saying that a number of readers had asked how modern technology and warfare had influenced the size of armies. The responding article, written by Colonel A. M. Iovlev, made clear the military view that modern weapons and the general international situation had not reduced the requirement for mass armies.

[14] Speech by Marshal R. Ia. Malinovskii to the XXIInd Congress of the CPSU, *Pravda,* October 25, 1961.

earlier judgment on the likelihood and feasibility of such a threat to Soviet security. In stressing the danger of surprise attack, Malinovskii also dwelt on the need to improve the posture of the Soviet armed forces for "breaking up the aggressive designs [of the enemy] by dealing him a crushing blow in time." This carefully phrased formula gave new cognizance to the idea of pre-emptive attack, which had not appeared in Khrushchev's January 1960 speech.[15]

Revival of the pre-emption theme on this occasion may well have been calculated for its political effect on the United States in connection with the Berlin situation. In this light, it did not, of course, betoken any immediate difference of view between Khrushchev and the military. However, one might note that a doctrine of pre-emption did pose issues of a troubling nature for Soviet military policy, which could become a source of contention, both between Khrushchev and the military, and among the military themselves. For example, it would tend to focus attention on the question of which branches of the armed forces should be strengthened and kept ready to assure a pre-emptive capability, and therefore, which claims on resources should come first. Since maintenance of a high state of readiness tends to be very expensive, this too could complicate decisions facing the Soviet leadership—as between expenditure for building up additional forces on the one hand, or for keeping forces-in-being at a high state of alert on the other.

The image of a future war in Malinovskii's exposition differed in a significant way from that drawn by Khrushchev. While both shared the view that a future war would "inevitably" be a missile-nuclear war, and that the use of such weapons in the initial period

---

15 Initial advocacy of the need for a pre-emptive capability was advanced in an earlier phase of the strategic dialogue in 1955 by Marshal Pavel Rotmistrov, one of the first open critics of Stalinist military doctrine. The subject subsequently dropped out of public discussion for several years, coming back into view in 1960–1961 in the professional military press. For example, in the *Voenno-istoricheskii zhurnal* (*Journal of Military History*), No. 4, April 1960, p. 119, Major General I. N. Rukhle argued that one of the first problems for military theory was to study how to "guarantee for oneself the advantages of successful delivery of a surprise first blow or the prevention of such a blow on the part of a probable enemy." In the same journal ("Questions of Soviet Military Science in the Works of V. I. Lenin," No. 3, March 1961, p. 10), the need to beat one's opponent to the draw in the event of war was discussed by General V. Kurasov, who cited Lenin as the authority for his views. However, Malinovskii's statement on pre-emption at the XXIInd Party Congress gave the subject an official cognizance that was absent in the earlier professional discussion. Further attention will be given later to the treatment of pre-emption.

would have decisive influence on the war's outcome, Malinovskii brought in a traditional notion conspicuously glossed over by Khrushchev, namely, that final victory could be assured only by "combined action of all arms and services." Malinovskii also affirmed that a future world war would be carried out by "mass, multi-million-man armed forces," which seemed to imply that it might turn out to be a protracted war rather than a short, decisive one. This important hedge by Malinovskii exposed a central issue that had been raised by Khrushchev's 1960 Supreme Soviet speech. If the Soviet Union could not rely on missiles and nuclear weapons alone to bring quick victory in a short war, but rather required large and diversified forces to wage nuclear war successfully, then Khrushchev's theorizing on the obsolescence of conventional arms and massive armies and his espousal of practical measures to reduce Soviet forces by one-third were inconsonant with Soviet security—as Malinovskii and presumably other key military leaders viewed it.

It should, of course, be noted that Khrushchev accepted the idea that larger forces might be needed in the event of war. In a sense, therefore, the central point at issue between Khrushchev and the military was over requirements for peacetime forces-in-being, which, in turn, implied a conflicting estimate of the effectiveness of Soviet deterrence of their opponents or, if deterrence failed, the likelihood of timely warnings. Khrushchev was saying, in effect, that even though Soviet forces might be less than adequate to fight a war, they were adequate to assure deterrence. The military leaders, on the other hand, were saying that deterrence might fail and therefore they must be in better shape to fight a war if one should occur—an attitude not unlike that which military men anywhere might hold.[16] The military apparently did not altogether agree among themselves, however, on what kind of a war they might have to fight and what forces would be needed for it.

Although Malinovskii's "theses" on military doctrine in October

---

[16] The difference in point of view between Khrushchev and the military might be described another way, with Khrushchev arguing essentially on the basis of his estimate of enemy intentions and the military on the basis of enemy capability. However, when seeking a rationale for strengthening the Soviet defense posture, the military also were obliged to go beyond the capabilities argument and to use the alleged intention of the West to start a preventive war to justify a claim on more resources, a higher state of readiness, larger forces, more attention to civil defense, and so on.

1961 served to illustrate the theoretical gap between Khrushchev's January 1960 views and those of the military, the gap had actually been narrowed appreciably under the pressure of intervening events by the time Malinovskii spoke at the XXIInd Party Congress.[17] In the summer of 1961, the troop-reduction program had been halted and the explicit military budget had been increased by one-third, while on the eve of the Party Congress itself, a resumption of nuclear testing—to include weapons of supermegaton yield—was announced. Although Khrushchev may have felt these moves were necessary mainly for their political-military effect during the Berlin crisis, they were, of course, favored by the military leadership. These concrete steps in a direction congenial to the military viewpoint had also been accompanied by Khrushchev's public retreat from some of the more extreme notions he had aired earlier, notably his views on the obsolescence of aircraft, ground forces, and the like.

The nexus of developments that led to a reframing of Soviet defense policies and a narrowing of the gap between Khrushchev's strategic formulations and the prevailing outlook of the military cannot be examined at length here. However, one might mention briefly such factors as the following:

> The U-2 episode in May 1960, which raised questions as to how seriously Soviet military security may have been compromised by loss of secrecy.

> General deterioration of the international situation following the abortive summit meeting in Paris in May 1960, which probably strengthened the hand of elements in the Soviet bureaucracy favoring sterner economic and defense policies than those with which Khrushchev had identified himself.

> Resentment and morale problems within the armed forces, notably in the officer corps, which accompanied initiation of the troop-cut policy in 1960.

---

17 In fact, Malinovskii's presentation to the Party Congress seemed to be meant to get the point across in public that the political and military leadership were now in accord on matters that had been under contention since the 1960 "new strategy" speech. This was especially suggested by the pains Malinovskii took to allude to the joint sanction of the Party Presidium and the government for the military establishment's obligation to "devote special attention to the initial period of a possible war." (For the full statement made by Malinovskii on this point see Note A to Chapter 1, pp. 96–98).

Status of the Soviet ICBM program, which in light of both technical and operational difficulties often associated with early generation systems may have raised doubts about over-reliance on such weapons and helped undermine Khrushchev's one-sided emphasis on them.

Technological developments leading to new evaluation of manned aircraft systems, such as Soviet development of a "stand-off capability" to deliver missiles from aircraft, and of very large-yield weapons, which in their early configuration might require delivery by aircraft.

U.S. reaction to revival of the Berlin crisis, taking the form in 1961 of U.S. defense budget increases, expansion of Polaris and Minuteman programs, measures to improve survivability and control of strategic forces, strengthening of conventional forces, etc.—all of which provided further pressure on the Soviet leaders for reappraisal of their military posture.

Concern within elements of the Soviet bureaucracy lest resource reallocation to improve consumer welfare and relieve such problems as the agricultural crisis be accomplished at the expense of defense requirements, with consequent pressure on Khrushchev to shift his policies.

In addition to the above factors, Soviet military policy considerations in the 1960–1961 period were probably affected to some extent by the Sino-Soviet dialogue, which became increasingly sharp from the fall of 1960 onward. While this dialogue did not immediately involve military doctrine in a narrow sense, it did bear on broad questions of the risk of war, the consequences of nuclear warfare, and the like. In general, the effect of the dispute with Peking may have been to bring Soviet military opinion and Khrushchev's thinking closer together to avoid leaving openings in the Soviet position that the Chinese could seek to exploit.

*Dialogue within the Military.* Concurrent with the unfolding of events that helped alter the dialogue between Khrushchev and the military in the period leading up to and following the presentation of Malinovskii's "theses" to the XXIInd Party Congress, a secondary debate ran on within the military itself. This debate has involved two identifiable schools of military thought, although the lines between them have often tended to be somewhat blurred. In general, one school might be said to represent "modernists" and "radical innovators," the other, "traditionalists" and those of more or less conservative bent. Neither school, however, professes any interest in a return to the doctrinal environment of the Stalinist period.

The central theme of the modernist school has been the need to discard old doctrinal views and to develop new concepts to exploit modern technologies of war. The more extreme adherents of this school argue that the technology of the nuclear-missile age has "cancelled out all previous concepts of the character of war." [18] They therefore hold that military-theoretical thought must lose no time in working out new concepts and methods to utilize modern weaponry. Radical innovation based on "scientific prediction" of the character of future war is favored by this school rather than relying too much on the "generalized experience of past wars." [19]

The traditionalist school, on the other hand, has tended to caution against extremes and to argue for a more moderate course of military innovation. While not denying the powerful influence of new weaponry on military doctrine and forces, and the need for change, adherents of this school hold that time-tested concepts and practices should not be lightly thrown overboard for the mere sake of embracing something new. As one traditionalist has put it: "Some of our comrades, under the influence of great technical advances, show a tendency to underestimate and even ignore the experience of past wars." [20] Theorists of this school in general favor an historical approach to working out a theory of future war, and they urge that development of new concepts should be combined with careful study of the past, especially of relevant lessons from World War II.[21]

In general, the modernist school, particularly the more extreme radical innovators among its adherents, might be said to represent

---

18 Colonel P. Sidorov, "To Tirelessly Strengthen the Country's Defense Capability," *Kommunist vooruzhennykh sil* (*Communist of the Armed Forces*), No. 12, June 1961, pp. 63, 65.

19 Colonel N. Sushko, *et al.*, "The Development of Marxist-Leninist Teaching on War under Modern Conditions," *Kommunist vooruzhennykh sil* (*Communist of the Armed Forces*), No. 18, September 1961, pp. 27–28.

20 General P. Kurochkin, "On Study of the History of Military Art under Contemporary Conditions," *Voenno-istoricheskii zhurnal* (*Journal of Military History*), No. 8, August 1961, p. 4.

21 Marshal A. A. Grechko, "Military History and the Contemporary Scene," *Voenno-istoricheskii zhurnal* (*Journal of Military History*), No. 2, February 1961, pp. 5–7.

a minority military outlook more sympathetic to Khrushchev's thinking than the majority viewpoint reflected by the traditionalist school. In fact, some of the radicals may be the conscious spokesmen of Khrushchev within the military. One military theorist who may belong in this category is Major General N. Talenskii, well known for his contributions to the doctrinal dialogue since the early post-Stalin period. It was Talenskii who in September 1953 took the first major step toward a revision of the Soviet view of warfare in the nuclear age with a ground-breaking article in the journal *Military Thought* entitled "On the Question of the Laws of Military Science." [22] He has since written periodically for both Soviet and international audiences, propagating through widely noted articles in 1960 and 1962 views on the character of nuclear warfare and its implications for international politics, which closely resemble those favored by Khrushchev.[23]

Among military men identifiable from their published views with one outlook or the other, the radical innovators as a rule appear to be less senior in rank than the traditionalists. However, a number of top-ranking officers in responsible posts, including Marshal Malinovskii, seem to have taken care not to become publicly identified too closely with extreme elements of either side, perhaps to preserve their freedom of action between political leaders like Khrushchev on the one hand, and their more conservative-minded military colleagues on the other.

As in the case of the dialogue between Khrushchev and the military, broad underlying pressures on Soviet strategy have been critical to the radical-traditionalist debate, even though the discussion has been carried on in the narrower idiom of military theory. One might say that these pressures come from three directions: economic, technological, and what the United States does or in future may do. The radical and traditionalist wings have, in general, expressed differing views in all three of these areas.

In the economic area, the traditionalists have tended to emphasize preferential heavy industry-defense policies, placing themselves in the van of general military opposition to Khrushchev's efforts in

[22] See Dinerstein, *op cit.,* pp. 36–49.

[23] Two of the widely circulated Talenskii articles were "Modern War: Its Character and Consequences," *International Affairs,* No. 10, October 1960; and "The 'Absolute Weapon' and the Problem of Security," *International Affairs,* No. 4, April 1962.

1960 and early 1961 to free a larger share of resources for other sectors of the economy. The radicals, on the other hand, seem to have felt that modern technology, even though expensive, offered the possibility of savings through reduction of large, traditionally oriented forces. Their position thus has tended to be more compatible with the economic development promises of the new Party Program announced in the summer of 1961 than that of the traditionalists. Within the sphere of military theory, these differences of outlook were reflected in 1960–1961 in a series of articles in the military press centering on such questions as the role of the economic factor in modern war and the problems of mobilization under nuclear conditions. In general, the prevailing line in this portion of the dialogue seemed to favor the traditionalist outlook. It was argued, for example, that modern military technology does not reduce the requirements for priority development of heavy industry and that economic preparation must be based on the expectation of supplying the country's military needs in a long war, rather than depending on strategic reserves prepared ahead of time.[24]

In the area of technology, the radical view has stressed the importance of not hobbling technological possibilities by waiting until technical advances become available in mass quantities before conceiving new ideas for their use. This has seemed to imply a radical leaning toward the notion that large investment of resources and scientific effort in research and development today will pay off handsomely in the future, and help compensate for the margin of U.S. industrial superiority. The traditionalist preference for maintaining large forces-in-being, by contrast, would imply a priority claim on presently available resources for this purpose.

With respect to the United States, both radical and traditionalist viewpoints have seemed to converge in cultivating an image of an enemy from whom only the worst can be expected, and hence, which allows no slackening of Soviet defense efforts. However, there has been some shading of view, with the radical outlook tending to reflect greater confidence in keeping the United States deterred from starting a war, or in breaking the U.S. will to resist by mass destruction attacks in case war should occur.

---

24 Colonel General N. Lomov, "On Soviet Military Doctrine," *Kommunist vooruzhennykh sil* (*Communist of the Armed Forces*), No. 10, May 1962, p. 15.

Down to the time when the collective authors of *Soviet Military Strategy* went to press in the spring of 1962, no clear-cut verdict had emerged for either side of the dialogue within the military between radical innovators and traditionalists. In fact, one might venture to say that as various practical decisions were taken in the defense policy area, they tended to be resolved in favor of what might best be described as a centrist viewpoint—roughly the ground occupied by Malinovskii between the radicals and tradi- tionalists.

*External Strategic Dialogue between Soviet-U.S. Leadership.* Concurrent with both streams of internal dialogue that have been mentioned above, but not necessarily in precise phase with either of them, so to speak, was a third, an external dialogue on the strategic power balance between Soviet and U.S. leaders. The Soviet side of this external dialogue antedated Khrushchev's January 1960 new strategy speech somewhat, picking up momentum in the 1957–1960 period following the first Soviet ICBM test shot and Sputnik launching in the fall of 1957. In this external dialogue, the main thrust of Khrushchev's argument was that strategic superiority had shifted to the Soviet side. He supported this claim by conveying an exaggerated picture of Soviet ICBM strength, while at the same time questioning the efficacy of U.S. strategic forces, which were still obliged to rely mainly, as he put it, on "obsolete" bombers.[25]

Khrushchev's technique of exaggeration was more suggestive than explicit. He avoided documented claims of Soviet ICBM numbers, leaving the arithmetic of the so-called missile gap mainly to specu- lation in the Western press. However, well before the Soviet Union could count on an operational ICBM force of any meaningful size,[26]

---

[25] Report by Comrade N. S. Khrushchev to the VIIth Session of the Supreme Soviet of the USSR, *Izvestiia,* May 8, 1957.

[26] The only specific figures that have been given for numbers of Soviet long-range missiles were interpolated in a January 19, 1963 speech by Khrushchev in East Germany. In referring to the withdrawal of Soviet medium-range missiles from Cuba, Khrushchev indicated that the United States was still covered by other missiles, by which he presumably meant ICBM's. The figure he used was "80, probably 120 missiles." Even so, his language as reported on this occasion (see *The Washington Post,* January 20, 1963) left some ambiguity as to whether he was referring to ICBM's aimed at the United States, or additional MRBM's. Incidentally, if Khrushchev's figure of 80 to 120 properly conveys the size of the Soviet ICBM force in 1963, then this further suggests that his claims of strategic superiority three years earlier were not founded on an ICBM force of ap- preciable size.

Khrushchev threatened that the USSR had the missile-nuclear capability to "wipe from the face of the earth" any countries that might dare to attack the Soviet Union or its allies.[27] This threat included the United States: "We have enough missiles for America, too," Khrushchev said.[28]

While Soviet military leaders associated themselves with the exaggerated missile claims Khrushchev was advancing down through early 1960 in the external dialogue with the West, they also may have been somewhat uneasy about these claims. One may venture to suppose that some of the military resistance to the new "Khrushchev doctrine" of January 1960 sprang from the feeling that it was stretching deterrence a bit thin.

After the U-2 episode in May 1960, there was an interesting shift in the tone of Khrushchev's claims of Soviet strategic superiority. He became somewhat more guarded with respect to the missile advantage claimed for the USSR, while, at the same time, asserting that the U-2 case proved that any bomber attacks against the Soviet Union were "doomed to failure." [29] He also displayed sensitivity to the implications for Soviet second-strike capabilities of loss of secrecy, first saying that American U-2 flights had not over flown operational Soviet ICBM sites, and then adding that even if the location of missile sites were known, "It is impossible to put a missile base out of commission with one, two, or several blows. Missile technology now assures means for dealing a retaliatory blow in any case." [30]

In the fall of 1961, the U.S. side of the strategic dialogue underwent marked change when the United States began to express new confidence in the margin of Western strategic superiority. Several official statements by Secretaries Gilpatric, McNamara, and others explicitly confirmed the downward revision of U.S. estimates of Soviet missile strength. From this time onward, Soviet claims of

---

[27] Speech by N. S. Khrushchev at a Meeting of Soviet Journalists in the Kremlin, November 14, 1959, *Izvestiia,* November 18, 1959; N. S. Khrushchev, Report to the Supreme Soviet of the USSR, *Pravda,* January 15, 1960.

[28] Interview of N. S. Khrushchev by the Editors of the Social-Democratic Newspapers of the F. G. R., May 5, 1959, *Pravda,* May 9, 1959.

[29] Speech by N. S. Khrushchev at the Czechoslovakian Embassy in Moscow, *Pravda,* May 10, 1960.

[30] Speech of Comrade N. S. Khrushchev at the Third Congress of the Romanian Workers' Party, *Izvestiia,* June 23, 1960.

strategic superiority have noticeably tended to be less extreme than those previously advanced by Khrushchev.

The main tendency of Soviet statements about the strategic balance has since been to argue for acceptance of strategic parity as the basis on which U.S.-Soviet policy should be conducted. For example, in an interview in January 1962 dealing specifically with the strategic balance, Malinovskii said: "Since our forces are equal, the American leaders should draw the correct conclusions and pursue a reasonable policy." [31] Khrushchev, in a speech in Moscow in July 1962, attacked an appraisal by McNamara three weeks earlier that the balance of forces favored the U.S.[32] However, Khrushchev did not reaffirm Soviet superiority; rather he asserted that the military power balance could be determined only during the course of a war and ultimately by its outcome, and that therefore the United States had no justification for trying to apply a "position of strength" policy in dealing with the Soviet Union.

A particularly interesting aspect of the Soviet response to revised U.S. appraisal of the strategic balance was a renewed effort to impress on European leaders that U.S. strategic power could not prevent their countries from being utterly destroyed in the event of war.[33] This line of response, somewhat more credible perhaps than attempting to intimidate the United States directly, indicated among other things that the concept of a "hostage Europe" was still a central element of Soviet strategic policy.[34]

Among other changes that appeared on the Soviet side of the strategic dialogue following revised U.S. estimates of Soviet ICBM numbers was a tendency to shift away from Khrushchev's "one weapon" emphasis on ICBM's and to allude more to the role and importance of other means of delivering nuclear weapons. Thus,

---

[31] Answers of Minister of Defense of the USSR Marshal R. Ia. Malinovskii to questions of correspondents of *Pravda* in response to a speech by Secretary of the Defense of the United States, R. McNamara, *Pravda,* January 24, 1962.

[32] "General and Complete Disarmament: The Guarantee for Peace and Safety for All People," speech by N. S. Khrushchev to the World Congress for General Disarmament and Peace, July 10, 1962, *Pravda,* July 11, 1962.

[33] Cf. Alastair Buchan, "The New Soviet Strategy," *The Reporter,* November 9, 1961, p. 28.

[34] Reporting on an interview with Khrushchev, Mr. Sulzberger of *The New York Times* wrote in 1961: "Quite blandly he asserts that these countries [Britain, France, Italy] are figuratively speaking hostages to the USSR and a guarantee against war." *Izvestiia,* September 9, 1961.

Soviet statements began to dwell more on diversified Soviet strategic capabilities, including long-range rocket-carrying aircraft, submarine-launched missiles, and surface vessels armed with missiles, as well as ICBM's. Along with this emphasis on diversified strategic forces, there was a new attempt to establish an image of Soviet primacy in novel forms of weapons. Supermegaton bombs, "global" missiles, and antimissile defenses fall into this category of claims. Supermegaton weapons in particular began to be treated in Soviet statements in such a way as to shift the focus of the dialogue from the relative size of U.S.-Soviet delivery forces to the greater destructive power of Soviet warheads.

On the whole, at the time the present volume was being prepared for publication, the Soviet Union was having some difficulty in holding up its side of the strategic dialogue with the United States. In a sense, the Soviet Union was laboring in the backwash of widely publicized and generally accepted assertions of Western strategic superiority, which no doubt generated further pressure on the Soviet leadership to repair the Soviet image in the world power balance.

## Relationship of Present Volume to the Strategic Debate

Viewed against the background of the strategic debate of the past few years—the internal and external aspects of which have been sketchily outlined above—the present volume would appear to represent a compromise balance of views on Soviet military doctrine and strategy, rather than a vehicle for bringing the debate to a close in a manner satisfactory to all parties concerned. This impression emerges not only from evidence internal to the book itself, but also from circumstances attending its publication and from continuing signs that doctrinal argument in the Soviet Union has by no means subsided since its appearance.

It must be recognized, of course, that the authors of *Soviet Military Strategy* were up against a difficult task from the outset. In bringing out a comprehensive work that would reflect the revisions and modifications of Soviet strategic thought in the post-Stalin decade, they were obliged to take account of two major doctrinal turning points: Khrushchev's "new strategy" prospectus of January 1960 and Malinovskii's outline of a Soviet military doctrine at the XXIInd Party Congress a year and a half later. As indicated above, these two sets of doctrinal guidelines were not altogether in harmony, and therefore the authors of the present work were left with the delicate task of dealing with any remaining divergencies between the postulates of Khrushchev's nuclear-age strategy and the military viewpoint summed up in Malinovskii's October 1961 presentation.[35]

As it turns out, it would appear that the authors have taken their guidance mainly from the Malinovskii theses outlined at the XXIInd Party Congress, fleshing out his main points on the character of a future war, the critical importance of the initial period, the danger of surprise attack, the primary task of being in constant readiness to repel or forestall such an attack, and his conspicuous hedge that despite the decisive role of nuclear-rocket weapons, final victory in modern war can only be achieved by combined action of all arms and services, requiring the employment of mass, multi-million-man armies. Moreover, out of an apparent desire to avoid opening new areas of controversy, a rather careful selective effort has been made in the present work to deny admission to special pleading for certain dissonant viewpoints occasionally sounded in other Soviet publications. For example, in one case, which has a somewhat interesting parallel in the Skybolt controversy in the West, Soviet Air Force officers and other aviation figures, like the well-known aircraft designer Andrei Tupolev, have been trying to argue for more air-to-surface missile carriers, and even suggesting that they were superior to ICBM's.[36] Such views have not been given a sympathetic hearing in the present work.

The net effect of this approach is to stamp the present work as a "centrist" compromise that perpetuates dissentient views from both sides of center and leaves a number of issues in the same state of uneasy equilibrium in which they stood before the work was undertaken. To mention but a few, among such issues are (a) The size

---

[35] The October 1961 presentation was not the only expression of the Malinovskii theses of a new Soviet military doctrine. For example, in *Kommunist,* No. 7, May 15, 1962, a major article by Malinovskii entitled "The CPSU Program and Problems of Strengthening the Armed Forces of the USSR" again laid out the main points of the new doctrine. This article, however, did not appear until the present volume had gone to press.

[36] In an article "The Missile-Aircraft Carrier," *Aviatsiia i kozmonavtika* (*Aviation and Cosmonautics*), No. 6, June 1962, Tupolev wrote about the virtues of air-to-surface missile delivery systems and argued, among other things, that such systems have "very important advantages over multi-stage missiles," p. 4.

of the armed forces: how large an army must be maintained and what priority claim on resources should be set for this purpose? (b) The nature of the initial period: just how "decisive" may this phase of a war prove to be and what are the practical implications for force posture, readiness, and pre-emptive capability? (c) The length of the war: will it be short or protracted; how critical are the effects of this factor on planning for military and economic mobilization? (d) The kind of strategy needed for dealing with the United States: what posture will best deter the United States; in case of war, what strategy will offer the best prospect of victory against an overseas power like the United States; can one count on breaking the U.S. will to resist with a nuclear attack on the U.S. homeland or will it be necessary to defeat the enemy's armed forces in detail and occupy his territory; in the absence of war, is an arms race against the United States a feasible long-term proposition or should other alternatives, such as a genuine arms control effort, receive serious consideration? (e) The escalation of small wars: are such wars likely and can they be kept limited, or is it "inevitable" that a local war involving the nuclear powers will quickly expand into global, nuclear war?

This canvass touches on only a few of the matters that the compromise formula in the present volume leaves in the category of unfinished business. Admittedly, issues of this sort are not susceptible to easy answers, and it is not at all surprising that they should be left essentially unsettled. However, it is the tendency of most compromise "solutions" to promise something for everybody. The compromise viewpoint reflected in the present volume appears to be no exception. The implications of this compromise approach point in many instances to very heavy defense expenditures. When the competitive demands on resources are great, which is certainly the case in the Soviet Union, the result can be to sharpen differences, rather than to smooth them out. Hence, this is another reason for supposing that the compromise reflected in the present volume on many of the issues under debate may prove to be unstable.

With regard to Khrushchev's running dialogue with the professional military, it is still by no means clear to what extent there remains a basic difference in outlook between them. One cannot, for that matter, be precise about how wide the difference was in

1960. Khrushchev was obviously prepared to go further in reducing the size of the ground forces than some military leaders, and he also seemed more ready to retire older weapons systems in favor of missiles with nuclear warheads. Quite possibly, Khrushchev had a lower expectation of the likelihood of war than the Soviet military leaders and, therefore, was primarily interested in the political capital he might be able to derive from conveying the impression of great military strength in the most modern weapons. By virtue of their professional preoccupation with the problem of *waging* nuclear war, the military leaders had to be concerned with weapons systems and forces that still had military utility, although they might become redundant at some future date. Now ostensibly, from some of the considerations mentioned earlier, and from what might be inferred from the synthesis laid down in *Soviet Military Strategy,* one might suppose that Khrushchev and the military have come closer on doctrine and on the underlying questions of defense policy.

What is not clear is whether the concessions on Khrushchev's part to the military point of view represent a wholehearted acceptance of that point of view, or whether the modifications in Khrushchev's point of view represent only a temporary response to an emergency situation. At the time Khrushchev had begun to alter his position and to adopt such measures in the summer of 1961 as suspension of the troop cut and an increase in the military budget, he had also, on several occasions, emphasized that these measures were "temporary" and "in the nature of a reply" to U.S. moves.[37] The implication was that Khrushchev might turn back to his previous program should an easing of tensions be achieved.

Moreover, while Khrushchev has publicly stepped away from his more extreme 1960 views on the one-sided dominance of missiles and nuclear weapons, and the obsolescence of conventional forces, he also continues on occasion to express opinions that leave some doubt as to where he stands on the role of various forces. For example, in early 1962 he said in a letter to President Kennedy that the outcome of a future war would be decisively settled by nuclear blows "before vast armies can be mobilized and thrown

---

[37] For example, his speech to graduates of Soviet military academies on July 8, 1961, and his television address on August 7, 1961. *Pravda,* July 9, 1961; *Izvestiia,* August 9, 1961.

into battle." [38] More recently, in an interview with W. E. Knox, the head of Westinghouse International, he repeated the claim that surface navies are obsolete and said that he was spending a great deal of his time "eliminating obsolete weapons from the Soviet arsenal." [39]

Khrushchev's somewhat contradictory position on the question of the destructiveness of a nuclear war and the Soviet Union's prospects of victory if war should occur also suggests an area of continuing difference with military opinion. On the one hand, Khrushchev has gone farther than have most military spokesmen to picture the *mutually* destructive character of nuclear war. One of his more recent statements on the subject, in a speech before the VIth Congress of the East German Communist Party on January 16, 1963, put likely casualties at 700–800 million and cast strong doubt on the possibility that even a communist society could be rebuilt on the radioactive rubble of a nuclear war.[40]

On the other hand, as leader of the Soviet state, Khrushchev has found it necessary to aver that if war should occur, the Soviet Union would, despite its suffering, inevitably come out on top. This ambiguity in his position, when translated into terms of developing a Soviet military posture, seems to put Khrushchev potentially at odds with the professional military. Whereas the latter are primarily oriented toward building up the military forces and urging the civil preparations needed to make good the promise of Soviet victory in the event of war, Khrushchev's bent seems to lie in the direction of concentrating on weapons with maximum political effect and a high probability of discouraging war from starting in the first place. This situation imputes neither more nor less virtue to either party, but it does have the implication that Khrushchev's criteria for weapons selection and expenditure of resources on the Soviet defense establishment are likely to differ from the opinions of many of his professional military advisers.

Khrushchev's tendency to speak disparagingly of professional mil-

---

[38] Message from the Chairman of the Council of Ministers of the USSR, N. S. Khrushchev to the President of the United States, John Kennedy, *Izvestiia,* February 24, 1962.

[39] W. E. Knox, "Close-up of Khrushchev during a Crisis," *The New York Times Magazine,* November 18, 1962, p. 129.

[40] Speech by Comrade N. S. Khrushchev to the VIth Congress of the German United Socialist Party, *Pravda,* January 17, 1963.

itary opinion has been tempered somewhat since his widely quoted remark in late 1959 that "I do not trust the appraisal of generals on questions of strategic importance," [41] but he still continues to stress his own competence in the field of defense. For example, in an interview with Gardner Cowles in April 1962, while discussing nuclear weapons, Khrushchev said:

> As head of government I have to deal with questions of defense, and consequently, questions of modern means of warfare, and I have occasion to watch them [nuclear weapons] being tested. This is why I have a perfectly clear idea of their effects.[42]

In light of indications that Khrushchev may not always hold the opinions of his generals in high regard, it is worth noting that the present volume suggests, in a number of ways, that the same may be true in reverse. One example occurs in a section of Chapter 8, which contains a curious and somewhat fulsome exposition of the role and qualities of the top Soviet professional military leadership. On the one hand, the account has the tone of an apologia for the military leadership; painting their qualities large, stressing that in the modern age they must be soundly informed on and must apply themselves to matters extending far beyond the battlefield. This suggests that the military may be seeking to defend themselves against criticism that they are encroaching on Khrushchev's political side of the house.

On the other hand, while stressing the close link of top Soviet generals with the Party and their responsiveness to the will of the people, the account also seems to hint that some affairs are best left in the hands of experienced military leaders, which might suggest that the military feel their own domain is being encroached on by Khrushchev. A particularly interesting passage in this connection (p. 496) makes the point that history affords no examples of an army "led by inexperienced military leaders successfully waging war against an army led by an experienced military leader."

There is other internal evidence in the present volume that may reflect a delicate species of in-fighting between Khrushchev

---

[41] This statement was made at a Kremlin press conference on November 8, 1959, where Khrushchev remarked that "strategy is enunciated by generals" before going on to say that he did not trust their opinions. Reported in *The New York Times,* November 9, 1959, p. 4.

[42] Interview of N. S. Khrushchev by American publisher G. Cowles, April 20, 1962, *Pravda,* April 27, 1962.

and the military. Throughout the work, for example, an ambivalent attitude can be found toward Khrushchev's individual contributions to Soviet military doctrine and strategy. While there are frequent references to him, care seems to be taken not to portray him as a uniquely endowed military genius. Indeed, in a significant passage on military doctrine that may have been written with Khrushchev partly in mind, the book emphasizes (pp. 130–131) that "military doctrine is not thought out or compiled by a single person or group of persons," but rather is the result of a "quite complex and lengthy historical process," and expresses "the general political line of the State's ruling social class" on questions of war and national defense.

This passage on military doctrine may point to a deeper unresolved issue between Khrushchev and the military than first meets the eye. To elaborate briefly, in the months following presentation of Malinovskii's theses of a new "Soviet military doctrine" in October 1961, there was a noticeable trend in the Soviet military press to expand on the military's share of credit for developing the new doctrine, and to emphasize the significance of the doctrine as a basis for state policy.[43] This appeared tantamount to arguing a case for increased military influence policy-making in an area traditionally reserved to the political leadership. The present work, which was in preparation during the same period, carries this line of argument forward by seeking to equate Soviet military doctrine with the most fundamental and durable conceptions of state interest and national security, and to divorce its formulation from the competence of individual leaders. This would appear to be a challenge that Khrushchev could hardly afford to let go unheeded, for it implies that the military leadership is seeking to put itself in a position to bend policy decisions in a direction responsive to its own concept of national interests.

Even though this challenge is more implicit than explicit in the present work, the volume itself represents, in a sense, a point scored for the military side of the argument by getting the military view-

---

[43] Among articles deserving note in this connection were: Colonel General N. Lomov, *op. cit.*, pp. 11–22; Colonel I. Sidel'nikov, "On Soviet Military Doctrine," *Red Star*, May 11, 1962; V. Siniagin, "Creation of the Material-Technical Base of Communism and Strengthening of the Defense Capacity of the USSR," *Kommunist vooruzhennykh sil* (*Communist of the Armed Forces*), No. 14, July 1962, pp. 8–16.

point on the record in the form of the first comprehensive exposition of the new doctrine. Khrushchev is thus put in a position where any future efforts to substitute his own strategic conceptions for those acceptable to the prevailing military outlook would be made more difficult. At the least, he would probably find it hard to dictate on technical military matters without winning some authoritative professional military opinion over to his side, which suggests a continuation of essentially the same sort of problem he has faced up to now.

From Khrushchev's standpoint, the very fact that he cannot simply knock military heads together to get agreement with his views means that it is to his advantage to stimulate discussion and debate among the military up to some point, precisely to avoid finding himself boxed in by a unanimous military viewpoint. The radical-traditionalist dialogue within the military thus serves his ends by preventing the formation of a solid front of military opinion with which he would have to contend. To the extent, therefore, that the present volume reflects a continuation of the radical-traditionalist dialogue, Khrushchev presumably would regard it as a not unwelcome addition to the library of contemporary Soviet military thought.

In this connection, the book itself and comment after its publication suggest continuing reservations toward some aspects of the compromise formula. From the traditionalist side, for example, it is interesting that the principal Soviet review of the book (by General of the Army P. Kurochkin in *Red Star,* September 22, 1962), although generally favorable, nevertheless offers a judicious mixture of praise and censure.[44] Kurochkin applauds the book for filling "a known gap in our military-theoretical literature" and for "substantiation of a whole series of new conclusions and tenets applied to the conditions of missile-nuclear war." At the same time, he finds it necessary to reproach the authors for concentrating on the importance of strategic missile forces to the neglect of the role of other forces, especially land troops:

> . . . having justifiably concentrated their main attention on the strategic missile forces, [the authors] have not given sufficient weight to and have not analyzed deeply enough the role and meth-

---

[44] This review, because of its intimate bearing on the book, is reproduced in its entirety in Appendix I.

ods of operation of other types of armed forces, particularly of the ground forces.

This would indicate that the traditionalist side of the house, to which Kurochkin obviously belongs, is not altogether happy with the compromise viewpoint that the authors, following Malinovskii, have sought to articulate. Kurochkin also censures the authors for having omitted mention of many important contributors to the development of Soviet strategic thought,[45] among whom he includes the name of one contemporary theorist, Lieutenant General S. N. Krasil'nikov.

As noted earlier, Krasil'nikov is one of the former "progressives" of the early post-Stalin period whose strategic views today appear to lie toward the traditionalist end of the spectrum. In one of his most recent published pieces, for example, he reflected the traditionalist viewpoint in arguing that a nuclear war would require mass armies, large trained manpower reserves, and that surprise cannot win a war or conclusively determine its course and outcome.[46] Besides implying that the omission of Krasil'nikov means that the traditionalist side of the argument has been slighted, Kurochkin may be suggesting here that, in his view, the book is slanted toward conveying the impression that everything new and progressive in Soviet military thinking has resulted from stimulus from the Party leadership. This could be his way of saying that military people should also be credited with having helped to break away from outmoded strategic conceptions of the Stalinist era.

There have been no reviews of the present work by Soviet military figures identified with the radical viewpoint, hence it is somewhat difficult to judge what grounds for complaint are felt most strongly from the radical side. However, a number of expressions of the radical viewpoint out of keeping with the middle-of-the-road

---

[45] Another briefer review of the book by Ya. Gorelik, which appeared in *Izvestiia,* August 24, 1962, made the same reproach about omission of many contributors to Soviet strategic thought, but it mentioned no names. In general, the Gorelik review, entitled "Valuable Scientific Work," anticipated the conservatively oriented comments of the fuller Kurochkin review.

[46] Lieutenant General S. N. Krasil'nikov, "On the Nature of Modern War," *Red Star,* November 18, 1960. In 1956, Krasil'nikov had also voiced the traditionalist view that "atomic or hydrogen weapons alone, and in general any single weapon, cannot determine the outcome of a war." See "On the Question of the Nature of Contemporary Warfare," *Marksizm-Leninizm o voine i armii (Marxism-Leninism on War and the Army),* Voenizdat Ministerstva Oborony Soiuza SSR, Moscow, 1956, p. 151.

approach that generally characterizes the work can be found in the book itself. One of these crops up in Chapter 7, dealing with "Preparation of a Country To Repel Aggression." This chapter is identified with Colonel General A. I. Gastilovich, described as a Doctor and Professor of Military Sciences, and curiously, the only contributor to be identified with a specific part of the work. The fact that he is singled out for mention at all may be meant to indicate that the editors wished to show that they had not ignored completely the holders of views inconsonant with the general tenor of the work. It can be inferred that Gastilovich probably lines up with nonconformists on the radical side of the dialogue from some of the propositions advanced in this chapter.

For example, he says (pp. 431–432) that preparations for war under contemporary conditions are influenced by:

> First, the availability of missiles and nuclear weapons of megaton yields, which reduce outlays on military preparations in peacetime, since they permit the possibility of considerable cutbacks of all other types of armament without lowering the firepower of the armed forces.

This idea, closely reminiscent of the argument earlier espoused but later dropped by Khrushchev, clearly runs counter to the traditionalist view of the need for continued peacetime maintenance of large, combined-arms forces. Another expression of concern for the economic burden of military preparedness—rather uncharacteristic of the prevailing military viewpoint—is also to be found in Gastilovich's discussion (p. 433) of the mobilization difficulties that would be created by a surprise nuclear attack. He says that:

> . . . It would seem advisable to have peacetime forces set up on such a basis as to achieve the basic objectives of the initial period of a war without additional mobilization.

This is a notion very similar to a position taken by Malinovskii in his article in May 1962 on the need for adequate forces-in-being.[47] However, Gastilovich then goes on to add a sobering conclusion that was not drawn by Malinovskii:

---

[47] R. Malinovskii, "The Program of the KPSS and the Question of Strengthening the Armed Forces of the USSR," *Kommunist,* No. 7, May 1962, p. 20. In this article, Malinovskii said: "Faced with the constant threat that the imperialists will unleash a war, the party is obliged to hold to the principle of maintaining a regular army of such size, composition, and training as to make it capable from the very start of a war of repulsing the aggressor's attack and routing him."

However, to maintain armed forces on such a basis is not within the economic capability of any, even the strongest, state.

Gastilovich continues this discussion by indicating which forces, given the necessity to live within economic constraints, are to receive priority in the peacetime military establishment—a contentious point on which Malinovskii did not elaborate. According to Gastilovich (p. 433), these forces, which should be maintained in a state of constant readiness are:

> . . . strategic forces and weapons of the amount and composition required for attainment of war aims, a nation-wide air defense system, and a certain portion of the other branches of the armed forces: ground troops, naval forces, air forces, and civil defense rescue and rehabilitation troops.

The latter branches of the armed forces, Gastilovich says, are "as a rule, increased at the outbreak of war by mobilization." While the Gastilovich formula thus falls short of specifying the precise proportion of each type of forces, it does at least indicate which forces in the mix should sit first at the resources table and which second. Part of the Gastilovich formula—the part stating that economic constraints limit the size and character of the peacetime forces that can be maintained prior to mobilization—can be found in an earlier chapter of the book (p. 338), but there the discussion stops even shorter of a prescription as to which branches of the armed forces should receive priority.

One notes a certain inconsistency in Gastilovich's contribution, which may indicate that he did not have an altogether free hand with the chapter. For example, the proposition that modern large-yield weapons will save money by permitting a cutback in other armaments is followed later (p. 433) by what seems to be an argument for a large and highly trained standing army—a notion congenial to the traditionalist school.

> In contrast to the covering forces of previous wars, the combat-ready part of the ground forces must in modern conditions be numerically much stronger to be capable of executing its assignments.

The inconsistency here may be more apparent than real, for Gastilovich was trying to make the point that one cannot count on massive post-outbreak mobilization of forces to meet the critical needs of the initial period of a future war. It is interesting, by the way, that this particular passage was singled out for approval by General Kurochkin, the rival theorist of the traditionalist school, in his *Red Star* review.

In addition to the discordant notes sounded in the chapter identified with Gastilovich, other comments of a radicalist tinge turn up here and there in the work. One example occurs in Chapter 6. While discussing the tendency of "bourgeois general staffs" to prepare for new wars with methods from past wars, the authors note that there should be no grounds for this kind of "conservatism" among Soviet military leaders. They then go on to say, however (p. 399), that:

> It cannot be denied that we have among us people so burdened with past experience and enamored of it that they are unable to see what is new.

Even on the question of combined forces—the hallmark of the traditionalist view—there is a rather curious reservation in one of the unattributed chapters of the book that seems to suggest that critics of the durability of this concept could not be altogether ignored. This reservation appears in a discussion of factors affecting force structure in Chapter 5. After noting somewhat cryptically that the principle of combined arms "remains in force at the present time," the authors add a statement on the necessity for change (p. 349) which seems to echo the credo of the radicalist school:

> It must be kept in mind, however, that trends in the development of armed forces are not constant. They always undergo, and in future will continue to undergo, various changes in response to the military and political situation, economic factors, and the development of technical means of warfare. Military strategy must study these changes in good time and take them into consideration in determining the organization and structure of the armed forces and methods for waging war.

Still another indication that the radical-traditionalist dialogue is being carried on within the pages of the present work, despite an ostensible effort to reduce the book's polemical content, can be found in Chapter 6 in a discussion of strategic operations and the role that ground forces can be expected to play in them in a future war. The anonymous contributors to this chapter observe that in the last war there were essentially only two types of strategic operations—strategic attack and strategic defense—in both of which ground forces played the major role, with all other forces used in their support. Modern weapons have changed the situation, they note, but "Some authors believe that the [old] situation remains essentially unchanged," and that nuclear operations of the strategic missile forces should be oriented around the proposed objectives of the ground forces, "paving the way to the front, as it were, with powerful nuclear strikes." They then go on (p. 401):

> This concept of how to wage modern war is incorrect. It is the result of overvaluing the experience of the past war and mechanically applying it to modern conditions.

An interesting aspect of this lecture on not keeping up with the times is that the authors chided for their backward views are named in a footnote. This is one of the rare occasions in the present volume where such a direct polemical note is introduced. The authors taken to task are Major General Smirnov and Colonels Baz', Kozlov, and Sidorov, whose views under criticism had been set down in a 1960 Ministry of Defense text, *On Soviet Military Science*. Since these writers had, in fact, tended to occupy ground ranging from the radical to the traditionalist ends of the spectrum, one may assume that the attack on them here is meant to suggest that a substantial segment of Soviet military thinking has not yet accommodated itself to the new doctrinal proposition that strategic missiles are the "main means of attaining the goals of a war" and that consequently the strategic missile forces are "the leading type of armed forces." Behind the polemical note introduced here on the question of force roles, as elsewhere in the present volume, lies one of the central issues over which the strategic dialogue has been waged—the size and composition of the armed forces, and how available resources are to be apportioned among them.

As the foregoing discussion indicates, publication of the present volume does not appear to have signaled the end of the strategic debate in the Soviet Union. Furthermore, following the book's appearance last year, various signs of a continuing polemic became evident. One of these was the inauguration of a series of special articles in *Izvestiia* in October 1962.[48] A foreword by the editors

---

[48] The series began on October 20, 1962, with an article by Tank Marshal P. Rotmistrov, "Modern Tanks and Nuclear Weapons." The second article by Chief Marshal of Artillery S. Varentsov, "Missiles: Formidable Weapon of the Ground

said a new section of *Izvestiia* was being set up to present the views of outstanding military leaders and theoreticians on military doctrine and employment of modern weapons and various types of forces. The rather unusual forum chosen for this purpose, an organ of the regular press, edited incidentally, by Khrushchev's son-in-law, suggests that the series relates to issues that are still very much alive.

Concurrent with the *Izvestiia* series, there have also appeared pronouncements by Marshal Malinovskii, General A. A. Epishev, Chief of the Main Political Directorate of the Ministry of Defense, and others, reported in *Red Star,* which have attacked military "conservatism" and unnamed fellow officers who give "lip service to innovation" but stick to "outmoded ways in practice." [49] The most interesting, and perhaps the most significant of all the articles in this press campaign was an interview with Marshal V. I. Chuikov in *Red Star* following the Cuban crisis.[50]

In this interview, in which he hammered on the theme of the dominant role of the party in military affairs, Chuikov cited a hitherto unpublished message from Stalin to Lenin during the Russo-Polish campaign of 1920, to the effect that "our diplomacy sometimes very effectively spoils the results achieved by our military victories." Chuikov then quoted from Lenin's reply: "Our diplomacy is subordinated to the Central Committee and will never spoil our victories." The point of this interview, during which Chuikov went on to criticize officers "who do not . . . maintain proper attitudes and opinions," appeared to be that the military should remember that it is subordinate to the Party and must accept the decisions of the political leadership, which understands the larger

---

Forces," appeared December 1962. Rotmistrov's article advanced the argument that despite the role of strategic nuclear weapons in the opening phase of a war, the tank/infantry team still makes a vital contribution to attainment of the final goals of a war. Varentsov's rather carefully worded article argued that tactical missile forces, which he commands, now could best perform many battlefield tasks which formerly fell to tanks, infantry, and aviation. He also gave adherence, however, to the formula that only combined action of all arms can assure victory.

[49] Speech by Marshal R. Ia. Malinovskii to All-Army Conference on Ideological Questions, *Red Star,* October 25, 1962; "To Go Further, To Achieve More," *ibid.,* November 29, 1962; General A. A. Epishev, "Increasing the Military Preparedness of the Troops: The Main Goal of Party Work," *ibid.,* December 1, 1962.

[50] Marshal V. I. Chuikov, "The Basic Fundamentals of Military Development," *Red Star,* November 7, 1962. This article took the form of an interview.

issues involved better than professional military circles. This hint that a new element has entered into the strategic debate—dissatisfaction in some military circles with the outcome of the Cuban affair—suggests that another phase of the ongoing dialogue is now opening.[51]

So far as the present volume is concerned, however, the fact that it contains many elements of compromise and a good deal of unfinished business should not obscure its significance as a major milestone in the evolution of Soviet strategic thought. It may therefore serve the reader at this point to turn attention to the principal features of the strategic doctrine that emerges from the work.

## Main Features of Current Strategic Doctrine Depicted in the Present Work

As previously noted, this volume registers a broad shift in the Soviet strategic outlook from primary preoccupation with continental land warfare to a central focus on the problems of global strategic war. In a sense, this shift of emphasis has paralleled a growing realization that Soviet military strategy must give greater attention than in the past to the problem of dealing with an adversary whose main bastion of military power lies beyond the confines of Europe.[52] At the same time, the heritage of a continental military tradition continues to run strongly through Soviet strategic thinking. These countervailing tendencies can be seen at work in the current strategic doctrine that emerges from the present volume. The main features of this doctrine are drawn together for the convenience of the reader in the synopsis below.

*General Character of a Future War.* As in other Soviet military literature, great stress is laid on the importance of correct analysis of the character of a future war to properly prepare the armed forces and the country for what is invariably described as "war with the aggressor." The authors of the present volume draw

---

[51] Another address to which this article may have been directed could be Peking, since the Chinese at this time were also expressing criticism of the Soviet leadership for the handling of the Cuban crisis. One might also speculate that a Soviet military or political faction showing some sympathy with the Chinese viewpoint had made its voice heard behind the scenes, but there is no evidence of this.

[52] Soviet perception of this problem may have been heightened by the fact that efforts to exploit Soviet military power politically have tended to run ahead of development of a suitable supporting military strategy.

on both Marxist-Leninist theory and analysis of technical and military factors to present an image of future war along the lines described below. Most aspects of this image appear to be accepted without question in Soviet doctrine today, although a degree of ambiguity attaches to some points.

First of all, with regard to the possibility of war in the calculable future, a generally somber view is reflected in the present work. The authors follow the now-orthodox Soviet line that although war is not inevitable, it cannot be excluded because of, among other things, "the aggressive policies" and the "intensified imperialist war preparations" (p. 312). Such preparations are cited at one point (p. 286) as the basis for the appreciation that (in the sixties) "the danger of world war breaking out has become particularly real."

This estimate of increased danger of war parallels a perceptible increase in Soviet propaganda charges that the West is preparing for a "preventive" war and a surprise attack on the Soviet Bloc— charges that have become more noticeable since they were embedded in the Party Program in the summer of 1961, and given further emphasis in Malinovskii's Party Congress speech. One finds it difficult to judge what the real, rock-bottom Soviet estimate of this danger may be. As noted earlier, the issue has certain controversial implications in Soviet internal politics. The more real the danger of war can be painted, the stronger is the case of those who want to put more resources into Soviet military preparations. At the same time, the issue is also involved in the dispute between Moscow and the Chinese Communists, with Khrushchev in a position where his policies are less vulnerable to Chinese attack if the danger-of-war issue is kept in a low key.

In this connection, it is interesting that Khrushchev's impromptu remarks have sometimes reflected considerably less concern about the danger of Western attack and the likelihood of war than the "official" view appearing in such authoritative sources as the Party Program, documents of the XXIInd Party Congress, and so on. For example, in some offhand remarks made in Bulgaria in the spring of 1962 (which were not, incidentally, reprinted in the Soviet Union), Khrushchev suggested that war threats from both sides were in effect helping to stabilize the situation, and that rather than increasing the likelihood of war, this meant that the situation could be considered good. His words were:

> They frighten us with war, and we frighten them back bit by bit. They threaten us with nuclear arms and we tell them: "Listen, now only fools can do this, because we have them too, and they are not smaller than yours but, we think, even better than yours. So why do you do foolish things and frighten us?" This is the situation, and this is why we consider the situation to be good.[53]

The authors of the present volume, in addition to reflecting the view apparently favored by the military on the increased danger of war in the sixties, also make an attempt (pp. 380–381) to erect a general theory of advance war preparation and surprise attack by "imperialist aggressors," basing this theory on historical analysis of past wars. The authors have difficulty, however, fitting the United States into this scheme, noting simply that during both world wars the United States "avoided entering them at their outset."

With regard to circumstances of war outbreak, the notion that a future war will begin with a surprise nuclear attack on the Soviet Union, probably during a period of crisis, certainly constitutes the favored view in the current doctrine expressed in this work. However, other possible war outbreak scenarios are also mentioned (p. 289). They include escalation from local war, "accidental" outbreak, and retaliation by the Soviet Union for an attack on another Bloc member. The latter would imply a Soviet first strike against the United States, but despite the crucial implications of this question for Soviet strategy, it receives no explicit attention in the work.

Closely related in Soviet strategic discourse to the circumstances under which war might start is the question of warning. Throughout the latter fifties the prevailing Soviet view had been that the USSR would receive ample long-range strategic warning to enable it to make preparations to deal with an attack, as well as to facilitate tactical warning by heightened vigilance measures. Increasing doubt as to the validity of these assumptions appears to have arisen in the past couple of years. The present volume reflects a somewhat divided

---

[53] Federal Broadcast Information Service (FBIS), Daily Report, USSR-East Europe, May 16, 1962, p. KK3. Khrushchev's speech was made in Maritsa, Bulgaria, on May 15, and broadcast on that date on the Sofia domestic service.

body of views on this question. While confidence is expressed in some portions of the book that a well-organized intelligence system will provide ample, long-range warning of a political and strategic character, the frequent discussion elsewhere concerning maintenance of forces at a constant, high level of combat readiness seems to include an expectation (p. 393) that strategic warning may not be forthcoming. Except for inference that a high state of readiness may ease tactical warning problems, little direct discussion of tactical warning appears in the book.

As to the nature of a future war, the image portrayed in the present volume suggests general acceptance of the proposition that a future war will take the form of a nuclear war of global dimensions in which missiles will be the primary means of combat. A typical passage (p. 299) states:

> One of the important tenets of Soviet military doctrine is that a world war, if the imperialists initiate it, will inevitably assume the character of a nuclear war with missiles, i.e., a war in which the nuclear weapon will be the chief instrument of destruction and missiles the basic vehicle for their delivery to target.

This formulation raises the question whether wars other than world war are considered politically and technically tenable. There is an area of ambiguity on this point, which will be taken up presently under the heading of local war possibilities. However, the standard Soviet doctrinal position on escalation of any armed conflict involving the nuclear powers is reasserted in the present volume, as in the following passage (p. 299):

> One must emphasize that the present international system and the present state of military technology will cause any armed conflict to develop, inevitably, into a general war if the nuclear powers are drawn into it.

Along with this doctrinal assertion of the inevitability of escalation goes the theme that a future war would instantly and automatically become a worldwide nuclear conflict. In the event war should be started by "American aggressive circles," according to the book (p. 299), both the United States and its military allies would immediately "suffer crushing blows" and "nuclear war would, in an instant, spread over the entire globe." This theme of the automaticity of global nuclear war seems calculated not only to reinforce the credibility of Soviet nuclear retaliation, but also to discourage the United States and its allies from entertaining the idea that ground rules of some sort might be adopted for limiting the destructiveness of a war if one should occur. Nowhere in the book, as in most other Soviet military literature as well, are there to be found signs of serious professional interest in concepts like controlled response and restrained nuclear targeting, which have been widely discussed in the West.

In keeping with the notion of the automaticity of global nuclear war, another frequently emphasized feature of the image projected in the present volume is the destructive character of a future war, in which "entire countries will be wiped from the face of the earth." It is interesting, however, that the authors do not edge as close to the "mutual destruction" theme as have some statements by the Soviet political elite, such as those by Khrushchev cited earlier. One gets the impression that the question of how badly the Soviet Union might fare in a nuclear exchange is one which must be handled with great delicacy. In the present work, direct discussion of the question of reciprocal damage to the Soviet Union is skirted for the most part.

For example, in a passage on page 300, the authors paint a picture of the devastation that nuclear weapons would bring to various countries in the West, using open data from British and U.S. sources to illustrate the losses in these countries. There is no mention here, however, of the damage the Soviet Union itself would suffer. After citing various dismal statistics from Western sources, the authors add that these figures, using an average weapons yield of five megatons, fall far short of conveying the probable result of an actual Soviet attack, which would not only be of larger scale than any pictured by the foreign statistics, but also more destructive, since the Soviet Union has "warheads of much greater yield than five megatons." This would appear to be one of many instances in which the present volume goes beyond the elucidation of doctrine for a Soviet audience to indulge in a form of psychological warfare against the West. It could also be meant to reassure Soviet readers as to Soviet military might.

Some care seems to be taken in the book, however, not to make overly specific the claims about what can be done to knock large countries out of a war with nuclear attacks. For example, the notion of "wiping entire countries off the face of the earth" is qualified to indicate (p. 400) that this applies *particularly* to countries "with a small, densely populated area," and by inference, not to large powers like the United States and the USSR.

The class nature of a future war is dwelt on at some length in the present volume. In keeping with a long-held tenet of Marxist-Leninist dogma, a future world war is pictured as a "decisive armed collision of two opposing world social systems" (p. 312) and also one in which class interests will cause each side to set for itself "the most decisive political and military goals." There is, interestingly, a departure from the standard view that all combatants would be ranged in ideologically opposed coalitions in a passage on p. 287 stating that a future war would find some "non-socialist states siding with the socialist camp, especially after the war had begun." Precisely which countries the authors may have had in mind is not stated. This passage, incidentally, carries the inference that some countries outside the Soviet camp might wish to jump on the bandwagon if it appeared that the Soviet side were winning.

The conflict in current strategic doctrine between the concepts of a short decisive war and a long one tends to cloud somewhat the image of a future war pictured in the present work. While placing great emphasis on military preparations designed to win a war "in the shortest possible time, with minimum losses," the authors also add the hedge (p. 314) that—"at the same time it is necessary to make serious preparations for a protracted war." Despite this concession to the long war possibility, it is interesting that the middle and terminal phases of a future war receive much less consideration than its initial period.

The middle phase of a war pictured in the book seems to be envisaged as a period in which theater battles and ground mop-up operations would be carried out in the wake of the initial nuclear exchanges, followed by a terminal phase in which occupation and political collapse of enemy countries would take place (pp. 302, 341, 428), but the duration, sequence, and interrelationship of these phases and their component phenomena are only sketchily indicated. The targeting philosophy in the book, to be mentioned in more detail later, seems to imply that the concept of a "broken-back" war may be held as the characteristic scenario for the terminal phase of a war, in the event that the enemy's will to continue has not been broken in the meantime. However, there is no detailed development of such a terminal scenario in the work.

Although a rather similar dearth of detailed attention to the terminal aspects of a future war can be found in Western military literature, the present volume would suggest that Soviet military thinking has been at least equally, if not more laggard, in addressing itself to the problems involved in bringing a future war to an end.

*Local War Possibility.*   The vista of future war that unfolds in this work has little room in it for local wars, so far as the Soviet armed forces are concerned. However, there are a few instances in which local war is treated in matter-of-fact terms indicating that the Soviet armed forces should be prepared to cope with such wars outside the framework of general war.[54] One such reference occurs on page 288, where, after noting that the Soviet armed forces must prepare themselves primarily for a world war, the authors go on to say that at the same time:

> . . . the armed forces of the socialist countries must be ready for small-scale local wars which the imperialists might initiate. . . . Soviet military strategy must study the methods of waging such wars too, in order to prevent their expansion into a world war, and in order to achieve a rapid victory over the enemy.

This statement, it may be noted, implies the belief that local wars can be kept from developing into global nuclear war, which seems to contradict the doctrinal assertion of inevitable escalation. Similar ambiguity attends the statement elsewhere (p. 396) that a local war, "if not nipped in the bud, can grow into a world war with unlimited use of nuclear weapons." This also seems to imply some reservations as to the inevitability of escalation.

Considerable stress is laid on the alleged functions of limited war in U.S. planning. In one place (p. 383), it is asserted that the United States plans to use limited war as a cover for "preparation of unlimited nuclear war against the socialist countries." Elsewhere

---

[54] While local and limited war has customarily received little attention in Soviet military literature, it has not been entirely ignored. The need for Soviet military science to study local war along with other kinds of possible wars was pointed out, for example, in an article by Colonel S. Kozlov, "The Creative Character of Soviet Military Science," *Kommunist vooruzhennykh sil* (*Communist of the Armed Forces*), No. 11, June 1961, p. 55.

(pp. 356, 396), it is charged that the United States wants to avoid the political stigma and the military risks of initiating a large-scale nuclear war by resorting instead to local wars in which limited use of nuclear weapons at the critical moment "would sharply alter the situation in their favor." A standard accusation is that the United States plans to incite local wars to suppress "national-liberation movements." Another accusation (p. 393) is that local wars are contemplated to prove out war plans and military readiness. Alleged U.S. planning at the present time for limited war in Europe is singled out for denunciation (p. 383), but there is no indication that the Soviets consider that a limited war in Europe would remain limited. On the contrary, the implication given, with two great coalitions face-to-face, as in Europe, is that a limited war would definitely expand into general war. Whether the Soviets regard local wars in other areas as less subject to the formula of inevitable escalation is not, as indicated above, altogether clear from the discussion in the present volume.

On the whole, while *Soviet Military Strategy* gives somewhat greater recognition to the need for Soviet preparation to deal with local wars than does other recent Soviet military literature, no doctrine of local war is developed in the book itself. Neither does the book deal with guerrilla operations and other forms of irregular warfare, as one finds such matters treated, for example, in the strategic writing of Mao Tse-tung. The authors come closest to the question of irregular warfare in a discussion (pp. 282–283) of Marxist-Leninist categories of possible wars. Among the categories mentioned are anticolonial revolutionary wars of "national liberation," which in Soviet literature customarily are associated with guerrilla warfare.[55] These "national liberation struggles" are said to be unavoidable "as long as imperialism and colonialism exist," and the authors repeat Khrushchev's pledge of Soviet support for them.[56]

However, the discussion does not indicate the role the Soviet

---

[55] For example, as pointed out by a Soviet writer on colonial problems: "Guerrilla warfare is the most typical form of armed struggle in national-liberation wars." Y. Dolgopolov, "National-Liberation Wars in the Present Epoch," *International Affairs,* No. 2, February 1962, p. 21.

[56] N. S. Khrushchev, "For New Victories of the World Communist Movement," *Kommunist,* No. 1, January 1961, p. 20. This is Khrushchev's report of January 6, 1961, on the Moscow Conference of Communist and Workers Parties in November–December 1960.

armed forces might be expected to play, if any, in support of national liberation uprisings, which, as Khrushchev put it in January 1961, "must not be identified with wars among states, with local wars." [57] By drawing this distinction, Khrushchev seemed to be saying that local war situations involving formal confrontation of Soviet and U.S. forces were dangerous and should be avoided, whereas national liberation struggles involving guerrilla and proxy forces might be supported without undue risk. The authors of the present volume do not elaborate on this distinction, but one may assume this is one of the things they have in mind when they note (p. 283) that Soviet military strategy faces a serious task in working out ways and means to deal not with modern wars in general, but with the conditions that apply to "a given particular war."

*Impact of Modern Weaponry.* A great deal of emphasis is placed in the present volume on the "revolutionary" impact of modern military technology on warfare and strategy. This factor has not only brought about a "pronounced improvement in combat capabilities" (p. 295), but it has also led, according to the authors:

> . . . to a radical break in the organizational forms of armed forces and methods of conducting military operations on every scale. Military strategy and military art as a whole, have undergone a revolution.

While both radical and traditionalist viewpoints in Soviet military thought would probably subscribe to this formulation in principle, its flavor seems nearer the radical end of the spectrum, as does the statement elsewhere (p. 326) that modern weapons technology is "the most revolutionary element of all" affecting armed forces and strategy.

The dominant role of nuclear weapons in modern warfare, for operations of all types, is repeatedly stressed in the current doctrine expounded in the pages of this work. A representative passage on page 297 states:

> In modern warfare nuclear weapons can be employed for various missions: strategic, operational, and tactical. . . . [They] permit the execution of military missions in a considerably shorter time than was possible in past wars.

Coupled with the importance ascribed to nuclear weapons are claims of Soviet nuclear superiority over the West, on the basis of

---

[57] *Ibid.*

supermegaton weapons. Thus, in giving on pages 296–297 a thumbnail history of the introduction of nuclear weapons and missiles into the Soviet armed forces, the authors say:

> Since the Soviet Union created a hydrogen weapon before the United States did, and most important of all, since the United States does not possess high-yield thermonuclear warheads of several megatons such as those possessed by the USSR, we consider our superiority in nuclear weapons over the Western bloc to be indisputable.

Elsewhere (p. 354), the authors mention that the Soviet Union possesses nuclear weapons of 100 megatons yield. They do not, however, anticipate the interesting observation made by Khrushchev some months after the publication of the present work that 100 megaton weapons are too large to be employed safely in Europe and that this yield represents the militarily useful limit of such weapons.[58] Neither, in asserting Soviet nuclear superiority, do the authors introduce numbers of nuclear weapons, as Khrushchev on the same occasion mentioned when he credited the United States with "40,000 nuclear bombs and warheads." [59] The question of comparative numbers in the nuclear stockpiles of the USSR and the United States is avoided by simply suggesting that both sides have accumulated large quantities.

In a further discussion on pages 296–297 of Soviet and Western build-up of nuclear stockpiles, the rather interesting point is mentioned that in the course of time "other states of both military groupings" are likely to acquire nuclear weapons. Whether, on the Soviet side, this refers to China acquiring nuclear weapons on her own, or Soviet intentions to furnish them to satellite countries, is not made clear. The discussion also expresses the expectation that as long as nuclear weapons remain in existence, both sides will, without doubt, employ them in a new war. The conclusion drawn is that solution of all problems connected with waging a nuclear war "must be considered the basic task of military strategy and the strategic leadership."

The prospect that belligerents might confine themselves to conventional warfare in any large-scale conflict does not seem to be

---

[58] Speech by Comrade N. S. Khrushchev to the 6th Congress of the German United Socialist Party, *Pravda,* January 17, 1963.
[59] *Ibid.*

entertained in current Soviet doctrine, even though the Soviet military establishment continues to maintain a dual capability for both conventional and nuclear warfare. One of the more striking aspects of the doctrine set forth in the present volume is its almost exclusive concentration on nuclear warfare. If a substantial body of doctrine dealing with non-nuclear war is extant, only the smallest corner of it is lifted in the present volume.

Although the authors devote comparatively little attention to conventional arms, the subject is by no means ignored. The continued place for conventional weapons is described in a representative passage on page 338, which states that conventional arms will find broad application in both local and world wars. This passage, incidentally, furnishes another indication that the Soviets may be thinking about local wars outside the framework of world war.

The development and improvement of conventional weapons apparently will continue together with the development of new types of weapons; the former have not yet lost their combat function and will be extensively employed in local and world wars, either independently or in conjunction with new types of weapons.

Together with nuclear weapons, missiles share first place in current Soviet strategic doctrine as the primary means of combat. The leading role ascribed to missile forces and their influence on the role of other forces receives more attention in the present volume than any other subject. The reader will note that a distinction is made between "strategic missiles" and what are called "operational and tactical missiles" (p. 299). The former, which include ICBM's and ballistic missiles of medium and intermediate range, such as were deployed to Cuba, are to be found in a separate branch of the Soviet armed forces, the "strategic missile forces." [60] The latter, as the book points out, are to be found in the armament of the air defense forces, the ground forces, the navy, and the air forces. Generally speaking, references to the primacy of missile forces in the present work pertain to the "strategic missile forces," although it is also indicated that missiles are becoming the basic means of firepower in other forces as well.

---

[60] Khrushchev's January 1960 Supreme Soviet speech first suggested that separate missile forces had been established. Malinovskii's October 1961 Party Congress speech confirmed that "a new type of armed forces has been created, strategic missile forces." A literal rendering of the Soviet term for these forces is "Rocket Troops of Strategic Designation."

The shift of focus in Soviet thinking to dominance of strategic operations over theater warfare between contending armies, which is closely linked in current Soviet doctrine with the introduction of modern weapons, is, as previously noted, a central feature of the present volume. A characteristic expression of this shift of emphasis appears in a passage on page 306, which states:

> . . . the relationship between the role and importance of armed combat waged by forces in direct contact with the enemy in the zone of military operations . . . and armed combat waged beyond this zone by strategic weapons of destruction, has changed sharply in the direction of increasing the role and importance of the latter.

In a future war, the text goes on, "massive missile and nuclear blows will be of decisive importance." Delivery of these strikes "cannot be made directly dependent on the course of battle between adversaries in direct contact on the land front." Development of modern weapons has changed the situation, the authors say (p. 402), so that:

> Today, the Strategic Missile Forces, which are the main weapon of modern war, will not accommodate their operations to those of the Ground Forces, but vice versa. The Ground Forces should exploit missile strikes fully in order to execute their own missions rapidly.

*Role of Ground Forces.*   The amount of emphasis given to strategic missile forces should not be taken to imply that the doctrine laid out in the present work writes off by any means the importance of ground forces and the significance of theater operations. Although the traditional primacy of land warfare doctrine is no longer sustained, there are strong specific arguments in the work for the continuing significance of ground forces and their role in military operations in land theaters. These arguments are linked with the notion that however important the activities of the strategic missile forces may be, final victory cannot be attained without ground forces meeting in theater battles. A representative passage (p. 341) reads:

> For final victory, it is absolutely necessary to defeat the enemy's armed forces and capture his military bases, if, for some reason, they have already not been destroyed. Strategically important regions must be occupied. In addition one must defend one's own

territory against invasion by the aggressor's ground armies, air forces and naval forces. Only modern ground forces, adequate in size, armament, and organization, can execute these and a number of other missions.

Discussions of theater warfare in the book concede that "the focal points of the war will be deep within belligerent countries" (p. 400), but the observation is also made that fierce, large-scale combat will also be waged "in military theaters near the front lines and borders."

The assessment that the "imperialist bloc is preparing vast ground forces, tactical air forces, and tactical missiles to achieve their aggressive aims in military theaters" (p. 410) is used to justify Soviet preparation for theater warfare on a large scale, even though the character of battlefield operations will differ greatly from the past.

The Soviet ground forces must possess firepower superiority over the enemy in both nuclear and conventional arms (p. 341), although, according to the authors (p. 341), tactical missile units organic to the ground forces will provide their main firepower and will clear the way for tanks and motorized infantry.

While the doctrine for ground forces calls for firepower superiority over the enemy and indicates that ground forces continue to represent the "numerically largest" branch of the armed forces, the question as to how large a ground forces establishment should be maintained is, as previously mentioned, one of the issues on which the authors of *Soviet Military Strategy* display an ambivalent attitude. Arguments for what would appear to be relatively modest-sized ground forces emerge in parts of the book where it is suggested that economic constraints will not permit massive forces on the old basis (pp. 338, 433), or that the enemy may capitulate before large ground battles are fought (pp. 94, 105). At the same time, the concept of small, technically well-equipped armies as a substitute for large forces is attacked (p. 338), and the repetitive argument is made that "mass, multi-million-man" armies are required. On balance, the concept of massive armies emerges as the dominant view in the book. The rationale for large forces rests on several points: theater warfare and mopping-up operations in Europe and Asia; replacement for large losses expected in nuclear warfare; occupation and control requirements in conquered areas; maintenance of internal order and security; and civil defense tasks (pp. 302, 310, 338, 341, 428, 438, 461, 462).

*Role of Air Forces.* The question of fitting the role of air forces into current strategic doctrine has obviously given the authors no less difficulty than assigning the proper weight to ground forces at a time when technological change and other factors are having a strong impact on the traditional doctrine for these forces. One has the impression, from the treatment in the book, that many decisions affecting the future development of air forces are pending or under debate, and that the authors therefore had to pick their way rather carefully over uncertain terrain. For example, they note (p. 346):

> Today, the air force is in a special situation. In recent years, there has been keen competition between bombers, missiles, and air defense weapons. In this competition, air defense weapons have gained the advantage over bomber aircraft. . . .
>
> Therefore, long-range bombers are rapidly yielding first place to intermediate-range ballistic missiles. Front line (tactical) bombers are also gradually being replaced by missiles.

After sounding this virtual requiem, however, the authors back off again (pp. 346–347), much as Khrushchev did in disavowing his earlier assertions that air forces had outlived their day:

> Of course, this process of replacement may take a long time, and if war breaks out bombers and missiles could be used simultaneously to attack targets located deep within enemy zones and theaters of military operations. This is all the more likely, since aircraft have still not completely exhausted their combat potential. By arming bombers with various types [air-to-surface] missiles capable of delivering blows at great distances, these bombers in a number of cases could operate beyond zones of active defense and execute combat missions effectively enough. In addition, some specific missions, for example, striking mobile targets could be executed more successfully by aircraft than by missiles.

In addition to giving bombers a further lease on life, the authors also foresee (p. 347) continued uses for tactical and fighter aviation, and a growing importance for the role of reconnaissance and transport aviation in modern warfare. At one point, in connection with airborne operations (p. 343), the statement is made that aerial envelopment best answers to the requirements of missile-nuclear war on the battlefield, by allowing quick maneuver and avoidance of contaminated zones.

*Role of Naval Forces.* While recognizing that in a future world war, with the United States as an enemy, greater responsibilities would fall on the Soviet navy than in the past (p. 420), the present work gives on the whole a rather summary and sketchy picture of the place of naval forces in Soviet strategy. Rather significantly, perhaps, no Soviet naval officers were among contributors to the work.

In ranking the wartime tasks of the navy in order of importance (p. 420), it is interesting that the authors place destruction of enemy carrier units ahead of destruction of missile-launching submarines. Another task foreseen for the navy is attack upon sea transport (p. 348). While there is mention of the possible use of Soviet missile-launching submarines for strategic attack on land targets, no marked interest in this capability is reflected in the book. Neither is serious attention given to the question of developing a seaborne capability for overseas projection of Soviet military forces.

The threat to the Soviet Union from Polaris subs is also treated in a rather minor key, although there is an exception in Chapter 2, concerning Western military preparations, of which more will be said later. In one representative passage in Chapter 6, the following statement on dealing with the Polaris threat is made (p. 409):

> Much has been said in the foreign press about nuclear submarines, armed with Polaris missiles. The assertion has been made that these are the most invulnerable means for the use of missiles. Actually, these weapons are vulnerable. Homing missiles launched by submarines and surface ships are an effective weapon against missile-carrying nuclear submarines.

In view of the difficulties that development of an effective anti-submarine warfare system against nuclear submarines of the Polaris type seems to present, one wonders to what extent Soviet naval thinking would endorse the rather optimistic view offered here by the authors.

*Active Defense Doctrine.* The present volume reflects a strategic doctrine calling for rather heavy reliance on active defense against nuclear attack. This emphasis on the value of active defense, which

Soviet thinking has consistently stressed [61] and which is reflected in Soviet efforts to build a strong system of air defense against strategic bomber forces, apparently carries over into the missile era. While the treatment of active defense in the present volume rather carefully avoids flat claims that effective antimissile defenses are already an accomplished fact, both antimissile and antiaircraft defenses are given an optimistic evaluation. A pertinent passage (p. 307) reads:

> Further improvement in antimissile and antiaircraft defense, primarily by automated control of antiaircraft missile complexes; the creation of effective means of combatting enemy ballistic missiles in flight and mastery of the techniques of using them; organization of a defense against weapons of mass destruction plus other measures—should maximally reduce losses from enemy nuclear attacks and should preserve the continued functioning of the interior of the country and the combat capacity of the Armed Forces.

Although this and similar treatment elsewhere in the book suggests that the Soviets hope their active defense efforts will pay off, one also gets the impression that they may not be altogether confident that this would in fact be the case. This impression is conveyed, for example, by a specific reminder accompanying the above-cited passage (p. 307) to the effect that available means of nuclear attack still definitely predominate over means of defense.

> But one must recognize that the present instrumentalities of nuclear attack are undoubtedly superior to the instrumentalities of defense against them.

The offense-versus-defense question is, of course, more than a matter of academic interest to Soviet strategic policy-makers, for on it may hinge decisions involving the direction in which very substantial resources are to be committed. In view of this, it is somewhat surprising that no real collision of opinions on the relative value of offensive versus defensive emphasis in strategic doctrine

---

[61] In addition to Khrushchev's various references to the subject, Soviet military theorists and commanders have frequently placed strong emphasis on the value of active air defense. For example, see Lieutenant General S. N. Krasil'nikov, "On the Nature of Modern War," *Red Star,* November 18, 1960; Marshal S. Biriuzov, "Soldiers of Peace Are on Guard," *Sovetskaia Rossiia (Soviet Russia),* October 3, 1961; Interview with Colonel General P. N. Kuleshov, *Red Star,* November 18, 1961; Colonel I. Sidel'nikov, "On Soviet Military Doctrine," *Red Star,* May 11, 1962.

appears to be evident in the present volume or other published Soviet military literature. Perhaps the reason is that both active defense and the concept that a good offense is the best defense are accorded a high value in Soviet strategic doctrine, and are thus able to coexist comfortably with each other. This point is illustrated by a passage (p. 417) that states that protection of the country from enemy nuclear attack is best achieved by one's own offensive blows against the enemy:

> . . . mainly by destroying the enemy's nuclear weapons where they are based. However, there is no guarantee that significant air and missile forces can be destroyed at their bases, especially at the outset of a war if the enemy attacks by surprise.

This recognition that one might not fully succeed in blunting the enemy's nuclear attack forces at their bases, and the consequent need for active defenses to deal with attacks from residual forces, apparently keeps the concept of active defense from clashing with offensive doctrine in Soviet strategic thinking.

*Civil Defense.*   As a footnote to Soviet thinking on active defense, it may be observed that the present volume reflects definite military interest in an effective system of civil defense. This is a subject on which there has apparently been some internal debate, as indicated by an article in early 1962 by Colonel General of Aviation O. Tolstikov, then acting head of the Soviet civil-defense service (*Grazhdanskaia Oborona*), in which Tolstikov referred to differences of view on civil defense that had been settled in favor of a vigorous civil defense program.[62] Some of these differences apparently concerned the value of shelters when multimegaton weapons are involved. Occasional public statements of Soviet leaders deprecating the value of shelters have sometimes been interpreted to indicate lack of Soviet interest in civil defense measures generally.[63] This view accords neither with the extensive civil defense indoctrination program that has been under way in the Soviet Union for some time, nor with the description of civil defense by

---

[62] Colonel General O. Tolstikov, "A Matter of Great Importance to the State," *Voennye znaniia (Military Knowledge)*, No. 2, 1962, p. 22.

[63] Statements questioning the value of shelters include remarks by Mrs. Khrushchev to a group of Western peace-marchers in Moscow in October 1961, and a statement by Marshal Malinovskii in an interview in January 1962. *New York Times,* October 7, 1961; *Pravda,* January 24, 1962.

various Soviet military men as being of "extraordinary" importance in strengthening the country's defense capability.[64]

The authors, in dealing with civil defense, throw no specific light on the question of shelter planning, other than to indicate (p. 459) that "building shelters" is a necessary feature of the civil defense program. However, the book does reflect the military view that civil defense is an integral part of the Soviet defense posture, supplementing active military measures for defense against nuclear attack. In this connection, the authors state (p. 420):

> . . . no matter how effective an antiaircraft and antimissile defense system may be, it is essential to have prepared civil defense forces to: rapidly eliminate the aftermath of nuclear attacks; evacuate population from regions subjected to nuclear attack; organize emergency medical aid; extinguish fires, re-establish order; and carry out other urgent measures.[65]

*Main Military-Strategic Goals of a Future War.*   In all past wars, according to the analysis in the present work (p. 304), the main military-strategic goals of the belligerents were the defeat of the enemy's armed forces, and thereafter, seizure and occupation of territory and governing centers. Under conditions of a future war, considering the "massive use of nuclear weapons for the purpose of achieving the annihilation or capitulation of the enemy in the shortest possible time," a new question is posed:

> What, under these conditions, will constitute the main military-strategic goal of the war: defeat of the enemy's armed forces, as was the case in the past, or the annihilation and destruction of objectives in the enemy's rear, for the purpose of disorganizing it?

> Soviet military strategy gives the following answer to this question: both of these goals must be achieved simultaneously. . . .

Two main factors are cited as the basis for this conclusion. First, the need to defeat the enemy decisively in the shortest possible time, for which "it will be necessary to deprive him simultaneously of the military, political and economic means of waging war." Second, the existence of modern weapons, which create "the real possibility of achieving these aims simultaneously."

[64] Speech by Marshal V. I. Chuikov at the 5th All-Union Congress of DOSAAF, *Sovetskii patriot* (*Soviet Patriot*), May 26, 1962.

[65] See Leon Gouré, *Civil Defense in the Soviet Union,* University of California Press, Berkeley and Los Angeles, 1962, *passim,* for a detailed account of Soviet civil defense up to the end of 1961.

This formula of military-strategic goals, the reader will note, attempts to bridge a gap that has been opened in Soviet strategic doctrine by two quite different conceptions of fighting a war. On the one hand, traditional doctrine has rested on the concept that the aims of combatants were to be achieved by defeat of the enemy's armed forces. On the other hand, a new concept has appeared, which also finds expression in the present work. In its less radical form this new concept holds that strategic nuclear forces can be used independently of other forces for attainment of major military-strategic goals, and that therefore other forces must learn to exploit strategic strikes. In its more sweeping form, the new concept suggests that war might be won by strategic attack on the enemy's economy and morale without full defeat of his armed forces. By proposing a formulation that combines the two conceptions, the authors have apparently sought to avoid having to render a judgment in favor of one or the other.

At one point in the work (p. 274) the authors assert that under modern conditions "the chances of achieving the most decisive political goals in armed combat are enormously improved." The discussion here might conceivably be taken as a veiled argument for another world war to complete the achievement of communist goals. However, as one might expect, the authors do not draw this conclusion. Rather, they turn to an attack on "bourgeois ideologists" for attempting to disguise the "horror of nuclear war" and to divert popular attention from "imperialist" war preparations.

*Targeting Doctrine.* Frequent general allusions to the targets for strategic forces occur in the work, and the targeting doctrine that emerges follows the same undeviating formula, combining counterforce, urban-industrial, and population targets. This is not a refined nor discriminate targeting doctrine, and, as noted previously, it suggests little interest in working out "ground rules" for restrained nuclear targeting.[66]

---

[66] One of the most vociferous Soviet military deprecators of this idea has been Marshal Sokolovskii, head of the collective team that prepared the present volume. In "A Suicidal Strategy," *Red Star*, July 19, 1962, Sokolovskii strongly scored what he termed "rules for waging a nuclear war" advanced by the United States. In the same article, Sokolovskii suggested that the Soviet Union enjoys a targeting advantage over the United States because the Soviet Union is able, according to him, "to shelter our nuclear weapons and missiles in such a manner as to make them invulnerable to enemy reconnaissance and strategic means of attack."

Several factors seem to underlie the lack of Soviet interest in a philosophy of selective or controlled targeting. One of these appears to be the doctrinaire assumption that the political aims of the belligerents in any general war between the communist and the Western camps would be unlimited, and that therefore neither side could be expected to limit the use of the weapons at its disposal. Another and perhaps more cogent reason is probably that the Soviet Union finds itself in an inferior strategic posture and consequently wishes to emphasize the deterrent value of its strategic forces by professing no interest in ground rules for restrained targeting.

At the same time, pure population attacks—the ultimate expression of disdain for militarily rational target selection—does not seem to be part of the targeting doctrine expressed in the book either. In fact, among the various target systems mentioned, a constant point on which emphasis is placed is that the nuclear delivery means of the enemy, "the basis of his military power," constitute the priority target system. Then, in the usual order given in the book, come other main groupings of the enemy's armed forces, his economic base, command and control system, and other "important strategic targets" (pp. 298, 400, 408).

Within the category of nuclear delivery means, strategic nuclear forces seem generally to be further singled out as the most important targets to be marked for destruction, on the grounds that these can hurt one the most. For example, on pages 399–400, it is stated:

> The decisive weapon in modern warfare is the strategic nuclear weapon. The long-range delivery vehicle for this weapon is located far from the front lines or the borders, at a great distance from the theaters of military operations. Unless these weapons are destroyed or neutralized, it is impossible to protect the country's vital centers from destruction, and one cannot count on successfully achieving the aim of the war even if the [enemy] troop formations deployed in the military theaters are destroyed.

The primary target for operations in theaters is identified (p. 411) as: "enemy nuclear weapons." Without their elimination, "one cannot expect nowadays to conduct any military operations successfully, offensive or defensive, in military theaters."

In a discussion emphasizing the importance of strategic attacks against the "military and economic base of the enemy" (pp. 409–

410), it is asserted that the economies of the Western countries, including the United States, are more vulnerable than those of the Communist Bloc to nuclear weapons, because of denser target concentration, exposed communications, and dependence on imports. This is cited as a reason why any nuclear war started by the imperialists "will undoubtedly be turned against them." Similar assertions have been made from time to time by Khrushchev and others that the Soviet Union would enjoy an advantage in the event of nuclear war because of its large territory, lower population density, dispersed industry, and so on.

The destruction of the enemy's economy will require "a large number of nuclear weapons" and it is poitned out, furthermore, that the "first massive nuclear missile strikes may not immediately influence the course of the war" (p. 409). This is one of the few cases in which the authors allude to the tactics of the missile strike in the initial period of the war.

*Decisive Importance of Initial Period.*   The present volume, as previously noted, strongly reaffirms the primary weight now given in Soviet military thinking to the decisive importance of the initial phase of a future war, and the consequent necessity for developing a strategy and force structure aimed at bringing the war to a close with minimum losses in the shortest possible period of time, mainly by means of massive missile attacks.

Three significant doctrinal points are emphasized with respect to the initial period: *first,* its decisive influence on war outcome, owing to the fact that modern combat means can achieve exceptionally great strategic results in the briefest time period; *second,* in view of the potentially disastrous consequences of nuclear surprise attack by the enemy, the overriding importance of successfully frustrating such an attack, including the use of pre-emption; *third,* the need for maintenance of a constant high level of combat readiness.

With regard to the first point, although current doctrine is fully agreed on the decisive character of the initial period, it is rather curious that no very precise definition of how long this period may be expected to last is given, nor is the degree of its "decisiveness" spelled out. Soviet military literature has never been very precise on either of these matters, although there have been past indications in military writing and in statements by Khrushchev that the initial phase might be measured in days, hours, or even minutes.[67]

No doubt, definition of this interval and its decisiveness is a matter at sharp issue, since it seriously affects the positions taken by various schools of thought on such basic questions as short versus long war, the size of forces-in-being that should be maintained, the merits of preattack and postattack mobilization, the connection between warning and readiness posture, and so on.[68] To some extent, the distinction between the decisive nature of the initial period and the attainment of final victory that is expected to come after an undefined interval of further warfare, hinges on the point that final victory requires complete control over the enemy.

A standard formulation in the present work on the decisive character of the initial period can be found in the following passage on page 308:

> In the very first minutes of the war, the belligerents may use up their carriers, missiles, and aircraft, accumulated in peacetime along with their stockpiles of nuclear weapons in order to destroy and devastate the enemy's most important targets throughout his entire territory, and to achieve their main political, military-strategic aims within a brief period of time and at the very outset of the war. Therefore the initial period of a modern missile war will obviously be the main and decisive period and will predetermine the development and outcome of the entire war. The fighting in this period obviously will be most fierce and destructive.

This statement sounds very close to a description of "lightning war." However, it is also a matter of considerable interest that in

---

[67] N. S. Khrushchev, Report to the Supreme Soviet of the USSR, *Pravda*, January 15, 1960; *Voenno-istoricheskii zhurnal (Journal of Military History)*, No. 8, August 1960, p. 53.

[68] In general, the prevailing view expressed officially by such leading military spokesmen as Malinovskii has tended, since publication of the present volume, to put still greater stress on the "decisive" character of the initial period and the new demands it imposes on Soviet military planning, as contrasted with the situation in the past under conditions of prolonged warfare. For example, in October 1962 Malinovskii wrote as follows: "In the past it was possible to step up one's efforts gradually in the production of equipment and weapons, in the training of cadres, and so on, in order to attain victory in the course of a prolonged war. Nowadays, with the availability of nuclear weapons and missiles, decisive results can be achieved in the initial period of a war itself. I am not far from the mark when I say that a great part of the effort which the country and the army formerly expended toward victory over a period of several years must now be invested in the initial missile-nuclear attack and the subsequent coordinated operations of all types of forces." *Pravda*, October 25, 1962.

treating the decisive influence of the initial period on the outcome of war, the authors avoid specific discussion of lightning war or blitzkrieg—a subject that has appeared in previous Soviet military literature. A major 1960 work, for example, had indicated that:

> Soviet military science does not deny the lightning method of the conduct of war. It does point out that a favorable combination of economic, political and military conditions is required for successful conduct of lightning war.[69]

Failure of the authors of the present work to explore this question in the context of discussion of the initial period would seem to provide a further indication that the degree of decisiveness of the initial period is a charged doctrinal issue on which disagreement persists. Whatever the case may be with respect to Soviet thinking about the possibility of a war being brought to an end by a lightning attack at the very outset, there seems to be no question that the requirement for frustrating a surprise nuclear attack is very high on the Soviet agenda.

Indeed, the second doctrinal point stressed in connection with the initial period deals precisely with this question. As put on page 314:

> . . . the main task of Soviet military strategy is working out means for reliably repelling a surprise nuclear attack by an aggressor.

The doctrine of pre-emption, a corollary of Soviet concern about the potentially decisive effects of a first strike against the Soviet Union, is ratified in the present work, but not spelled out in detail. The authors stick close to the carefully phrased formulation employed by Malinovskii at the XXIInd Party Congress in October 1961, stating (pp. 313–314) that:

> . . . the initial period of a future war as well as the means of breaking up the aggressive plans of the enemy by dealing him a crushing blow in time will be of decisive significance for the outcome of the entire war.

---

[69] Smirnov, *et al., op. cit.,* p. 243. This is the book whose authors were taken to task in Chapter 6 of the present work for holding backward views on the influence of nuclear-rocket weapons on warfare. Subsequent to the May 1960 book which gave lightning war a place in Soviet military science, one of its authors, Colonel S. Kozlov took an opposite position, suggesting differences between the authors of the book. Kozlov said, in an article in *Kommunist vooruzhennykh sil (Communist of the Armed Forces)*, No. 11, June 1961, p. 53, that overvaluation of missiles and nuclear weapons could lead to "one-sided" notions like blitzkrieg, which he inferred were mistakenly held by "some comrades."

Considerable interest attaches to the guarded treatment of pre-emption in this work. Since the XXIInd Party Congress, the subject has been addressed in Soviet military literature from time to time in terms indicating that "study and practice" of ways to improve the Soviet pre-emptive posture are matters that deserve the closest attention.[70] Furthermore, the question obviously has great bearing on a strategy intended to frustrate a surprise first strike, particularly for a strategically weaker power that professes to fear such an attack. While many aspects of Soviet thinking about pre-emption and the problem of repelling a surprise attack presumably would not be disclosed in an open publication, it is still rather surprising that in this major work on military strategy the subject has not been exposed to somewhat more discussion.

The question of pre-emption involves a number of considerations, both political and military, which may account for its guarded treatment in the present work. For one thing, it raises the politically delicate problem of distinguishing between *pre-emptive* action (taken in response to an enemy's initiative) and *preventive* action (where one takes the initiative into one's own hands). For obvious reasons, military discussion that might lay the Soviet Union open to charges of harboring preventive war designs would not fit the Soviet political line.

A second consideration counseling careful treatment of the subject is that a pre-emptive capability is essentially the resort of a strategically inferior power. Militarily, it offers the prospect of blunting an enemy attack, but it is not the basis for a strategy that holds much promise of a favorable war outcome. In the Soviet case, this means that too searching a scrutiny of the implications of pre-emption could lead to internal doubt and questioning about the Soviet military posture.

At the same time, a declaratory policy of pre-emption must bear an important load so far as Soviet political strategy is concerned.

---

[70] For example, by Colonel I. Sidel'nikov, "On Soviet Military Doctrine," *Red Star,* May 11, 1962; Captain B. Demidov, "The Decisive Conditions for Creative Development of Soviet Military Science," *Kommunist vooruzhennykh sil* (*Communist of the Armed Forces*), No. 9, May 1962, p. 25. The latter wrote: ". . . the main task of the armed forces in their combat and operational training . . . is the study and practice of ways of reliably beating off an enemy surprise nuclear attack, of ways of anticipating his aggressive intentions by means of striking a devastating blow in time. It is this task that determines the direction of military-theoretical thought at the present time."

In effect, it must remain sufficiently credible to cause the United States to worry that in the event of a really serious crisis the Soviet Union might pre-empt. In this connection, it is significant perhaps that official revival of the pre-emption theme by the Soviets in the fall of 1961 came at a time when the Soviet Union may have feared that the United States was bent upon exploiting its superior strategic position for political gains in the Berlin situation. Later with regard to Cuba in the fall of 1962 the threat of Soviet pre-emption failed to meet the credibility test, with consequent damage to Soviet political strategy. The point is, so far as this discussion is concerned, that the political function of pre-emption in over-all Soviet policy is too touchy to allow the subject to be exposed publicly to very much technical inquiry.

In the present volume, the principal answer offered to the problem of repelling a surprise nuclear attack is that Soviet forces, "especially strategic missile forces" (p. 314) and long-range air forces (p. 411), must be kept in a high state of training and combat readiness, prepared, presumably, to launch a pre-emptive blow if preparations for a surprise attack on the Soviet Union were detected. However, no criteria for situations that would justify a momentous decision to pre-empt are explored. Neither is another possible avenue ever mentioned—resort by the Soviet Union to a surprise first strike on its own account. While this "solution" would turn the problem around, and is certainly one on which some attention must be bestowed in Soviet strategic thinking, it has not, for obvious reasons, found its way into this book.

The closest approach to thinking along these lines occurs in a passage on page 159 in which the authors pose the following hypothetical question:

> If general nuclear war is dangerous to both sides, then what must be done so that it can lead to the attainment of the desired objectives, that is, the destruction of the enemy with the least possible losses and destruction for oneself?

The proposed "solution" is attributed to the "imperialists": first, to achieve nuclear, missile, and space superiority; then, to launch a surprise attack that may paralyze the enemy and decide his fate "within the very first days of the war." This "solution," while attributed to the West, may reveal what some Soviet theorists feel is the preferred answer, but which would be exceedingly awkward to put down on paper if describing their own strategy.[71]

While the notion of pre-emption and the singling out of readiness of the strategic missile forces would suggest that the main thrust of present doctrine on dealing with surprise attack is in the direction of attempting to destroy the enemy's striking forces on their bases by one's own offensive blows, the possibility that one might not beat the opponent to the draw is also recognized. It is here that additional reliance is placed on active defenses to blunt the weight of an initial enemy attack, although, as previously noted, it is not at all clear, despite their strong adherence to the doctrine of active defense, how much confidence the Soviets really attach to the prospects of active defense in the face of what they describe as the predominance of modern offensive weapons over defensive means.

*Military Uses of Space.*   Current Soviet strategic thought, as reflected in the present work,[72] is focused mainly on the problems of war as a terrestrial phenomenon. The brief treatment of military uses of space is couched largely in terms of alleged U.S. plans for exploitation of space as "the strategic theater of tomorrow" (p. 424). Veiled acknowledgment of a Soviet military space program can be inferred from statements (p. 427) that the Soviet Union must give attention to ways of using space for defense purposes and to ensure that the West does not "gain any superiority in this field." No indication is given of what kind of military space projects the Soviets may have in mind.

*Chemical and Biological Warfare.*   Reference to the anticipated use of chemical and biological weapons in a future war occurs several times in the present work (pp. 304, 337), linked with the allegation that the United States intends to use them in combination with nuclear weapons. Although there is no discussion of specific employment by Soviet forces, the implication is plain that the Soviets would be prepared to do so.

*Wartime Strategic Leadership.*   The present volume offers an outline of the possible top structure of Soviet strategic leadership in a future war which is of particular interest, because little hint as to current Soviet thinking on this subject has appeared in the open

---

[71] This would be consistent with the emphasis on the importance of destroying enemy strategic weapons before they are employed (p. 399).

[72] One of the authors of the present volume, Lieutenant Colonel V. Larionov, has written elsewhere on the prospects of space warfare. See, for example, "Missiles and Strategy," *Red Star,* March 18, 1962.

military literature. The arrangements envisaged follow very closely those of World War II except those relating to co-ordination of satellite armed forces with the Soviet war effort, for which there was no World War II parallel.

According to the description given on pages 494–495, over-all wartime leadership of the country and the armed forces might be vested in an agency similar to the State Defense Committee of World War II. It would be headed by the First Secretary of the CPSU and the head of government, to whom could "also be entrusted the functions of Supreme High Commander of all the armed forces." Thus, under present circumstances, if war should come, Khrushchev would assume a role similar to that of Stalin in World War II. Only such "an organic relationship between the leadership of the country and the armed forces" can, according to the book, provide the most efficient employment of the country's resources and its armed forces to achieve victory.

Direct leadership of the armed forces would be exercised by the Supreme Headquarters (Stavka) of the Supreme High Command (VGK), as was the case in World War II. The Stavka, as described in the book, "will represent a collective organ of leadership under the chairmanship of the Supreme High Commander." The General Staff, as before, would be the basic agency of the Stavka to provide direction of all branches of services.

With respect to coalition leadership, it is suggested that the Political Consultative Committee of the Warsaw Pact could be "the highest political agency for co-ordinating all efforts of the countries in the socialist camp." Military direction would be handled somewhat differently, with military units of various satellite countries integrated in joint "fronts" in the combat theaters. Command of these fronts would be, as the authors put it, "entrusted to the Supreme High Command of the Soviet armed forces." Interestingly enough, the discussion of coalition arrangements seems to make no provision for inclusion of Communist China.

Whether a contemplated revival of the World War II leadership structure indicates Soviet satisfaction with it as a model for present-day conditions, or whether the authors merely preferred to tread on known ground in this area, it is difficult to say.

*Achievement of Superiority.*   While some Soviet elite statements and actions suggest that the Soviets would like to win acceptance, at least at the present time, for a doctrine of strategic parity with the

West, the main thrust of the strategic doctrine expressed in the present volume is clearly in the direction of achievement of superiority. The notion of the necessity of gaining superiority can be found not only in connection with strategic forces as such, but also as it touches on other elements of national strength. Both qualitative and quantitative superiority are to be sought.

There is some ambiguity on the matter of qualitative versus quantitative superiority. In some passages, they are said to be of equal importance; in others, quantity is the criterion stressed, as when speaking (p. 409) of the "large number" of nuclear weapons required for successful attack on the enemy's economy. On the other hand, the statement is also made (p. 335) that "at the present time, in gaining superiority in nuclear weapons, their quality and the technique for their employment are more important than their number."

In a discussion (p. 340) of strategic missile forces and the need for "constant attention to their development and improvement," the assertion is made that attainment of qualitative and quantitative superiority in these forces is one of today's "most important problems in organizing and developing the armed forces."

Another statement that relates the achievement of superiority to keeping close watch on enemy developments and on countering them appears on page 349. This statement also implies that across-the-board, not merely selective, superiority is the Soviet desideratum:

> In organizing and developing the armed forces, one must also evaluate the directions in which the enemy is developing in order to find an appropriate countermeasure for each new enemy weapon. Here, the main thing is to maintain constant superiority over the enemy in the basic branches of the armed forces, weapons and ways of waging war. It is especially necessary to have constant superiority over the enemy in firepower, troop mobility, and maneuverability.

The "material prerequisites of victory" receive considerable attention in the book in connection with attainment of superiority. These lie in the ability of the economy to provide the necessary tools of war at the appropriate time. Incidentally, the stress in current doctrine on the initial period of a war is reflected in Soviet thinking on the role of economic strength in war. Whereas emphasis once lay on the ability of the economy to support the wartime mobilization of large forces and resources for a lengthy war, the key criterion now stressed (p. 314) is the ability of technology and industry to provide powerful and modern peacetime forces-in-being for successfully meeting the critical early phases of a war:

> The ability of the country's economy to mass produce military equipment, especially missiles, and to establish superiority over the enemy in modern weapons are the material prerequisites of victory. *The ability of the economy to assure the maximum power to the Armed Forces for dealing an annihilatory blow to the aggressor in the initial period of the war will be decisive for the outcome of a future war.*

At the same time, however, peacetime preparation of the economy should also provide (p. 326) for meeting military needs if the war should be prolonged. In addition to superiority in economic and technical support of military forces, emphasis is placed (p. 314) on ability to organize the defeat of the enemy, to utilize effectively the available means of combat.

One might say that while Soviet military thought seems to be agreed on the desirability of attaining across-the-board superiority over the United States, the question of how this is to be achieved, given the relative resources of the two countries, is a central problem to which no answer is forthcoming in this book. In effect, the superiority doctrine sketched is a potential source of further strain within the Soviet bureaucracy, insofar as it tends to blur priorities by which the claims of competing sectors on available Soviet resources could be measured.

*Victory in a Future War.*   As suggested by the foregoing discussion, the concept of "no victor" in a future war is not admitted to a place in the doctrine revealed in this work. It is held (p. 313) that the socialist camp will be the victor in a future war because "the real relationship between the political, economic, and military forces of the two systems" is claimed to have changed in its favor: "However, victory in a future war will not come of itself. It must be thoroughly prepared for and secured in advance" (p. 313). Conclusive or "full defeat" of the enemy is an accepted article of the doctrine expressed in the book.

So far as a world war between the "imperialist and socialist camps" is concerned, the doctrine holds (p. 282) that it would be "the decisive armed clash between two opposing world social systems," thus seeming to allow no room for such a war to end short of full defeat of one or the other. "Full defeat" is defined to include crushing the enemy's armed forces, seizure of his territories, and eradication of his social-political system. In a passage on page 287, the West is charged with holding such war aims toward the Soviet camp, which means that:

> To protect the achievements of socialism, the Soviet Union and the peoples democracies will be compelled to aim for results no less conclusive: to destroy completely the enemy's armed forces, at the same time to disorganize his homeland, to crush his will to resist, and to help the people free themselves from imperialist oppression.

The latter part of this formula seems to imply that Soviet expectation of victory rests partly on the concept of class conflict in the West and the assumption that "peace forces" there would arise to help overthrow their governments. No details of the kind of political settlement that would be imposed on the loser are spelled out. However, it is stated in connection with the role of ground troops (p. 410) that one of their functions would be to facilitate "the establishment of the appropriate order and the peaceful regulation of all postwar questions. . . ." Judging from past performance, it is not difficult to imagine the "appropriate order" to which the presence of Soviet troops on a loser's territory would be expected to lead.

As for the military path toward attainment of the "decisive political and military goals" set for the Soviet Union and its allies in a future war, the formula laid down in the present volume again reflects the ambivalence in current strategic doctrine as regards the concepts of a short decisive war and a long one.

On the one hand, the prospect is offered (p. 94) that "modern strategic weapons . . . make it possible to achieve decisive results in winning victory in war sometimes even without resort to tactical and field forces and their weapons," and that (p. 105) a country subjected to "massive missile blows may find it necessary to surrender even before its armed forces have suffered decisive defeat." As pointed out previously, these views reflect a departure from traditional Soviet doctrine, and suggest that at least some Soviet strategists may count on destroying the will of the enemy as the key to victory.

On the other hand, it is also argued that however significant may be the role of strategic forces in a future war it will not be enough to rely on them to destroy the enemy's means of nuclear delivery, to rout his main forces, and to disorganize his rear. Rather, for final victory:

> . . . it will be absolutely necessary to smash the enemy's armed forces completely, deprive him of strategic areas of deployment, liquidate his military bases, and occupy his strategically important regions [p. 302].

All these and other tasks leading to final victory can only be accomplished by ground forces. What the doctrine seemingly fails to provide is a formula calling for development of the overseas capabilities required by these forces to accomplish such tasks against the principal enemy, the United States.

Thus, two conceptions of the military road to victory vie with each other in the strategic doctrine expounded in the present volume, but each appears to have its flaws. The first, embodying the concept of quick victory by crushing the will of the enemy, involves great risk. Many things could go wrong. Against a powerful enemy, this strategy might cut the other way. As a strategy for the side with inferior strategic forces, it might afford some hope of salvaging victory in the event a war had to be fought, but it would hardly offer the margin of assurance on which a bold policy could be based. The second conception, while more orthodox and less risky, proposes a strategy peculiarly ill-adapted to closing with a transoceanic enemy, and what is more, calls for a formidable drain on resources, which even a country richer than the Soviet Union would find it hard to bear. It seems clear, in short, that the problem of formulating a war-winning military strategy remains an unfinished item on the Soviet agenda. Which is all the more reason, perhaps, for supposing that Soviet political strategy will seek further ways to carry the day.

## Soviet Image of the West

In contrast to customary Soviet lore on the "imperialist enemy," the present volume provides an unusually candid and generally accurate account of U.S.-NATO military developments and strategy. To be sure, the account is not free of serious distortions, especially with regard to Western motives and intentions, and it thus conveys an image of the West that one finds impossible to accept.

Nevertheless, the book marks a departure from the standard Soviet picture of the West that is worth noting in a number of respects, especially the material presented in Chapter 2.

Perhaps, the most arresting feature of this chapter is the realistic presentation it gives of U.S. military power, mainly by bringing together in one place a considerable body of cold figures on U.S. forces. While the material has apparently been drawn from open U.S. sources, it goes beyond what has been available to Soviet readers in any broadly circulated Soviet publication to date on the size and composition of U.S. strategic weapons systems, both existing and as planned through 1966 (pp. 171–179). In particular, the projected figures for 1966 are new in Soviet military literature.

The projected U.S. strength figures used in the table (on p. 177) have undergone some change since the Soviet authors gathered material for this work. Nevertheless, one can surmise that the figures will have a significant impact on many Soviet readers, for they picture a very formidable opponent indeed. The image of an America being rapidly left in the backwash of superior Soviet military power will be a little hard to sustain in light of the straightforward treatment here of presently operational and projected U.S. striking forces. Comparative figures for Soviet strategic forces are not given, of course, and this could, to some extent, soften the impact on the average Soviet reader, who may take comfort in his government's assurances that Soviet military power remains unmatched.

From the viewpoint of the Soviet military, the picture given in the present work of a U.S. military threat of great magnitude may have certain self-serving aspects, for it could strengthen the position of those who feel that the Soviet military establishment should get an even larger slice of available resources than it has received in the past. Incidentally, the book was sent to the press, though perhaps only by coincidence, in May 1962 at the same time the government was announcing such guns-versus-butter measures as increases in prices of milk and meat, and when Marshal Malinovskii in a *Kommunist* article went out of his way to make an explicit justification of heavy military spending.[73]

The authors of the present volume, particularly in Chapter 2, show a tendency to credit the United States with a greater capacity

---

[73] R. Malinovskii, "The Program of the KPSS and the Questions of Strengthening the Armed Forces of the USSR," *Kommunist,* No. 7, May 1962, p. 17.

for strategy formulation and with a better understanding of the link between politics and military strategy than has customarily been the case in Soviet military literature. While the work still boasts of the superiority of Marxist-Leninist thought in the area of military strategy, it no longer leaves the impression that Western strategists are unable to perceive important political-strategic truths. For example, warning that it would be a mistake to underestimate the capabilities of "bourgeois military thought," the book states (p. 205):

> The enormous scientific and technical advances of the principal capitalist countries facilitate to a certain extent the development of a military strategy responsive to the changing conditions of war.

Considerable attention is given to the place of weapons system selection in U.S. strategy. The authors observe (p. 206) that in the American view "the main task of modern strategy is the proper selection of appropriate weapons systems for the next 10 to 15 years or more." They then go on to say (p. 207):

> . . . it is recognized [by the U.S. command] that military strategy must seek the most rational utilization of budgets and resources to attain the military aims of the state (or coalition), and that the appropriate military decisions must be made only after an economic analysis of the various alternatives.

The tone of the discussion here seems neither patronizing nor disparaging, and one has the impression that the authors may be speaking obliquely to some of their own people on whom they hope the lesson will not be lost.

A lengthy description of the debates in the United States between 1953 and 1961 over defense policy and strategy is also given in Chapter 2 (pp. 151–171). The account includes a reasonably accurate discussion of how the United States dropped the strategy of "massive retaliation" and took up that of "flexible response," although the reasons for change are given a characteristic communist twist to picture the West as plotting aggression against the Soviet Bloc, attempting to suppress national-liberation movements, and so on.

In discussing U.S. strategic policy evolution, the authors stress (p. 168) that while the United States is preparing for both general nuclear wars and limited wars, the main efforts under the new strategy are still devoted to the former. U.S. attempts to change the balance of conventional strength between West and East should not obscure the fact, they note, that the main emphasis as before is on build-up of strategic nuclear forces.

It is rather difficult to judge whether the Soviets find the new trends in U.S. strategy more complicated to deal with than the old, because specific preferences are not voiced. There does appear, however, to be a definite shift in previous Soviet assertions that the United States is one-weapon oriented. The authors note (p. 170) that while the United States sees little possibility any longer for use of strategic nuclear forces in limited wars, its nonstrategic as well as its strategic forces will both be employed for general war. In fact, they say, the United States considers that victory in a general nuclear war can only be attained by joint effort of all arms, even though strategic means may have the central role. This concept is close to the one the Soviets have claimed as their own.

In dealing with over-all Western strategy, the authors assert (p. 151) that while "the strategies of the principal capitalist countries bore a distinctly national character," they have now been merged into a single global strategy designed to serve U.S. ends. The concepts of interdependence and balanced armed forces within the aggressive military blocs of the West are analyzed (p. 168) as devices used by American ruling circles to ensure that various national forces of the Western alliance will be responsive to American needs.

American possession of the bulk of strategic forces is asserted to be a means for the United States to exert political and military pressure on its allies to U.S. advantage. Opposition of some allies, notably France and Germany, to this American dominance in the strategic field has led (p. 168) to their demands for nuclear sharing. While the temper of this discussion is critical of U.S. relations with its allies, the authors appear to consider that the United States has nevertheless succeeded in welding together a unified coalition strategy on a global scale.

## Doctrinal Lacunae

As the reader of *Soviet Military Strategy* will presently discover for himself, there are some notable gaps in the strategic doctrine developed in the work. Some of these have been mentioned in the preceding discussion, such as the lack of definition concerning decisiveness of the initial period of a war; the vague treatment of pre-emption problems and criteria; the absence of attention to the terminal phases of a war; the relatively minor consideration accorded nonnuclear and limited war; and the sketchy handling of air and naval doctrine. In terms of an over-all strategic design, however, perhaps the most significant doctrinal gap shows up in the failure of the work to lay out a promising formula for winning a war against the United States if such a war should have to be fought.

On the one hand, although giving great weight to strategic forces, the current doctrine expounded still holds to the tenet that long-range strategic delivery forces alone cannot bring victory. On the other hand, the doctrine is mute on how the land forces of a continental military power like the Soviet Union are to invade and occupy the main bastion of a powerful transoceanic enemy. The only apparent prospect of winning a war with the United States, given the present relationship of forces, would appear to rest on the hope that either (a) U.S. morale would collapse early in the war; or (b) that if the war should drag on, the Soviet system would prove itself the more durable under the rugged conditions prevailing in a seriously disrupted world. Both of these possibilities are suggested in the present volume, but not with the conviction that either holds sufficient promise to constitute the backbone of a winning military strategy.

There are, of course, other possible avenues out of the Soviet strategic dilemma. The present volume suggests that one way might be the achievement of overwhelming superiority over the West, but again, there is a wide gap between a doctrine of superiority and its actual realization against a powerful opponent who declines to co-operate in his own demise. In fact, Soviet doctrine appears torn in several directions on this question, such as whether to place Soviet bets on technological superiority tomorrow or large forces-in-being today. Another quite different path for the Soviet Union might be to seek genuine coexistence with the West and give up communism's expansionist ideology altogether, but this would involve a fundamental change of context in the world situation at which the present volume does not even hint, and which one would not expect such a work to interest itself in.

Within the context of the situation as it exists, the framers of Soviet military strategy must not only deal with the question of how to conduct a war successfully if one should occur, but of no less importance, how to improve the Soviet strategic posture to best deter war and support Soviet political strategy generally. In this regard, the strategic doctrine laid out in the present work probably can be judged a good deal more successful than the effort to formulate a war-winning strategy. Even so, current Soviet strategic doctrine and the military posture it prescribes would appear to leave something to be desired as a back-up for Soviet political strategy. The framers of Soviet strategy evidently are so aware, although the pages of the present work have not been used to expose the full range of their thinking on how shortcomings in the Soviet posture might be met.

To cite a conspicuous example, there seems to be no hint in this comprehensive work on Soviet military strategy of a theoretical foundation for the kind of "forward strategy" the world witnessed recently in the abortive deployment of Soviet missiles to Cuba. Indeed, so far as declared doctrine goes, the Soviet contention has been that there was never any need for strategic missiles in Cuba, since ICBM's based on Soviet territory could reach their targets in any case.[74]

Yet, a strategic gamble of considerable dimensions was attempted in Cuba. Along with the patent political aims of the Soviet move, it is apparent that significant strategic ends would have been served had the build-up of Soviet MRBM/IRBM capabilities in Cuba succeeded. This radical step, unheralded in published Soviet strategic doctrine, would have helped to redress the strategic imbalance at one stroke. It seems hardly likely that the framers of Soviet strategy had hit on this strategic *tour de force* in a moment of absent-mindedness. In fact, they may have come to it slowly and painfully, by way of realization that the doctrine and policies governing the creation of Soviet strategic forces were failing to produce a posture suitable to Soviet needs in the power contest with the United States. Possibly, the establishment of a Cuba bridgehead was even visualized as the first tentative step in a new strategic conception, aimed

---

[74] *Pravda,* September 11, 1962, and subsequent Soviet statements directed to this point, including Khrushchev's speech to the Supreme Soviet of the USSR, December 12, 1962, *Pravda,* December 13, 1962.

at staging Soviet military power progressively into the Western Hemisphere and thus into closer proximity to the main enemy. If so, however, no traces of the development of this conception are to be found in the present volume.

Another area in which an obvious gap shows up in the present work has to do with the integration of disarmament policy with military strategy. Although Soviet disarmament proposals are a major element in Soviet strategy, designed to improve the Soviet military position as well as to serve immediate political and propaganda ends, nothing is said in the work on this subject, apart from a few ritual bows to Soviet advocacy of general disarmament. This absence of attention to disarmament and arms control may be explained by the fact that the Soviets perceive them essentially as political matters beyond the competence of a treatise on military strategy.

However, even as a technical problem of interest to military planners, the subject of arms control is completely ignored. There is no discussion, for example, that parallels Western interest in arms control techniques to lower the risks of accidental war, to improve command and control arrangements, and to help cool off crisis situations. Neither is there any equivalent of Western discourse in which various concepts of deterrence, arms control, and strategic postures are treated as interrelated aspects of the military security problem. If Soviet military theoreticians are interested in such questions, they have seldom seen fit to discuss them in Soviet professional military literature, and the present volume is no exception.

A further indication that there are a number of problems of Soviet military doctrine and strategy that have not received a full airing in the present work is given in General Kurochkin's *Red Star* review of the book. After remarking that the book raised "a large number of problems," which could not be touched on within the space of a newspaper article, Kurochkin noted that these problems "deserve a special discussion." This might suggest that he had in mind some less public forum than the pages of a book or a newspaper for carrying on the discussion. However, when all is said and done, one is prompted to observe that *Soviet Military Strategy* remains a positive vehicle for the Soviets precisely because it does serve to point up doctrinal gaps and unresolved problems to which the further efforts of Soviet military thought may be addressed.

With that, it is now time to release the reader from this background introduction to *Soviet Military Strategy* and let him see for himself what its authors have to say.

# ВОЕННАЯ СТРАТЕГИЯ

*Под редакцией Маршала Советского Союза*
*СОКОЛОВСКОГО В. Д.*

ВОЕННОЕ ИЗДАТЕЛЬСТВО
МИНИСТЕРСТВА ОБОРОНЫ СССР
Москва—1962

The present study was written by the following committee of authors: Marshal of the Soviet Union V. D. Sokolovskii (chairman); Colonel A. I. Belaev; Doctor of Military Sciences Professor Colonel General A. I. Gastilovich (worked on Chapter 7); Colonel V. K. Denisenko; Major General I. G. Zav'ialov; Major General V. V. Kolechitskii; Candidate of Military Sciences Colonel V. V. Larionov; Colonel G. M. Nyrkov; Candidate of Military Sciences Colonel I. V. Parot'kin; Major General A. A. Prokhorov; Colonel A. S. Popov; Colonel K. I. Sal'nikov; Colonel A. N. Shimanskii; Major General M. I. Cherednichenko; Colonel A. I. Shchegolev.

Helpful advice was given by Lieutenant General P. Ia. Mordvintsev, Lieutenant General S. P. Platonov, Major General A. N. Strogii, Major General N. P. Tsygichko.

The book was prepared for the press by Candidate of Military Sciences Colonel V. V. Larionov.

# Introduction

The XXIInd Congress of the Communist Party of the Soviet Union [which met in October 1961], a new and historic landmark in the development of Marxism-Leninism and of the entire international Communist movement, has outlined a program of struggle for the building of a Communist society in the USSR.

In assigning glorious tasks to the Soviet people in the sphere of economic, political, and cultural development, the Communist Party has proclaimed the chief aim of its foreign policy to be the assuring of peaceful conditions for the building of Communism in the USSR and for the development of the world socialist system. As in the past, the guiding principle of the Party's and Soviet Government's foreign policy is the struggle for peaceful coexistence of states with different social systems, for general and complete disarmament, and for the abolition of world war from the life of society. In line with this, the CPSU [Communist Party of the Soviet Union] proceeds from the premise that growing forces exist in the world which are capable of preserving and strengthening peace, and that there are indications of a growing preponderance of the forces of socialism and peace over those of imperialism and war. Having outstripped capitalism in a number of important branches of science and technology, socialism has put powerful material means for curbing imperialist aggression into the hands of peace-loving peoples.

At the same time the Party, fully cognizant of its responsibility for the fate of the world, exposes the danger inherent in the existence of

81

the world imperialist system. Contemporary state-monopoly capitalism is advancing a clearly stated militaristic program and is intensifying all the basic aggressive tendencies of world imperialism.

The successes of the world socialist system, which have become a decisive factor in the development of human society, the bankruptcy of the superannuated colonial system, the insoluble contradictions in the capitalist camp, and the desire of peoples for peace clearly show the imperialists that their intentions to dominate the world cannot be realized. All this causes the imperialists, and primarily the American imperialists, to make greater efforts to ward off their inevitable destruction and, by means of war, to change the course of world events now so unfavorable to them. This is the reason that contemporary imperialism poses a threat to peace and the security of nations.

The imperialist states openly proclaim their insane plans to liquidate the Soviet Union and other socialist states by a new world war. To this end, they are conducting a frenzied arms race, allocating additional funds to their military budgets and taking practical measures to prepare an attack on the USSR and other countries of the socialist commonwealth.

Taking all this into account, to assure the security of the USSR the Party is strengthening the defensive might of our Motherland and raising the level of combat readiness of the Soviet Armed Forces to the utmost.

The Program of the CPSU adopted at the XXIInd Congress states:

> The Soviet Union needs no army for internal purposes. But because the danger of war coming from the imperialist camp persists and because general and complete disarmament has not been achieved, the CPSU considers it necessary to maintain the defensive might of the Soviet state and the combat readiness of its armed forces at a level assuring the decisive and complete defeat of any enemy who dares to encroach upon the Soviet Motherland.

In the light of these requirements, the thorough study of Marxist-Leninist theory on war and the army and the mastery of all military fields of knowledge by Soviet military personnel are of particularly great significance. One of the urgent tasks of the military and theoretical training of military personnel under present conditions is the study of the theory of military strategy as the main branch of the art of war.

At the same time one should note the obvious dearth, in the open Soviet military literature, of works that give a general understanding of military strategy in all its numerous facets. Actually, not one work by Soviet military authors, devoted to problems of military strategy as a whole, has been issued in the Soviet Union since the publication of *Strategy* by A. Svechin in 1926; the latter did not give a correct Marxist interpretation of the character and content of military strategy, and contained many methodological shortcomings.

It must also be taken into account that views expressed in our press on many fundamental aspects of Soviet military strategy, especially during the postwar period, were greatly influenced by the cult of personality of J. V. Stalin, who deliberately distorted the presentation of numerous questions of military strategy in order to justify his miscalculations and errors during the Great Patriotic War. He erected into general principles the following propositions: the belief that the non-aggressive [i.e., socialist] countries will unavoidably be poorly prepared for war; the theory of active defense, which was used ex post facto to justify the retreat of our army deep into the country and the abandonment of large territories to the enemy; and the allegation that counterattack is the inevitable form of strategic operation in wartime, and a number of other propositions.[1]

The appearance of weapons of mass destruction in the armament of modern armies and in particular the development and perfection of missiles with nuclear warheads have necessitated a fundamental review of many tenets of military strategy. However, this phenomenon which normally follows weapons development is much easier to comprehend when one takes account of earlier views on strategy and if one has studied the development of military strategic theory. The needs of a wide circle of Soviet readers, and the military and theoretical training of young officers call for the publication of a book that will present the general ideas of military strategy and illuminate the character and conduct of modern war, the preparation of the country and the armed forces for war, and the development of the armed forces. Such a work would certainly be useful as a manual.

These considerations have guided the authors in the preparation of this work.

The book contains eight chapters which examine the following topics in sequence: the development of the concept of military strategy, and its relation to politics; economic, morale, and political factors; and the essential content of the military strategy of the contemporary imperialist states, which is directed toward the preparation of a third world war. The book provides a brief description of the development and status of Soviet military strategy, modern weapons, the military, political, and economic principles underlying the military strategy of the leading capitalist states, and the views of bourgeois military theorists on the nature of modern war and the principles of its conduct. There is a discussion of the organization of the armed forces, preparations for

---

[1] U.S. ED. NOTE—See Note A, p. 84.

war, and the agencies and methods of strategic direction of the armed forces. The role of various branches of the armed forces and types of troops in a modern war is demonstrated.

The authors wish to express in advance their sincere gratitude to all readers wishing to offer criticism of this book, which is intended for a wide circle of readers.

### U.S. EDITORS' NOTE A: SOVIET VIEWS ON DEFENSIVE OPERATIONS IN WORLD WAR II

[Since his death in 1953, Stalin's military theories and his leadership during World War II have been frequently criticized in the Soviet Union. This criticism has centered on Stalin's failure to heed the numerous warnings of the coming German attack on the Soviet Union, on the inadequate preparations of the Red Army for war, on his judgment in directing military operations, and on his subsequent efforts to represent these shortcomings as the products of great wisdom. Although prewar Soviet strategic doctrine had envisaged a war of offensive operations on enemy soil, there were extensive Soviet retreats in the early part of the war. These were later explained away as part of a deliberate "active defense" strategy, planned and executed by Stalin to draw the Germans deep into the Soviet Union where they would be more vulnerable to Soviet counterattacks.

In 1941, in actual fact, Stalin had attempted to hold every foot of Soviet territory and this inflexible strategy had led to the encirclement and destruction of very large elements of the Red Army. The concept of a defensive strategy was not made an explicit part of Soviet military doctrine until 1942, and provisions regarding the possibility of strategic retreats were not added to the Field Regulations of the Soviet Armed Forces until 1944. See, for example, N. S. Khrushchev, "Secret Speech, Delivered at the XXth Congress of the Communist Party of the Soviet Union, February 25, 1956," in *The Anti-Stalin Campaign and International Communism,* Columbia University Press, New York, 1956, pp. 1–89; Lieutenant General S. Shatilov, "A Double-edged Weapon," *Literaturnaia gazeta* (*Literary Gazette*), May 28, 1955; Captain 1st Rank, B. Demidov, "The Decisive Conditions for a Creative Development of Soviet Military Science," *Kommunist vooruzhennykh sil* (*Communist of the Armed Forces*), May 1962, pp. 16–26; R. L. Garthoff, *Soviet Military Doctrine,* Free Press, Glencoe, Illinois, 1953.]

1

# General Concepts

## General Information regarding Military Strategy

*How the Concept of Military Strategy Arose.* The modern conception of military strategy as a science was not formed all at once. As we know, the advent of any conceptual system is preceded by the accumulation of knowledge; V. I. Lenin pointed out that man goes from experience to theory in his knowledge of the world.

Military experience gathered over many years, which was the source of man's knowledge of military phenomena, stimulated the development of military strategy.

With the division of society into classes and the appearance of professional armies, war became an inevitable phenomenon in the life of nations. Often the head of the state also assumed the functions of a military leader. At first, his military expeditions, victories, and defeats were merely recorded by chroniclers. Later, as military experience accumulated and the events of military history could be compared, the regularity of certain phenomena of war permitted generalization and the formulation of rules and principles. However, at first these generalizations were not put into systematic form. Despite the fact that generals of classical antiquity, such as Alexander the Great, Hannibal, Julius Caesar, and others, already entertained definite concepts of the art of war, these concepts never transcended partial generalizations and conclusions.

The first attempt to arrange accumulated military knowledge into some system was made in the fifth century A.D. By that time the

85

ancient Oriental military thinkers, Confucius, Sun Tsu, and Wu Tsu, had already propounded certain basic principles for the conduct of war: the road, or the unity of the people and the leader; the sky, or the time factor; the earth, or the geographic conditions of the theater of war; and finally, the skill of the general.

In ancient Rome and Greece, the first military works bearing on problems of strategy appeared at approximately the same time.* These included Onisander's *Instructions to Generals* and Vegetius' *Brief Exposition of the Principles of Military Action.* Even though these works dealt mainly with the training of troops and the art and mastery of tactics, they devoted a certain place to the art of war in general.

The Middle Ages, until the sixteenth century, contributed little to the formulation and development of military strategy as a science. F. Engels characterized this as the "barren period."

At the beginning of the sixteenth century, the Italian, Machiavelli, made a serious attempt to discuss the factors pertaining to the art of conducting war. His work, *Dell' Arte della Guerra,* was based upon generalizations drawn from the experience of generals of classical antiquity. This treatise, which is in the form of an original dialogue, made recommendations concerning the organization and principles of a national militia to replace mercenary armies, the role and formation of cavalry and artillery, and certain general requirements for military leaders. The author felt it essential that a general be familiar with geography, the theater of operations, and the art of war.

However, bourgeois military history usually attributes the birth of military science to the middle of the eighteenth century, when the Englishman Henry Lloyd, who was serving in Russia, systematized and summarized a number of general theoretical concepts and principles of military strategy in his introduction to the history of the Seven Years' War. From this time on, strategy was described in military literature with increasing frequency as a system of knowledge embracing the most general concepts of war; strategy was identified with military science.

Thus, just as in philosophy, which initially encompassed man's entire knowledge of nature and society, military strategy was initially an all-inclusive science in the area of military knowledge, and until approximately the end of the nineteenth century it was defined as the "synthesis and integration of the entire military art, its generalization and philosophy." †

---

* The word "strategy" is derived from the Greek "strategiia," i.e., "military leader," and means "leadership of troops."

† Leer, *Strategiia* [Strategy], Vol. I (6th edition), St. Petersburg, 1898, p. 2.

By this time, the process of differentiation was already well under way in other social sciences. This lag was quite typical of bourgeois military science, which attributed all military theory solely to the creation of individual geniuses.

The appearance of a new methodology in the study of military phenomena was related to the birth of the Marxist dialectic method, which uncovered great opportunities to elucidate the rules governing changes in the nature of war and the methods of its conduct.

The founders of this scientific method, K. Marx and F. Engels, showed that industrial development, railroad construction, and the appearance of new types of weapons and equipment caused changes in army organization and in the development and expansion of theoretical military concepts, and, consequently, the necessity for a more concrete study of the problems of war.

In contrast to bourgeois military concepts, experience soon showed that all of the problems of preparing and conducting armed combat could not be subsumed under strategy alone; by the middle of the nineteenth century, independent sciences had already begun to develop within the realm of military science. As a result of this process, strategy first developed from an all-encompassing military science into tactics, artillery, and fortifications. Later, the increased geographical scope of wars prompted the separate development of military geography. Military administration evolved even later. The theory of operations, which incidentally has been clearly elucidated only in Soviet military science, developed at the beginning of the present century.

Thus, the problems in the sphere of military strategy were gradually determined and the concept of military strategy as a science evolved.

The formulation of military strategy as a discipline was the direct result of the experience of military leadership in preparing and conducting wars on a strategic scale. Military strategy, however, is not only the result of generalized experience, but also includes the theoretical prediction of the possible conditions, methods, and leadership of future warfare. For this reason, strategic theory today is inseparable from practice.

The theory of military strategy is constantly being augmented and developed by the practical experience of the leaders of armed forces and by changes in military equipment and weapons, as well as by training and maneuvers. The constant application of strategy enables it to serve as a criterion for the validity of newly advanced concepts and also determines its future development.

Thus, the unity and interrelation of strategic theory and practice are of decisive importance in the dialectic process of their mutual enrichment and development.

Such unity is most clearly expressed in wartime, when the theory of preparing and conducting military operations on a strategic scale merges with the practical strategic conduct of war.

*The Role of Strategy in Military Science.* The complexity and diversity of the phenomena of armed combat studied by military science require an exact scientific classification of military disciplines, i.e., a determination of how each of them fits into the general system of military knowledge.

The modern classification of military sciences is based upon the principle of classifying each branch [of the military sciences] according to the scale of military operations and according to the branch of the armed forces being discussed.

Hence, the principal discipline in this systematized body of knowledge is the theory of military art, which concerns the nature and methods of military operations of various scope as a whole, as well as in reference to each branch of the armed forces and to each type of troops in particular.

The theory of military art, as applied to military operations of various scope, is divided into strategy, operational art, and tactics.

In bourgeois military science these divisions correspond to grand strategy, strategy, and tactics. For instance, in the British Field Service Regulation, grand strategy is defined as "The art of the most effective application of the entire might of the state."

Strategy occupies a leading position in the theory of military art.

The theory of strategy deals with the mobilization of all the forces and instruments of a state in wartime. This means that one of the problems of military strategy is the development of general principles for utilizing various branches of the armed forces and co-ordinating their efforts in the accomplishment of a single military-political aim. At the same time, the theory of strategic utilization of each branch of the armed forces develops concrete forms and methods for utilizing them, since it is based on general principles of a unified strategy.

Strategy is closely allied to the operational and tactical arts. Military strategy predominates over them since it determines the general aim of military operations, the forces employed, and the means and methods for solving the problems at hand. The interdependence of the component parts of the theory of military art and the dominant position of strategy are due to the fact that in wartime each individual action is subordinate to the general aim. For this reason, tactical principles must correspond to operational goals, which in turn are determined by strategic aims. Strategy uses tactics and operations to verify its assumptions and conclusions.

Modern strategy cannot be developed without taking into account economic, political, and scientific and technical factors. Its predictions must be based on modern accomplishments in mathematics, physics, chemistry, cybernetics, and other sciences. Without these, the problems of preparing and utilizing the armed forces in wartime cannot be solved in modern times. Therefore, military strategy is also closely allied to other social, natural, and physical sciences.

The close relationship between strategy and other sciences is also necessitated by the fact that some physical sciences—those more closely related to military production than others—receive general, and sometimes even specific, tactical and technical strategic assignments, such as the construction of new types of weapons and military equipment.

*The Content of Military Strategy.* The content of strategy varies. It is modified by the strategic aim at a given time, by the problems put to it by state policy, as well as by material and morale potential, i.e., the forces and means at the disposal of strategy.

In accordance with the political aims of war, one of the problems of military strategy is the study of the laws of armed combat by means of a theoretical analysis of military experience on a strategic scale, giving due consideration to the state of the military art. One of the main missions for strategy is to study the conditions and nature of a future war and to develop the methods and forms of its conduct. Hence, strategy must determine the composition of forces and the instruments necessary for attainment of its goals and thus the general development of the armed forces and their preparation for war. Another problem of strategy is the development of the material and technological base for armed combat and the leadership of the armed forces. Military strategy must study all of these problems, taking into account the attitudes and capabilities of the potential enemy. Thus it is the function of strategy also to study the enemy's strategic views.

Considering the above, the scope of the theory of military strategy includes:

The general rules governing armed combat
The conditions and nature of a future war
Theoretical principles of preparing the country and the armed forces for war, and the principles of planning war
The branches of the armed forces and the basis of their strategic utilization
The methods of conducting armed combat

The material and technological base for armed combat
The principles of directing the armed forces and war in general
The strategic views of potential enemies.[1]

In order to give a more complete exposition of the content of military strategy, the problems which comprise each of the enumerated subdivisions should be clarified in brief.

Military strategy cannot claim the status of a science if it is not actually based on knowledge of the historically developed laws of war as armed combat.

Proof that the development of weapons and techniques of armed combat is subject to definite laws was given as early as 1851 by F. Engels, who wrote: "A prerequisite of the Napoleonic method of conducting war was an increase in productive forces; new productive forces will also be a prerequisite for each new improvement in the conduct of war." *

The laws of strategy are objective and apply inexorably and to the same degree to all belligerents.

This can be confirmed by the strategic principles which V. I. Lenin formulated in his time. The general propositions he advanced apply in equal measure to all belligerents: that war is a comprehensive test of the material and spiritual resources of each nation, that wars are won by those nations which possess the greatest resources and whose populations are strongest and have most endurance, and that each war yields final victory to those nations whose masses, shedding their blood on the field of battle, are endowed with the strongest spirit.

A knowledge of the general rules governing armed combat makes it possible for the military leader to foresee the nature of military events in a future war and to use these laws successfully in the intelligent direction of the operations of the armed forces. This is the subjective aspect of using objective laws.

Thus, the clarification and study of the rules governing armed combat have great practical value for military leadership in the preparation and conduct of military operations on a strategic scale.

The next important element in the content of military strategy is the problem of the nature of a future war. Here strategy includes the conditions and factors that determine, at the given historical moment, the nature of a future war, the distribution of military and political forces, the quality and quantity of weapons, the military and economic poten-

---

[1] U.S. ED. NOTE—See Note A, p. 97.

* F. Engels, *Izbrannye voennye proizvedeniia* [*Selected Military Works*], Voenizdat, Moscow, 1957, p. 636.

tial, the probable composition and strength of the opposing coalitions and their geographical distribution.

Concerning the nature of the war itself, strategic analysis devotes attention to the basic means of its conduct, its duration, intensity, and geographical scope.

As for the nature of a future war, military strategy includes the means and methods of preparing the armed forces for war, where the problems receiving primary attention will be the following: scientific planning of war preparations, taking into account political requirements, economic potential, and scientific and technical accomplishments; the organization of strategic intelligence; the composition of the armed forces necessary for solving strategic problems; the composition and preparation of strategic reserves; the accumulation of material reserves, and the preparation of the country as a theater of military operations.

With respect to the branches of the armed forces, military strategy includes the factors which determine their structure and interrelation, the requirements put upon them in view of the changing nature of political and strategic war aims and of the conditions under which war is conducted, their purpose and tasks in a future war, and the principles and prospects of their future development.

The study of techniques for conducting war occupies an important place in military strategy. Concerning these problems, strategic theory develops general concepts concerning the techniques of conducting war and their dependence upon the factors which most strongly influence their change and development.

Military strategy directs primary attention to the study of how a future war may break out and to a detailed study of the particular features of strategic deployment of the armed forces, methods of delivering the first blow [2] and conducting initial operations, and strategic utilization of the different branches of the armed forces.

Material requirements are studied with respect to war as a whole and to the needs of different types of strategic operations. Attention is given to the organization of the strategic rear areas, including the location of rear agencies of the armed forces, and to the principles of planning and the execution of concrete measures to guarantee the material and technological base for armed combat.

For examining the principles of leadership of armed forces, military strategy bears, in the first order, upon war leadership as a whole. It determines possible agencies of strategic leadership, their organizational

---

[2] U.S. ED. NOTE—See Note A, pp. 96–98.

structure and functions, and the principles and methods of directing the armed forces of each individual country as well as those of a military coalition.

As for the strategic views of the potential enemy, military strategy focuses attention on what his military and political aims may be in a future war and what his economic, military, and morale potentialities are for such a war. In addition, strategy also takes into consideration the enemy's views on the nature and techniques of waging war; the organization of armed forces; and the preparation of the economy, the population, and the country's territory for war.

These are the problems embraced by the theory of military strategy and its component parts. Careful analysis of each specific problem will enable strategic theory to develop scientifically based recommendations for practical direction of the armed forces during preparation for war and its conduct.

The practical aspects of military strategy deal with the activity of higher military and political leadership, the supreme military command and the higher staffs in preparing the country for war, and the organization and execution of strategic operations of the armed forces, both in war as a whole as well as during various stages of war and in theaters of military operations. On the basis of theory and the actual strategic situations, these agencies put into effect a whole series of measures aimed at the preparation and successful conduct of armed combat. The following are included in these measures:

> Strategic decisions and practical implementation of plans for preparing the country for war
> Practical guidance for preparing the armed forces for war
> Leadership of the armed forces during the entire course of the war

In summary the following definition of military strategy can be given:

> *Military strategy is a system of theoretical knowledge dealing with the rules governing war as armed combat for definite class interests. Strategy, using as a basis the military experience, military and political conditions, economic and morale potential of the country, new weapons and the views of the potential enemy, studies the conditions and the nature of a future war, the methods for its preparation and conduct, the branches of the armed forces and the basis for their strategic utilization, as well as the material and technological base and leadership for war and the armed forces.*
>
> *At the same time, this is the area of practical activity of the higher military and political leadership, the supreme command and the higher headquarters, with respect to preparing the country for war and waging armed combat under concrete historical conditions.*

*The Content and Nature of Military Strategy in Modern Nuclear and Missile Warfare.* As is generally known, the development of weapons technology has had a basic influence on the nature of war and military strategy.

The appearance of missiles and nuclear weapons radically changed previous concepts of the nature of war. Modern missile warfare is incomparably more destructive and deadly than previous wars. The massive use of missiles and nuclear weapons makes it possible, within a short time, to eliminate either one country or a number of countries from the war, even those with relatively large territories, well-developed economies, and populations of the order of tens of millions.

The geographical scope of modern warfare has increased immeasurably. The almost unlimited capacity to deliver nuclear weapons over any range lends unlimited scope to modern warfare, so that boundaries between front lines and the rear are erased, thus changing previous concepts about theaters of operations.

*In modern warfare, military strategy has become the strategy of missile and nuclear strikes in depth along with the simultaneous use of all branches of the armed forces in order to achieve complete defeat of the enemy and the destruction of his economic potential and armed forces throughout his entire territory; such war aims are to be accomplished within a short period of time.*

In view of this definition, a whole series of previous principles, norms, and rules considered definitive as late as World War I and II have undergone radical revision or have lost their significance altogether.

*The principle of concentrating forces and weapons in a decisive area,* which has existed since ancient times, requires extensive modification. In all previous wars, the main efforts were channeled in a principal area by concentrating manpower and equipment and by their close deployment on a relatively limited sector of the ground front; today this [end] can obviously be accomplished by massive missile attacks.

The concentration of troops at breakthrough areas and the formation of high troop densities in these relatively narrow front sectors, practiced as recently as World War II, are fraught with grave consequences. Moreover, there is no longer a need for such concentration, since continuous fronts have become a thing of the past and the concept of penetration of the front has lost its former significance. It is not the direction of the main blow [on the ground front as in the past] which is now of most importance, but rather the areas where force is applied, since nuclear strikes can be delivered simultaneously to targets in many areas throughout an entire enemy territory. Also of great importance is an accurate estimate of the forces and weapons needed for the targets as well as the sequence and timing of the destruction of these targets.

In missile and nuclear warfare,[3] *the strategic principle of the economy of forces* appears in a new light. Obviously, when the very outcome of the war depends largely upon the extent and the effectiveness of the application of force at the very beginning of the war, it is hardly reasonable to count upon the state's potential capabilities and to reserve a large number of forces for conducting military operations later in the war. The overwhelming majority of military theoreticians in advanced countries are arriving at this conclusion.

Military strategy in previous wars assigned an important place to *the principle of partial victory*. It was considered irrefutable that general victory in war consisted of a number of partial successes on various fronts and in various spheres of military operation. Modern strategic weapons, which are directly subordinated to the high commands, make it possible to achieve decisive results in winning victory in war sometimes even without resort to tactical and field forces and their weapons. This lends support to the proposition that today partial successes can be replaced by successes of a general strategic nature.[4]

The strategic changes brought about by the introduction of new weapons not only bear upon the principles and rules governing military strategy, but also upon the basic categories of strategy.

Thus, the concept of the *theater of military operations* is changing completely. The classical concept of a theater of military operations was that of a territory or body of water upon which direct military opera-

---

[3] U.S. ED. NOTE—The question of whether the Soviet Union must rely primarily on forces and weapons in being at the outbreak of a war or whether it can expect to mobilize additional forces and to continue war production in the course of the war has been a major point of disagreement among Soviet military writers. These disagreements are reflected to some extent throughout this book. Until October 1961 when Malinovskii laid particular stress on the decisive character of the first phase of nuclear war, some Soviet writers not only denied the possibility of a speedy conclusion of a war between great states but spoke of the need for continuing industrial production under war conditions.

[4] Assertions that victory in a war can be attained solely by strategic nuclear attacks against an enemy's homeland without the use of other types of armed forces, are unusual in Soviet military literature (see also p. 105). Soviet writers generally reserve such claims for war with relatively small and densely populated countries, but deny or leave it ambiguous whether such action can win a war against a large and highly industrialized state. Khrushchev has frequently denied that the United States could win a war against the Soviet Union by a nuclear attack. Nevertheless, the possibility of such a victory appears to be implied in the current Soviet emphasis on the decisive influence which a surprise attack or the "first phase of the war" would have on the further course and outcome of the war. (See Marshal R. Malinovskii, *Pravda*, October 25, 1961.) However, Soviet doctrine makes a distinction between "decisive results in winning victory" and "final victory" in a war. The attainment of the latter is said to require the use of all types of forces, while the former may essentially mean the destruction of the enemy's capability to offer effective resistance with strategic weapons.

tions developed. The boundaries of the theater were determined by the range of the weapons, which until World War II seldom reached beyond the operational rear areas. Thus, the belligerents' strategic rear and their entire territories which lay beyond these boundaries [of the operational rear] were not included in the theater of military operations.

The development of long-range (strategic) bomber air forces, and the appearance of nuclear weapons, especially intercontinental missiles, significantly changed the concept of a theater of military operations.

The modern concept of a theater of military operations may include the entire territory of a belligerent or coalition, whole continents, large bodies of water, and extensive regions of the atmosphere and outer space. Thus the zone of military operations is no longer limited to the firing range of weapons, since the latter is almost unlimited. This zone is limited only by the location of strategic targets subject to attack.

*Strategic offense and strategic defense* as forms of strategic operations have lost their previous significance in the conditions of missile and nuclear warfare. They played a major role when the main war aims and missions were accomplished by ground forces with the aid of aircraft (in coastal areas with the navy), and the conduct of war was based upon operations on the ground front. In a missile war, the main war aims and missions will be accomplished by strategic missile forces, which will deliver massive nuclear strikes. Ground forces in conjunction with aircraft will perform important strategic functions in modern war. By rapid and forceful offense movements ground forces will completely annihilate the remaining enemy formations, occupy enemy territory, and prevent the enemy forces from entering one's own territory. The strategic operations of the other branches of the armed forces will consist of the following: the National PVO will protect the country from enemy nuclear attacks; the navy will execute military operations in naval theaters, aimed at the destruction of enemy naval formations and naval communications, and the defense of our own communications as well as coastal areas from naval attack.

Strategic offense and strategic defense as forms of strategic operation may retain their significance in certain types of local wars where military operations are conducted by conventional weapons. The probability of such wars cannot be completely excluded at the present time.

Missiles and nuclear weapons have introduced substantial changes in the concept of *strategic deployment*.

Until World War II, the strategic deployment of armed forces consisted of a complex of measures instituted in the threatening period or at the start of the war to screen, mobilize, concentrate, and deploy the armed forces in the theater of operations and executed systematically according to a plan. This concept has now obviously become obsolete.

Today most of these measures can be implemented in advance, and they need only be completed in the period when war threatens.

Thus the new concept of strategic deployment is a process of creating strategic formations of armed forces prior to the outbreak of war, according to a plan of war and according to how it breaks out. A high state of combat readiness in the armed forces is an important part of this process.

Perfection of the delivery vehicles for nuclear weapons and their increased range and ability to retarget the nuclear attack rapidly have altered the previous concept of *strategic maneuver*. Previously this was defined as the creation of the most favorable concentration of forces and weapons in a military theater of operations or in a strategic area. Today it will obviously consist, in essence, of the creation of favorable conditions by shifting and concentrating nuclear strikes in order to accomplish the main aims of war as well as the strategic objectives by all branches of the armed forces.

In the last war, strategic maneuvers were accomplished by moving large commands and units by rail and motor transport from one front or theater of operations to another. Given the great vulnerability of communications [in a future war] and insufficient time for such reconcentration, these maneuvers will be difficult to execute and, in a number of cases, ineffective.

Consequently, strategic maneuver in missile and nuclear warfare can be described as the shifting of the [main] effort from one strategic direction or target to another, mainly by the fire-maneuver of nuclear weapons. Maneuver in the former sense may be undertaken by the ground forces, air forces, and navy primarily on an operational scale, within theaters of military operation.

The basic principles and categories of military strategy discussed above confirm the fact that basic changes have been inevitably introduced into strategy by the appearance of new weapons.

These are the general principles of military strategy, bearing upon the definition of its concepts, the position of strategy in military science, its content, and those changes which it has undergone in connection with the appearance of missiles and nuclear weapons.

## U.S. EDITORS' NOTE A: SOVIET VIEWS ON THE ROLE OF ENEMY STRATEGY AND THE FIRST STRIKE

[As pointed out in the Analytical Introduction, Soviet military strategy today emphasizes that the principal war aims of the belligerents in a future war will be achieved by means of massive use of strategic missiles. This view was crystallized in Khrushchev's speech to the Supreme Soviet on January 14, 1960, in which he stated that, henceforth, Soviet military power would be based primarily on missiles while the role of other forces and weapons would be markedly reduced.[5] Khrushchev also said that modern weapons had radically changed the nature of war, and that, therefore, "war would begin differently, if it should occur, and would develop differently."

Khrushchev's formulation, as discussed in the Analytical Introduction, was one of the landmarks in the prolonged doctrinal debate which has been carried out in the Soviet Union. Because of the eventual recognition of the decisive character of modern weapons, Soviet military doctrine had to pay increasing attention not only to the military capabilities of a possible enemy, but also to the way in which these capabilities might be employed against the Soviet Union. It is noteworthy that the discussion in this chapter of the range of factors that concern Soviet strategy is more explicit than that found in earlier Soviet writings.[6] While the more traditional formula states that Soviet strategy "studies the means and techniques of armed combat of probable enemies, their economic, morale and military capabilities . . ."[7] the present work puts more emphasis on the need to take into consideration the "strategic views of potential enemies" (p. 90). The book also reflects the new concern of Soviet strategy with the study of conditions of war initiation (p. 91) and with the "methods of delivering the first blow and the conduct of initial operations" (p. 91). As indicated in the Analytical Introduction, the stress in Soviet military thinking on the initiative and on the first phase of a war was made especially explicit in Marshal Malinovskii's speech to the XXIInd Congress of the Communist Party of the Soviet Union on October 23, 1961, where he stated that

> the Presidium of the Central Committee of the Party and the Soviet Government have demanded and continue to demand of us that we devote special attention to the initial period of a possible war. The importance of this period lies in the fact that the first massive nuclear

---

[5] *Pravda*, January 15, 1960.

[6] See, for example, the article on "Military Strategy," in *Bol'shaia sovetskaia entsiklopediia (Great Soviet Encyclopedia)*, 2nd edition, Vol. 41, Gosudarstvennoe Nauchnoe Izdatel'stvo, Moscow, 1956, pp. 65–66 (hereafter cited as *BSE*). Major General M. V. Smirnov, *et al.*, *O sovetskoi voennoi nauke (On Soviet Military Science)*, Voenizdat Ministerstva Oborony Soiuza SSR, Moscow, 1960, pp. 276–283. Lieutenant Colonel I. Seleznev, "Concerning the Foundations of Soviet Military Science," *Sovetskaia aviatsiia (Soviet Aviation)*, April 16, 1957.

[7] *BSE, op. cit.*, p. 66.

blows can to an enormous extent determine the entire subsequent course of the war and result in losses in the homeland and among the troops which could place the people and the country in a difficult situation.[8]]

## Strategy and Politics

*The Dependence of Military Strategy on Politics.*   In defining the essential nature of war, Marxism-Leninism proceeds from the proposition that war is not an aim in itself, but rather a tool of policy.

In his remarks on Clausewitz's book *Vom Kriege [On War]*, V. I. Lenin stressed that "politics is the guiding force, and war is only the tool, not vice versa. Consequently, it remains only to subordinate the military point of view to the political." *

The acceptance of war as a tool of politics determines the relationship of military strategy to politics and makes the former completely dependent upon the latter.

The representatives of the bourgeois metaphysical approach to war, who deny its class essence, have attacked and are still attacking these scientific Marxist propositions. They do not perceive the cause of any war to be in the policies followed by the state before the war, but rather in the "psychological makeup" of man, the overpopulation of the earth (Malthusians and neo-Malthusians), and in racist geopolitics.

Such theories have always played into the hands of extreme militarists, who deny the dependence of military strategy upon politics. This idea was exemplified by the German military writer F. Bernhardi, who asserted that policy must "adjust its demands to what is militarily expedient and feasible." † The German military ideologists of World War I, Schlieffen and Ludendorff, in justifying their militaristic aspirations, argued that politics, having accomplished its aim by starting the war, becomes a passive observer at the beginning of military operations.

The views of bourgeois military theoreticians of the past find adherents even among the present-day military ideologists of modern imperialism.

Thus, the English military theoretician Kingston-McCloughry writes with regard to the Clausewitz formula:

But take his most famous pronouncement that "war is the continuation of policy by other means," viz., by force, and consider it in the

---

[8] *Pravda,* October 25, 1961. See also Marshal R. Malinovskii, "The Program of the Communist Party of the Soviet Union and the Question of Strengthening the Armed Forces of the USSR," *Kommunist,* No. 7, May 1962, p. 19.

* See V. I. Lenin, *Leninskii sbornik [Lenin's Collected Works],* XII, 2nd edition, 1931, p. 437.

† F. Bernhardi, *Sovremennaia voina [Modern War],* Vol. II, St. Petersburg, 1912, p. 148.

light of present-day conditions. Nothing would seem further from the truth in the event of nuclear warfare. Such a war if wholly unleashed, would be the end of all policies and an utter mutual annihilation.*

He is echoed by the West German military theoretician Rendulič, a former Nazi general, who, in the article entitled "Armament Changes Politics," declares that ". . . the nuclear weapon introduced radical changes in the form of warfare and its relation to politics. . . . Nuclear war has lost its significance as a political instrument." [9]

It is quite evident that such views are the consequence of a metaphysical and anti-scientific approach to a social phenomenon such as war and are the result of idealization of the new weapons. It is well known that the essential nature of war as a continuation of politics does not change with changing technology and armament. The imperialist ideologists require contrary conclusions to justify their preparations for a new war and to subordinate the development of economics, science, and technology to the requirements of military organization. In their opinion, it is not the civil but rather the military organization which, with science, has taken over the leadership.

At the same time, regardless of such declarations by individual authors, bourgeois military science recognizes the dependence of war and military strategy on politics. True, bourgeois politics in this case is presented as the expression of the interests of the entire society, which in reality is not the case. Thus, the class content is removed from politics and it is represented as a national [classless], primarily foreign, policy. However, such a policy cannot be pursued in a society consisting of antagonistic classes since, as V. I. Lenin pointed out, neither nonclass nor supraclass politics exist.

The dependence of military strategy on politics finds most varied expression. Political influence is manifested in the determination of general and particular strategic aims, in the general nature of state strategy, and in the selection of the method and form of waging war.

V. I. Lenin declared that the nature of the political aim has a decisive influence on the conduct of war. Indeed, it is the political aim which determines whether the war is just or unjust that has a basic influence on strategy. In one case [of a just war] the wholehearted endorsement of the war aims by the people reinforces the strategy, and in the other case [of an unjust war] the people may not share these aims, and the extent of their participation in the war is sharply reduced.

The decisiveness of political war aims will vary with the depth of

---

* E. J. Kingston-McCloughry, *Global'naia strategiia,* Voenizdat, Moscow, 1959, p. 290 [English edition *Global Strategy,* Praeger, New York, 1957, p. 248].

[9] U.S. ED. NOTE—It has not been possible to locate the original article.

the contradictions between states or coalitions of states in the war. The most decisive political and, consequently, strategic aims are pursued in civil or revolutionary class wars. Wars between states with different social systems are particularly decisive, inasmuch as these are a higher form of the class struggle. In wars between states with the same social system, when there are no social contradictions between the antagonists, the political and strategic aims are usually limited. In such wars, compromises of various types are possible long before the belligerents are economically and militarily exhausted. This type of strategy is characteristic of participants in imperialist wars in which both sides pursue predatory aims.

The subordination of military strategy to state policy not only determines the nature of the strategic aims, but also the general nature of strategy.

For example, the policy of imperialism as an outmoded social system is to attempt to forestall its inevitable downfall and to prevent the historically determined development of socialism in the world.

Being reactionary and adventuristic by nature, the policies of imperialist countries also produce a military strategy founded on adventuristic calculations. By their character, such strategies ignore the laws of armed combat, the permanently operating factors and the role of the popular masses, and expect to exploit a combination of political and strategic situations in order to attack treacherously in violation of international treaties and agreements.

The general nature of military strategy is strongly influenced by the guiding idea or general line of state policy. The existence of such an idea renders military strategy firm and consistent. For example, the general political line of the CPSU, whose essential nature was so graphically expressed during the XXIInd Party Congress, is the building of a communist society. In achieving this goal, our country has to sustain various battles, some of them, as shown by historical experience, with weapons in hand. Such a clear and noble idea imparts the necessary drive and consistency to Soviet military strategy.

Another example could be cited where [state] policy cannot provide strategy with a guiding idea, or where this idea is essentially reactionary.

For more than half a century (1799–1863), the policy of Tsarist Russia was guided by the reactionary idea of combating the bourgeois revolution. Hoping to preserve the outmoded, feudal, serf-holding system, Russia became the *gendarme* of Europe. Even though Russia waged many wars during this period, some successfully, its military strategy nevertheless remained inconclusive and inconsistent since all of these wars could not or did not prevent the inevitable downfall of feudalism.

Such factors as general, historical, national, and political traditions of the state often influence the nature of military strategy. For example, in its foreign policy Great Britain has always adhered to a clearly defined policy of watchful waiting, double dealing, and having someone else pull the chestnuts out of the fire. This was also manifested in its military strategy, which avoided decisive engagements, refused to take even reasonable risks, and always looked for devious, indirect roads to victory. Naturally the concept of "the strategy of indirect action" is widespread in Great Britain. This does not mean, of course, that Great Britain has not pursued and does not pursue an aggressive policy intended to unleash wars.

However, the influence of politics on military strategy is not limited to the determination of the general nature of strategy. The solution of many concrete strategic problems depends directly upon state policy. One such problem is the method of conducting war.

The methods of waging particular wars, as is known, are determined by the level of development of productive forces, the characteristics of the armaments and military equipment, and the composition and nature of the armed forces. For this reason, state policy must always ascertain that the methods employed in the conduct of war correspond to the military and economic potential of the state, the level of the technical equipment of the armed forces, and the nature of the war. Under modern conditions, for example, if a state does not have nuclear weapons at its disposal, then no matter what method of conducting war is advanced by state policy, it could hardly achieve a victory in a war with an opponent who did possess such weapons.

Nevertheless, in spite of this, at times policy exerts a very evident influence upon the selection of methods of warfare.

F. Engels, in stating that the victorious proletariat will device new methods of conducting war, stressed that the revolutionary change in social structure itself presupposed the creation of new and more progressive methods of conducting military operations. "The actual liberation of the proletariat, the complete elimination of all class differences, and the total socialization of all means of production . . ." * are, in his words, the prerequisites for new methods of conducting war.

Politics manifests its influence on the conduct of war in a variety of ways.

---

* F. Engels, *Izbrannye voennye proizvedeniia* [*Selected Military Works*], Voenizdat, Moscow, 1957, p. 635.

Everyone knows that the Anglo-French command pursued a passive and defensive strategy during the "Phony War" in the West (1939–1940), when it acted in accord with the will of imperialist policy in encouraging Hitler's aggression against the USSR and transforming the existing war into an anti-Soviet war.[10]

Certain American and British circles exerted considerable influence on the Anglo-American methods of conducting World War II in order to achieve the economic and military exhaustion of the USSR and Germany. This was the reason behind the Anglo-American strategy of scattering forces along secondary fronts and prolonging military operations.

The military strategy of the capitalist countries, guided by this policy, refused to deal the main blow in France in 1942 and 1943, which would have led to a quick German defeat. In an effort to preserve the rule of imperialism in Central and Southeastern Europe, the British political leaders delayed by all possible means the landing of the Allied forces and the opening of a second front in France, insisting instead on a landing in the Balkans.

Present-day theories of "limited war," "massive retaliation," and "global war," advanced in such profusion by bourgeois military theoreticians, are also fruits of imperialist policy, serving as yet another proof that the techniques of conducting war depend upon policy.

*Policy Creates Favorable Conditions for Military Strategy.* State policy usually does not limit itself to a presentation of strategic aims, but also strives to bring about the conditions favorable to the realization of these aims. Inasmuch as it controls all the [state] machinery, policy is used to mobilize the maximum human and material resources in order to assure the operation of the armed forces. In doing so [state] policy takes into account strategic requirements and considerations as well as the capabilities of the state, seeking to make the aims commensurate with the available means and forces.

Favorable diplomatic, economic, morale, and political conditions must be created in order that the military forces may carry out their assigned missions successfully. The state prepares for war in all of these realms. The preparation of foreign policy for war includes such measures as concluding alliances, forming coalitions of states, ensuring the neutrality of neighboring states, etc. This opens a wide field for diplomacy

---

[10] U.S. ED. NOTE—This interpretation of the "Phony War" reflects a standard Soviet propaganda policy. See, for example, N. N. Iakovlev, *SShA i Angliia vo vtoroi mirovoi voine* (*The United States and England during the Second World War*), Gosizdat, Uchebno-Pedagogicheskoe Izdatel'stvo Ministerstva Prosveshcheniia RSFSR, Moscow, 1961, p. 55. A more realistic interpretation of Franco-British strategy is given in Chapter 2, pp. 144–146, of this translation.

which, in striving to consolidate the international position of its state, constantly takes into account the state's security interests, in conformity with the requirements of military strategy.

In concluding alliances, bourgeois diplomacy is usually guided primarily by financial considerations and advantages. In selecting allies it usually takes into account their forces, their stake in the war, and their geographic location, which is particularly important to military strategy.

The history of bourgeois diplomacy shows that because the main aim of alliances among capitalist states is the strengthening of one alliance and the weakening of another, these alliances, allegedly formed for mutual defense in the event of war, in reality always led to war.

"Peaceful alliances," wrote Lenin, "prepare the ground for wars and, in turn, are products of wars; the one is the condition for the other. . . ." *

This is the reason that the Soviet Union, true to its peaceful policy, basically opposes the formation of military alliances. It is only the creation of aggressive military blocs by imperialist states, which threaten socialist countries, that forces the Soviet Union to unite with [other] socialist states in the military alliance brought about by the obligation of the Warsaw Defense Pact of 1955.

In military strategy it is sometimes important to assure the neutrality of one or more countries; this is the task of diplomacy.

For example, prior to the Franco-Prussian war of 1870–1871, Prussia secured the neutrality of Russia, which enabled Prussia first of all to avoid simultaneous fighting on two fronts, and second, to commit the majority of its forces to battle, leaving only one division in the rear of its army.

It is well known that in World War II, Soviet diplomacy made considerable efforts to assure the neutrality of Japan. To a certain extent, this made it possible for the Soviet Supreme High Command to shift part of its forces from the Far East and to concentrate them on the Soviet-German front.

The above examples show that the creation of favorable conditions by foreign policy plays quite an important role in military strategy.

[State] policy prepares war and creates favorable economic and ideological conditions for the benefit of strategy; this is examined in detail in the following sections of this chapter.

*The Special Nature of the Relationship of Politics to Strategy during Wartime.* The particular features of this relationship result from

---

* V. I. Lenin, *Sochineniia* [*Works*], Vol. 22 [4th edition], p. 282. [Hereafter, unless otherwise indicated, the 4th edition of Lenin's works is cited.]

the fact that in wartime the political struggle shifts basically from a non-military to a military form. Policy, as is said, "exchanges the pen for the sword," and new relationships and laws obtain.

"Once military operations on land and sea have begun, they are no longer subject to the desires and plans of diplomacy, but rather to their own laws which cannot be violated without endangering the entire undertaking." *

Consequently, if policy violates or ignores the laws of military strategy, this can lead to the defeat of the army and to the destruction of the state. In wartime, therefore, strategic considerations often determine policy. Cases even arise when the military factor not only predominates, but even acquires decisive significance. During the Civil War in the USSR, V. I. Lenin pointed out that the outcome of the Revolution depended entirely upon who won the Civil War.

During war, policy must, therefore, often adjust its position to conform to the requirements of strategic aims, which, in the final analysis, lead to the wartime accomplishment of political aims. Naturally, diplomatic and economic struggle do not cease in wartime, but these forms of political struggle are entirely dependent upon the decisive form, i.e., armed combat, and at times they are also conducted by such means.

For example, in an all-out diplomatic effort to facilitate the attainment of strategic aims, an alliance may be made with a country which heretofore has been in the enemy camp. This is undoubtedly an important factor in military strategy and facilitates the carrying out of its assignments. Thus, in the Great Patriotic War, Soviet diplomats concluded [armistice] agreements with Bulgaria and Romania, which put the Fascist German army in a very difficult position on the southern flank of the Russian front. To ensure the success of this diplomatic step, the Red Army had to deliver a crushing blow to the Fascist German and Romanian armies, which confronted them with military disaster. These successes were achieved only as a result of the combined efforts of Soviet strategy and diplomacy. This is a striking example of the complete concurrence of diplomacy and strategy unified in a single aim.

The economic struggle, which during wartime is dependent on military strategy, sometimes may be conducted by military means, so that special strategic operations may even be undertaken for economic benefit.

When we consider the experience of the Great Patriotic War, we can see that shortly before the surrender of Fascist Germany, her economy was still fully capable of supporting successful military operations. This

---

* F. Engels, *Izbrannye voennye proizvedeniia* [*Selected Military Works*], Vol. II, Voenizdat, Moscow, 1936, p. 34.

is evidenced by the production index of Germany's main armaments in January 1945, i.e., three months before her surrender. Although as a whole it did have a tendency to decline, nevertheless, when compared to the production index in January 1942 taken provisionally as 100, the 1945 production index was quite high.

|  | January 1942 |  | January 1945 |
| --- | --- | --- | --- |
| All types of weapons | 100 |  | 210 |
| Aircraft | 100 |  | 210 |
| Ammunition | 100 |  | 200 |
| Tanks | 100 | approx. | 600 |
| Artillery and small arms | 100 |  | 300 |
| Warships | 100 |  | 150 |
| Gunpowder and other explosives | 100 |  | 160 * |

As these data show, Nazi economic capacities three months before surrender were even higher than when their armies were successful. However, the destruction of the German armed forces by the Red Army brought Germany to disaster.

Thus, it was not so much the economic struggle and economic exhaustion that caused the defeat of Nazi Germany, as armed combat and the defeat of its armed forces.

"The heroic Soviet Army not only accelerated the 'economic exhaustion' of Nazi Germany but also was the cause and main force which undermined the economic foundations of the enemy." †

In modern warfare, when the massive use of missiles can lead to the destruction of the most important industrial targets and economic regions and to the disruption of the entire economy of an enemy country or coalition, a somewhat different picture emerges. A country plunged into catastrophe by massive missile blows may find it necessary to surrender even before its armed forces have suffered decisive defeat.[11] However, we must remember that such results can only be accomplished by force, i.e., by weapons.

By evaluating military and political factors, policy selects the most propitious moment to start a war, taking into account strategic considerations. The importance of proper timing in starting a war can be judged from the fact that when the time is properly selected, strategy usually

---

* The data was taken from the book *Promyshlennost' Germanii v 1939–1944* [*German Industry from 1939–1945*], Izdatel'stvo Inostrannoi Literatury, Moscow, 1956, p. 117.

† N. Voznesenskii, *Voennaia ekonomika SSR v period Otechestvennoi voine* [*The Military Economy of the USSR during the Patriotic War*], Ogiz, Moscow, 1948, p. 173.

[11] U.S. ED. NOTE—See note 4, p. 94.

obtains great military successes and policy reaps the greatest rewards from them.

Thus, in 1866 the Prussian Chancellor Bismarck started the war with Austria at a time when Austria, which had not recovered from its unsuccessful Italian campaign of 1859, was carrying out a reform of its entire military system. As a consequence of Hungary's desire for independence, Austria's internal situation was also unstable. Prussia at this time, however, had a well-organized army and a rather strong ally in Italy. All of these circumstances enabled her to achieve victory almost entirely because of proper timing.

Another example, from the Russo-Turkish war, also confirms the important role of policy in timing the initiation of military operations and creating favorable conditions for military strategy from the very beginning of the war.

By the middle of the nineteenth century, a national liberation movement had arisen in the Balkan countries subjugated by Turkey. This movement was supported in Russia by Slavophiles and the Tsarist government, which was pursuing its private capitalistic interests in the Balkans. Turkish oppression of the population further inflamed this movement. A war was brewing between Russia and Turkey. Great Britain assumed the part of mediator, all the time pursuing her own selfish interests, in fear that a Turkish defeat would allow Russia to capture the Bosporus and the Dardanelles. While allegedly supporting Russia, Great Britain at the same time encouraged Turkey to be obdurate. Russian diplomacy was unable to resolve the Balkan contradictions under these circumstances, and on November 1, 1876, Russia declared a partial mobilization.

Had military operations followed immediately, the timing would have been most unsuitable for Turkey and Great Britain. The former was tied down by a war with Serbia and Montenegro and needed to reform her army. The latter, being militarily weak at that time, was unable to dictate any terms to Russia. In addition, it was very important for Turkey to wait until the beginning of the winter storms on the Black Sea, which would hinder the operation of the Russian Navy.

In these conditions, Turkey and England resorted to a delaying diplomacy. And when on April 12, 1877, Russia was nevertheless forced to begin warring with Turkey, the favorable moment had passed; England had gathered her forces, and Turkey, having concluded peace with Serbia, had put her army in order.

Thus, as a result of poor timing in beginning the war, strategic activity was fettered, and policy did not reap all the possible gains from military success. Even though Russia was victorious, the subsequent peace treaty did not achieve her original political aims. Strategy was also hindered by treaty limitations. Instead of attempting to achieve complete destruction of the Turkish army and the occupation of Constantinople, which the Russian army could have done at that time, Russia was compelled to restrict herself to the occupation of Bulgaria, at that time part of the Turkish empire.

A more recent example could also be given. The timing of the Nazi attack in 1941, which was extremely unfavorable for our country, was responsible for the initial success of the Nazi troops. Our country was insufficiently prepared for war, and the army, which was not fully mobilized, was in the process of reorganization and rearmament.

All of these examples point to the close relationship of strategy to politics at the outset of war.

Politics also plays an exceptionally important role and has a great influence in military strategy at the end of war since a country's international position after a war depends to a great extent on the country's situation during the concluding phases of the war.

*Particular Features of the Relationship of Politics to Strategy in Coalitions.* The present epoch is one of coalition wars. In coalition wars, the relationships of policy to strategy have some special features. Actually, to achieve victory in a coalition war, the states of a coalition must completely concur in strategy. However, such a strategy can arise only from a policy strengthened by unity of purpose among the coalition members; this is difficult to achieve in alliances of predatory imperialist states. Also, the strategy of each individual country is determined by its economic potential, geographic location, national character and traditions, etc. Consequently, strategy possesses clearly defined national features in each country. At the same time, the allied strategy cannot be simply the sum of the strategic doctrines of the various countries.

Because of this, a unified plan of strategy among capitalist states in a coalition war can be achieved only by compromises, mutual concessions, or dictation by the strongest countries. American dictation creates the unified strategy of present-day imperialist coalitions, whose primary purpose is to satisfy American military and political aims. Quite understandably the irreconcilable contradictions inherent in capitalist society make it impossible to achieve complete strategic unity in imperialist blocs and coalitions. Experience shows that where the development of a unified strategy for the alliance is concerned, each country tries to get more from the alliance and contribute less than the others. As V. I. Lenin remarked, in capitalistic alliances ". . . two tendencies exist: one which makes the coalition of all imperialists inevitable, and the other which makes for opposition among the imperialists; neither of these is based on sound foundation." *

This is confirmed by the contradictions within modern aggressive military blocs of imperialist states.

In the past, very bitter disputes have arisen in NATO during discussions of a strategic plan for "the defense of the West." The French and West German military leaders insisted upon the concept of "continental strategy" and demanded that the United States participate in the "defense" of the European continent. The "peripheral strategy" propounded by the American and British military leaders did not provide for the "defense" of Europe by the noncontinental countries and proposed instead the creation of a defense zone along the periphery of the European continent, on the islands of the Atlantic Ocean, in the Mediterranean, and in the North Sea. And although it would seem that the proponents of the "continental strategy" won, subsequent events demonstrated that the agreement reached in 1955 was illusory. During the regular session of the NATO Council in 1959, the basic disagreements of the allies reappeared with new strength. The United States, refusing to finance the armament of the West European armies to the degree that it had previously, demanded increased contributions for armaments from the allies, which they refused.

All these examples confirm that British Field Marshal Montgomery was correct in declaring that instead of a "lake of unity," NATO had "approximately thirty political puddles."

President Kennedy's message to Congress also confirmed this fact:

> In Europe our alliances are unfulfilled and in some disarray. The unity of NATO has been weakened by economic rivalry and partially eroded by national interests." †

In a coalition of socialist countries, the co-ordination of military strategy is the result of the unity of the political aims, which unite all the countries into an alliance of equal partners. In V. I. Lenin's words: "*We* . . . [in our Civil War against the bourgeoisie] shall unite and merge the people *not* by the power of money *nor* with a big stick nor force, but by *voluntary* agreement, and the solidarity of the workers against the exploiters." ‡

The absence of contradictions between policy and strategy in socialist coalitions assures the harmonious correlation of the international and

---

* V. I. Lenin, *Sochineniia* [*Works*], Vol. 27, p. 333.

† *Pravda*, January 31, 1961. [President Kennedy, "State of the Union," January 30, 1961, in *Documents on American Foreign Relations, 1961*, Harper, New York, 1962, p. 19.]

‡ V. I. Lenin, *Sochineniia* [*Works*], Vol. 23, p. 15.

national aspects of the military strategies of the different countries. The common interest in the defense of the socialist camp from attacks by imperialist aggressors not only assumes military co-operation among the armies of the socialist countries, but also a unity of strategic views.

The Warsaw Pact on military defense, which was signed by the socialist countries, unites all of its participants in the single aim of defending the accomplishments of socialism in their countries from imperialist aggression. Its freedom-loving aims assure tremendous advantages to this coalition if war breaks out, since "the basis for the relations of countries in the worldwide socialist system and of all the Communist and Workers' Parties are the principles of Marxism-Leninism, and the principles of proletarian internationalism, which have been tested by experience." *

## U.S. ED. NOTE B: SOVIET VIEWS ON WAR AS AN INSTRUMENT OF POLICY

[Soviet doctrine distinguishes between the political character of war in general and the rationality of a particular war as an instrument of state policy. As was pointed out in the Analytical Introduction, the fundamental communist view maintains that all wars are by definition political acts because they are waged by the belligerents to achieve specific political aims. For example, Lenin wrote: "The ruling class also determines policy in war. War is in its entirety politics; it is the continuation by this class of the pursuit of the same aims by other means." [12] Consequently, "the warring states formulate the political aims of the war. The nature of the political aims decisively influences the conduct of the war," [13] that is, the scale and intensity of the war.

Since the war aims of a country reflect the interests of its ruling class, wars between countries with different social systems are bound to be more intense because the war aims tend to be less limited. Khrushchev has repeatedly warned that the "logic of war" would require that "all means, intercontinental ballistic missiles, submarine missiles, and other means which now exist will be used in case of armed conflict." [14]

---

* *Deklaratsiia stran-uchastnits Varshavskogo pakta* [*Declaration of the Countries Participating in the Warsaw Pact*], Gospolitizdat, Moscow, 1957.

[12] V. I. Lenin, *Sochineniia* [*Works*], Vol. 25, p. 19.

[13] Colonel G. A. Fedorov, "The Nature of Wars and Their Causes," in *Marksizm-Leninizm o voine i armii* [*Marxism-Leninism on War and the Army*], Voenizdat Ministerstva Oborony Soiuza SSR, Moscow, 1961, p. 43. See also T. Kondratkov, "Concerning the Interdependence of War and Politics," *Sovetskii flot* (*Soviet Fleet*), January 8, 1958.

[14] *Pravda*, November 29, 1957. See also *Pravda*, January 15, 1960, and July 11, 1962.

Because of this fundamental Soviet view on the nature of war, Soviet theoreticians reject the argument that nuclear war is no longer a political act and that politics plays no role in such a war. They argue that a war between the West and the Soviet Union would be the most intense form of the ongoing struggle, begun in 1917 with the Communist seizure of power in Russia, between two antagonistic social systems. In such a war each side would seek to destroy the other's political, economic, and social system, and the finality of this aim would in turn determine the intensity of the war and the military strategies of the belligerents.

> In the course of the war, the imperialist states will choose theaters of military operation, determine the targets for their nuclear attacks and their priority, direct the action of their armed forces—air force, missile units, navy and ground forces—in accordance with their counterrevolutionary aims. Consequently, politics will play a dominant role in a nuclear and missile war as it has in previous wars.[15]

One reason for the greater role of the political leadership in a nuclear war is said to be the highly centralized control over modern strategic weapons, which will facilitate direct employment of these weapons in accordance with the political aims of the ruling class.[16]

While arguing that nuclear war remains a political act, Soviet writers and spokesmen recognize that it may not be "reasonable, from the point of view of a particular state, to initiate war"[17] if that state knows in advance that it will suffer devastating retaliatory attacks. Thus, according to one Soviet military writer:

> The process of development of technology for the extermination of people has led to a situation which makes it impossible to use weapons to solve political problems, as was done for thousands of years. A nuclear and missile war is not only extremely dangerous for the side subject to attack but suicidal for the aggressor himself.

> In our opinion, from the military-technology point of view, war as an instrument of policy is outliving itself. But this, obviously, does not in the least exclude the possibility that an aggressor may nevertheless unleash war, as the advancement of military technology, taken alone, cannot guarantee peace on earth.[18]

---

[15] Fedorov, *op. cit.,* p. 51.

[16] *Ibid.,* pp. 49–50.

[17] *Ibid.,* p. 51.

[18] Major General N. Talenskii, "Contemporary War: Its Character and Consequences," *Mezhdunarodnaia zhizn'* (*International Affairs*), No. 10, October 1960, p. 34.

"As long as capitalism survives in the world," Khrushchev has said, "the reactionary forces, representing the interests of the capitalist monopolies, will continue this drive toward military gambles and aggression and may try to unleash war." [19] This basic position was incorporated into the Program of the Communist Party of the Soviet Union, adopted in October 1961.[20]]

## Strategy and Economics

*The Role of the Economic Factor in War.* Every war is the product of social and economic relations. In this demonstration of the mutual dependence of war, as a form of coercion, and the material basis of this coercion, i.e., weapons and troops, F. Engels stated that war is not a simple act of volition: ". . . the triumph of force is based on arms production and this, in turn, on production in general and therefore on 'economic power,' on the economic order, and on the *material* means which force has at its disposal." *

However, war in general is dependent not only upon economic conditions, but also upon "the combat methods of the army," i.e., the methods by which war is conducted, in other words, strategy.

Initially, this dependence was not very noticeable. The influence of economics upon war and strategy was not very sharply defined in slave-owning and feudal societies and during the initial development of capitalism. During the time of small scale wars, states could war even when their economy was disrupted. This is quite evident from military history. Before the French Revolution, the Bourbon dynasty had brought France to complete economic exhaustion so that Napoleon undertook his initial campaigns literally with an empty treasury. However, in spite of a twenty-year period of continuous war, the Napoleonic Empire in 1811 had a reserve of 200 million francs. Another example is pre-revolutionary Russia which, in spite of being backward and completely dependent upon foreign capital, was militarily strong because of its vast human resources.

Such was the case until the inception of capitalism, which gave impetus to the development of trade, industry, and means of communication. This provided the basis for wars of increased scope and, consequently, increased their material requirements. World War I showed

---

[19] N. S. Khrushchev, speech at the XXth Congress of the CPSU, *Pravda*, February 15, 1956.

[20] *Programme of the Communist Party of the Soviet Union*, Supplement to *New Times*, No. 48, November 29, 1961.

* F. Engels, *Anti-Diuring*, Gospolitizdat, Moscow, 1953, pp. 155–156 [F. Engels, *Herr Eugen Dühring's Revolution in Science (Anti-Dühring)*, Lawrence & Wishart, London, England, 1943, p. 18].

a sharp increase in material cost in comparison with preceding wars. For example, the cost of one year of war conducted by Russia in the nineteenth and twentieth centuries increased progressively from one war to the next and amounted to the following (in millions of gold rubles):

| | |
|---|---:|
| The Patriotic War of 1812 | 80 |
| The Crimean War (1853–1856) | 190 |
| The Russo-Turkish War (1877–1878) | 450 |
| The Russo-Japanese War (1904–1905) | 1,420 |
| World War I (1914–1917) | 12,000 |

In the wars of the monopoly-capitalist era, the percentage of expenditures for military equipment as compared to the total cost of the war increased similarly. For example, in the Russo-Turkish War, for Russia it was 25 per cent, whereas in World War I it increased to 60 per cent.

World War II showed an even larger increase in the role of equipment. Whereas in 1914 there was an average of ⅓ horsepower in motor equipment for every soldier mobilized in all of the countries, in World War II this came to 20 horsepower. These indexes will undoubtedly increase much more in a present-day war.

The increasing material requirements for conducting war naturally call for an increased industrial potential in the belligerent countries. The comparative table provided below shows the increase in annual industrial production of basic weapons and military equipment of the main participants of World War I and World War II.

Production in the Main Belligerent Countries,
Yearly Average (in Units)

| | World War I | World War II (1941–1944) |
|---|---:|---:|
| Airplanes | up to 45,000 | 130,000 |
| Tanks | 9,000 * | over 91,000 |
| Artillery pieces and mortars | 37,000 | up to 510,000 |
| Machine guns | over 250,000 | over 1,660,000 |

These indexes indicate that industrial growth and the development of productive forces inescapably lead to an increasing role of the economic factor in war.

*The Nature of the Relationship of Strategy to Economics.* Strategy is related to economics in that strategic concepts develop and change completely because of their dependence on the economic conditions and the level of productive forces achieved at a given time.

Although economic development is subject to its own laws, strategic

---

* Produced in the countries of the Triple Entente by the end of the war.

considerations are taken into account in directing the economy [in peacetime]; and in war, military requirements dominate almost completely. Strategy and economics do not influence each other directly, but rather through the agencies of state administration.

Let us examine in sequence how these particular features are manifested in various aspects of the relationship of strategy to economics.

The entire history of development of strategic theory is a clear example of the determining influence of economics upon the nature of military strategic concepts. Apart from the epoch whose character is always reflected in these concepts, and the national character of the strategy, there is one general law formulated by F. Engels: "Armaments, the composition of forces and their organization, tactics and strategy depend above all on the state reached at the time in production and communication." *

This dependence is a result of evolutionary development and gradual changes in industrial methods, as well as basic revolutionary changes. Change in the whole social and economic structure, and individual discoveries and inventions influence strategy. For example, the invention of gunpowder and firearms led to the creation of the extended formation on battlefields. Rifled artillery led to greater depth of unit deployment and the destruction of the enemy at a great distance. The invention of radio and the organization of the first radio-telegraphic military units, which provided communication over distances of 80 kilometers [50 miles] or more, transformed radio communication into an instrument of strategic command. With the appearance of aircraft the strategic theory of [winning] air supremacy was born and earlier concepts of ground operations were changed. The nuclear weapon marked the beginning of a new stage in the development of strategy, based upon entirely new principles.

It should be noted, however, that it is not only discoveries and inventions in specialized fields, but also the general level of technical progress, comprising all the main branches of the economy, which change the concepts of military strategy. For example, the gradual increase in tonnage of ocean-going vessels increased the capability to move and concentrate troops by sea. This in turn made the navy an instrument of strategic concentration and deployment. In another example, metallurgical improvements led to higher quality steel, which made it possible to design and produce rapid-firing artillery and machine guns. The introduction of these weapons into the army not only affected the execution of tactical and operational missions, but also the conduct of war as a

---

* F. Engels, *Anti-Diuring*, p. 156 [*Anti-Dühring*, p. 188].

whole. The massive introduction of tanks and other motor vehicles into armies caused basic changes in military and strategic ideas; this in turn made possible the development of ways of waging wars of maneuver.

Strategy was enormously influenced at one time by extensive railway construction, which considerably accelerated transport and increased its volume, thus facilitating the concentration of troops. Further extension of railroad networks, improved railroad technology, the increase in the load capacity of the rolling stock and in the traffic capacity of the system made possible large and rapid troop concentrations in the theaters of military operation, thus increasing the opportunities for strategic maneuver.

All this had a great influence in changing strategic concepts. The density and location of railroad networks began to affect the formulation of strategic war plans as well as single operations, since the mobilization and deployment schedules of the armed forces depended upon railroad networks. For example, before World War I Germany and Austria, which had a highly developed railroad system and trunklines along their eastern borders, planned to complete their strategic deployment according to the following schedule: Germany, 13 days after the proclamation of mobilization, and Austria, 16 days. At the same time, Tsarist Russia which had no well-developed railroad system or trunkline along its western border, could complete its deployment only after 24 days, according to the calculations of the Russian general staff.

This is the first aspect of the relationship of military strategy to economics.

In spite of the fact that economic development is governed by its own special laws, its development has some particular features which derive from its responsibilities to strategy.

The economy of any country cannot be developed without taking into account strategic considerations, as well as the most rational use of the country's resources for defense. For this reason, strategic requirements are considered in the formulation of the economic development plan. In addition, a country must be able at any minute to reorganize its economy for war production in the event of war. Consequently, the economic structure of a country is usually to some extent adapted to facilitate conversion to a war economy.

Economic administrative agencies pay most careful attention to strategic considerations when planning the geographic distribution of industry, agricultural production, and the construction of communication lines.

When discussing the relationship of military strategy to economy, one must not neglect the responsibilities of the former to the latter.

When military strategy presents its economic requirements, it must outline very clearly the entire course of mobilization of the national economy, the actual capabilities, schedules, and conditions necessary for the development of defense production, as well as difficulties that may arise.

Strategy must furnish the economy with accurate information on the requirements of at least the first year of war, as well as the expected rates of supply and losses and replacement of material and technical equipment. Strategy must develop and implement measures to protect economic installations as well as to attack the enemy's economy.

In order to attack the enemy's economy according to strategic plans, special operations are often carried out to capture or destroy strategically important regions and sources of raw materials. A case in point is Hitler's Operation "Blue Fox," whose main purpose was to capture the Kola Peninsula nickel deposits.

In order to wage war each state usually puts its economy on a war footing. This reorganization in various countries differs with the economic organization of the society. However, as war experience has shown, it must include the following measures:

Mobilization of industry, agriculture, transport and communication
Construction of new defense-industrial installations, and evacuation [of industry] from threatened regions of the country
Construction of a road net
Organization and redistribution of the labor force, and the training and retraining of industrial workers
Mobilization of all food resources of the country and strict control over food distribution
The institution of financial measures in the country; issuing paper money, levying of additional taxes, and floating internal loans
Reorganization and reorientation of foreign trade
Reorganization of economic administration

Once military operations begin, strategic plans exert an increasing degree of influence upon economic development. Correspondingly, strategic plans are always based upon material and technical capacities. Military history shows that the initiation of many large-scale operations has to be timed with the arrival of military equipment at the front. The Soviet counterattack during the Battle of Stalingrad, in 1942–1943, was a perfect example of this.

The subsequent actions [after the initiation of an operation] of the strategic leadership also frequently depend upon the availability of materiel. For example, the Russian High Command in 1915 had to halt its successful Carpathian offensive and to withdraw its troops because of lack of ammunition.

We shall briefly treat the interrelationships of strategy and economics.

As was pointed out, the relationship of one to the other is most often indirect, i.e., through the agencies of state administration. This is understandable, since military leaders cannot issue direct orders to a trust, industrial aggregate, or factory, thus creating anarchy in production. Therefore, even a capitalist state tries to regulate and co-ordinate the action of its strategy and economy through the agency of the state administration, even though it is not always successful. The wartime centralization of economic administration permits military leaders to deal with a single responsible agency or office which takes both military and economic interests into consideration.

The organization and functions of the state agencies that handle strategic requirements and provide the necessities of the armed forces vary in different countries. However, these agencies have something of a common purpose. They usually perform the following functions: make an account of the country's economic potential and the probable requirements of war; plan the economic preparation of the country and the provision of the armed forces with all necessities in the event of war; co-ordinate current economic measures with the requirements of military strategy; eliminate structural imbalances should they arise; prepare and carry out the mobilization of industry, transportation, and communication; and allocate resources to the homeland and front.

*Strategy and Economy in the Socialist and in the Capitalist State.* Social and economic conditions exert a basic influence upon the relationship of strategy to economy. This became quite evident in the epoch of imperialism. In 1904, in an article entitled "The Fall of Port Arthur," V. I. Lenin stated: "Never before has the military organization of a country had such a close bearing on its entire economic and cultural system." *

In the socialist state, the relation between strategy and economics is largely determined by public ownership of the means of production, by the planned development of the national economy, and by the leadership of the party of the working class.

Public ownership of the means of production excludes all unhealthy competition in the economy and permits all efforts to be concentrated on the attainment of the general aims of the state.

The absence of private ownership of the means of production enables Soviet military strategy, in its determination of the relative importance and the direction of development of one branch or another of the armed forces, to base itself exclusively upon a scientific analysis of the nature of the modern warfare, since it is not necessary to consider the interests of large monopolies, as in capitalist countries.

---

* V. I. Lenin, *Sochineniia* [*Works*], Vol. 8, p. 36.

Planning improves the economic organization of the society and permits the rapid and efficient utilization of all the productive resources of a country. Thus, in a socialist state, strategic calculations are based upon precisely known capabilities and clearly defined prospects of economic development.

The unified leadership of the party of the working class assures agreement between the aims and action of strategy and economy.

One of the advantages of a Soviet socialist state over a bourgeois state is that the socialist system assures a more perfect organization of the society, which is of critical importance to the state's defensive might. Superior economic organization permitted the Soviet government during the Civil War, when the economy was destroyed, to make effective use of the meager material resources then at the disposal of the young Soviet Republic and to organize the country's defense successfully. The management by the Communist Party of the country's defense and the high degree of popular discipline made it possible even in those days to successfully implement Lenin's slogan: "Everything for the front, everything for the victory!"

The highly organized Soviet economy played an even greater role in the Great Patriotic War. The reorganization of industry on a war footing was accomplished twice as fast in the Soviet Union as in the capitalist countries of the anti-Hitler coalition. At the same time the rate of growth of military production [in the USSR] greatly exceeded all the previous rates for a socialist economy. Thus, by December 1942, the production of aircraft in the USSR was 3.3 times that of December 1941, and the production of tanks was twice as great. These high rates of production, combined with the efficient organization of labor and production, made it possible for the Soviet economy to achieve a greater annual production of aircraft, tanks, guns, and mortars than the enemy, in spite of a lower output of steel, cast iron, coal, and other materials.

During the four years of the Great Patriotic War, the Soviet Union produced annually an average of 11.3 million [metric] tons of steel, 7.8 million tons of pig iron, and 113.7 million tons of coal, whereas Nazi Germany and its satellites produced 33.4 million tons of steel, 24.5 million tons of pig iron, and 537.7 million tons of coal. On the basis of this output, the Soviet Union had an average annual production of 27,-000 airplanes and 23,774 tanks and self-propelled artillery pieces, while Nazi Germany produced 19,720 airplanes and 12,400 tanks and self-propelled artillery.

One of the principles of socialist economy is the harmonious, proportionate development of the national economy to satisfy the growing needs of the population and the requirements of increasing the country's defense potential.

In 1924 M. V. Frunze [21] wrote on this principle in an article entitled "The Front and the Rear in a Future War": "In every new undertaking, economic, cultural, etc., one must always ask the question: How will the results of this undertaking fit into the defense of the country? Is there a chance to ensure also the attainment of definite military purposes without detriment to peacetime requirements?" * The principle of combining the development of the economic interests with an increase in the country's defense power makes it simultaneously possible: to bring industry closer to the sources of raw materials and to consumers; to develop the economy of backward regions of the country; to distribute the labor force according to a systematic territorial plan among the economic regions and in accordance with the plans for the development of economic complexes within each economic region; to facilitate strategic deployment; and to provide for the needs of the armed forces for equipment and materiel and to assure their constant high combat readiness.

These are, in brief, the particular features of the relationship of strategy to economy in a socialist state.

An entirely different picture meets the eye in a capitalist state, where economic development to a considerable degree is subject to the unbridled forces of competition. Private ownership of the means of production gives rise to a bitter struggle for profits. This has a serious effect on military industry, and consequently on the development of the different branches of the armed forces and on the development of strategic concepts and theories. Private capitalist interests often slow up the development of branches of defense industry that are not very profitable even if indispensable from the military point of view. The attempts of a bourgeois state to co-ordinate [these matters] are not always successful, since government officials act for the benefit of the monopolistic armament suppliers, whose interests they protect in the government. To prove this, one need only consider the new American administration. The present Secretary of State, Dean Rusk, is the president of the Rockefeller Fund; Secretary of Defense Robert McNamara is a former president of The Ford Motor Company and a director of the Scott Paper Company; the Postmaster General, Edward Day, is a former vice-president of the Prudential Life Insurance Company; and the Secretary of the Treasury, Douglas Dillon, is one of the directors of the Dillon-Reed Company.

---

[21] U.S. ED. NOTE—Michail Vasil'evech Frunze (1885–1925), a prominent early Soviet military leader and theoretician, held high military posts in the Red Army, such as Peoples' Commissioner for Defense, Chief of Staff of the Red Army, and Chief of the Military Academy. He was also Candidate-Member of the Politburo. See *BSE,* Vol. 45, pp. 614–616.

* M. V. Frunze, *Izbrannye proizvedeniia* [*Selected Works*], Voenizdat, Moscow, 1951, p. 260.

In order to favor business in a bourgeois state, even strategic concepts are based upon considerations of economic advantage. Experience has shown that during a war private capitalist interests often guide military operations. Thus, during World War II, the American companies General Motors and Ford, which were closely affiliated with German automobile and tank manufacturing firms, prevented the German plants from being bombed by the American air force.

Capitalists are prepared to justify and support any strategic doctrine for the sake of profits. World War I earned the Rockefellers $450,000,-000 in net profits. The capital of the Rockefellers increased by $2,127,-000,000 as a result of World War II. In pursuit of profits, the capitalist monopolies do not hesitate to betray the national interests of their own people. It is known that more than 60 American companies located on German soil during the war produced armament for Hitler's armies, which was then used against the allied armies. The American firm, General Motors, produced through the German Opel company one-half of all the motor vehicles manufactured in Germany during the war to equip the German army. During World War II the Rockefellers gave the German concern, I. G. Farbenindustrie, patents for the preparation of synthetic rubber, vitally needed by Hitler's armies, and withheld these patents from American manufacturers.

One cannot completely deny the role of bourgeois state agencies in the relation of strategy to economics in capitalist countries. For example, in countries with a totalitarian fascist regime, as experience has shown, the state played a strongly regulating role. This was particularly evident in wartime.

However, it should not be forgotten that economic regulation by a bourgeois state in the interest of strategy can often assume the most monstrous forms. Thus, in the past war the German and British governments compelled the liquidation of medium-sized and small industrial firms by law in order to achieve great concentration of industry. In Germany, a government decree forbade small businessmen with a capital less than 500,000 marks to develop any kind of production. In England by the middle of 1943, allegedly because of shortages of labor, equipment, and raw materials, 32,000 small firms were forcibly closed, or one-third of those in existence at the beginning of the war.

In the final analysis, these measures produced some benefits in effective industrial organization and increased defense production of needed items. But again, this was done to the advantage of the large monopolists, who were thus aided by the government in their competition with the smaller firms. Bourgeois governments, when co-ordinating strategy and the economy, are able only to take into account the peculiarities of capitalist economic development and to devise strategic plans on this basis.

The governments of imperialist states cannot bring about a more rational geographic distribution of economic installations. It is not accidental that almost the entire economy of capitalist countries is concentrated in large industrial and administrative centers, and nothing is done to develop the economy of the peripheral regions. For example, in the United States, 80 per cent of the ferrous metal industry and two-thirds of the electrical power industry are concentrated in the northeastern industrial region, which comprises 30.9 per cent of the territory of the United States.

In Great Britain, 55 per cent of the petroleum products, 63 per cent of the steel and pig iron, and over 60 per cent of the entire defense production are concentrated in fifteen large industrial districts. In West Germany, the Ruhr industrial region accounts for 90 per cent of the coal production and 85 per cent of the production of the steel, chemical, and defense industry.

Thus, although the capitalist economy as a whole is directed to the preparation for war, bourgeois military strategy cannot be based on planned economic development, and often the development of the economy cannot be clearly anticipated since everything is dominated by chaotic economic competition.

### U.S. ED. NOTE C: THE ROLE OF ECONOMICS IN THE SOVIET VIEW OF MODERN WAR

[According to Soviet military writers, the economic strength of a country plays a critical role in contemporary wars: According to two Soviet military analysts:

The role of economic factors in a missile war has not only considerably increased, but has become essentially different in comparison with previous world wars. The exceptional role which will be played by nuclear strikes against the enemy's vital regions in the initial stage of the war does not contradict the thesis that the outcome of such a war will be to a decisive extent determined by the results of the competition of the economies of the warring states. At the same time, the peculiarities of a missile war lead to very important conclusions. The stocks of nuclear weapons and means of delivering them to targets, especially missiles of various types and other modern weapons, acquire an exceptional and paramount strategic significance. The significance of the reserves of the more important strategic materials which are stocked in peacetime is considerably increased.[22]

---

[22] Colonel I. N. Levanov and Colonel G. A. Fedorov, "The Economic and Social-Political Bases of the Military Might of a State," in *Marksizm-Leninizm o voine i armii* (Marxism-Leninism on War and the Army), Moscow, 1961, p. 272.

See also Colonel A. Lagovskii, *Strategiia i ekonomika* (Strategy and Economy), Voenizdat Ministerstva Oborony Soiuza SSR, Moscow, 1961, p. 33.

Hence economic defense potential of a country is of decisive importance in determining the military strength of that country. In a message to Chancellor Adenauer, Khrushchev wrote: "I assess power not by the number of weapons and divisions but by the level of economic development. This is the main thing. Whoever has a strong economy has the ability, if he so wishes, to create also a strong army." [23]

Different Soviet writers give somewhat varying accounts of the factors that make up a country's economic potential. One rather conservative definition lists the following factors: the size of the population, its cultural level, and its political attitude and morale; the economic system and the economic organization of the state; the capacity of industry and especially of heavy industry; the density, distribution, and condition of transportation routes; the level of development in agriculture; the availability of mineral resources and their exploitation; the degree of dependence of the economy on foreign imports and the reliability of means of communication with foreign suppliers; the speed with which the economy can be placed on a war footing; the effectiveness of the use of the economic resources; the degree of labor productivity and its growth; and the availability of various national reserves.[24]

Other Soviet publications indicate the need to bring this definition more closely in line with the conditions of a nuclear and missile war. According to one such publication, the economic defense potential comprises the following factors: the total volume of production of all economic elements which contribute to the defense effort, including the availability of natural resources, the size of the population and the number of technically trained personnel, and the effective use made of all these resources; the speed with which the economy can be put on a war footing; the rate of growth in defense production in wartime and the capacity of industry to mass-produce new military equipment; the ability of the economy to survive nuclear attack, which will depend on the organization of production, the geographic distribution of important industrial centers and the vulnerability of their lines of supply, and the speed of rehabilitation and recovery of the destroyed industrial facilities.[25]

The relative vulnerability of the opposing economies to nuclear attack is vital because: "The necessity to weaken the economic poten-

---

[23] *Pravda,* August 27, 1959.
[24] Lagovskii, *op. cit.,* p. 31.
[25] Levanov and Fedorov, *op. cit.,* pp. 272–273.

tial of the aggressor by all available means of armed combat is one of the most important rules governing modern war." Consequently, it is also important to study the enemy's economy not only to assess his military capability but also to "discover the strong and weak sides of his economy," so that in the event of a war this information can be used in formulating plans for military operations against the enemy's economic potential.[26]

Khrushchev and the Soviet military writers all agree that in a war both sides would concentrate much of their strategic nuclear efforts against economic targets.[27] Such a nuclear exchange, it is said, can lead to a fundamental change, even a reversal, in the balance of the opposing economic potentials. Consequently, "There arises the very important problem of how to preserve the vitality of the economy during the entire period of military action, how to locate industry rationally throughout one's own territory, how to create the essential state reserves, etc." [28] The question of industrial vulnerability and dispersal has received considerable attention in Soviet literature and Khrushchev has claimed that the Soviet Union is less vulnerable to attack than the Western powers because of the greater dispersal of its industry.[29]

While Soviet writings stress the importance of prewar production and stockpiling, they also retain the notion of conversion of industry to war production and of economic mobilization after war breaks out. This appears to reflect Soviet indecision on whether a war would be of short or long duration. The emphasis on the need to attack economic targets in a war and on the question of industrial vulnerability and rehabilitation suggests Soviet concern with the possibility of a "broken-back" war after the initial nuclear exchange. In such a war the relative degree of economic survival and rates of recovery of the belligerent countries could decisively influence the final outcome and determine which side would be victorious.

It has been Soviet practice to take defense requirements into account in planning economic development. This fact has been repeatedly stressed in Soviet official statements. For example, in 1957 Khrushchev told a foreign correspondent, concerning the newly instituted decentralization of industrial management, that "the reorganization of

---

[26] Lagovskii, *op. cit.*, p. 32.

[27] See, for example, *Pravda*, January 15, 1960.

[28] V. Siniagin, "The Creation of the Material-Technical Base of Communism and the Strengthening of the Defense Capacity of the USSR," *Kommunist vooruzhennykh sil* (*Communist of the Armed Forces*), No. 14, July 1962, p. 9.

[29] *Pravda*, January 15, 1960.

industry we have carried out ensures a more autonomous management of industry, which is also a strategic gain." [30] According to its current program the Party "will continue to give unflagging attention to the growth of heavy industry, which ensures the development of the country's productive forces and defense capacity," and "the chief task of heavy industry is to meet the needs of the country's defense in full . . . as well as to satisfy other economic needs." [31]]

## Strategy and Morale and Political Factors

*The Role of the Morale Factor in War.* Marxism-Leninism defines the morale factor as one of the decisive elements of any war, since victory, to a considerable extent, depends on ". . . the spirit of the masses who shed their blood on the battlefield." [*]

High morale among troops engaged directly in military operations is inconceivable without a high political morale throughout the entire nation. This has become particularly obvious under current conditions, when enormous masses of the population of the warring countries participate in the armed struggle and when the distinctions between the front and the rear are erased.

Modern wars are conducted with mass armies whose morale is determined by the mood of the entire nation, that is, by the ideas which emanate from the homeland. A military strategy that does not take this most important factor into account and that is based only upon the superiority of its material resources risks losing even this advantage. In times of war, as F. Engels pointed out, the element of morale is immediately transformed into a material force.

F. Engels considered the morale of soldiers and the socio-political composition of the army to be the most important factors influencing military strategy. He stressed that the victories of the French Revolution resulted largely from the fact that its revolutionary army was composed of people liberated from the feudal yoke, which could not be said of the enemies of the revolution, who maintained discipline in their troops only by means of a stick [i.e., by flogging]. Engels also pointed out that a member of a socialist society will always fight with inspiration, fortitude, and courage, against which the mechanical drill of bourgeois armies will have no chance of success.

In discussing the reasons for our victories in the Civil War, V. I. Lenin wrote: ". . . our proletariat, weak in numbers, exhausted by

---

[30] *Pravda,* November 19, 1957.
[31] *Pravda,* July 30, 1961.
[*] V. I. Lenin, *Sochineniia* [*Works*], Vol. 31, p. 115.

calamity and privation, was victorious because it was strong in morale." *

In order to evaluate the role of the morale factor in war correctly, it is necessary to proceed from an objective analysis of military history and the conditions and nature of modern war. Both the underestimation of this factor and its overestimation are equally harmful to military strategy. One must realize that in different epochs, the role of the morale factor in war has been evaluated differently.

For a long time, generals have understood the importance of morale in war. Napoleon himself said that victory depends three-fourths upon morale factors and only one-fourth upon others.

Modern bourgeois military theoreticians are even inclined at times to overestimate the significance of these factors in war. For example, English Field Marshal Montgomery stated in one of his speeches that he considers "morale to be the most important and only factor in war. Without high morale no success can be achieved, no matter how good the strategic and tactical plans and the rest." †

One could cite many examples of bourgeois ideologists' recognition of the important role of the morale factor in war. However, at the same time, it is essential to know what is meant by morale and what elements, in the opinion of the military ideologists of imperialism, go into its creation.

The bourgeois idea of army morale is usually confined to the sum of the psychological and biological qualities of soldiers and officers. Consequently, social and economic conditions and class interests are not considered to be the basis for the morale potential; its basis is considered to lie [rather] in the biological, racial, and psychological characteristics of man instead, which result from national customs and habits.

The British Field Marshal Slim, in the article entitled "What Is Morale?" defines morale as follows: "Morale is the intangible spirit of men and women. Just as bravery, morale is a state of mind, a mixture of feelings and reason." ‡

Correspondingly, bourgeois military ideologists do not believe that morale is rooted in the conditions of life and the social structure, but rather in the peculiarities of the national character. Some bourgeois theoreticians maintain that man's striving for self-preservation, his gregarious instincts, his racial solidarity, etc., are the sources of morale.

It is quite obvious that national characteristics of the people play a certain role in creating an army's morale, just as do the individual char-

---

* V. I. Lenin, *Sochineniia* [*Works*], Vol. 32, p. 252.

† M. A. Mil'shtein and A. K. Slobodenko, *O burzhuaznoi voennoi nauke* [*On Bourgeois Military Science*], Voenizdat, Moscow, 1957, pp. 184–185.

‡ *Information Journal*, July 1948 [unverified].

acteristics of each person (heroism, self-sacrifice, initiative, and intelligence). However, this is not the main source of morale. History shows that a military strategy based only on strong patriotism and the readiness of people for self-sacrifice often proves shortsighted. Only the total material, political, and spiritual resources of the people as a whole determine the course and outcome of the war. In pointing this out, V. I. Lenin stressed that morale itself has an economic basis: "They refer constantly to the heroic patriotism and the marvelous military valor of the French in 1792–1793. However, they forget the material and historical-economic conditions, which alone made these wonders possible." *

The social and state systems are a most important source of army morale. A belligerent country's social and state system plays a decisive role not only in creating popular and army morale, but also in maintaining these at the necessary level during wartime.

What is political morale?

*Political morale, as a wartime phenomenon, is the totality of all the elements of morale expressing the ability of the people and the armed forces to withstand all the trials of war, even those requiring a maximum exertion of physical and spiritual strength. It is also the ability of the state to provide materially and politically for maintaining constant high morale in the army and people.*

Policy, which creates the necessary ideological and economic conditions, plays a decisive role in the formation of political morale. But even the highest morale does not guarantee victory; it merely increases the chances of gaining victory over the enemy. These chances must still be transformed into reality, which is the task of military strategy.

*The Mutual Relation and Interdependence of Strategy and Political Morale.* To assure the success of military operations one needs not only a high level of political morale in the entire nation, but also high combat morale of the troops directly engaged in battle. Military history often shows that victory is possible with equal and sometimes even smaller forces than the enemy if the armed forces have a high combat morale.

Thus, the relationship of strategy to political morale in war is most often manifested in the interdependence of strategic success and troop morale as one of the elements of political morale.

Social and political equality in the homeland and a unified spirit among all strata of the population are most important sources of high military morale. As one might expect, the army in whose homeland

---

* V. I. Lenin, *Sochineniia* [*Works*], Vol. 25, p. 335.

class unity is the rule has the strongest morale. One must recognize, however, that in individual cases, high steadfastness of army morale can be attained even without such unity. Such a situation arises when a belligerent country is united by feeling of national solidarity, and when the class contradictions are temporarily less pronounced than ideas of national independence and sovereignty.

In other cases, the troops may perform well in battle, even when there is no class unity, as a result of false but well-directed propaganda. One must never underestimate the ability of the ideological apparatus of an imperialist state to fool its people, intoxicate them with the narcotic of nationalistic ideas, and whip up emotions in order to achieve selfish imperialist aims. The shameless role of Hitler's propaganda in playing upon the German peoples' national and racial feelings during World War II is well known.

However, as experience shows, such a spurt in morale is of short duration. The nationalistic fervor of the German people, who were intoxicated by the military successes in the West, disappeared as soon as Fascist Germany met defeat on the Eastern Front.

Here the mutual relation and dependence of strategy and political morale were manifested most strongly. As this example shows, military success or defeat decisively affects the morale of the army and the people.

The victories of the Red Army at the battles of Moscow and Stalingrad are also instructive in this respect. They not only raised Soviet popular morale, but also that of the peoples in all the countries of the anti-German coalitions. In spite of the efforts of bourgeois falsifiers of history to minimize the psychological significance of these victories, they will remain the most important military and psychological victories of the entire war.

Even the German military historian K. Tippelskirch refuted the statement of the Anglo-American historians who assigned primary significance in World War II to the events in Africa.

"In spite of the fact that within the context of war as a whole, the North African events received greater attention than the Battle of Stalingrad, the catastrophe at Stalingrad shook the German army and German people far more, because it was far more immediate and tangible. Something [for generations [32]] inconceivable had occurred there, something not experienced since 1806; the annihilation of an army encircled by the enemy." *

---

[32] U.S. ED. NOTE—The Soviet authors omitted these words, found in the German original, without indicating an ellipsis.

\* K. Tippelskirch, *Istoriia vtoroi mirovoi voiny* [*History of the Second World War*], Izdatel'stvo Inostrannoi Literatury, Moscow, 1956, p. 256.

Thus military success has a considerable influence on popular and army morale, which, in turn, determines the nature of strategic plans as a whole as well as individual operations.

Morale is important in strategic planning. Thus if policy, as a whole, represents the interests of the mass of people, strategic plans which reflect policy are supported by the people and the army. If not they are built upon sand. For example, the leaders of the countries of the Entente [33] initially thought it possible to defeat the young Soviet Republic with twenty or thirty thousand well-armed soldiers.[34] However, the high morale of the young Red Army, as well as popular resistance within the Entente countries, showed how completely inadequate these plans were.

Because the Red Army during the Civil War showed such exceptionally high revolutionary steadfastness and enjoyed the moral support of the majority of the population, the interventionists,[35] even with hundreds or thousands of troops and huge amounts of military equipment, could not accomplish their predatory aims.

Strategic plans often depend upon army morale since such plans must often be adapted to troop morale at the given moment. History furnishes many examples of how low troop morale forced strategic leadership to eschew offensive plans.

To estimate accurately an army's combat potential it is always necessary to have a clear idea of its morale, i.e., as Engels stressed, to know what can and cannot be demanded from the army without risk of demoralization. Strategic plans must reckon not only with prewar army morale, but also wartime morale. An army's morale changes substantially with the onset of war because war sharply intensifies contradictions, particularly those in a country with class differences.

As Lenin pointed out, in a capitalist state during wartime the contradictions are intensified between the people and the government, the people and the army, and the army and the government. In a socialist state, on the other hand, the government, people, and the army achieve even greater solidarity in wartime, which generates new political morale in the entire society. Past wars have shown that the harder the trials of a state, the more graphically these opposing tendencies are manifested. For this very reason present-day bourgeois military theoreticians, afraid to upset the balance of their country's social groupings (which has been achieved with such difficulty and is so often imperfect even in peace-

---

[33] U.S. ED. NOTE—Soviet historiography tends to use the term "Entente" loosely to describe the Allied powers in World War I, including the United States.

[34] U.S. ED. NOTE—Apparently a reference to the Allies' Archangel Expedition of 1918–1919.

[35] U.S. ED. NOTE—The reference here is to the intervention of the Allied powers in Russia during 1917–1922.

time), seek strategic concepts and methods of conducting war which guarantee its most rapid conclusion and prevent their population from [openly] opposing the war. In adapting their military strategy to limited morale resources, bourgeois military theoreticians advance various theories, such as "limited war" and "small professional armies." The real political reasons for these theories are to convince the public that war will not require sacrifices and that it will allegedly be limited in scope, methods of conduct, and aims, so that it can be won by a small professional army without mobilizing the entire nation.

In addition, certain militarist strategists of the capitalist countries are not opposed to "blitzkrieg." The basis for this is that in a short war the political morale advantages of the socialist camp would supposedly not have sufficient time to manifest themselves as in a prolonged war.

However, some imperialist military strategists are not only interested in the preparation of their own military and political morale for war. Imperialist strategic plans devote an important place to ideological work among the opponent's troops and population, to so-called psychological warfare. This method of warfare, along with the operations of the ground forces, air forces, and the navy, is considered to be an independent type of operation. In theory, "psychological warfare" is often transformed into the concept of delivering a "demoralizing blow," which, according to bourgeois military theoreticians, should result in final victory within a short time.

The idea of the "demoralizing" blow was hatched by Hitler, who attempted, on the basis of Fascist German [successful] experience in the West, to sow panic in the rear of the Red Army. However, by the Germans' own admission, what was readily accomplished in France and Belgium proved to be unattainable on the Russian front.

John Fuller admits that "strangely enough, there was little or no panic within or behind the Russian front." *

This illustrates the fact that "a demoralizing" blow and "psychological warfare" will be successful only in combat with an opponent with poor morale.

### U.S. ED. NOTE D: CHANGING ASSESSMENTS OF THE INFLUENCE OF MORALE IN NUCLEAR WAR

[Soviet military doctrine has always ascribed critical importance to the morale and political attitude of the population and of the armed forces. Stalin had included these attitudes among his "permanently

---

* J. F. Fuller, *Vtoraia mirovaia voina 1939–1945* gg [*The Second World War*], Izdatel'stvo Inostrannoi Literatury, Moscow, 1956, p. 161 [English edition, *The Second World War 1939–1945*, Duell, Sloan and Pearce, New York, 1949, p. 120].

operating factors," or principles of war which "determine the course and outcome of war." [36] The advent of nuclear weapons and of missiles has not lessened Soviet emphasis on morale.

One reason for the increased importance of morale in a future war is that armed combat will be more difficult, mobile, and rapid, and will entail greater casualties than in previous wars. Hence the soldier must have high morale and determination if he is to fight effectively under conditions of nuclear warfare.[37] This requires discipline, training, and confidence in the military and political leadership and in the objectives for which the war is fought.[38]

The morale of the soldiers will also depend on the morale and political attitudes of the population, which, in a future war, will become a major target for enemy nuclear attacks.

> In contemporary war the aspiration to break down the morale of the enemy's population and to give rise to a mood for capitulation, is one of the characteristics of the strategy of the warring sides.[39]

Consequently a great deal will depend on the population's ability to bear the effects of a nuclear war without "becoming panicky or desperate." [40]

> From a military point of view the morale potential of a group of allied countries means the ability of the population to bear in the cause of the war enormous strains, difficulties, losses, calamities, even defeats, and under contemporary conditions, to bear the catastrophic consequences of nuclear attacks without losing the will to win. The higher expression

---

[36] Raymond L. Garthoff, *Soviet Military Doctrine*, Free Press, Glencoe, Ill., 1953, p. 34. J. V. Stalin, *On the Great Patriotic War of the Soviet Union*, Foreign Languages Publishing House, Moscow, 1946, p. 45.

[37] *Markisizm-Leninizm o voine i armii (Marxism-Leninism on War and the Army)*, Moscow, 1961, pp. 331–333; Colonel General V. F. Tolubko, "New Weapons and Psychological Training," *Red Star*, August 26, 1962.

[38] Marshal M. V. Zakharov, "Raise the Educational Significance of Disciplinary Practices," in *K novomu podemu partiino-politicheskoi raboty v sovetskoi armii i flote* (*Toward a New Increase in the Party-Political Work in the Army and Navy*), Voenizdat Ministerstva Oborony Soiuza SSR, Moscow, 1960, pp. 70–72. Colonel A. O. Baranov, *Voennaia tekhnika i moral'no-boevye kachestva voina (Military Technology and the Morale and Fighting Qualities of the Soldier)*, Voenizdat Ministerstva Oborony Soiuza SSR, Moscow, 1961, p. 5. *Marksizm-Leninizm o voine i armii (Marxism-Leninism on War and the Army)*, Moscow, 1961, pp. 332–333.

[39] Colonel M. G. Zhuravkov, Colonel B. A. Belov, Colonel I. V. Maryganov, *Moral'no-politicheskii faktor v sovremennoi voine (The Morale-Political Factor in Contemporary War)*, Voenizdat Ministerstva Oborony Soiuza SSR, Moscow, 1958, p. 162.

[40] *Marksizm-Leninizm o voine i armii (Marxism-Leninism on War and the Army)*, Moscow, 1961, p. 304.

of the will to fight and to win is expressed in the active determination
of the masses to win at any price, in the readiness to devote to this
end the greatest energy, to make any sacrifices, to show courage,
steadfastness, and heroism.[41]

Since wartime morale is said to be largely determined by the state
of class relations within each country, the classless Soviet society, it is
claimed, will be better able to bear the effects of a nuclear war than
the divided capitalist societies. Khrushchev has frequently asserted
that, while the Soviet system would survive a nuclear war, the capitalist
system would collapse because the peoples would hold it responsible for
the war and would overthrow it.

The recognition in this book, however, that the capitalist nations
are also capable of displaying national unity in war and Khrushchev's
assertion that a nuclear war could lead to the death of seven or eight
hundred million persons and to the destruction of "all big cities" [42]
suggest that the Soviet leadership may not in reality place great reliance on the alleged superiority of Soviet morale. In its debate with
Peking, *Pravda* pointed out that "the International Communist Movement knows very well that imperialism is on the decline, that it has
historically outlived itself, but it also knows that it has atomic teeth
which it can bring into action." [43] Despite the inherent weakness attributed to the capitalist system, the security of the Communist bloc has
been entrusted primarily to its nuclear armament.]

## Strategy and Military Doctrine

Military doctrine expresses the views accepted by the state on: the
political evaluation of a future war, the attitude toward war, the nature
of war, the measures necessary to prepare the country economically
and spiritually for war and the problems involved in organizing and
preparing the armed forces, as well as in the methods for conducting
war. Consequently, military doctrine is the officially approved system
of concepts on the basic, fundamental problems of war.

Military doctrine depends directly upon the social system, on the
state's general purpose in foreign and domestic policy, and the economic, political, and cultural state of the country.

Military doctrine is not thought out or compiled by a single person
or group of persons; it comes out of the vital activities of the state
as a whole, and is the result of a quite complex and lengthy historical

---

[41] *Ibid.,* p. 295.
[42] *Pravda,* January 17, 1963. See also *Pravda,* July 11, 1962.
[43] *Pravda,* January 7, 1963.

process of the creation and development of official ideas. Therefore, military doctrine is based on the entire state. There can be no single military doctrine for all states, since the general political line of the state's ruling social class and the economic and morale resources at its disposal determine military doctrine.

The geography of the country, which must be considered in conjunction with national interest, has a certain influence on the content and the nature of a military doctrine.

The influence of the state's geographical location and the position of neighboring states and relations with them must be studied along with other economic and political factors.

The influence of particular national characteristics on capitalist military doctrine is losing its earlier significance. In their struggle to suppress their own country's democratic forces and to strengthen their own position, the bourgeoisie of one country will come to terms with the bourgeoisie of another stronger capitalist state, often to the detriment of their national interests.

Military strategy is subordinate to military doctrine. Military doctrine determines general positions and principles, whereas military strategy, proceeding from these general positions, develops and studies concrete problems bearing upon the nature of a future war, the preparation of the country for war, the organization of the armed forces, and the techniques of conducting war.

## The Essentially Class Nature of Bourgeois Military Strategy

When one discusses the essentially class nature of bourgeois military strategy, one cannot ignore imperialist foreign policies, since this is just where imperialist class interests are expressed, and it is foreign policy that determines the content of military strategy and its essential nature.

At its present stage, the United States of America provides the economic and ideological foundations for imperialism, setting the tone and, in many respects, determining the foreign policy of all imperialist states.

American imperialism aspires to world domination, as evidenced by former President Eisenhower's statement: "America's vital interests are worldwide, embracing both hemispheres and every continent," and the United States deems it necessary to take upon itself a high role in world affairs: "a role of vigorous leadership [. . . .]" *

---

* *Pravda,* January 12, 1957. [President Eisenhower's State of the Union Message, *American Foreign Policy 1957,* Department of State Publications, Washington, D.C., 1961, pp. 7, 4.]

In attempting to conceal the predatory, aggressive nature of the foreign policy of the United States, the ruling circles resort to lies, declaring that they extend economic aid to underdeveloped countries and comprehensive assistance to their partners in various blocs and alliances in defense against communist aggression. The President of the United States, Kennedy, hypocritically declared in connection with his meeting with N. S. Khrushchev in Vienna in June 1961 that economic assistance to underdeveloped countries is "a historic opportunity for the United States to help these countries build their societies" and that for this purpose the United States "can train and equip their forces." [44] In the same declaration Kennedy stated that "the United States even now supports many countries from Northern Europe to the Middle East to Saigon." [45] Essentially, this declaration again confirms the American aspiration to dominate the world and proves that the economic relations of American imperialism with other countries are clearly colored by military-political considerations.

The policies of the United States, Great Britain, France, and West Germany reflect the aspirations of reactionary militarist circles to impose their will upon other countries by economic and political pressures, threats and provocations. [46]

Such a policy has been called negotiating "from a position of strength." It expresses the aspiration of the most aggressive circles of modern imperialism to dominate the world, to suppress labor, democratic, and national liberation movements, and to prepare military ventures against the socialist camp.

It is not accidental that American military and political literature

---

[44] U.S. ED. NOTE—The President's full statement was: "On the contrary we have a historical opportunity to help these countries build their societies until they are so strong and broadly based that only an outside invasion could topple them, and that threat we know can be stopped. We can train and equip their forces to resist Communist-supplied insurrections." President Kennedy's Report to the Nation on His Visit to Paris, Vienna and London, June 6, 1961, *Documents on American Foreign Relations, 1961,* Harper, New York, 1962, p. 94.

[45] U.S. ED. NOTE—The original full sentence reads: "I know that there is a great deal of feeling in the United States that we have carried the burden of economic assistance long enough, but these countries that we are now supporting stretching all the way along from the top of Europe through the Middle East, down through Saigon are now subject to great efforts internally in many of them to seize control." *Ibid.*

[46] U.S. ED. NOTE—There is no precise English equivalent for the Russian usage of the term "provocation." It means to manipulate an opponent into committing an act which then serves as a pretext for counteraction. Thus Tsarist police agents within the revolutionary movement in nineteenth century Russia assassinated high officials in order to justify the state's action against the revolutionary parties. In the Soviet view, "provocation" is a common technique of aggressive states,

devotes special attention to the cult of power as a most important element in the execution of its foreign policy.

In numerous military and political publications that have appeared in the United States in recent years, the principle of power is regarded as the only possible principle for the relations of the United States with other states. Thus, the American military theoretician G. F. Eliot asserts that "the only realistic policy for Americans is to maintain its power at an unequalled level," and that foreign policy must be based on "an actively aggressive principle." * [47] Another author, Spykman, in his book *America's Strategy in World Politics,* tries to show that only power can solve international problems and that only power can accomplish the aims of foreign policy. "In international society," he writes, "all forms of coercion are permissible including wars of destruction." Spykman calls upon the government to "impose its will upon those who have no strength, and force concessions from those who are weak." † [48]

The policy of negotiating "from a position of strength" consists of international provocation, espionage and sabotage, the disruption of international economic and cultural ties, and deliberate aggravation of international relations.

According to official declarations by United States political leaders, the policy of negotiating "from a position of strength" is a policy of pressure and dictation, supported by the army, the air force, and the navy. It is based upon and revolves around the nuclear weapon.

Among Western statesmen the opinion is widespread that this policy supposedly makes a new war impossible, since it assures "a balance of forces" in the world arena.

---

* G. F. Eliot, *The Strength We Need* [Viking Press], New York, 1946, pp. 9, 30, 31, 40–42.

[47] U.S. ED. NOTE—The citation of Eliot's book appears to be in error. On p. 9 Eliot wrote: "It is therefore a book about a period of paradox: a period in which we work for peace with better prospects of attaining it than ever before, yet a period in which we must maintain greater and more immediately ready armaments than ever before." On p. 30 he calls for "an active, not a passive policy" in breaking down the "artificial barriers to truth and knowledge" and on p. 42 he states that "unity of command and the offensive principle still form the twin pillars of Anglo-American strength."

‡ N. I. Spykman, *America's Strategy in World Politics* [Harcourt, Brace], New York, 1942, p. 18.

[48] U.S. ED. NOTE—Spykman was describing the state of international relations following the failure of the League of Nations. He did not "call upon the government" to "impose its will upon" others, but stated: "Power means survival, the ability to impose one's will on others, the capacity to dictate to those who are without power, and the possibility of forcing concessions from those with less power."

Speaking in Chicago, former Secretary of State Dulles defined the two directions of American policy: military blocs and the arms race.[49]

The armaments race has already assumed enormous proportions in the United States. An increasingly large share of the national revenue is expended for the maintenance of huge armies and the arms race. The projected budget of the United States for 1962–1963 provides for direct military expenditures of 55.1 billion dollars, which represents approximately 60 per cent of the entire budget. In the United States, more than one-third of all scientists and engineers are engaged in military industry, and no less than five million people are directly and entirely engaged in the armament program. Military production comprises 15 to 20 per cent of the total production of large capitalist countries.

The military and strategic methods employed to carry out the foreign policies of modern imperialist states are manifested in the seizure of bases, the occupation of foreign territories, and the setting up of aggressive military blocs and alliances.

In pursuing aggressive ends and fulfilling the requirements of military strategy, the United States government has created large military bases on the territories of states thousands of miles from the United States. These are part of the plan for military operations against the Soviet Union and other socialist countries.

American military bases, which are build-up areas for launching an aggressive war against the socialist countries, also create opportunities to intervene in the internal affairs of the countries on whose territories they are located. In addition, by locating its military formations and units on the territory of its allies and equipping them with nuclear weapons, the United States pursues a provocative aim, to deflect from itself a retaliatory strike in case of attack against the Soviet Union and the other countries of the socialist camp.

The ideologists of American imperialism do not conceal the true purposes of these bases. For example, Kieffer writes: "Tomorrow's battlefield is the world, today's problem is to secure as many of the strategic locations of the world as may be possible and to train our troops to hold those areas." *

---

[49] U.S. ED. NOTE—Dulles said: "The free nations have adopted and implemented two interrelated policies for collective security. The first policy is to give clear warning that armed aggression will be met by collective action. The second policy is to be prepared to implement this political warning with deterrent power." "The Foundation for a Firm Peace," address by the Secretary of State before a meeting of the Illinois Manufacturers' Association, Chicago, December 8, 1955, *American Foreign Policy, 1950–1955,* Vol. I, Department of State Publications, No. 6446, Washington, D.C., 1957, p. 123.

* T. Kieffer [John E. Kieffer], *Realities of World Power* [David McKay], New York, 1952, p. 109.

The military correspondent for the American magazine, *Saturday Evening Post,* Hanson Baldwin, gives a more complete description of the reasons for creating these bases. He writes that the military bases of the United States "serve many purposes [besides giving us warning and time [50]]. They are essential as offensive springboards against the Russian heartland. . . . But the economic necessity which drives us beyond the seas is perhaps even more important than the military. . . . We must have access to the raw materials of the earth and we must be able to export some of our farm surpluses and our manufactured goods * [if American prosperity is to endure and—more important—if we are to win other cold or hot wars [51]]."

In practice, the creation of numerous bases on foreign soil becomes actual occupation of these countries. Thus, for example, according to the United States-Greek agreement on military bases, ". . . the Government of the United States of America may bring in, station and house in Greece United States personnel. United States Armed Forces and equipment under their control may enter, exit, circulate within and overfly Greece and its territorial waters † [subject to any technical arrangements that may be agreed upon by the appropriate authorities of the two governments [52]]."

New military blocs and alliances are being formed in preparation for a new war. Thus, during the last fifteen years the following have been formed under the aegis of American imperialism: "Western Hemisphere Defense Pact" [Rio Pact] (1947); the Baghdad Pact (1948); The Western Alliance [WEU] (1948); The West Eurpean Alliance (1954–1955); The North Atlantic Treaty Organization Pact [NATO] (1949), including Great Britain, France, Italy, Belgium, Holland, Luxembourg, Canada, Iceland, Norway, Denmark, Portugal, Greece, and Turkey, and from 1955 on, also West Germany; ANZUS—The Pacific Pact (1951); SEATO with the participation of the United States, Great Britain, France, Australia, Thailand, and Pakistan; the Near East Bloc [CENTO] with the participation of England, Turkey, Pakistan, and Iran. In addition, there are a number of bilateral aggressive military

---

[50] U.S. ED. NOTE—Omitted in Russian translation, without indication of an ellipsis.

* *Pravda,* February 8, 1955.

[51] U.S. ED. NOTE—Omitted in Russian translation, without indication of an ellipsis. Hanson W. Baldwin, "Let's Quit Talking Nonsense about the Cold War," *Saturday Evening Post,* September 11, 1954, p. 155.

† *Pravda,* October 14, 1953.

[52] U.S. ED. NOTE—Omitted in Russian translation, without indication of an ellipsis. "United States Use of Defense Facilities: Agreement between the U.S. and the Kingdom of Greece, October 12, 1953," *American Foreign Policy, 1950–1955,* Vol. II, p. 2188.

pacts: the Chiang Kai-shek American Agreement, the American-Korean Pact, and the "Security Pact" between the United States and Japan.

The participation of small countries in military and political blocs and alliances often leads to their direct occupation.

In serving the aggressive policy of their state and carrying out their orders, bourgeois military theoreticians formulate a military strategy for the capitalist countries which directs human genius against man himself, and transforms scientific discoveries into terrible weapons of annihilation. Thus, the scientific discovery of nuclear fission was immediately used by American military strategy to make atomic bombs.

In serving the militaristic aspiration of the American imperialists, reactionary scientists have developed inhuman theories which differ little from Hitler's delusions. Thus, the President of the University in Tampa, Dr. Nance, declared: "I believe that we must be totally prepared, and proceed from the law of the jungle. Everybody must learn the art of killing. I do not believe that war should be restricted to armies, navies, and air forces, or that there should be any limitation with regard to method or weapons of destruction. I would approve of bacteriological warfare, the use of poison gas, atomic and hydrogen bombs, and intercontinental missiles. I would not ask mercy for hospitals, churches, schools, or any groups of the population. . . ." * [53]

Some "scientists" are calculating how many hydrogen bombs are necessary to annihilate all life on the earth. Dr. Leo Szilard of the University of Chicago declared: "How many neutrons or how much heavy hydrogen do we have to detonate to kill everybody on earth by this particular method? Well, I come out with about fifty tons of neutrons being needed to kill everybody which means about 500 tons of heavy hydrogen." †

Reactionary theories find practical application in American military strategy and foreign policy. The colossal apparatus of the White House, the Pentagon, NATO, SEATO, CENTO, and the entire practical activity of the United States government is directed toward the implementation of these theories.

Reactionary scientists in various disciplines—sociologists, economists,

---

* *Pravda,* August 6, 1950.

[53] U.S. ED. NOTE—In the full text of the speech (supplied by Dr. Nance), the remarks cited were prefaced by the following: "No one in our country wants to attack Russia or any other country, but in the light of history and the threats of Russia against the United States and the Western World, I think we should be prepared to defend ourselves should Russia attack us." "Hydrogen bombs" is an insertion by the Soviet editor and does not appear in the original.

† *Izvestiia,* August 22, 1952. [*New York Times,* February 27, 1950.]

and military theoreticians—who reflect an imperialist aspiration to world domination, develop various theories and doctrines in military strategy. In the pages of the bourgeois press, we see flashing by as in a kaleidoscope: "brinkmanship," "the strategy of massive retaliation," "the strategy of deterrence," "graduated strategy," "doctrine of containment," "doctrine of liberation"; and recently, since the United States' loss of its nuclear monopoly, particular interest in so-called limited or small wars has arisen in many capitalist countries.

The appearance of a theory of limited war is not accidental. Observing the colossal success of the Soviet Union and other socialist countries in economic development, science, technology, and culture, the imperialists began to be convinced not only of the impossibility of crushing the socialist system, but also of the fact that a new world war would inevitably be disastrous for capitalism. However, the achievement of political aims in capitalist society is inconceivable without war. The military theoreticians of imperialism scurry about in search of solutions of military and political problems which, on one hand, would avoid the destruction of the capitalist system, and on the other hand, would lead to the realization of expansionist aims. Limited war, in the opinion of American military theoreticians, is most responsive to these aims. In advocating the theory of limited war, American strategists thus try to keep the United States safe from retaliatory nuclear strikes, to suppress movements of national liberation, to preserve the colonial system, and to create additional stimuli for its economy in order to extract maximum profits.

In the imperialist plans, limited war is also particularly important as a pretext for starting wars against the socialist countries.

Bourgeois strategy is reactionary in its social and political aims since it serves the interests of imperialist aggressors, who conduct unjust and predatory wars in order to seize foreign territories, to suppress national liberation movements, and to enslave the people of other countries.

Bourgeois military strategy is reactionary, not only in its political content, but in its ideological, theoretical and philosophical bases as well, because it appraises social phenomena, including war, by means of an anti-scientific bourgeois sociology and an idealistic and metaphysical philosophy.

The military strategy of imperialist states is intended to preserve and to extend [the life of] the capitalist system, which has outlived itself, to preserve the rotten system of colonialism, and to combat the most advanced and most progressive system of human society, the socialist system.

## The Class Nature of Soviet Military Strategy

The peace-loving policy of the Soviet Union, which the Soviet government constantly follows in its international relations, is determined by the particular features of the economic system which has triumphed in the USSR, as well as by the fundamental economic law of socialism. The essential features and the requirements of this law are the maximum fulfillment of the constantly increasing material and cultural requirements of the whole society by means of continual growth and improvement of socialist production. The fundamental economic law of socialism is the objective law by which a socialist society develops. This fundamental law is the basic principle, which, in the final analysis, essentially determines the foreign policy of a socialist state.

The Marxist-Leninist teachings on the determining role of economics are of fundamental importance in providing a scientific basis for the peace-loving foreign policy of the Soviet state, and also [explains] its basic differences from imperialistic foreign policy.

The determining role of economics in relation to politics is that social ideas and theories are rooted in the material conditions of the life of society. They must be sought in economics, since new political ideas and institutions emerge during the development of the material life of society.

V. I. Lenin developed the Marxist teachings on foreign policy within new historical conditions. Leninism is based upon the objective economic laws of social development, and provided a comprehensive foundation for the peace-loving foreign policy of the future proletarian state long before the victory of the proletariat in Russia. Lenin proceeded from the particular features of the new socialist system and its new objective laws arising after the victory of the socialist revolution.

The Communist Party of the Soviet Union is the great directing and guiding force of the Soviet state. Guided by Marxist-Leninist theory and objective economic laws, it scientifically solves most important problems in the building of communism. In the area of domestic policy the party considers one of its important tasks to be an unremitting effort for the utmost satisfaction of the constantly increasing needs of the Soviet people. In the area of foreign policy, the Communist Party and Soviet Government follow a consistent course of preserving and strengthening peace between nations, and developing co-operation and trade with all countries on a basis of mutual interest and equal rights. During its entire existence, the Soviet Union has never conducted a single war with aggressive aims.

The congresses of the Communist Party and the decisions of its plenums and conferences constantly emphasize that the foreign policy of the Communist Party and the Soviet Government is fundamentally aimed at eliminating war from the life of the society and strengthening peace throughout the world. The entire practical activity of the Soviet state in the international arena stems from these decisions and is guided by them.

The Communist Party, the Soviet Government, and the entire Soviet people do not consider peace and national security to be a matter of tactics and diplomatic maneuvers. It is the general line of Soviet foreign policy as it has been manifested during all the years of the Soviet state.

The efforts of the Soviet state in this direction are bearing fruit. The people believe increasingly in the possibility of liberating mankind from world wars. The elimination of world wars from the life of the society is a realistic task. All the necessary objective conditions are ripe for it. K. Marx wrote: ". . . mankind always sets itself only such tasks as it can solve; since looking at the matter more closely, it will always be found that the task itself arises only when the material conditions for its solution already exist or are at least in the process of formation." *

The real possibilities for solving this problem lie in the fulfillment of the Soviet Union's and other socialist countries' national economic plans, which will secure and increase their defense potential.[54]

In spite of the growth of the Soviet state's military might, it is waging an increased struggle to stop the armaments race, to prohibit nuclear weapons and testing, to bring about total and general disarmament, to eliminate foreign bases and remove troops from foreign territories, and to eliminate world war from the life of the society.

New scientific discoveries and technological accomplishments in socialist society are being used to strengthen peace and security.

Nuclear energy and ballistic missiles are being used by the Soviets to benefit mankind and conquer nature. The Soviet Union was the first to build nuclear power stations and a nuclear icebreaker. It launched the first artificial earth satellite, the first interplanetary stations [deep space probes], and, finally, the first man to blaze a trail in space.

Quite evidently the Soviet Union has left the United States far behind in the conquest of space. However, this advantage is being used by the

---

* K. Marx and F. Engels, *Izbrannye proizvedeniia* [*Selected Works*], Vol. 1, Gospolitizdat, Moscow, 1952, p. 322.

[54] U.S. ED. NOTE—The Soviet argument rests on the proposition that world peace and disarmament will be possible only when the imperialists give up their attempts to change the situation by war, i.e., when they realize that the Communist bloc is too strong militarily for them to risk opposing the Soviet Union and social-political change in the world by means of war.

Soviet Union for peaceful and scientific aims to the benefit of all mankind.[55]

The Soviet Union has had intercontinental missiles since 1956.[56] The strategic importance of these missiles can scarcely be overestimated. They can deliver nuclear or hydrogen warheads of essentially unlimited destructive power to any point on the globe. However, the Soviet Government did not utilize this advantage to solve problems of foreign policy. On the contrary, the Soviet Government insists upon outlawing war, stressing the complete irrationality of solving international disputes under present conditions by war. History offers only a choice of peaceful coexistence or catastrophic war.

The lofty and noble aims of the Soviet Government and Armed Forces determine the nature and essence of Soviet military strategy. Soviet military strategy serves the interests of the most advanced progressive social system, directs all its efforts toward increasing the defense potential of the Soviet state, and organizes its Armed Forces for the successful repulsion of aggression. This is essentially the class nature of Soviet military strategy.

Soviet military strategy is guided by the progressive, consistent, and completely scientific Marxist-Leninist theory, and by the philosophy of dialectical and historical materialism, which makes possible scientific knowledge and correct use of the objective laws determining victory in modern war.

---

[55] U.S. ED. NOTE—Concerning Soviet interest in the military use of space, see p. 424.

[56] U.S. ED. NOTE—The Soviet Government announced the first successful test of a multistage intercontinental ballistic missile on August 26, 1957. *Pravda*, August 27, 1957.

★ 2

# Military Strategy of Imperialist States and Their Preparation of New Wars

## Military Strategy of Principal Capitalist States during the Two World Wars

The predatory and aggressive policy of monopoly, which was essentially the same for the principal imperialist states, influenced the form of the military strategy of those states. Thus, the strategies of the imperialist countries had much in common.

Each country's strategy, however, had a certain special character resulting from indigenous political, economic, geographic, and national factors, as well as from purely military factors.

Bourgeois military strategy changed and developed according to changes in the foreign policy of the ruling circles of these countries, the balance of forces in the international arena, economic potentials, the development of new weapons, as well as other factors.

This chapter gives a brief analysis of the development of British, American, French, German, and Japanese military strategy during the two world wars, and of the military strategy of the present-day imperialist coalition headed by the United States.

In entering World War I, Britain, America, France, and Germany pursued similar predatory aims, but realized them differently. Thus, for example, Great Britain adhered to its traditional policy of getting others to do its fighting. Former Prime Minister Lloyd George described the essential nature of British military strategy by stating, with the greatest candor:

141

We conceived our participation in the war in accordance with the traditional British role in continental wars. Our fleet would dominate the sea in the interests of the allies. Our wealth would help finance their purchases abroad. Our army was to play a secondary role in the war.*

However, the British Government was compelled to revise its views at the very beginning of the war, after realizing that the outcome of the war would be decided on the continent rather than on the sea and that massive ground forces would be required. As a result of the reassessment in the course of the war of the role and purpose of the armed forces under a coalition in a continental war, the British Government organized a large, well-equipped land army. By the beginning of 1918 the British Ground Forces already contained 90 divisions, most of them involved in operations on the [European] continent, whereas the initial plans had called only for an expeditionary corps of seven divisions for continental operations.

Before World War I, America's military strategy resembled that of Britain. It was based upon the policy of the American imperialists who sought to expand their sphere of influence. Having achieved the world's greatest industrial potential at the beginning of the twentieth century, the United States began to strive for world domination. Its intentions were to exploit the war [in Europe] to achieve this goal.

In view of America's geographical position (the United States shared no common boundaries with great powers) and the possibility of a prolonged war, American ruling circles planned to organize a large army gradually and to wait for a favorable moment to enter the war. Consequently the United States devoted primary attention before the war to the development of its navy, and less attention to the development of ground forces.

French military strategy on the eve of World War I reflected both the cowardice of the French bourgeoisie and their desire for territorial expansion. The desire to regain the lost provinces of Alsace-Lorraine forced the French General Staff to plan active operations particularly in that region. However, the French war plans had a passive, temporizing character because France feared German military power, intending to strike the main blow only after the first encounters with the enemy [when conditions seemed favorable].

The French recognized the possibility that Germany might invade France through Belgium, but considered it unlikely because they believed the German forces to be inadequate for [such a task].

---

* Lloyd George, *Voennye memuary* [*War Memoirs*], Vols. I–II [translated from English], Gosekonomizdat, Moscow, 1934, p. 473. [For English text see *War Memoirs of David Lloyd George, 1915–1916,* 2 vols., Little, Brown, Boston, 1933, p. 60.]

Germany, occupying a central position on the European continent, primarily feared a fatal war on two fronts (i.e., against Russia and the Western Powers). To win such a war with an economic and military potential inferior to that of her enemies, Germany's operations had to be rapid and conclusive; the enemies had to be destroyed one at a time, without giving them time to mobilize and bring their enormous resources to bear. Thus the war plan developed by the German General Staff was based on a "lightning war," first against France and then against Russia. In planning the first blow against France, the German General Staff assumed that Russia would not be able to initiate operations prior to completing the mobilization and concentration of her troops; the Germans expected this to require at least forty days, during which they could finish the war with France.

The strategic aims of German imperialism determined the decisive and offensive character of the operation of her armed forces. During the initial stages of the war, such strategy and tactics met with considerable success. However, the adventuristic policies and strategy of German imperialism subsequently brought Germany to disaster.

The experience of World War I has demonstrated that bourgeois military strategy could not understand and evaluate the new conditions in which war in the machine age was to be conducted.

When the war began, most of the capitalist states were convinced that it would be short and would end in a few months. Schlieffen expressed this most graphically in his statement that the war should be over "by the time the leaves begin to fall" [i.e., the fall of 1914]. Consequently the German General Staff only planned the initial operations, during which it was expected to destroy the enemy forces and bring the war to a conclusion. No provision was made for organizing and training reserves or mobilizing industry for war, since the ammunition and weapons stockpiled in peacetime were considered sufficient to wage and win the war.

However, the war upset all these plans. For well-known reasons, it became prolonged and required the organization and continual reinforcement of armies, each comprising millions, as well as the conversion of industry to the production of tremendous quantities of weapons, ammunition, equipment, uniforms, and other military supplies.

New weapons appeared in the course of this war, and fundamental changes took place in troop organization and the nature of combat operations. The war acquired an exceptionally destructive and exhausting character.

World War I concluded with the complete military defeat of Germany and its allies. However, it not only failed to resolve the conflicts existing among the large capitalist powers, but served to intensify them. The Versailles Treaty system, which came about as a result of World War I, proved so unstable that it generated another world war.

The entire capitalist system suffered a severe defeat as a result of World War I. One of the largest countries was eliminated from the general system of world capitalism as a result of the victory of the Great October Socialist Revolution in Russia. The world became divided into two opposing social systems, capitalism and socialism.

The appearance of the first socialist state of workers and peasants on the international scene created a serious obstacle to world domination by the imperialist powers. Consequently, during the period between the two world wars, the British, French, and American imperialists set themselves two tasks: first, to destroy or at the very least weaken the Soviet Union, and second, to eliminate their former rivals, Germany and Japan, from the struggle for world domination. To this end, Britain, France, and the United States for a long time conducted a policy aimed at inciting Germany and Japan against the USSR, hoping to destroy the USSR by proxy and then to eliminate war-weakened Germany and Japan from the world markets. To realize these plans, Germany was granted the large credits necessary to revive its economy and to modernize its defense and heavy industries, and everything was done to further Hitler's aggressive policies.

However, contrary to the plans of international reaction, the conflicts among the large imperialist powers during this period proved to be greater than those between the USSR and the imperialist states. This led to the formation, on the eve of World War II, of two groups of imperialist states. One included the United States, Britain, and France, which sought to strengthen their ruling position in the world. The second group, whose aim was to redivide the world, consisted primarily of Germany, Italy, and Japan.

By 1939 the Fascist states had built up their economic and military potential to such an extent that they began to see a genuine possibility of destroying their competitors before initiating war against the Soviet Union. Thus the German military machine, created with the direct and active assistance of the United States, England, and France, was turned against them in 1939–1940.

During the period between the wars, bourgeois military leaders had feverishly sought the best way of waging war. To this end, all the countries intensively studied World War I and searched for new strategic concepts.

Some bourgeois military ideologists (von Seeckt in Germany, Fuller and Liddell-Hart in England, De Gaulle in France, and others) advanced the theory of small, highly mechanized, professional armies and argued that contemporary military technology obviated the need for massive armed forces.

The theory of a professional army derived from the bourgeoisie's fear of armed masses of workers. The victory of the Great October Socialist Revolution in Russia, the demoralization of the armies, and the growth of the revolutionary movement in the countries which had participated in World War I revealed to the bourgeoisie the danger it faced in conducting war with massive armed forces.

Other such theories also existed, in particular that of the Italian General Douhet, who insisted that the only form of war was "air war." Douhet believed that air attacks by large bomber forces upon the enemy's most important industrial and political centers would make it possible to achieve victory within a short time without the use of massive armies and navies.

The imperialist powers entered World War II with different strategic concepts.

The French bourgeoisie, frightened by the enormous manpower losses of World War I (over 1.5 million killed), expected to avoid large losses and to win a future war with fewer forces by purely defensive operations in conjunction with heavy fortifications on their eastern border.

The French General Staff seriously believed that it could win the war against Germany by defense along the Maginot Line. Progressive attrition of the enemy by a naval blockade was to be an important supplement to the strength of the Maginot Line. Consequently, the French army and its General Staff prepared for a positional war like that of World War I. The passive defense strategy of France was also reflected in the organization of its armed forces, the training of military personnel, and later, in strategic deployment and methods of conducting war. Therefore, it was not surprising that the French armed forces, which numbered more than three million men, were utterly routed during the war in a month and a half.

It should be emphasized also that the French imperialists hoped until the very last moment that Fascist Germany would attack the USSR and would not initiate decisive operations in the West.

The ruling circles of Britain and the United States, who for well-known reasons found themselves in the same coalition as the Soviet Union, continued to pursue their imperialistic interests during the war, although covertly.

American and British ruling circles intended to undermine the power of Germany, Italy, and Japan—their principal competitors—but to preserve the regimes existing in these countries.

The political aims of the United States and Britain toward the Soviet Union found concrete expression in the military objectives pursued by the imperialist circles of those countries: to conduct the war as much as possible at the expense of the USSR, to weaken the USSR in the course of the war, and to prevent the Red Army from entering the Balkans and Central Europe. Because of this policy, they delayed in all sorts of ways the opening of the second front, and made plans to launch Anglo-American operations in the Apennine Peninsula and in the Balkans, instead of in France where they would have hurt Germany the most.[1]

These strategic aims, directed at prolonging the war in every way, also were responsible for the combat methods employed by British and American troops, and for the slow, passive, and indecisive nature of their operations.

The political plans and the principal military strategic tasks of Fascist Germany were different. In order to destroy Germany's enemies, who jointly possessed a considerably superior potential, Fascist leaders and the German General Staff relied primarily upon extensive use of surprise and the destruction of the countries of the opposing coalition by lightning blows, one at a time. In fact, this strategy differed very little from German strategy prior to World War I. However, it was better supported by large numbers of mobile troops, i.e., armored and motorized divisions, and a fairly large air force, which did not exist at the beginning of World War I.

Ludendorff formulated the essence of the "lightning war" theory. According to this theory, the largest possible forces and equipment were to be concentrated for the initial attack. Mobilization and concentration of the armed forces were to be carried out in advance and secretly. The "lightning war" theory was based on the following: throw the enemy off balance by surprise, lull his vigilance, invade and penetrate the country rapidly, take ruthless measures of terror against the population, make use of a previously prepared "Fifth Column," paralyze the enemy's will to resist, and force him to surrender.

However, as is known, this theory failed in the war against the Soviet Union because Nazi Germany did not possess the political, economic, and particularly the military capabilities to conclude the war in its favor in a short period of time.

---

[1] U.S. ED. NOTE—See Note A, pp. 148–149.

Prior to World War II, the aggressive program of Japanese imperialism was most completely formulated by a prominent representative of the Japanese military, General Tanaka. On July 25, 1927, he presented a memorandum to the Emperor of Japan outlining a plan to conquer China and to attain world domination.[2] The memorandum stated that, in order to conquer China, Japan would have to do the following:

> . . . first conquer Manchuria and Mongolia. In order to conquer the world, we must first conquer China. If we succeed in conquering China, all the other small Asian countries, India as well as the countries of the South Sea shall fear us and will surrender to us. The world will then realize that East Asia belongs to us and will not dare to question our rights. . . . Having in our possession all the resources of China, we shall proceed to the conquest of India, the South Sea countries, and later to the conquest of Asia Minor, Central Asia and finally Europe.*

Aggression against the Soviet Union was an integral part of General Tanaka's plan. "The Program of our national development," the memorandum states, "apparently includes the necessity of crossing swords with Russia again." †

Japan's imperialist aims and her desire to dominate the world produced an aggressive and determined military strategy.

However, the Japanese military recognized the relative weakness of their economy and always foresaw a thorough and lengthy preparation for expansion, which was to start at a time when the international situation was favorable to Japan and the great powers were at war or burdened by contradictions as a result of war and hence unable to oppose Japanese aggression.

The same causes (economic weakness and inadequate military potential) produced the second principle of Japanese strategy, i.e., surprise attack which eventuated in the most disgusting treachery.

The Japanese maintained the view that the ground forces were basic

---

[2] U.S. ED. NOTE—General Giichi Tanaka (1863–1929), Japanese officer and statesman, Prime Minister and Minister of Foreign Affairs in 1927, was the alleged author of the "Tanaka Memorial" or "Tanaka Memorandum." The full text of the document was first published by the Chinese periodical *China Critic* in 1931. Although it was once believed to be authentic, the majority of historians today believe the document to be a falsification. See, for example, Klaus H. Pringsheim, "Das Tanaka-Memorandum: weder von Tanaka noch ein Memorandum," *Nachrichten,* 85/86, 1959, pp. 73–79; Mamoru Shigemitsu, *Japan and Her Destiny,* E. P. Dutton, New York, 1958, *passim;* Robert A. Scalapino, *Democracy and the Party Movement in Prewar Japan,* University of California Press, Berkeley, 1953, p. 236; *Time* magazine, March 21, 1932.

* *Istoriia voiny na Tikhom Okean* [*History of the War in the Pacific*], Vol. 1, Izdatel'stvo Innostrannoi Literatury, Moscow, 1957, pp. 338–339.

† *Ibid.,* p. 344.

to the organization, development, and combat deployment of the armed forces. At the same time, Japan's insular position induced her to maintain a large navy and to attach special importance to amphibious operations.

World War II did not resolve the imperialist contradictions, but sharpened and intensified them instead. It did not strengthen the foundations of the capitalist system but on the contrary loosened and weakened them.

The reactionaries of the world, especially the Wall Street bosses, failed to realize their hopes that Hitler's war machine would deal a mortal blow to the Soviet Union during World War II. The USSR destroyed the Fascist German Army, overthrew Nazi Germany, and emerged victorious from the war.

## U.S. ED. NOTE A: THE SOVIET IMAGE OF ALLIED STRATEGY IN WORLD WAR II

[The interpretation of Western strategies and policies during the First and Second World Wars, given above and elsewhere in the book, is in general accord with the established public Soviet views on the subject. Certain questions, such as the postponement of the Allied landings in France until 1944, have been the subject of considerable debate between Soviet and Western governments and historians. The distortions and historical inaccuracies in the Soviet interpretation of past Western policies are more than mere calculated propaganda. They are based on an ideologically conditioned view of the West which assumes that the latter constantly seeks the weakening and destruction of the Soviet Union. Consequently, according to the standard Soviet interpretation, the British, French, and U.S. governments prior to World War II sought to have the Axis powers attack the Soviet Union, and during World War II planned their military campaigns to put the main burden of the fighting on the Soviet Union in the hope of completely exhausting both Germany and the Soviet Union. Soviet literature, therefore, usually discounts the contribution made by Western Allies to the victory in World War II, and minimizes or omits any reference to Anglo-American aid to the Soviet Union.

Despite this official Soviet position, which most Soviet writers feel obliged to adopt, the Soviet authorities have translated and published a considerable number of Western histories, memoirs, and theoretical works.[3] Furthermore, the Soviet reader also has available to him exten-

---

[3] See Appendix II.

sive Russian studies devoted exclusively to detailed descriptions of Western military doctrines and strategies, and these, despite some inevitable political bias, attempt to be more comprehensive. See, for example, Colonel V. A. Vasilenko, *et al.,* Sovremenaia imperialisticheskaia voennaia ideologiia *(Contemporary Imperialist Military Ideology)*, Voenizdat Ministerstva Oborony Soiuza SSR, Moscow, 1958; Major General M. A. Mil'shtein, Colonel A. K. Slobodenko, O *burzhuaznoi voennoi nauke* (On Bourgeois Military Science), 2nd edition, Voenizdat Ministerstva Oborony Soiuza SSR, Moscow, 1961.]

## Contemporary Military Strategy of the United States and NATO

The destruction of German Fascism and Japanese militarism greatly influenced the progressive movements in Europe, Asia, Africa, and Latin America and created favorable conditions for further strengthening and expanding the forces of socialism. Socialism has grown beyond the boundaries of a single country and has become a world system embracing more than one-third of the world population.

The capitalist world also changed substantially as a result of the Second World War. England, having lost her former power, emerged from the war considerably weakened. France and other European countries, which were occupied for a prolonged period by the Fascist-German armies, were almost completely ruined. The other capitalist countries that had participated in the war in the anti-Hitler coalition (with the exception of the United States and Canada) found themselves in difficult economic circumstances.

The United States, which had reaped fabulous profits during the war, exploited the postwar situation to strengthen its economic, political, and military position. The political aims of the American imperialists were and still are to enslave economically and politically the European and other capitalist countries and, after the latter are transformed into obedient tools, to unify them in various military-political blocs and groups directed against the socialist countries. The main aim of all this is to achieve world domination.

American leaders have repeatedly proclaimed the aspirations of aggressive American imperialist circles to dominate the world. Thus, in 1945, shortly after the conclusion of World War II, the former Chief of Staff of the American Army, General Marshall, wrote in a report to the Secretary of Defense that the United States possessed the necessary "power to secure a leading role in the future development of mankind." * [4] The notorious ex-President Truman stated this idea more clearly in his message to Congress in December 1945. He asserted that victory in World War II allegedly ". . . has placed upon the American people the continuing burden of responsibility for world leadership." † Finally, the new president, John Kennedy, in his special message to the American Congress on May 25, 1961, concerning "The Urgent National Needs," noted that "the government must consider additional long-term measures . . . , if we are to sustain our full role as world leaders." [5]

During the first postwar years, American ruling circles attempted to encircle the socialist countries with a system of hostile military-political groups and blocs of capitalist states and to unite the latter into a single anti-Communist coalition. This policy was most clearly expressed in the organization of numerous military, air, and naval bases around the countries of the socialist camp; in the adoption by the American Congress of the essentially expansionist "Truman Doctrine"; in the "Marshall Plan," which made it possible for the United States to establish control over the economies and policies of the European countries; and in the "Eisenhower Doctrine," aimed at the enslavement of the Near and Middle Eastern countries.

Aggressive military blocs were formed with the direct and active participation of the United States: in 1949 the North Atlantic Treaty Organization (NATO) in Europe; in 1954 in Southeast Asia—SEATO; in 1955 in the Near and Middle East—CENTO. In 1954 at the fourteenth session of the NATO Council in Paris, the United States pushed through a military agreement that made possible the rebirth of West German militarism and its transformation into the NATO striking force. In particular, at the London and Paris meetings the Western powers decided to terminate the occupation regime in the Federal German Republic, to remilitarize it, and to bring it into NATO. In addition, the

---

* *The War Report,* Washington, 1945, p. 143.

[4] U.S. ED. NOTE—The original passage reads: "Never was the strength of American democracy so evident nor has it ever been so clearly within our power to give definite guidance for our course into the future of the human race." General G. Marshall, General H. H. Arnold, Admiral E. King, *The War Report,* J. B. Lippincott, Philadelphia, 1947, p. 143.

† *Pravda,* December 23, 1945. [Message to Congress by President Truman on "The Unification of the Armed Forces," December 14, 1945, *Congressional Record,* Vol. 91, Part a, November 29–December 21, 1945, p. 12398.]

[5] U.S. ED. NOTE—President Kennedy's complete sentence reads: "The government must consider additional long-range measures to cure this unemployment and increase our economic growth, if we are to sustain our full role as world leader." *Documents on American Foreign Relations, 1961,* Harper, New York, 1962, p. 73.

Americans concluded a number of military-political treaties with their vassals.

Thus, shortly after the conclusion of World War II, the United States had created a closed ring of aggressive military groups around the Soviet Union and the other socialist countries. As a result, the American imperialists received the right to use the territories of the signatory countries as military bases. They also assumed control of almost the entire military and economic potential of these countries, including the organization, preparation, and possible use of their armed forces, in order to transform their partners into obedient instruments of their will.

The formation of aggressive military-political blocs under the aegis of the United States signifies the almost complete loss of political sovereignty of the countries participating in these blocs, and to a considerable extent the loss of the [independent] national character of their foreign policy and strategy.

In contrast to prewar years, when the strategy of the principal capitalist countries bore a distinctly national character, the postwar period has been characterized by a tendency toward uniformity in national military strategies and their combination into a single global military strategy, intended to assure the realization of American foreign policy aims. Therefore, under present conditions it is no longer possible to conceive of independent military strategies for the British, French, West German, or Japanese, for example. Bourgeois strategy is now unified; each country participating in one bloc or another contributes its own proposals, additions, or changes, on the basis of its national interests; this is not accomplished without sharp disputes, of course. However, when dealing with the political or ideological aspects of the struggle against the Soviet Union and other countries of the socialist camp, the imperialist circles, motivated by hatred of the socialist countries, always find a common basis for reaching agreement. This is even evident, for example, in the declarations of the present Secretary General of NATO, Stikker, who states that there are disagreements and contradictions in NATO only "on tactical problems." When the matter concerns the struggle against the Soviet Union, "our alliance functions well." * [6]

The end of World War II coincided with the appearance of nuclear and, subsequently, thermonuclear weapons. This fact facilitated the consolidation of the imperialist forces under the leadership of the United

---

* Report of France Presse, February 1, 1962.

[6] U.S. ED. NOTE—Dr. Stikker's full statement was: "When it is a question of a direct threat from the side of the Soviets our alliance functions well." *Le Monde*, February 2, 1962.

States, and exerted considerable influence on the development of a unified imperialist military policy and strategy determined by American ruling circles. In the initial postwar period the American imperialists also initiated the policy of negotiating "from a position of strength" in their dealings with the Soviet Union and other socialist countries. This policy on strategy was also reflected in official directives in which military strategy was defined as ". . . the art and science of using the armed forces of the country to achieve the aims of national policy by the application of force or the threat of force." * [7]

From this it follows that the American imperialists plan to attain their main political aim—world domination—by means of aggressive wars.

Until approximately the end of 1960, American leadership adhered to the strategy of so-called massive response, which derived from the policy of "deterrence," and acknowledged the possibility of conducting only total nuclear war against the Soviet Union. The strategy of "massive response" or, as it was also called, "massive retaliation" was adopted by the U.S. Government and the military command in 1953 at the beginning of the Eisenhower administration. Its official adoption was announced on January 12, 1954, by Secretary of State Dulles, who declared in a speech to the Council on Foreign Relations in New York: "The basic decision was to depend primarily upon a great capacity to retaliate, instantly, by means and at places of our own choosing." †

The terminology "massive response" and "massive retaliation" serves to conceal the general aggressive nature of American strategy. American imperialists, while hiding behind such phrases and terms, are really preparing a surprise nuclear attack on the Soviet Union and the other socialist countries. American political and military leaders have repeatedly stated this, directly or indirectly.

Thus, the former Chief of Staff of the American army, General Taylor, wrote in 1960 that in the opinion of the U.S. Air Force "in strategic air warfare a strong offense is the best defense." ‡

Taylor stated further: "If we take into account the possibility of an unsuccessful use of our forces, the *retaliatory* attacks of the enemy. . . ." §
(Our emphasis—[*Soviet*] *ed.*) [8] This clearly shows who will attack first.

---

* *The Joint and Combined Staff Officer's Manual,* 1959, p. 175.

[7] U.S. ED. NOTE—It has not been possible to verify this quotation.

† *New York Times,* January 13, 1954.

‡ M. Taylor, *Nenadezhnaia strategiia* [*Unreliable strategy;* U.S. edition entitled *The Uncertain Trumpet,* Harper, New York, 1960, p. 103], Moscow, 1961, p. 120.

§ *Ibid.,* p. 154.

[8] U.S. ED. NOTE—The original English sentence reads: "After due allowance has been made for aborts, enemy actions and failures, both human and mechanical, the number of atomic vehicles needed to destroy this target system can be determined by simple arithmetic." *The Uncertain Trumpet,* p. 148.

In May 1959 the Commander of the American Strategic Air Command, General Power, was even more frank on this subject: "We must never find ourselves in a situation where we cannot begin a war ourselves. . . . We must have the capability to deliver the first strike." *

As is known, the strategy of "massive retaliation" was based on the assumption that the United States had overwhelming superiority over the Soviet Union in nuclear weapons and especially in strategic aircraft. Therefore, the United States could be sure of attaining its political and military aims only by threatening to initiate a general nuclear war, which the countries of the socialist camp could not risk because of their inferiority in offensive nuclear forces.

In accord with this strategy, the American government placed the main emphasis on the development of strategic and tactical nuclear weapons, to the detriment of conventional armed forces, especially ground forces; this resulted in sharp disagreement between the Army on the one hand, and the Air Force and, to some extent, the Navy on the other. Undoubtedly, such a trend in the development of the armed forces could not fail to cause great dissatisfaction among the representatives of the ground forces and the groups of monopolists who supplied these forces with arms and equipment. The victory of the proponents of the "massive retaliation" strategy was not only a victory for the Air Force and the Navy, but also for the monopolies producing armaments for the Air Force and Navy.

The strategy of "massive retaliation" was adopted not only by the United States but also by the other NATO countries. In December 1954 they began for the first time to plan war operations using nuclear weapons, and later they officially adopted the above strategy, according to which the countries of the North Atlantic aggressive bloc were to use nuclear weapons in any situation, whether or not the opponent used them. Indeed, it was assumed that the NATO countries could not entertain the idea of waging limited war against the Soviet Union in Europe. The possibility of waging limited (local) wars was envisaged only "in the less-developed areas of the world outside Europe. . . ." †

Thus, according to American and NATO aggressive schemes, the mere threat to resort to nuclear weapons was supposed to be a sufficient deterrent, and their use in any conflict was presumed to reduce the offensive capability of the Soviet Armed Forces to nought. However, these hopes were not to be realized.

As a result of the spectacular Soviet success in the field of missile construction and in the conquest of space, the strategy of "massive retaliation" collapsed. Being completely unrealistic in its assumptions, it was

* *Survival* [No. 2, May–] June 1959, p. 57.
† Taylor, *op. cit.,* p. 37 [p. 8 in English text].

soon rejected by its own creators. Dulles himself declared as early as October 27, 1957, that the United States and its allies must take necessary steps if a local conflict occurred, "without provoking by our actions a general nuclear war." *

In this connection, during 1957–1960 the United States and other Western countries began to study the reasons for the failure of the "retaliatory" strategy and to search intensively for a new strategy which would correspond, from the standpoint of the American aggressors, with the changed balance of forces between the West and the East. This study was conducted by various military and civilian agencies and organizations, such as the scientific-research RAND Corporation,† The Johns Hopkins Washington Center for International Studies, and the Gaither and Rockefeller committees, as well as Harvard, Princeton, Chicago, Pennsylvania, and other American universities. Various American and Western European military leaders have also worked on this problem.

As a result, a considerable number of reports, books, and articles dealing with questions of foreign policy, war, and strategy were published in the United States, England, and other countries.

Thus, in December 1959, the Senate Foreign Affairs Committee published a special report, "Developments in Military Technology and Their Impact on United States Strategy and Foreign Policy," which was prepared by The Johns Hopkins Washington Center for International Studies and became an official Congressional document. Furthermore, the following books were published in the United States: *Limited War* by R. Osgood; *Strategy in the Missile Age* by B. Brodie; *The Uncertain Trumpet* by General M. Taylor; *The Necessity for Choice* by H. Kissinger; *The Future U.S. Strategy* by several authors; in England, a book by Air Marshal Kingston-McCloughry, *Defense, Policy and Strategy*; and a number of other books.

The authors of these books and reports agreed, in view of the altered

---

* *Developments in Military Technology and Their Impact on United States Strategy and Foreign Policy: A Study Prepared at the Request of the Committee on Foreign Relations, United States Senate,* December 6, 1959, p. 102. [Hereafter cited as *A Study.*]

† The RAND Corporation (from the English RAND—Research and Development) was formed by the U.S. Air Force in 1948 and employs more than 800 prominent scientists. It is charged with the task of determining the types of weapons that satisfy the requirement of contemporary strategy. Other similar organizations are The Johns Hopkins University's Operations Research Office (ORO) which does similar work for the Army, the Navy's Operations Evaluation Group at MIT, and the Institute for Defense Analyses which receives its assignments from the Joint Chiefs of Staff and the Secretary of Defense of the United States.

situation, in their negative evaluation of the "massive retaliation" strategy and the proposed methods of preparing an aggressive war against the socialist countries and other areas of the world. A considerable number of the studies mentioned above were prepared at the behest of U.S. governmental and military agencies and therefore exerted a certain influence on the formulation of the official views of American ruling circles.

The most up-to-date publications that clarify the nature of current Western military strategy are the report of the U.S. Senate Committee on Foreign Relations, General M. Taylor's *The Uncertain Trumpet,* and Professor H. Kissinger's book, *The Necessity for Choice.**

The main reasons for the failure of the strategy of "massive retaliation" were the overestimation of American strength and capabilities, and the obvious underestimation of the economic, technical, scientific, and military capabilities of the Soviet Union. As a result of the Soviet Union's significant superiority in intercontinental ballistic missiles, a real threat to American territory had arisen.[9] Therefore, American political and military leadership was compelled to reassess its strategic position and capabilities.

The report of the Senate Committee on Foreign Relations noted that "termination of the American nuclear monopoly and growing Soviet strategic capabilities have increased the difficulties of maintaining a military posture appropriate to the pursuit of established American objectives." † This report was quite sober in its assessment of the resources of the United States and the Soviet Union with respect to the size of their territory, population, and industrial potential, as well as to the continuance of the traditional advantages derived by America from a secure continent. The Committee noted that "the military position of the United States has declined . . . from one of unchallenged security to that of a nation both open and vulnerable to direct and devastating attack." ‡

An even more unfavorable appraisal of the United States position was given by H. Kissinger, who proposed that illusions about American invulnerability be abandoned.

---

* In 1961, Taylor and Kissinger were appointed special military and political advisers to President Kennedy, and nearly everything that they proposed in their books has been or is being put into practice. Prior to his appointment, Kissinger was a consultant to the Joint Chiefs of Staff of the United States. [General Taylor is at present Chairman of the Joint Chiefs of Staff.]

9 U.S. ED. NOTE—This refers to the Soviet claims to general military and specifically strategic-missile superiority over the United States. These were most clearly stated by Khrushchev in January 1960 (*Pravda,* January 15, 1960).

† *A Study,* p. 1.

‡ *Ibid.,* p. 3.

In referring to the tremendous influence of the Soviet Union and the Chinese People's Republic on the course of world social development, he bitterly admitted that "the success of Moscow and Peiping will have the same kind of attraction as the accomplishment of Europe in the nineteenth century. No amount of economic assistance will avail against the conviction that the West is doomed." *

It is significant that in his book, *Nuclear Weapons and Foreign Policy,* published in the United States in 1957, Kissinger still argued for a strategy based on the threat of unlimited use of nuclear weapons, i.e., in favor of initiating a general nuclear war. However, the events of the past four years have forced him to arrive at diametrically opposite conclusions, involving the necessity for a choice, as he has expressed it, "between humiliation and general nuclear war."

Even President Kennedy himself was forced to admit the increased military strength of the Soviet Union and the loss of alleged American superiority in strategic weapons, when he stated in Seattle in November 1961 that the United States was neither omnipotent nor omniscient.†

Thus, under the conditions of today, when there is a "balance" (approximate "equality") in strategic weapons and Soviet superiority in conventional armed forces, the American strategists are forced to reevaluate their previous attitude toward general nuclear war.‡ [10]

They understand that when both sides possess very large stockpiles of nuclear weapons and various means of delivering them to targets, primarily strategic means, a general nuclear war holds great risks of complete mutual annihilation.§ Consequently, the greater the stockpiling of weapons of mass destruction, the greater becomes the conviction that it is impossible to use them. Thus the growth of nuclear-missile power is inversely proportional to the possibility of its use. A "nuclear

---

* Henry A. Kissinger, *The Necessity for Choice* [Harper, New York], 1961, p. 7.

† *New York Times,* November 17, 1961.

‡ By "balance" of forces the Americans understand "albeit an approximate, shifting and sometimes unstable equilibrium, in which neither side has, or believes it has power sufficient to impose its will on its adversary by the threat or use of force." (*A Study,* p. 31.)

[10] U.S. ED. NOTE—In his speech in Moscow to the World Congress for General Disarmament and Peace, Khrushchev said: "In reality under the banner of the 'doctrine of balance of forces' plans are made [in the West] for the initiation of a preventive war." *Pravda,* July 11, 1962. However, from August 1961 and repeatedly in 1962 Khrushchev insisted that the United States had acknowledged that Soviet strategic power was equal to its own. See, for example, *Pravda,* August 8, October 18, 1961; January 17, 1963.

§ At a press conference on November 29, 1961, President Kennedy declared: "Now, while we rely on our nuclear weapons we also, as I have said, want to have a choice between humiliation and holocaust." [*New York Times,* November 30, 1961.]

stalemate," to use the Western expression, had arisen; on the one hand a tremendous increase in the number of missiles and nuclear weapons, and on the other hand the incredible danger of their use. Under these conditions, according to the evaluation of American and NATO political and military circles, both sides had attained the position of so-called "mutual deterrence."

All this led to the conclusion that the strategy of "massive retaliation" was inflexible and could no longer assure the attainment of the political aims of the American imperialists. Whereas previously the United States could, with almost complete impunity, threaten unlimited use of nuclear weapons in any situation, even the possible outbreak of a local (limited) military conflict, the change in the balance of forces had made it dangerous to engage in "nuclear blackmail" and to risk the security of one's own country.

This circumstance has had an especially strong effect on the European satellites of the United States. In particular, by the end of 1959 the Western European Alliance had already openly noted in its decisions that the European countries could no longer rely exclusively on the strategic nuclear forces of the United States, as they had previously. There was no reason to expect that the Americans would automatically become involved in an armed conflict in which there was a risk of exposing themselves to a nuclear blow from the Soviet Union. Thus the European countries raised the question of creating their own independent strategic nuclear forces.

On the basis of their assessment of the new situation, American political and military leaders began to consider the so-called strategy of "flexible response" more acceptable and expedient. In their opinion, this would permit the conduct of either general nuclear war or limited wars, with or without nuclear weapons.

The strategy of "flexible response" was formulated by General Taylor in the book mentioned above, *The Uncertain Trumpet,* where he reveals the essence of this strategy and the mode of its conduct:

> The strategic doctrine, which I would propose to replace massive retaliation, is called herein the Strategy of Flexible Response. This name suggests the need for a capability to react across the entire spectrum of possible challenge, for coping with anything [. . .].*

In other words, the strategy proposed by Taylor is suitable, in his opinion, for all contingencies and provides an answer to any situation.

In an article entitled "Security Will Not Wait," published in the January 1961 issue of the American journal *Foreign Affairs,* Taylor formu-

---

* Taylor, *op. cit.,* p. 38 [p. 6 in the English text].

lated the basic principles of this strategy and the general military program of the U.S. Government in the following manner:

(a) The creation of an invulnerable strategic missile force, capable of delivering a crippling blow to the enemy "even after absorbing a surprise nuclear attack."

(b) The formation of adequate and properly equipped mobile forces for limited wars, "i.e., armed conflicts short of general atomic war between two nuclear power blocs."

(c) The formation of an effective system of military alliances.

(d) The assurance of the most favorable use of resources allocated to the military program.

The new strategic concept of the United States and NATO, therefore, was already essentially determined by the time Kennedy came to power, and the new President became its most fervent exponent.

In his messages to Congress on March 28 and May 25, as well as in his televised appearance on July 25, 1961, President Kennedy described aspects of the new strategic concept and the military program of the United States in some detail.

The strategic concept, the message of March 28, 1961, stressed, "must be both flexible and determined" and must prepare for the conduct of any war: general or local, nuclear or conventional, large or small. This concept is based upon the same idea as a "retaliatory strike," the only difference being that, whereas previously the threat of such a strike implied the unlimited use of nuclear weapons regardless of the scale of [the existing] conflict, i.e., a general nuclear war, now the "retaliatory strike" must be appropriate to the nature of the potential conflict.

The message noted that the United States must increase the capability of its armed forces "to respond swiftly and effectively" to any enemy action. In a world war this would mean that such a capability must be retained by that part of the armed forces which "survives the first strike." The message pointed out the prime importance of the ability to survive the enemy's first strike and to deliver a devastating retaliatory strike "in order to inflict unacceptable losses upon him." The President stressed that the ability to deter an enemy attack depended not only on the number of missiles and bombers but also on their state of readiness, their ability to survive attack, and the flexibility and sureness with which they were controlled to achieve strategic objectives.

Referring to the possible conduct of limited wars, the message stated that the United States and its allies must be capable of waging such wars with conventional weapons. If the forces with conventional weapons are unable to achieve the desired objectives, however, nuclear weapons could be used. At the same time, the probability of a limited war expanding into a general war was not denied, but it was stressed that all necessary measures must be taken to localize the conflict and to prevent it from causing the outbreak of a general nuclear war.

The U.S. military program outlined by President Kennedy in his messages and speeches provided for the organization and preparation of the armed forces for general nuclear war as well as for limited wars.

Thus, the strategy of "massive retaliation" which existed prior to 1961 in the United States and NATO, and which provided for the preparation and conduct only of general nuclear war against the Soviet Union and the socialist countries, has become obsolete and is being replaced by the strategy of "flexible response," which provides for the preparation and conduct not only of general nuclear war but also of limited wars, with or without the use of nuclear weapons, against the socialist countries.

At first glance the following may seem strange. On the one hand, American and NATO political and military leaders believe a general nuclear war to be implausible, or more precisely, unpromising, in the sense that it would lead to mutual annihilation, [a belief that explains] why the former strategy was rejected. On the other hand, the newly adopted strategy, while more flexible, again provides primarily for the capability and readiness for general nuclear war. But this is only an apparent contradiction.

The admission of the possibility that they might conduct a nuclear war, despite its unlikelihood, proves that the American imperialists are ready to embark upon any monstrous crimes against mankind to prevent their own inevitable destruction. Such a war would be an extreme measure; it might be initiated by the aggressors when all other measures had failed to give tangible results in the struggle with the socialist camp.

The question is this: If general nuclear war is dangerous to both sides, then what must be done so that it can lead to the attainment of the desired objectives, i.e., the destruction of the enemy with the least possible losses and destruction for oneself? The American imperialists and their Western European allies answer this question as follows: first, sharply step up the arms race, especially missiles, and nuclear and space weapons; and second, [achieve] surprise. The first [measure] must assure overwhelming quantitative superiority over the enemy in the most advanced strategic weapons, primarily missiles, and nuclear and space weapons, in order to make possible a continuing policy of "intimidation" [11] toward the Soviet Union and to facilitate negotiations with it from a "position of strength."

---

11 U.S. ED. NOTE—The Western notion of deterrence is rendered in Russian either by the word, *ustrashenie* (intimidation) or *sderzhivanie* which means "holding in check." Although both terms are used to characterize American policy, only the latter is used to describe Soviet policy.

Surprise assures the seizure of initiative, the rapid destruction of the enemy's armed forces, in particular his strategic forces and weapons, the disruption of his control over troops and the country as a whole, the undermining of his economy, and the demoralization of the people. It is believed [by the Western powers] that the enemy could be paralyzed in all respects by a powerful attack and that his fate would be determined during the very first days of the war.

The U.S. Senate Foreign Relations Committee has made a complete appraisal of the role of surprise in contemporary war. Rejecting any talk of "peacefulness," [the document] openly calls for a surprise nuclear first strike against the Soviet Union and the other countries of the socialist camp:

> The advent of the nuclear-missile weapons generation [heralded by the Soviet ICBM test of August 1957 [12]] brought a drastic compression in the time required for the delivery of nuclear explosions at intercontinental ranges and a corresponding reduction in the attack-warning time . . . [available to the victim of strategic aggression [13]]. These effects, added to the fact that there is as yet no active defense whatsoever against an intercontinental missile in flight, have gravely increased the temptation to strike first in a nuclear war.*

Thus it is no accident that American military theorists are carefully studying the advantages and disadvantages of preventive war, a first strike, and a pre-emptive attack.

The theory of preventive war was first advanced at the end of the 1940's by the most reactionary representatives of the American political and military leadership, when America possessed a monopoly of nuclear weapons. However, propaganda for this theory subsided when the Soviet Union also acquired such weapons. Now the American military leaders and scientists have returned to the study of preventive war, viewing it as a possible and acceptable choice. What is meant by preventive war? B. Brodie gives the following definition in his book, *Strategy in the Missile Age:*

> I am using the term to describe a premeditated attack by one country against another, which is unprovoked in the sense that it does not wait upon a specific aggression or other overt action by the target state, and in which the chief and most immediate objective is the destruction of the latter's over-all military power and especially its strategic armed forces. Naturally, success in such an action would

---

[12] U.S. ED. NOTE—The Soviet authors omitted these words, without indicating an ellipsis.

[13] U.S. ED. NOTE—The Soviet authors omitted these words, but indicated an ellipsis.

\* *A Study,* p. 3.

enable the former power to wreak whatever further injury it desired or to exact almost any peace terms it wished.*

In Brodie's opinion, arguments in favor of preventive war are based primarily on two premises: first, that in a strategic air and space war with nuclear weapons the one who strikes first will undoubtedly gain an important advantage, which with reasonably good planning will almost surely be conclusive; and second, that total war is inevitable.

Brodie emphasizes that:

> The least that can be said is that our plan for strategic attack, whatever it is, would have its best chances of being carried out if we struck first, and that these chances would be brought to a very low minimum if the enemy struck first. If we thought *only* [italics in English edition only] about maximizing our chances of survival, the above circumstances might be considered reason enough for going ahead with preventive war.†

This is how frankly the American theorists speak in favor of preventive war and surprise attack. Brodie is an associate of The RAND Corporation; consequently his statements not only reflect his personal views but also those of the leaders of the Air Force and other American military agencies in whose interests The RAND Corporation works. The conclusions and recommendations made by members of this corporation are not simply "voices in the wilderness"; they are listened to and adopted, since otherwise the corporation's activity would be meaningless.[14]

However, American officials, such as government and military representatives, who agree with the conclusions reached by their expert scientists and who implement them, prefer to use other terms to persuade the peoples of the world of their "peaceful intentions." Even Brodie is compelled to acknowledge this when he states that the partisans of preventive war employed by the government consider it "impolitic" to express their views publicly on this subject.‡ Therefore, even though these officials always assert that preventive war is "incompatible" with the principles of American "democracy" and "morality," they fully share these views.

---

* B. Brodie, *Strategiia v vek raketnogo oruzhiia* [*Strategy in the Missile Age*], Moscow, 1961, fn. 2, pp. 249–250 [English edition, Princeton University Press, Princeton, New Jersey, 1959, pp. 227–228].

† *Ibid.*, p. 253 [p. 231 in English text].

[14] U.S. ED. NOTE—In his book *Strategy in the Missile Age*, Brodie describes the preventive war thesis only in order to take issue with it. He points out that "it would be presumptuous and reckless in the extreme to base so cataclysmic an action on the thesis that total war is inevitable or nearly so." *Ibid.*, p. 232 in English text.

‡ *Ibid.*, p. 251 [p. 229 in English text].

Thus it follows that there is a very real threat of a preventive war being unleashed by the American imperialists against the Soviet Union and other countries of the socialist camp. The slogan of such a war is: "What was inevitable had better come early rather than late . . . because it would be less devastating that way." * This slogan has many temptations for them, since the aggressor picks the time he thinks most favorable to begin the preventive war. The American imperialists believe that the military potential of the United States is much more capable of destroying the Soviet Union now than it will be in the future, particularly by preventive war.[15]

Some military ideologists such as Kissinger substitute the term "surprise (first) strike" for the term "preventive war." This is a purely formal distinction, since the first strike can also mean the beginning of preventive war. But no matter what the attack is called, its main feature is the achievement of maximum surprise.

Surprise can and must be achieved in a pre-emptive blow. Such a blow is defensive, according to American military theorists, since it is dealt to an enemy who is ready to attack (to initiate a preventive war or deal a first blow). It is considered to be the final and only means of avoiding disaster.

This is how they assess the factor of surprise, which can be achieved by initiating a preventive war and by dealing a first or pre-emptive blow.

The United States simultaneously devotes considerable attention to defensive measures. Moreover, American leaders consider two matters to be of decisive importance: the time factor and, above all, the invulnerability of their strategic forces and weapons.

It is generally acknowledged immensely important to receive warning of an attack in good time, to remove the armed forces, especially the strategic, from the [vicinity of the expected] blow, to prepare a retaliatory strike, to alert the population for civil defense purposes, etc.

In September 1960, Kennedy, while still a presidential candidate, formed a temporary committee under the chairmanship of Senator Symington (former Secretary of the Air Force) to study the organization of the American military command and its suitability in the prevailing military, political, and strategic conditions. In early December of 1960,

---

* *Ibid.*

[15] U.S. ED. NOTE—This refers to the reassessment by the United States in the fall of 1961 of the strategic military balance which, the Department of Defense indicated, favored the United States. (See speech by Deputy Secretary of Defense R. L. Gilpatric at Hot Springs, Virginia, on October 21, 1961, *New York Times,* October 22, 1961; Secretary of Defense R. S. McNamara's testimony before the U.S. Senate Armed Services Committee, *New York Times,* January 20, 1962, and speech in Chicago on February 17, 1962, *New York Times,* February 18, 1962.)

the committee submitted a report to Kennedy, entitled "Plan for Broad Revision in the Defense Set-Up" [16] of the United States," which emphasized that any evaluation of America's military position would have to take into account "one salient factor [which] stands out above the rest." At the prevailing level of technical development, this factor was time; according to the committee, time was important for the following three reasons:

(1) The unprecedented strategic value of time in assuring the ability to react instantly in the present nuclear-space age. According to the committee, the United States had at least eighteen months for its preparations prior to entering World Wars I and II; however, in a general nuclear war the available reaction time would be at most eighteen minutes.

(2) Time is of crucial importance in the United States vs. Soviet arms race. The committee emphasized that a sufficiently up-to-date weapons system must be chosen and that the lead time between conception and use [i.e., operational readiness] of weapons must be minimized.

(3) Time affects defense costs. Regardless of how much the United States spends for military purposes, "time cannot be bought." Thus it is important to keep in mind the costly effect of building weapons which have become obsolescent as a result of delay.

At present, when missiles have "fantastically reduced the time necessary to deliver nuclear warheads from one continent to another," reaction time is literally measured in minutes. For example, a missile would require only thirty minutes to fly from America to the Eurasian continent, or vice versa; even less time may be required in the future.

Consequently, American political and military leaders seek all possible ways and means to gain additional time. The solution of this problem is believed to lie in the launching of special artificial satellites that can detect launchings of intercontinental ballistic missiles and signal this information back to earth. In addition, the Americans are building radar stations to track launchings of ballistic missiles.

Another equally important problem is to ensure the relative invulnerability of the armed forces, especially strategic forces and weapons. American and NATO political and military leaders believe that this problem can be solved by the creation of a large variety of strategic weapons instead of a single weapon: solid-fuel intercontinental and medium-range ballistic missiles, missile-carrying nuclear submarines, medium and heavy bombers armed with ballistic air-to-ground long-range missiles, and, in the near future, special space weapons.

One such measure is the construction of underground and mobile

---

[16] U.S. ED. NOTE—*New York Times,* December 6, 1960.

launchers for solid-fuel intercontinental and medium-range ballistic missiles, in order to make their detection and destruction more difficult. In addition, all combat-ready intercontinental and medium-range ballistic missiles, as well as a significant portion of the Strategic and Tactical Air Force Commands, are to be maintained on a fifteen-minute alert, and the number of airborne heavy bombers carrying nuclear bombs will be increased. A reliable system of communication, guidance, and warning is to be created.

It should be noted that the maintenance of a significant number of strategic and tactical weapons on a fifteen-minute alert and the increase in the number of airborne heavy bombers secure a double advantage: first, considerable preparedness to deliver a surprise attack, and second, quick launching in order to avoid destruction and deliver a retaliatory (counter) strike. However, an immediate retaliatory strike, if it were possible, could be delivered only by surviving missile forces, which would include missile-carrying nuclear submarines, aircraft carriers, and airborne heavy bombers on patrol. The remaining strategic and tactical aircraft that had taken off to escape the blow would have to land again on the surviving airfields to refuel and to pick up nuclear weapons before proceeding to execute their mission.

The United States military command today is seriously concerned over the vulnerability of its strategic air force. For this reason it is carrying out measures to disperse and protect its aircraft, and is further increasing the forces on alert on airfields and in the air. In order to shorten the reaction time required for [launching] a strike, the Americans are studying the possibility of maintaining airplanes loaded with nuclear bombs on ground alert.

Missile-carrying nuclear submarines are considered the most invulnerable [strategic weapon carriers, while close behind these are] underground and mobile launching installations for intercontinental and medium-range ballistic missiles, carrier planes, and, in the future, space weapons.

## U.S. NOTE B: THE SOVIET ASSESSMENT OF RECENT
## U.S. STRATEGIC CONCEPTS

[The true Soviet views on Western strategies and intentions are difficult to assess on the basis of public Soviet statements, which usually serve the tendentious purpose of attributing aggressive intentions to the West. The propaganda motive results in a certain amount of inconsistency in the public Soviet interpretations of Western strategies. For example, it is argued that the growth of Soviet military power has forced the West to give up its reliance on a general war strategy and to develop instead limited-war and "flexible response" doctrines, yet it is also alleged that the latter reflect a Western intention to initiate a preventive general nuclear war against the Soviet Union.

Public Soviet interpretation of Western strategies, especially as expressed by Khrushchev has undergone marked changes over the years. From the emergence of the Soviet Union as a nuclear power Khrushchev showed an increasing tendency to stress the growing effectiveness of Soviet military power as a deterrent of Western aggression, and to de-emphasize the danger of a rational premeditated attack by the West against the Soviet Union.[17] In 1956, for example, Khrushchev had reversed Leninist theory by asserting that, because of the growth of the moral and material strength of the socialist camp and of worldwide forces favoring peace, war was "not fatalistically inevitable."[18] By 1959, it was said that the West increasingly recognized the deterrent effect of Soviet military power. In May of that year Khrushchev declared:

> The imperialists know our strength. To attack us is tantamount to suicide; one would have to be insane to do this. I do not believe they are as stupid as all that; they understand the consequences which the unleashing of war against the socialist countries may have for them. . . .[19]

A few months later he asserted that the West would "hardly dare to launch a war against our motherland" and that "our forces and those of our socialist allies are colossal, and in the West, apparently, this is now understood."[20] Although war might still be unleashed by a madman, Khrushchev asserted, such an attempt could be "cut short" and "a straightjacket" found for the culprit.[21] As indicated in the Analytical Introduction, Khrushchev's public confidence in the deterrent effect of Soviet arms reached a high point in his speech to the Supreme Soviet in January 1960. In this speech, Khrushchev claimed that in missiles the Soviet Union had a five-year lead over the United States and that "the Soviet Army today possesses such combat means and fire power as no army has ever had before," sufficient "literally to wipe the country or countries that attack us off the face of the earth."[22] Consequently, Khrushchev said, "the Soviet people can be calm and

---

[17] See A. L. Horelick, *"Deterrence" and Surprise Attack in Soviet Strategic Thought,* The RAND Corporation, RM-2618, July 1960.
[18] *Pravda,* February 15, 1956.
[19] *Pravda,* June 1, 1959.
[20] *Pravda,* July 30, 1959.
[21] *Pravda,* October 15, 1958; January 28, 1959.
[22] *Pravda,* January 15, 1960.

confident: the Soviet Army's modern equipment ensures the unassailability of our country." A few months later Khrushchev boasted that "the Soviet Union is now the world's strongest military power." [23] Khrushchev used these claims to buttress his demands for a settlement on Soviet terms of various issues in dispute with the West.

Following the American reassessment of the strategic balance of power in the fall of 1961, the Soviet interpretation of U.S. strategy and intentions changed. Already, during the second half of 1961, Soviet public statements had placed more emphasis on Western aggressiveness. However, Soviet statements no longer emphasized the irrationality of a Western attack on the Soviet Union, but accused the West and especially the United States of preparing a preventive war. This interpretation of U.S. intentions was voiced first by Marshal Malinovskii [24] and then by Khrushchev [25] after the publication in March of a statement by President Kennedy in which the President said: "Of course, in some circumstances we must be prepared to use nuclear weapons at the start, come what may—a clear attack on Western Europe for example." And again: "In some circumstances we might have to take the initiative." [26]

Soviet spokesmen no longer claimed over-all strategic superiority over the United States, but strategic parity or qualitative superiority on the basis of missile technology and the large yields of some of their nuclear weapons.[27] Accordingly, they called for a further strengthening of the Soviet Armed Forces.

After the Soviet edition of this book had gone to press, in a speech at Ann Arbor on June 16, 1962, Secretary of Defense McNamara announced adoption of the so-called counterforce strategy.[28] "Given the current balance of nuclear power, which we confidently expect to maintain through the years ahead," said McNamara, "a surprise nuclear attack is simply not a rational act for an enemy." He continued:

> The United States has come to the conclusion that to the extent feasible, basic military strategy in a possible general nuclear war should

[23] *Izvestiia,* March 2, 1960.

[24] *Pravda,* May 1, 2, 1962.

[25] *Pravda,* July 11, 1962.

[26] Stewart Alsop, "Kennedy's Grand Strategy," *The Saturday Evening Post,* March 31, 1962, pp. 11, 13.

[27] See Khrushchev in *Pravda,* October 18, 1961, and Marshal Malinovskii in *Pravda,* January 25, 1962; Malinovskii, "The Program of the CPSU and the Question of Strengthening the Armed Forces of the USSR," *Kommunist,* No. 7, May 1962, p. 14.

[28] *Vital Speeches of the Day,* August 1, 1962, pp. 626–629.

be approached in much the same way that more conventional military operations have been regarded in the past. That is to say, principal military objectives, in the event of a nuclear war stemming from a major attack on the Alliance, should be the destruction of the enemy's military forces, not of his civilian population.

The very strength and nature of the Alliance forces make it possible for us to retain, even in the face of a massive surprise attack, sufficient reserve striking power to destroy an enemy society if driven to it. In other words, we are giving a possible opponent the strongest imaginable incentive to refrain from striking our own cities.

In a subsequent statement Secretary McNamara denied that this implied the adoption by the United States of a first-strike strategy:

What I said meant exactly the opposite. Because we have a sure second-strike capability, there is no pressure on us whatsoever to preempt. . . . One point I was making in the Ann Arbor speech is that our second-strike capability is so sure that there would be no rational basis on which to launch a preemptive strike.[29]

The public Soviet assessment of the "counterforce" strategy was in accord with the previous Soviet official interpretation of the "controlled response" strategy. Soviet commentators flatly rejected any Soviet commitment to restrict the use of nuclear weapons and denied the feasibility of avoiding the destruction of cities, especially if the Soviet Union were to use its 50- and 100-megaton weapons according to "McNamara's rules." The United States Government, according to Soviet comments, was trying to establish "rules" of nuclear war in order to make it more acceptable to the American people. It was asserted that "McNamara's statement shows concrete and practical evidence of preparation for a preventive war." [30] Khrushchev expressed similar views in his speech of July 10, 1962, and asserted in addition that the new strategy represented an attempt to divert the main weight of Soviet nuclear retaliation to American overseas bases and forces.[31]]

[29] Stewart Alsop, "Our New Strategy," *The Saturday Evening Post,* December 1, 1962, p. 18.

[30] Marshal Sokolovskii, "A Suicidal Strategy," *Red Star,* July 19, 1962. See also Major General M. Mil'shtein, "Certain Strategic Military Concepts of the American Imperialists," *Mirovaia ekonomika i mezhdunarodnie otnosheniia (World Economics and International Relations),* No. 8, August 1962; Major General N. Talenskii, "Preventive War—Nuclear Suicide," *International Affairs,* No. 9, August 1962, pp. 10–16. Colonel General A. Rytov, "The USSR Air Force Day," *Kommunist vooruzhennykh sil (Communist of the Armed Forces),* No. 15, August 1962, p. 14; Chief Air Marshal K. Vershinin, "Aviation in Modern War," *Izvestiia,* December 23, 1962.

[31] *Pravda,* July 11, 1962. See also January 17, 1963.

## Preparation of New Wars by Imperialist States

*Development and Growth of the Armed Forces.* The United States and NATO are developing their armed forces along lines determined by the strategic concepts they adopted in 1961 and by their views on the possible nature of present-day war. This development is based on the so-called principle of "interdependence" of the political, economic, and military spheres of the NATO countries, a principle that was advanced by American ruling circles in 1950. Later the principle was extended to include countries participating in other military and political alliances.

The basic aim of this principle imposed by the Americans is to create "balanced" military forces within the framework of the aggressive military blocs, and hence to define the responsibility of each participating country or group of countries in the development of whatever national armed forces the United States may deem necessary.

The United States and to a certain extent Great Britain have taken over the task of developing, preparing, and using primarily offensive strategic weapons, including nuclear weapons, because these countries have the greatest military, economic, and technical potential. The remaining countries of NATO and the other military blocs have undertaken principally the development of ground forces, and of small air forces and navies intended to support the operations of the ground forces and to execute auxiliary tasks.

The American imperialists, who have all the strategic weapons at their disposal, exert political and military pressure on their allies to force them to pursue policies advantageous to the United States.

Hence this so-called "interdependence" does not sit well with some NATO countries, primarily France and West Germany, which are attempting to play a greater military and political role than that assigned to them. French, and particularly West German, ruling circles object to the complete domination of the Americans, and to some extent of the British, over the [Western] military blocs, and insist upon a revision of the principle of "interdependence." They demand that nuclear weapons and the strategic means for delivering them be put in their hands.

At the present time, the organization and preparation of the armed forces of the countries in NATO and other aggressive military blocs are designed for limited wars, wherever they may break out, as well as for general nuclear war. However, the principal efforts still emphasize the preparation for general nuclear war.

The American plans, which President Kennedy presented in messages to Congress in 1961 and early 1962, provide for an increased rate of deployment of strategic missiles and space weapons in the countries of NATO and other alliances, and of well-equipped and mobile conventional forces, especially ground forces. In his message to Congress on May 25, 1961, Kennedy remarked that the American government was then particularly desirous of seeing its NATO allies devote their main efforts to the development of conventional armed forces, especially ground forces, in order to adapt to conditions arising from the changing East-West balance of power.[32]

It must be emphasized, however, that even though the United States has begun to devote greater attention to conventional armed forces, the main direction of its war effort remains the same. The principal efforts are being concentrated on the creation and improvement of nuclear forces and strategic weapons. This is evident from the above-cited military program of the new American administration as well as from the statements of prominent American military leaders. For example, the [former] Chairman of the Joint Chiefs of Staff, General Lemnitzer, declared on October 28, 1961: "In recent times, public attention has been centered on the measures we have taken in regard to conventional armed forces. I want to state clearly that this in no way indicates any decreased significance of the strategic nuclear potential. We are continuing to apply our main efforts to the improvement of our strategic forces for delivering a retaliatory blow." * [33]

The accelerated development of nuclear offensive forces and strategic weapons continues to furnish the main basis for the military strength of the countries of NATO and the other aggressive military blocs as a whole. The considerable attention devoted to strengthening conventional armed forces has naturally led to a sharp increase in military expenditures in several capitalist countries and to a continued arms race.

As a result of measures instituted in 1961, the NATO countries, especially the United States, have increased the numbers and fighting

---

[32] U.S. ED. NOTE—*Documents on American Foreign Relations, 1961,* pp. 77–78.

* Address of General Lemnitzer in Boston (Massachusetts) Oct. 28, 1961, at the 55th Anniversary Celebration of the "West End House" organization.

[33] U.S. ED. NOTE—Lemnitzer's actual words were: "The actions which have attracted most public attention, however, have been those we have taken with regard to other types of military forces. I would like to make it clear that these increases in no way reflect a downgrading of the importance of the strategic nuclear capability. Rather, they represent additions to the flexibility with which we can deal with military threats of varying degrees of intensity." Department of Defense, Office of Public Affairs, News Release No. 1211-61, p. 4.

strength of their national armed forces and have raised the strength of units and formations and the general combat readiness of their ground forces, air forces, and navies. The armed forces of the European NATO countries have also been strengthened.

In view of the fact that American imperialist circles are preparing to unleash different types of wars, they consider that the armed forces must now correspond more closely to their prescribed purpose. The traditional division of the armed forces into ground forces, air force, and navy no longer fully satisfies present requirements. Therefore, it is considered more expedient to organize the armed forces on the basis of strategic requirements for a general nuclear war and/or the possible need to wage limited wars.

However, it should be emphasized that, whereas it is almost impossible to use strategic weapons in a limited war, the forces intended for limited wars on the contrary must be used in a general nuclear war. For this reason it is believed that victory in such a war can be achieved only by the combined efforts of all the armed forces, but that the main role will naturally belong to the strategic forces. Consequently, the typical division of armed forces [into branches] is necessary for limited wars, whereas for general nuclear war they must be combined as much as possible.

In the opinion of the American military leaders, the need to maintain unity of purpose dictates the utility of developing the armed forces according to prescribed missions; however, centralized leadership is necessary, since only this can ensure that the various forces are used efficiently and purposefully to attain a unity of operation.

Historically, the following situation developed. The U.S. Air Force and Navy commands, which are charged with the development of their respective armed forces, have developed and continue to develop their own strategic weapons almost independently of each other: the Air Force has created heavy and medium bombers, intercontinental and medium-range ballistic missiles, and special space weapons; the Navy has created missile-carrying nuclear submarines. The same holds true for the operational and tactical weapons and the antiaircraft weapons.

The plans for utilizing these weapons, particularly the strategic ones, are developed by the command of the appropriate branch of the armed forces. Although these plans are co-ordinated, they do not have the organic unity inherent in centralized planning.

In early 1962, the American government and military leaders completed their study for improving the strategic leadership of the armed forces whose organization is determined on the basis of their assigned missions; on the basis of recommendations made by the committees of

Senator Symington and retired General Partridge.* The armed forces were consequently unified according to the following assigned missions:

1. Strategic offensive forces for conducting general nuclear war consist of units and formations of intercontinental ballistic missiles, missile-carrying nuclear submarines, heavy and medium bombers as well as tanker planes and, possibly in the near future, special space weapons.

2. The air defense and antimissile defense (space defense) forces for the American continent.

3. General purpose forces consisting of ground, tactical air, and naval forces (excluding missile-carrying nuclear submarines). These are intended for operations in conjunction with strategic offensive forces in a general nuclear war, and for independent operation in limited wars which may or may not involve the use of tactical nuclear weapons.

4. The forces and equipment needed to transport strategic troops by sea and air, including all necessary air and naval transport craft for rapid transfer of troops and armaments from the United States to other parts of the world in case of an armed conflict.

5. Armed forces reserves.

*The Strategic Offensive Forces.* American and NATO political and military leaders are of the opinion that strategic offensive forces cannot be restricted to one particular weapon system. Within reasonable limits, various types of systems are needed to assure flexibility and, above all, relative invulnerability and survivability.

At present, the strategic offensive forces include intercontinental and intermediate-range ballistic missiles,† nuclear submarines equipped with Polaris missiles, and heavy and medium bombers, some equipped with air-to-ground missiles. Special space weapons are planned for the near future.

*Intercontinental ballistic missiles* are in the possession of only the United States [among the Western powers] and are located on American territory. Units are armed with ballistic, liquid-fuel, Atlas and Titan missiles, and in 1962 will begin to receive solid-fuel Minuteman missiles.

By early 1962, the U.S. Air Force had seventeen [missile] squadrons, eleven equipped with Atlas missiles and six with Titans.

----

* Besides Senator Symington's committee, an *ad hoc* committee, formed early in September 1961 by order of the Secretary of Defense and headed by General Partridge (former Chief of the North American Defense Command), also studied this problem. In November 1961, the committee presented a secret report to the Secretary of Defense on the reorganization of the armed forces leadership (*New York Times,* November 29, 1961).

† In the European NATO countries.

Thirteen Atlas squadrons with 132 launching sites are planned by the end of 1962.

According to the Unit Equipment [schedule], the six Titan squadrons have 54 launching sites (nine per squadron). Plans have been made to increase the number of Titan squadrons to twelve by the end of 1963, with 108 launching sites. All of these missiles are to be underground.

The Minuteman missile, with its increased invulnerability, is considered the most promising. On the basis of test results the United States is trying to improve its reliability, accuracy, range and re-entry capability, and is speeding up its test program to obtain more operational data. The 1961–1962 budget provides for doubling the capacity to produce these missiles and to create the necessary reserve production capability.*

The U.S. command has decided to create sixteen such [Minuteman] squadrons with a total of 800 launching sites by the end of 1966.†

All of these missiles are to be underground.

It is possible that a number of the launchers will be mobile (for example, on special railroad flat cars) to increase their chances for survival; these are the so-called mobile missiles presently under study.

The following data [table on the opposite page] illustrates the general status and prospects for development of intercontinental ballistic missiles.

*Intermediate-range ballistic missiles,* though they are also developed and produced in the United States, are intended for transfer to the NATO member countries and possibly to other military blocs. By early 1962, two types of liquid-fuel rockets, Thor and Jupiter, were located in England, Italy, and Turkey.

The Thor squadrons are part of the British Air Force and are under British control; the Jupiter squadrons are under the dual control of Italy and Turkey on the one hand, and of the NATO command in Europe on the other. All of the missile launching sites in Great Britain, Italy, and Turkey are maintained on a fifteen-minute alert. However, these countries do not have missiles with nuclear warheads; such warheads are under the control of the American command.

The NATO plans provide for approximately 500 launching installations for intermediate-range ballistic missiles in Europe by 1966, not counting the British Thor missiles. These missiles are to be under the

---

* President Kennedy's message to Congress, March 28, 1961. [*Documents on American Foreign Relations, 1961,* p. 57.]

† Statement by the Secretary of Defense of the United States concerning the RS-70 airplane, reported in the press on March 16, 1962. [This particular statement by the Secretary of Defense made no mention of the number of Minuteman squadrons or launching pads. *New York Times,* March 17, 1962.]

| Squadrons (launching installations) | Planned | | | | | |
|---|---|---|---|---|---|---|
| | By early 1962 | By end of 1962 | By end of 1963 | By end of 1964–65 | By end of 1966 | Total by end of 1966 |
| Atlas missile | 11(108) | 13(132) | — | — | — | 13(132) |
| Titan missile | 6(54) | . | 12(108) | — | — | 12(108) |
| Minuteman missile | — | . | . | . | 16(800) | 16(800) |
| Total | 17(162)* | 13(132) | 12(108) | . | 15(800) | 41(1040) |
| Launching installations with rockets ready for combat | 63* | . | . | . | . | 990 |

Note: The dot indicates absence of data.

* In addition, there were 6 launching sites for Atlas, 5 installations for Titan, and 6 installations for Minuteman located at three test ranges, which if necessary could be used to launch combat rockets.

unified command of the European bloc. With this in mind, U.S. military leaders decided early in January of 1962 to develop a new intermediate-range missile (2,800 kilometers [1,500 miles]) using solid fuel and intended for the NATO countries. Presumably it will be lighter, more mobile, and consequently less vulnerable.

*Missile-carrying Nuclear Submarines.*    The Polaris (solid-fuel) intermediate-range ballistic missile carried by nuclear submarines ranks next in importance to the Minuteman intercontinental ballistic missile. The ability of these submarines to cruise submerged for a prolonged period and to launch missiles while submerged assures high mobility and good concealment and makes them practically invulnerable to enemy ballistic missiles.

By early 1963 the U.S. Navy had six nuclear submarines, each equipped with sixteen Polaris missiles. Five nuclear submarines with Polaris missiles, based at the Holy Loch, Scotland, patrol the waters of the northeastern Atlantic. They are constantly at combat readiness.

With the advent of the Kennedy administration, the United States reviewed its construction program for Polaris-equipped nuclear submarines in order to accelerate their production. Previously, 45 such submarines were to be built by 1970; the revised plan provides for the construction of 41 by 1966.*

By early 1962, 23 submarines were under construction, of which ten were started in 1961 alone.† From mid-1963 on, twelve missile-carrying nuclear submarines are to become operational annually, instead of the five envisaged in the original program.‡

The missile-carrying nuclear submarines are being equipped with Polaris A-2 missiles which have a range of 2,800 kilometers [1,500 miles]; by 1962–1963, they will be equipped with Polaris A-3 missiles which have a range of up to 4,000 kilometers [2,500 miles]. The development of Polaris A-3 has been accelerated in order to obtain [the weapon] one year sooner, at the expense of Polaris A-2 production.§

Equipping nuclear submarines with the Polaris A-3 missile, which because of its greater range can penetrate deep into the enemy's homeland, considerably increases the combat potential of these submarines and makes them less vulnerable to shore-based antisubmarine weapons.

*The Strategic Air Force.*    At the present time, the strategic air force remains the principal striking force of the United States and its allies

---

* Message of President Kennedy to Congress, January 18, 1962, concerning the 1962/63 budget. [*New York Times,* January 19, 1962.]

† Message of President Kennedy to Congress, March 28, 1961. [*Documents on American Foreign Relations, 1961,* p. 56.]

‡ *Ibid.*

§ *Ibid.* [p. 57].

in the aggressive military blocs. It includes heavy and medium American strategic bombers and medium British strategic bombers.

By early 1962 the United States had more than 600 heavy B-52 bombers, 1,100 medium B-47 bombers, and up to 60 medium super-sonic B-58 bombers.* In addition, it possessed more than 1,000 tanker planes capable of refueling large numbers of heavy and medium bombers in the air.

The main formation of the Strategic Air Force, including all of the heavy bombers and more than 900 medium bombers, is based in the United States. The remaining bombers are based in Europe, the Pacific, and Alaska.

Up to 50 per cent of the combat-ready strategic aircraft are kept on fifteen-minute ground alert to deliver strikes against pre-planned targets, and for quick take-off to avoid an enemy attack. At the same time, up to fifteen heavy bombers carrying nuclear bombs are engaged in a round-the-clock patrol of the northern coasts of Greenland, Canada, and Alaska, as well as of the Mediterranean region. If necessary, the number of heavy bombers on airborne alert can be increased to 70 or 80 and, under extraordinary circumstances, all of the operationally ready heavy and medium strategic bombers can become airborne.† [34]

The American military leaders believe that the accelerated growth [of the number] of intercontinental ballistic missiles does not eliminate the need for manned strategic bombers. Therefore it is planned to im-prove further the capability of the air force by increasing the number of heavy bombers and equipping them with air-to-surface missiles.

Plans are being made to maintain 700 heavy bombers within the next few years, most of them armed with Hound Dog guided missiles (air-to-surface) with nuclear warheads and a range of 800 kilometers [480 miles].[35] Subsequently, it is planned to equip these bombers with solid-fuel Skybolt ballistic missiles with nuclear warheads and a range up to 1,800 [1,000 miles]. It is believed that the successful development

---

* *The Military Balance 1961–1962*, November 1961. [The actual numbers cited were 1,000 B-47, 600 B-52, 30–40 B-58. *The Communist Bloc and the Western Alliances: The Military Balance 1961–1962*, The Institute for Strategic Studies, London, November 1961, p. 8.]

† Messages of President Kennedy to Congress, March 28 and May 25, 1961.

[34] U.S. ED. NOTE—In the cited speeches, President Kennedy, while recommend-ing improvement in the airborne-alert capacity of the Air Force, did not specifically mention 70–80 bombers. *Documents on American Foreign Relations, 1961*, pp. 51–66, 70–78.

[35] U.S. ED. NOTE—In the cited speeches, President Kennedy merely mentioned that, as to its range, the Skybolt missile was "far superior to the present Hound Dog missiles." *Ibid.*, p. 58.

and production of these missiles can extend the useful life of heavy bombers and thus assure their effective use in the missile age.*

It is planned to reduce considerably, over a period of time, the number of medium strategic bombers. By the end of 1966, it is expected that only the B-58 medium range strategic bomber will be in use; the B-47 medium bomber is to be withdrawn.

Work continues in the United States on the development of the new strategic B-70 bomber with a range of 13,000 kilometers [8,000 miles], a maximum speed of Mach 3, and a ceiling of 25,000–30,000 meters [82,000–98,000 feet]. A test model is to be built in 1962. If accepted, the B-70 will not be placed in operation before 1966.

The United States has spent fifteen years, and more than one billion dollars, in an attempt to develop a nuclear-powered plane. However, the American military leadership believes that the chances of developing a plane suitable for military purposes in the near future are very slight.

By early 1962 Britain had slightly more than 120 medium bombers; she plans to have approximately 150 medium bombers by 1965, a large number of which are to be equipped with the American Skybolt air-to-ground ballistic missile.

At present, France has several medium Mirage IV A strategic bombers. By 1964 she plans to have approximately fifty of these planes, economic conditions permitting.

*Space weapons,* which include various types of space devices, are by their very nature considered strategic weapons, or are intended to assure the successful utilization of other strategic weapons in wartime.

The U.S. Air Force directs the development, research, and testing of almost all types of space systems designed for reconnaissance, warning, radio navigation, communication, defense against ballistic missiles and enemy satellites, and nuclear strikes against strategic targets on the ground.

Activities concerned with the development, production, and testing of prototypes of space systems, their mass production and assignment to the armed forces are (with a few exceptions) under the control of the [Air Force] Systems Command, which in turn is responsible to the U.S. Air Force Chief of Staff. This command has 60,000 military and civilian employees, among them many scientists and engineers.

From 60 to 120 billion dollars are to be allocated to this command during 1960–1975 for the development of new types of space, ballistic, and electronic systems, and for aerodynamic flight equipment (aircraft and guided missiles).

---

* *Ibid.*

By early 1962, a number of military space satellites were in the experimental stage or being designed; these presumably will be turned over to the armed forces in 1962–1965. The main satellite systems are designed for reconnaissance of ground targets, meteorological forecasting, very long-range detection of intercontinental ballistic missile launchings, warning of missile strikes, and also for radio navigation and radio-satellite communication to assist the command and control of the armed forces.

Plans are also being made for the development and utilization of space systems to destroy ballistic missiles in the powered phase of flight, to identify and destroy enemy military satellites, etc.

It should be noted that by early 1962 the United States had launched more than one hundred different space satellites, among them up to forty for purely military purposes. Plans are being made to increase substantially the number of satellites in space and to launch approximately one thousand satellites by 1975, of which approximately six hundred are for military purposes.

Thus, the status and prospects of development for all the strategic offense weapon systems up to 1966 can be summarized in the following data:

| Types | In existence by early 1962 | Planned by the end of 1966 |
|---|---|---|
| Launching installations for intercontinental ballistic missiles | 162 * | 1040 |
| Launching installations for intermediate-range ballistic missiles | 105 | 560 † |
| Missile-carrying nuclear submarines (missiles) | 6(96) | 41(656) |
| Heavy strategic bombers | 600 | }900 ‡ |
| Medium strategic bombers | 1300 | |
| Active space weapons (for destruction of ballistic missiles and enemy satellites, and the delivery of nuclear strikes) | — | 34 § |

* Of these, 63 are combat ready (with missiles). In addition, there are 17 pads at test centers.
† A rough approximation.
‡ A rough approximation. A considerable number of these bombers will be equipped with air-to-ground ballistic missiles with a range of 1,600–1,800 kilometers [1,000–1,100 miles].
§ By end of 1964.

Planned Launchings of American Military Space Vehicles (Satellites)
According to a Fifteen Year Program

| Name of System | Mission | Number of launchings | | | |
|---|---|---|---|---|---|
| | | 1960–64 | 1965–70 | 1970–75 | Total for 15 yrs. |
| Samos | Reconnaissance of ground-target objects 6 to 18 meters in over-all length (later 0.7–18 meters); radio reconnaissance | 49 | 38 | 30 | 117 |
| Midas | Warning of missile attack 30 minutes before missiles reach their targets | 33 | 50 | 40 | 123 |
| Transit | Radio navigation of submarines and missile-carrying aircraft with an accuracy of 100–200 meters | 26 | 48 | 40 | 114 |
| Advent Rebound | Active \} global network of radio communica-Passive \} tion (Army, Air Force, and Navy) | 8 26 | 3 30 | 15 30 | 26 86 |
| Nimbus and Aeros | Global network of meteorological reconnaissance | 7 2 | 9 14 | 30 15 | 46 31 |
| Bambi | Destruction of ballistic missiles in the power phase of flight | 6 | 36 | 30 | 72 |
| Saint | Identification and destruction of military satellites | 20 | 36 | 30 | 86 |
| Dyna-Soar | Destruction of ground targets by nuclear weapons; reconnaissance | 8 | 6 | 10 | 24 |
| Anna Sekor | Linking geodetic networks | . | . | . | . |
| | Total | | | | Approx. 1000 |

[Apparently the dot indicates absence of data.]

178

From these data it appears that the number of general strategic weapons is to be increased by one half and the number of missiles by six to seven times, by the end of 1966. Missile forces will occupy the predominant position in American and NATO armed forces by 1966. President Kennedy declared in his Message to Congress on March 28, 1961: "By that time we expect to have a large number of intercontinental ballistic missiles completely tested and on the launching pads, as well as a powerful fleet of manned bombers, equipped primarily with air-to-surface missiles. Space weapons will occupy an important position during 1965–1975." [36]

*Antiaircraft and Antimissile Defense.* The American and NATO commands believe that air defense against manned aircraft will continue to be important during the immediate future in spite of the accelerated development by both sides of strategic missiles that will also require the development of an appropriate defense. In his Message to Congress on March 28, 1961, President Kennedy stated: "For the next several years at least, however, we shall have to continue to provide a defense against manned bomber attacks."

Since mixed types of strategic offensive weapons, such as intercontinental ballistic missiles and strategic bombers, now exist side by side, the United States is planning a parallel development of defense systems against both aircraft and missiles; however, the principal efforts are to be concentrated on creating a reliable defense against missiles.

The imperialist bloc has set up its air defense according to geographic regions: North America, Europe, and the Pacific. These systems are unified, particularly the North American and European systems.

The North American air defense system is the most highly developed and unified; it covers the continental United States, Canada, Alaska, Greenland, and Iceland.

North American Air Defense Command includes American and Canadian air force and ground force units equipped with fighter planes and guided antiaircraft missiles. In addition, some American naval and tactical air force interceptors are stationed in the United States and available for air defense.

An integral part of the air defense is the unified detection and guidance system which includes a long-range [i.e., distant early] warning network and a short-range [i.e., close-in] control and warning network. The early warning network, in combination with air and radar picket

---

[36] U.S. ED. NOTE—The quoted statement by President Kennedy was not made in the Message cited. See *Documents on American Foreign Relations, 1961,* pp. 51–66.

ships, forms three lines for detection of manned aircraft along the distant approaches to the continental United States from the north, west, and east.

The first early warning line (DEW Line) is located 2,500–3,000 kilometers [1,500–2,000 miles] north of the American border and passes through Iceland, Greenland, and the northernmost regions of Canada and Alaska. The overlapping radar stations on this line can fully monitor the polar air space and provide warning to the air defense commands, within two to three hours, of the approach from the north of enemy aircraft, including low-flying types.

The second early warning line runs approximately along the 55th Parallel. It is built, organized, and manned by the Royal Canadian Air Force; its purpose is to give more precise information about detected targets. The radar stations along this line can provide warning to the American air defense units, within forty to fifty minutes, of the approach of enemy aircraft to the northern borders of the United States.

The third early warning line (Pine Tree) runs along the southern border of Canada and provides ten to fifteen minutes' warning of the approach of enemy aircraft to American territory.

The close-in aircraft control and warning network is distributed throughout the United States, including the east and west coasts and the country's southern regions where it monitors the air space south of the Mexican border and south of the Gulf states. A major portion of the close-in control and warning network is part of the automated SAGE system, which makes it possible to co-ordinate more than 70 per cent of the active air defense weapons. There are more than twenty SAGE centers in the United States for rapid collection and evaluation of air data.

The Americans believe that the existing system of air defense, undergoing continuous improvement, will prove sufficiently reliable against manned enemy aircraft.

The United States is devoting considerable effort to the development of antimissile and antispace weapons. Many practical measures have been taken in this direction. In particular, three early warning radar centers exist for detecting ballistic missile launchings—in Greenland (near Thule Air Base), in Alaska (Clear), and at Fylingdales in Great Britain (under construction). These radar stations have a range exceeding 5,500 kilometers [3,300 miles]. Their purpose is to detect intercontinental ballistic missiles as soon as they leave the atmosphere and to provide fifteen to seventeen minutes' warning before the missiles strike. High-speed computers receiving data from the radar stations automatically determine the origin and destination of the missiles by analyzing their trajectories.[37]

In addition, the United States has a number of shorter range radar stations on the island of Shemya (in the Aleutians), in Turkey, in Canada, and on its own territory. Their main function is to provide continual monitoring of Soviet missile test sites. If necessary, they can be used as intermediate stations for the early detection of ballistic missiles.

The United States has built the SPADAT radar system to detect and track all enemy space devices; the center of this system is located at the North American Air Defense Command Headquarters. In early 1962 this system included more than 125 military and civilian observation sites equipped with up-to-date electronic equipment for detection and observation of devices in space.

The proposed orbiting of large numbers of Midas satellites to detect intercontinental ballistic missile launchings and to give thirty-minute warning will help strengthen antimissile and antispace defense.

In addition, the development of the Nike-Zeus antimissile missile is being accelerated. When this is adopted, it will be the primary means of defense against enemy ballistic missiles.

Late in 1961 the United States created a division for defense against space weapons, including antimissile defense, which operates the detection and warning system for ballistic missiles, artificial satellites, and other space devices.

Initially the division will receive, process, and report data on the space situation and on ballistic missile launchings. In the future, as weapons against ballistic missiles, artificial satellites, and space devices are developed, this division will also receive the means for defense against space weapons.

The air defense system of the European NATO countries is divided into four zones: the Northern Zone (Norway and Denmark), the British Zone (British territory), the Central Zone (West Germany, France, Belgium, the Netherlands, and Luxembourg), and the Southern Zone (Italy, Greece, and Turkey).

Fighter planes are the European NATO countries' main weapons of defense. However, many of these planes are outdated and have no guided air-to-air missiles. The air defense of the European NATO

---

[37] U.S. ED. NOTE—In a speech on March 16, 1962, Khrushchev claimed the development by the Soviet Union of a "global missile" capable of bypassing the early warning systems located in the North by circling the earth and striking from a different direction. "The early warning systems have lost their significance in view of the existence of global missiles." *Pravda,* March 17, 1962.

countries also has American antiaircraft guided missiles of various types to protect their most important economic and political centers and troop formations.

In order to control the active instruments for detection and warning in all four zones, a large number of centers and posts for control and warning have been established. These include a large number of radar stations of various kinds, which are intended to furnish warning of aerial targets at a distance of 500 kilometers [300 miles].

A single automated system of observation, warning, and control similar to the American SAGE system is planned for each of the European air defense zones.

Pacific air defense is also unified. It includes South Korea, Japan, the Philippines, the Hawaiian Islands, and the most important areas of the Pacific. Both the United States and the above countries provide forces and weapons for the air defense of this zone; planning and general direction are under the American Command in the Pacific.

Thus [our most] probable enemies have created a strong air defense for strategically important regions, particularly North America. The European and Pacific air defense zones are essentially the front lines of American defense. One must expect that in the future the air defense of these three most important geographic regions will probably be consolidated into a single system with the greatest degree of centralized direction. In addition, American military leaders continue to take significant measures for antimissile and antisatellite defense, from the viewpoint that the side which first develops a defense against missiles and space weapons can threaten war or even initiate it without fear of strong retaliatory blows.

*General Purpose Forces.* These include ground forces, tactical air forces, and naval forces (excluding missile-carrying nuclear submarines).

*The ground forces* of the countries participating in the aggressive military blocs (NATO, CENTO, SEATO), as well as those of Japan, South Korea, and the Kuomintang clique on Taiwan,* early in 1962 consisted of about five million troops and over 160 regular army divisions.

These ground forces are located mainly in the geographical regions encompassed by their respective blocs. The composition of these troops varies; they do not all possess the same amount of armament and

---

* Japan, South Korea, and the Kuomintang clique are included with the above three blocs among the imperialist military coalitions headed by the United States, since they have similar mutual defense agreements with the United States.

military equipment, and their personnel do not receive uniform training. Consequently, they vary in combat capability.

The ground forces of the NATO countries are the most important with respect to size and, particularly, quality. By early 1962 they included more than 90 regular army divisions and a large number of independent units and subunits, particularly those equipped with tactical missiles.

In the development of the NATO countries' ground forces, especially the unified ground forces, the main efforts are directed toward increasing their fire power, striking potential, mobility, and self-sufficiency to carry out combat missions. In addition, an effort is being made to attain uniform divisional organization.

The fire and striking power of the ground forces are being increased by providing them with the means for delivering tactical nuclear weapons, and re-equipping them with the most modern conventional weapons and combat equipment.

It is planned to increase in the near future the number of guided and unguided missiles available to the forces of the NATO countries.

In addition to existing means of nuclear delivery in the hands of the ground forces, new means are being developed, particularly various types of guided and unguided missiles which are considerably smaller than existing models; these will provide greater mobility and reliability, and a more speedy battlefield employment, both in limited war and in general nuclear war.

The American and NATO commands are both re-equipping their ground forces with more modern conventional weapons and combat equipment. Thus in 1961 American and British ground forces were being equipped with an improved type of M-60 medium tank and with the Centurion tank, which has an increased range (up to 400 kilometers [240 miles]) and improved armament (105 mm. howitzer); these tanks are expected to replace a large number of the older models of medium tanks. Ground forces are also being equipped with self-propelled, 105 mm. and 155 mm. artillery. These guns have greater range, accuracy, and mobility (up to 1,000 kilometers [600 miles]). Almost all of the European countries are equipping their ground forces with automatic rifles and multipurpose machine guns of standard NATO 7.62 mm. caliber.

American ground forces are being equipped with mobile radio relay stations for multichannel communication between one operational tactical headquarters and another. These stations are designed for round-the-clock operation and can be rapidly deployed under field conditions.

Attention continues to be directed toward further improvement of troop organization for limited war as well as general nuclear war. At present the main efforts are directed at achieving uniform organization of all the divisions of the NATO countries on the basis of brigades. Britain, France, West Germany, Belgium, and the Netherlands have already adopted the brigade structure. In 1962 the United States and several other NATO countries will begin [*sic*] to adopt this organizational structure for their divisions.

The training of the NATO countries' ground forces, in particular the unified forces, is generally carried out through a uniform program that applies throughout the entire bloc and terminates annually in major exercises or maneuvers. These troops are the most combat-ready, since they possess sufficient quantities of modern weapons, highly trained personnel, the necessary administrative services, etc., and can conduct active military operations in limited wars as well as in general nuclear war, in conjunction with tactical air forces and naval forces.

The NATO countries, especially the United States and Great Britain, are devoting considerable attention to preparing their reserves, as well as increasing the effectiveness and combat-readiness of the regular ground forces. The United States continuously maintains thirty-five reserve divisions (National Guard and Army Reserves)* and Britain maintains ten divisions (Territorial Army). Several months are required, after mobilization has been declared, to arm these divisions and bring them up to strength. These reserves are organized in a manner similar to regular army divisions, and the American and British military leaders are attempting to make the reserves nearly as combat-ready as regular troops.

In his Message to Congress on May 25, 1961, President Kennedy stated that the U.S. Army Command was developing a plan for rapid deployment of reserve divisions within three to eight weeks after the declaration of mobilization, depending on how complete the mobilization of these divisions.[38] It is now assumed that in an emergency, ten divisions would be combat-ready in less than two months, whereas this previously required almost nine months.

Other NATO countries also maintain a small number of reserve divisions and trained reserves.

The ground forces of the CENTO countries (excluding Turkey) consist of approximately twenty divisions (twelve Iranian and seven Pakistani); those of SEATO, Japan, South Korea, and the Kuomintang clique have more than fifty divisions. Although these troops are considerably inferior to NATO troops in equipment, training, and combat-readiness, the imperialist aggressors, particularly the United States, are

---

* In addition, the Army Reserves have thirteen training divisions.

[38] U.S. ED. NOTE—*Documents on American Foreign Relations, 1961,* p. 80.

making a considerable effort to increase their combat potential. Furthermore, three American divisions and one British division are also located in the Far East.

In a general nuclear war, if the imperialists start one, the ground forces of SEATO, CENTO, Japan, South Korea, and the Kuomintang will primarily conduct defensive operations and limited wars with the support of American and British tactical air and naval forces.

*The Tactical Air Force.* The air forces of the NATO countries (except the United States and Great Britain), CENTO, SEATO, Japan, South Korea, and the Kuomintang consist of tactical and air defense forces [only]. The American and British air forces also include strategic air forces.

The tactical air force is intended for delivery of nuclear strikes in conjunction with strategic forces to a depth of 1,000 kilometers [600 miles], for interdicting military operations, supporting ground forces, and performing other missions in a general nuclear war, as well as supporting ground forces in limited wars with or without nuclear weapons.

The air forces of the NATO countries account for about 75 per cent of all tactical aircraft. The main force is in Europe, where more than 3,000 combat aircraft are concentrated, many of which can carry nuclear weapons. There are also forty-eight launch sites for tactical guided missiles. This force is the most combat-ready.

The tactical aircraft forces in Europe vary according to the international situation. During the second half of 1961, for example, American tactical aircraft in Europe were considerably reinforced by the deployment of a number of squadrons from the United States.

The tactical air forces of the majority of European NATO countries are equipped mainly with American aircraft. In recent years, the NATO Command has taken measures to standardize the types of aircraft, i.e., it has recommended the best types of planes for adoption by the countries in the bloc. The latter are adopting these planes in their armament and arranging for their joint production. Thus several European NATO countries have arranged to produce the American F-104G fighter, the French transport plane, *Atlantic,* and the Italian G-91 light fighter.*

Since 1961 the American and NATO commands have altered their views toward tactical air power to a certain extent. Previously there was a tendency to attach less importance to the role of tactical aircraft in the air forces, because of the increased development of intermediate-range and ground force missiles; now that the possibility of limited wars has been recognized, the importance of tactical aircraft has increased.

---

* *The Military Balance 1961–1962,* November 1961 [p. 10].

Since a considerable number of obsolete fighter planes are supposed to be withdrawn from service by 1965 and since the dwindling number of remaining aircraft are becoming obsolete, an improved tactical fighter plane is being developed which is not intended to deliver nuclear weapons. The necessary funds have already been allocated; however, until a tactical fighter plane that meets the above requirements is developed, Kennedy has recommended that funds be allocated for modifying the F-105 tactical fighter plane to improve its performance when used with conventional weapons and its ability to operate from airfields of all types.

In view of the importance of increasing the strategic mobility of its armed forces, especially the ground forces, the American military leadership is taking steps to expand the air transport capability, i.e., to accelerate and expand the production of transport aircraft, which should assure the necessary volume of air transport.

The second most important tactical aircraft formation, composed mainly of American planes, is located in the Far East. The aircraft of the CENTO countries (except Turkey) and of SEATO, Japan, South Korea, and the Kuomintang are mostly obsolete American planes capable of carrying out missions in limited wars only.

A large part of the tactical air force is located in the United States, and is designed to support units and formations deployed to Europe and the Far East.

*Naval Forces.*    The main mission of naval forces in a general nuclear war is to win naval supremacy, in conjunction with strategic offensive forces and tactical air forces, by delivering nuclear strikes on enemy missile installations, on naval and air forces in bases or at sea, and on other military and industrial targets. A considerable portion of the naval forces can also be used for the conduct of limited wars.

By early 1962 the naval forces of NATO, CENTO, SEATO, Japan, South Korea, and the Kuomintang contained approximately 1.4 million men,* more than 4,000 warships, and 10,000 planes and helicopters, including reserve ships and planes.

The basic naval power of the coalition is provided by the U.S. Navy, and to a lesser extent by the British Navy, which have substantial means for delivering nuclear weapons. The naval forces of the other capitalist countries possess mainly obsolete warships; they only supplement the U.S. and British navies and are intended for security and support tasks.

By early 1962 the American and British regular naval forces included over 900 warships,† among them 21 attack carriers, 5 submarines

---

* *The Military Balance 1961–1962,* November 1961 [pp. 14–23].
† *The Military Balance 1961–1962,* November 1961 [pp. 17–18].

armed with Regulus missiles, 15 nuclear submarines armed with torpedoes, and 27 ships with guided antiaircraft missiles, as well as up to 3,000 combat planes.

The main striking power of the American and British navies is provided by carrier aviation.

The most combat-ready American naval forces are the United States Sixth Fleet in the Mediterranean, which has two attack carriers with approximately 160 planes (75 per cent are [bomb] carriers), and the Seventh Fleet in the Far East, with three attack carriers and 230 planes.

The British attack carriers are also well prepared for combat; one is located in the Mediterranean, one in the Far East, and two in the Northeast Atlantic.

If necessary, the forward carrier strike forces can be reinforced by deploying attack carriers from the United States to the Northeast Atlantic, Mediterranean, and Far East. This could be done under the pretext of maneuvers or of rotating ships to European and Far Eastern waters.

The Americans believe that the importance of surface ships, especially aircraft carriers, is increasing in view of possible requirements for waging limited wars. Consequently they have accelerated the construction of various types of surface vessels, especially aircraft carriers. The latter are considered capable of carrying out various types of missions, especially in limited wars. They can perform air reconnaissance, deliver strikes to small targets, and provide direct support for ground forces and amphibious forces. This is the reason that the Americans are making continued efforts to re-equip their aircraft carriers with modern planes and to build new aircraft carriers.

At the same time, a considerable number of postwar warships are being modernized, particularly fleet destroyers, patrol vessels, and submarines, which are being equipped with new antiaircraft and antisubmarine weapons.

The U.S. Navy also transferred more than twenty transport ships from the reserve fleet to the active fleet in 1961 in order to increase the navy's capability to transport ground forces from America to Europe, the Far East, and other areas. Up to the middle of 1961, the available navy transport ships could carry approximately one and a half divisions at one time; with the additional ships it will now be possible to carry two divisions at once. The navy's transport capabilities will be further increased by the construction of new transport and landing vessels.

In 1961 the American leadership initiated a series of changes in the Navy and Marine Corps organization to increase the combat-readiness of the naval forces as a whole. The First and Second Fleets were put

on full operational status.* Prior to this there were the fleets' headquarters and command personnel, and ships, aircraft, and marines were
assigned to them only during training periods. In the reorganization, the
First Fleet (Pacific) and the Second Fleet (Atlantic) were assigned
forces and definite zones of operation. Each of these fleets has attack
carrier task forces, carrier-based antisubmarine forces, amphibious
forces, and supply and service forces. The fleet commanders and their
staffs were transferred from shore headquarters to their respective flag-
ships.

A reorganization of the Marine Corps is still in progress; new units
and formations are planned, and a proposal has been made to increase
the fire-power and striking potential of marine divisions by assigning
them tank battalions, batteries of missiles (unguided), and howitzers.

British naval forces have concentrated their efforts on building submarines and ships with guided antiaircraft missiles. The fleet is being
reinforced by equipping its aircraft carriers with nuclear weapons and
providing the naval air force with new aircraft.

In 1961 the naval forces of the other imperialist countries directed
their main efforts toward building ships with conventional armament,
primarily for antiaircraft and antisubmarine defense.

*The Preparation of Military Theaters for War.*   One of the principal
measures taken by the imperialist countries in planning general nuclear
war is to prepare likely military theaters and the continental United States
in an appropriate manner before the outbreak of war.

The influence of new weapons upon the conduct of war has been
taken into account when preparing military theaters and American territory. Whereas formerly the main efforts were directed toward creating
fortified lines and developing railroad systems and highways for the
deployment and combat operations of ground forces, now these efforts
are primarily directed toward assuring the necessary conditions for
effective use of missile and air forces. Launching pads for all types of
missiles are being constructed in [prospective] military theaters, as well
as missile and nuclear-weapon storage facilities. Networks of air bases
and airfields are being improved, as well as naval bases, ports, and
debarkation sites for troops and equipment. New fixed air defense and
radar installations are being constructed, reliable systems of communication, control, and warning are being organized, pipelines are being
laid, etc.

The American and NATO commands believe that these measures

---

* *The Military Balance 1961–1962*, November 1961. [No mention of this appears in the referenced source.]

should guarantee the possibility of delivering surprise nuclear strikes by missile, aircraft, and naval forces on strategically important targets in the Soviet Union and other socialist countries.

Another characteristic is that, whereas each country used to prepare its territory independently before the war, now territories are prepared systematically and in the interests of the military blocs. The most extensive measures to prepare NATO operational theaters have been taken both in Europe and in the United States. The American continent is being readied, above all, as a build-up area for strategic offensive weapons—intercontinental ballistic missiles and strategic aircraft. The European operational theaters are being prepared for the use of intermediate-range ballistic missiles, tactical aircraft, naval forces, and large formations of ground forces.

The following Atlas intercontinental ballistic missile launching sites existed by early 1962: Vandenberg, Offutt, Warren, Fairchild, and others. According to the American press, there are to be twenty operational locations in the United States for launching Atlas, Titan, and Minuteman intercontinental ballistic missiles by the end of 1963. Four more bases for launching Minuteman missiles are to be built by 1966. By that time the twenty-four operational missile bases are to have more than 1,000 launching pads.

The American command is attempting to reduce the vulnerability of missile sites on American soil by considerably dispersing the launchers and putting them underground. Thus all Titan and Minuteman sites planned or under construction, and all future Atlas sites, are to have underground launchers, and the launchers at each site are to be 15–60 kilometers [9–35 miles] apart.

American military leaders also devote considerable attention to improving and expanding the network of air bases necessary for the strategic air force. In order to safeguard the mobility, diminish the losses, and improve the survivability of air units, air bases are being constructed not only within the continental United States, which is the principal basing area of the strategic air force, but also beyond its borders. By early 1962, there were more than eighty bases for American strategic aircraft, most of them in the continental United States (up to fifty) and more than twenty in Europe and North Africa. However, even this number is considered insufficient. Consequently American leaders have developed a plan to use large civilian airports in the United States for medium bombers in case of a war threat.

Bases for launching intermediate-range ballistic missiles are being constructed in the European military theaters of operation. By early

1962, sixty Thor launch sites were ready for operation in Britain and thirty Jupiter launch sites in Italy. At the same time, sixteen Jupiter launch sites were under construction in Turkey.

NATO's unified air force requires one airfield for each squadron. From 1951 to 1960 more than two hundred airfields were built according to NATO plans.* In addition, the NATO unified air force command intends to use the airfields of the NATO countries' national air forces.

In constructing and rebuilding naval bases and ports, the NATO and American commands aim to create a system of naval bases able to assume the reliable defense of naval communications in the Atlantic, Mediterranean, and Pacific area and to support naval offensives in these maritime theaters as well as joint ground-force and tactical aircraft operations in ground theaters.

There are more than one hundred naval bases and anchorages in the North Atlantic and in the Mediterranean basin; these are the areas where NATO expects the fleet's main combat operations to develop. This number of bases is acknowledged to be quite adequate (taking into account the use of medium and small ports in order to disperse the ships) for the unified NATO naval forces and for the national navies.

The countries of the imperialist coalition have numerous well-equipped ports capable of handling the necessary volume of foreign and domestic transport in peacetime and in war. In the North Atlantic and the Mediterranean basin, which are the areas of greatest maritime traffic, there are more than 600 ports; 150 of these ports have an average annual turnover of more than one million tons of cargo.

Considerable attention is devoted to dispersing naval bases and loading points in order to protect the system of bases and anchorages from nuclear weapons. Medium and small ports are to be used for this purpose. Some of them are presently being appropriately prepared: dredging operations are in process and access to the ports is being improved; loading equipment (especially portable equipment) is being developed; protected warehouses are under construction; and underground pipelines are being laid from the piers to liquid-fuel storage tanks and consumers. To assure adequate facilities for submarine forces widespread use of floating bases is expected.

Extensive work is in process in all theaters of military operation to organize a reliable communication, control, and warning system, and particularly to organize radio, radio-relay, tropospheric, and ionospheric communication systems, underground and underwater cable lines and submarine cables, communication centers and command posts, a radar

---

* *The Military Balance 1961–1962,* November 1961. [The actual number of NATO operational air bases is given as 220, p. 9.]

coverage system, etc. By early 1962, a communication system that extends over more than 42,000 kilometers * was created in the European NATO countries.

In view of the considerable increase in the liquid-fuel requirements of the armed forces, primarily those of the air force, the U.S. and NATO commands pay considerable attention to the development of pipelines and to the creation of large stores of fuels and lubricants, especially in European theaters. Thus, by early 1962 in accordance with the plans of the NATO command, 8,000 kilometers [5,000 miles] of pipelines †️ had been laid in the European countries, and storage facilities with a total capacity of over 2 million cubic meters had been constructed for fuels and lubricants. The dense network of commercial pipelines in the United States substantially facilitates the laying of pipelines to the more important air bases.

Thus the United States and NATO commands are undertaking large-scale measures to prepare probable theaters of military operation. Tremendous sums are being spent to construct intercontinental and inter-mediate-range ballistic missile bases, air bases, and naval bases; to stockpile weapons; to organize systems of communication, guidance, and control; and to lay pipelines.

*Economic Preparation for War.*   During the postwar period, bourgeois military science began to devote special attention to the most effective utilization of economic resources and to the preparations of the economy for war.

Even before World War II, the military strategy of the principal capitalist countries took into account the necessity for the preparation in good time of an extensive military industry capable of producing large amounts of weapons and military equipment. The general staffs of the main capitalist countries developed detailed mobilization plans for industry and weapons production.

In Nazi Germany, long before the war, a system of government agencies was created to direct the economy and develop military production. Government control was established over all spheres of the country's economic activity. From 1934 to August 31, 1939, 59 per cent of the entire budget of Fascist Germany was allocated to the preparation for war.

Germany expected a short war, and her economic mobilization plans did not provide for sufficient reserves, especially of strategic raw materials. As a result less than 15 per cent of Germany's gross industrial

---

* *The Military Balance 1961–1962,* November 1961. [The length of the communication system is given in the source as 26,500 miles, p. 9.]

†️ *Ibid.*

production in 1940 was for military purposes; in 1941, 19 per cent; in 1942, 26 per cent; in 1943, 38 per cent. Only in 1944 did it reach 50 per cent.

Having developed a high military industrial potential, the Germans could not use it to the fullest extent. The principal limiting factors were the severe shortage of several minerals and the limited domestic labor resources.

England began its economic preparation for war late, mainly after the Munich Agreement. During the initial stages, the main attention was given to the development of the aircraft and shipbuilding industries. The industries providing armaments for the ground forces were developed during the war. After the destruction of the British Expeditionary Force by the Germans at Dunkirk in May 1940, the ground forces were essentially without arms and British industry needed approximately three years to supply sufficient armaments for the ground forces.

Although Britain had essentially the highest degree of economic mobilization in comparison to the other capitalist states, her own production still could not fill all the arms requirements of her forces during the course of the war, and she depended greatly upon shipments from the United States. The United States provided more than one half of Britain's tank requirements, 18 per cent of fighter aircraft, 60 per cent of military cargo planes, 38 per cent of ships and landing craft, 21 per cent of small arms, and 6 per cent of artillery.

France, in effect, had no time to develop its economy to supply the needs of the armed forces, and its industrial mobilization plans remained on paper.

The inadequate war preparations of Nazi Germany's principal Western European opponents afforded Germany certain advantages in the beginning of World War II.

The United States also had plans for industrial war preparation. The last plan, adopted in 1938, provided for 9,500 industrial enterprises to be involved in defense production, with a total planned output of armaments and equipment of the order of 6.7 billion dollars per year.

One characteristic of the American plan was that private enterprises were to convert to war production, and only a relatively small [amount of government owned] military industry was to be maintained.

The war upset these calculations and forced the American ruling circles to create a large specialized defense industry during the course of the war. In addition, the extent of conversion of private industry exceeded prewar plans by a factor of approximately 2.5. Approximately

45 per cent of the gross national product was used to satisfy war requirements in 1944.

During World War II, the principal capitalist countries created large defense industries. The maximum annual production of the main types of armaments in these countries are shown by the following data (in thousands of units).

| Types of Armaments | United States | England | Germany |
|---|---|---|---|
| Bombers | 35.0 | 7.9 | 6.5 |
| Fighter aircraft | 38.8 | 10.7 | 28.9 |
| Tanks and self-propelled guns | 38.6 | 8.6 | 18.9 |
| Artillery (75 mm. and larger) | 16.7 | 3.0 | 40.7 |
| Mortars | 39.2 | 25.1 | 30.8 |
| Warships (thousands of tons of standard displacement) | 1402. | 233.9 | No information available |

The above armament production rates were attained by the countries named in early 1944, i.e., almost three years after the beginning of the war for the United States and four years for Germany and England.

The experience of World War II, and in particular its final outcome, provided the modern imperialist countries with extensive data on strategic planning and economic mobilization for war.

Today the military strategy of the principal countries in the Anglo-American coalition is based upon the principle that in future wars they will have little time to develop defense industry and very little time to organize mass production of the most important types of weapons. Consequently the United States and Great Britain, when carrying out their postwar demobilization, conserved their military industrial potential in such a fashion as to assure, in an emergency, the production of large amounts of the principal types of armaments and military equipment.

The military strategy of the Western countries is based on the fact that the imperialist coalition consists of countries with different levels of economic development. This is shown by the following data [first table, p. 194] on the production of the main capitalist countries in percentages of world capitalist production.

More than four-fifths of the entire capitalist production is concentrated in NATO countries. The United States accounts for more than one half of the production, though this percentage is continually decreasing. From 1950 to 1960, the industrial production of West Germany increased by a factor of almost 2.5, that of Italy by 2.2, France by 1.9, while that of the United States and Britain only by 1.4. This is a manifestation of the law of uneven economic development of capitalist countries in the epoch of imperialism.

| Country | 1937 | 1948 | 1955 | 1960 |
|---|---|---|---|---|
| United States | 41.4 | 56.4 | 50.5 | 46.9 |
| West Germany | 9.0 | 4.3 | 9.3 | 10.4 |
| England | 12.5 | 11.7 | 8.5 | 7.7 |
| France | 6.0 | 4.1 | 4.4 | 5.1 |
| Italy | 3.0 | 2.1 | 3.3 | 4.1 |
| Canada | 2.7 | 3.6 | 3.5 | 3.4 |
| Japan | 4.8 | 1.5 | 2.3 | 4.1 |
| Total | 79.4 | 83.7 | 81.8 | 81.7 |
| Remaining countries | 20.6 | 16.3 | 18.2 | 18.3 |

The main strength of capitalist heavy industry is concentrated in the countries of the North Atlantic bloc. These countries have large fuel and power industries, metallurgical and chemical industries, and highly developed machine-building industries. The extent of production in various branches of heavy industry in the NATO countries is shown by the following data:

| Types of production | 1937 Absolute production | 1937 Per cent of world capitalist production | 1950 Absolute production | 1950 Per cent of world capitalist production | 1955 Absolute production | 1955 Per cent of world capitalist production | 1960 Absolute production | 1960 Per cent of world capitalist production |
|---|---|---|---|---|---|---|---|---|
| Coal (million tons) | 948.9 | 88.8 | 962.9 | 87.1 | 932.3 | 84.4 | 831.5 | 77.3 |
| USA alone | 448.3 | 41.9 | 505.3 | 57.0 | 442.4 | 40.0 | 392.7 | 36.5 |
| Petroleum (million tons) | 173.8 | 71.4 | 272.6 | 57.0 | 388.9 | 56.4 | 383.1 | 43.3 |
| USA alone | 173.0 | 71.1 | 266.7 | 55.8 | 336.0 | 53.0 | 346.0 | 39.1 |
| Electrical energy (billion kilo-watt hours) | 292.5 | 76.6 | 648.2 | 79.7 | 1024.8 | 80.3 | 1282.8 | 70.3 |
| USA alone | 164.5 | 38.3 | 388.7 | 47.8 | 629.0 | 49.3 | 840.4 | 46.0 |
| Steel (million tons) | 99.4 | 88.1 | 137.0 | 89.7 | 179.6 | 86.7 | 192.7 | 82.3 |
| USA alone | 51.3 | 45.5 | 87.8 | 57.4 | 106.2 | 51.3 | 90.0 | 38.4 |

From 1937 to 1960, the production of electrical power in the NATO countries increased by a factor of 4.4, that of petroleum by 2.2, and that of steel by 1.9. The output of coal fell by 12 per cent; this is explained by the continuous decrease in the importance of coal in producing power in the above countries, and by a corresponding increase in the importance of petroleum and gas.

The appearance of new, complex, and expensive weapons and military equipment has immeasurably increased economic demands. At present only economically strong countries with large and highly developed industries, particularly defense industries, and considerable scientific, research, experimental, and developmental facilities can develop their armed forces independently and equip them with all the necessary modern weapons. Among the capitalist countries, only the United States, Great Britain, and to a certain extent France and West Germany are able to do this. West Germany, now second in economic development in the capitalist world, is steadily expanding its capabilities. The remaining countries in the Anglo-American coalition are not in a position to provide their own armed forces with modern weapons and military equipment. The extent and the nature of economic preparations in these countries are determined by their economic capabilities and the role assigned to them in the coalition.

Since the organization of armed forces for war and economic preparations for it are interdependent, the principal strategic weapons are produced in the United States and Britain; these countries also produce considerable quantities of the principal conventional weapons in order to equip countries that have insufficient defense industries. Other industrially developed countries in the coalition produce only conventional arms in limited quantities.

The extent of various countries' participation in defense preparations can be judged by their share in the military expenditures of NATO. In 1961, direct military expenditures [by NATO countries] amounted to 69.2 billion dollars. Four countries accounted for 90 per cent of this amount: the United States—73.8 per cent; Britain—6.9 per cent; France—5.7 per cent and West Germany—4.6 per cent. The other eleven countries accounted for only 9 per cent.

NATO's political and military leaders are taking measures to make comprehensive use of the material and financial resources of NATO countries for war preparations. With this aim in mind there have been formed a number of regional alliances and unions within the bloc to facilitate economic war preparations. This is also the reason for such bodies as the Organization for Economic Cooperation and Development, the European Coal and Steel Community, the Franco-German-Italian Military Industrial Alliance, and Euratom, as well as for the co-operative production of operational and tactical missiles and aircraft equipment by several states.

In 1959, West Germany, France, Italy, Belgium, and Holland formed an association for the production of Hawk air defense missiles. By the end of the same year, West Germany, Norway, Holland, Greece, and Turkey united to produce air-to-air Sidewinder missiles. West Germany, Belgium, Holland, and Italy are planning to produce American F-104 fighter planes within the European community.

All of these associations are designed to secure the extensive participation of West German capital in the production of modern weapons and to assure it a leading position in this industry.

In their economic war preparations during the last decade, the major countries of the Anglo-American coalition have devoted their primary attention to the creation of a large, well-equipped defense industry capable of producing modern strategic weapons as well as other weapons. As we noted before, the United States and Great Britain possess the most highly developed military industry and are capable of organizing mass production of armaments within a short time. The remaining countries of the Anglo-American blocs are provided with aircraft, missiles, and tanks by the United States and, to a certain extent, by Great Britain and Canada.

West Germany has considerable capabilities for producing weapons and military equipment. The West German government is developing its military production to an increasing degree. Its industry now receives large defense orders. Production of small arms and artillery, armored troop carriers, jet fighter planes, trainers, and cargo aircraft has already begun. Preparations are being completed to produce tanks, and warships are already under construction.

Particularly intensive development took place in U.S. defense industry during the partial mobilization for the Korean War.

The plan [then initiated], which was essentially fulfilled by early 1956, provided for an increased industrial potential capable of producing, if necessary, up to 50,000 military planes and 35,000 tanks per year. It also provided for extensive development of nuclear and military-chemical industries, particularly in order to produce new toxic agents.

During this time, over 400 government reserve defense plants were reactivated, many new defense installations were built, and approximately 1,500 private firms were drawn into the production of armaments.

Defense plants were fully renovated, and their equipment was largely modernized to produce all types of new weapons.

From 1956 to 1960, the United States Government continued to carry out a broad program of military and economic measures to prepare the country for war. Primary attention was directed to equipping all the armed forces with still more strategic offensive weapons, nuclear weapons, strategic bombers, intercontinental and intermediate-range ballistic missiles, new warships, and air defense weapons for both the continental [United States] and troops [in the field].

The high level of defense expenditures during this period permitted the operation of a large war industry and the production of a considerable number of modern weapons. Simultaneously, the capacity to produce missiles and nuclear weapons increased.

In 1960, U.S. defense industry employed more than four million people; approximately two million were directly involved in military production.

The United States has devoted particular attention to the expansion of its nuclear industry, whose potential is still increasing at the present time. By early 1961, the United States had five important centers for producing fissionable materials (uranium 235, plutonium, and lithium deuteride), fourteen plants for producing strategic and tactical nuclear weapons, and many other supporting enterprises. The nuclear industry employs 122,000 people.

American ruling circles attach tremendous importance to the development of their missile industry. More than 170 firms employing 400,000 people are engaged in the production of missiles. Primary attention is directed toward the accelerated development and production of strategic missiles.

The extent of American efforts to develop strategic missiles can be judged by the expenditures for their development and production, which have been constantly increasing. During the 1960–1961 fiscal year they amounted to almost 4.4 billion dollars. During the eight-year period from 1953–1960, more than 14.8 billion dollars were spent for this purpose. By the end of 1965, American industry is to produce a minimum of 135 Atlas missiles, 108 Titan missiles, and 800 Minuteman missiles, in addition to 656 Polaris missiles for missile-carrying nuclear submarines. However, the total production of these missiles apparently will be somewhat higher. According to the press, approximately 1,000 Polaris missiles are planned for the 41 missile-carrying nuclear submarines to be constructed.

The United States also produces a considerable number of tactical missiles. During the 1960–1961 fiscal year, 3.5 billion dollars were spent on the development and production of these missiles. The industrial base already in existence not only meets the requirements of the American armed forces, but also makes it possible to supply considerable numbers of these weapons to other capitalist states.

The United States has a large aircraft industry consisting of more than two hundred companies employing almost 600,000 people. During the 1960–1961 fiscal year, approximately six billion dollars were spent on the production of aircraft equipment. However, the production of military aircraft has steadily decreased. In 1953, 10,626 military airplanes were produced, whereas only 2,700 were produced in 1960.

During the postwar period, the armored vehicle industry was considerably expanded by rebuilding and reactivating government defense plants. Six large tank-manufacturing plants with an annual production capacity of 30,000 to 35,000 tanks comprise the basic part of this industry. In addition, three plants produce self-propelled artillery and three, armored troop carriers. In wartime, other private companies can be converted to the production of armored equipment.

The American chemical war industry was created during World War II. It consists of twenty-two large plants that produce gunpowder and explosives and four plants that produce chemical munitions. The main plants of the chemical war industry were reactivated during the postwar period. The production capacity for solid and liquid missile fuels continues to increase. At present, a considerable number of chemical war plants are not producing.

The United States has a highly developed shipbuilding industry. During World War II the United States raised its annual shipbuilding production to 3.2 million standard displacement tons of war shipping and 12.5 million registered tons of commercial shipping.

At present the shipbuilding industry is carrying out an extensive program of military shipbuilding. On August 1, 1961, ninety-five ships and auxiliary vessels were under construction, including three attack carriers, one nuclear cruiser, fifteen frigates with guided antiaircraft missiles, seventeen fleet destroyers with guided antiaircraft missiles, twenty-four missile-carrying nuclear submarines, fifteen [torpedo-carrying] nuclear submarines, three helicopter carriers [amphibious assault ships], and seventeen other vessels.

Shipbuilding expenditures during the 1961–1962 fiscal year will amount to more than two billion dollars. The naval command has particularly pushed the construction of missile-carrying nuclear submarines. By the middle of 1963, the submarine construction rate is to reach twelve annually, so that twenty-nine Polaris-equipped nuclear submarines will be in service by the end of 1964.

This brief review of the present status of American defense industry indicates that its principal branches are kept highly mobilized and in case of war can assure the production of a considerable amount of armaments without further mobilization. In addition, we can also conclude from this survey that a real threat exists to the security of nations, and we can gauge the intensity of the arms race in the principal countries of the military imperialist coalition, which confirms the aggressive imperialist plans for preparing a new world war.

British political and military leaders base their economic war preparations on the premise that Britain's economic capabilities are insufficient to satisfy completely the needs of modern war, even though the official view is that the economy must be totally mobilized. In organizing its armed forces, as well as in its economic preparations for war, the British government relies on the fact that it will only enter a war as a member of a coalition in which the decisive role is played by the United States, with its vast economic and military potential.

Britain is third in industrial production among the capitalist countries, coming after the United States and West Germany.

The British military economic potential is broadly based. The great majority of its productive forces are concentrated in industry; agriculture is minor and provides only about half of the country's needs.

The country possesses practically no basic natural resources except iron and coal.

This is the reason that the British economy is so dependent upon the world capitalist market; the latter is indispensable for the export of Britain's industrial production and for providing the country with raw materials and foodstuffs.

In the development of British defense industry since World War II, considerable attention has been devoted to the creation of a nuclear industry, improvement of the aircraft industry, reorganization of the armored vehicle industry, and maintenance of shipbuilding at a high level.

Britain's nuclear industry consists of nine enterprises; these include four plants for producing fissionable materials, two plants for producing nuclear weapons, and three supporting companies. The British have been stockpiling atomic weapons since 1954, and thermonuclear weapons since 1957. It should be noted, however, that the American nuclear industry is almost eleven times as large as the British.

Britain has a large aircraft industry, second only to that of the United States in the capitalist world. The British aircraft industry currently consists of 67 aircraft plants; 41 of these are engaged in the construction of aircraft and 26 in the construction of aircraft engines. Approximately 200,000 people are employed in the aircraft industry. The plants currently in operation have an annual production capacity of several thousand planes. At present the aircraft industry is producing a small number of "V" type, medium strategic bombers, and carrier-based attack and fighter aircraft. A total of 560 military airplanes were produced in 1960.

The relatively weak spot in British defense industry is its missile production, which consists of ten enterprises. Only antiaircraft and air-to-air missiles are mass-produced in Britain; surface-to-surface and tactical missiles are still in the testing stage.

The British were also engaged in the development of the surface-to-surface Blue Streak intermediate-range ballistic missile; however, this work was stopped because of insufficient funds. Consequently, the British intend to equip their forces with American missiles of this type. Britain has already received sixty Thor missiles. In addition, it is receiving the tactical Corporal missile from the United States.

Four plants exist for the production of armored vehicles; two of them are in operation and two are held in reserve. These plants have a production capacity of approximately 4,000 tanks per year. In the event of war, a number of private machine-building factories are to be converted to the production of armored equipment. At present a small number of heavy Centurion tanks are being produced.

Britain's shipbuilding industry consists of 250 shipbuilding and ship repairing companies, which have a production capacity of 500,000 standard displacement tons of military shipping and over two million registered tons of commercial shipping [per year]. Nearly one and one-third million registered tons of commercial shipping were built in 1960. By the middle of 1961, twenty-eight ships were under construction, including four fleet destroyers equipped with guided antiaircraft missiles, one nuclear submarine, seven [conventional] submarines, and sixteen frigates.

The artillery enterprises are not as highly developed. They consist of four government plants and several private companies.

The specialized companies that produce explosives and gunpowder are not capable of fulfilling the wartime requirements of the armed forces. New plants would have to be built in order to meet these needs. The production of chemical munitions can be carried out at six specialized plants.

Thus the British have a rather large and well-prepared defense industry capable of producing the principal strategic weapons as well as many other types. Missile production is the weak link in the chain.

Postwar French defense industry has been required to supply the needs of colonial wars. The production of conventional arms has been maintained at a high level, but limited funds have constantly hindered an increase in the production of the most modern weapons. Only in 1960 did France begin to re-equip her armed forces. She then adopted a five-year plan (1960–1964) for providing the armed forces with new weapons and "nuclear striking forces." Twelve billion new francs were allocated to this program: 4.1 billion for the development and production of nuclear weapons, 1.1 billion for missiles, almost 4.5 billion for aircraft equipment, 0.8 billion for military shipbuilding, and 1.5 billion for armored equipment.

An additional 19 billion francs from the annual budgets will be spent for the production of arms and military equipment during this five-year period.

The adopted program calls for an expanded nuclear industry, serial production of nuclear weapons, and the building of about five hundred aircraft of various types, including one hundred light bombers capable of carrying nuclear weapons. Six warships are to be built, including two carriers and three fleet destroyers with guided antiaircraft missiles, and construction is to begin on a missile-carrying nuclear submarine. In addition, 650 combat vehicles equipped with antitank guided missiles are to be built, as well as a considerable amount of other combat materiel.

France has one nuclear industrial center for producing fissionable materials, which can supply up to 140 kilograms of plutonium per year. Two nuclear power stations and a gas diffusion plant for producing uranium 235 are under construction.

The aircraft industry is one of France's most highly developed defense industries. It consists of about seventy-five enterprises employing 85,000 people. During the last few years, 500–600 military aircraft have been produced annually.

In France, most of the missile production is carried out by aircraft plants, though several specialized plants are being built. The French have been most successful in producing guided antitank missiles, which they supply in large quantities to other NATO countries. Antiaircraft missiles and air-to-air missiles are also in production. A medium-range surface-to-surface missile is under development.

The tank industry consists of three specialized tank plants which primarily produce light, thirteen-ton tanks and combat vehicles.

The French shipbuilding industry consists of twenty-two large private shipyards and four state naval yards employing approximately 40,000 people. The productive capacity is estimated at 600,000 registered tons. About half of this capacity can be used for military shipbuilding.

West Germany ranks next to the United States in economic potential for modern war. By 1954, West Germany had reached an industrial production level equal to that of the whole of prewar Germany, and by 1961 it significantly exceeded this level and took first place among the European capitalist countries. In 1960, West Germany produced 30.3 million tons of steel, 126 million tons of coal, 114.9 billion kilowatt hours of electricity, 23.7 million tons of petroleum products, 1.1 million registered tons of commercial shipping, and over 2 million automobiles. West Germany's industrial production is now almost 2.5 times what it was in 1950. It possesses the most powerful economic base for defense production among the European capitalist states.

West Germany's entrance into the aggressive North Atlantic bloc in May 1955 assured the extensive participation of West German capital in the arms race and in preparations for a new war. More than 75 billion marks were allocated to military preparations in 1955–1961; of this amount, 25.2 billion marks were allocated to domestic arms production and purchase of weapons abroad. At present, orders for weapons and war materiel totaling more than 20 billion marks have already been placed, of which more than 60 per cent went to foreign firms.

The lack of existing domestic designs for modern weapons compelled the West German government to purchase weapons abroad during the first stages of the Bundeswehr's formation. Thus 460 F-104 fighter planes, 750 M-48 medium tanks, 24 Matador missiles, 300 antiaircraft Nike missiles, and 312 unguided Honest John missiles had been ordered from the United States by early 1961. West Germany has ordered 1,000 armored troop carriers and 7 patrol ships from Britain; 300 light tanks, approximately 2,000 armored troop carriers, and 20,000 antitank missiles from France; and 225 fighter planes from Canada. Orders for artillery, ammunition, and other war materiel have also been placed abroad.

In addition to purchasing weapons abroad, measures are being taken to develop domestic arms production. The best foreign designs for military equipment are being adopted for production, while domestic designs are simultaneously undergoing development.

The Germans are devoting their greatest attention to rebuilding their aircraft industry. Considerable funds and privileges have been extended to this industry. By the middle of 1961, aircraft plants had produced approximately 900 military aircraft, primarily trainers and transport planes. Having gained experience in the production of aircraft equipment, West German factories began to produce American F-104G and Italian G-91 Fiat fighter planes early in 1961. West German aircraft plants will participate in the production of 560 of the 949 F-104G fighters to be co-operatively produced by several NATO countries. In addition, these same West German plants will produce 232 G-91 Fiat fighters.

Increasing military orders have led to the expansion of plants and to an increase in the number of employees. By early 1961, West Germany had twelve main aircraft plants employing 25,000 people.

West Germany is also taking steps to develop its missile production. Until recently missiles were purchased from the Americans. However, after 1960 the Germans began to set up their own production of anti-aircraft and air-to-air missiles in co-operation with other countries. They have already received an order for 8,000 air-to-air Sidewinder missiles. Eight West German firms are preparing to produce the American Hawk air defense missile. In 1959 West Germany began serial production of model "810" antitank missiles of its own design.

Twelve West German plants are engaged in producing armored equipment; three of these plants produce armored troop carriers and the others military vehicles. Orders are being filled for 1,600 Hispano Suiza and 600 Hotchkiss armored troop carriers.

West Germany does not yet manufacture tanks, but preparations are being made to do so. In 1960, the Germans completed the development of a domestic medium tank. Its serial production is planned for the immediate future. The Ministry of Defense has already ordered 105 mm. howitzers for this tank from Britain.

West Germany is already producing light artillery systems and small arms. The Germans purchase heavy artillery systems abroad.

Eager to acquire its own nuclear weapons to assist its revanchist plans, West Germany already has created the research basis for a nuclear industry. A program adopted in 1958 calls for the construction of experimental nuclear electric power stations. Beginning in 1957, the United States agreed to supply West Germany for the next ten years with 2,500 tons of uranium [ore], while Canada will supply 500 tons. Approximately 260 German firms are engaged in nuclear energy research.

West Germany has a large shipbuilding industry, which consists of 170 enterprises and employs more than 100,000 persons. In 1960, the shipyards built 200 commercial vessels totaling 1.2 million registered tons. According to information for the middle of 1961, West German shipyards had orders for the construction of 131 military ships and 29 auxiliary vessels, including 4 fleet destroyers, 15 [conventional] submarines, 6 patrol ships, 40 torpedo boats, 18 coastal minesweepers, and 30 inshore minesweepers.

Thus the West German defense industry in its present state will soon be able to mass-produce many types of modern weapons. West Germany will have the largest military industry of any of the European countries. This is the reason why peace-loving European nations see a potential aggressor in Germany and strongly reject the territorial claims of the West German revanchists.

Since the principal capitalist countries are dependent upon the import of many strategic raw materials, fuels, and foodstuffs, and because many strategic raw material sources are quite distant from metropolitan areas, and maritime communications vulnerable, the economically strong countries have been compelled to stockpile large quantities of strategic materials.

Immediately following World War II, the United States enacted a number of laws dealing with the stockpiling of large reserves of strategic raw materials and industrial equipment. Initially the reserves of strategic raw materials were designed for a five-year war. In 1957, the program was reviewed and it was decided to create reserves for a three-year war. The stockpiling of the required reserves is now essentially completed. At the same time, the United States maintains a large stock of industrial machinery comprising several tens of thousands of units. More than five hundred defense plants and their supporting facilities have been given reserve status.

Smaller stockpiles of strategic raw materials and foodstuffs have been built up in Great Britain and other European capitalist countries.

American strategy for a considerable time assumed that the United States would be a principal and relatively invulnerable industrial base for supplying armaments and war materiel to other capitalist countries. The loss of America's strategic invulnerability has compelled her political and military leaders to revise their views on economic war preparations and to abandon the classic formula for the wartime deployment of defense industry during the first, second, and third years of the war; according to [this formula] a considerable portion of defense industry was to be kept in reserve with the intention of activating it in the first nine to thirteen months of the war.

Up to 1956 American economic war preparations were based upon the principle of forming a so-called broad mobilization base, which would guarantee that a maximum number of enterprises would be drawn into the production of weapons and war materiel in the course of the war. It was planned to carry out the industrial mobilization during the first two or three years of war.

These views were revised during 1955–1957, because [by then] defense industry could suffer substantial losses from enemy nuclear strikes during the initial and most critical period of the war; this could seriously affect the provision of the armed forces with the most important types of weapons: nuclear weapons, missiles, strategic bombers, and antiaircraft weapons. Consequently, industry was to be organized to assure continuous production of the above weapons and to increase their production even under the most adverse conditions in the United States. To accomplish this, the principal plants must be kept in operational readiness even in peacetime, and must be prepared to revert to mass production of the main types of weapons within two or three months. [In the future] production is to be organized so that weapons can still be produced even if the country's internal transportation and communication systems are disrupted and the labor force and available industrial equipment are diminished. The production of various types of weapons and equipment is to be at least doubled.

In the opinion of the Americans, the new principles governing industrial preparations for war are designed to secure a considerable increase in the readiness for mobilization of the main branches of defense industry. They are also designed to reduce the effect of a surprise attack, to preserve as much as possible the most important production facilities, and to assure the uninterrupted production of nuclear weapons, strategic missiles, strategic bombers, and other important weapons, especially during the critical initial stages of the war.

The development of imperialist military strategy has been influenced by objective and subjective factors—political, economic, and purely military.

However, due to its class limitations, bourgeois military thought cannot fully comprehend and evaluate these factors; this has often led to major miscalculations. At the same time, it would be incorrect to assume that modern bourgeois military thought is generally incapable of scientific investigation of military problems, including military strategy. The enormous scientific and technical advances of the principal capitalist countries facilitate to a certain extent the development of a military strategy responsive to the changing conditions of war.

The postwar balance of forces in the world arena has led to basic changes in all spheres of imperialist activities. Because of the unification after the war of many capitalist countries into a single anti-Communist political and military coalition under American leadership, these countries lost almost all of their national independence and, consequently, the freedom to determine their foreign policies and strategies. This led to their economic, political, and military subordination to the United States. Whereas prior to World War II the strategy of the main capitalist countries had a clearly defined national character, now with the creation of postwar aggressive military and political blocs and alliances the military strategy of the imperialist countries is becoming increasingly unified; it is determined and co-ordinated by the United States throughout the entire capitalist coalition. Therefore, rather than speak of the military strategy of Western capitalist countries, it is more correct to call it the United States and NATO military strategy.

The development of American and NATO military strategy has been influenced primarily by the East-West balance of strategic forces and weapons. Within a relatively brief postwar period of slightly more than fifteen years, the military strategy of the United States and NATO has changed twice, in 1953 and in 1961.

In 1953, the United States and later NATO adopted the so-called strategy of "massive retaliation," which provided for the preparation and conduct of only general nuclear war against the countries of the socialist camp.

However, with the Soviet Union's magnificent success in building missiles and in the conquest of space, the United States and NATO military strategy, which was nothing but a strategy of "nuclear blackmail," suffered complete defeat. Within a few years (1957–1960) it underwent a serious crisis. After the change in the balance of strategic offensive forces, the American aggressors were compelled to review their previous attitude toward general nuclear war.

In 1961, after the advent of the Kennedy administration, the strategy of "massive retaliation" was replaced by the so-called strategy of "flexible response."

American political and military leaders consider the main task of military strategy to be the proper selection of appropriate weapon systems for the next 10 to 15 years, or more. At the same time, the functions [of U.S. strategy] still include the determination of the most expedient distribution of forces on a global scale, the selection of a direction for the main blow (the determination of the most advantageous targets for destruction by strategic weapons), the evaluation of the importance of the strategic surprise that can be achieved by initiating a preventive war, the delivery of a first or pre-emptive blow, the determination of the time factor so as to ensure invulnerability of the strategic forces, etc.

In the present missile and space age, however, when the rapid development of science and technology continually exerts a tremendous influence on military questions, the American leadership considers its principal and most difficult task to be the selection of the most effective and economically advantageous combination of weapons that is suited to modern strategy. The difficulty of the task is due to the extreme technical complexity of modern armaments, the prolonged periods necessary for their development, and the large expenditures connected with development and production. Consequently, the best types of weapons cannot be acquired immediately in final form; they must be developed continuously on a selective basis. The solution of this problem is considered to lie in guiding scientific research and development rather than following [where it leads].

In view of the importance assigned to the proper selection of the necessary weapon systems, it is recognized that military strategy must seek the most rational utilization of budgets and resources to attain the military aims of the state (or coalition) and that the appropriate military decisions must be made only after an economic analysis of various alternatives. In order to maintain an increasing military potential in a country (or coalition) over an extended period, a powerful economy is vital since it bears the continual burden of an unprecedented arms race. Therefore, all activities which weaken the country's economic potential and lower its effectiveness will weaken the military potential since the latter, in the final analysis, depends upon the state of the economy.

Consequently, modern military strategy must have a firm economic basis. However, it must also have an appropriate political basis. American leadership believes that under current conditions military policy and strategy are organically united with foreign policy as never before. In his Message to Congress on March 28, 1961, President Kennedy stated: "Diplomacy and defense are no longer distinct alternatives, one to be used when the other fails; both must complement each other." [39]

The increasing ties between modern military strategy and the technical, economic, social, and political activities of the state (or coalition) inevitably lead to a decrease in the importance of the purely military functions of strategy. This casts doubt upon the ability of military specialists to solve strategic problems unaided. The military, because of their "professional limitations," are no longer considered to be in a position to grasp and evaluate all the technical, economic, social, and political factors that exert such a vast influence upon modern military strategy.

American leaders believe that this problem can only be solved by the concerted efforts of civilian scientists in various disciplines and the most able representatives of the armed forces. Consequently, it is not surprising that in the United States all of the main problems of military policy and strategy are being worked out by civilian scientists with the necessary aid and co-operation of the appropriate military agencies. These scientists, who number several hundred prominent specialists in various fields, are primarily members of research organizations established soon after the conclusion of World War II and attached to the headquarters of the armed services, the Joint Chiefs of Staff, and the Department of Defense. These organizations are primarily concerned with the evaluation and selection of weapon systems that are responsive to [the needs of] modern military strategy. Consequently, the

[39] U.S. ED. NOTE—*Documents on American Foreign Relations, 1961*, p. 52.

scientists not only create weapons and military equipment but also play an important role in solving problems of foreign and military policy and strategy.

In accordance with the United States and NATO military strategy described above, the imperialist countries, especially the United States, are making extensive preparations for various types of wars against the socialist countries, particularly general nuclear war. Since this [kind of] war entails a tremendous risk of mutual annihilation,[40] the American aggressors are exerting every effort, if war does start, to assure victory with minimum losses and destruction. They see the possibility of such an outcome of the war through the creation of strong and fully combat-ready armed forces, significantly superior in equipment (especially space weapons) to the armed forces of the enemy, and through the attainment of surprise.

The American aggressors, however, must take into account the might of the Soviet Armed Forces and the persistent demands of all the peoples who protest nuclear war and actively support the Soviet Government's proposals for prohibition of nuclear weapons, general and total disarmament, and the attainment of peace on earth.

---

[40] U.S. ED. NOTE—Flat statements about possible mutual annihilation are unusual in Soviet literature. According to the official line, the Soviet Union is less vulnerable to nuclear attacks than the Western powers and would emerge victorious in such a war. However, as noted in the Analytical Introduction, in some of his speeches Khrushchev has come close to admitting the possibility of mutual annihilation. *Pravda,* March 15, 1958; July 11, 1962; January 17, 1963.

# ★ 3

# Development of Soviet Military Strategy (1917-1945)

## Soviet Military Strategy during the Civil War and Foreign Military Intervention (1917–1922)

The birth and development of Soviet military strategy followed that of the armed forces of the Soviet state. The theoretical basis of Soviet military strategy and military science as a whole is in the Marxist-Leninist teachings on war and the army.

The most important concepts of Soviet military science and strategy were developed in the brilliant works of V. I. Lenin, which were devoted to the political struggle of the working class, armed uprising, and proletarian revolution.

V. I. Lenin defined the nature of wars in the imperialist epoch, demonstrated the historical conditions and causes of these wars, revealed trends in the development of military science, and gave a profound scientific analysis of the state of Russian military science of the early twentieth century.

In developing and establishing the Marxist concepts of armed conflict, Lenin developed the thesis of just and unjust wars and the thesis of the transformation of imperialist wars into civil wars and the workers' wars against the exploiters. In doing this he armed the working class and its advance guard, the Communist Party, with a clear program of action in the struggle to liberate the working people from capitalist slavery.

Lenin thus deserves great credit for the development of Marxist mili-

209

tary theory. Soviet military theory is based on Lenin's theoretical concepts.

Soviet military strategy has absorbed the most important political strategic concepts of the Communist Party and the experience of the armed struggle of the working class.

"The political question," Lenin wrote, "now bears completely upon the military question. . . . The political task is also the military task: the organization of headquarters, the concentration of material strength, and supplying the soldiers with everything they need. . . ." * This is the principal reason that Soviet military strategy is based on the most important concepts of political strategy of the Communist Party, those dealing with the importance of the proper choice of the direction of a main effort, the importance of achieving superiority of forces and weapons in the direction of the chosen blow, the importance of changing the form and method of combat depending on the situation, the dependence of troop organization on methods of warfare, and the importance of strategic reserves and leadership.

In following Lenin's teachings on the importance of knowing the fundamental laws of each war, Soviet military strategy also makes use of the experience of past wars, especially those of the imperialist epoch, as well as the most important theoretical concepts of bourgeois military science in the field of strategy.[1]

In spite of the economic and political backwardness of Russia and the retarding influence of Tsarism on the solution of a number of military problems, Russian military theory in the nineteenth century and early part of the twentieth century was, as is well known, more advanced than that of other countries. Since it developed independently, it was not limited to the national [Russian] experience but made skillful use of the best examples of the military experience of other countries.

Because of its particular historical development, Russia organized a large national army and developed the principles for its use much sooner than Western European countries.†

------

* V. I. Lenin, *Sochineniia* [*Works*], Vol. 26, pp. 235– 236.

[1] U.S. ED. NOTE—Although Soviet military doctrine has been influenced by foreign concepts (see Raymond L. Garthoff, *Soviet Military Doctrine,* The Free Press, Glencoe, Ill., 1953, pp. 51–58), the admission that Soviet strategy has something to learn from Western strategic doctrines is rarely made, since in theory the classless Soviet society is asserted to make possible the development of new ways of waging wars, see pp. 90, 212).

† The Russian army in the eighteenth century was similar to armies formed in the West after the first half of the nineteenth century, with respect to recruiting, composition, and numbers.

Long before the Napoleonic wars, Suvorov [2] used massed troops very successfully instead of the linear tactical and strategic deployment that prevailed in Western European armies.

At the beginning of the nineteenth century, Kutuzov [3] elevated Russian military strategy to a new and higher level. His strategy, as well as that of Suvorov, was characterized by rapid and decisive operations and was aimed at the complete annihilation of the enemy. The characteristic features of Kutuzov's strategy were the effective use of all types of military operations unified by a general strategic plan, skillful leadership of troops, the creation of strategic reserves and their correct utilization, and strategic pursuit of the enemy until his final annihilation.

The conduct of war changed rapidly in the epoch of imperialism, with the adoption of mass armies equipped with new weapons. Military theory was confronted with the task of developing a strategy that was responsive to the changing conditions of war.

N. P. Mikhnevich, V. F. Novitskii, A. A. Neznamov [4] and others played an important role in the development of Russian military theory during this period. The best work was *Strategy,* by N. P. Mikhnevich, which was published in 1899–1901. In this work the author attempted to illustrate the development of methods for strategic breakthrough and defense, as well as to show the interrelation of policy and strategy and the influence of the economic factor on the conduct of war. Mikhnevich's strategy was more concrete than the idealistic theory of Leer, [5] which prevailed throughout the Russian army. However, since he did not understand the political and class nature of war, Mikhnevich and the other military theorists of his time were unable to provide a correct solution to the problem of the origin of wars and the relationship between war and politics. These problems received a truly scientific solution only in the works of classical Marxism-Leninism, which revealed the class nature of wars.

----

[2] U.S. ED. NOTE—Aleksandr Vasil'evich Suvorov (1730–1800) was a famous Russian military leader and generalissimo of the Russian army. *Bol'shaia sovetskaia entsiklopediia* [*The Great Soviet Encyclopedia*], Vol. 41, pp. 189–193 (hereafter cited as *BSE*); Garthoff, *Soviet Military Doctrine,* pp. 49–50.

[3] U.S. ED. NOTE—Mikhail Illarionovich Kutuzov (1745–1813) was a famous Russian military leader and field marshal of the Russian army. *BSE,* Vol. 24, pp. 145–148; Garthoff, *Soviet Military Doctrine,* p. 50.

[4] U.S. ED. NOTE—Mikhnevich, Novitskii, and Neznamov were Russian officers of the nineteenth and early twentieth centuries who wrote on military questions and also directly contributed to the development of the military doctrine of the Red Army in the 1920's.

[5] U.S. ED. NOTE—Genrich Antonovich Leer (1829–1904) was a general of infantry and a leading Russian military theoretician and author of a book, *Strategy* (1898), and other works on military problems. *BSE,* Vol. 24, p. 443.

The development of Tsarist Russian military science was severely hampered by the technical and economic backwardness of the country, and especially by its reactionary feudal system.

"Tsarism," wrote Lenin, "has proved to be a hindrance to the organization of up-to-date efficient warfare, that very business to which tsarism dedicated itself so wholeheartedly. . . ." *

In prerevolutionary Russia, military thought was not systematic, theory was divorced from practice, and reactionary views prevailed in military science. But the military leaders of the Russian national school could not understand this, even though they had taken a significant step forward in understanding those problems in military science that had arisen during World War I.

During World War I, Russian military strategy gained experience in carrying out strategic offensives, strategic defense involving utilization of the rear defense lines, and in conducting counteroffensives with several armies on two adjacent fronts. Russian military leaders also solved the important problem of breaking through the positional front by a method previously unknown to the military art. In 1916, a new form of operational maneuver was used on the southwestern front, a simultaneous breakthrough in several sectors of the opponent's front lines. Simultaneous blows along a broad front tied down enemy reserves and made possible a breakthrough to a depth of 75 kilometers [46 miles].

World War I confirmed the unusual survivability of modern mass armies, the impossibility of destroying a strong opponent with a single offensive, and the impossibility of concluding a war with one or two major battles, as well as the need for unified political and strategic leadership and strategic co-ordination of the fronts.

Thus World War I confronted military strategy with a number of new and important problems, which Soviet military strategy solved during the Civil War and, particularly, during the Great Patriotic War of 1941–1945.

Marxism-Leninism teaches that social revolutions cause revolutions in military science. The working class that comes to power gives new content to military views and creates a new military science. The creation and development of Soviet military science and, consequently, military strategy were based on the further consolidation of the new social relationships and the technological and industrial progress brought about by the revolution.

In spite of the fact that Soviet military strategy on the whole used the means and methods of combat inherited from the old regime, from

---

* V. I. Lenin, *Sochineniia* [*Works*], Vol. 8, p. 35.

the very first year of its existence it had a special character since it was the strategy of a socialist state.

Soviet military strategy during the Civil War was particularly distinguished by its vigor, purposefulness, and determination—the natural product of the class nature of the war and the character of its political aims.

The nature of political aims, as is well known, decisively influenced the conduct of wars and thus military strategy.

Both war as a whole and military strategy bear the imprint of classes whose interests are reflected in the war. The extent of the political differences between the contestants caused them to aim for far-reaching and conclusive results.

During the Civil War, the political aim of the working classes of the Soviet Republic was the total destruction of the interventionists [6] and the White Guard; [7] this required a very active and determined strategy. Only bold, decisive action could achieve victory, and thus create the conditions for the peaceful construction of socialism.

During the Civil War, the Soviet Armed Forces were imbued with the decisiveness of their strategic aims and the determination to accomplish them within the shortest possible time. This characterized all the principal operational and strategic plans of the Red Army against Kolchak, Denikin, the White Poles, and Wrangel. [8]

When an operation was planned for one of the fronts, the strategy did not pursue limited objectives but the total destruction of the enemy in the area involved and the capture of all the territory he occupied.

Thus the strategy had a sharply defined, decisive nature, since there could be no possibility of coming to terms with the class enemies.

Soviet military strategy was particularly careful to assess the economic, political, and morale factors as well as the balance of forces; this

---

[6] U.S. ED. NOTE—See Chap. 1, note 35, p. 127.

[7] U.S. ED. NOTE—Reference is made to the Russian anti-Soviet forces, which fought against the Soviet regime during the Russian Civil War (1917–1920).

[8] U.S. ED. NOTE—Anti-Bolshevik leaders and forces active during the Russian Civil War (1917–1920). Aleksandr Vasil'evich Kolchak (1873–1920) was a Tsarist admiral who established an anti-Bolshevik government in Siberia after the October Revolution. He was captured and shot in 1920. Anton Ivanovich Denikin (1872–1947) was a Lieutenant General of the Tsarist army and one of the organizers of the White (anti-Bolshevik) Army in Southern Russia. His army was evacuated in 1920 to Turkey. Baron Piotr Nikolaevich Wrangel (1878–1928) was a Tsarist general who succeeded Denikin in command of the White forces in Southern Russia in 1920. The "White Poles" were Polish forces of the newly created Polish state, which invaded the Western Ukraine in 1919–1920. Michael T. Florinsky, ed., *McGraw-Hill Encyclopedia of Russia and the Soviet Union,* McGraw-Hill Book Company, Inc., New York, 1961, pp. 130, 280, 612.

was one of its greatest advantages over the strategy of the interventionists and the White Guard.

In taking note of the importance of a careful assessment of military and political conditions and the balance of forces, Lenin wrote: "We can by no means limit ourselves to one strategic maneuver. Everything depends upon the balance of forces. . . ." *

The Soviet Republic was surrounded by a fiery ring of fronts. The enemy, with superior forces and weapons, pressed from all sides and attempted to reach the country's vital centers. Meanwhile, limited manpower and material resources prevented the Red Army from conducting concurrent broad offensives with decisive objectives on several fronts.

Consequently, one of the most important strategic problems was to select the critical front from among the many that existed.

The Party's Central Committee, headed by Lenin, successfully solved this problem during the Civil War by its profound scientific comprehension of the interrelation of policy and military strategy, and by a careful calculation of the balance of forces.

The individual fronts varied in importance during the Civil War according to the general military and political situation.

Thus, during the summer and the first half of autumn of 1918, the eastern front was recognized to be more important than the southern, Caspian-Caucasian, northern, and western fronts in the Republic. By the end of 1918, the southern front had become the most important, and by the spring of 1919 the eastern front again; by the middle of the summer of 1919, the southern front again, etc.

Thus the Red Army directed its main efforts first against one enemy and then another, concentrating the main mass of its troops, according to the needs of the military and political situation.

These military operations were conducted, not only to destroy the enemy's manpower, but also for raw materials sources, grain, and fuel, without which the country could not exist.

Therefore, the most important strategic aims of the Civil War included economic missions as well as the destruction of the White Guard and interventionist forces.

It was characteristic for Soviet military strategy to identify and solve successfully the primary strategic tasks, to identify principal danger areas and the choice of a direction for the main effort, and to concentrate forces and weapons decisively in the direction chosen from the main effort.

Lenin stated in his writings: "The 'law' of military success is to have

---

* V. I. Lenin, *Sochineniia* [*Works*], Vol. 27, p. 96.

an overwhelming superiority of forces at the decisive moment and place." *

This was quite difficult to accomplish because of the general lack of weapons and forces during the Civil War. These were successively concentrated at the critical front at the expense of severely weakening the other fronts.

Although this made it possible to realize the main strategic aims established by policy, well-known instances occurred during the Civil War when the other fronts were so weakened that our troops were forced to retreat or even suffer temporary defeat in order to strengthen the principal front.

This occurred, for example, at the end of 1918 and beginning of 1919 when the concentration of principal forces on the southern front severely weakened the eastern front.

The principle of massive concentration of forces and weapons in the area of the main efforts also found extensive application on the various fronts. Soviet military strategy strictly adhered to this principle in the conduct of major offensive operations. Thus, 49,000 infantry and cavalry troops with 152 pieces of artillery were concentrated on a 200 to 220 kilometer [120–135 miles] sector in the area of the main assault to be dealt by the southern group of the western front; this left 22,500 infantry and cavalry troops with 70 pieces of artillery along the 700 kilometers [440 miles] of the southern group's remaining front. During the offensive of the western front in July of 1920, three armies and one cavalry corps totaling 60,000 infantry and cavalry troops were concentrated in one area for a main blow along a 120 kilometer [75 miles] sector, while only one army and a small operational group remained on the support sector of approximately 300 kilometers [190 miles].

However, the principle of massed concentration of forces in one area for a main blow was not always observed during individual operations in the Civil War, which often impaired the outcome of the operation. Such was the case, for example, in the August 1919 offensive of the troops on the southern front and the May 1920 offensive of the troops on the western front.

During the Civil War, Soviet military strategy made use of numerous types of armed combat. Following Lenin's dictum that "the methods of struggle against the enemy must vary with the situation," † Soviet military leaders exhibited exceptional flexibility in their selection of combat methods depending on the situation.

Along with offensive operations, which were the principal and most

---

* V. I. Lenin, *Sochineniia* [*Works*], Vol. 30, p. 235.
† V. I. Lenin, *Sochineniia* [*Works*], Vol. 27, p. 219.

important form of combat operation in the Civil War, there were also defensive operations and retreats. Defense and retreat, which were forced, temporary types of operations, would be followed by counter-attacks or a general offensive on one or two fronts.

The Red Army's offensives aimed at the total and conclusive defeat of the enemy and in some cases were conducted to great depth without any operational pauses. Large-scale offensives, as a rule, consisted of a series of successive operations aimed at the attainment of a single strategic objective in a given area, each operation being a link in a chain leading to final accomplishment of the objective of the entire operation.

The broad and maneuverable fronts of the Civil War made it possible for the enemy to withdraw after the first defeats of his troops and organize new defense lines or even offensives from his rear positions. Total destruction of the enemy was achieved only after repeated blows by continuous and successive operations. The strategic operations of the Civil War typically combined continuous offensives with relentless pursuit.

Thus, the offensive of the forces on the eastern and southern fronts against the armies of Kolchak and Denikin included several successive operations having a single objective. The Buguruslan, Belebey, Ufa, Zlatoust, and Chelyabinsk operations were executed to a total distance of 900 to 1,000 kilometers [550–600 miles] during the offensive from the Volga to the Urals (April 1919 to July 1919) and the first Tobolsk, Petropavlovsk, and Omsk operations were carried out from August to November. From November 20, 1919, to March 8, 1920, the troops of the eastern front pursued the armies of Kolchak from Omsk to Irkutsk, that is, a distance of 2,500 to 2,800 kilometers [1,550–1,700 miles].

The strategic offensives used by the army of the southern front to destroy Denikin's forces also consisted of several successive operations unified by a general objective; these were the Orlovsk-Kromy, Voronezh-Kastornoye, Kharkov, Donbas, and Rostov operations. During these operations (from October 10, 1919, to January 8, 1920), the troops of the southern front advanced a distance of 850 to 900 kilometers [500–550 miles]. During the liquidation of Denikin's armies (from February 10, 1920, to March 27, 1920), the Soviet troops advanced an additional 450 to 500 kilometers [270–300 miles].

In the majority of cases, the Red Army major strategic offensives were conducted on a wide front, but the main attacks ordinarily were delivered over narrow sectors comprising 25 per cent to 28 per cent of the front.

Strategic offensives were ordinarily conducted by the forces of a single front operating in a given strategic direction and numbering two to six armies, each containing from two to five divisions. In individual operations (against Denikin in the autumn of 1919 and the White Poles in 1920), the offensive was carried out by the forces of two fronts.

The operations of the Civil War, which were wide in scope, differed substantially from those of World War I.

Table 1 presents data on the scope of some of the strategic operations.

It is evident from Table 1 that the Red Army's operations during the Civil War were continuous and extended to great depth; they were also of long duration (some of them lasted several months).

It should be kept in mind that uninterrupted offensives during the Civil War were often carried out without all the necessary supplies from distant rear areas. Thus, the offensives against the forces of Kolchak and Denikin proceeded on the principle that "the [supply] bases are ahead of us," that is, by the use of local supplies; this was characteristic of Soviet strategy during the Civil War.

An exceedingly flexible strategy in organizing units and using available forces and weapons was necessary to achieve the conclusive aims of the offensives. During the Civil War, up to 75 per cent of the Red Army forces carried out strategic redeployments from one front to another; some divisions were transferred from one front to another up to five times.

Under conditions of a war of maneuver with only limited forces and weapons, defense became very important. As is generally known, the offensives were conducted on the principal front, where the main forces and weapons were concentrated, whereas defensive operations were primarily carried out on other fronts; the Red Army even retreated in some regions. Thus, during the offensive operations of the forces on the eastern front against Kolchak, the forces of the southern front were forced to abandon the Donbas and withdraw to the central regions of the country, and the forces of the western front were compelled to conduct a stubborn defense in the Petrograd area.

In the autumn of 1919, when the struggle with Denikin's armies on the southern front entered its decisive phase, the forces of the eastern front retreated under the pressure of superior enemy forces to the Tobol River, and the forces of the western front again resumed a stubborn defense in the Petrograd region.

When an unfavorable balance of forces was encountered, defensive and offensive operations were combined on one front. This occurred in the military operations on the eastern front in the spring of 1919, when, in addition to a counterattack on the central sector of the front, both flanks engaged in stubborn defensive battles.

The Red Army's defensive operations during the Civil War were of

# TABLE 1

## The Extent of the Most Important Strategic Operations of the Red Army during the Civil War

| Operation | Number of Forces and Means Participating in the Operations | | Width of the Offensive Sector (km) [1 km = 0.6 mi.] | Depth of the Offensive (km) | Duration of the Operation (days) | Average Rate of Advance per Day (km) |
|---|---|---|---|---|---|---|
| | Divisions | Infantry and Cavalry Troops | | | | |
| Counter attack of the southern group of the eastern front: | | | | | | |
| on the entire front | 8 | 73,500 | Up to 1000 | Up to 400 | April 28, 1919–June 19, 1919 (53 days) | 7–8 |
| in the direction of the main blow | Approx. 6 | 49,000 | 200–220 | | | |
| The offensive of the southern front against Denikin: | | | | | | |
| on the entire front | 20/5* | 95,000 | 1400 | 850–900 | October 10, 1919–January 10, 1920 (92 days) | 8–10 |
| in the active sector | 13/5 | 70,000 | 600 | | | |
| The offensive of the western front against the White Poles: | | | | | | |
| on the entire front | 20/2 | 89,000 | 500 | 700–750 | July 4, 1920–August 15, 1920 (43 days) | 16–18 |
| in the direction of the main blow | 13/2 | 60,000 | 140 | | | |

* The first figure shows the number of infantry divisions; the second shows the number of cavalry divisions.

a highly active nature and were accompanied by decisive counter-attacks against the enemy's flanks and rear. The army's aim was to exhaust and weaken the enemy, to deprive him of his freedom to maneuver, and to prepare the conditions for counteroffensives. Examples of such operations were the defense of Tsaritsyno during the summer and autumn of 1918 and of Petrograd during the summer and autumn of 1919.

During the Civil War, Soviet military strategy gained valuable experience in co-ordinating fronts and army groups. Thus, the defeat of Kolchak's army required the joint operation of the southern and northern groups of the eastern front, and the battle against Denikin involved joint operation of the southern and the southeastern (Caucasian) fronts.

However, there were instances in the history of the Civil War when the operation of the fronts failed to be co-ordinated. It is well known that one of the reasons for the unsuccessful outcome of the Warsaw operation was a lack of co-ordination between the western and southwestern fronts.

The Red Army used various forms of operational and strategic maneuver during the Civil War, such as development and encirclement of the enemy by rapid flanking attacks in combination with deep breakthrough by the cavalry to the enemy's rear. Flanking attacks were widely used by our troops in destroying the armies of Kolchak, Denikin, and Wrangel.

In the counterattack on the southwestern front against the White Poles, a double envelopment maneuver was used with simultaneous penetration of cavalry to the enemy's rear, which resulted in the encirclement of a large enemy force near Kiev.

In addition to flanking attacks and deep envelopments, the Red Army also used such operational and strategic maneuvers as the deep salient thrust, first used in the autumn of 1919 to destroy the Denikin army.

It was specifically during the Civil War that Soviet strategy successfully solved the problem of penetrating the entire depth of the enemy's front by the massive use of cavalry organized into cavalry armies.

Cavalry armies, supported by artillery, armored vehicles, infantry and aircraft, were used to strike powerful blows at the enemy's rear areas and to combat his operational reserves.

Thus various forms of operational and strategic maneuver were used extensively during the Civil War, depending on the situation, whereas the interventionists and White Guards made primary use of frontal attack on a wide sector. The majority of the operations of the interventionists and White Guards were characterized by frontal offensives along an extended line.

General economic and political factors exerted considerable influence on the nature and objectives of strategic operations during the Civil War.

Soviet strategy planned its major offensive not only on a basis of military considerations, but also on the necessity to solve general political and economic problems. In a number of cases, these factors determined the main aim of an operation. Thus, in the report that the Supreme Command presented to V. I. Lenin on October 7, 1918, concerning the Republic's strategic position, it was noted that "by directing our efforts primarily toward the south, we will more rapidly obtain the necessities of life, without which the center of the country cannot exist." *

A characteristic feature of the Civil War was the extremely limited amount of essential strategic reserves at the disposal of the Soviet military leaders.

In spite of the fact that the Red Army made extensive use of the advantages provided by internal lines of communication in its operations, the war required a considerable amount of strategic (operational) reserves. However, until 1920 the reinforcement of fronts that were involved in the principal strategic operations was accomplished primarily by transferring troops from other less active fronts; this entailed tremendous difficulties.

The difficulties encountered by Soviet military strategy due to the great lack of reserves can be judged by the following report of the Supreme Command to Lenin in March of 1919 during the Kolchak offensive: "The troops at the front have been fighting in their positions without any relief for approximately a year. As a consequence of the extreme length of the combat sectors (frequently one division covers 200 versts [9]) and of direct enemy pressure, no army reserves or even front reserves could be created. The troop formations, which are constantly in the front lines, have had no opportunity to be organized, draw reinforcements, or to form proper combat units. The strategic transfer of units from one front to another has often been accomplished by taking them directly from the front lines, leaving the burden of defense on neighboring units, which resulted in an extreme weakening of the front." †

To create reserves, the Red Army Supreme Command planned late

---

* Ts GASA. Form 4, List 1, Report 39, Lines 43 to 50. [The reference is to Soviet archival materials.]

[9] U.S. ED. NOTE—A "verst" is a unit of measurement equal to 0.66 miles.

† Ts GASA. Form 2, Report 125, Line 37.

in 1918 to form eleven infantry divisions in the interior military districts. With the formation of these divisions by the spring of 1919, the Red Army Supreme Command could muster a reserve of 150,000 to 200,000 infantry troops. However, the deteriorating military situation on the southern and eastern fronts made it impossible to carry out this measure. Seven of the eleven divisions were sent to the front even before they were fully organized. As a result, when the Kolchak offensive began in 1919, the Soviet Supreme Command had only approximately 60,000 infantry; these reserves were not fully prepared because the units and formations lacked artillery and machine guns.

Because of insufficient reserves, regrouping of forces within the front was of great importance in achieving the planned strategic objectives. During the entire course of the Civil War, the Soviet military leadership often transferred forces from secondary sectors to the areas of main attack in order to achieve significant superiority in forces and weapons.

The Central Committee of the Party, headed by V. I. Lenin, devoted considerable attention to the preparation and use of reserves. The measures carried out during the Civil War by the Central Committee of the Party were part of a broad program to form manpower as well as materiel reserves.

From the second half of 1919 on, reserve armies were formed, which played an important role in the preparation of the reserves. Thus, from July of 1919 to December of 1920, the reserve army of the Republic stationed in Kazan supplied 34 per cent of the replacements sent to all fronts, and up to 40 per cent of those sent to the most active fronts. Special replacement centers were formed at headquarters of the fronts for bringing up to strength, organizing and training of troops in order to create their own reserve units.

The centralized system of preparing manpower reserves made possible the rapid replenishment of units and formations at the front and aided in the creation of striking forces.

Mobilization of Party, Komsomol (The Young Communists League), and trade unions played a very important role in reinforcing the fronts.

Along with mobilization of the Party and trade unions, local mobilization of workers from liberated territories played an exceedingly important role in providing replacements for the army in the field. For example, by the time the armies of the eastern front had crossed the Urals, its personnel had been almost completely replaced by additional workers from the Ural regions.

By August of 1919, the 5th Army of the eastern front, on the Tobol River, numbered 24,000 men; by October of 1919, in spite of its losses, its numbers had increased to 37,000 through local mobilizations. Such a build-up in forces was characteristic of all the armies of the eastern front during their offensive against, and pursuit of, the Kolchak army. The same was observed in the armies of the southern front during the defeat of Denikin's forces.

During the Civil War, Soviet military strategy was characterized by the skillful co-ordination of the Red Army's military operations with partisans at the rear of the interventionists and White Guards.

The White Guard established a terroristic military dictatorship with the active co-operation of British, French, and American imperialists in those territories that it had temporarily captured. This caused widespread rebellion and resentment among the working masses. In spite of cruel terror, oppression, and persecution, the workers and peasants, under the leadership of underground Bolshevist party organizations, waged decisive battle against the interventionists and the White Guard.

The widespread partisan movements that developed in the rear of Kolchak's and Denikin's forces played an important part in the destruction of their armies. The partisans paralyzed the functioning of the White Guard rear by rapid surprise attacks, and disrupted the supply system of the front and control over the troops. The partisan struggle at the rear of the interventionists and the White Guard assumed large proportions. Thus, in September of 1919, there were a total of 80,000 active partisans in Siberia. A partisan army of 25,000 was active in the Far East in the Amur region. Large partisan forces also existed in the eastern Transbaikal, Maritime, and Priamur regions.

By the fall of 1919, the partisan movement embraced vast regions in the rear of Denikin's forces.

During the Civil War, the Soviet military leaders closely co-ordinated the combat operations of the Red Army with partisan activities in planning and conducting major offensives. An important role was thus assigned to uprisings in the rear of the White Guard during the operations of the forces of the southern front on the Don against Krasnov [10] and Denikin in the autumn of 1918.

In preparing a counteroffensive by the forces of the southern front in October of 1919, the Central Committee of the Party instructed the Central Committee of the Ukranian Communist Party to call upon Ukranian partisans to give extensive support to the Red Army.

---

[10] U.S. ED. NOTE—Piotr Nikolaevich Krasnov (1869–1947) was a Tsarist general and leader of the anti-Soviet Cossacks during the Civil War. Florinsky, *op. cit.,* p. 289.

The Zafrontbiuro * accordingly issued detailed directives to the Ukranian partisans calling for immediate initiation of military operations against Denikin, the capture and retention of the most important strong points and railroad lines, the cutting of the enemy's lines of retreat, and the prevention of enemy destruction of railways, bridges, and other major railroad communication in the path of the advancing Red Army forces.

Accordingly, the Ukranian partisans stepped up their attacks on Denikin, and at the approach of the Red Army, directly joined the latter and assisted in its advanced units. In December of 1919, according to the Commander in Chief, G. A. Kolos, the numerical strength of partisan units and forces directed by the Revolutionary Military Council [*Revvoensovet*] [11] reached 50,000.†

The military operations of the Soviet forces were also closely co-ordinated with partisan activity during the destruction of the armies of Kolchak, Miller,[12] Iudenich,[13] and Wrangel.

The selfless and heroic struggle of the toilers under the leadership of the Communist Party, at the rear of the interventionists and the White Guard, played an important role in the victorious outcome of the Civil War.

The strategy of the Civil War was closely co-ordinated with the policy of the Soviet state. Both Soviet military strategy and policy were inspired with a single aim and supported by the firm and united leadership of the Party's Central Committee headed by V. I. Lenin.

---

* The Zafrontbiuro (Rear Area Bureau) of the Central Committee of the Ukranian Communist Party was formed in July of 1919 to direct the underground communist organization of the Ukraine and, through it, labor strikes and partisan movements in the enemy's rear. S. V. Kosior, the Secretary of the Central Committee of the Ukranian Communist Party, directed the Zafrontbiuro. The Central Committee of the Russian Communist Party approved the creation of the Zafrontbiuro on September 8, 1919.

[11] U.S. ED. NOTE—The Revolutionary Military Council was formed in 1918, under the chairmanship of the People's Commissioner for War, Trotskii, to co-ordinate all operational, administrative, and supply activities relating to the Red Army. It existed, under a different name, until 1934. *BSE*, Vol. 36, p. 185; Merle Fainsod, *How Russia Is Ruled*, Harvard University Press, Cambridge, Mass., 1953, p. 392.

† *Istoriia grazhdanskoi voiny v SSSR* [*History of the Civil War in the USSR*], Vol. 4, Gospolitizdat, Moscow, 1959, p. 315.

[12] U.S. ED. NOTE—Eugene Miller was a Tsarist general and head of an anti-Soviet North Russian Government and army based in Arkhangelsk. William H. Chamberlin, *The Russian Revolution, 1917–1921*, Vol. II, The Macmillan Company, New York, 1935, pp. 158, 401, 405.

[13] U.S. ED. NOTE—Nikolai Nikolaevich Iudenich (1862–1933), a Tsarist general commanding anti-Soviet forces in the Baltic, led an abortive offensive on Petrograd in October 1919. Florinsky, *op. cit*, p. 617.

The Party's Central Committee was the battle staff that organized and inspired the Soviet people in the battle with the interventionists and the White Guard.

The Central Committee of the Party studied all the most important problems bearing on the conduct of the war: the organization and strengthening of the armed forces, the strategic war plans, the organization and distribution of reserves, the appointment of commanders, etc. The strategic plans of all the important campaigns of the Civil War and all the measures connected with their execution were developed under Lenin's direct leadership and were fully discussed at the plenums and sessions of the Party's Central Committee. Thus, the preparation and conduct of the major strategic operations to destroy Kolchak's army were studied at the plenums of the Central Committee of the Russian Communist Party on April 13 and May 4 of 1919, at the session of the Politburo on April 24, and at the joint session of the Orgburo [14] and Politburo on April 29, 1919.

The operation to destroy Denikin's army was based on decisions made at the July and September plenums of the Central Committee of the Russian Communist Party, and the Politburo of October 15, November 6 and 14, 1919.

The plenums and sessions of the Party's Central Committee developed the general strategic plans of the operation, outlined measures for increasing the country's defense potential, improving the supply of the armies in the field, strengthening the control over the fronts and armies, strengthening the political organs and party organizations, and increasing the political party work among the troops and population.

In a speech at a closed session of the VIIIth Congress of the Russian Communist Party on March 21, 1919, Lenin remarked that "the questions of military organization were discussed literally at every session of the Central Committee. There was not one question of strategy that had not been evaluated and put into execution by the Central Committee or a bureau of the Central Committee." *

The fighting at the fronts was only one activity of the Party's Central Committee. In addition to directing battles, the Central Committee was charged with the [political] organization of the Republic. Thus the history of the Civil War is inseparable from the history of the entire country. The close unity of the army and the people was one of the strongest

---

[14] U.S. ED. NOTE—Organizational Bureau of the Central Committee of the CPSU directing the organizational work of the Party. Fainsod, *op. cit.,* pp. 154–155.

* *VIII S"ezd RKP(b). Protokoly* [*VIIIth Congress of the Russian Communist Party (Bolshevik), Protocols*], Gospolitizdat, Moscow, 1959, p. 14.

advantages of Soviet military strategy over that of the interventionists and the White Guard.

In directing the country's defense, the Central Committee took into account all aspects of national activity in creating favorable internal and external conditions for the political aims of Soviet military strategy.

By its vast organizational and political activity, the Communist Party transformed the country into a single military camp and mobilized the greatest possible manpower and material resources for the Red Army.

The Defense Council of Workers and Peasants,[15] headed by V. I. Lenin, played an important part in mobilizing all the country's forces and means. The Council of Defense had plenary powers to mobilize forces and instruments in the defense of the country. It co-ordinated and directed the activity of all agencies to assist the Red Army, directed and controlled the work of the Revolutionary Military Council of the Republic, the Supreme Command, the People's Commissar of Naval Affairs, and the Russian General Staff. The organization of the country's defense and the material provision of the Red Army were constantly on the agenda of the Defense Council's sessions.

The appeals of the Central Committee to the Party, to the Soviet and trade union organizations, and to the entire Soviet people played an extremely important role in mobilizing all the country's forces and means to destroy the enemy. The Central Committee's slogans such as "The socialist Fatherland is in danger!" and its communication entitled "Everything for the fight with Denikin!" its theses like "The Polish front and our tasks," as well as other documents, provided a militant program of operation for all Party and Soviet organizations and for the working masses of the country.

Scrupulous centralization in the administration of all internal resources and their proper use according to the situation at the front lines enabled the Red Army to conduct major strategic operations.

In spite of the exceptional difficulties that existed during the Civil War, the Communist Party organized a regular Red Army that was solidly unified, strong in class consciousness, very well disciplined, and highly dedicated to its people.

"By the fall of 1918, the Red Army had mobilized over 800,000 men. Within a short time the army numbered one million. This made possible a considerable increase in the number of active troops at the front." *

---

15 U.S. ED. NOTE—The Council was organized in November 30, 1918, and was charged with the mobilization of manpower and resources for defense. *BSE*, Vol. 39, p. 472.

* *Istoriia grazhdanskoi voiny v SSSR* [*History of the Civil War in the USSR*], Vol. 3, Gospolitizdat, Moscow, 1957, p. 224.

In October of 1918, Lenin ordered the formation of an army of three million men. "We decided to have an army of one million men by spring," Lenin wrote. "Now we need an army of three million men. We can have it. *And we shall have it!*" *

By March of 1919, the Red Army numbered about a million and a half men, of which approximately 700,000 were at the front. On the average, the fronts required a total of 150,000 to 200,000 replacements per month, of which approximately 100,000 were sent to whichever was the main front at that time. During 1919, the Red Army grew by almost 200,000 men every month, and by January 1, 1920, it numbered three million men. At the end of the Civil War, as is known, the Red Army numbered five and a half million men.

More than 120 infantry and cavalry divisions were formed during the Civil War. Table 2 shows the increase in the number of Red Army divisions (excluding nondivisional units and formations).

TABLE 2

*Numbers of Organized and Disbanded Infantry and Cavalry Divisions during the Civil War (1918–1920)*

| Type of Division | 1918 | | | 1919 | | | 1920 | | | Number of divisions by the beginning of 1921 |
|---|---|---|---|---|---|---|---|---|---|---|
| | Number of divisions by the beginning of the year | Number of divisions organized during the year | Number of divisions disbanded during the year | Number of divisions by the beginning of the year | Number of divisions organized during the year | Number of divisions disbanded during the year | Number of divisions by the beginning of the year | Number of divisions organized during the year | Number of divisions disbanded during the year | |
| Infantry | — | 47 | 3 | 44 | 31 | 11 | 64 | 10 | 24 | 50 |
| Cavalry | — | 3 | — | 3 | 11 | — | 14 | 15 | 7 | 22 |
| Total | — | 50 | 3 | 47 | 42 | 11 | 78 | 25 | 31 | 72 |

In addition to creating a regular Red Army, the Communist Party also performed the huge task of providing the army with weapons, ammunition, supplies, and food.

Increasing amounts of armaments were required by the expanded military operations and the increasing number of Red Army personnel.

* V. I. Lenin, *Sochineniia* [*Works*], Vol. 28, p. 84.

"However, by the second half of 1918, the weapon and ammunition reserves consisted only of about 3,000 artillery pieces, over 10,000 machine guns, 1.3 million rifles and approximately 800 million rounds of rifle ammunition. These quantities could not satisfy the growing needs of the Red Army." *

The material base for producing armaments and ammunition was also quite inadequate. By the autumn of 1918, about 3,500 of the 5,402 factories capable of filling military orders were in enemy occupied territories. The interventionists and the White Guards controlled the regions that produced 90 per cent of the coal, 85 per cent of the iron ore, and approximately 75 per cent of the pig iron and steel produced in Russia. A severe shortage of fuel and raw materials seriously hampered industry and railway transport.

In spite of these tremendous difficulties, the Communist Party exercised all possible means to arouse the enthusiasm of the workers, and succeeded in organizing defense production.

By the end of 1918, the defense factories had already attained a monthly production of 60,000 rifles, 600 machine guns, up to 50 artillery pieces, over 30 million rounds of rifle ammunition, and more than 90,000 artillery shells.

Table 3 shows the production of armaments and ammunition during the Civil War.

TABLE 3

*Production of Arms and Ammunition by the Industry of the Soviet Union during the Civil War (1918–1920)*

| Items | Production of Armaments for the War Years † | | | |
|---|---|---|---|---|
| | 1918 | 1919 | 1920 | Total |
| Rifles | 380,239 | 470,155 | 425,994 | 1,276,388 |
| Machine guns | 4,650 | 6,270 | 4,459 | 15,379 |
| Field artillery pieces | na | 540 | 213 ‡ | 753 |
| Artillery shells | na | 184,000 | 16,267 ‡ | 200,267 |
| Rounds of rifle ammunition, in thousands | na | 357,260 | 411,365 | 768,625 |

* *Istoriia grazhdanskoi voiny v SSSR* [*History of the Civil War in the USSR*], Vol. 3, Gospolitizdat, Moscow, 1957, p. 306.

† *Istoriia grazhdanskoi voiny v SSSR* [*History of the Civil War in the USSR*], Vol. 4, Gospolitizdat, Moscow, 1959, p. 388.

‡ Information on the production of arms and ammunition for 1920 is given only for the first half of 1920.

The inadequate material and technical base did not permit the production of armaments on a scale large enough to completely satisfy the Red Army's requirements. Consequently, there were severe shortages of armaments, especially rifle ammunition, during the Civil War. Thus, the 125 infantry and 9 cavalry brigades formed in 1919 were short 239,000 infantry rifles (35 per cent), 837,000 carbines and cavalry rifles (87 per cent), 14,500 machine guns (65 per cent), and 2,650 guns of various calibers (60 per cent).

The minimum level of supply for rifle ammunition was set at 306,-226,000 rounds (500 rounds per rifle and 10,000 per machine gun), but this supply constantly was short about 80 million rounds.*

The Communist Party performed a tremendous task in supplying the Red Army with clothing and food during the Civil War.

The peace-loving foreign policy of the Communist Party and Soviet government, which they pursued steadfastly and consistently from the first victorious days of the Socialist Revolution in our country, played a major role in the victory over the interventionists and the White Guard.

This policy assured the Soviet Republic widespread sympathy and support from the working masses of the capitalist countries, furnished us the opportunity of withdrawing from World War I after the Brest Peace Treaty, and disrupted the plans of the imperialist Triple Entente for drawing into the war the small states bordering the Soviet Union.

These were the basic features of Soviet military strategy during the Civil War.

## Theory of Military Strategy during the Period of Peaceful Construction (1922–1941)

The interval between the Civil War and the Great Patriotic War proved to be an important period in the organization of Soviet Armed Forces and the development of our military theory; these activities were closely allied to the economic and political consolidation of the Soviet state.

With the industrialization of the country and the collectivization of agriculture, the Soviet Union became a strong, advanced industrial power with a large mechanized agriculture. During the prewar five-year plans, approximately 9,000 major factories were built, and new branches of industry were developed; these included the tractor, automobile, aircraft, and chemical and machine-building industries. This made possible a further strengthening of the country's defense potential.

---

* See *Voenno-istoricheskii zhurnal* [*Journal of Military History*], No. 11, 1960, p. 6.

The industrial development of the country's eastern regions also strengthened the military and economic base of the Soviet Union. In 1940, these regions produced 28.5 per cent of the pig iron, 32 per cent of the steel, 32.1 per cent of the rolled iron, 36 per cent of the coal, and over 12 per cent of the petroleum.* This not only decreased the vulnerability of our homeland, but also made it possible to conduct a war on two fronts simultaneously, should the need arise.

The increase in government reserves and war stockpiles of strategic materials also strengthened our military and economic base. These were sufficient to supply the economy for about two to three months, and even up to four months in some types of materials.

Finally, the strengthening of the country's military and economic base was greatly aided by the increased cultural level and technical knowledge of the Soviet people. This was highly important for the economy and its conversion to war, as well as for manning the Red Army [with competent personnel].

These facts clearly indicate that the Communist Party and the Soviet government were strictly guided in their practical activities by Lenin's teachings that a truly strong, well-organized homeland and a well-armed, well-provided army are essential for the conduct of war.

The successes achieved in the industrialization of the country made possible the rapid and complete re-equipping of the Soviet Armed Forces, without which it would have been impossible to successfully strengthen our country's defense capacity. Lenin pointed out that in modern war ". . . he who has the best equipment, organization, discipline, and machinery will triumph . . . it is impossible to exist in modern society without machines and without discipline; one must either master advanced technology or be crushed." †

During the prewar five-year plans, the Red Army had become a first-rank army in quantity and quality of weapons, combat materiel and combat training, and was fully prepared for fighting wars of that time. From 1934 to 1938 the number of Red Army tanks increased almost threefold, the number of planes increased 2.3 times, artillery almost 80 per cent, and the size of the Red Army almost doubled.‡

The increase in size was accompanied by improvement in the Red Army's organization. The striking and fire power of the infantry were considerably increased. In order to meet the growing threat of war

---

* See *Dostizheniia Sovetskogo Soiuza za 40 let v tsifrakh* [*Achievements of the Soviet Union over 40 Years, in Figures*], Gospolitizdat, Moscow, 1957, pp. 87, 92.
† V. I. Lenin, *Sochineniia* [*Works*], Vol. 27, p. 167.
‡ *XVIII S"ezd VKP(b). Stenograficheskii otchet* [*XVIIIth Congress of the All-Union Communist Party (Bolshevik), Stenographic Report*], pp. 191–195.

and to further strengthen the country's defense, to increase the combat readiness of the forces, and to eliminate the inconsistencies between the level of technical equipment of the army and the territorial organization of our forces, it was decided in 1938 to shift to a cadre organization of the Armed Forces. Simultaneously, new formations and units of all branches of the Armed Forces continued to be organized. As a result of these measures, the over-all size of the Armed Forces increased more than 2.5 times from 1939 to 1940, while the number of armored troops increased 4.8 times, and that of the Air Forces 2.1 times.

Along with the increase in size and the improvement in the Armed Forces organization, there was intensive scientific development of Soviet military strategic theory. It was based on Marxist-Leninist teachings on war and the army, the political and economic state of our country, and a critical evaluation of past war experiences.

It was pointed out in Soviet military strategy that a future war would be global in scope; in view of the existence of two opposing social systems, the imminent war was expected to be primarily a coalition war of capitalist countries against the Soviet Union. The intensive class nature of this war predetermined the extreme decisiveness of its military and political objectives and excluded any possibility of compromise.

It was anticipated that the future war would be prolonged and highly mobile, requiring mass armies and placing the utmost strain on the economic and organizational resources of each nation, and that victory could not be achieved by one blow. M. V. Frunze pointed out that "modern armies have a tremendous ability to survive. . . . Even the complete defeat of an enemy army at a given moment does not assure final victory as long as the defeated forces are supported by an economically and morally strong rear." *

In accordance with the view that final war aims could not be accomplished by one blow, our military theorists believed that a series of successive campaigns and operations would be necessary.

The highly mobile nature of the forthcoming war was predetermined by the extensive mechanization and motorization of the forces and large-scale adoption of new, powerful offensive weapons, such as tanks and aircraft, which made it possible to break through defenses successfully and to advance to a great depth.

In accordance with Lenin's dictum that the methods of warfare must be altered with the situation, prewar Soviet theory adopted the view

---

* M. V. Frunze, *Izbrannye proizvedeniia* [*Selected Works*], Voenizdat, Moscow, 1951, p. 253.

that various methods of armed combat, namely offense, defense, and retreat, could be used during the war.

Nevertheless, our military doctrine gave definite preference to the conduct of offensive operations, which alone achieve the total destruction of the enemy. M. V. Frunze wrote, "only he will win, who will have the determination to attack . . ." and thus "first and foremost . . . is the preparation and training of our army in the spirit of mobile large-scale operations." *

Our theory held that the enemy forces in a given theater of operation were the main target of strategic operations. This was based on the indisputable principle that total victory could be achieved only by delivering a decisive defeat to the enemy's armed forces.

Our prewar regulations and directives, war games, and field exercises all reflected the conduct of war by active offensive methods. The Soviet doctrine of offense was most succinctly and clearly expressed in the *Draft Field Service Regulations of 1939. "Every enemy attack against the Union of Soviet Socialist Republics will be met by a crushing blow with the entire might of our armed forces. . . .*

*"If the enemy forces us into a war, the Workers' and Peasants' Red Army will be the most aggressive army that ever existed.*

*"We will wage an offensive war, and carry it into the territory of the enemy.*

*"The combat operations of the Red Army will be aimed at the annihilation and total defeat of the enemy. . . ."* †

Although Soviet strategy considered the offensive operation to be the main method of conducting armed combat, the defensive operation was also accepted as a wholly proper method of combat. However, our prewar theory had not fully worked out the problems of organizing and conducting defense. It was believed that defense would play a subordinate role to offense, and would be resorted to only in isolated areas within the context of strategic advance rather than on the entire front. In principle, our prewar theory acknowledged the possibility of the forces having to retreat in individual sectors. However, no theoretical or practical work was done on the problem of withdrawing large forces from enemy attack.

Our prewar military theory correctly anticipated how the future war would break out. It took the view that modern wars as a rule

---

* M. V. Frunze, *Izbrannye prolzvedeniia* [*Selected Works*], Vol. II, Voenizdat, Moscow, 1957, pp. 17–18.

† *Polevoi ustav RKKA (proekt)* [*Field Service Regulations of the Workers' and Peasants' Red Army (Draft)*], Voenizdat, Moscow, 1939, p. 9.

would begin by surprise, without formal declaration. However, no correct conclusions on the content and nature of the initial period of the war were drawn. The initial period of the war was understood as the interval of time from the beginning of military operations to the commitment of the main mass of the armed forces.

It was anticipated that the initial period of the war would last fifteen to twenty days after the beginning of hostilities. During this interval, the army was expected to conduct combat operations with covering forces and to wage the battle for air superiority, while the main forces were being mobilized, concentrated, and deployed. Thus, only limited military operations were envisaged for the initial period. This erroneous view, as it proved to be, of the nature of the initial period of the war adversely affected our Armed Forces' preparations for war.

The period between World War I and II was characterized not only by the further improvement of existing armed forces, but also by the appearance and rapid development of new types of armed services and forces. The air forces were transformed from an auxiliary force into an independent branch of the armed forces, while new types of troops, armored, antiaircraft and airborne troops, were developed in the ground forces.

Consequently, Soviet military theory devoted considerable attention to determining the question of the role and place of the various armed forces in a future war. In solving this question it was assumed that victory could be achieved only by co-ordinated and united efforts of all the branches, and kinds of troops, of the armed forces.

The main role in armed combat was assigned to the ground forces, since it was anticipated that a future war would take place primarily on land. However, the ability of large armored formations to carry out independent missions was underestimated, because of incorrect conclusions drawn from the Spanish Civil War.

The air force was primarily intended to support ground forces directly on the field of battle, but it could also conduct independent operations. However, the theory of such operations had not been developed by the time the war began; thus, bomber capabilities were underestimated, and insufficient attention was given to their development.

The navy was to co-operate with ground forces operating in coastal areas, and to carry out independent operations on the high seas. However, serious errors were made in evaluating the importance of the various naval forces. Because preference was given to the surface fleet, independent operations carried out by surface vessels were considered to be the main type of naval combat operations. This in turn led to emphasis on the construction of large and expensive surface ships. The role of the submarine fleet and naval aviation in the future war was underestimated.

By our extensive construction program for surface ships we aimed at achieving superiority over the fleets of our likely enemies, because at that time our surface fleet was qualitatively and quantitatively inferior to those of the capitalist countries. However, no consideration was given to the fact that two of our fleets were based in closed seas [the Baltic and Black Seas], while the Northern and Pacific Fleets faced great difficulties in reaching the open seas. In this situation, the main emphasis should have been on a submarine fleet and naval aviation. Thus, our theory on the strategic use of the navy was under the influence of already outdated concepts of the character of naval operations and of the predominant role of the surface fleet.

Our prewar theory devoted an important place to the use of airborne troops for deep penetration and rapid operations. These troops were regarded as instruments of the higher command and were intended for operational and tactical missions in the enemy's rear, and for maintaining pressure on the entire depth of his defenses. However, these valid theoretical concepts could not be realized in practice, because the use of airborne troops was limited by the inadequate development of air transport.

The further development of aviation, particularly the bomber force capable of delivering powerful strikes, not only against troops, but also against economic and political centers deep within the country, made the problem of air defense of troops and installations in the rear very acute. This problem was to be solved by co-ordinating the operations of the PVO forces and air force that were under the control of the local commanders of the PVO. The PVO was based on the principle of protecting individual targets.

As a whole, prewar PVO was adequate against the existing means of air attack; however, its weakness lay in the absence of unified control over fighters and antiaircraft artillery in air defense zones, and in the inadequate provision of the most modern detection and control equipment to the PVO forces.

It was anticipated that the coming war against the Soviet Union would be a coalition war; consequently, strategy was based on a defeat of the coalition in stages. The main efforts would be directed each time against the most dangerous enemy under the given conditions, whose destruction would result in major military and political advantages that would decisively influence the subsequent course of the war.

Soviet prewar theory devoted considerable attention to the problem of strategic co-operation. This was understood as the co-ordination of operations of all branches of the armed forces and types of troops with respect to aims, timing, and location. Strategic co-operation was not only worked out on a theoretical basis, but was also tested in practice in tactical games and maneuvers.

Lenin's dictum that "in war he wins who has the larger reserves, the greater sources of strength, and whose masses have greater endurance" * guided Soviet military theorists in developing a strategic theory that devoted particular attention to the problem of the creation, use, and replenishment of strategic reserves. The concept of "strategic reserves" not only included the troop formations at the disposal of the Supreme High Command, but also the country's manpower and economic resources, which would be necessary for the conduct of an intense and prolonged war. However, errors were made in the practical solution of this problem, which were reflected in the fact that, in spite of the constant threat of war, we did not create the necessary reserves of weapons and combat materiel for the mobilization needs of our Armed Forces.

## Soviet Military Strategy during the Great Patriotic War (1941–1945)

The Great Patriotic War was one of the most difficult and intense wars ever endured by our Motherland. It was a severe test of the moral and physical strength of our people. The Soviet Union's historical victory in this war, which was of world importance, was a clear and convincing proof, not only of the stability and vitality of the Soviet society and government, but also of the might of the Soviet Armed Forces and the highly developed level of Soviet military art. Soviet military art, which is based on Marxist-Leninist teachings on war and the army, developed systematically during the war and was enhanced by valuable experience in organizing and conducting armed combat under various military and political conditions.

The continuous development of Soviet military art was the natural result of the superiority of our socialist system, which assured the rapid mobilization of all the nation's forces to repel the enemy, and the systematic growth of the quality of the technical equipment of our Armed Forces. Thus, by early 1945 the army in the field had one and a half times as many rifles and carbines, three times as many submachine guns, eight times as many tanks and self-propelled artillery, and five times as many combat planes as in December 1941. During this period there was a marked improvement in the quality of the Red Army's weapons

---

* V. I. Lenin, *Sochineniia* [*Works*], Vol. 30, p. 55.

and combat materiel. The development of Soviet military art was brought about not only by an increase in the quantity and quality of weapons and combat materiel, but also by improved troop organization, which further strengthened our Armed Forces.

One of the most important factors in the development of military strategy was the high combat morale of Soviet soldiers and officers, which was due in turn, to the moral and political unity of our people. During the Great Patriotic War, approximately eleven thousand members of the army and navy received the high award of Hero of the Soviet Union and more than seven million soldiers and officers received Soviet orders and medals.*

Finally, the development and perfection of Soviet military art were assured by the wise policy followed by the Communist Party. Guided by Lenin's concepts of the defense of the Socialist Motherland, the Party correctly determined the military and political aims for the war against Nazi Germany, organized and inspired the Soviet people and soldiers in the just war against the German aggressors, unified political and military strategy in the struggle against the enemy by the motto "Everything for the front, everything for victory!" and made skillful use of all the country's resources to achieve victory against a strong and dangerous enemy.

As military art developed, strategy—its most important component— also developed and perfected itself. This development was most clearly manifested in the organization and conduct of strategic offensives.

The past war fully confirmed the validity of the basic concepts of Soviet military doctrine: that only by a decisive offensive would it be possible to defeat the enemy forces, occupy his territory, crush his will to resist, and achieve final victory. The Soviet Armed Forces conducted several major offensives to realize this general war aim. Each offensive achieved a major military and political goal, which was part of the general war plan. The following aims were most characteristic of the strategic offensives: destroying the main enemy forces in the one or two most important sectors; liberating economically and politically important areas; eliminating Nazi Germany's allies from the war (Finland, Romania, and Hungary), and finally, freeing the occupied territories and subjugated peoples of the countries of Central, Eastern, and Southeastern Europe from German occupation. Soviet strategy successfully solved the problem of organizing and conducting major strategic operations during the war. In spite of the difficult conditions under which armed combat took place, the Soviet military leadership was able to solve all

* Data cited from *Istoriia SSSR, Epokha sotsializma* [*History of the USSR: The Epoch of Socialism*], Gospolitizdat, Moscow, 1957, p. 641.

the problems involved in preparing and conducting strategic operations on the basis of a critical evaluation of the experience of the war. Beginning with the second period of the war, strategic operations became the main method of conducting strategic offensives. During the third period of war, up to 70 per cent of the frontal offensives were conducted as strategic operations.

In defining the aims of its strategic operations, the Soviet Supreme High Command always took into consideration the general political aims of the war, the economic potential and morale of the belligerent country, and the strategic situation existing at the beginning of each strategic operation.

During the Great Patriotic War, the Soviet military leadership successfully solved the important strategic problem of choosing the proper area for the main effort. Taking into consideration the military and political aims of the particular period of the war, the strategic situation at the front, and the balance of forces along the entire front and in strategically [critical] areas, the Soviet Supreme High Command in the last war chose the area for the main blow. It considered where the enemy was most vulnerable and which [blow] would assure the decisive defeat of the largest or most dangerous enemy forces and a favorable change in the strategic situation on the entire front in favor of the Red Army. Moreover, care was exercised so that the areas chosen provided the necessary operational space for deploying large masses of forces and great quantities of equipment, and permitted extensive maneuver along the front and in depth.

In the winter operations of 1941–1942, the Soviet forces struck the main blow against the largest enemy formation, which was attempting to capture Moscow. The defeat of these forces not only resulted in a radical change in the military and political situation on the Soviet-German front, but also compelled Japan and Turkey to refrain from openly entering the war against the Soviet Union.

During the operations of the second period of war and the winter of 1944, the Red Army delivered its main attack in the southwest area. The shifting of the area of the main attack from the west to the southwest was due to the fact that the most powerful and active enemy formation was operating in that southwestern area. The defeat of this force brought about a radical change in the situation on the entire Soviet-German front and led to the liberation of such economically important areas as the Stalingrad industrial region, the northern Caucasus, the Donbas, the Krivoy Rog region, Kerch, and the Ukranian regions west of the Dnieper River. The results of these operations greatly influenced the entire course of the Great Patriotic War and World War II.

During the summer operations of 1944 and the winter operations of 1945, the Red Army's main efforts were concentrated in the western area. The shift of the main effort to the western area made it possible for the Soviet forces to strike that section of the front most dangerous to the enemy, to reach German territory within a short time, and to complete the defeat of Germany.

In choosing the area for the main attack, the Stavka considered political and economic requirements as well as those of strategy. The relationship among strategy, politics and economics was completely evident. Thus, in directing the main attack against the southern flank of the Soviet-German front during the second period of war and the winter operations of 1944, the Stavka was compelled to take the following important conditions into consideration. First, a main advance on this sector of the front would result in the expulsion of the enemy from such economically highly developed regions as the Northern Caucasus, the Donbas, Krivoy Rog, Nikopol, and the Western Ukraine; liberation of these areas would increase the economic potential of our country. Second, the approach of Soviet forces to the borders of Romania would increase the contradictions between Nazi Germany and her satellites in southeastern Europe and create favorable conditions for eliminating Romania and Bulgaria, which were allies of Nazi Germany, from the war.

The proper choice of the area for a main strategic attack attested to the skill of the Soviet Supreme High Command in foreseeing the future course of the war and selecting the vital link in the entire chain of military events.

Once the area for the main attack was chosen, the Stavka concentrated large masses of troops and combat materiel in this area. The accompanying strategic operations were characterized by superior concentration of troops and combat materiel and the formation of powerful offensive dispositions considerably stronger than those that operated in other areas. These operations, which were carried out in sectors constituting 20 to 37 per cent of the entire length of the Soviet-German front, involved from 20 to 50 per cent of the personnel, 25 to 52 per cent of the guns and mortars, 20 to 70 per cent of the tanks and self-propelled artillery, and 30 to 90 per cent of the air force of the field army.

The concentration of large forces and weapons in the area of the main attack made it possible to break up strong, deeply echeloned enemy defenses within a short period, to penetrate rapidly in depth, and to destroy major enemy formations. We need only refer to the following examples: During the winter offensives of 1941–1943, the Soviet troops destroyed two German army groups, Group "B" and Group "Don," including the Italian 8th, the Hungarian 2nd, the Romanian 3rd and 4th, the 4th tank divisions and the 6th army as well as the "Hollidt" combat group. A total of 100 enemy divisions were destroyed during these operations, 98 of which were located in the area of the main attack.

In the summer and autumn operations of 1944, our troops directed their main effort against, and destroyed, two German army groups, "Center" and "North Ukraine" and their component 9th, 4th, and 2nd field armies; the 1st, 2nd, 3rd, and 4th tank armies; and the 1st Hungarian army. A hundred and thirty-seven divisions located in the area of the main attack were destroyed, or more than one third of all the divisions destroyed during the strategic offensive. Enemy losses were just as great in the main area of our attack during the operations of 1945 in the Central European theater. Here our troops destroyed the German "Visla" and "Center" army groups with their component 2nd, 11th, 9th, and 17th field armies as well as the 3rd and 4th tank armies. A total of 191 divisions were destroyed in this area, or more than half of the divisions destroyed during the course of the offensive on the entire Soviet-German front. The destruction of such large forces in the area of the main attack, to which the enemy had been compelled to transfer reserves as well as considerable numbers of troops from other sectors of the Soviet-German front, created favorable conditions for Soviet offensives in other areas.

Decisive political and strategic objectives during a given stage of the war were achieved by conducting several successive operations along the front and in depth, or by a simultaneous strategic operation on the entire strategic front according to a single strategic plan.

The methods of strategic offense selected by the Stavka were those that best corresponded to the military and political situation, our economic capabilities, the combat capabilities of the Soviet troops, and that in the final analysis was most likely to achieve the desired objectives.

When the Red Army forces were not decisively superior to those of the enemy, the Soviet Supreme High Command executed its strategic offensives by conducting successive strategic operations along the front and in depth. This type of offensive made it possible to accumulate the necessary amounts of materiel, ammunition, and fuel for subsequent operations, and to create strong striking formations in the chosen area, as well as to achieve superiority in forces and weapons over the enemy in all operations. This method of strategic offensive also made it possible for us to defeat the enemy in stages, enabling us to choose the most convenient and advantageous time and place for the next blow.

To counter the successive Soviet attacks, the German military leadership was compelled to transfer its reserves from one area to another. This weakened the enemy forces in the areas selected for the next attack. The sequence of offensive operations in different areas led to rapid extension of the strategic offensive front. Whereas initially the active front of strategic operations comprised some 500 to 600 kilometers [300–370 miles], when our forces began offensives in other areas, the area of combined operations increased up to 2,000 to 3,000 kilometers [1,250–1,860 miles], i.e., the offensives were conducted simultaneously on a front comprising 50 to 70 per cent of the entire strategic front.

During the winter operations of 1945, which took place in an entirely different military and political situation from those of the preceding war periods, Soviet strategic offensives took the form of powerful simultaneous attacks on the entire Soviet-German front. The development of a simultaneous offensive in a number of adjacent strategic areas was made possible by the further strengthening of the Soviet Union's military and economic base and by a considerable shortening of the entire front.

The advantage of this type of strategic offensive lay primarily in the fact that the enemy's strategic front was split and broken up most rapidly, and his formations were simultaneously surrounded and defeated in several strategic areas. Thus, the enemy was prevented from maneuvering along the front to create large defensive formations to counter our blows. This made it possible for the Soviet troops to achieve rapidly major military and political success in the 1945 operations.

The Stavka took several factors into careful account when selecting the form of a strategic offensive operation. The most important of these factors were the composition of the Soviet forces, particularly the existence among them of mobile units and formations; the configuration of the front lines; the composition of enemy forces and the weak and strong points in his defense; and the character of the theater of military operations. Although various forms of strategic operations were used, predominant use was made of encirclement and destruction of major enemy units.

The following main forms of strategic operations were employed during the past war: the encircling of large enemy units and their subsequent destruction; the splitting of the enemy's strategic front; and the breakup of the enemy's strategic front and subsequent isolation of enemy formations.

Different techniques were used to encircle major enemy formations. The most characteristic were simultaneous strikes in two areas, enveloping the flanks of the enemy forces and advance in depth in converging directions (Stalingrad, Lvov, Yassko-Kishinev, and other operations), and one strong enveloping attack aimed at trapping the enemy forces against hard-to-cross natural barriers (the liberation of the Northern Caucasus, and the East Prussian operation). In some cases, the encirclement of large enemy formations was accomplished by penetration of the front at several points with subsequent development of offensives along converging directions and encirclement of enemy troops throughout the operational depth (Byelorussian and Berlin operations).

Strategic offensive operations to split the enemy's strategic front were executed by having adjacent fronts deliver attacks in depth throughout the entire strategic disposition of the enemy formations (the liberation of the Western Ukraine and the East Pomeranian operation).

The enemy's strategic front was broken up by a series of powerful blows at several points, and by development of an offensive along a broad front on parallel or even diverging lines. This broke up the enemy's defensive front, which facilitated the destruction of the isolated enemy formations that had lost operational contact (Vistula-Oder operation).

These were, in brief, the most typical forms of strategic offensive operations. However, it should be remembered that strategic operations often took more complex forms. The forms were sometimes combined in various ways or developed from one into another.

Soviet military strategy made successful use of strategic surprise as one of the means of achieving desired objectives in the Great Patriotic War. Strategic surprise was achieved by the following measures, which were aimed at misleading the German military leadership about our plans:

1. The development of a major offensive in the area least expected by the enemy. This was the case during the winter of 1942–1943, when the Red Army delivered its main attack at Stalingrad, while the enemy expected an attack in a western area; and in the summer of 1944, when contrary to the enemy's expectations, the Red Army delivered its main attack in Byelorussia instead of to the south.

2. Concealment of the preparation for the offensives, as was the case at Kursk, and keeping the plans of the Soviet leadership secret.

3. Providing the enemy with false information to mislead him concerning the location, time, and strength of our attack. The Soviet Command used this measure particularly during the third period of war; it proved to have considerable influence on the successful conduct of strategic operations.

It should be noted, however, that the Soviet military leadership was not always completely successful in achieving strategic surprise. This was particularly the case during the summer of 1943 and the winter of

1944, when the enemy discovered the Soviet leadership's plans in advance, since we were not able to conceal from the enemy the concentration of our strategic reserves (summer of 1943), the regrouping of troops, and the creation of assault formations at the front. The dissemination of false information concerning preparations for the offensives in the Western Ukraine was badly handled, which also resulted in the German military leadership discovering the actual regrouping and being able to determine the regions of pretended troop concentrations.

The scope of the strategic operations and offensives during the Great Patriotic War increased steadily. This was primarily manifested by the expansion of the front and by the increased number of forces and weapons involved in strategic attack (Table 4).

TABLE 4

*The Extent of Strategic Offensives in the Great Patriotic War*

| Time of Offensive | Extent of the Soviet-German Front at the Beginning of the Offensive | | Number of Active Fronts | | Depth of Advance of Soviet Forces (km) |
|---|---|---|---|---|---|
| | Total (km) [1 km = 0.6 mi] | Offensive Sector (km) | Total | Acting in Combination during the Offensive | |
| Winter, 1941–1942 | 4,000 | 1,000 | 10 | 7 | 200–400 |
| Winter, 1942–1943 | 6,000 | 3,200 | 12 | 8 | 200–700 |
| Summer and fall, 1943 | 4,300 | 2,000 | 11 | 7 | 200–600 |
| Winter, 1944 | 4,400 | 2,900 | 11 | 10 | 300–500 |
| Summer and fall, 1944 | 4,250 | 4,250 | 12 | 10 | 600–1,100 |
| Winter, 1945 | 2,400 | 2,100 | 10 | 8 | 400–700 |

It is evident from Table 4 that the offensive fronts during 1942–1945 were two to three times as long as those of the winter of 1941–1942; the number of fronts simultaneously engaged in the offensive increased almost by a factor of 1.5, and the depth of the advance 2 to 2.5 times. The zone of advance in strategic operations also increased considerably and, in the concluding period of war, reached 1,000 to 1,400 kilometers [600–800 miles]. The increased scope of the strategic operations was also manifested in the more rapid rate of advance. Thus,

whereas in the strategic operations of the initial war period the average
rate of advance of Soviet troops was 4 to 5 kilometers [2.4–3.1 miles]
per day, in the operations of 1944–1945 it reached 15 to 20 kilometers
[9.3–12 miles].

The increase in the scope of strategic operations during the war is
also evident from the increased amounts of forces and weapons engaged
in strategic operations. This is indicated by data in Table 5.

TABLE 5

*The Number of Troops and Weapons Involved in Strategic
Offensive Operations in 1941–1945 (The Forces and Weapons
Engaged in the Moscow Counteroffensive Are Taken as 100 per cent)*

| Operation | Divisions (%) | Manpower (%) | Guns-Mortars (%) | Tanks and Self-propelled Guns (%) | Aircraft (%) |
|---|---|---|---|---|---|
| Moscow counter-offensive | 100 | 100 | 100 | 100 | 100 |
| Stalingrad counter-offensive | 80 | 100 | 190 | 128 | 108 |
| Orel operation | 69 | 80 | 238 | 339 | 250 |
| Belgorod-Kharkov operation | 61 | 96 | 183 | 385 | 125 |
| Liberation of the Western Ukraine | 176 | 215 | 384 | 371 | 200 |
| Byelorussian operation | 171 | 209 | 500 | 860 | 666 |
| Lvov-Sandomirsk operation | 74 | 97 | 207 | 314 | 266 |
| Yassko-Kishinev operation | 84 | 114 | 233 | 264 | 162 |
| Vistula-Oder operation | 155 | 209 | 423 | 950 | 466 |
| East Prussian operation | 122 | 152 | 341 | 491 | 250 |
| Berlin operation | 179 | 227 | 520 | 894 | 666 |

Table 5 shows that the number of forces and weapons engaged in
strategic operations had a general tendency to increase. There is a
particularly pronounced increase in the amount of combat materiel.

It is evident from the table that during the war the number of troops engaged in strategic operations increased by a factor of 2, that of guns and mortars by a factor of 3 to 5, tanks by 3 to 9, and aircraft by 3 to 6.

The increased amounts of combat materiel at the fronts and in the armies caused qualitative changes in the ground forces as the main means of destroying enemy forces. The continuous increase in the technical and tactical capabilities of artillery and tanks and the further motorization of the ground forces resulted in greater firepower, and increased their striking power, their range of advance, as well as their mobility and maneuverability. These qualitative changes in the ground forces brought about an increase in the decisiveness and effectiveness of strategic offensives, which made possible the destruction of large enemy formations and the liberation of vast territories containing important economic areas and political centers. Table 6 presents data on the decisiveness and effectiveness of the strategic operations.

TABLE 6

*The Effectiveness of Strategic Offensive Operations
during the Great Patriotic War*

| Operation | Number of Enemy Divisions | | Enemy Divisions Destroyed ( % ) | |
| --- | --- | --- | --- | --- |
| | Taking Part in Combat | Destroyed in the Course of the Operation | With Respect to the Number of Divisions Taking Part in the Operation | With Respect to the Number of Divisions Active on the Soviet-German Front |
| Moscow counter-offensive | 74 | 25 | 34 | 13 |
| Stalingrad counter-offensive | 65 | 49 | 75 | 18 |
| Kursk counter-offensive | 92 | 39 | 33 | 13 |
| The offensive in the Western Ukraine | 135 | 76 | 56 | 31 |
| Byelorussia operation | 114 | 76 | 68 | 32 |
| Vistula-Oder operation | 70 | 58 | 83 | 32 |
| Berlin operation | 116 | 100 | 90 | 55 |

It is evident from Table 6 that the major strategic operations resulted in the destruction of 34 to 90 per cent of the opposing enemy
divisions.

As a rule, a strategic operation was executed by the combined forces
of several fronts, and included long-range [strategic] air force and in
the coastal regions naval forces. The use of several fronts in a strategic
operation appeared as a new feature in Soviet military art during the
Great Patriotic War. During prewar years, our theoretical literature
maintained the view that offensive operations with strategic objectives
were to be conducted by one front and that offensive operations could
best be developed within a front capable of achieving major strategic
missions.

As the Soviet Armed Forces grew in strength and became experienced
in organizing and directing the offensives of the Great Patriotic War, the
strategic operation involving several fronts gradually came into existence.

The start of combined operation by a group of fronts dates back to
the period of the Moscow counteroffensive carried out by the forces of
the Kalinin and western fronts together with the right wing of the southwestern front. Later, there was the Stalingrad offensive conducted by
three fronts. With the Kursk counteroffensive in 1943, the combined
strategic operation by a group of fronts became firmly established in
Soviet military practice.

During the Great Patriotic War, a combined operation of a group
of fronts was prepared, supplied and controlled under the direct leadership of the Stavka, with the active participation of headquarters of the
fronts. Centralized control of the operation by the Stavka assured co-
ordination of the efforts of the various fronts with respect to time, place,
and objective, especially under conditions of radical and serious changes
in the situation; in the final analysis, it assured the accomplishment of
major military and political aims.

The increased scope of the strategic operations was primarily due to
further strengthening of the Soviet Union's military and economic
base, which made it possible to raise the technical capability of the
Armed Forces and to increase troop mobility and artillery range. The
increased scope was also strongly influenced by the motorization of supply transport and the accelerated rate of railroad restoration, which
made possible more systematic supply of the forces with ammunition and
other materiel during operations.

Another highly important accomplishment of Soviet military strategy
was the solution of the problem of breaking through the enemy's strategic
front. During the Great Patriotic War, the Red Army repeatedly broke

through the enemy's strategic front. This was achieved once in the winter of 1942–1943, once in the winter of 1944, twice in the summer of 1944, and once again in January 1945 in the direction of Berlin.

Penetration of the enemy's strategic front opened the way for the Soviet forces to develop offensives in great depth.

The German military leadership required considerable time and large forces to close the gap and to form a new defensive front. To do this, it was compelled to withdraw its troops a considerable distance (500 to 600 kilometers [310–370 miles]) and to transfer to the breakthrough sector from thirty to sixty divisions from other sectors of the Soviet-German front or from Germany and occupied countries. The enemy's new defense line was usually located along major natural barriers such as rivers or mountains.

The successful penetration of the enemy's strategic front was accomplished by forming major strategic groupings, which could deliver a strong initial blow and defeat the opposing enemy forces within a short time, and by reinforcing the development of the offensive in depth, especially by introducing large armored forces. The rapid rate at which the Soviet troops advanced also aided breakthrough of the enemy's strategic front. The Soviet troops were more mobile than those of the enemy and prevented the enemy from organizing temporary defense lines. The availability to the Soviet military leadership of a sufficient quantity of strategic reserves and their proper employment as well as the skillful choice of the form of strategic operations also contributed to success.

In the Great Patriotic War, the front was very long, and a variety of problems arose during the course of armed combat. Soviet military leadership was required to solve the most complex problems, e.g., the strategic co-ordination of major groups of armed forces operating in different areas in accordance with a unified plan. Essentially, strategic co-operation consisted of the co-ordination of the time, place, and purpose of the efforts of formations and units of various types of armed forces participating in strategic advances—all aimed at gaining the strategic goals of the operation. When the Stavka developed the plans for an operation, it established the basic features of the strategic co-ordination. They became manifest in the missions assigned to major formations of Soviet forces, in the determination of the role and function of each front in the strategic operation, in the conduct of the strategic offensive, in the sequence of the tasks assigned to the fronts, and in the missions assigned to the various types of armed forces as well as the methods of their execution.

Several techniques were used to achieve strategic co-operation. In some cases this was done by co-ordinating strategic formations of Soviet troops, which were operating in different areas and carrying out independent missions (this was used successfully during the winter operations of 1942–1943, in the summer and autumn operations of 1943, and in the concluding stages of the war in 1945). In other cases, it was accomplished by conducting successive operations by groups of fronts in various theaters of military operation in contiguous strategic areas. This method of strategic co-ordination was widely used in almost all offensives, but was especially successful in the summer and autumn operations of 1944, when the Red Army delivered six successive powerful assaults against the enemy. These assaults not only tied down the enemy over an extended front, but also prevented him from using his reserves and undertaking any serious countermeasures. Each attack created favorable conditions for a succeeding attack in a different area.

In strategic defense, strategic co-ordination combined defensive and offensive operations in several strategic areas. This hampered the enemy's ability to strengthen his main formation by transferring forces from other sectors of the front and enabled us to slow down the enemy offensive, thus giving us time to assemble reserves for a counteroffensive.

The Ground Forces co-operated with the Navy in carrying out combined operations in the coastal areas (Odessa, the Crimea, Petsamo-Kirkenes, and the East Prussian operations), in protecting the sea flanks of the Ground Forces, and in maintaining their lines of communication.

Strategic co-operation between fronts, groups of fronts, and the National PVO was achieved by co-ordinating the efforts in the battle against the enemy's air force.

However, the Soviet Command also committed serious errors in the important problem of organizing and achieving strategic co-ordination. Thus, during the winter offensives of 1941–1942 the Soviet Supreme High Command failed to properly co-ordinate the Kalinin, western, and Bryansk fronts in the western area with the forces of the Leningrad and Volkhov fronts around Leningrad. This was one of the reasons for the unsatisfactory outcome of the winter operations of 1941–1942 and for the difficult situation in which our forces found themselves during the spring of 1942. There was no real strategic co-ordination during the Kharkov offensive in May of 1942; as a result, the offensive of the southwestern front directed at Kharkov proved to be isolated and lacked active support by adjacent fronts. This enabled the enemy to maneuver his forces successfully and deliver strong blows to the flanks of the southwestern front assault formations, which resulted in the defeat of our advancing forces. There were also inadequacies in the co-ordination of the Ground Forces with the Navy. Thus, in destroying the enemy's Kurland formation, the Soviet military leadership failed to blockade the enemy from the sea, a failure that not only hindered the destruction of this enemy formation but also complicated the military operations of our forces during the winter of 1944–1945 in the area of Berlin, where the enemy transferred ten divisions from Kurland.

The success of a strategic offensive and the expansion of its scope depended to a considerable degree on the availability and utilization of strategic reserves. These reserves were organized and replenished in different ways, depending on the availability of forces and the conditions of combat. During the first and second stages of the Great Patriotic War, the Stavka reserves were primarily created from new units. Subsequently, the strategic reserves were mainly replenished by withdrawing units and formations from fronts that were concluding operations in various areas (the 4th Ukrainian front after the liberation of the Crimea, and the Karelian front at the conclusion of hostilities with Finland), or from units on those fronts that, because of changing conditions, were able to achieve their missions with smaller forces (the 1st and 2nd Baltic fronts blockading the enemy's Kurland formation).

During the Great Patriotic War, the major portion of the strategic reserves was used in principal [battle] areas, where the Stavka sent from 50 to 70 per cent of its reserves.

At certain stages of the war, the Stavka reinforced the front with 16 to 155 infantry divisions, 5 to 16 cavalry divisions, 57 to 68 infantry brigades, 24 to 25 tank brigades, 3 to 22 tank corps, and 4 to 10 mechanized corps from its reserves.

It should be stressed that strategic reserves were used to solve the most diverse problems during the Great Patriotic War:

1. To create strategic formations in the preparation of operations; thus, in the summer operation of 1944, five armies, two tank armies, and two air armies were used for this purpose; in preparing the winter offensive of 1944–1945, eleven armies and four tank armies were used.

2. To strengthen the fronts for counteroffensives, which was the case at Moscow when the western front was reinforced by four armies.

3. To build up forces for an offensive in the area of the main assault; during the summer offensive of 1943, the Stavka transferred nine armies and two tank armies from its reserves to the fronts for this purpose.

4. To protect the flank of the main assault forces by launching an offensive in an adjacent sector; thus, during the winter of 1943–1944, to safeguard the flank of the main assault formation conducting the offensive in the Western Ukraine, the Stavka organized a second Bye-

lorussian front at the boundary of the first Ukrainian and first Byelorussian fronts, and transferred to it two armies and one air army from
the reserves.

5. To strengthen the fronts for contingencies arising during a strategic
offensive, such as the Byelorussian operation, when the first Baltic front
was reinforced by two armies after a change in the situation.

6. To strengthen the forces operating along the outer line of an
encirclement; for this purpose, the Stalingrad front, battling the German Kotelnikov counteroffensive, was reinforced by the Second Guards
Army in December of 1942.

7. To reinforce the fronts for offensive operations after halting an
enemy counteroffensive; the First Guards Army was thus used at Zhito-
mir in December of 1943 and the Ninth Guards Army in the region of
Lake Balaton in March of 1945.

It is evident from the experience of the past war that the Stavka,
which constantly followed the development of the armed conflict, carried
out the necessary regroupings and provided strategic reserves in proper
time to those sectors where reinforcements would have the greatest
effect and most influence on the development of the offensive. The use
of large strategic reserves guaranteed the necessary superiority in forces
and weapons over the enemy, made possible the build-up of forces for
developing offensives along the front, as well as in depth, and also made
it possible for the front to solve new problems arising during the course
of an operation. However, serious errors were also committed in the
utilization of strategic reserves. This applied primarily to the first stage
of war, when the Soviet military leadership, attempting to develop offensives in all the main strategic areas, scattered its forces and weapons,
which made it impossible to achieve decisive superiority in any area.

The Great Patriotic War provided very valuable experience in solving the very real and complex problem of conducting armed combat
during the initial period of war. The difficulty of solving the problem was
aggravated by the suddenness of the enemy attack; the latter was due
to miscalculation of the time when Nazi Germany would attack the
Soviet Union.

The experience of the initial period of World War II demonstrated
quite clearly that the aggressor had prepared for the invasion by organizing strong, well-prepared armies during peacetime. The existence of
such armies made it possible for the enemy to start war suddenly and
immediately develop decisive air and ground operations. From the very
first days of the war, the countries under attack were forced to resist
the assault of the enemy's main armies under extremely unfavorable
conditions, and simultaneously to mobilize and deploy their armed forces

and to shift the economy to a war footing. However, Soviet military strategy failed to draw the appropriate practical conclusion from this lesson.

The political and higher military leadership of the Soviet Union had the necessary information concerning Germany's planned aggression against our country long before the war. They knew about the preparatory concentration and deployment of German forces along our borders. Thus, it was possible to conclude that the threat of war was genuine and imminent and to take the measures necessary to increase the level of force combat readiness and the level of readiness to mobilize the country to be ready to repel an aggression and prevent a sudden enemy attack.

However, Stalin's strong preconceptions in evaluating the military and political situation on the eve of the war led to serious errors in the preparation of the country and Armed Forces for the forthcoming war.

The error of our prewar theoretical views on the meaning and nature of the initial war period also played a negative role in this. Our military theory did not take sufficient account of the fact that a sudden attack by a previously mobilized enemy army, and the massive use of tanks and aircraft in the early stages of the war for a combined strike in great depth, would radically change the requirements for strategic concentration and deployment of the armed forces of countries under attack, and consequently would change the entire nature of their operations during the initial period of war.

As a result of errors committed by our higher military leadership, orders were not issued prior to the outbreak of the war to increase the combat readiness of forces stationed in the border regions or to move forward and deploy covering armies along the planned forward defense lines.

The Soviet military leadership knew that the enemy could forestall our strategic concentration and deployment, but it lacked a realistic view of the actual situation; it underestimated the enemy's potential and overestimated our own. As a result, the Soviet military leadership did not display the necessary flexibility in directing the Armed Forces (in anticipation of the probable area of enemy attack) to organize appropriate defense formations capable of repelling the initial massive enemy attacks. This would have ensured the complete mobilization, concentration, and deployment of our Armed Forces.

The General Staff's directive, sent on the night of June 22,[16] to alert the troops stationed in the border areas, was very belated and

---

[16] U.S. ED. NOTE—Reference is made to a directive issued in the early hours of June 22, 1941, the day Germany launched its attack against the Soviet Union.

could not change the unfavorable situation. In addition, many units and formations of the military districts along the border received this directive only after the German forces had launched their attack.

The delay in the decision to alert the troops of the Western military district and direct them to occupy defense lines specified by the plan for the protection of the state border was one of the serious miscalculations of the initial period of the Great Patriotic War. The forward deployment of our troops under conditions of ongoing combat operations and of German air supremacy led to unjustifiably great losses.

The serious situation of our troops in the military districts on the western border was aggravated by considerable inadequacies in the operational and unit rear areas. The latter were not capable of supplying the troops under the difficult conditions that prevailed during the initial period of war.

This predetermined, to a considerable extent, the unfavorable outcome of armed conflict for the Soviet Armed Forces during the initial period.

The country was confronted with the need to mobilize, concentrate, and deploy its Armed Forces to repel an enemy who was already invading our territory.

Because of the incompleted deployment of the forces in border military districts, their disposition at the beginning of the war was extremely disadvantageous for us.

The defense lines along which the divisions of the first echelon of the Western military districts were to be deployed were extremely close to the border, which exposed them to enemy attack and greatly hampered their deployment. The more powerful troop formations of the Western and Kiev military districts, which were being deployed in the Bialystok and Lvov salients, were widely enveloped by the enemy and immediately subjected to flanking attacks. At the same time, the areas of the most probable enemy attacks were covered by insufficient forces. In addition, these groups were far from fully assembled by the beginning of hostilities. More than 35 per cent of the units of the first strategic echelon did not have time to reach their assigned areas. In general, the forces of the military districts of the Western border were widely scattered along the front and in depth; as a result, their operations were poorly co-ordinated.

The enemy was able to bring all his strength to bear on the weak Soviet forces located near the border, and then to engage the major covering forces. Then, after penetrating in depth, he was able to attack the second echelon forces of the border military districts.

The assaults of the Fascist air force and artillery and the powerful blows of the enemy's ground forces caused high losses among our troops, particularly to the air forces, and resulted in serious destruction to border towns, communications and control points, disorganizing the control of troops from the very first moment.

As a result of this disorganization, the front commanders could not properly evaluate the full seriousness of the situation and make appropriate decisions. The higher military leadership, lacking a true picture of the developments, attempted to execute the prewar defense plan. The latter provided, in the event of German attack against the Soviet Union, for a powerful retaliatory attack in the direction of Suwalki and Lublin, and subsequently, for seizing the strategic initiative. With this in view, at 8:30–9:00 a.m. on June 22, 1941, the People's Commissariat for War sent Directive No. 2 ordering the ground forces and air forces of the border districts to destroy enemy forces that had crossed the state border. By the evening of June 22, the troops were assigned an even more decisive mission: to encircle and destroy the Suwalki and Sokalski enemy formations and to occupy the regions of Suwalki and Lublin by June 24. However, the attempt to carry out these orders was completely unsuccessful. Already by the fourth day of the war there arose a real threat of enemy mobile forces reaching the West Dvina River. It became evident that the covering armies were incapable of liquidating the enemy forces, which had penetrated and advanced to a great depth. The offensive plans that the Soviet military leadership had attempted to put into operation were thwarted by the entire course of events. A radical revision of strategic concepts was needed.

Under the existing circumstances, the Stavka decided on June 25 to establish a defense line, using the troops of the northwestern and western fronts along the West Dvina and Dnieper Rivers. The Stavka created a group of reserve armies composed of the 22nd, 20th, 21st, and 19th Armies to prepare and occupy defense positions along a line from Sushchevo, Vitebsk, Chernigov, the Desna River, and the Dnieper River to Kremenchug.

However, our troops did not succeed in organizing a continuous defense front.

The enemy forestalled our occupying the above defense lines by capturing a bridgehead on the West Dvina River on June 29 and cutting the lines of retreat for the main forces of the western front in the region west of Minsk, and then approached Bobruysk.

To prevent an enemy breakthrough toward Moscow, the Stavka decided to create a deeply echeloned defense in the Moscow area. The Stavka reserve army group were to move forward and establish a defense line along Kraslava, the Polotskii fortified region, Vitebsk, Orsha, and the Dnieper River up to Loyev. The 16th Army was transferred there from the Ukraine. The 24th and 28th Armies were to be deployed some 180 to 200 kilometers [110–120 miles] east of this line. At the same time, one of the Stavka reserve army groups joined the western front, which in effect meant the creation of a new western front. The armies composing the front were still concentrating by the end of June. Thirty-nine out of fifty divisions arrived at the Idritsa-Loyev defense line, while the others were still en route.

The mobile enemy forces reached the Soviet defense line from Disna to Zhlobin late on July 9, having seized a bridgehead in the area of Disna and having captured Vitebsk.

In the southwestern area, our troops offered stubborn resistance to the enemy and launched repeated strong counterattacks. However, by July 10, they were forced to retreat to the line along Korosten, Proskurov, Mogilev Podolsk, and the Prut River.

Thus, the Great Patriotic War began with the commitment of the major forces of both sides. Within the first ten to twelve days, 70 to 80 per cent of the ground forces, and the entire air forces of both sides were engaged in bloody combat. These operations were rapid, intense, and involved broad maneuvers of forces and weapons.

The unfavorable outcome of the initial period of the war was greatly influenced by the fact that we had not worked out the problems of strategic leadership of the Armed Forces by the beginning of the war. As a result, leadership in the command of the armed forces was quite inadequate during the initial period of the war.

The experience of the Great Patriotic War enriched Soviet strategy in the field of the organization and conduct of strategic defense. As we mentioned before, in our prewar theoretical views, strategic defense was envisaged as a form of combat accompanying strategic offense. It was presumed that strategic defense would be used in areas of secondary importance to conserve manpower and materiel for organizing strong assault formations in decisive areas or in theaters of military operation.

The Soviet military leadership used this technique three times during the Great Patriotic War. In two cases, during the summer of 1941 and 1942, it was a forced measure, and in one case, during the summer of 1943, it was planned. However, in each case the objective was to repel (retard) the enemy offensive, to exhaust and decimate his troops, to gain time and to prepare the conditions for a decisive counteroffensive. But the reasons for the transition to strategic defense were different. Thus, during the summer of 1941, the strategic defense was made necessary by sudden enemy attack and the loss of strategic initiative because of the unfortunate outcome of the initial war period, which led to a radical change in the balance of forces in favor of the enemy. By this time, a considerable portion of the strategic reserves (five out of nine armies) had already been committed. The strategic defense of the Red Army during the summer of 1942 was the result of the defeat of our forces in the Crimean operations and at Kharkov, during which the Red Army sustained tremendous losses, totaling approximately seven armies. At the same time, the enemy transferred an additional 24 divisions to the Soviet-German front. This changed the balance of forces in the enemy's favor.

The transition to strategic defense during the summer of 1943, unlike the changes in previous years, was planned. The Soviet military leadership, which by the summer of 1943 held the strategic initiative and had large reserves (nine armies, two tank armies, and a number of independent formations: 63 infantry divisions, 10 mechanized corps, 13 tank corps, and 5 cavalry corps), was able to forestall the enemy and take the offensive. However, it was decided to pass temporarily to the strategic defense to compel the enemy to initiate the offensive and to exhaust and drain his assault formations by defensive combat; then, having moved up fresh strategic reserves, to launch a decisive counteroffensive.

Soviet military strategy solved the following highly important problems of strategic defense during the war: determining the area of the major enemy attack, organizing a strategic defense and re-establishing an [unbroken] strategic front, devising methods of conducting defense and using strategic reserves, and creating the conditions for a counteroffensive.

The success of the strategic defense in 1941 depended to a great extent on the correct determination of the areas for concentrating the main effort of the Armed Forces. Already in the very first days, the Stavka reached the correct conclusion that the western area was the most important and decisive of the three strategic areas, since it was in this very area that the enemy committed his strongest formations and delivered his main assault. This area was also important in that it was the shortest route for the German forces to reach the central industrial region and the capital of our country, Moscow. To a considerable extent, the stability of the entire strategic front was determined by our troops' successful defense in this area. This is the reason that the Stavka sent the main portion of its reserves to reinforce the western front: 150 infantry divisions and 44 infantry brigades, or 52 per cent of the divisions and 47 per cent of the brigades, were sent to the army in the field between June 22 and December 1, 1941. Such effective utilization of the reserves enabled the Soviet military leadership to halt the enemy advance and to shift the balance of forces in our favor in this most important area, thereby decisively influencing the outcome of the struggle in 1941.

In the defensive campaign of 1942, the Soviet Supreme High Command initially assumed that the enemy's main attack would be in the western area and the secondary attack in the southwest area from the Donbas toward Rostov and further on to the Northern Caucasus. To a certain extent, this opinion was based on the fact that the most powerful formation of German forces, organized during the winter operations of 1941–1942, was located in the western area by the spring of 1942; it was also based on the fact that Moscow was the capital of the country and an important economic and strategic center.

However, the events during the summer of 1942 demonstrated that the Soviet Supreme High Command had not correctly anticipated the enemy's intentions. Although the enemy maintained a strong formation in the central, or Moscow, area, he concentrated his main efforts on the southern flank of the front and, as is known, delivered his main assault during the summer of 1942 in the southwest area.

The enemy assault in this area led to the defeat of our forces, the withdrawal of our entire left flank beyond the Don River, and the invasion of the Northern Caucasus by the enemy. The Soviet military leadership had not anticipated the amount of forces and weapons needed to hold if the German forces invaded this area.

It was not until early July of 1942, when the German offensive toward Voronezh was already under way, that the Soviet Supreme High Command realized that the enemy was making his main attack in the southwest area instead of the west.

The Soviet Command showed real skill in strategic prediction during the preparation of the summer operations of 1943. The Nazi plans to launch their main operations in the Kursk area were estimated quite accurately two to two and a half months before the battle of Kursk; this made it possible for our forces to make complete preparations for repelling the enemy.

In the Kursk sector of the front, which comprised 13 per cent of the entire length of the Soviet-German front, we concentrated 28 per cent of the personnel, 20 per cent of the guns and mortars, over 40 per cent of the tanks and self-propelled artillery, and 33 per cent of the combat aircraft available to the army in the field by the summer of 1943.

Depending on the strategic situation, available forces and weapons and time, the depths of Soviet strategic defense in the past war, including manned defense lines as well as prepared [reserve] lines of defense, varied from 250 to 600 kilometers [150–360 miles]. In 1941 (during the middle of July), it reached 250 to 300 kilometers [150–180 miles] on the Moscow area from the upper Dnieper to the Mozhaysk line of defense. In the Leningrad area, the depth of defense varied from 100 to 120 kilometers [60–72 miles] and involved the creation of the Luga defense line, the Krasnogvardeysk fortified region, and the defense lines directly on the outskirts of Leningrad. With the advance of the German forces from the Dnieper to the east, the depth of the defenses were increased by creation of the Moscow defense zone and also by the construction of state defense lines east of Moscow.

However, the effective use of the prepared lines of defense was not possible. First, the enemy, who had superior mobility, usually prevented us from occupying these lines of defense. Second, our troops, which were retreating from the front because of great losses, were usually unable to organize a strong defense on the prepared rear lines, and the Soviet military leadership lacked the strategic reserves necessary to occupy these defense lines in advance. Of the 291 infantry divisions and 66 infantry brigades transferred from the Stavka reserve to the army in the field during the summer operations of 1941, only 66 divisions and 4 brigades were used to man the [reserve] defense lines in advance.

By the summer of 1942, the total depth of the fortified defense line, including the rear defense line in preparation on the Volga, increased 500 to 600 kilometers [300–360 miles]. During the summer of 1943, though, when the Soviet military leadership held the strategic initiative and was planning a powerful offensive with decisive aims after repelling the enemy advance, the depth of the prepared defense zone did not exceed 300 to 350 kilometers [180–210 miles].

During the initial period of war, Soviet troops gained considerable experience in re-establishing a strategic defense front. During this time, as is known, the enemy succeeded in penetrating our strategic front four times to a depth of 300 to 500 kilometers [180–300 miles]. The creation of a continuous and stable strategic defense front after it was penetrated in the summer of 1941, when the Soviet forces were considerably weakened and continuously retreating under enemy attack, was possible only because the Stavka had considerable strategic reserves and sent them to the front at the right time. Thus, during the period from June 27 to July 10, 1941, the Stavka placed five armies from its reserves at the disposal of the commander of the western front to re-establish the strategic defense front. Later, an additional thirteen armies were sent to create a large strategic formation in the western area. The stabilized front in the areas of Leningrad and Kiev was also made possible by the reserves of the Stavka which sent there 140 infantry divisions and 50 infantry brigades.

In the summer of 1942, the strategic front on the southern flank [of the over-all front] was re-established by strategic reserves. To form a continuous front along the Don and in the Northern Caucasus, the Stavka sent to the appropriate fronts, during July and August of 1942, six armies, two tank armies, and a number of independent formations with a total of 26 infantry divisions, 25 infantry brigades, up to five tank corps, and one cavalry corps.

In some cases, the strategic defense front was re-established by re-grouping forces and weapons of the active fronts, and by using the retreating forces. Thus, after the October 1941 enemy breakthrough of the defense of the Bryansk, Reserve [sic], and western fronts, the strategic front was re-established along the Mozhaysk defense line by regrouping the left flank of the northwestern front and the right flank of the western front, and by using the Stavka reserves.

Thus, only the strategic reserves at the disposal of the Stavka made it possible to re-establish a deeply echeloned strategic defense front (from 250 to 500 kilometers [150–300 miles]), and to form large strategic formations in the most important strategic areas, and thus ensure the success of the defensive operations.

One of the most characteristic features of the Red Army's strategic defense was its active nature. Stubborn defense of prepared lines and major towns was combined with strong counterattacks and offensive operations in several areas by the forces of one or two fronts. Thus, for example, stubborn defense in 1941 of prepared lines in the most important strategic areas, such as Moscow, Leningrad, and Kiev-Rostov, was combined with strong counterattacks conducted during the battle of Smolensk and the Luga and Kiev defensive operations, the Tikhvin and Rostov counterattacks, etc. In 1942, stubborn defense of prepared lines was combined with strong Soviet counterattacks in the area of Voronezh, Stalingrad, and the Northern Caucasus, and with the offensive operations of the troops of the Leningrad and Volkhov fronts in the Leningrad area, the troops of the northwestern front against the Dem-yansk enemy formation, and the forces of the Kalinin and western fronts in the Smolensk area. During the defensive actions of summer and autumn of 1941, and in 1942, the Red Army conducted more than 30 operations by whole fronts. The highly active nature of our defense, even during the initial period of the war, made it possible to retard the offense of the enemy and slow his rate of advance. Thus, whereas during the first 18 days of the war the Germans advanced at an average daily rate of 20 to 30 kilometers [12–18 miles], subsequently, in September and October of 1941, their average daily rate of advance in the northwestern area was reduced from 20 to 5 kilometers [3 miles], in the western area from 30 to 2.5 kilometers [1.5 miles], and in the southwest area from 20 to 6 kilometers [3.6 miles]. Because of our stubborn and highly active defense, the enemy was forced to hold significant forces [in reserve] to parry our attacks, which weakened his own assault formations, considerably influenced the rate of his advance, and frustrated his plan for waging a "Blitzkrieg war." The German forces sustained tremendous losses. During the first six months of the war alone, according to the data of the German High Command, the German ground forces lost more than 800,000 troops on the Soviet-German front.

Defensive operations in the most important strategic areas were conducted simultaneously by several co-ordinated fronts. This involved the participation of long-range air forces and in coastal regions the co-operation of the naval forces. The length of a defensive front, in specific strategic areas, varied from 450 to 800 kilometers [270–480 miles]. As the Soviet Armed Forces increased in strength and the balance of forces changed in our favor, particularly after the Soviet offensives during the winter of 1941–1942, the enemy, no longer able to conduct offensive operations along the entire strategic front, could conduct offensives only in individual strategic areas. Consequently, the length of our fronts in strategic defense operations constantly diminished.

Whereas in the summer of 1941, defensive operations were carried out along the entire 4,000 kilometer [2,400 miles] front, as early as the summer of 1942 the Red Army conducted defensive operations on a 750 to 2,100 kilometer [450–1,260 miles] front and in the summer of 1943, on a front only 600 kilometers [360 miles] in length. The conduct of defense along considerably smaller sectors of the front enabled the Supreme High Command to make more effective use of its strategic reserves for strengthening the defense and delivering counterattacks in these areas.

The larger strategic defensive operations were those of Smolensk, Leningrad, Moscow, Stalingrad, the Caucasus, and Kursk. Some of these operations for a variety of reasons, as is known, ended in the defeat of our troops. This was due mainly to the overestimation of our own capabilities and underestimation of that of the enemy, particularly the mobility of his tank groups and armies, which, in a number of cases, led to the encirclement of our forces. Another cause was the unjustifiable retention of frontline troops in defensive positions in the face of a threat of encirclement, which was the case in June of 1941 with the forces of the western front in the Bialystok salient, and in September of 1941 in the defense operation of the forces of the southwestern front on the left bank of the Dnieper. Inadequate operational and strategic co-ordination and the poor provision of the forces were also contributing factors. An example of the latter was the defensive operations of the forces of the Central, Bryansk, and southwestern fronts in August of 1941, and the defensive operations of the forces of the Bryansk and southwestern fronts in the area of Voronezh in July of 1942. The Kursk defensive operation was better planned, prepared, and executed by the Soviet military leadership with regard to conducting the operation as well as materiel and equipment. During this operation the German forces sustained tremendous losses and could not penetrate our operational defense, while on the seventh to the tenth day after the start of the enemy offensive, our troops launched a counterattack, which resulted in the defeat of the enemy.

In spite of the unfavorable outcome of the initial period of war, the Red Army was nevertheless able to cope with the organization and conduct of strategic defense. By conducting a strategic defense and skillfully co-ordinating its operations, the Soviet military leadership was able to exhaust and decimate the enemy, and prepare the conditions for a radical change in the course of the war. As a result of its active method of strategic defense, the Soviet military leadership gained a wealth of experience in organizing and conducting offensive as well as defensive operations.

These were the primary lessons of the Great Patriotic War in organizing and conducting strategic defense.

Strategic utilization of the various branches of the Armed Forces was also accomplished successfully during the Great Patriotic War. Soviet military strategy was based on the principle that victory in war can be achieved only by the combined efforts of all the branches of the Armed Forces; accordingly, the problem of most effective use of the strongest characteristics of each branch was fully investigated. At the same time, the role and significance of each branch of the Armed Forces, and consequently, its relative importance in the composition of the Armed Forces, did not remain unchanged during the last war. During the war, these varied according to the increase in our military and economic potential, scientific and technological developments, and the changing nature of the tasks confronting the Armed Forces.

During the Great Patriotic War the largest branch of the Armed Forces was the Ground Forces. They contained from 80 to 86 per cent of the entire personnel of the Armed Forces. Theirs was the main role in the conduct of war, since they formed the basis of our strategic formations. The most important tasks confronting the Soviet Armed Forces during the last war were mainly accomplished by the Ground Forces. In defense, they were the force that broke up the enemy assault. In stubborn battle, they exhausted and decimated the enemy, re-established the strategic front, and delivered powerful counterattacks against the enemy. In offensives, they were the decisive force for breaking up the enemy's strategic front, destroying his formations, and capturing his territory.

The Ground Forces were extensively developed during the Great Patriotic War, primarily by increasing their striking potential and firepower as well as their mobility.

The infantry, which was the main element of the Ground Forces, manifested high combat capabilities and the ability to operate in any terrain, at any time or season, and, in conjunction with tanks, artillery, and aircraft, to execute successfully the most complex missions. The infantry's main method of operation was close-range fire, which resulted in high losses of personnel during the last war.

The armored forces were the main striking power of the Ground Forces during the last war. The appearance of large tank formations and units decisively changed the nature of operations. In addition to carrying out important independent operational missions, they made possible rapid penetration through the entire depth of enemy defenses, the encirclement and destruction of large enemy formations, and rapid pursuit of the enemy to great distances.

The next most important branch of the Ground Forces was the artillery, which became even more important during the war. It became the principal and decisive means of firepower for neutralizing and destroying the enemy in defensive as well as offensive operations. The extensive development of rocket artillery in the Red Army, which made it possible to create a high concentration of fire within a very short time, significantly contributed to increase the firepower of the artillery. The use of artillery in the past war was characterized by marked increase in the volume of fire per unit of time, high mobility on the battlefield, the destruction of the enemy's defense to a great depth, and, finally, the destruction and neutralization of the enemy throughout a large area.

At the same time, the Great Patriotic War demonstrated that our Ground Forces, as the main branch of the Armed Forces, required further improvement in mobility and firepower.

The Air Force was the second most important branch of the Armed Forces during the past war. It was used extensively for both defense and offense. The main efforts of our Air Force were directed at supporting the operations of the Ground Forces and destroying enemy troops and equipment directly on the field of battle. Such missions accounted for more than 46 per cent of the total sorties flown by our Air Force during the past war.

During the past war, the question of the participation of the Air Force in joint offensive operations with the Ground Forces and Navy was successfully solved by means of air offensives. This type of support for offensive operations fully proved itself during the war. The first air offensive was planned and partly executed during the Stalingrad counteroffensive. It was used during the battle of Kursk and in the operations of 1944–1945, by which time this support had been fully developed.

The next most important strategic problem involving the use of the Air Force was the battle for air superiority. Approximately 35 per cent of all the sorties flown during the past war were for this purpose.

The main technique used in the battle for air supremacy during the past war was aerial combat by fighter planes. The destruction of enemy aircraft on airfields by special air operations did not find extensive application during the war, even though this method was the most effective. An average of 30 sorties were required for each German airplane destroyed in the air, whereas only 5 sorties were required for each airplane destroyed on airfields. The relatively small proportion of Soviet air operations against enemy airfields was due to the numerical and qualitative inferiority of our bombers, the complexity of this type of operation, and considerable underestimation by some air commanders of the effectiveness of strikes against airfields.

During the Great Patriotic War, the Air Force also carried out independent missions by means of special air operations. These were primarily to destroy large enemy air formations. These operations employed not only the long-range air force, but also the [tactical] air armies of the fronts.

Independent air operations were also conducted to neutralize and destroy enemy economic and political centers. However, because the Soviet Air Force lacked the necessary means to do this during the past war, such operations were rare and conducted with limited forces; they were not able to exert any major influence on the course of the armed conflict.* Consequently, during the war we really were not able to solve the problem of destroying the enemy's deep strategic rear areas or to undermine his economic potential and national morale. The long-range Air Force flew a total of only 215,000 sorties; of these only 3.9 per cent were aimed at enemy economic centers.

---

* During these operations, our air force flew only 6,607 sorties, which comprised only 0.2 per cent of the total sorties flown by our air force during the war.

And finally, independent air operations were conducted to disrupt enemy railroad and naval transport and to assist partisan forces. Such operations were mainly conducted in 1943–1944.

Thus, during the past war the operations of the Soviet Air Force were primarily tactical in nature. The tactical air force played the decisive role in these operations; it carried out more than 76 per cent of all sorties flown by the Soviet Air Force.

Aerial reconnaissance, particularly of the strategic type, reached full development during the war. The great need for air reconnaissance information and the lack of a special reconnaissance plane compelled our command to use fighter, attack and bomber forces for this purpose, which flew up to 80 per cent of all reconnaissance sorties.

One weakness of the Soviet Air Force was the absence of special military air transport capability, although some was constructed during the course of the war. This limited the use of airborne troops and the organization of air supply for rapidly advancing forces, particularly in the concluding stages of strategic operations.

The National PVO played a very important role in the Great Patriotic War. The war demonstrated that the organization of reliable air defense for rear targets in the country was an important task. Not only did the uninterrupted functioning of the country depend on the successful defense of these targets from air attacks, but also the morale of the people, and consequently the course of the entire armed conflict. Therefore, the PVO devoted its main efforts to the defense of large political and administrative centers, and important industrial regions and facilities. In 1941–1942, this required the use of 60 to 87 per cent of the fighter force and from 60 to 80 per cent of the antiaircraft artillery of the National PVO. Later, when the Red Army began its strategic offensive, the number of forces and weapons assigned to the defense of rear facilities considerably diminished.

The next most important mission of the National PVO during the past war was to provide cover for attack formations and important targets at the front and army rear, and most important of all, to protect the front lines of communication at least up to a distance of 300 to 500 kilometers [180–300 miles] from the front. This was necessary, first, because the German military leadership used its air force almost exclusively over the battlefields and in the forward areas, and second, because our fronts usually were not provided with sufficient PVO forces and weapons for reliable protection from enemy air strikes against the numerous targets in the rear areas of the front and sometimes even against our assault formations.

The third important problem involving the use of the National PVO was the battle for air supremacy. This task was carried out in close co-operation with the [tactical] air forces of the fronts.

The National PVO also took part in antiaircraft operations. The PVO troops conducted these operations independently, as well as in conjunction with the fighter air force and antiaircraft artillery of the fronts and the naval forces.

In individual cases, the air units of the National PVO were also used to cover naval convoys and to escort bombers; however, this was not a typical function.

The war provided very instructive experience in the strategic use of the Navy.

As is generally known, our prewar theory took the view that in a future war, naval operations would primarily be confined to independent operations by large groups of surface vessels. However, the war upset these views. In strategic operations, the Navy ordinarily did not operate independently, but rather in conjunction with the Ground Forces and the Air Force. The Navy's principal efforts were directed at co-operating with the Ground Forces for the main task of defeating Nazi Germany and her armed forces.

The Navy carried out a variety of tasks when participating in joint strategic operations. The most important of these were the covering of the coastal flanks of the Ground Forces, coastal defense, amphibious landings on beaches and rivers, blockade of encircled formations from the sea, and assisting in the regrouping of Ground Forces.

In addition to participating in combined strategic operations with the Ground Forces and the Air Force, the Navy also carried out a number of independent strategic operations during the war, by attacking the enemy's maritime communications lines and defending our own communication lines on the seas, lakes, and rivers. The enemy's maritime communications were attacked to disrupt the supply of strategic materials to Germany (nickel from Finland, iron ore from Sweden, etc.), and to disrupt the supplying of enemy groups along the coast and to prevent their evacuation. During the first and second stages of the war, the battle against the enemy's naval communications was mainly conducted as a routine naval operation. However, combat experience demonstrated that this technique was not sufficiently effective and would not always guarantee execution of the task assigned to the naval forces.

After the second half of 1943 as a result of the improvement of our naval air forces by the introduction of [new] torpedo-aircraft, attack air units, and radar equipment, and when our naval personnel had gained more combat experience, special operations were employed against the enemy's maritime communications. This resulted in a marked increase in the effectiveness of naval combat operations. The number of enemy vessels sunk in 1944 was two and a half times greater than the number sunk in 1942.

Operations to protect our communication lines on the sea and lakes were another form of independent naval operations. The Great Patriotic War demonstrated that although the Soviet Union depended less on external communications than did other states, nevertheless, maritime communications were of extreme importance to us. More than 105 million tons of various types of cargo were transported during the course of the war.

The Northern Fleet played a particularly important role in securing naval communications. It is sufficient to indicate that it protected the passage of 1,624 convoys during the war, involving 4,414 different vessels. During the war, 1,022 convoys with 3,223 transport ships were escorted in the Baltic Sea.

All types of naval units were used in combat operations to protect maritime communications. In some operations, even the air forces assigned to the fronts and to the National PVO were drawn into this task.

Mine-laying operations should also be included among the Navy's independent operations. More than 40,000 mines were laid during the war.

On the whole this measure was justified and played a positive role, particularly in defending the sea approaches to Leningrad. However, the naval leadership did commit errors in carrying out this task for it was not justified in laying mine fields in the Black Sea in 1941. In view of the absence of major enemy naval forces in this theater, there was no practical need for this measure. These mine fields subsequently greatly hampered the operations of the Black Sea Fleet, causing more damage to us than to the Germans.

The roles of various types of naval forces were redefined during the Great Patriotic War. Before the war, naval aviation had been regarded as a supporting type of force; however, because of its combat capabilities and achievements it came to occupy a leading position *in the fleet*. Next in importance were submarines, which, in conjunction with the Air Force, were the basic weapons of armed conflict in naval theaters of operations. However, large surface vessels, which before the war were considered to be the mainstay of the fleet, lost their dominant position in carrying out naval missions.

During the Great Patriotic War, one of the most important strategic tasks was the constant improvement of the Armed Forces' organization.

The successful solution of this problem depended primarily on our country's economic capabilities to supply the Armed Forces with weapons and materiel.

The concept of military science that guided the Soviet Supreme High Command in organizing its Armed Forces during the war was that such organization was not arbitrary, but must correspond to the forms and methods of conducting armed combat. Changes in the organization of the Armed Forces were determined to a considerable extent by the development of new weapons and the improvement of military equipment already in use.

During the war an intensive effort was made to develop the organization of the Armed Forces, and types of forces that were most appropriate to our economic capabilities, to changes in the nature of military operations, to the solution of strategic problems during various stages of the war, and to the new types of weapons and combat equipment.

In organizing its Armed Forces during the Great Patriotic War, the Soviet Supreme High Command did not rely exclusively on any one branch or service of the Armed Forces. It proceeded on the principle that the strategic use of each branch of the Armed Forces must be based on the assignments that can be most effectively carried out by that branch.

When the Soviet Armed Forces entered the war, their organizational structure was basically suited to the requirements of modern warfare. However, because of the loss of economically important regions and the evacuation of industry to the east at the beginning of the war, the country's production of weapons and military equipment declined. It became extremely difficult to replace materiel losses and to equip the new formations. All of this made changes necessary in the organization of the forces.

Consequently, the infantry corps were disbanded and the infantry divisions were reorganized during the first months of the war. Some of the artillery was removed from the divisions. New types of infantry units and formations were organized, such as independent infantry brigades and regiments, as well as areas of field fortifications [sic]. Independent tank brigades and battalions were formed to replace the disbanded tank and mechanized divisions; the former were intended primarily for co-operation with the infantry. During this period a decision was made to form powerful artillery reserves for the Supreme High Command from units of disbanded infantry corps and by temporarily weakening the artillery of the infantry divisions. These reserves could be shifted to strengthen the forces in the most important area or sectors of the front.

During the period of strategic defense, the changes in the organizational structure of the Ground Forces also included the formation of special forces, including also the engineering forces. In the autumn of 1941, strong engineering reserves were necessary to build rear defense lines in the most important strategic areas. Ten armies [*sic*] of field engineers were formed and placed at the disposal of the Supreme High Command. When the situation changed, these armies were disbanded in the middle of 1942 and their personnel were used to form engineering units and formations.

The change in Air Force organization at the beginning of the war was manifested in the reduction of the number of planes in the regiments and number of regiments in divisions. Air Force regiments were reduced to a strength of between 32 and 22 aircraft instead of 61. The number of regiments in a division was decreased from 4 or 6 to 2. New attack and light night-bomber regiments were formed.

The PVO forces' lack of a unified control system at the beginning of the war necessitated the introduction of a new air defense system and PVO organization. In November of 1941, the post of Commander of the National PVO was created. This Commander was given control over all the National PVO, including fighter planes previously under the orders of the air force commanders of military districts. Except for the Southern and Far Eastern districts, the air defense zones in the districts were replaced by corps and divisional air defense regions.

From November of 1941 to January of 1942, the air defense of the air force was organized. This made possible the unified command and control of the air units of the PVO.

These measures played a positive role in the control of the PVO and made possible a more flexible and prompt solution of the problems involved in defending the most important targets and achieving the necessary maneuverability in the PVO.

In 1942, a new period began in the development of Soviet Armed Forces' organization as a result of the transition of the economy to a war footing.

The production of arms and combat materiel began to increase steadily from 1942 on owing to the measures taken by the Communist Party and the great efforts of the Soviet people. During this same year, the Red Army embarked on a counteroffensive after difficult and intense defensive operations. The forces had to be reorganized according to the changes that had occurred in the methods of conducting warfare. It was highly important that the Armed Forces be organized in such a way as to secure the possibility of co-ordinated action in solving strategic, operational, and tactical problems during offensives.

During the organization of the Armed Forces in this period, the chief attention was devoted to improving their quality and increasing their combat capabilities to the utmost.

Ground Force organization was improved, and its firepower, striking potential, and mobility were increased by all possible means.

Infantry corps were re-established in 1942–1943, which aided troop command and control and the co-ordination of various types of troops. The amount of automatic weapons, artillery, and mortars in the infantry divisions was increased, which greatly increased their firepower. After 1942, the infantry brigades were disbanded or reorganized into infantry divisions.

Artillery was organized by creating breakthrough artillery divisions and corps, antiaircraft artillery divisions and antitank artillery brigades. This made it possible to concentrate artillery in the most important areas and to clear the path more effectively for infantry and tanks; it also provided more reliable cover from enemy aircraft for the troops.

The organization of the tank troops was changed by the creation of more powerful tank units and formations. Tank corps were created in the spring of 1942, and mechanized corps in the autumn of the same year; however, these corps still lacked supporting units. Their organization and armament was continually improved, and their firepower and striking power were increased. This was expressed in the increased number of tanks, and the increase in quality and amount of artillery for the armored units.

Mixed tank armies (tank corps and infantry divisions) were formed in 1942, but the offensive operations at Stalingrad demonstrated that this type of organization for tank armies was not successful. Consequently, in 1943 we changed from mixed tank armies to tank armies consisting of tank corps and mechanized corps. The army received appreciable amounts of artillery. This measure greatly increased the mobility of the tank armies and their combat potential for the solution of major operational problems.

In addition to the organization of tank armies, tank regiments and brigades continued to be formed to provide the infantry with direct tank support. The offensive operations of the Soviet troops demonstrated that tanks and infantry greatly needed continuous artillery support; consequently, regiments and brigades of self-propelled artillery were created.

In general, the improvement of the organizational form of the tank troops, which had been brought about by the Red Army's shifting to extensive offensive operations, greatly increased the Ground Forces' striking potential and their capability to penetrate enemy defense and rapidly develop an offensive in depth.

Major organizational changes were made in the engineering forces after the end of 1942. The units and formations of the Supreme High Command's reserve were particularly developed. The role of the engineering forces in supporting offensive operations increased as the Soviet Armed Forces' operations became more active. The engineering forces began to participate directly in penetration of enemy defenses. Assault engineering brigades were organized among the engineering troops to carry out this task; from 1944 on, they included tank-engineer and tank flame-thrower regiments.

Important changes took place in the organization of the Air Force when the Red Army shifted from strategic defense to offense. The Air Force was organized for the best possible support of the Ground Forces' offensive operations.

In 1942, the entire tactical aviation was removed from the armies and combined into air armies under the direct control of the front commanders. The creation of the air armies was a major stage in the organizational development of the Air Force. The front commanders thus received strong support for the Ground Forces. In addition, the possibility of concentrating aircraft in decisive areas was greatly increased. At the same time, air corps and divisions were created in the Supreme High Command reserves to reinforce the air armies of the fronts in the most important areas. The Long-range Air Force under the direct control of the Stavka was organizationally included in the Air Force.

The shift from mixed units and formations to uniform air divisions and regiments of bomber, attack, and fighter aircraft proved to be an important measure in the development of the Air Force's organizational structure during the war; this increased the flexibility of air units in solving operational problems and facilitated co-ordination with the Ground Forces.

The numerical increase in the National PVO, which was caused by the need to defend important industrial targets, resulted in the operational unification of the PVO for armies and fronts. The air regiments included in the PVO were consolidated into divisions and corps. In 1943, simultaneously with the organization of PVO for armies and fronts there were created commands to direct the fighters of the PVO of the fronts as well as a [special] fighter army for the defense of Moscow. The organization of antiaircraft artillery was also considerably changed. In the summer of 1943, antiaircraft artillery divisions were formed in the PVO, and in the spring of 1944, antiaircraft brigades.

The organization of the PVO during the war assured flexible command and rapid concentration of forces and weapons in the most important areas for protecting troops and the country's most important targets from enemy air attacks.

During the Great Patriotic War, combat operations in the naval theaters were conducted on a relatively small scale and were confined mainly to supporting the operations of the ground forces. Consequently, there were no major changes in naval organization. The organization of surface vessels and submarine formations was improved slightly to suit operational missions. The organization of naval aviation, just as in the Red Army Air Force, was changed from composite to single-type formations. The need for an efficient, unified system of air defense resulted in the creation of base PVO regions instead of PVO districts. This significantly increased the possibilities of organizing air defense throughout the entire zone of a naval base or in a definite region of the naval theater.

Thus, during the Great Patriotic War, Soviet strategy, after carefully examining the economic and political situation, and the forms and methods of conducting war, introduced changes in the organization of the Armed Forces that were best suited to the requirements of war.

# ★ 4

# The Nature of
# Modern War

One of the primary tasks of the theory of military strategy is to study and define the nature of wars: their characteristic military strategy and technical features. The correct scientific solution of this problem is attainable primarily through the Marxist-Leninist analysis of the actual conditions of historical and social development (which make it possible to establish the essential socio-political nature of various wars), why and how wars break out, and the material base upon which they are waged.

The scientific forecast of the nature of a future war is important because only thus can the political and military leaders correctly and optimally direct the development of the armed forces and successfully and forcefully execute the mission of preparing the whole country for war with an aggressor.

At present, accurate anticipation of the nature of the initial period of a war is exceptionally important for the theoretical and practical problems of military strategy. In this initial period, the effect of the armed conflict upon the course and outcome of modern war will be fundamentally different from that of the past. Consequently, grave new demands already confront the armed forces, the state, and the people.

## The Marxist-Leninist Concept of the Essential Meaning of War in the Present Epoch

The question: What is the essential meaning of war? is decisive for the solution of all basic theoretical and practical problems in military

269

strategy. It is also crucial for clarifying the nature of any particular war. The tenets of historical materialism; the Marxist-Leninist study of war; and the more important documents of the program for the Communist and Workers' Parties, defining their theoretical, political, and practical activity, at present provide an exhaustive answer to this question. The military events of our epoch are convincing proof of the correctness of the Marxist-Leninist concept of the essential meaning of war and the causes and conditions which give rise to it.

This proposition [on the essential nature of war] should be particularly emphasized. In recent years, as the ideological struggle has become sharper on an international scale, revisionists and various schools of dogmatists, encouraged by reactionary imperialist forces, have attacked Marxism-Leninism with renewed vigor in an attempt to prove that it has become obsolete and unresponsive to actual, contemporary social conditions. In their attacks, the revisionists even address themselves to military and political questions. In the West, the military ideologists of imperialism promote, with increasing intensity, various "new" military and philosophical theories that serve the imperialist interests and justify aggressive wars as anticommunist.

Marxism-Leninism teaches that war is a socio-historical phenomenon arising at a definite stage in the course of social development. It is an extremely complex social phenomenon, whose essential meaning can be revealed solely by using the only scientific method: Marxist-Leninist dialectics. When discussing the use of Marxist epistemology in the study of war, V. I. Lenin stated that "dialectics require a comprehensive study of a given social phenomenon as it develops, as well as a study of information which is seemingly extraneous to basic motive forces, to the development of productive forces and to the class struggle." *

Historical experience shows that even the greatest world war, no matter how all-encompassing it may seem, represents only one aspect of social development and completely depends upon the course of that development and upon the political interactions between classes and states.

V. I. Lenin insisted that *war is part of a whole and that whole is politics*. He also stated that war is a continuation of politics and that politics also "continues" during war. Lenin's proposition is extremely important and basic; it takes note of bourgeois theories of the comprehensive, all-encompassing nature of war, and of "class peace" during war. It explains that even during war, politics continues; that is, class

---

* V. I. Lenin, *Sochineniia* [*Works*], Vol. 21, pp. 193–194.

relations do not cease, and the class conflict continues in every way and by every means (ideological, political, economic, etc.).

The correct understanding of these basic propositions also permits the discovery of the essential nature of war. "The basic proposition of dialectics as applied to war . . .," V. I. Lenin wrote, "is that *war is simply a continuation of politics by other* (namely, violent) *means. . . .*" And this was always the very point of view held by Marx and Engels, who considered *every* war to be a *continuation* of the politics of the given interested powers—and of the *various classes* within them—at a given time.* As is generally known, it was Clausewitz, the German military theoretician, who said: "War is simply a continuation of politics by other means." V. I. Lenin, however, introduced a basic correction by adding "namely, violent" means, which fundamentally altered the statement of the problem. One should emphasize that for Marxist-Leninists, the word "violence," when used in a military context, has always meant weapons, the armed forces, and the entire military organization as an instrumentality of war. F. Engels wrote in his work *The Theory of Force* that the army and the navy represent force at the current time, and he explained that [the use of] force is a political act. N. S. Khrushchev has pointed out that in relations between states, violence is war.

On this Marxist-Leninist basis, war can be defined as armed violence: organized armed conflict between different social classes, states, groups of states and nations, in order to achieve definite political goals.

In peacetime, classes, states, and nations have always attempted to attain their goals by the most diverse means and forms of struggle: ideological, political, economic, and others. When antagonisms were sharply aggravated, they resorted to forms of armed conflict—to war.

All of this demonstrates that war is only one form of political and class conflict. V. I. Lenin showed, in particular, that "civil war is the most acute form of class conflict, when a series of economic and political clashes occurring repeatedly, gather momentum, spread, become more intense, and are transformed into acute and armed conflict. . . ." † Another of Lenin's ideas is that: "In certain periods of acute economic and political crises, the class struggle ripens into a direct civil war, i.e., armed conflict. . . ." ‡

The meaning of Lenin's explanation (that war is the continuation of politics by other—violent—means) is that war is not synonymous with

---

* V. I. Lenin, *Sochineniia* [*Works*], Vol. 21, pp. 194–195.
† V. I. Lenin, *Sochineniia* [*Works*], Vol. 26, p. 11.
‡ V. I. Lenin, *Sochineniia* [*Works*], Vol. 11, p. 192.

politics in general but comprises only part of it, and that politics, in addition to war, commands a large arsenal of various nonviolent means which it can enlist to attain its goals, without resort to war. This now closely guides the Communist Party of the Soviet Union and the Soviet government in its summons to the Western powers to solve all international disputes by negotiation and not by war.

The theory of Soviet military strategy also takes into account another aspect of the problem, namely, that war has a special and concrete character in contrast to other political means. A special system, a military organization, is created to wage war; military equipment is produced; and methods of combat are developed. The conduct of war itself has always been a special form of human activity, where each opposing side has directed its efforts toward the defeat of the other, toward the capture of enemy territory, or to holding its own territory, striving thus to attain its political goals.

In this epoch, society's power to produce has grown enormously, thus generating new, superpowerful and superlong-range instruments of destruction. The formation of a world socialist system has also caused radical changes in the terms of political struggle. Hence in a future world war, the participants will achieve their political goals not only by the defeat of the armed forces but also by the complete disruption of the enemy's economy and the demoralization of his population. *For this reason, the essential meaning of war, as a continuation of politics with the instruments of armed violence, and its concrete character now stand out even more prominently than in the past, and the modern instruments of violence become increasingly important.*

Thus, armed conflict has become an even more characteristic form of human activity. The causes are the following: first, enormous masses of people are drawn into modern war as armed forces increase and the civilian population is enlisted on a large scale to cope with a number of the military and semimilitary problems of defending the rear.[1] Second, the complexity of the widely available modern military equipment requires special military knowledge and skills. And finally, modern war, as never before, demands the utmost use of the economy to provide for the needs of war and, simultaneously, requires the existence of a large defense industry as well as a special material and technological base, which are specially created to satisfy the needs of the armed conflict.

However, even though hundreds of millions of people are drawn into it, war is only one aspect of political life, one particular form of political and class struggle. Social development, on the other hand, and the inter-

---

[1] U.S. ED. NOTE—Civil defense is apparently what is meant by "the semimilitary problems of defending the rear."

actions of classes, countries, and nations are much more inclusive phenomena. Obviously, therefore, no world ("total" or "global") war can contain all these phenomena. And simultaneous with war, an uncompromising class struggle does and must go on. Thus it is improper to confuse and identify two such social phenomena as war and class struggle, or war and politics.

This has always been the Marxist-Leninist understanding of these problems. It applies to the present situation as well.

Various foreign military publications have recently said that it was wrong to consider war as a continuation of politics with the instruments of violence, and that not only military forces but also various "nonmilitary" means of conflict—ideological, political, psychological, economic, financial, commercial, diplomatic, scientific, subversive, etc.—must be considered as instruments of war. On this basis they concluded that war is a conflict involving all the instruments of politics, a "complex" of all the modes and instruments of struggle. Thus, in essence, they equate war, politics, and the class struggle, as a whole, with each other.

The military ideologists of imperialism cannot ignore the fact that a new, nuclear world war initiated by imperialists will inevitably lead to the collapse of capitalism as a social system. Fear for the fate of capitalism and dread of their people, who oppose war, make these ideologists try to justify war, as though it were no longer violent. The British military theoretician, Liddell-Hart, in his book *The Strategy of Indirect Approach,* asserts that instruments of war now not only refer primarily to the armed forces but also to various "nonmilitary" instruments of conflict: economic pressure, propaganda, diplomacy, subversion, etc.

The Yugoslav revisionists also keep step with the military ideologists of imperialism. In his slanderous book *Socialism and War,* Edvard Kardelj [2] tries to whitewash the aggressive American imperialist policy and to hide the real source of war which threatens the world. In spite of the historically proven teachings of Marxism-Leninism, Kardelj does not consider war to be a continuation of politics with the instruments of violence, and he ignores the relationship between war and the class struggle.

As a social phenomenon and as the extreme means of realizing the policies of certain classes and states, war is not isolated from other phenomena of political life. The experience of modern wars shows that when they arise, countries strive for the maximum mobilization of their

---

2 U.S. ED. NOTE—Edvard Kardelj is a secretary of the Central Committee of the Yugoslav Communist Party and a vice-president of the Executive Council of the Yugoslav government.

resources and strength in order to gain victory. V. I. Lenin showed that once it comes to war, everything must be subordinated to its interests.

The role and importance of various instrumentalities of conflict that execute policy change in peace and in war according to the situation. During war, the armed forces and armed combat are the basic and decisive instruments of policy. All other instruments are directed primarily toward supporting the armed forces and the other military formations, created by extensive enlistment of masses of the population, in order to attain political goals by armed violence.

Quite obviously, only armed combat is the distinguishing characteristic of war; its beginning and end actually define the beginning and end of war itself.

It is necessary to emphasize once again that Lenin saw the essential nature of war and its concrete character as the continuation of politics by violent means, by waging armed combat and by military operations.

It was precisely as a result of military operations—armed combat and violence, rather than by some kind of "nonmilitary" and "indirect" action—that 10 million people perished and more than 20 million were wounded and maimed in World War I. World War II took almost 50 million lives. Many countries suffered enormous material losses. In the Soviet Union alone, over 70,000 hamlets and villages and 1,710 towns were either partially or completely destroyed and burned.

Such is the actual reality, reflecting the essential nature of war as armed combat. A future war in which the basic instrument of violence is the nuclear weapon—a weapon of mass destruction—would lead to immeasurably more casualties and devastation.

With the rapid development of productive forces, science, and technology, the instruments of war have become so powerful that the chances of attaining the most decisive political goals in armed combat are enormously improved. Consequently, reliance upon "nonmilitary" means of conflict will not suit the requirements of a future war, nor conform to the laws governing its development. Some Western ideological efforts to promote "nonmilitary" methods of waging war are designed to draw a veil over the horrors of a future nuclear war and to divert the attention of the general population from imperialist war preparations.

The XXth [January 1956], XXIst [January 1959], and XXIInd [October 1961] Congresses of the Communist Party of the Soviet Union, the new Program of the Communist Party of the Soviet Union, the documents of the conferences of the Communist and Workers' Parties, and the statements of N. S. Khrushchev and other prominent Party and government figures of the Soviet Union and the countries in the socialist camp have contributed to the creative development of the Marxist-Leninist teachings on war. Of particular importance are the propositions on the nature of the present epoch, on categories of wars, on the absence of the fatal inevitability of war and on the possibilities of preventing world war, on the peaceful coexistence of states with different social systems, on the military function of a socialist state in present-day conditions, on the development of the world socialist system and the further decline of imperialism, on the outcome of a future war between them being favorable to socialism, and on the means of waging war.

The propositions developed by the Communist Party on the nature of coexistence between the two world systems are very important for a correct understanding of the basic problems of war.

"Peaceful coexistence," N. S. Khrushchev stated at a workers' meeting in Novosibirsk, October 10, 1959, "must be correctly understood. Coexistence is a continuation of the struggle between the two social systems, but a struggle by *peaceful means,* without war. . . . We consider this to be an economic, political and ideological struggle, *but not a military one.*" (Italics ours—[Soviet] editor.)

The perfectly clear and absolutely fundamental, logical conclusion is that the concept of "war" does not include peaceful, "nonmilitary" means of conflict.

N. S. Khrushchev's statements on the means of waging war are also extremely important. Speaking at the National Press Club in Washington on September 16, 1959, on the question of disarmament, he said that the best and most reliable way to make war impossible was to make certain that no state—without any exceptions—possessed *the means for waging war;* in other words, to *solve* the problem of disarmament.

In his address to the United Nations General Assembly on September 18, 1959, N. S. Khrushchev treated this problem in greater detail, stating that if states disarm completely and have no *means of waging war, i.e., no nuclear weapons or missiles, armies, navies, or air forces,* then all international problems would be solved peacefully rather than by force of arms. With the destruction of weapons and the abolition of armed forces, states will have the *material capacities* only for the conduct of a peaceful policy.

To summarize what has been said, it should be emphasized that (1) war is violence in the relations between states; (2) the state's armed forces, it goes without saying, are the instruments of violence or the instruments to wage war; (3) Lenin's concept of war as a continuation of class politics with the instruments of violence and the concept of war as armed combat for definite political goals still remain valid in the present epoch.

Bourgeois ideologists, in denying the class nature of politics and war, always try to portray politics as an extension of the common interests of the state and the people.

The present-day ideologists of imperialism and their agents in the international workers' movement—the revisionists—preach the reformist theory of "class peace"; deny the class struggle; and distort the Marxist-Leninist propositions on war, on the defense of the socialist Fatherland, and on proletarian internationalism.

The American bourgeois ideologists and reformists assert in particular that modern American capitalism is not the capitalism about which Karl Marx wrote, but rather a people's capitalism, humane and peaceful.

The Yugoslav revisionists assert that the modern bourgeois states have a supra-class nature, that they protect the interests of all classes, and that their politics are those of the people as a whole.

The Program of the Communist Party of the Soviet Union points out that the defenders of the bourgeois system, in striving to hold the masses in spiritual captivity, continually invent new "theories" which mask the exploitative nature of capitalism and dress it up. They assert that modern capitalism has changed its essential nature and that it has become a "people's capitalism," where classes disappear and class contradictions are erased. In reality, the development of modern capitalism confirms the correctness of Marxist-Leninist teachings on the growth of contradictions and antagonisms in capitalist society.

Certain military writers try to show that in the capitalist world of today war is waged by the *entire state—all the people—*and that war has now been transformed into *conflict between one armed people and another,* where all of their military, labor, and spiritual forces are directed toward the defeat of the enemy.

All of these theories depart from objective reality, conceal the class contradictions of modern capitalism, and mask the real and essential nature of war and its class-contradictory character. "War in our time," V. I. Lenin wrote in 1914, "is a people's war. From this truth it does not follow that it is necessary to drift with the 'popular' current of chauvinism but that in wartime, in the war and in a military atmosphere, class contradictions will continue to exist and manifest themselves, creating strife among the people." *

The example of the United States—the richest capitalist country— actually confirms Lenin's thesis. The most extensive strike movement

---

* V. I. Lenin, *Sochineniia* [*Works*], Vol. 21, p. 23.

in that country developed during the last war. Thus, in 1941, there were 4,288 strikes in which 2.4 million people participated; in 1943, there were (during 11 months) 3,425 strikes in which 3.5 million people participated, and in 1944, there were 4,956 strikes with 2.1 million participants.

The refusal of a group of capitalists to retool their factories for war production is evidence of the "unity" of the American people and the country during wartime. "Capitalists," wrote William E. Foster on this subject, "even arranged the peculiar 'Italian' strike and continued it until the government accepted their usurious conditions." *

The experience of imperialist wars proves that genuine popular unity is inconceivable in such wars. It is another matter when a just war is waged. Speaking of the reasons for Soviet victory over the foreign enemy during the period of foreign intervention and Civil War, Lenin stated that so great a number of people had never before been attracted to active support of the war and that "no other political regime had a tenth as many [people on its side] as the Soviet regime." † The Great Patriotic War of the Soviet Union against Nazi Germany proved this even further.

The Marxist-Leninist propositions on the class nature of wars and on war as a continuation of politics with the instruments of violence are basic assumptions of Soviet military strategy. They help prepare the armed forces and the people for war with an aggressor and make it possible to discover the nature of modern wars and the methods of their conduct. They also solve other important problems in the theory and practice of strategy.

## Wars in the Present Epoch and the Conditions and Causes That Give Rise to Them

Marxism-Leninism teaches that it is impossible to understand a war without understanding the epoch [in which it occurs]. Some of the most important documents of our times, such as the Declaration and Appeal of the 1960 Conference of Representatives of the Communist and Workers' Parties, N. S. Khrushchev's speeches at the fifteenth session of the United Nations General Assembly, and the Program of the Communist Party of the Soviet Union which was adopted by the historic XXIInd Congress of the Communist Party of the Soviet Union, have given a thoroughly scientific and comprehensive exposition of the

---

* William E. [Z] Foster, *Ocherk politicheskoi istorii Ameriki* [*Outline: Political History of the Americas*], Izdatel'stvo Innostrannoi Literatury, Moscow, 1955, p. 614.

† V. I. Lenin, *Sochineniia* [*Works*], Vol. 31, p. 467.

characteristics of the present epoch. These outstanding theoretical and political documents make it possible to understand correctly both the true nature of modern wars and how they start and develop.

The Leninist approach to the characteristics of an epoch is that all great historical events can be correctly understood only if two factors are taken into account: first, the conflict between the two basic historical trends—capitalism and socialism—and, second, the particular historical balance of forces between them, i.e., taking into account the ineluctable growth and consolidation of the socialist position.

At the beginning of the twentieth century, capitalism, which was the only all-embracing system, held sole sway in the international arena, started war when it pleased, and thus provoked revolutionary uprisings against itself. Under these conditions, the Marxist-Leninists correctly posed the problem as that of the "epoch of imperialism, wars, and revolutions."

The Great October Socialist Revolution opened a new era in the history of mankind—the era of the downfall of capitalism and of the consolidation of communism. The victory of the socialist revolution in Russia was directly related to the first imperialist world war. Socialist revolutions in European and Asian countries were the outcome of World War II and led to the formation of the world socialist system.

Today, the countries of the world socialist system occupy more than 26 per cent of the earth's territory and comprise about 35 per cent of its population. They possess vast natural resources and produce almost one-half of the world's supply of grain and more than one-third of the world's industrial output. The time is not far off when the socialist countries will produce more than half of the world's industrial output. The world socialist system, taken as a whole, has already caught up with the world capitalist system in industrial output per capita. The socialist method of production, as is increasingly evident, demonstrates its obvious supremacy over that of capitalism. In the present epoch, the international balance of forces has developed in favor of socialism, and this predetermines the course and character of international relations.

National liberation revolutions, which destroy the colonial system of imperialism, are a most important factor in contemporary times. The international revolutionary movement of the working class is spreading.

The Program of the Communist Party of the Soviet Union states that the present epoch, whose main content is the transition from capitalism to socialism, is an *epoch of struggle between the two opposing social systems,* an epoch of socialist and national liberation revolutions, an epoch of the downfall of imperialism and the liquidation of the colonial system, an epoch of the transition of more and more peoples to the socialist path, an epoch of the *triumph of socialism and communism on a world scale*. The central factor of the present epoch is the international working class and its main creation—the world socialist system.

In characterizing the present epoch, Marxist-Leninists emphasize the new fact that the present is not the epoch of imperialism and war but the epoch of the decay of imperialism as a world system, the epoch of revolutions and the triumph of socialism and communism on a world scale. This fundamental characteristic of the epoch is decisive for explaining the basic problems of war and peace.

In our time, imperialism has entered a period of decline and collapse; it has irrevocably lost its domination over the majority of mankind. Today, the world socialist system and the forces which battle against imperialism for the socialist reconstruction of society determine the main content, direction, and features of man's historical development.

World War I and the Great October Socialist Revolution initiated the general crisis of capitalism. The second stage of capitalism's crisis developed as a result of World War II and of socialist revolutions in a number of countries. Today, world capitalism is entering a new stage, the third in this crisis.

One of the manifestations of this crisis is the further, unprecedented intensification of militarism. The imperialist countries have built up huge armed forces on which they spend an increasingly large portion of their national budgets. The imperialist states are becoming militarist and military-political states.

In the course of one generation, imperialism has plunged mankind into two world wars in which tens of millions of people have perished. A new world war, prepared by world reactionaries, threatens the nations with terrible disasters—the deaths of many hundreds of millions of people and the destruction and devastation of cities.

Now, as a result of the uneven development of capitalism, the economic, political, and military center of imperialism has shifted from Europe to the United States. American monopoly capital has seized the basic sources of raw material, the markets and spheres of capital investment: It has created a surreptitious colonial empire and has become the biggest international exploiter. American imperialism today plays the role of world gendarme, opposing democratic and revolutionary changes and launching aggression against peoples fighting for independence.

The American monopolists and their English and French allies in NATO have again aided West German imperialism to rise after its defeat. Thus a dangerous breeding ground for war and for new aggressive forces that menace the peace has been created in the heart of Europe.

In the Far East, where American monopolists are reviving Japanese militarism, another dangerous breeding ground for war is being created.

The areas where the imperialists will most likely initiate aggressive wars are in the Near and Middle East, where the colonial powers and the people fighting for their independence are in sharpest conflict and clash most; in Korea, inasmuch as numerous armed forces (particularly American) are maintained in South Korea; in Taiwan, occupied by the United States, where the latter incites Chiang Kai-shek to provocative actions against People's China; in Vietnam, where as a result of the American violation of the Geneva agreements, the South Vietnamese government constantly embroils itself with democratic North Vietnam.

Thus, Soviet military strategy must consider it possible that the imperialist aggressors will unleash new *wars of conquest* at the most diverse points on the globe.

One also cannot discount the possibility of *wars between the imperialist, capitalist countries* during the present epoch. Actually, the capitalist world is rent by deep-rooted contradictions. There is an acute internecine struggle for markets, spheres of investment, and sources of raw material. This conflict is becoming particularly acute because the territorial sphere of capitalist domination has been greatly narrowed. The contradictions between the principal imperialist powers are increasing, such as those between England and America, France and America, France and Germany, Germany and America, England and Germany, and Japan and America. Political crises arise periodically in the imperialist military blocs.

The past is of some interest in this context, for example, the statements of the former Nazi general, Kammhuber, presently inspector of the air force of the West German Bundeswehr. In "The Art of War," an article published in a West German magazine, he wrote that if the Nazis had had the atomic bomb, they would have completely destroyed England and France and would have won World War II.[3] It must be assumed that now, too, there is no guarantee that the Bonn revanchists, having obtained atomic weapons, will not use them against their present partners in NATO—England and France—and will not embark upon crimes even more savage and infamous than those committed during the last war. As R. Edwards, the English labor leader, writes in the pamphlet *America—Ally or Boss?*, the West German revanchists are persuading the United States that France has too many communists and England too many socialists and that, therefore, both England and France are very unreliable military allies. This is advanced as an argument for the necessity of providing the West German army with nuclear

---

[3] U.S. ED. NOTE—It has not been possible to verify this statement.

weapons, so that in unusual circumstances it could "neutralize" England and France.

World-wide historical victories of the international revolutionary movement of the working class are characteristic of the times. In the capitalist countries, social forces, whose size and determination are growing, are called upon to guarantee the victory of socialism. These countries are constantly shaken by class strife. The ruling circles use the armed forces to suppress strikes. The imperialists create military blocs and bases, not only to battle the socialist countries, but also to crush revolutionary workers' movements and national liberation movements.

According to Marxism-Leninism, socialist revolutions are not necessarily connected with war, although socialist revolutions concluded both world wars (which were initiated by the imperialists). In the present epoch, the magnificent goals of the working class can be realized without world war and without civil war—by peaceful means.[4] However, when the exploiting classes resort to violence against the people, one must keep in mind the possibility of a non-peaceful transition to socialism. And this means that revolutionary wars and popular uprisings are not excluded.

The present epoch is characterized by one violent national liberation revolution after another, sweeping away colonial systems and undermining the foundations of capitalism.

The imperialists are making every effort to preserve their rule in the colonies. To this end they employ every possible means: colonial wars, economic pressure, subversion, conspiracy, terror, and bribery.

The colonialists do not grant nations independence voluntarily. For this reason, colonies are liberated by stubborn struggle, including armed combat. And as long as imperialism and colonialism exist, *wars of national liberation and revolutionary wars are unavoidable.*

---

[4] U.S. ED. NOTE—In 1905 Lenin wrote: "The revolutionary army is needed because great historical questions can be solved only by violence and the organization of violence in the modern struggle is a military organization." (V. I. Lenin, *Selected Works,* Vol. III, International Publishers, New York, 1943, p. 313.) In recent years, however, Khrushchev has argued that a world communist system can be achieved without war and that war is not a necessary or desirable midwife of revolution. However, the appropriate passage in the 1961 Party Program appears to show some uncertainty on this question. The Party Program states: "Communists have never held and do not hold that the road to revolution *inevitably* lies through wars between states. Socialist revolution *is not necessarily* linked with war. Although both world wars, which were started by the imperialists, culminated in socialist revolutions, revolutions are *quite* possible without wars. The great objective of the working class can be realized without world war." (Italics added.) *Programme of the Communist Party of the Soviet Union,* Supplement to *New Times,* Moscow, No. 48, November 29, 1961, p. 18.

Socialist, national liberation, anti-imperialist, and popular democratic revolutions; broad peasant movements; popular struggles to overthrow fascist and other despotic regimes; and general democratic movements against national oppression—all these merge in our epoch into a general world revolutionary process which is undermining the foundations of the imperialist camp.

Revolution cannot be externally imposed upon a nation; it comes as a result of the profound internal and international contradictions of capitalism.

Together with the other Marxist-Leninist parties, the Communist Party of the Soviet Union states in its Program that it considers it its international duty to summon the peoples of all countries to unite and mobilize all their internal forces to prevent the imperialists—with the support of the power of the world socialist system—from interfering in the affairs of the people of any country which rise in revolt or to repulse the imperialists decisively. The Communist Party of the Soviet Union also considers it its international duty to assist countries which are on the road to winning and consolidating their national independence and to assist all nations fighting for complete destruction of the colonial system.

Whatever path the nations which have thrown off the yoke of colonialism may choose—capitalist or noncapitalist—is their internal affair. With the present balance of world power, however, and the real possibility of powerful support from the world socialist system, the former colonial peoples can solve this problem in their own interests.

It is necessary to begin with all these Marxist-Leninist propositions to understand correctly the essential social-political nature of modern wars.

In its study of the nature of these wars, Soviet military strategy assumes the theoretical possibility of the following fundamental types of war in the present epoch.[5]

*World War.* If a world war between the imperialist and socialist camps is not prevented, it will be, because of its essentially political nature, the decisive armed clash between the two opposing world social systems. Such a war would be aggressive, predatory, and unjust for the imperialists, but liberating, just, and revolutionary for the socialist commonwealth.

---

[5] U.S. ED. NOTE—The characterization of the various categories of wars was made by Khrushchev in his report on the Moscow Conference of Representatives of Communist and Workers' Parties on January 6, 1961. N. S. Khrushchev, "Toward New Victories of the World Communist Movement," *Kommunist,* No. 1, January 1961, pp. 17–19.

*Small imperialist wars* on a local, limited scale, are undertaken by the imperialists in order to suppress national liberation movements, seize or hold on to colonies. Small local wars between the imperialist states, too, are not excluded. All these imperialist wars are also predatory, unjust, and against the interests of the people.

The purpose of *national liberation wars, civil wars,* and other popular wars is to repulse the aggressive, predatory, imperialist assaults and to fight for freedom and independence. Such wars are just, liberating, and revolutionary.

The communists have always been the most determined opponents of world wars, as well as opponents in general of wars between states. Only the imperialists need such wars to seize foreign territories and to enslave and rob nations.

The Program of the Communist Party of the Soviet Union states that the Communist Party of the Soviet Union and the entire Soviet nation will also continue to oppose any and all predatory wars, including wars among the capitalist states, and local wars to strangle national liberation movements; they also consider it their duty to support the sacred struggle of oppressed nations and their just wars of liberation against imperialism.[6]

Naturally, each time they occur, wars in these categories will break out and develop quite differently.

The military, political, and strategic goals of the contenders and the instruments and methods of such wars will be very different. This imposes upon military strategic theory an important task: to study and work out the problems of modern war in concrete terms applicable to a given, particular war rather than to some generalized kind of war.

The distinctive and special features of the present epoch permit Marxist-Leninists to make a fundamentally fresh approach to the questions of war and peace.

On the basis of a Marxist-Leninist analysis of the fundamental

---

[6] U.S. ED. NOTE—In his report on the Moscow Conference of Representatives of Communist and Workers' Parties, Khrushchev characterized the national liberation wars as revolutionary wars and said that the communists would support them. *Kommunist,* No. 1, 1961. The Party Program adopted in 1961 states: "The CPSU regards it as its international duty to assist the peoples who have set out to win and strengthen their national independence, all people who are fighting for the complete abolition of the colonial system." *Programme of the Communist Party of the Soviet Union,* p. 23. On September 11, 1962, the Soviet Union went beyond this commitment when it declared: "We have said and we do repeat that if war is unleashed, if the aggressor makes an attack on one state or another and this state asks for assistance, the Soviet Union has the possibility from its own territory to render assistance to any peace-loving state and not only to Cuba. And let no one doubt that the Soviet Union will render such assistance. . . ." *New York Times,* September 12, 1962.

change in the balance of power between the two world systems and in the total international situation, the XXth Congress of the Communist Party of the Soviet Union concluded that, since the world socialist camp has become converted to a powerful political, economic, and military force and since the forces of peace have gained world-wide strength, war is no longer a fatal inevitability.

In developing this position, the XXIst Congress of the Communist Party of the Soviet Union noted in its resolutions that a genuine possibility is emerging for excluding world war from the life of society even before the complete world-wide victory of socialism, and while capitalism still survives in parts of the world. This conclusion rests on the fulfillment of the seven-year plan, adopted by the Congress to build a communist society. [Such an economic success] will profoundly influence the entire international situation and strengthen the forces of peace and weaken the forces of war, producing not only vast changes in our own country but also throughout the world. It will radically advance socialism's role in international economic life. And economics, as is well known, is the main area in which the peaceful competition between socialism and capitalism will take place.

The XXIInd Congress of the Communist Party has defined the general Soviet strategy for the next historical period—the period of full-scale construction of communist society. The main tasks of this period are to create the material and technological base for communism, to satisfy more completely the needs of the populace and, simultaneously, to strengthen further the economic and defensive might of the USSR. During this period the historical task of overtaking and surpassing the most advanced capitalist countries in per capita production will be accomplished.[7] The key task is to make maximum gains in the next seven years in the peaceful economic competition between socialism and capitalism.

In international relations, the XXIInd Congress of the Communist Party of the Soviet Union has determined to conduct a consistent foreign policy whose object is to preserve and to strengthen the peace and the security of nations. [This policy is] based on the Leninist principle of the peaceful coexistence of states with different social systems. The Congress stated that it was necessary to end the "cold war," to

---

[7] U.S. ED. NOTE—The Program of the Communist Party of the Soviet Union states: "In the current decade (1961–1970), the Soviet Union, in creating the material and technical basis of communism, will surpass the strongest and richest capitalist country, the USA, in production per head of population. . . ." *Programme of the Communist Party of the Soviet Union,* p. 28.

ease international tensions, and to strengthen to the utmost the world socialist system and the commonwealth of fraternal nations.

In the present epoch, the struggle for peace and the fight to gain time depend above all on an unremitting increase in Soviet military power and that of the entire socialist camp, based on the development of productive forces and the continuous growth of its material and technological base. To accomplish this vitally important task is an historical necessity because while imperialism exists, the economic basis for war remains and reactionary forces representing the interests of monopoly capital will continue military adventures and aggression. Our military strategy must accept the fact that there is still danger of the imperialists' initiating new predatory wars and attacking the socialist countries, particularly the Soviet Union, despite the growing influence of factors ensuring the preservation of peace.

The Program of the Communist Party of the Soviet Union stresses that the imperialist camp is preparing a terrible crime against mankind— world nuclear war, which can cause unprecedented destruction to whole countries and annihilate whole nations. The problem of peace and war has become a problem of life and death to hundreds of millions of people.

This is why the Communist Party of the Soviet Union and the Soviet government regard the prevention of nuclear war as their main task. This task can be performed because the combined forces of the powerful socialist camp, the peace-loving nonsocialist states, the international working class, and all advocates of peace are interested in its accomplishment. Having outstripped capitalism in the most important branches of science and engineering, socialism has placed powerful instruments for curbing imperialist aggression at the disposal of peace-loving peoples.

In considering the nature of modern wars and how they break out, Soviet military strategy acknowledges that two world social systems exist and are in conflict: the socialist, which is building communism and conducts a policy of peace; and the capitalist, which is entering the third stage of its general crisis and pursues an aggressive policy of initiating new wars.

Peaceful coexistence of the two world systems—socialism and capitalism—continues the international class struggle of these opposing social systems. But it is a struggle by peaceful means, without the use of force. However, despite the persistent socialist policy of peaceful coexistence, the imperialist bloc may adventurously try to attain its aggressive goals by force of arms, i.e., by war.

At present, the principal threat of war is from aggressive American imperialism, which expresses American monopoly's capitalistic desire to dominate the world.

The aggressive temper of imperialist policy expresses itself in the following ways: The ruling circles of the United States and other countries in the aggressive military blocs have constantly opposed the peaceful settlement of international problems and the liquidation of the vestiges of World War II. They proclaim the so-called "policy of liberation" of Eastern European countries; they continue the arms race without cease; they stockpile nuclear weapons; they establish missile, air, and naval bases around the socialist states; they intensify military training and prepare future theaters of military operation for nuclear war. The Western powers try to get all the new states into military blocs, to combine the existing aggressive alliances, such as NATO, SEATO, and CENTO, into a single bloc under American leadership, and to form new antisocialist blocs.

The aggressiveness of this policy may be seen in the ever-increasing militarization of the economy and of science, in the increased political and economic enslavement of underdeveloped countries, in the attempts to preserve the remnants of colonial rule by armed force, and in the planned provocation of military conflicts in various parts of the globe, including the socialist camp. Imperialist aggressiveness is also expressed in the military and ideological preparation for a future war conducted under the guise of an anticommunist struggle.

The ruling circles of the United States, Great Britain, and France want to revive West German militarism, restore its military economy, develop its armed forces, provide it with missiles—in sum, a policy especially dangerous for peace. The United States, leading the aggressive imperialist blocs, maintains large armed forces in Western Europe and numbers of missile bases directed openly against the USSR and other other regions of the world close to the borders of socialist countries, keeps numerous air and naval bases in readiness, and builds increasing socialist countries.

In pursuit of these imperialistic policies, Western leaders of the armed forces and their general staffs are preparing detailed plans for a military attack on the USSR and other countries of the socialist camp. The aims and content of these plans are clearly aggressive.

The threat of a military attack on the USSR is thus by no means eliminated. Moreover, at the present time (in the sixties) the danger of a world war breaking out has become particularly real. The imperialist forces can initiate war against the Soviet Union and the socialist camp together, either by a direct attack on the USSR or other socialist countries, or as a consequence of an aggressive local war against one of the nonsocialist countries that affects the basic interests of the socialist states and creates a threat to world peace. In any of these cases, a war initiated by the aggressor will obviously lead to a new world war in which the countries in the socialist camp will be on one side and the imperialist countries and their dependent capitalist states, combined into aggressive military blocs, will be on the other. An overwhelming majority of the countries of the world would be drawn into this war. This would be a war of world coalitions.

It is possible that a future war would find some nonsocialist states siding with the socialist camp, especially after the war had begun. It is possible to create a coalition of states with different social-political structures, as shown by the history of World War II when the Soviet Union and a number of capitalist countries joined in an antifascist coalition.

A war between the socialist and imperialist camps, if an aggressor succeeds in starting it, will be the extreme solution of the historical problem—armed combat between the socialist and capitalist social systems.

Soviet military strategy clearly reflects the view that the sharp class nature of such a war will compel the belligerents to aim at conclusive political and military decisions. Furthermore, the widespread use of weapons of mass destruction will make the war destructive and annihilating as never before. Our Armed Forces must be prepared for a severe, strenuous, and exceptionally violent war.[8]

In a new world war the imperialist bloc will try to destroy utterly the armed forces and the homeland of the socialist states, to liquidate their social and political systems, to replace them by capitalist regimes, and to enslave the peoples of these countries.

To protect the achievements of socialism, the Soviet Union and the peoples' democracies will be compelled to aim for results no less conclusive: to destroy completely the enemy's armed forces, at the same time to disorganize his homeland, to crush his will to resist, and to help the people free themselves from imperialist oppression.

Evaluating the true balance of all the political, economic, and mil-

---

[8] U.S. ED. NOTE—This characterization of a future general war is standard in Soviet literature. For example, in September 1961, Marshal Malinovskii stated: "The world war of the future, if the imperialists unleash it, will be in political essence a decisive armed clash between two opposing social systems. It must be completely clear to us that the distinct class nature of such a war will foreordain the extremely decisive nature of the military and political goals of the belligerents. On the other hand, the use of weapons of mass destruction will impart to the war an unprecedentedly destructive aspect. It is for such an intense, difficult, and exceptionally violent war that we must prepare our armed forces." *Pravda,* September 14, 1961.

itary forces of the two world systems, our military strategists believe that the socialist camp has at its disposal everything necessary to repulse successfully any aggressor's attack and to defeat him completely. The basis of this conclusion is the complete and final victory of socialism in the USSR, the strengthened unity of the socialist countries, the speedy development of their economies and science and technology, and the continual growth of their military might. In addition, the socialist camp in its just struggle against the forces of aggression can count upon the active support of the colonial and dependent countries, which are battling courageously against imperialism and colonialism, and also upon the support of people in capitalist states who are vitally interested in preserving peace. Our over-all evaluation of the military-strategic situation of both camps is that the socialist position is significantly more advantageous and ensures victory in case of aggression.

Obviously, both gigantic military coalitions in such a decisive world war will deploy massive armed forces, will employ on a huge scale all modern, powerful, long-range weapons, including missiles and nuclear weapons, and will use the most efficacious forms of military operations. To ensure that such a war is [successfully] waged, tremendous moral and economic exertions are required.

Consequently, the Soviet state and all the socialist countries and their armed forces must be prepared above all for a world-wide war against a militarily and economically powerful imperialist coalition. Surprise attack is the most probable way for the imperialist bloc to initiate such a war against the socialist states and is of the gravest danger.

While preparing for a decisive struggle with the aggressor in a world war, the armed forces of the socialist countries must also be ready for small-scale local wars which the imperialists might initiate. The experience of such wars, which have broken out repeatedly in the postwar period, is that they are waged with different instruments and by other methods than world wars. Soviet military strategy therefore must study the methods of waging such wars, too, in order to prevent their expansion into a world war and in order to achieve a rapid victory over the enemy.[9]

In order to understand correctly how wars break out, one must distinguish the causes of wars from the pretext of their initiation.

The causes of modern wars are to be found in the law of unequal and spasmodic capitalist economic and political development, the contradictions inherent in the capitalist system, and the struggle of the imperialists for world domination. The immediate reason for wars in the

---

[9] U.S. ED. NOTE—See Note A, pp. 289–293.

present epoch is the aggressive, imperialist, and predatory nature of the policies that the United States and other large capitalist powers direct primarily against the Soviet Union and other socialist countries.

The most diverse events can serve as the pretext for initiating a war. Ordinarily the ruling classes of the aggressive imperialist states, as historical experience teaches, simply fabricate the pretext for an attack. At present, the increased possibility of a so-called accidental outbreak of war complicates this problem considerably.

In a frenzied arms race, there is a serious danger that even a small miscalculation by the statesmen of one country or another can lead to the initiation of a new war.

A nuclear weapon can be launched, not only by order of a government, but also at the initiative of persons at the weapons control panels.

Malfunction in the operation of a radar system can cause an incorrect interpretation of instrument readings and lead to the beginning of military activities. A misunderstood command, or the mental derangement of an American pilot on a routine flight in a bomber loaded with nuclear bombs, can lead to the bombs being dropped on the territory of another state. A defect in the electronic equipment of armed missile combat systems can also lead to the beginning of a war. All of this requires the greatest vigilance of our Armed Forces and enormous wisdom and sagacity of our national, political, and military leadership so that a war is not allowed to start for any such accidental reasons.

These are the basic problems relating to the categories of war and of how and why they break out under contemporary conditions.

## U.S. ED. NOTE A: SOME SOVIET VIEWS ON LIMITED WAR

[As was pointed out in the Analytical Introduction, the Soviet authors of this book have paid scant attention to the question of limited wars, and Soviet literature as a whole gives no indication of the existence of a limited-war doctrine. Since most Soviet public discussion of this subject is intended to condemn Western limited-war theories and deter possible Western initiation of such wars, it is not possible to determine the real Soviet views on this subject. However, the reader may be interested in acquainting himself with the nature of Soviet statements on limited war, a generous sampling of which is presented below.

Soviet discussion of limited war began in the early 1950's largely in response to growing Western interest in this problem, notably following the publication of Henry Kissinger's book, *Nuclear Weapons and Foreign Policy*. The basic Soviet theme was that limited wars were impossible in the nuclear era or that such wars would unavoidably expand into a general nuclear war. For example, a prominent Soviet military writer, Major General G. I. Pokrovskii, declared in 1955 that: "the era of local wars is over." [10] Bulganin, in a letter to President Eisenhower on December 11, 1957, concerning the possibility of limited wars, wrote:

> It should be stressed, most emphatically, that this theory not only is utterly inconsistent from the military point of view but is extremely dangerous politically. . . . Can one seriously count on the possibility of localizing war in our time when there exist in the world two opposing military groupings comprising scores of countries in various parts of the world and when the effects of modern types of weapons know no geographical limits? [11]

Similarly, Khrushchev told a group of Brazilian newsmen that "one must not think that under present conditions minor wars would remain localized. Should such a war break out, they could soon grow into a world war." [12]

This theme has also been repeated in more recent years. For example, Major General N. Talenskii wrote in 1960: "It has been proven that under present-day conditions local or limited wars would be nothing but the prelude to a general missile-nuclear war, and one of the forms of unleashing [such] a war." [13] He also asserted that the occurrence of limited wars in the past could not serve as a guide for the future, because: "Limited wars were possible under totally different economic, political, and strategic conditions. As a rule, the limited scale of such wars was the result of insufficient forces and means for waging them." [14] On a number of occasions Khrushchev has mentioned the high probability of a local war's expanding into a general nuclear war but has claimed that the West's opportunity for initiating local wars has declined because of the restraining influence of the Soviet power and the "forces of peace." [15]

However, Soviet military authorities, writing in publications addressed to military audiences, have been less inclined to deny the

10 *News*, No. 7, April 1, 1955, p. 7.

11 *Pravda*, December 12, 1957. For a similar statement by Khrushchev see his letter to the British Labor Party in October 1957. *New York Times*, October 16, 1957.

12 *Mezhdunarodnaia zhizn'* (*International Affairs*), No. 12, December 1957, p. 6.

13 Major General N. Talenskii, "Modern War: Its Character and Consequences," *Mezhdunarodnaia zhizn'* (*International Affairs*), No. 10, October 1960, p. 36.

14 *Ibid.*

15 See, for example, Khrushchev, "Toward New Victories of the World Communist Movement," *Kommunist*, No. 1, January 1961, p. 18; *Red Star*, May 16, 1961.

possibility of limited wars even under modern conditions. For example, Lieutenant General Krasil'nikov wrote in 1956: "Soviet military science believes that under modern conditions, as before, there may occur wars of different types. . . . By their scale, modern wars can be local or worldwide." [16]

Another Soviet military theoretician, Colonel I. S. Baz', wrote that it would be "incorrect" to conclude that future wars could only be general in character, because local wars had occurred in the postwar period and "may also occur in the future." [17]

The possible or even likely occurrence of limited wars was also recognized by Khrushchev in his 1961 report on the Conference of Representatives of Communist and Workers' Parties. As indicated in this chapter, he divided such wars into two categories: limited wars initiated by the West, which the Soviet Union opposed, and national-liberation wars, which it approved.

However, Soviet political as well as military spokesmen have cited various reasons for the increased danger of the expansion of limited wars into general wars. Those most frequently mentioned are: the existence of nuclear and long-range weapons in the armed forces of both power blocs, the opposing alliance systems, especially in Europe, and the probable unwillingness of a great power or alliance to lose a limited war. For example, one military writer stated:

> The possibility of an expansion of a small war into a large scale war is as old as war itself. It has always existed. But in our times this possibility is particularly great, especially as a result of the widespread equipping of the armed forces with various weapons of long-range and very long-range capability, which permit one to strike powerful blows at distances of hundreds and even thousands of kilometers.[18]

Soviet spokesmen and writers have refused to make any distinction between the possible use of tactical and strategic nuclear weapons in a limited war. For example, Major General Talenskii wrote in 1955 that ". . . there is no difference in the tactical and strategic use of atomic weapons, nor could there be any." [19] Several writers have

---

[16] *Marksizm-Leninizm o voine i armii (Marxism-Leninism on War and the Army)*, Voenizdat Ministerstva Oborony Soiuza SSR, Moscow, 1956, p. 145.

[17] Colonel I. S. Baz', "Soviet Military Science on the Character of Contemporary War," *Voennyi vestnik (Military Herald)*, No. 6, 1958, p. 24.

[18] *Ibid.*

[19] Major General N. Talenskii, "About Atomic and Conventional Weapons," *Mezhdunarodnaia zhizn' (International Affairs)*, No. 1, January 1955, p. 25.

warned that if nuclear weapons are used, "any 'small' war will inevitably grow into a 'big' war."[20]

The obligation of members of alliances to come to each other's aid in the event that one of them becomes involved in a war in another factor frequently cited as increasing the danger of local wars' expanding. This danger is said to be especially great in the event of a local war in Europe. For example, a Soviet military radio commentator said:

> Are little wars at all possible under present conditions in Europe? No, they are impossible from the political and from the military point of view. In the center of Europe, along the frontiers between the NATO powers and the members of the Warsaw Pact, there are two military groupings whose members have undertaken obligations of mutual military aid.[21]

As early as 1955, the Supreme Soviet of the USSR had issued a statement warning that if Europe became "an arena of war," such a war "would inevitably develop into another world war."[22]

Similarly, Soviet writers have repeatedly stated that an "attack on any of the socialist countries will be viewed as an attack on the USSR, or the whole socialist camp."[23] Khrushchev has used this threat on several occasions when discussing the possibility of a Western attempt to use military force to maintain access to Berlin. The Soviet Union has also threatened general war in the event of an American attack on Cuba and has promised to defend any state which requests assistance against Western aggression.[24]

Finally, Khrushchev has warned that, in the event of a conflict involving the major powers, both sides would expand the conflict rather than accept defeat. For example, Khrushchev said:

> But it would be criminal frivolity on the part of the American leaders
> if they were seriously expecting that once they had unleashed a war

---

[20] Colonel V. Mochalov and Major V. Dashichev, "The Smoke Screen of American Imperialism," *Red Star*, December 27, 1957. See also V. Kamenev, "The Big Lie about 'Small' Atomic Wars," *Mezhdunarodnaia zhizn'* (*International Affairs*), No. 3, March 1957, pp. 94–97; Colonel V. Glazov, "What Is Local War?", *Red Star*, May 16, 1961; Major General M. Mil'shtein and Colonel A. Slobodenko, "On the Military Doctrine of the United States," *Red Star*, February 6, 1963.

[21] Foreign Broadcast Information Service (FBIS), *USSR and Eastern Europe*, December 9, 1957. See also *Red Star*, December 17, 1957.

[22] *Izvestiia*, February 10, 1955.

[23] Lieutenant General S. N. Krasil'nikov, "On the Nature of Modern War," *Red Star*, November 18, 1960. See also Major General A. Prokhorov, "The Possibility of Preventing Wars and the Danger of the Outbreak of Wars," *Red Star*, December 26, 1962.

[24] See, for example, *Pravda*, September 11, 1962; February 23, 1963.

against the socialist states it could be kept within certain bounds. If there is a clash between the two giants—the Soviet Union and the United States—that possess powerful economies and big stocks of nuclear weapons, neither side, of course, will want to concede defeat before resorting to the use of all weapons, including the most devastating ones.[25]

In its simplest form, the Soviet argument, which is also made by the Soviet authors of this book (p. 299), states that any armed conflict between major nuclear powers will inevitably expand into a general war.

Some Soviet writers, however, recognize that the scale of a war is not determined by the existing level of military technology alone. Thus a publication of the Military-Political Academy of the Armed Forces declares: "The scale of wars as well as their intensity are determined by the political objectives" of the belligerents.[26] Khrushchev, as is noted above, expressed approval of the wars of national liberation waged by colonial and dependent peoples and predicted that they would continue to occur as long as colonialism survives. Furthermore, although he condemned limited wars allegedly initiated by the Western powers, their repeated occurrence since the Korean War had led him to recognize that ". . . they may occur again in the future." [27]

However, since the Soviet Union is asserted to have no aggressive intentions and since one of its major policy objectives is to deter Western use of military force against the communist bloc of nations as well as against underdeveloped states friendly to the Soviet Union, the Soviet leaders are unlikely to publicize a Soviet limited war doctrine which, in their views, might weaken the restraints on Western use of its military power.]

## Modern Means of Armed Combat and Their Effect on the Nature of War

The present epoch is one of tremendous growth in productive forces and scientific development. Mankind is entering a period of the greatest scientific and technological revolution, resulting from mastery of nuclear energy and the conquest of space, the development of chemistry, automation of industry, electronic equipment, and other notable achievements in science and technology. These developments will largely deter-

---

[25] *Pravda,* August 8, 1961.

[26] *Marksizm-Leninizm o voine i armii (Marxism-Leninism on War and the Army),* Moscow, 1958, p. 44. See also the 1961 edition of this book, for a similar statement on p. 45.

[27] *Kommunist,* No. 1, January 1961, p. 18.

mine the nature of a future world war, if the imperialists succeed in initiating it.

For this reason, military strategy cannot fail to take into account the status and prospects of the development of science and technology when investigating the possible nature of modern warfare.

Particularly favorable conditions have been created in the Soviet Union for the development of science and technology. The primary economic task of the Party and the nation (as set forth in the Program of the Communist Party of the Soviet Union) is the creation of a material and technical base for communism. A major role is assigned to science, which, as it continues to develop and expand its connection with the practical construction of socialism, should become in the fullest sense a direct productive force.

The creation of a material and technical base for communism means the following: complete electrification of the country with concomitant improvement in equipment, technology, and organization for the production of consumer goods in industry and agriculture; comprehensive mechanization of production with more complete automation; widespread use of chemistry in the national economy; the greatest possible development of new, economically effective branches of industry; new sources of energy and materials; a close union of science and industry, and a rapid rate of scientific and technical progress, with a high cultural and technical level among workers; and finally—the most important condition for the victory of communism—a substantial superiority in labor productivity over that of the most highly advanced capitalist countries.

The creation of the material-technical base of communism will at the same time solve also the problem of strengthening and developing the material and technical base necessary to provide our Armed Forces with the required amount of modern military equipment. A first-class heavy industry, already created in the Soviet Union, is the basis for further technical progress and for increasing the economic power and defense capacity of the country. The Communist Party of the Soviet Union has taken measures to develop heavy industry, a reliable guarantee that the defense needs of the country will be fully met. Further achievements in our science—which occupies an advanced position in world science—will aid this process considerably.

Soviet science already occupies the world's leading position in a number of important fields. The discoveries of our physicists in atomic theory and the theory of nuclear particles, in low-temperature physics, and in other fields, rank among the greatest achievements in physics. The country has an advanced atomic industry, and the way is open for research in controlled thermonuclear reactions. Important investigations have been carried out in mathematics, and significant progress has been achieved in building electronic computers.

Achievements in science and technology enabled the Soviet Union to be the first to make peaceful use of atomic energy, blaze a trail into space, launch artificial earth and solar satellites as well as powerful space rockets and interplanetary space ships. The Soviet Union also accomplished the world's first flight around the globe and was the first to build a hydrogen bomb and an intercontinental ballistic missile.

The achievements of modern science, technology, and industry in creating and producing nuclear warheads, missiles of various types and purposes, and military electronic gear are the basis for all the equipment of a modern army. And this in its turn determines the nature of a future war, the methods of its conduct, and the basis for the organization of the armed forces.

Historical experience shows that as productive forces (particularly industrial production), science, and technology increase, there is also a steady development of weapons and military equipment in general, which play an increased role in warfare. Moreover, the development of weapons inevitably produces changes in the methods of conducting military operations as well.

Weapons have been continuously developed and improved over the many centuries of the existence of human society. However, never before in history has this development been as intensive as in the middle of the twentieth century, particularly at the beginning of its second half. Rapid progress in science and industry and the outstanding discoveries in physics, chemistry, and other natural sciences are the primary explanation. Weapons development is also affected by the aggressive, anti-socialist imperialist states, which have intensified the arms race.

The distinguishing feature of weapon development under current conditions is the appearance of *qualitatively new types of weapons and military equipment* and their rapid and massive introduction into the armed forces. This has led to a pronounced improvement in the latter's combat capabilities, a radical break in the organizational forms of armed forces and methods of conducting military operations on every scale. Military strategy and the art of war as a whole have undergone a revolution.

In World War II, ground forces consisting primarily of nonmotorized infantry, armored troops, and special support forces played the main role. Then the chief means of fire on an opponent were artillery and aircraft, both of which had a relatively modest range and power. The methods used for conducting military operations at that time also corresponded to the existing armed forces and weapons.

Military operations occurred mainly in ground theaters, where the results, in the last analysis, determined the outcome of the entire war. The war was characterized by mutual destruction of armed forces at the front lines and the simultaneous execution of missions for capturing or holding territory. The available means of destruction did not make it possible to achieve a rapid change in the relationship of forces between sides; therefore, military operations developed relatively slowly. World War II, although it was more mobile than World War I, nevertheless retained static forms of combat, and to some extent troop deployment and combat operations were conducted on continuous fronts. Action by the belligerents against the enemy's deep rear was negligible, owing to the absence of appropriate means of destruction, and did not significantly affect the outcome of the war.

What was fundamentally new in weapons development during World War II was the use, at the end of the war, of long-range missiles (V-1 and V-2), especially for destroying targets in the enemy's rear, as well as the use of a powerful new explosive weapon—the atomic bomb. This heralded the appearance of completely new weapons for armed combat that should have—and actually did—bring about a basic revolution in military affairs, a revolution immeasurably greater than that caused by the appearance of gunpowder and firearms.

The first half of the twentieth century ended with the technical solution of the problem of utilizing the enormous energy reserves of the heavy atomic nuclei of uranium and thorium. The achievement of nuclear fission led to the creation of the atomic bomb. In the opinion of scientists, the second half of the twentieth century will be the century of space and thermonuclear energy, which cannot fail to affect the development of corresponding means of destruction.

Nuclear weapons appeared in the Soviet Union at the end of the forties and the beginning of the fifties, first in the form of atomic and then hydrogen bombs, and somewhat later in the form of nuclear warheads for missiles of various types and for torpedoes. By the sixties, all branches of the Soviet Armed Forces (Strategic Missile Forces, Ground Forces, the Air Force, Navy, and the PVO) were already equipped with nuclear weapons. Moreover, our Armed Forces received nuclear weapons with explosive yields of from several tons [28] to tens of millions of tons. Since the Soviet Union created a hydrogen weapon before the United States did, and most important of all, since the United States does not possess high-yield thermonuclear warheads of several tens of megatons, such

———

[28] U.S. ED. NOTE—The claim that the Soviet Union possesses nuclear weapons of such extremely low yield is highly unusual.

as those possessed by the USSR, we consider our superiority in nuclear weapons over the Western bloc to be indisputable.[29]

As far as the level of development of our nuclear munitions industry is concerned, its output is assured on a scale sufficient to solve all the problems of a possible large-scale war. The creation of nuclear [weapons] stocks and their widespread introduction into all the branches of the Armed Forces enable the strategic command to use these weapons simultaneously to inflict great losses on the aggressor's armed forces and to destroy his material and technical base for the conduct of the war and so disrupt his national and military administration.

In modern warfare, nuclear weapons can be employed for various missions: strategic, operational, and tactical. From a purely military point of view, a nuclear weapon is incomparably more effective than a conventional weapon. It permits the execution of military missions in a considerably shorter time than was possible in past wars. For this reason, experts believe that the nuclear weapon is the most powerful and effective instrument by which to destroy an opponent in any type of operation, or in war as a whole. The introduction of this weapon into the Soviet Armed Forces markedly increased their combat capabilities and put a powerful instrument in the hands of Soviet military strategy for curbing an aggressor, protecting the achievements of socialism, and assuring peace.

The aggressors also equip their armed forces with nuclear weapons on a large scale. The United States is the main nuclear power in the West. England has a certain supply of nuclear weapons, and France is beginning to create them. Revanchist West Germany is especially feverish in its efforts to obtain nuclear weapons from the United States and to organize its own production.

It is not impossible that in time some other states of both military groupings will have nuclear weapons.

The nuclear industries in the Soviet Union and the United States have achieved such a level that each country has enormous stockpiles of nuclear weapons.

If nuclear weapons are not eliminated and if the aggressors initiate a world war, then both sides will undoubtedly use these weapons. The aggressors' intentions in this respect are well known. The French Marshal Juin, the former Commander-in-Chief of NATO's armed forces in the central zone of Europe, quite typically stated in an interview on November 4, 1960, that NATO would use nuclear weapons in the event

---

[29] U.S. ED. NOTE—The reader will note that the text avoids the question of superiority in numbers of missiles, confining the claim to priority and large yields.

of war even if the enemy did not resort to them at the beginning of military operations.

From this, we conclude that the Soviet Union's Armed Forces and those of the other socialist countries must be prepared above all to wage a war where both antagonists make massive use of nuclear weapons. Therefore, the key task of strategic leadership and theory is to determine the correct, completely scientific solution to all the theoretical and practical questions related to the preparation and conduct of just such a war.

In addition to nuclear weapons, military missiles of various types and purposes have been rapidly developed during the last decade, especially missiles for destroying targets on the ground and in the air. At the end of the fifties, massive introduction of missiles into the Soviet Armed Forces began.

The rapid development of the missile is due to its extremely advantageous characteristics. This weapon has unlimited range, enormous speed and high trajectory, great accuracy and maneuver of fire, and can carry a nuclear warhead of any yield. Ballistic missiles, employed en masse, are still practically invulnerable to existing means of air defense, and their employment is almost independent of weather conditions. Only as special instruments of antimissile defense are developed will it be possible to combat the massive use of missiles in the air. All of these characteristics provide missiles with a capability of inflicting surprise blows and simultaneously of destroying, rapidly and reliably, a large number of targets both deep in the rear and on the front. No other weapons can do this.

These properties give missiles first place among all other instruments of war. The development of missiles has forced a careful re-evaluation of the role of bombers and artillery, which were the principal means of destruction in the last war.

The employment of strategic missiles has greatly influenced the character of war as a whole. The Soviet Union has strategic missiles in such quantity and of such quality that it can simultaneously destroy the required number of the aggressor's targets in the most distant regions of the globe and eliminate entire countries from the war by massive missile attacks.

The intensive development and enormous military effectiveness of strategic missiles have led to the creation of a new branch of the Soviet Armed Forces: Strategic Missile Forces. These forces can, if necessary, be used to carry out the main missions of war: the destruction of the aggressor's means of nuclear attack—the basis of his military power—and the defeat of the main formations of his armed forces, as well as the destruction of the basic, vitally important enemy targets.

Execution of these missions by the Missile Forces will create the conditions for the successful operations by the other branches of the Armed Forces, for defending the rear of the country against the enemy's nuclear blows, and for the rapid achievement of the military, political, and strategic war aims and final victory.

The Strategic Missile Forces now have so many launchers, missiles, and nuclear warheads, including multimegaton warheads, that they can completely carry out their missions.

Besides strategic missiles, operational and tactical missiles are being developed for the National PVO, the Ground Forces, the Navy, and the Air Force. These missiles, now becoming the principal means for destroying targets on the ground, in the air, and on the sea, are radically changing the character of all the previous types of Armed Forces and have immeasurably increased their military effectiveness.

Thus missiles are the most effective and promising instruments of armed combat. Their massive employment with nuclear warheads radically alters the methods of conducting war and its nature, making it decisive and destructive to the nth degree.

One of the important tenets in Soviet military doctrine is that a world war, if the imperialists initiate it, will inevitably assume the character of a nuclear war with missiles, i.e., a war in which the nuclear weapon will be the chief instrument of destruction, and missiles the basic vehicle for their delivery to target.

The massive employment of atomic and thermonuclear weapons and the unlimited capabilities of missiles to deliver them to any target within minutes will make possible the most decisive military results at any distance, over an enormous area, and within an extremely brief period.

One must emphasize that the present international system and the present state of military technology will cause any armed conflict to develop, inevitably, into a general war if the nuclear powers are drawn into it.

The logic of war is such that if American aggressive circles initiate a war, it will be transferred immediately to the territory of the United States of America. All weapons—intercontinental ballistic missiles, submarine-launched missiles, and other strategic weapons—will be used in this military conflict.

Countries on whose territory NATO and American military bases are located and countries which build these military bases for aggressive purposes would suffer crushing blows in such a war. A nuclear war would, in an instant, spread over the entire globe.

The enormous destructive power of already existing types of nuclear weapons is well known. If one multiplies this force by the massive use of nuclear weapons and the reliable and accurate means of delivery provided by missiles, an idea of the nature of a missile-nuclear war is obtained.

The currently existing types of hydrogen bombs are several times more powerful than all the explosives used in World War II and even in the whole history of mankind. It is sufficient to say that whereas English and American aircraft, in huge numbers of air raids from 1940–1945, were able to drop about two million tons of bombs on targets in Germany and German-occupied countries, now one strategic missile can deliver a nuclear charge many times greater than the total explosive power of the ordinary explosives contained in these two million tons of bombs.

According to calculations made by scientists, if one hydrogen bomb is detonated in an industrial region, up to 1.5 million people may be killed outright and about 400,000 more people will perish from the subsequent fall-out. Even an average hydrogen bomb is sufficient to wipe a large city from the face of the earth.

British scientists have concluded that four bombs with megaton yields, one each dropped on London, Birmingham, Lancashire, and Yorkshire, will annihilate a minimum of 20 million people.

Soviet and foreign experts have calculated that approximately 100 nuclear bombs of 2 megatons each, detonated within a short space of time, would be sufficient to turn all the industrial regions and administrative-political centers of an industrially developed state of about 300–500 thousand square kilometers into a pile of ruins, and its territory into a wasteland contaminated with deadly radioactive substances.

The data on possible American losses are particularly interesting. According to calculations presented to Congress by American experts, the expected losses in the United States after a twenty-four-hour nuclear war would amount to 50–75 million people.

An official American congressional document states that if, in the initial phase of a war, the main targets in the United States were struck by 263 thermonuclear bombs, averaging 5 megatons each, then according to the authors' calculations, these blows would destroy 132 large military targets, many important industrial plants, and 71 large cities. Almost half of the nation's territory would be contaminated by radioactivity. Consequently, 50 per cent of the American population would be casualties of nuclear weapons.[30]

According to U.S. Department of Health calculations, only 135 million Americans out of 188 million would survive a nuclear attack on

---

[30] U.S. ED. NOTE—The reference is to the report of the Joint Committee on Atomic Energy, Congress of the United States, *Biological and Environmental Effects of Nuclear War, Summary-Analysis of Hearings June 22–26, 1959,* August 1959, U.S. Government Printing Office, Washington, D.C., 1959.

American cities. The dead alone would amount to 53 million. Moreover, it is believed that the majority of the cities would be destroyed by the nuclear blow, 90 per cent of the water supply would be disrupted, and large amounts of medical supplies would become unusable. Naturally, under these conditions, widespread, catastrophic epidemics would be inevitable.

These data give some idea of the inevitable destruction and casualties in a nuclear war. Moreover, it should be emphasized that the numbers cited were taken largely from foreign sources and fall short of reflecting the probable results of nuclear blows. Actually, if the Soviet Union is forced to fight, it will have the sufficient means to deliver nuclear strikes to a much larger number of any aggressor's various targets, and to use warheads of much greater yield than 5 megatons. Obviously, the use of superpowerful thermonuclear warheads, which are being further developed, will increase the destructive, annihilating character of a future war to a colossal degree.

Now, in addition to nuclear weapons and missiles, still another new and very important military and technical factor has emerged which undoubtedly will exert a marked influence on the nature of war. We refer to the use of electronic gear, in particular, electronic computers and various other types of equipment, by the armed forces, and other devices for automatizing and mechanizing control and command over weapons and troops as a whole.

The further development and massive introduction of the latest military electronic gear, primarily electronic computers, into the armed forces will substantially increase the military effectiveness of the armed forces. This, in turn, will alter the methods and character of military operations, making them more flexible and mobile.

Electronic equipment and automation in modern warfare are exceptionally important primarily because they are components of missile control systems; neither the development nor the use of this decisive weapon is possible without them. N. S. Khrushchev has stated: "Now we need press only one button and . . . whole cities will be blown up, and whole countries can be destroyed. Such is the enormous destructive power of modern weapons. . . ." * Missiles with nuclear warheads are such weapons, and electronic devices, figuratively speaking, are the "buttons."

Military electronic equipment is of use, not only for the employment of missiles and other military equipment, but also for the control of

---

* N. S. Khrushchev, *Velichestvennaia programma Kommunisticheskogo stroitel'-stva v nashei strane* [*The Magnificent Program of Communist Construction in Our Country*], Gospolitizdat, Moscow, 1958, p. 29.

military forces and weapons as a whole. It is basic to the problem of the automation of complex and diverse staff activities. Without such automation, effective command of the armed forces in a modern war cannot be assured.

The development and introduction of missiles, nuclear weapons, and electronic equipment have led to fundamental changes in almost all other weapons. As a result, the relative importance and strategic purpose of the various branches of the armed forces and their military employment have so changed that a war of a wholly new nature is foreordained.

Regardless of the future wartime role of such instruments of strategy as the Strategic Missile Forces, victory over the aggressor can be achieved only by the combined exertions of all the war-waging forces, namely: the Ground Forces, the National PVO, the Air Force, and the Navy, with the active participation of the people.

In a future war, the socialist coalition will aim at conclusive political and military goals. To attain these goals, it will not be enough just to destroy the enemy's means of nuclear attack, to defeat his main forces by missile blows and to disorganize his rear. For final victory in what would clearly be a class war, it will be absolutely necessary to smash the enemy's armed forces completely, deprive him of strategic areas of deployment, liquidate his military bases, and occupy his strategically important regions. In addition, the enemy's air and naval forces must not be permitted to make landings, and his ground forces must be prevented from invading the territories of the socialist countries. These territories must be held, and the internal security of the socialist states must be protected against enemy subversion. All these and a number of other problems can be solved only by the Ground Forces.

For this reason, the Ground Forces will undoubtedly play an important role, along with the Missile Forces, in achieving the final goals of the war.

The Ground Forces, equipped with operational and tactical missiles carrying nuclear warheads, have new military effectiveness, and an increased ability to defeat enemy formations in ground theaters. The necessity of conducting military operations with large masses of infantry in close formation is decreased.

The basic fire power of the Ground Forces is now in its operational [medium range] and tactical missile divisions and regiments, which are armed with nuclear missiles and other missiles with a range of several to many hundreds of miles. In addition, conventional weapons, especially artillery, also play an important role in the Ground Forces. Soviet military strategy envisages the most extensive use of conventional weapons even in a missile war, and they should be skillfully employed in conjunction with, and to supplement, nuclear weapons.

Let us note the following fact. A Soviet motorized infantry division now has considerably fewer personnel than at the end of the last war. On the other hand, the weight of one of its volleys [total weight of one round fired by all weapons], not including missiles, is more than four times as great. Moreover, Soviet motorized infantry and tank divisions now have more tanks than either a corps in the Great Patriotic War or a similar division of any NATO country.

The possibility that the probable aggressor will inflict massive nuclear blows upon vitally important centers of the socialist countries and upon the main formations of their armed forces leads to the conclusion that the air defense and antimissile defenses of the country will assume an increasingly important role in a future war.

Air and antimissile defense is currently being equipped with anti-aircraft missiles of varying range, new types of fighter planes, long-range search radars, and automated control systems. This has resulted in a marked increase in the military effectiveness of the defense against current forms of air attack.

The rearming of the National PVO with antiaircraft missiles instead of antiaircraft artillery has brought exceptionally important military advantages. The following case illustrates the point. During the last war, an average of 400–600 antiaircraft shells were required merely to destroy a single enemy airplane. On the other hand, a modern plane with enormous speed and a ceiling twice that of antiaircraft shells can be downed by one or, at most, two missiles.

A study of the present status and prospects of modern weapon development indicates that the wartime role of the Air Forces differs from that of the last war. At that time, aircraft was by far the longest range instrument of destruction in the combat zone and the only means for striking targets deep in the enemy's rear. Aircraft, by comparison with armaments, also had the most powerful explosives.

The situation has now changed radically. Missiles have the longer range and are more powerful and effective instruments of destruction. Moreover, it has become difficult for bombers to penetrate air defenses. Because this role of the bomber has changed considerably, aviation itself has also undergone extensive modernization.

Obsolete piston-engine planes have been completely replaced by modern jet planes, including supersonic long-range bombers. Aircraft cannon and machine guns have also been replaced by missiles. In recent years, the speed and ceiling of military planes have been increased 1.5 to 2.5 times. Missile-carrying aircraft, capable of dealing nuclear blows to an aggressor from a great distance without penetrating the zone of antiaircraft defense, are being introduced in increasing measure.

In a future war, air missions like reconnaissance and the transport of troops and supplies will occupy an important place.

The development and large-scale introduction of missiles into the Armed Forces have also led to a reappraisal of the Navy's wartime role and significance. The Navy's over-all wartime importance will be determined by the new missions assigned to it, especially combat with the enemy's navy, whether the latter is at sea or in port.

The chief weapons of the Soviet Navy are various types of submarines, which are incomparably more effective than surface ships in a missile war. Moreover, strategy views nuclear [powered] submarines armed with powerful missiles with nuclear warheads as the core of the submarine fleet. Missile-carrying naval aircraft will fight in combination with submarines.

Our naval strength has grown considerably because it has been equipped with new weapons. It can now carry out active missions far from Soviet shores. Modern submarines are capable of striking vital centers with ballistic and homing missiles, as well as destroying ships of any enemy's navy.

The development of the branches of the Armed Forces will be considered in detail in Chapter 5.

A brief survey of the status of the principal modern weapons and their effect on the nature of war permits the well-founded conclusion that a future world war, from the weapons point of view, will be primarily a *missile and nuclear* war. It will be conducted primarily with massive employment of missiles by all branches of the armed forces, but mainly by the Strategic Missile Forces. One must expect the aggressor to use chemical and bacteriological weapons in conjunction with nuclear weapons.

## Military and Strategic Features of a Future World War

The use of qualitatively new weapons in a future missile world war will naturally lead to basic changes in the military and strategic aims of both sides and will cause a radical break in the methods of conducting war and military operations.

In all previous wars, the belligerents sought principally to defeat or weaken the enemy's armed forces and, consequently, to capture and occupy vitally important regions or administrative and political centers. Once such goals were achieved, the political goals of the war were usually also realized.

The adversaries therefore conducted offensive and defensive operations, or a combination of both, in accordance with their political and strategic goals and the capacities of their armed forces. The main events took place in military theaters of operation (ground or naval), both sides being in direct contact, since no long-range destructive instruments of strategy then existed.

In World War II, the introduction of the strategic weapon of the long-range bomber made it possible for the belligerents not only to inflict deeper blows on the opponent's armed forces but also to attack targets within his homeland. As a result, aerial bombardment with the purpose of disrupting operations far behind the lines was added to direct battlefield action.

Here one must stress that blows on targets deep in the territory of the belligerents were not at all decisive for the course and outcome of World War II. The defeat of the enemy's armed forces in the theaters of military operation and the seizure of his administrative political centers and other vital regions actually accomplished the war's strategic aims.

What will be the characteristic strategic aims of a future war and how will it be conducted?

Assuming that the belligerents of both camps strive for the goals described above, they will employ the most decisive instruments of war—above all, many nuclear weapons—in order to annihilate the opponent or force him to surrender in the shortest possible time.

The question arises: Given such conditions, what is the main strategic goal of war? Is it, as in the past, the defeat of the opponent's armed forces or is it the annihilation and devastation of targets deep within a country in order to break up the organization of the country?

Soviet military strategy answers as follows: The attainment of both these goals must be simultaneous. The annihilation of the opponent's armed forces, the destruction of targets deep in his territory, and the disorganization of the country will be a single, continuous process of the war. The two chief reasons are, first, the need to defeat the aggressor as thoroughly and as quickly as possible, which requires that he be deprived of the military, political, and economic capacity to wage war; and, second, the use of military instruments [now] at hand might well accomplish these [military, political, and economic] aims simultaneously.

The probable enemy's targets, which comprise his economic, moral, and political potential and his military might, are located over an enormous area, often deep within his territory and on other continents. To destroy them, long-range strategic weapons above all will be required, together with appropriate methods of armed combat. The proportion of such [long-range] military operations in the whole struggle will greatly increase. At the same time, military operations on a relatively shallow front, where the opponent's ground forces are concentrated, will be much less important in a future war, and chiefly ground forces in contact with the opponent's troops will conduct these operations.

All this shows that the relationship between the role and importance of armed combat, on the one hand, waged by forces in direct contact with the enemy in the zone of military operations and employing tactical and operational weapons of destruction, and of armed combat, on the other hand, waged beyond this zone by strategic weapons of destruction has changed sharply in the direction of increasing the role and importance of the latter.

Thus, the mission of strategic weapons, whose action is beyond the range of tactical and operational weapons, has become much more important than that of troops in direct contact with the opponent.

Thus, the instruments acting on the opponent, the techniques of their use, and the way in which the war of the future will be fought will differ radically from previous wars, including also the past world wars.

Massive missile-nuclear blows will be of decisive importance in attaining the goals of a future world war. Such blows will be the principal and decisive means of conducting the war, and their delivery cannot be made directly dependent upon the course of the battle between adversaries in direct contact on the ground front.

Armed combat in ground theaters will also be different. Missile attacks will be the primary means of defeating the opponent's ground forces, of destroying his missiles, planes, and nuclear weapons. All this will lead to numerous completely destroyed, devastated, and radioactively contaminated zones. Considerable opportunities for extensive offensive maneuvers with highly mobile mechanized troops are thus opened. Positional warfare evidently has become a thing of the past. Rapid combat maneuvers conducted simultaneously or consecutively in different places and at different depths in the zone of military operations will replace positional warfare.

Whereas in the last war the main problem of the offensive was systematically to break through deeply echeloned, strongly fortified defense zones, the opportunity of using missile weapons obviates this problem.

Formerly, an attack was ordinarily carried out slowly on a continuous front, in close battle formations, against a defending enemy who assumed the same operational disposition. Now, it will be carried out by mobile assault formations in the direction of the principal thrusts, at great speed, and with rapid and deep penetration of the enemy's position. In the past, attacking forces had to seize the entire area within the zone of advance;

now they need only capture particular regions and centers of vital importance not destroyed or demolished by missile attack.

The techniques of defense operation by troops are also changing fundamentally. Defense will be based upon missile attacks, swift maneuver of highly mobile troops, and counterattacks in conjunction with stubborn defense of vital regions. The defense will try to hold the main regions in the most likely places of enemy attack. A linear defense based on continuous zones evidently will not be used.

Fundamental changes occur in the techniques of naval operations. It is instructive that even in World War II aircraft caused up to one-half of all naval losses. If strategic missiles are widely used, they will execute the main naval missions. Of the naval forces, only missile-carrying submarines and, to some extent, missile-carrying naval aircraft will be used in conjunction with these weapons. The naval operations of large surface formations will disappear from the scene, as well as the surface ships themselves. In a future war, missile strikes from the ground and from submarines on maneuvers, operating together with missile-carrying aircraft, will try to defeat enemy naval formations, his carrier task forces, and his missile-carrying submarines both in port and at sea, to disrupt his maritime and ocean communications, and to destroy important targets in coastal regions.

Since the potential enemy believes that the best way to his goals in a future war is by "nuclear attack" and strategic bombers, and "surface-to-surface" and "ship-to-surface" missiles are the best delivery vehicles, one of the primary Soviet strategic missions is to protect the rear from nuclear attack by antimissile and air defenses.

Further improvement in antimissile and antiaircraft defense, primarily by automated control of antiaircraft missile complexes, the creation of effective means of combating enemy ballistic missiles in flight and mastery of the techniques of using them, and the organization of a defense against weapons of mass destruction plus other measures should maximally reduce losses from enemy nuclear attacks and should preserve the continued functioning of the interior of the country and the combat capacity of the Armed Forces.

But one must recognize that the present instrumentalities of nuclear attack are undoubtedly superior to the instrumentalities of defense against them. Consequently, the threat of a massive nuclear surprise attack by the enemy remains.[31]

The possibility that the enemy will attack by surprise and with massive use of nuclear weapons immeasurably increases the need for the

---

[31] U.S. ED. NOTE—See Note B, pp. 315–316.

Armed Forces to be in constant combat readiness. In some instances, the time required to bring troops to combat readiness should be measured not in days, and in a number of cases, not even in hours. For many units and formations it is now only a matter of minutes. This applies above all to the Missile Forces, the main instrument for dealing massive nuclear blows to the aggressor, and it also applies to the National PVO, whose mission is to repel any enemy air attack and to protect the country's most important regions and installations, including the Armed Forces, from nuclear attacks. Troops in border districts, fleets, and air forces must be in constant combat readiness. Every unit, every formation must be ready at a signal or upon command to execute its combat mission immediately. Only with such an exceptionally high degree of readiness can an aggressor's attack be successfully foiled and his surprise blows repelled.

To achieve the most decisive results in the shortest time in a future world war, the Soviet Armed Forces and those of the entire socialist camp will have to employ their main military forces from the very outset of the war, literally during the very first hours and minutes. This is a strategic requirement because the enemy's first massive nuclear assaults could cause such civilian and military losses that the people and the country would be put in an extremely difficult situation. Therefore, not only is a high degree of combat readiness required of the Armed Forces but the entire country must also be specially prepared for war against the aggressor.

War conducted in such a way can fundamentally alter former concepts of how fighting develops during various stages of a war. At the same time, it attests to the extraordinary increase in the importance of the *initial period of the war.*

In the very first minutes of the war, the belligerents may use up their carriers, missiles and aircraft, accumulated in peacetime along with their stockpiles of nuclear weapons in order to destroy and devastate the enemy's most important targets throughout his entire territory, and to achieve their main political and military-strategic aims within a brief period of time and at the very outset of the war. Therefore the initial period of a modern missile war will obviously be the main and decisive period and will predetermine the development and outcome of the entire war. The fighting in this period obviously will be most fierce and destructive.

A future war characteristically will extend over an *enormous geographic expanse*. The conduct of hostilities will reflect the fact that the adversaries will aim for conclusive results. Hostilities will be conducted, not only in the zone where the two sides are in military contact, but everywhere on the territory of the warring coalitions, since both sides

will try to completely break up the organization of the enemy's homeland. The large numbers of weapons and their great strategic maneuverability and range will mean that all the enemy's territory, including the
remotest regions, will be under fire. The enormous size of the belligerents' territories and their geographic relation to each other mean that the
war will engulf almost all the continents of the world. War will be waged,
not only on land and sea, but also over the long lines of communication.

The enormous geographic expanse of a future war requires the development and improvement above all of those weapons which can
execute missions at any range: strategic missiles, atomic-powered missile-carrying submarines, and, to a certain extent, missile-carrying aircraft.

The Leninist teachings on *the role of the popular masses in war* are
of fundamental importance for the correct elucidation of the special
features of modern war.

Writing about Tsarism's defeat in the Russo-Japanese War, V. I.
Lenin said: "Wars today are fought by peoples; this brings out more
strikingly than ever a great attribute of war, namely, that it opens the
eyes of millions to the disparity between the people and the government,
which heretofore was evident only to a small class-conscious minority." *
In modern wars the disparity between the national interest and the
aggressive policy of the imperialistic governments stands out even more
clearly. The masses of the people, depending on their level of political
maturity and all the circumstances of the predatory wars conducted by
their governments, either passively resist this continuation [of imperialist
policy] or struggle actively against it. As a result of the class contradictions which, in Lenin's phrase, tear peoples to pieces in unjust predatory
wars, there never has been nor will there be unity within the imperialist
states, and [therefore] no chance to pull all the people into support of
the war.

The political goals of the just wars of liberation, in defense of a socialist
state, are intelligible and dear to the broadest masses, who therefore
will conscientiously and actively support and execute their government's
policies. Here, the socialist states have an indisputable and reliable advantage over capitalist countries.

A future war will be a clash of two military coalitions with enormous
human resources. The socialist coalition has a population of over 1
billion. About 650 million people make up the imperialist blocs. These
data show how great a mass of people could be drawn into a third
world war.

---

* V. I. Lenin, *Sochineniia* [*Works*], Vol. 8, p. 34.

A future war will require a different approach, from that in the past, to the use of the state's human resources. Modern complex military equipment requires large numbers of operating personnel, particularly engineers and technicians.

The proportion of engineering and technical personnel in all armies is continuously increasing. At the end of the last war, in the Soviet Armed Forces, the ratio of engineering and technical personnel to command personnel in the Table of Organization was 1 to 4.2. In the Ground Forces, the ratio was 1 to 5.7. Since the war, the situation has changed sharply. Now the ratio of engineering and technical personnel to command personnel in the Armed Forces as a whole is 1 to 1.5, and 1 to 3 in the Ground Forces. By the beginning of 1960, the engineering and technical staff made up almost 38 per cent of all officers, i.e., twice as many as in 1941. Typically, for every 100 officers in the Missile Forces, there are 72 engineers and technicians. The number of engineers and technicians in our Armed Forces is being increased, undoubtedly because of the complexity of modern military equipment and because the Armed Forces are getting more of this equipment.

The increase in engineering and technical personnel will be determined to a considerable extent by the wide introduction of nuclear and missile weapons and military electronic equipment in the Armed Forces. The appearance [of these new weapons] has led to the creation of special units, both combat and maintenance, and also to [special] staffs in the armies and the headquarters of the Armed Forces.

In a future war, the extensive use of weapons of mass destruction will cause heavy losses of military personnel. Large numbers of militarily trained reserves to provide replacements for the armies in the field and to form new units will be needed. Not only the armies in the field and the strategic reserves but the civilian population, too, will suffer serious losses from weapons of mass destruction. For this reason, large contingents of medical personnel will be required, along with various specialists to organize public health measures and to deal with the consequences of a nuclear, chemical, and bacteriological attack by an aggressor.

Enormous manpower losses by the belligerents characterized even past world wars. During World War I, the German army lost 7.5 million men, the Russian army lost 7 million men, the French army lost 4.6 million men, and the British army lost 3.1 million men.

According to the Western press, Germany lost 12 million men during World War II, primarily on the Russian front.

Our former allies' losses in this war are quite interesting. The United States had only 417,000 dead and Great Britain, 771,000. This, by the way, demonstrates strikingly how passively the American and British armed forces conducted military operations against the fascist bloc.

Experience shows that the large-scale introduction of increasingly complex and highly effective equipment causes increase in numbers of the armed forces generally, as well as of those troops that make use of technical equipment. [This increase takes place] for troops with primary combat missions and also for maintenance units, directorates, staffs, etc. On this basis, Soviet military strategy has concluded that, in spite of the extensive introduction of nuclear weapons and the latest types of different kinds of military equipment, a future world war will require *massive armed forces*.

The armed forces will be of very great size, moreover, because a large number of countries on both sides will be involved in the war and because the geographical scope of the war will be extended. Enormous territories in the deep rear [of the combatant countries] and communications of all types and of tremendous length will have to be protected and defended.

In this connection, one must draw attention to the complete bankruptcy of modern bourgeois theorists who advocate small professional armies with a high level of technical equipment, because they are afraid to arm the masses for class reasons. Similar theories have been advanced in the past. Before World War I, some general staffs, in official documents and military literature as well, tried to prove that, given the increasing power and rate of fire weapons, the forces composed of the already mobilized cadres and reserves and the weapons stocks accumulated in peacetime would be sufficient [to fight the war]. However, as is known, reality upset all these calculations.

During the present epoch, the largest capitalist states maintain massive armies even in peacetime. The United States had more than 2.5 million men in the armed forces at the end of 1961.

These data show that modern armed forces are already of tremendous size and may be considerably increased if the imperialist states unleash an aggressive war.

Thus, a future world war between the imperialist and socialist coalitions of states will undoubtedly be conducted with massive armed forces, even though these forces have very extensive technical equipment and employ missiles of enormous combat effectiveness.

Obviously, in a future war, only countries with large populations can organize armed forces in the millions. But there is more to the matter. The rational use of the country's human resources, both for call up to the Armed Forces and to work in the economy, depends greatly on the character of the social and political system and on the level of development and the particulars of economic organization and planning. The experience of the Civil War and, in particular, of the Great Patriotic War showed that the Soviet socialist system possessed an indisputable and important advantage over the capitalist systems in this respect.

Not only the capacity of states to mobilize but the quality of military personnel, too, depends on the nature of the social and political system. The level of popular well-being and education determines the quality of the personnel, which is extremely important, both in the physical preparation and, in modern war, in technical preparation.

When the armed forces include tens of millions of men and when war becomes more intense and violent than at any time in the past, the importance of the soldiers' combat morale increases. With the widespread use of nuclear weapons, the [military] personnel will be required to strain their moral and physical capacities to the utmost; to exhibit exceptional organization, discipline, courage, steadfastness, and the ability to fight effectively under any, even the most difficult, conditions; and to make maximum use of military equipment.

As the Great Patriotic War showed, the personnel of the Soviet Armed Forces possess these qualities in full measure. They are united around the Communist Party and are ready to endure any privations and make any sacrifices to defend their socialist achievements and their socialist Fatherland from encroachments by any aggressor.

An analysis of the essential nature of modern war, how it breaks out, the instruments and the methods with which it is fought, permits the following basic general conclusions on the possible nature of a future war.

In the present epoch (in spite of the absence of a fatal inevitability of war and in spite of the unrelenting struggle for peace by the Soviet Union, the entire socialist camp, and all men of good will), the outbreak of war is not excluded. This conclusion derives from the insoluble economic and political contradictions of imperialism, the bitter international class struggle, the aggressive policy of world reaction, particularly of the American monopolists, and the intensified imperialist war preparations.

If the imperialist bloc initiates a war against the USSR or any other socialist state, it will inevitably become a *world war,* with the majority of the world's countries participating in it.

In its political and social essentials, *a new world war will be the decisive armed collision of two opposing world social systems. This war will inevitably end with the victory of the progressive, communist social and economic system over the reactionary, capitalist social and economic system, which is historically doomed to destruction.* The true balance of political, economic, and military forces of the two systems, which has changed in favor of the socialist camp, guarantees such an outcome of war. However, victory in a future war will not come of itself. It must be thoroughly prepared for and secured in advance.

A new world war will be a *coalition war.* The capitalist military coalition will be on one side; the socialist coalition on the other.

Given the acute class nature of a future world war, in which each side will aim for conclusive political and military results, the peoples' relation to the war will be of very great importance. In spite of the fact that large quantities of new kinds of military equipment will be used, *massive armed forces* will engage in combat. Many millions of people will be needed to meet war needs and to work in the economy. Therefore the attitude of the masses of the people toward the war will inevitably exert a decisive influence on the outcome of a future war.

From the point of view of weapons, a third world war will be a *missile and nuclear war.* The massive use of nuclear weapons, particularly thermonuclear, will make the war unprecedentedly destructive and devastating. Entire states will be wiped off the face of the earth. Missiles carrying nuclear warheads will be the main instruments for attaining the war's aims and for accomplishing the most important strategic and operational missions. Consequently, the leading branch of the armed forces will be the Strategic Missile Forces, and the role and mission of the other branches of the armed forces will be essentially changed. However, final victory will be attained only as a result of the combined efforts of all the branches of the armed forces.

The basic method of waging the war will be by massive missile blows to destroy the aggressor's instruments for nuclear attack and, simultaneously, to destroy and devastate on a large scale the vitally important enemy targets making up his military, political, and economic might, to crush his will to resist, and to attain victory within the shortest possible time.

*Under these conditions, the center of gravity of the entire armed struggle will be transferred from the zone of military contact, as in past wars, to deep within the enemy's land, including the remotest places. As a result, the war will be of unprecedented geographic scope.*

Since modern weapons permit exceptionally important strategic results to be achieved in the briefest time, both the *initial period of the war* and the methods of breaking up the opponent's aggressive plans by dealing him in good time a crushing blow will be of *decisive significance* *for the outcome of the entire war.** [32] Hence, the main task of Soviet military strategy is working out means for reliably *repelling a surprise nuclear attack by an aggressor.* To execute this mission successfully requires first of all a high state of combat readiness of the Soviet Armed Forces, particularly of the Strategic Missile Forces. In accordance with the decisions of the XXIInd Party Congress, this is the chief mission of the Armed Forces. It must never be forgotten by the command and staff at all levels and by those in the political and Party apparatus.

The enormous capacities of missiles and nuclear weapons make it possible to achieve the purposes of war within relatively short periods of time. Therefore, in the interest of our Motherland, it is necessary to develop and perfect the instruments and methods of combat with a view to *attaining victory over the aggressor, above all in the shortest possible time,* with minimum losses; but at the same time, it is necessary to make serious preparations for a protracted war.

The ability of the country's economy to mass produce military equipment, especially missiles, and to establish superiority over the enemy in modern weapons are the material prerequisites of victory. *The ability of the economy to assure the maximum power to the Armed Forces for dealing an annihilatory blow to the aggressor in the initial period of the war will be decisive for the outcome of a future war.*

Victory in war is determined not only by superiority in the military and technical sense, which, in turn, depends on the superiority of a nation's social, economic, and political system, but also by the ability to organize the defeat of the enemy and make effective use of available

---

* Speech of Marshal of the Soviet Union R. Ia. Malinovskii at XXIInd Party Congress. [October 23, 1961. *Pravda,* October 25, 1961.]

[32] U.S. ED. NOTE—As was noted in the Analytical Introduction, the reference here to the concept of pre-emptive attack is neither discussed in detail nor given as much emphasis as it was in Malinovskii's speech to the XXIInd Congress (where he mentioned it twice) or in subsequent statements by other military writers. Khrushchev, too, on a few occasions has made similar statements, as in his speech to the graduates of military academies, in July 1962, when he said: "We shall not allow anyone to take us by surprise. We have a reliable guard which will be able to seize in time the hand of those who would try to destroy our cities and villages. Such a reliable guard is the Armed Forces of the Soviet Union and of all the socialist countries." (*Red Star,* July 6, 1962.) However, in an article published in May 1962, Marshal Malinovskii omitted his earlier reference to anticipating an aggressor by dealing him a blow "in time." Instead, he seemed to imply the possibility of frustrating "the opponent's aggressive intentions" without initiating war. "The defensive might of a state is determined by its capability to reliably defend the country from aggression. This means that our defensive might must be such as to be able to instill in the aggressor uncertainty as to the outcome of the war planned by him, to nip in the bud his criminal designs, and finally, if war should become a fact, decisively to destroy the aggressor." (*Kommunist,* No. 7, May 1962, p. 15.)

weapons. For this purpose, the country must be thoroughly and scientifically prepared for war against the aggressor; and a high level of military skill must be required of the command staff and troops. Success in a future war will also depend on how far the level of development of military strategy meets the demands of modern war.

## U.S. ED. NOTE B: SOVIET STATEMENT ON ANTIMISSILE DEFENSE

[The Soviet authors have been more sober in their assessment of the effectiveness of antimissile defense than have public Soviet claims. In his talk with Arthur Sulzberger, of *The New York Times,* in September 1961, Khrushchev said: "I can only tell you that at the same time we told our scientists and engineers to develop intercontinental rockets, we told another group to work out means to combat such rockets. We expressed our great satisfaction with the work of the experts who produced the ICBM's. At the same time, we remain very satisfied with the work of those who produced the means for combating such rockets." [33] In his address to the XXIInd Congress of the CPSU, Marshal Malinovskii claimed that "the problem of destroying missiles in flight has been successfully solved." [34] This claim was repeated by Khrushchev. In a statement to visiting American newspaper editors in July 1962, Krushchev asserted that Soviet antimissile missiles could "hit a fly in outer space" and that he had planned to show a documentary film of the test explosion of a Soviet antimissile missile but had been advised against it. [35] Later in 1962, Soviet military spokesmen announced that the Soviet Union had built antimissile "complexes." For example, in a speech published in October 1962, Marshal Malinovskii said: "We have successfully solved the problem of destroying enemy missiles in flight. Our scientists have developed and our engineers, technicians, and workers have built and prepared complexes of numerous means for the defense of our country against enemy missile attacks." [36] This claim was repeated by Marshal S. S. Biriuzov, formerly Chief of the Soviet Air Defense Forces and presently Chief of the Strategic Missile Forces. [37]

Concerning Soviet defenses against submarines armed with Polaris missiles, Malinovskii said in a speech on February 22, 1963: "I must

---

[33] *New York Times,* September 8, 1961; *Izvestiia,* September 9, 1961.

[34] *Pravda,* October 25, 1961.

[35] *Izvestiia,* July 19, 1962.

[36] "Speech at the All-Army Conference on Ideological Questions," *Red Star,* October 25, 1962.

[37] *Red Star,* December 4, 1962; "Guarding the Motherland," *Voennye znaniia (Military Knowledge),* No. 1, January 1963, p. 4.

declare in all responsibility that this will not give the leaders of the Pentagon the military advantages which they expect to have. Our navy, in co-operation with missile troops and the air force, is capable of coping equally well with both land and submarine missile bases."[38]

The importance of developing an effective air and antimissile defense is often stressed in Soviet literature and is said to be "at the center of attention of our Party and government."[39] In this connection it is interesting to note a statement by the prominent Soviet physicist P. Kapitsa, who wrote in 1956: "In the struggle for the prevention of atomic war, it is essential to take into account the possibility that there will be found a reliable defense against nuclear weapons. If this is achieved by a country with aggressive intentions, then being itself protected against the direct effects of nuclear weapons, it can much more easily decide to launch an atomic war."[40]

[38] *Pravda,* February 23, 1963.
[39] Colonel I. Sidel'nikov, "On Soviet Military Doctrine," *Red Star,* May 11, 1962.
[40] "The Task of All Progressive Mankind," *Novoe vremiia (New Times),* No. 39, 1956, p. 10.

# ★ 5

# The Problem of Organizing and Developing the Armed Forces

## Factors Determining the Organization and Development of the Armed Forces

In order to organize and develop the armed forces, the problems of recruitment, organizational structure, weapons, personnel training, mobilization, and combat preparedness of troops must be solved. The social system, economic capacity, and guiding policy of the state are primary in the solution of these problems.

The nature and purpose of the state's armed forces reflect its social character and policy. This applies especially to the composition and aims of the armed forces, and to recruitment and training methods, particularly during modern times.

Armed forces appeared when the state did and represent one of its most important instrumentalities. The capitalist bourgeois state employs them as an instrument to extend its rule and suppress the popular masses, to seize foreign territories and enslave other peoples, and to defend itself if attacked by stronger and more aggressive capitalist states. V. I. Lenin wrote that militarism serves two purposes: ". . . as a military force to be used by capitalist states in their external conflicts . . . and as a weapon for the ruling classes to suppress any kind of (economic and political) proletarian movements. . . ." *

In brief, the armed forces of capitalist states, in the hands of the ruling classes, are tools of oppression, robbery, and violence.

---

* V. I. Lenin, *Sochineniia* [*Works*], Vol. 15, p. 169.

This concept is particularly relevant today. In a number of imperialist states, especially the United States, because of the increased coalescence of the capitalist monopolies with the military-bureaucratic state apparatus, the armed forces are becoming increasingly dependent upon the major monopolies and are being transformed into their obedient minions. As a result, they are becoming more reactionary, aggressive, and anti-popular—the tools of reaction, the servants of capital in its battle against labor, and the executioners of popular freedom inside as well as outside the country.

The essentially class nature of the capitalist states' armed forces and their function and designation as imperialist instruments predetermine even recruiting procedure and the entire training system.

At present, the armies of the capitalist states are ordinarily recruited by universal conscription; all classes of the population are drafted. This does not mean, however, that class selection and class divisions are without effect. The bourgeoisie, fearing their own people, employ veiled techniques of class selection when recruiting for the armed forces. "All governments in the world," Lenin wrote, "have come to fear a national army open to peasants and workers; they take secret measures of all kinds to select special military units from the bourgeoisie and provide them with particularly advanced military equipment." *

Selectivity in manning was a regular procedure of the Nazi Army, which followed this principle in forming the SS troops, tank formations and commands, air forces, and other special troops. In modern capitalist armies, the bourgeoisie select the most reliable units and formations for missile and nuclear forces, special aviation units, paratroops, and other special troops. For example, one could point to the special selection of the most reliable soldiers and sergeants to man the American Strategic Army Corps [Strac]. This corps is intended to suppress popular revolutionary uprisings in other states and movements for national independence in colonies and dependent countries. For this reason, the personnel selected for such a corps are those who will carry out any orders of their masters without hesitation. French paratroopers employed in the "dirty Algerian war" are an example of this kind of manning. Their officers were selected with particular care.

But a special system of class selection in manning the capitalist armed forces is only one of the ways [used] to convert them into obedient imperialist tools. The chief efforts to this end are made when the personnel, particularly the soldiers and sailors, are trained and indoctrinated. The former American Secretary of Defense, McElroy, stated

---

* V. I. Lenin, *Sochineniia* [*Works*], Vol. 31, p. 171.

that "the first and most important question is the struggle for men's minds. Everything else depends on this struggle." And indeed, the struggle for men's minds, which has been carefully conceived and organized in all the capitalist armies, is conducted in a thoroughgoing manner.

The entire system of training and indoctrination in capitalist armies is directed toward eradicating class consciousness among the soldiers; the army is represented as a supra-class organization intended, it is alleged, to carry out the will of the entire people and nation. Using tricky ideological methods in working over the personnel, the bourgeois ideologists try to smooth over contradictions between the social origins [class interests] of army personnel and their designated functions. Even before being drafted, youth in capitalist countries are educated in a militaristic, chauvinistic spirit, and this "education" is reinforced when they are drafted. This is most typical of the American army. The ideological training of its personnel represents a carefully conceived system of propaganda and influence designed to keep bourgeois ideology dominant among the troops and to prepare soldiers and sailors for war against the Soviet Union and other socialist countries. Anti-Soviet and anti-Communist propaganda, the preaching of militant chauvinism, slander against socialism, and the fomenting of hatred toward the Soviet people are prominent in this training.

At the same time, the army's propaganda organization tries to embellish the façade of decrepit capitalism. The soldiers are instilled with the idea that they are allegedly protecting "the popular system," "the society of universal prosperity," "people's capitalism," "the free world," etc. Slogans of equality, freedom, and brotherhood are shamelessly propagated. The imperialist military forces, particularly the American, are glorified in every possible way, and justifications of all kinds are invented for the alliance with the West German revanchists and for the existence of aggressive imperialist blocs.

American soldiers and sailors are indoctrinated with the desire for domination, profit, and private ownership; attempts are made to cultivate the lowest instincts among these troops and to poison them with bourgeois nationalism, chauvinism, and racism. The ideas that the American way of life is exceptional, that the American army has a special mission, and that the American nation is superior are continually drummed into their heads. Supposedly the United States has been called upon to lead the whole world and manage the destiny of nations.

The ideological conditioning of soldiers in other capitalist armies is conducted along the same lines. In the West German Bundeswehr, hatred of mankind reigns once more. Former Nazi generals and officers try to re-establish the worst traditions of the defeated Fascist German army.

The imperialists, directly interested in predatory wars, try to inculcate a private interest in war into the soldiers of their armies and to transform them into professional marauders. This typified the Nazi Army, which not only satisfied the predatory desires of the German militarists, but also indulged in violence and open plunder of local populations in occupied territories.

The imperialists use various techniques to influence their soldiers and to convert the armed forces into passive instruments of class and national oppression, militarism, and reaction, which seriously threaten peace and security.

However, these instruments do not always pass the test of war and often betray the imperialists. Soldiers regain their class consciousness under the difficulties of war; they begin to realize that war is conducted in the interest of a handful of imperialists and that it brings suffering and want to the vast majority.

Then the military machine of the capitalist states begins to creak, weaken, and fall apart. This is what happened to many armies in World Wars I and II, and will happen in a third world war, which the imperialists are preparing against the socialist countries.

The idea of aggression, plunder, and enslavement of other peoples cannot serve as a reliable foundation for high morale in belligerent armies. V. I. Lenin stated that "The masses cannot be led in a war of plunder . . . and their enthusiasm cannot be relied on." *

In the socialist states, the nature of the social system also determines the organization and development of the armed forces. But this system is completely new, advanced, and progressive. Predatory wars of conquest against other nations are alien to it. The foreign policies of socialist states are based on principles of peace, equal rights, national self-determination, respect for the independence and the sovereignty of all countries and peoples, and the peaceful coexistence of states with different social systems. The socialist system is the natural center of gravity for all the peace-loving forces in the world.

Consequently, even the armed forces of the socialist states are of an entirely new type. These are armed forces of the people, liberated from capitalist slavery and summoned to protect the nation's freedom and independence from encroachment by imperialist aggressors.

Armies are not formed in socialist countries to cope with the internal situation, but primarily to protect the state against attack by external enemies and from the danger of war emanating from the imperialist camp. Only this compels the Soviet Union to maintain Armed Forces

---

* V. I. Lenin, *Sochineniia* [*Works*], Vol. 25, p. 337.

and to keep them at a level of combat-readiness which will ensure the conclusive and complete defeat of an enemy who dares encroach upon the Soviet Motherland. This is also true of the armed forces of all the other socialist countries.

In contrast to the capitalist armies, the armed forces of the socialist countries are not the tools of the exploiting classes, but the instruments of an entire people liberated from capitalist slavery. These are true peoples' armies. They are of the people, inseparably attached to them, and they protect the magnificent conquests of socialism, the freedom and independence of the socialist countries, and their state interests. These are armies [that epitomize] the friendship and brotherhood of socialist peoples; they are imbued with the spirit of socialist internationalism,[1] and trained to respect peoples of other countries and to extend fraternal aid to peoples struggling for liberation from class and national oppression.

Such is the social nature and purpose of socialist armed forces, which determine how they are manned, trained, and indoctrinated. In socialist states, military service is the honorable duty of every citizen. Here there is no class selection; all citizens have the same rights and the same obligation to defend their state. There is also none of the class antagonism between enlisted men and officers which is typical of capitalist armies. Whereas in capitalist armies the officer is a servant who executes the will of the imperialists, in the socialist countries an officer is a servant who executes the will of the entire people. The basic criterion for selecting the officer corps is not class affiliation, but devotion to the people and to the Socialist Motherland, high political morale, efficiency, and the individual's personal qualities.

In the socialist armies the entire training system is directed toward developing the high moral and political qualities characteristic of the new man who is a member of the most progressive society. [All this is done] to strengthen the standards of Communist morality which is the most humane in the world.

In the socialist states the personnel of the armed forces are imbued with a high level of political consciousness, a great love for their Motherland, a sanctified hatred of the enemy, boundless devotion to the people, selflessness in fulfilling their military obligations, genuine humanity and comradeship in their relations with one another and in their dealings with civilians, a high sense of military discipline and courage, and respect for human dignity and the rights and customs of the people whose

---

[1] U.S. ED. NOTE—In Russian a distinction is made between *internatsionalizm*, i.e., the relations between the nationalities within a state, and *mezhdunarodnyi*, i.e., the relations between states. The first usage is employed above.

countries they enter during war or peace to carry out the obligations of allies.

The very humane moral code of the Soviet individual and of the [people of] other socialist states is also compulsory for all the personnel of their armed forces. This code is instilled in officers and men by the whole system of civil and military education.

The fundamental principle in organizing and developing armed forces in the Soviet Union and other socialist countries is that of leadership by the Communist and Workers' Parties. The Parties carefully train the armed forces, improve their combat capacity and fighting readiness, and inspire them to great military deeds in the interest of all the peoples of the socialist states.

The armed forces of the socialist states are strong in their acceptance of their high duty to the people; they are not daunted by any of the difficulties or adversities of war. This has been proved to the world more than once by the Soviet Armed Forces, particularly in World War II.[2]

These are the two completely contrasting bases for the origin, manning, and indoctrination of the armed forces in capitalist and socialist states. [The contrast] derives from essential differences between the [two] social and political systems and their domestic and foreign policies.

Another important factor in determining how the armed forces are to be organized is the condition of the national economy. The differences between the social systems of states, however, are much more important. Whereas the difference between the capitalist and socialist social systems produces sharply contrasting practices in the selection of personnel for the armed forces and in their indoctrination, the economy exerts an influence on the organization and development of the armed forces in both capitalist and socialist states which is, in principle, the same. This affects two things: the size of the armed forces and their military equipment. In short, the stronger the economy of the state, the more numerous its population, the higher its cultural level, the more developed its industry, agriculture, science, and technology, and the better able it will

---

[2] U.S. ED. NOTE—Various Soviet writers have expressed concern over the inadequate psychological preparation and training of Soviet soldiers. According to the First Deputy of the Chief of the Missile Forces, Colonel General V. F. Tolubko, "It is a secret for no one that there are fearful, indecisive, inattentive, unskillful soldiers and sergeants, with little endurance," and that some of them argue that they can do little in a future nuclear war where everything will be decided by missiles launched from thousands of miles away ("New Weapons and Psychological Training," *Red Star*, August 26, 1962). The low morale, poor living conditions, and inadequate state of readiness of Soviet soldiers, especially in the ground forces, have been the subject of a high-level military "Conference on the Living Conditions in the Soviet Armed Forces," which met in Moscow on June 4–9, 1962. (*Red Star,* June 5–9, 1962.)

be to maintain armed forces and provide them with the latest weapons and other military equipment. The economy, through its influence upon weapons and personnel, also affects the techniques of conducting military operations. However, whereas an increase in the might of any large imperialist power is invariably accompanied by an intensification of its aggressive aims, which leads to an increased threat of war, an increase in the strength of the socialist states, on the contrary, remains a reliable guarantee for preserving peace and increases the possibility of preventing war.

Capitalism has imposed its rule by fire and sword; the weapons of socialism, on the other hand, are superiority to the capitalist system in social organization, government, and the economy, in raising the standard of living and in the spirit and quality of the people. Thus the capitalist economy is the main source of the aggressiveness of its armed forces, whereas the socialist economy is the basis for the peace-loving aims of socialism, which are supported by the great military power of the army and the navy.

The economy of the state has always been the material basis for organizing armed forces and has determined their size and quality. Here it is useful to recall the well-known thesis of Engels: "All the organization and combat methods of armies . . . depend on materiel, i.e., economic conditions: either on human resources or weapons; consequently, on the size and nature of the population and technology." *

These words, spoken by Engels more than eighty years ago, are especially significant today. They refer to a period when armies were comparatively small and consisted only of ground forces and navies, when advances in military equipment, which depended upon the general level of production, were relatively slow and when it was not necessary to create large reserves of materiel to conduct war, since the outcome of a war ordinarily was decided by one or sometimes several general engagements. Then as now, however, the expenditures for maintaining armies and buying weapons and other military equipment exhausted state treasuries and placed a heavy burden on the shoulders of the people.

As the predatory aspirations of the capitalist states grew, their conflicts of interest became more intense and, as a result, their armed forces were continuously enlarged; advances in military equipment became more rapid and armies came to depend increasingly upon the level of production and the economic potential of the state. Whereas in the recent past armies were mainly equipped with rifles and cannons, their equipment now includes the most complex and expensive machinery—the last word

---

* F. Engels, *Anti-Diuring* [*Anti-Dühring*], Moscow, Gospolitizdat, 1952, p. 160.

in science and technology: missiles and nuclear weapons, missile-carrying nuclear submarines, supersonic jet aircraft, and complex electronic equipment, not to mention tanks, trucks, armored troop carriers, truck tractors, the newest artillery systems, combat engineering equipment, and other complex military equipment. The latest achievements of science and technology are used primarily for the production of armaments, and tremendous resources are expended for this purpose.

As military equipment has been developed and perfected, its cost has become exorbitant and state expenditures for army equipment have increased many times over. The Martin American bomber cost $38,000 in 1920; the B-29 cost $680,000 in World War II; the modern B-52 bomber costs $8.5 million and the B-58, $17.6 million. Each American Atlas missile costs the country $1.5 million; and according to the London *Times,* a nuclear submarine costs 35 million pounds while the sixteen Polaris missiles with which it is armed cost 6 million pounds.

The nature of military expenditures has changed with the increase in the cost of military equipment. Before World War I, more than 80 per cent of the military budget was spent on personnel, and the portion for weapons and other military equipment did not exceed 11 to 15 per cent. At present, however, the main portion of military expenditures goes for army equipment. In 1944, for example, the United States spent $60.2 billion of the $89.7-billion military budget on armaments, equipment, and military stores for the army, i.e., 67 per cent, while $29.5 billion or 33 per cent of all military expenditures were for personnel, etc.

The nature of military expenditures has also changed basically even in peacetime. During the 1961–1962 fiscal year, the United States spent about 43 per cent of the military budget on personnel for the armed forces. In the 1962–1963 fiscal year the allocations for personnel are planned to be about 28 per cent of the military budget, in spite of the fact that the armed forces have considerably increased in size over the past few years. In 1959, the United States spent 56 times as much on armament and weapons research as in 1938, and England spent 38 times as much.

Tremendous sums of money are spent to maintain armed forces. In peacetime military expenditures in many imperialist states consume more than 50 per cent of the entire state budget, while in wartime these increase to 70 per cent and more of the general budget. War and expenditures for war have become a real burden for the people and most profitable for capitalist monopolies, which run their businesses on the blood and suffering of millions.

The Program of the Communist Party of the Soviet Union states: "The imperialist states maintain enormous armed forces even in peacetime. Military expenditures absorb an increasingly greater share of the state budget. . . . By enriching individual groups of the monopoly bourgeoisie, militarism impoverishes nations, ruins peoples languishing under a burden of taxes, and increases inflation and high prices." In the United States, the military expenditures of the 1962–1963 fiscal year are 50 times greater than in 1936. During the last five years, the direct military expenditures of the United States have exceeded $220 billion; the expenditures of all the NATO countries in the arms race during the past ten years amount to more than $500 billion. In general, the capitalist countries spent 15 to 20 per cent of their entire national income for weapons and armed forces.

The capitalist states have built up a powerful military industry to prepare for war and equip armies; this industry is developing the most modern instruments for slaughtering people and destroying the values they have created. Many branches of nonmilitary industry are committed in some degree to the same purpose, and the greatest achievements in science and technology are used for these same ends. In the United States, for example, 48 per cent of all government allocations to science are for research related to war preparations. The trend to war has become a constant element of the capitalist economy.

The declaration of the Moscow Conference of Representatives of the Communist and Workers' Parties pointed out that only a negligible handful of monopolists and war speculators, who extract fabulous profits from war production are interested in the arms race. According to official data, the clear profits of American monopolies increased from $3.3 billion in 1938 to $43.4 billion in 1957; i.e., they increased by a factor of more than 13. In France, 32 capitalist companies received profits of over 32 billion francs in 1957, 40 billion in 1958, and about 46 billion in 1959. The clear profits of British monopolies increased from 1,242 million pounds in 1951 to 2,210 million in 1959.

The capitalist monopolies manufacturing nuclear weapons have earned the greatest profits. The General Dynamics Corporation increased its profits within ten years from 1.8 to 91.8 million dollars, and General Electric from $177 million in 1947 to $500 million in 1959.

Former President Eisenhower has acknowledged the existence of a sinister alliance between the colossal military organization and the huge military industry which employs millions of people and controls billions of dollars. Its pervasive influence—economic, political, and even psychological—is felt in every city, state government, and branch of the federal government. This union, or as Eisenhower called it, "the military and industrial complex," actually determines the entire domestic and foreign policy of the United States.

Once the war starts, state military expenditures increase even more steeply than in the past. The entire economy of the belligerent is converted to the needs of war, so that the population is provided with only a minimum of the bare necessities. The cost of war to mankind is very high. Entire countries are devastated, thousands of towns and villages are destroyed, and the labor of many generations is lost.

According to the calculations of the French economist, A. Claude, the war damage in Europe during World War II came to $260 billion, 50 per cent of it in the USSR. The direct military expenditures of all states participating in this war amounted to 1 trillion, 117 billion dollars, and the total cost of material damage resulting from the war reached the astronomical figure of $4 trillion. Such is the price mankind paid for imperialism's policy of plunder.

Only states with stable social and governmental systems enjoying popular support, and with highly developed economies able to maintain full-time armies of millions and to multiply them in the event of mobilization for war, can bear the enormous burdens of modern warfare. These armies must be equipped with all the latest weapons for the rapid execution of strategic missions and also for the conduct of a prolonged war. In a word, a modern economy must be able to equip its armed forces rapidly with maximum quantities of modern weapons and to ensure their regular provision with all the needed accessories in case the war is prolonged. To do this, the economy must be prepared during peacetime.

The economy of the state, which is the base on which the armed forces are developed, even determines the principles for their organization. The stronger the economic system of a state and the more highly developed its industry, science, and technology, the more easily can that state equip its army rapidly with sufficient high-quality weapons; these in turn determine how the armed forces are to be organized, and also how the war is to be conducted, that is, tactics, operations, and strategy.

The level of military art is important for the organization and development of the armed forces. The military art develops according to the laws of dialectics. One of the laws determining the progress of the military art is the interrelationship and mutual interdependence of military equipment, the organization of the armed forces, and the techniques for conducting combat operations. These factors are in constant flux. They develop reciprocally. As one or another factor changes, the others must change too. The determining factor in this interrelationship and interdependence is a product of industry or the economy—military equipment, primarily weapons. It is the most revolutionary element of all, and has a direct influence on how war is waged and on how the armed forces are developed and organized.

The development of military science affords concrete examples of this. The appearance of gunpowder and the subsequent development of firearms completely revolutionized military activity and ushered in a new epoch in the development of the military art and in the development and organization of the armed forces. As a result of the introduction of these arms into the army, and of their acceptance as basic weapons, the mass formations of troops that had been used for centuries disappeared forever. A new, extended formation, requiring more flexible troop organization, replaced them. The subsequent adoption by the army of rifled weapons, which have greater range and accuracy than smooth-bore weapons, contributed to the development of a new method of combat using riflemen in extended firing lines. The invention of automatic weapons and the development of combat engineering equipment produced group combat formations and furnished one of the principal reasons for positional types of warfare. Airplanes, tanks, and the many types of mobile artillery led to new mobile forms of combat operations. And finally, the modern nuclear weapon has brought about a complete revolution in military activity, making it necessary to revise principles of the military art that have been accepted for centuries; these new weapons required the search for and the elaboration of completely new methods of combat and troop organization.

The appearance of a new weapon not only influenced the [general] methods of offense and defense, but often produced a new type of combat operation for defense against this [specific] weapon, for example, antichemical defense, antiaircraft and antitank defense, defense against weapons of mass destruction, antisubmarine defense, etc. This process has introduced basic changes in control of troops, the organization of materiel, technical and medical supply operations, and many other areas of combat activity.

The new combat methods generated by new weapons have directly influenced the organizational structure and posture of the armed forces. These methods of combat have given rise not only to corresponding subdivisions, regiments, and units, but even to entire branches and types of armed forces. This applies particularly to air forces, PVO troops, and missile troops, which have not only pressed upon the heels of traditional types of armed forces (ground and naval forces) but in some cases have become dominant.

At the same time, the older types of armed forces have also changed markedly in structure, organization, size, and character because of the advent of new types of weapons and troops. Individual branches of the armed forces that previously played a rather considerable role in war have gradually lost their importance and have often completely disappeared from the scene. When World War I began, the ground forces of all the fighting armies had rather large cavalry forces, which played an important role in combat operations; in World War II, the only remaining cavalry was to be found, in small quantities, in the Soviet Armed Forces. Now cavalry no longer exists as a branch of the armed forces of any country. The horse as a means of maneuver has been replaced by the truck, tank, armored troop carrier, automobile, and prime mover. The wartime role and purpose of various types of armed forces and weapons have essentially changed. This will continue to be true in the future; obsolete forms of weapons will give way to new ones. Such are the dialectics of development.

Meanwhile, the conduct of combat operations and the army's organization of troops are not unaffected by weapons. As the former changes, new requirements are established for military equipment, weapons, and troop organization, which compel military and scientific thought to continue their development and improvement.

Production, which is fundamental to the development of weapons, even affects the methods of conducting war: tactics, operations, and strategy, the organizational form of the armed forces, and their posture. This effect is transmitted through the influence of production upon man and military equipment. The appearance of new forms of troop organization and new techniques for the conduct of war influence, in turn, the development of military equipment, and through it, the development of industry. There is a continuous process of historical development in the military art, and it revolves about man.

Indeed, it is man, with his reason and will, knowledge and ability, who creates the weapons for his own destruction and determines techniques for using these weapons, and methods for conducting war with the weapons that he has created. The higher the level of [political] consciousness or, more accurately, class consciousness in man, and the greater his understanding of his historical mission, the more effectively will he use the weapons he has created against the reactionary and aggressive forces of the old order, and against imperialist states if they start wars. In the final analysis he will eliminate war itself and guarantee the victory of the new Communist society, in which war will only be a historical relic from a difficult period in the past.

However, objective laws in nature and in society, including those governing the development of the military art, are not eternal in their operation, but apply only in certain conditions. Weapons do not always introduce basic changes in the conduct of war or in the organization and development of the armed forces. This only happens when a new weapon possesses fundamentally different and better military properties than older types, when it is produced and supplied to the armies en masse and thus becomes a basic, or one of the basic, combat weapons. When a new weapon radically changes the combat capacities of the armed forces so that they cannot be reconciled with the old ways of waging war, that is when weapons and ways of waging war are not in correspondence, contradictions are produced.

Accordingly, any attempt to use a new weapon within the framework of obsolete combat methods, or to use these obsolete methods without reference to the altered combat capacity of the troops, will be doomed to failure, or at best will not produce the required effect. Thus, during the Franco-Prussian War (1870–1871) the opposing armies were equipped with new rifled weapons, which had greater speed of fire, range, and accuracy than smooth-bore weapons. Neither side, however, drew the proper conclusions: they did not make the necessary changes in army organization or in combat methods and, as before, they attempted to fight with massed troop formations, using company and battalion columns in line formation. This inevitably led to great troop losses, and the men, often against the will of the officers, broke the obsolete battle formations and found new formations more suited to combat against rifled weapons. In this war the company and battalion columns broke under rifle fire and the men instinctively found a more appropriate form of combat: deployment of riflemen in extended fire positions.

Another example: When tanks appeared at the end of World War I, they were used within the limits of existing combat methods, which did not permit full exploitation of their combat potential and which led to only local tactical successes. Some operations during the final period of World War I, however, particularly the Battle of Cambrai and the Amiens operation, showed that even the tanks of that time, which were far from modern, could make major and decisive gains against the enemy if their full combat potential was used and if they were massed in one main area.

The history of war and the military art demonstrate that, when a weapon no longer matches the ways of waging war, the discrepancy will not be remedied by using the new weapon with the old techniques; this would be a step backward. Instead, methods of armed combat and troop organization must be sought which will make possible the most complete and effective use of the new weapon's combat potential. New forms of troop organization and combat methods do not develop at once, but gradually within the framework of previous types. As a rule, older forms of troop organization and ways of conducting combat operations are adapted to the new weapon, or vice versa; gradually, new methods are developed and improved until they give rise to other, still more effective weapons.

Any new weapon goes through a certain period of development and assimilation. During this period the combat properties of the weapon are studied and mastered, and appropriate forms of troop organization and combat methods are investigated. This period varies in length. It depends upon the industrial level of the country and its economic status. The higher this level and the greater the economic potential of the state, the less time required to master the use of the new military equipment and to furnish it to the armed forces. After that, new forms of troop organization and combat methods are investigated. For example, firearms first appeared in Western Europe in the first half of the fourteenth century. However, it took approximately four centuries to perfect these weapons so that they became the basic means of combat and completely revolutionized military operations. About three hundred years were required to develop rifled weapons to the point where they replaced smooth-bore weapons, began to play a decisive role in warfare, and caused the development of new forms of troop organization and combat methods.

As industry grew, less time was required to develop and test new weapons and to devise appropriate troop organization and combat methods. This has been particularly true of the twentieth century. Machine guns were first used, to a small extent, by the British army during the Boer War (1899–1902); twelve years later, in World War I, both belligerent sides used them extensively. In conjunction with fortifications, they reinforced defense to the point where the war rapidly acquired a positional nature. Aircraft were first used as a means of combat during this war, and tanks appeared at the end of the war; twenty years later, in World War II, tanks and aircraft became very important weapons of warfare and produced changes in combat methods that brought them to a high degree of perfection. Finally, in 1945, the American Air Force dropped two atomic bombs; after ten to twelve years, these terrible weapons have been developed to the point where they are indisputably the principal means of destruction in all modern armies.

The appearance of the nuclear weapon, like the invention of gunpowder and firearms, marks the beginning of a new era in the development of armed forces and the military art. Nuclear weapons and the modern means (missiles) for delivering them to targets are essentially unprecedented instruments of war. They have tremendous destructive power: for the first time in history weapons have been converted from a means which supports and secures troop combat operations into a means which independently executes operational and strategic missions. Strategy, operations, and tactics have acquired a powerful new weapon whose combat characteristics require that military operations be conducted differently and that troops be organized differently. These weapons leave their imprint on all the problems of organizing and developing armed forces in modern conditions.

The widespread introduction of nuclear weapons and other new military equipment into armed forces has altered the character of the latter radically, so that they have already outgrown the established methods of waging war. [The new character of weapons] imperiously demands, not the modification of the established methods, but the creation of new methods more appropriate to the combat capacity of modern weapons. At present, the military art is in a period of developing and assimilating nuclear weapons, and of investigating new ways to conduct combat operations, new forms of troop organization, and new directions in the organization and development of the armed forces. The salient feature of this period is the short time it has taken to develop nuclear weapons and establish them as the basic instrumentalities of combat. Because of their tremendous combat potential, these weapons have rapidly established themselves in this role. However, the search for new combat methods, new forms of troop organization, and new avenues of development of armed forces appropriate for these powerful weapons has proved to be a difficult problem over whose solution theoreticians and practitioners of the military art both here and abroad are laboring persistently.

One can sketch in outline how economics influences the development and organization of the armed forces and the development of the instruments and techniques for waging war.

War, however, does not break out independently. All the policies of the states and [social] classes involved have prepared the war, which is a continuation of those policies by other than peaceful means. Hence, it would be quite incorrect to assert that only the economic capacity of states determines the size and nature of the armed forces. The policies of the states and social classes involved exert just as much influence. Their policy establishes the strategic missions and determines the size and nature of the armed forces appropriate for the execution of these missions.

The stronger the economy of a capitalist state, the more aggressive is its policy and the more conclusive are the results at which its predatory strategy aims. But strategic war aims must always correspond to the combat capacity of the state's armed forces and to the ability of its economy to supply the armed forces with all the necessities for the conduct of war, and to maintain the state and its population at the necessary level of activity.

When the state's strategic war aims do not correspond to the weapons at its disposal, this leads to adventurism in war and policy, and finally to defeat. The sad lesson of Germany in two world wars is an obvious example.

In World War I, German imperialism pursued essentially adventuristic aims. War on two fronts was beyond the strength of Germany and her allies. The inability of the German economy to support prolonged strain led the Kaiser's army to an ignominious end.

In World War II, the Nazi armed forces were no stronger than the total armed forces of the other Western European countries, but the German army was many times stronger than the armed forces of each of these countries taken separately. Employing the strategy of defeating the enemy in stages, Nazi Germany rapidly brought almost all of Western Europe to its knees, and used the Western European economy for its own purposes. In this case, the Nazi German war aims corresponded to the forces, weapons, and the methods of combat used by Germany.

The Nazi attack on the Soviet Union created an entirely different situation. Here [Germany] encountered the more powerful Armed Forces of a state which was economically and politically stronger. The established aim of Nazi Germany—to enslave the Soviet Union—was not in consonance with Germany's weapons or economic capacity.

The predatory aspirations of Nazi Germany shattered against the fiery patriotism, staunchness, and courage of the Soviet people. The war quite convincingly demonstrated the power and invincibility of socialism.

The increasingly predatory aspirations of the imperialist states compel them to expand their armed forces continually and to expend tremendous resources to maintain them; the major part of their economy is devoted to this aim. This inevitably leads to an uninterrupted arms race in the capitalist states, to the search for new and more powerful weapons, and to the improvement of troop organization and combat methods. Such a one-sided military development of the economy of these states cannot continue forever. It will either lead to war, or, as the result of these unproductive military expenditures, to economic bankruptcy and complete subservience to another, stronger capitalist state. Such a process was typified by the experience of Germany, Italy, and Japan. At present, the United States, England, France, West Germany, and several other countries, combined in aggressive imperialist blocs, are following the same course.

Greece, Turkey, Iran, Pakistan, and several other states, being completely dependent upon the United States, exemplify the subservience of some capitalist countries, which have entered into aggressive imperialist blocs, to other more powerful imperialist states. Pakistan, for example, spends two-thirds of its budget for military purposes; consequently, the country's national industry is not developing, and foreign capital rules there as if in its own domain.

The socialist states are peace-loving by nature. Wars, as a method of achieving policies by violent means, are alien to them. Their policy is to pursue peaceful aims, and is based on the principle of peaceful coexistence of states with different social systems. However, the arms race and the aggressive predatory policies of the imperialist states, which are openly directed against the socialist countries, particularly the Soviet Union, compel the latter to take appropriate and sufficient measures to strengthen its own armed forces and maintain the defense capacities of the [socialist] states at the required level. In the present circumstances, the Soviet Union and the other socialist states are compelled to keep sufficient Armed Forces at a level of combat readiness which will completely guarantee the security of all the socialist countries from any aggressive imperialist actions. In his report to the Central Committee at the XXIInd Congress of the Communist Party of the Soviet Union, N. S. Khrushchev stated: "World reaction is increasingly oriented to dealing a blow to the socialist states, to re-establishing the rule of capitalism throughout the world by means of war, or at least to retarding the development of socialism. . . . For this reason . . ., as long as imperialist aggressors exist, we must be on the alert, keep our powder dry, and perfect the defense of the socialist countries, their armed forces, and agencies of state security." [3]

Consequently, even in the socialist states, policy is one of the principal factors affecting the organization and development of the armed forces. But this policy is one of peace, and the armed forces are not intended to seize foreign lands and enslave weaker peoples, but rather to guard over the peaceful toil of the peoples of the socialist states and to keep them free and independent.

Thus, policy and economy are determining factors in the size and nature of armed forces.

Whereas the quality of the armed forces depends primarly on the

---

[3] U.S. ED. NOTE—In Russian this phrase is used only to refer to security police.

level of industrial and scientific development, their size is limited largely by the number of able-bodied people available in wartime for duty in the armed forces and [taking into account the labor requirements of] the economy, which provides for the needs of war and the vital functions of the state.

In capitalist countries, the monopolies that produce various types of weapons with the aim of getting government contracts for them hardly lack influence in determining the nature of the armed forces. For example, in the United States the constant battle between the three branches of the armed forces for increased allocations, when the military budget is being discussed in Congress, is in fact a battle between the capitalist monopolies who stand behind each branch of the armed forces and try to grab the lion's share of profits from weapons production.

Apropos of the fact that [a country's] policy and economy determine the size and nature of the armed forces, it must always be borne in mind that strategy's concern is precisely the concrete solution of these problems.

## Basic Directions in the Organization and Development of the Armed Forces

The question of how the armed forces are to be organized and developed is essentially the question of what war is like and how it is to be waged. What forces and weapons a state has in hand [determine] the way the war is waged. The larger the armed forces and the more powerful their weapons, the more conclusive the results they aim for and the more active and determined their methods of combat.

All states throughout their history have preferred, when organizing and developing the armed forces and their branches, to develop and perfect those forces and weapons which they believed would gain their political aims in war. Typically, the sea powers gave preference to the development of their navies, while the land powers gave preference to ground forces. Each such branch of the armed forces was developed to make use of the most powerful weapons available, in order to achieve superiority in firepower over the enemy. Military equipment with a potential for improvement was chosen so that the firepower superiority could be most effectively employed.

Artillery, until recently, was the basic weapon of all branches of the armed forces. It was rightly regarded as the "god of war," since it provided the main firepower of the armed forces. In the last war, aerial bombing and automatic weapons played a leading role along with artillery. Consequently, all military equipment was adapted to be used most effectively with artillery, aircraft, and automatic weapons. Transport, control, engineering, and other military equipment was also developed along these lines. Consequently, the development of the armed forces was based on a combination of great firepower and rapid troop movement under continuous and firm control.

Now let us examine how the situation today has changed and what are the possible directions in which the armed forces of today may develop as regards their technical equipment.

At present, the basic weapon for the execution of primary war missions on land, sea, and air is the nuclear weapon, and consequently this is of first importance in the development and organization of the armed forces. The colossal destructive power of this weapon and the ability to deliver nuclear strikes over any distance now permit the accomplishment of strategic missions and the attainment of strategic war aims, not by the successive destruction of enemy armed forces on the battlefield and the capture of his territory, but by simultaneous action against the most vulnerable targets in the whole of enemy territory and against major formations of his armed forces. The targets for destruction will now include not only armed forces deployed in theaters of military operations, but also the economies of the belligerents, their systems of governmental control, communications, and strategic weapons deployed outside of military theaters.

Since combat weapons now affect the entire territories of the belligerents, the boundaries between the front and the rear in a future war will be erased and there will be genuine possibilities for the rapid defeat and elimination from the war of entire countries, particularly those of small size. Nuclear-armed missiles, especially strategic missiles, will be the main instruments in realizing these possibilities.

It is this very weapon that now determines the direction in which the armed forces are organized and developed and how the future war will be waged. The accelerated introduction of [the nuclear weapon] into all branches of the armed forces has radically changed their quality; it has increased their firepower and combat potential, changed the role and purpose of conventional weapons, and necessitated the supply of more technical equipment to the armed forces and improvements in their organizational structure. It requires the use of basically new methods of combat. The firepower of all branches of the armed forces is now based on nuclear weapons. The main task, now, in organizing and developing armed forces, both in peace and war, is to be superior to the enemy in nuclear weapons and the technique of their employment. It should be noted here that, at the present time, in gaining superiority in nuclear weapons, their quality and the technique for their employment are more important than their number. According to the

American National Security Council, the United States and the Soviet Union now have vast amounts of nuclear munition of various calibers and types. The American scientists, Harrison Brown and James Real, stated in their brochure entitled *The Community of Fear* that the United States and the USSR together possess an amount of explosives equivalent to approximately 30 billion tons of TNT, or about 10 tons for each inhabitant of the earth. In such a situation, naturally, the deciding factor will not be their quantity but rather their quality, the vehicles for their delivery to target, and the technique for their employment.[4]

Because of the enormous destructive power of the nuclear weapon, the unlimited distances at which it can be applied, and the complexity of combating ballistic missiles, the view has begun to prevail more and more in military theoretical literature, particularly in the West, that the aims of war can be achieved by using only nuclear weapons, and that all the other instruments for waging war will allegedly play an insignificant role. The proponents of this view believe that massive nuclear strikes can so disrupt the economy and disorganize the vital functions of even large states that other military operations will not really affect the outcome.

For example, Professor Bernard Brodie, the well-known author of many articles and books on military strategy and an associate of the American scientific-research RAND Corporation, writes: "When we say that strategic bombing will be decisive, we mean that if it occurs on the grand scale that existing forces make possible, other kinds of military operations are likely to prove both unfeasible and superfluous." *

On this assumption, he advocates and pushes preventive war against the Soviet Union and advances the idea of a pre-emptive blow as a variant of such a war. This idea is enormously dangerous not only to the Soviet Union, but to all mankind as well, since American militarism daily becomes more brazen, stomping up and down America and loudly pro-

---

[4] U.S. ED. NOTE—In his speech in Berlin in January 1963, Khrushchev said: "Foreign scientists and military experts estimate that the United States has at the present time approximately 40,000 nuclear bombs and warheads. As is known, the Soviet Union, too, has more than enough of this stuff." *Pravda,* January 17, 1963. However, Soviet political and military leaders frequently claim that their very high-yield nuclear weapons and "global missiles," and the reliability and great weight lifting capability of their missiles, give them a qualitative superiority in strategic weapons over the United States. See, for example, Marshal Malinovskii, "The Program of the CPSU and the Question of Strengthening the Armed Force of the USSR," *Kommunist,* No. 7, May 1962, p. 14. Colonel P. Astashenkov, "Strategic Missile Forces," *Sovetskii Patriot (Soviet Patriot),* January 9, 1963.

* B. Brodie, *Strategiia v vek raketnogo oruzhiia,* Voenizdat, Moscow, 1961, p. 190. [B. Brodie, *Strategy in the Missile Age,* Princeton University Press, Princeton, New Jersey, 1959, p. 166.]

claiming that complete eradication of the Soviet system should become the national goal of the United States.

It is well known that nuclear weapons have terrible destructive power and are capable of wiping from the face of the earth entire states with small but densely populated territories. Enormous damage can also be done to large states, particularly if massive nuclear blows are dealt to the most densely populated industrial regions. In order to gain complete victory over an enemy, however, it is still necessary to eliminate his power to resist, to destroy all his means of nuclear attack, and to deprive his fleet of naval bases. This can be accomplished only by completely defeating the enemy's armed forces and capturing his territory, including the regions where strategic weapons are reliably protected.

It is not possible to accomplish all this solely by the use of nuclear weapons. Other types of weapons will also be needed, as well as the most diverse types of military equipment. In particular, in a future war one may expect the employment of chemical and bacteriological weapons to whose development great significance is accorded in the Western countries, particularly the United States.[5]

The question of warfare in the ether [electronic warfare] has been sharply posed by the fact that electronic equipment has been widely introduced into the armed forces and is used extensively in all areas of military activity.

Electronic equipment is used in this warfare to completely cancel or limit the effectiveness of enemy electronic equipment (i.e., electronic countermeasures) and to assure successful use of one's own electronic equipment and protect it from enemy electronic countermeasures.

One of the main missions of such warfare is to disrupt the direction and control of troops and weapons by active radio interference and destruction of the enemy's most important electronic systems and installations. This involves destruction or jamming of the electronic fuses of bombs and missiles by electronic radiation; interception of radio signals and generation of interference in the electronic equipment of enemy air-

---

[5] U.S. ED. NOTE—Soviet literature pays considerable attention to chemical and bacteriological weapons which, together with nuclear weapons, are generally called "weapons of mass destruction." The possible use of chemical and bacteriological weapons in a future war has been mentioned by various Soviet military writers and a great deal of attention is paid in Soviet civil defense to measures for protecting the population against such weapons. (See, for example, L. Gouré, *Civil Defense in the Soviet Union,* University of California Press, Berkeley and Los Angeles, 1962, pp. 12–13.) In a message to the Pugwash Conference in August 1959, Khrushchev pointed out that "we share the concern of the scientists, who justly point out that the employment of these [chemical and bacteriological] weapons could have no less terrible consequences than the employment of atomic and hydrogen weapons." *New York Times,* August 26, 1959.

planes and missiles; interdiction of enemy use of electronic equipment for aerial reconnaissance, navigation, bombing, and in-flight missile guidance; and disruption of the operation of the enemy's ground-based electronic equipment for troop control.

Merely to list the uses of electronic warfare is to show how widespread are electronic countermeasures and defense against enemy countermeasures, and how serious the consequences [of such measures] can be. For this reason, the development of electronics has now acquired the same importance as the development of missiles and nuclear weapons, which cannot be used without electronic equipment.

The development and improvement of conventional weapons apparently will continue together with the development of new types of weapons; the former have not yet lost their combat utility and will be extensively employed in local and world wars, either independently or in conjunction with new types of weapons.

These are the tendencies one notes in the development of modern armament and other military equipment. They permit the statement of some propositions concerning the paths which the development of armed forces will follow and about the basic direction of their organization and development.

The appearance of missiles and nuclear weapons and the development of aircraft and other instruments of armed combat, as described above, again revived the notorious theory of the possibility of waging war with small but technically well-equipped armies. The advocates of such armies fail to consider that the new equipment, far from reducing the requirements of the armed forces for personnel, increases them. For this reason, massive armies of millions of men will be needed to wage a future war.

Moreover, massive armed forces, well trained in the use of modern military equipment, will be required from the very first days of the war, since the belligerents will attempt to achieve their strategic military and political aims in the shortest possible time. Combat operations, employing nuclear weapons extensively, will immediately develop on a tremendous scale, on land, on sea, and in the air; and these operations will be most fierce and decisive. In such conditions, one can hardly count on a more or less extended period, as in previous wars, to mobilize fully and to deploy one's armed forces. At the same time, not even the economically strongest states can today keep their armed forces fully deployed during peacetime.

Obviously, the best solution of this problem would be the peacetime maintenance of such armed forces as would be able to secure at least certain proximate strategic war aims while the remaining echelons were being fully mobilized and put into operation. Thus it is not accidental that the most aggressive imperialist states, primarily the United States, West Germany, and the other members of NATO, already maintain enormous armed forces, at a high level of combat-readiness, which surround the socialist countries with a dense ring of missile, naval, and air bases. Instead of reducing their armed forces, they continually increase their combat potential, especially in nuclear weapons. Moreover, in order to obtain certain advantages in the use of nuclear weapons, the American armed forces are on constant combat alert: missiles are in the launching position, strategic bombers are aloft carrying nuclear bombs of enormous destructive powers, and nuclear submarines are at sea carrying Polaris missiles. Of course, to agree to disarm totally, or even to reduce their armed forces, would mean that the United States and its allies in the imperialist blocs would have to give up their aggressive, predatory aims and the rapacious policies dictated by the capitalist monopolies. They would hardly do this voluntarily. They can only be compelled to do so by the combined efforts of all peace-loving peoples and all the forces of peace and progress.

But whatever types of armed forces exist during peacetime, they cannot solve all the problems of war even by using nuclear weapons. Troops will still have to be mobilized in order to supplement peacetime forces and execute the subsequent strategic missions of war. This [mobilization] apparently will take place partially during the threatening period while international tensions are mounting, and will continue on a full scale during the active military operations of the initial period of the missile and nuclear war.

Strategic missile troops will be the basic troops of modern massive armed forces. They are the decisive force at the disposal of supreme commands, since it is primarily these troops who will be charged with carrying out the principal war aim: destruction of enemy strategic and operational nuclear weapons distributed throughout his territory, destruction of his military economy, disorganization of his civil and military leadership, disruption of his communications, and destruction of his strategic reserves. At the same time, missile troops will also carry out a number of missions in theaters of military operations, particularly destroying major formations of ground forces and aircraft, operational nuclear weapons, naval forces in port, and supply bases, and disrupting the command and control systems of the enemy. The execution of all these missions will create favorable conditions of combat for the ground forces and other branches of the armed forces, to help them attain the goals of the war.

Strategic missile troops are comparatively more ready for combat than other branches of the armed forces and can rapidly destroy enormous numbers of targets over a wide area at any distance. They can cause the enemy irretrievable losses, and in some cases even force him to surrender. All this ranks missile troops first among the branches of the armed forces, and requires constant attention to their development and improvement.

Regardless of whether strategic missile troops are an independent branch of the armed forces, as in our country, or whether they are a component part of other branches, as in the United States, theirs is the main role in executing the chief missions of a future war. Consequently, one of the most important problems in organizing and developing armed forces today is to create and maintain quantitative and qualitative superiority in missile troops over the enemy and to use them in a superior fashion. In the most highly developed countries, the evolution of the armed forces is following this trend.

Along with the development of strategic missile troops, missiles and nuclear weapons are being widely introduced into other branches of the armed forces. Just as strategic missile troops are the decisive instrument of the armed forces in general, the missile troops and missiles of other branches of the armed forces are the basic means of combat for each of these branches.[6]

Understandably, the modern missile, just like any other new weapon, must be perfected. Its practical and technical features need further improvement, and its combat use must be simplified. It must be made more efficient, more accurate; its launch readying time must be reduced and its reliability and launching equipment improved. Missiles must be developed for use with highly efficient fuels that are easy to prepare and handle. The simplest and most suitable methods must be developed for delivery to the field of missiles, fuel components, and warheads by all types of transport, including air transport.

It has been seen that no matter how great a role strategic missile troops play in a future war, they still cannot carry out all the missions of the war. To triumph in war, it is not sufficient to destroy the military

---

[6] U.S. ED. NOTE—In discussing the firepower of Soviet ground forces, Soviet military writers frequently emphasize that "the basis of their power is now tactical missile formations and units." Lieutenant General N. Sbytov, "The Revolution in Military Affairs and Its Results," *Red Star*, February 15, 1963. See also Colonel General S. M. Shtemenko, "Ground Forces in Contemporary War and Their Combat Preparation," *Red Star*, January 3, 1963; Colonel P. Astashenkov, "The Main Force of the Ground Forces," *Sovetskii patriot* (*Soviet Patriot*), January 16, 1963. Similar claims are made for the Soviet Navy. See, for example, Commander in Chief of the Soviet Navy, Fleet Admiral S. G. Gorshkov, "True Sons of the Motherland," *Pravda*, July 29, 1962, and "The Great Tasks of the Soviet Fleet," *Red Star*, February 5, 1963.

potential of the aggressor, his strategic combat instruments, the main formations of his armed forces, and his civil and military controls. For final victory, it is absolutely necessary to defeat the enemy's armed forces and capture his military bases, if, for some reason, they have not already been destroyed. Strategically important regions must be occupied. In addition one must defend one's own territory against invasion by the aggressor's ground armies, air forces, and naval forces. Only modern ground forces, adequate in size, armament, and organization, can execute these and a number of other missions. Theirs is the extremely important role of achieving the final war aims. For this reason, the ground forces remain the largest of the various branches of the armed forces and to them falls the execution of many war missions in ground theaters.

The organization and composition of the ground forces are continually improved according to changes in the nature of war. The basic characteristics of modern ground forces are the following: high firepower, mobility and maneuverability, the ability to execute long marches over considerable distances, with or without roads, and the adaptation of the units and formations to maneuver by air. The ground troops have great striking power and can conduct military operations even when nuclear weapons are used extensively. In organizing these forces, attention has been directed mainly toward developing troops and weapons with the above-mentioned characteristics, so that they will be suited to the nature and meet the needs of modern missile and nuclear war.

To succeed in combat, it is absolutely essential for ground troops to surpass the enemy in firepower. Consequently they must have the nuclear and conventional weapons to destroy any target, whatever the depth of the operational zone, regardless of weather, visibility, or enemy countermeasures.

Hence missile troops receive priority in the ground forces as well as in other branches of the armed forces. In time they will become the basic force, capable of carrying out any operation to destroy enemy targets. To a considerable degree they will replace artillery and aviation in bombarding the front; for some purposes they will completely replace artillery and aviation.

The missile forces provide basic firepower for the ground troops. They will be the main means used to clear the way for tank and motorized troops to carry out broad maneuvers and rapid penetration in depth. When necessary, these forces will create obstacles in the path of advancing enemy troops, consisting of vast zones of destruction and radioactive contamination, which can become an insurmountable barrier on the ground. In order to carry out such tasks, the missile forces of the ground troops must be sufficiently large and independent and must have high mobility coupled with the ability to carry out maneuvers in conjunction with tanks and motorized infantry, and to co-operate closely, when necessary, with strategic missile forces.

Among the conventional fire-support weapons, the ground forces need one that can simultaneously provide a large volume of fire to neutralize the enemy's nuclear weapons, missiles, and centers of resistance, as well as destroy his tanks. The main weapons of this kind are rocket artillery and antitank missiles which obviously must be developed further.

The proportion of tank troops in the ground forces will apparently be increased further. Tanks are better able to withstand the effects of nuclear weapons, have a high cross-country capability, and can move quickly without roads. They are able to execute rapid maneuvers and deliver strikes to great depths. They can quickly cross enemy zones of radioactive contamination and rapidly exploit the results of their own side's nuclear strikes.

Tank units and formations have high artillery firepower and are able, just like artillery, to destroy and neutralize exposed and protected targets. With proper organization, they can not only effectively exploit the results of nuclear strikes, but by armored attack and fire from their numerous guns can eliminate from their path the surviving remnants of the opposing forces. They can also deal rapid and forceful blows to the enemy's flanks and rear and can advance great distances without pausing. Of all the service branches, tank troops are best suited to missile and nuclear war.

It must be kept in mind, however, that existing tanks have become very vulnerable to antitank weapons, whose development is now in advance of that of tanks.[7] The continued improvement of tanks will tend to increase the effectiveness of armor against antitank weapons and penetrating radiation, to enhance the power of their armament, their range, mobility and maneuverability, and to raise their cross-country capability.

In general, the problem of increasing the speed and maneuverability of ground forces has acquired primary importance under modern conditions.

The capability of the ground forces to move rapidly and execute swift

---

[7] U.S. ED. NOTE—The importance of armored forces as those best suited for exploiting nuclear strikes in ground warfare is stressed in Soviet literature. Some Soviet officers appear to believe that modern tank forces, in co-operation with nuclear strikes, can overcome all enemy resistance. See, for example, Chief Marshal of the Tank Forces, P. Rotmistrov, "Modern Tanks and Nuclear Weapons," *Izvestiia,* October 20, 1962.

maneuvers must exceed that of past world wars. To achieve victory in a future war, it will not be sufficient to have nuclear weapons and the means to deliver them very accurately on target; it will also be necessary that the ground forces be able to move rapidly into regions which have been subjected to nuclear strikes. Only when this problem is solved will it be possible to speak of the effective exploitation of nuclear strikes by tanks and infantry in conclusively defeating the enemy, or of carrying out extensive maneuvers and decisive advances in depth. The old principle of combining firepower and troop mobility under continuous control has acquired new and even greater importance. Today, along with the increased speed, mobility, and cross-country capability of tank forces, there is also a need to provide motorized troops with fast, cross-country, and transportable vehicles of high endurance. These will not only make it possible to cover great distances, but also to carry out sustained combat operations in the most difficult situations and terrain. If required, the vehicles should be transportable by air along with the troops.

In a future war, an attack on foot will apparently be a rare phenomenon. Destruction of the enemy will be achieved primarily by nuclear-weapon fire. In close combat operations, when it is impossible to use nuclear weapons, conventional weapons will be used, particularly tanks, aircraft, artillery, and infantry, all possessed of high mobility and maneuverability. It must be kept in mind that under modern conditions, success in combat and operations often will be achieved by using nuclear weapons to destroy individual enemy formations along a wide front and in great depth, and then, with rapid penetration of tank and motorized troops to a great depth, by striking suddenly at the flank and rear areas of still resisting enemy formations.

In addition, it must be taken into account that troops carrying out maneuvers in a future war may encounter insurmountable obstacles such as vast zones of destruction and radioactive contamination created by nuclear strikes. Therefore, speed in carrying out ground maneuvers at the high tempos of modern combat will not always ensure the execution in time of the tasks assigned to infantry. If we also take into account the necessity of frequent troop movements into the far rear lines of the enemy, then it becomes obvious that air maneuver will best meet the requirements of missile and nuclear war. It is this type of maneuver which is most suited to modern warfare. In order to make timely and most effective use of the results of nuclear strikes, it is necessary to shift troops to the appropriate areas rapidly enough to prevent the enemy in these areas from reorganizing or transferring troops from other areas. Hence modern motorized infantry, with the exception of units and subunits armed with heavy weapons, is being adapted to rapid air transport over short or long distances. This has become as ordinary a procedure for the infantry as railroad or automobile transport.

The solution of the problem of transporting armored troops and motorized infantry by air does not eliminate the necessity of having in the composition of the ground forces special airborne troops, which are prepared to make parachute drops and carry out missions in the enemy's rear. Moreover, it should be expected that the role of airborne troops in a future war, and the proportion of the ground troops they represent, will increase considerably. This is a result of the changing nature and increased number of tasks to be performed by them. Whereas, in the last war, the airborne troops were mainly used to assist the ground forces to defeat enemy formations, now their additional functions will include independent execution of such missions as capturing and holding or destroying missile, air, and naval bases, and other important targets deep within the military theaters of operation.

Because of the fact that tactical air forces in many armies are one of the main means for delivering nuclear weapons, air defense troops are becoming increasingly important to the ground forces. They will have the main task of repelling any nuclear air strikes on ground-force formations and targets in the operational rear. For the Field PVO to be able to solve these problems, antiaircraft missiles will have to be improved to the point where they will reliably intercept and destroy enemy airplanes and tactical missiles at sufficiently great ranges and at low and medium altitudes. It is important that the fighters of the air defense have the tactical and technical qualities, and the missile and electronic equipment, to enable them to reliably destroy enemy aerial targets at any altitude and at ranges that will protect the troops from enemy air attacks.

The development of the ground forces involves not only the introduction of new equipment and the improvement of older military equipment, but also extensive improvement of their organizational structure. It is well known that troop mobility and maneuverability depend not only upon the means of transportation, but also upon the organization of units, the system of command, the combat methods employed, and finally the training and co-ordination of combat formations and the political morale of the troops.

With the development of weapons of air attack, particularly nuclear-armed missiles, the role and importance of the National PVO have increased immeasurably. This branch of the armed forces provides air defense and antimissile defense for the country. Its functions include cooperation with Field PVO to prevent enemy air weapons from penetrating the country's air space and to prevent nuclear attacks on the country's most important regions and targets, including concentrations of the armed forces, missile, air, and naval bases, strategic reserves, storage areas, control points, and communications. If missile troops in a future war will play the main role in dealing nuclear blows to targets all over the enemy's territory, the National PVO will play the principal role in protecting our territory from such blows and repelling enemy nuclear assaults. The National PVO can also play an important part in protecting the operations of other branches of the armed forces.

To execute these missions, the National PVO will need highly effective means of detecting, tracking, and destroying aerial targets. Active air defense is now based on air defense troops whose weapons have considerable range and high accuracy in destroying enemy aircraft.

In addition to the range of antiaircraft missiles, it is important that their ceiling also be increased in order to destroy enemy aircraft at a distance and height which prevent the use of their air-to-surface missiles against important targets.

Fighters will evidently play a considerable role in the National PVO system in the coming years. By increasing their speed, altitude, and range, and by improving their missiles and radar, fighters can continue to combat enemy bombers successfully. A modern air defense fighter plane must be able to remain aloft for a prolonged period, execute radar patrols, and shoot down enemy aircraft at any altitude if they appear.

The rapid development of nuclear-armed missiles and their adoption as the basic means for delivering nuclear blows to targets deep within the country have sharply posed the problem, for all states, of creating an effective antimissile defense capable of destroying enemy ballistic missiles in the air. In principle, a technical solution to this problem has now been found. In the future this form of defense must be perfected.[8]

Warfare against artificial satellites, which can be launched for the most diverse purposes, even as vehicles for nuclear weapons, has now become an important problem.

Radar troops have become increasingly important in the country's air defense system. They detect and track aerial targets and guide antiaircraft missiles and fighter aircraft to them. To assure the execution of these defense missions, it is necessary to have a continuous radar coverage as far as possible beyond the country's borders and from the targets to be protected. This will provide the necessary time to prepare active air defense against enemy air strikes. The radar coverage assures detection and guidance at all altitudes used by modern enemy air weapons.

---

[8] U.S. ED. NOTE—See Note B, Chapter IV, pp. 315 ff.

Electronic countermeasures must be highly developed in the air defense system. These can be used effectively against the guidance [systems] of manned and unmanned aerial weapon carriers.

A most important problem in developing the PVO is the improvement of automated systems of tracking, target designation, and control of antiaircraft missiles, fighters, and radar.

Air defense must be improved in efficiency, reliability, and range, and antiaircraft and air-to-air missiles must be made less susceptible to interference. Command and control of [air defense] troops must be extensively automated in order to be sure of destroying aerial targets at any altitude, even when there is [radar] interference, and with a minimum expenditure of air defense resources.

Not only the military equipment of the National PVO must be improved, but their organization as well; this will enable them to make full use of their combat potential. The simultaneous solution of these problems will assure the existence of an antiaircraft and antimissile defense that cannot be penetrated by all the enemy's modern aerial weapons, or at least, a defense that will reduce to a minimum the possibility of their reaching the country's protected targets.

Today the air force is in a special situation. In recent years there has been keen competition between bombers, missiles, and air defense weapons. In this competition, air defense weapons have gained the advantage over bomber aircraft. Long-range bombers have become especially vulnerable; it is impossible to conceal them when delivering strikes deep within enemy territory. Since they cover considerable distances at relatively low speeds, long-range bombers will often have to remain in active air defense zones for extended periods. Thus it is doubtful that they can reach the assigned enemy targets.

Consequently, long-range bombers are rapidly yielding first place to intercontinental and intermediate-range ballistic missiles. Front line (tactical) bombers are also gradually being replaced by missiles.[9]

Of course, this process of replacement may take a long time, and if war breaks out bombers and missiles could be used simultaneously to attack targets located deep within enemy zones and theaters of military operations. This is all the more likely, since aircraft have still not completely exhausted their combat potential. By arming bombers with various types of [air-to-surface] missiles capable of delivering blows at great distances, these bombers in a number of cases could operate beyond zones of active defense and execute combat missions effectively enough. In addition, some specific missions, for example striking mobile

---

[9] U.S. ED. NOTE—See Note A, pp. 351 ff.

targets, could be executed more successfully by aircraft than by missiles. Further improvement of aircraft missiles could somewhat improve the effectiveness of bombers on the battlefield. The nature of their missions and the way they are executed, however, will obviously be changed. The depth of their operations will be determined by the combat potential of enemy air defense and the range of the missiles [they carry].

In the coming years, tactical fighters and fighter-bombers will obviously still be able to support ground troops on the battlefield effectively and to co-operate with antiaircraft missile troops to protect troop formations and important targets from enemy air strikes against the rear areas of the front. But to do this their speed and altitude must surpass those of enemy aircraft. Front line aircraft can be particularly effective in destroying enemy nuclear weapons, especially missiles, on the battlefield. By "free hunting" [reconnaissance strikes], and even using conventional weapons, they can disorganize the operation of enemy missile troops and if not spoil, at least seriously reduce the effectiveness of their nuclear strikes.

Aircraft still have the important mission of aerial reconnaissance for all branches of the armed forces, especially missile troops. Hence reconnaissance aircraft and instruments of aerial reconnaissance are continually being improved with respect to their ability to detect enemy targets traveling at high speeds and altitudes at any time of day and in any weather. Reconnaissance data will be automatically transmitted directly from the airplane to the appropriate headquarters over great distances.

As we have already mentioned, modern warfare places particularly great demands on aerial transport. Among these are high load-carrying capacity and a capability for mass troop movements, for carrying large loads over any distances, and for utilizing either the most simple types of landing strips or none at all.

In the discussion of the general development of aviation, it should be recognized that aircraft have not completely exhausted their combat potential for modern warfare. If one takes into account trends in the development of aircraft-associated missiles and of electronic equipment, along with the introduction of types of aircraft not requiring airfields and improvement of flight control techniques, then one can significantly increase the combat capability of aircraft in the battle zone and in the deep rear of the enemy territory.

Of the future development of the air force, it can be said that, although the development of modern military equipment has qualitatively changed the earlier significance of this branch of the armed forces, in a future war it will still have a number of important missions. Today the main purpose of the air force is to co-operate with all branches of the armed forces in the execution of their combat missions. In the future, aircraft will still have such responsible tasks as aerial reconnaisance, air communications, particularly troop and materiel transport, and the evacuation of the wounded and sick. Air power must become strong enough to operate on any scale [required of it].

The direction in which navies, like the other branches of the armed forces, are to develop is determined not only by the nature of weapons and other military equipment, but also by the missions to be assigned to them in a future war. The imperialist states, pursuing an aggressive policy directed against the USSR and other socialist countries, have powerful navies at their disposal, comprising carrier task forces, missile-carrying surface vessels, and submarines capable of dealing nuclear blows to important coastal targets as well as targets deep within the territory of the socialist states. Hence the navy's basic mission in modern warfare will be to combat enemy naval forces at sea and in port.

A second but no less important naval mission in a future war will be to destroy or disrupt enemy maritime transportation, since the enemy is highly dependent on it for waging war in the ground theaters of military operations.

These missions can be most effectively executed by submarines and aircraft armed with nuclear missiles and torpedoes. A certain number of surface ships will also be needed to support the operation of submarines and to perform secondary missions such as the protection of naval communications and co-operation with the Ground Forces in coastal operations.

The most important qualities that submarines need are: great autonomy, high speed, the ability to fire missiles when submerged, sufficiently large supplies of combat missiles and torpedoes, high defensive capabilities, particularly great depth and speed of submersion, and the ability to remain submerged for extended periods.

These qualities will permit the submarine forces to engage in successful combat with an enemy navy and, if necessary, to deliver nuclear strikes to coastal targets.

Naval aircraft must be able to make strikes on enemy warships at sea before the ships' carrier aircraft and missiles are close enough to deal blows against targets in the socialist states. Our naval aircraft will also have the mission of destroying enemy transports at sea and in port.

Naval combat operations require adequate numbers of reconnaissance and antisubmarine aircraft, and of special ships for antisubmarine and air defense, radar patrol, trawling operations, etc.

Naval organization must correspond to the projected methods of warfare at sea and to the requirements of a future war.

In discussing the organization and development of the Armed Forces, whether as a whole or branch by branch, it must be recognized that a most important principle of the Soviet military art still obtains: Victory in war is gained by the combined efforts of all branches of the Armed Forces and all their weapons with maximal employment of their military capabilities. Basic to the organization and development of the Armed Forces, therefore, is the need to develop further and to improve all the branches of the Armed Forces, all types of troops, weapons, equipment, organization and training. Nevertheless, basic reliance must be placed on the forces and weapons to be used to execute the major missions and to achieve the main war aims, i.e., those which will play the most active role in war. It must be recognized that, in the course of the war, the role and relative importance of some branches of the Armed Forces and of troops and weapons may vary according to the course of the war and the nature of their missions at various stages of the war.

In our opinion, these are the main directions in the organization and development of the Armed Forces. These directions are determined by the present military and political situation, by economic factors, and by the development of weapons and other military equipment. They now more or less characterize the evolution of the armed forces of all highly developed countries.

However, it must be kept in mind that trends in the development of armed forces are not constant. They always undergo and in the future will continue to undergo various changes in response to the military and political situation, economic factors, and the development of technical means of warfare. Military strategy must study these changes in good time and take them into consideration in determining the organization and structure of the armed forces and the methods for waging war.

In organizing and developing the armed forces, one must also evaluate the directions in which the enemy is developing in order to find an appropriate countermeasure for each new enemy weapon. Here, the main thing is to maintain constant superiority over the enemy in the basic branches of the armed forces, weapons, and ways of waging war. It is especially necessary to maintain constant superiority over the enemy in firepower, troop mobility, and maneuverability.

Merely having technically well-equipped armed forces, however, does not solve all the problems of their organization and development. It is necessary for the armed forces to master their equipment completely and be able to employ it in war for victory over the enemy with minimum loss of personnel. Military equipment can be rapidly repaired and restored to service or new equipment can be produced, but it is impossible to restore lost personnel to life.

The most important qualities of the armed forces under current conditions are a high level of combat-readiness and the ability promptly to initiate and conduct combat operations in any, even the most difficult, circumstances if an aggressor unleashes war. These [qualities] are assured by the entire system of organizing and developing the armed forces, by the proper manning of units and formations and their provision with modern military equipment, and by maintaining high morale and a combative spirit among the personnel. Troops must be constantly well prepared for action when modern weapons of destruction of all types might be used, particularly nuclear weapons. Their disposition and deployment must ensure the rapid initiation of combat activities. A high level of combat-readiness among the armed forces is assured by the advance creation of a command system that meets the needs of modern war, and by highly trained commanders and command agencies which can provide firm and continuous command of troop combat operations.[10]

The high combat-readiness and combat potential of the troops must be maintained in peacetime as well as in wartime. War is the most demanding and severe test of armed forces. The suitability of their organization can only be evaluated by the results of war.

The Soviet Armed Forces have twice sustained such a severe test— in the Civil War and the Great Patriotic War. The results of these wars, the victories achieved in them, and the entire history of the Soviet Armed Forces are vivid proof of the correctness of the principles followed in their organization and the validity of the direction selected for their development during all stages of their history.

This was achieved by the steadfast support of the Armed Forces by the Communist Party. The Party is the organizational and guiding force of the entire existence and activity of the Soviet Army and Navy. The Party stood at the cradle of our Armed Forces and now the latter, by

---

[10] U.S. ED. NOTE—As indicated in the Analytical Introduction, no precise information has been published in the Soviet literature concerning the minimum response time underlying Soviet readiness requirements, or the expected duration of the first phase of the war. In his speech of January 1960, Khrushchev mentioned that in the event of a Western attack, the Soviet Union would carry out retaliatory strikes "in the first minutes" of the war (*Pravda,* January 15, 1960). In describing a firing exercise by strategic missiles, a Soviet article states that they were ready within minutes of the alert. (Major A. Shichalin, Major E. Udovichenko, "The Strategic [Missiles] Are on Alert," *Red Star,* October 7, 1962.) Colonel General S. M. Shtemenko, Chief of Staff of the Soviet Ground Forces, has declared that "the readiness of units and sub-units must be counted literally in minutes, and that of the missile forces even in seconds." ("The Ground Forces in Contemporary War and Their Combat Preparation," *Red Star,* January 3, 1963.) However, most Soviet statements on this subject speak only of the need for readiness to respond "immediately" or "in the shortest possible time."

the will of the Party, have been transformed into a most formidable power which deters the imperialist aggressors from unleashing a new world war.

## U.S. ED. NOTE A: CHANGING SOVIET ATTITUDES ON THE ROLE OF THE MANNED BOMBER

[As pointed out in the Analytical Introduction, Soviet views on the role of the strategic manned bomber have changed repeatedly over the years. Khrushchev started to downgrade the bomber as soon as the Soviet Union succeeded in launching its first earth satellite. For example, Khrushchev told two British Members of Parliament in 1957 that the era of the bomber had passed and that these planes could be destroyed without further ado.[11] He also told James Reston of *The New York Times*: "Military specialists believe that both bomber aircraft and fighters are in the twilight of their existence." [12] In his speech on January 14, 1960, Khrushchev again stated that bomber aircraft were being phased out of the Soviet Air Force: "Almost the entire military air force is being replaced by missiles. We have by now sharply reduced, and probably will further reduce and even discontinue the production of bombers and other obsolete equipment." [13]

Marshal Malinovskii told the Supreme Soviet in January 1960 that missiles were superior to planes because "the building of large, expensive airfields with complicated equipment is not required for launching missiles." [14] Following the U-2 incident, in May 1960, Khrushchev claimed that "not a single bomber could get through to its target." [15] However, he did not repeat this claim in later speeches.

Despite these claims, which were designed to emphasize Soviet missile superiority and the vulnerability of U.S. strategic bomber forces, Khrushchev took a more sober attitude when he addressed military audiences. In 1958, for example, he told graduates of the aircraft engineering schools that "the role of winged aircraft piloted by individuals is somewhat reduced" but that it was necessary to "perfect" and "master the new jet and missile technology." [16]

The Soviet Air Force, not surprisingly, emphasized the continuing

---

[11] "Khrushchev's Triumph," *Neue Zürcher Zeitung*, October 10, 1957.

[12] "Answers to the Questions of the Chief Diplomatic Correspondent of the American Newspaper, *The New York Times*, J. Reston, October 7, 1957," *Pravda*, October 11, 1957.

[13] *Pravda*, January 15, 1960.

[14] *Pravda*, January 15, 1960.

[15] *Pravda*, May 29, 1960.

[16] *Vestnik vozdushogo flota (Herald of the Air Fleet)*, No. 4, April 1958, p. 6.

utility of aircraft rather than their obsolescence. For example, following Khrushchev's speech to the graduates of aircraft engineering schools, the daily organ of the Soviet Air Force published an article which declared that aircraft would not only continue to be important in joint operation with ground and naval forces "but could also annihilate the opponent's strategic targets," and that the development of missiles did not mean "that aircraft have outlived their day and that missiles will completely replace them in the near future." [17]

During 1961 and 1962 Soviet publications increasingly referred to the equipment of Soviet bombers with air-to-surface missiles so that the bombers could stay outside the enemy's air defense zones. It was pointed out that these bombers could inflict "powerful blows jointly with the strategic missile forces." [18]

Khrushchev, too, reflected this new appreciation of the virtues of aircraft and retreated from his earlier denigration of their value. In his speech to the XXIInd Congress of the CPSU, Khrushchev said: "In equipping the armed forces with missiles and an atomic submarine fleet, we are not leaving the air force out of our reckoning; we are continuing to develop and improve it." [19] In his address to the same Congress, Marshal Malinovskii mentioned further improvements in Soviet military aircraft and declared that the Soviet Air Force was ready to "strike powerful nuclear blows in conjunction with the strategic missile forces." [20] A similar statement on the role of the strategic bombers was made a year later by the Chief of the Soviet Air Force, Chief Air Marshal Vershinin.[21] Another article asserted that "missile carrying aircraft, capable of dealing nuclear blows on the aggressor from a long way off without penetrating the enemy's air defense zone, are fast gaining in importance." [22]

There is some evidence, indeed, to suggest that the Soviet Air Force would like to upgrade aircraft even further. For example, the First Deputy Commander of the Soviet Air Force, Air Marshal S. Rudenko, has written that the Air Force is "one of the most flexible and effec-

---

[17] Colonel A. Lapenin, "Aircraft in Modern War," *Sovetskaia aviatsiia (Soviet Aviation)*, June 3, 1958.

[18] Colonel General A. N. Ponomarev, "Air-to-Air and Air-to-Surface," *Red Star*, November 18, 1961. See also Chief Air Marshal K. A. Vershinin, "The Air Force of the Powerful Soviet State," *Pravda*, August 18, 1962; Air Marshal S. I. Rudenko, "Heroic Mission," *Red Star*, August 18, 1962.

[19] *Pravda*, October 18, 1961.

[20] *Pravda*, October 25, 1961.

[21] K. A. Vershinin, "Aviation in Modern War," *Izvestiia*, December 23, 1962.

[22] Lieutenant General N. Sbytov, "The Revolution in Military Affairs and Its Results," *Red Star*, February 15, 1963.

tive means in the struggle with an aggressor."[23] A. Tupolev, the Soviet aircraft designer, was even more outspoken, possibly because of his privileged position. He claimed that aircraft were superior to missiles:

> Missile-carrying aircraft can be viewed as the first stage of a multi-stage system that has significant advantages in comparison with multi-stage missiles. It [the system] does not require a stationary launch site or expensive and complex launching installations. Its first stage, the piloted aircraft, can be used repeatedly. If necessary, by decision of the flight commander, the plane can change its target. If the target has moved, the crew can make its own decision and still carry out its combat mission. Only missile-carrying aircraft possess these properties.[24]

One might speculate that in the competition for resources the Soviet Air Force is running a poor second to the Soviet Strategic Missile Forces and that it is arguing for the indefinite retention of its strategic mission.]

[23] Air Marshal S. Rudenko, "The Make-up of the Combat Readiness of the Air Force," *Red Star,* January 11, 1963.

[24] A. Tupolev, "The Missile-Carrying Aircraft," *Aviatsiia i kozmonovtika (Aviation and Cosmonautics),* No. 6 ,1962, pp. 4–5.

# ★ 6

# Methods of Conducting Warfare

In his report to the XXIInd Congress of the Communist Party of the Soviet Union, Premier Khrushchev stated: "We now have an extremely reliable precision-instruments industry and specialized metallurgical, nuclear, electronic, and missile industries; also jet aviation, a modern shipbuilding industry, and production facilities for automation equipment." * On this base our Armed Forces have been completely rearmed with nuclear weapons and missiles. Our Armed Forces are equipped with intercontinental and medium-range ballistic missiles, anti-aircraft missiles, missile-carrying nuclear submarines, operational and tactical Ground Force missiles, air-to-surface and air-to-air missiles in the Air Force, and other modern military equipment. Missiles of all classes have nuclear warheads of various sizes including warheads of tremendous power up to 50 and 100 megatons. Thus we have the necessary material requisites to wage war successfully if the aggressors initiate it against the socialist countries.

To defeat an aggressor conclusively, however, the mere possession of modern weapons is not enough; it is also essential that the Armed Forces know how to use these weapons effectively to execute military, political, and strategic missions—in other words, to work out and master the best way to conduct the armed conflict.

---

* N. S. Khrushchev, *Otchet Tsentral'nogo Komiteta Kommunisticheskoi Partii Sovetskogo Soiuza XXII S"ezda partii* [*Report of the Central Committee of the Communist Party of the Soviet Union, at the XXIInd Congress of the Party*], Izdatel'stvo Pravda, Moscow, 1961, p. 52.

There have been many instances in history where states with powerful, well-equipped armed forces were defeated in war because they lacked effective methods of warfare. For example, the British and French bloc at the start of World War II had large armed forces equipped in approximately the same manner as those of Nazi Germany; however, Germany's superior military skill made it possible for her to achieve considerable initial success in 1940.

By methods of warfare we mean all the techniques and methods of conducting military operations, methods of using weapons, branches of the armed forces, units, formations, and special types of troops, all of which execute political, military, strategic, operational, or tactical missions.

This chapter will examine methods of conducting modern warfare on a strategic scale and due attention will be devoted to operational art and tactics.

Marxism-Leninism teaches that the basic factors determining the development of methods of warfare and military science are the creation and introduction of new weapons and military equipment into the armed forces. This [development], in turn, depends on the state of the economy, the level of production, and the degree of scientific development. Engels noted that "achievements in technology—almost violently and often against the will of the military leadership—change and even revolutionize combat methods." *

The causes of any war should be sought in the economic and political system of society. These causes, however, are not an automatic and spontaneous product of the economy. Each war is deliberately prepared by classes and states pursuing certain political aims. Consequently the methods of warfare, like the art of warfare, depend upon the political aims pursued by given classes and states in war, the world balance of forces, and the international political situation.

The geography of the area of military operations also exerts considerable influence on methods of warfare. Methods of warfare can only be properly determined and used skillfully by taking account of all these factors and conditions in each case. There have never been two wars, no matter how close in time, conducted by exactly the same methods. Consequently, the methods for conducting war must be evaluated "on the basis of the specific case, of each war taken individually." †

N. S. Khrushchev has pointed out that "under present conditions, the most probable wars are not likely to be between capitalist, imperialist countries, although the possibility is not to be excluded. The imperialists

* F. Engels, *Anti-Diuring* [*Anti-Dühring*], Gospolitizdat, Moscow, 1952, p. 160.
† V. I. Lenin, *Sochineniia* [*Works*], Vol. 26, p. 134.

are preparing wars mainly against the socialist countries, and primarily against the Soviet Union as the most powerful of the socialist states." *

Thus, the aggressive imperialist forces led by the United States may initiate a nuclear world war against the USSR and the other socialist countries. Moreover, some imperialist circles, fearing that a world war might mean complete disaster for capitalism, insist on the conduct of local wars and point out their political advantages. Such a war might also be foisted upon the socialist countries. Therefore Soviet military strategy should study methods of conducting both world and local wars.

The methods for conducting these two kinds of wars are essentially different, especially at the beginning of the war. This must be taken into account, in theory and practice, when training our Armed Forces. The present chapter concentrates on the methods of waging nuclear world war between coalitions of capitalist and socialist states, inasmuch as this kind of war is the most complex and dangerous.

In order to clarify interrelationships and basic historical trends in the development of methods of warfare, it is necessary, if only in general outline, to review historical experience and master the most important lessons in this area of the military art.

## Development of Methods of Warfare

War appeared, when society divided into classes, as a means to resolve irreconcilable conflicts between classes. Wars have accompanied the development of mankind through many centuries.

Under capitalism, wars became a constant phenomenon, acquiring unprecedented scope and violence. World wars are monsters born of imperialism. No other ruling or exploiting class has committed such crimes against mankind. Consequently it will be useful to give a brief analysis of the methods used to wage the most important wars during the era of capitalism, especially during its last stage—imperialism.

The methods by which wars were conducted during the early stages of capitalism are still important today. As is generally known, the French Revolution completely revolutionized military affairs. V. I. Lenin noted: "Within the country itself, the revolutionary French people displayed an enormous revolutionary energy such as had not been seen for centuries, and in the war at the end of the eighteenth century they displayed equally enormous revolutionary creativity when they initiated an entirely new system of strategy that broke through all the old rules and traditions of warfare, creating new, revolutionary people's armies and new methods

---

* N. S. Khrushchev, "Toward New Victories of the World Communist Movement," *Kommunist*, No. 1, 1961, pp. 17–18.

of warfare." * Napoleon employed the methods of warfare generated in the French Revolution and brought them to perfection during his predatory wars for the hegemony of Europe.

Napoleon assigned decisive importance in war to the general battle whose purpose was to crush the enemy armed forces in one single effort. For this purpose large numbers of infantry, cavalry, and artillery were concentrated in a main area. The enemy was first struck by heavy artillery fire and then subjected to an attack in columns and extended formations. At that time such an attack stunned the enemy and brought Napoleon victory in many wars.

However, Napoleon's strategy was not effective in Russia, although he made careful preparations for [his campaign there], deployed his armed forces in advance, and attacked the Russian Army without declaring war.

The decadent serf-owning class of Tsarist Russia and the cowardly, ungifted Tsar Alexander I had not prepared the Russian Army to repel aggression. Scattered over a vast territory and unprepared, the army was compelled to withdraw deep into the country. It had to stand fast and find new combat methods to oppose the Napoleonic strategy of a general battle.

To the [strategy of] general battle, the well-known Russian commander Kutuzov opposed [that of] successive engagements, maneuver, and partisan warfare, which weakened and exhausted Napoleon's army. Thus Russia, at the beginning of the nineteenth century, was very advanced in the military art and had developed the most modern methods of warfare of that period.

By the middle of the nineteenth century, however, the situation had changed. Russia's increasing economic backwardness, the decadence and impotence of the feudal system, and Nicholas I's reactionary methods of national leadership led Russia to defeat in the Crimean War of 1853–1856. The Russian army was poorly prepared for war and equipped with obsolete weapons. Although during the first stages of the war the Russian troops enjoyed some success in the Balkans and the Transcaucasus, in the major war theater—the Crimea—they were forced into a passive, defensive strategy which resulted in defeat. The inept Commander-in-Chief, Menshikov, permitted the British and French troops to land in the Balaklava [sic] region unopposed, deploy their troops in battle positions, and win their first success at the Alma River. The Russian Army was pushed back to Sevastopol and actually cut off from

---

* V. I. Lenin, *Sochineniia* [*Works*], Vol. 24, p. 364.

the rest of the country. It was forced to defend itself though unable to maneuver, and was in dire need of ammunition, arms, and food. And yet, under these difficult conditions, the Russian troops withstood the onslaughts of well-equipped and superior enemy forces for 349 days. The British and French troops actually were unable to break the resistance of the defenders of Sevastopol. The Russian defense of their fortress proved stronger than the British and French onslaughts.

The nineteenth century is distinguished as the era of the first proletarian attack against the bourgeoisie, and the first proletarian revolutionary wars. These enriched the military experience of the proletariat. Marx and Engels made generalizations about this experience, which played an enormous role in developing proletarian revolutionary struggle in the next epoch. Marx's rules for the armed uprising, as an art combining the offensive, the superiority of forces, leadership of the revolution, and mastery of the techniques of revolt, are still valid today.

By the end of the nineteenth century, capitalism had entered the last stage of its development—imperialism. The struggle of the rapacious imperialists to divide the world was the main cause of wars unprecedented in scale and violence.

One of the first wars of the present age was the *Russo-Japanese War of 1904–1905*. This war exemplified, on the one hand, the treacherous, aggressive Japanese imperialist strategy and, on the other hand, the decadence of Russian autocracy and the economic and political backwardness of Tsarist Russia, which produced an indecisive military strategy and a conservative choice of methods of warfare.

Russia's preparations for war were slipshod, although the government had information on Japan's preparations for military attacks. The Russian Army was poorly equipped technically. It had no mountain artillery, howitzers, or technical communications. The Russian Navy was inferior to the Japanese Navy in speed and rate of fire. The limited capacity of the Trans-Siberian Railroad made it impossible to concentrate enough troops in the Far East in advance. Fortifications were built slowly, particularly in Port Arthur. No study had been made of the theater of military operation, and there were no topographical maps of a major part of the theater. Strategic reconnaissance was poorly organized. The Russian Army forces, led by stupid and ignorant generals and admirals, like Kuropatkin, Alekseev, and Rozhestvenskii, were not prepared for military operations against an active enemy. The army was trained to make a frontal attack in compact waves without adequate fire preparations, whereas the armies of some other states deployed their infantry for attack in [extended] waves, and engaged in maneuvers on the battlefield.

The Russian armed forces were not deployed at the beginning of the war, but were scattered over a vast territory, including Manchuria, the Primorye and the Amur regions, and the Transbaikal. It was not planned to deploy the ground forces until six months after military operations had begun.

Gross miscalculations were made in the disposition of naval forces. The main forces of the First Squadron, based at Port Arthur, could not carry out tactical operations. The forces in Vladivostok were weak. Individual ships were scattered in Korean and Chinese ports. The Second Squadron was located in Baltic ports.

In preparing for war, Japan had attained a significant superiority over Russia. She had practically completed her planned program for building up her armed forces, particularly the navy. At the beginning of the war, Japan was prepared to land sizable infantry forces in Manchuria and Korea, and her fleet was more skillfully deployed. Japan strove to get command of the seas before beginning infantry landings.

Japan started the war by surprise. This took the Russian military leaders unaware.

Having won command of the seas, Japan then began to land her Second Army on the Liaotung Peninsula. Although sufficient Russian Army forces were concentrated in Southern Manchuria at this time, the Russian Commander, General Kuropatkin, did not oppose the landing since he intended to attack only after final concentration and deployment of the Russian Army had been accomplished, i.e., six months after the war had begun. Thus the initiative in the ground theater of operations was voluntarily handed over to the Japanese.

The Russian Army employed an extremely passive and conservative strategy in the ground theater during this war. Its operational plans were defensive; it dispersed armed forces over a vast front; in shifting to attack, it committed forces piecemeal; and it underestimated the importance of artillery support, thus considerably reducing the effectiveness of its own offensives. The war also demonstrated the backwardness of Russian naval science at that time.

The Russo-Japanese War introduced many innovations in methods of warfare. The beginnings of static combat methods appeared in this war; machine guns and magazine rifles were used, which strengthened the defense. The troops began to dig in and to create a continuous defensive front extending over a distance, which hindered envelopments and encirclements. Consequently, it was necessary for advancing troops to break through the defensive front, and hence to overcome enemy firepower with artillery. Attack and defense were the basic types of military operation, but withdrawal was also employed. Large battles developed in naval theaters. The basic form of naval combat operations consisted of fire fights between large surface ships—battleships and cruisers.

World War I was the next important stage in the development of methods of warfare.

*The First World War,* an outgrowth of imperialism, was a clash between the interests of two powerful imperialist groups. This war involved thirty-six states and more than 60 per cent of the world's population. More than seventeen million men were mobilized to fight.

The strategic views of representatives of the German General Staff—Schlieffen, and the younger Moltke—reflected the aggressive aspirations of German imperialism and exerted considerable influence on the development of methods for conducting the war. In his book, *Cannae,* Schlieffen first advanced the idea of a massive surprise strike with concentrated forces. This is still the basic strategic doctrine of the imperialists and revanchists. He also developed a plan of war for attacking France through Belgium. His successor, the younger Moltke, developed a war plan calling for the encirclement of the main Anglo-French forces by a flanking move of a large German Army formation through Belgium and the Paris region. This plan was basically adventuristic, since Imperial Germany did not have the requisite forces to carry it out rapidly.

The Anglo-French bloc countered the Germans with an inept plan for a frontal attack in the center of the strategic front.

In planning the war, the Russian General Staff proved to be completely incapable. Although it was possible at the very beginning of the war to deliver the main blow against Germany from Russia's western borders, the Russian commanders concentrated their major forces on a secondary area, i.e., against the Austro-Hungarian Army in Galicia.

Both sides expected the war to be short; consequently only modest reserves were stockpiled [for subsequent] mobilization. Russia did not even plan to convert her industry to military production. Both sides expected to achieve their aims by an offensive, and in a general battle; defense was considered almost a disgrace. This was a symptom of the inability of the general staffs of the belligerents to foresee the nature, scope, and methods of the war.

The deployment of forces began before the war and continued during its initial period.

Thus the war developed in classical form.

The main events of World War I developed on the Western and Eastern Fronts of the European ground theater. The first months of the war demonstrated the errors in prewar views about methods for conducting [war].

By the end of 1914 the gross miscalculation of the general staffs in counting on a short war was evident. It became an extended war of attrition. Continuous fronts developed, first in the West and then in the East. When the period of maneuver ended in the West and the war became static, Germany transferred her main forces to the eastern front. The Russian Army was compelled to shift to the defensive. At first the Germans succeeded in breaking through the Russian front and gained some victories, but by the end of 1915 that front had also become stabilized from the Baltic Sea to Romania.

Thus positional forms of combat, which first arose in the Russo-Japanese war, predominated in World War I.

The machine gun and the magazine rifle made defense more powerful than offense. The open battlefield became empty as the infantry went underground. Troops of the belligerents occupied the entire length of the front, creating a multizone and multipositional defense that consisted of trenches and communication trenches protected by several lines of barbed wire barriers. Only a frontal breakthrough could overcome such a defense.

Both sides tried to break through in every possible way, even if only on an operational scale. Since the means to overpower and destroy were not perfected, the [breakthrough] problem was not solved in World War I.

First the contestants tried to solve the breakthrough problem with artillery and with mortars that appeared at that time [*sic*]. Before the breakthrough, there was prolonged artillery fire, sometimes for seven days. But the result was only a breakthrough in one or two positions, since the defenders could regroup in new positions and the assault would fail.

The German imperialists, violating international agreements, tried to get out of the blind alley of static warfare by using chemical agents. The British and French tried to solve the breakthrough problem by using a new weapon, the tank. However, neither poison gases nor tanks were yet sufficiently developed to be employed strategically or to exert a significant influence in breaking through a static front.

The Russian Army, it is true, had some success in penetrating static positions. In the summer of 1916, the southwestern front, commanded by General Brusilov, simultaneously attacked in several directions, broke the Austro-Hungarian front army and penetrated 75 kilometers [40 miles]. However, this operational success was not translated into a strategic success because The Imperial Stavka did not consider the southwestern area to be of major importance, and the front was not supplied with ammunition. The ineptitude of the Russian High Command and the disintegration of the military rear areas did not permit the Russian Army to get out of the blind alley of positional warfare, in spite of the success of the Brusilov breakthrough.

Thus World War I remained essentially a positional war to the end.

In World War I, military operations in naval theaters were of secondary importance. The contestants, at the beginning of the war, believed that capital ships—battleships and [battle]cruisers—were basic weapons of naval warfare. Several so-called [battle]cruiser actions were conducted during the war; their outcome was determined by exchanges of fire between formations of surface vessels.

Even at the very outset of the war, however, a new naval weapon, the submarine, demonstrated its high combat potential. At the beginning of 1915 Germany inaugurated a ruthless submarine war against her enemies. By 1917, German submarine operations had placed England in a critical position. World War I demonstrated the great potential of submarines for naval combat operations.

Both sides made considerable use of air forces in World War I. They were used, in conjunction with artillery, as infantry support and also for aerial reconnaissance. Germany even tried to deal blows from the air upon British and French targets in the homeland first with dirigibles and then with airplanes. British and to a lesser degree French air defense, however, was more efficient than the German air offensives. Consequently, the German air raids did not cause serious damage in Great Britain and France. On the whole, air forces did not have any noticeable effect on methods of warfare since aircraft technology was not sufficiently advanced. Nevertheless, World War I demonstrated the great potential that aircraft had to deliver blows deep within enemy country. Air defense also began during this war.

Thus World War I introduced many innovations in methods of warfare. The general battle, as the way to attain basic war aims, passed into history. War became a prolonged affair involving armies of many millions and considerable military equipment. Numerous campaigns were necessary to achieve the aims of war; these campaigns involved military operations both on land and sea. The main target of the operations was the armed forces in the military theaters. War came to mean the mutual annihilation of field troops or naval forces. Air raids and submarine operations against maritime communications sought to destroy the economy and the systems of government in this war. Strategic operations were essentially offense and defense in ground theaters, and fire fights between surface vessels on the seas. The strategic offensive was executed in the main in a brief maneuver. The defensive then regained the advantage and both sides shifted to strategic defense.

During World War I, the Great October Socialist Revolution occurred in Russia. The experience gained in preparing and conducting the armed uprising in the October days influenced the development of the methods of warfare in an important way.

The Bolshevik Party, headed by V. I. Lenin, prepared the armed uprising meticulously. Lenin worked out the plans for it in detail and laid down the political and economic platforms that would follow the successful conclusion of the uprising.

Immediately after the Revolution, international imperialism joined Russian counterrevolutionaries to prepare a military assault against Soviet Russia. In 1918, without declaring war, the imperialists began the military intervention, which marked the start of the Civil War that lasted three years and cost our people enormous sacrifices.

*The Civil War* was a just war on the highest level and a very acute form of the class struggle. It continued the policy of the proletariat in the socialist revolution—the policy of overturning the bourgeoisie and landowners.

V. I. Lenin developed the most important principles of Soviet military strategy and combat methods for waging the Civil War. The strategic plans for waging the war, which brought victory over a strong enemy, were developed under his guidance. V. I. Lenin personally directed the armed conflict during the entire Civil War.

Armed combat developed over a vast territory. Moreover, the armed forces of the Interventionists and the White Guard occupied peripheral positions throughout the entire war, which gave them lines of communication to the outside world and enabled them to obtain supplies and military equipment and to deliver concentric strikes into our country. The Soviet Republic, occupying a central position, was blockaded on all sides, but its army could maneuver on interior lines.

There was no continuous front, and operational units and formations operated over wide expanses. However, forces and equipment were concentrated in the main areas and regions. The objectives of the struggle were primarily cities, railroad centers, and other important installations and districts. Offensives were often conducted along railroad lines. Typical of the military operations were high mobility, the extensive use of wide envelopments, encirclements, strikes against the rear and flank of enemy formations, brief engagements, and pursuit of the enemy.

Cavalry under the direction of the front command was a mobile means of delivering deep strikes into the main areas and played an important role in defeating the Interventionists during the Civil War. Infantry units and groups were most often used to penetrate organized enemy defenses, but cavalry often carried out the same task. After breaking through the defense, the cavalry penetrated to the enemy rear and executed maneuvers over a wide area. However, breakthrough of defenses was not always employed. The absence of a continuous front permitted the assembly of large offensive forces, particularly cavalry, to maneuver around the enemy flank and in his rear. The armored train played an important role in maneuver.

In the Civil War, partisan warfare was of unprecedented importance. The most diverse types of partisan warfare were used, from surprise raids by small units, and harassing operations, to large operations by partisan armies.

These were the most important methods of waging the Civil War. The Soviet military art developed during this war was the most advanced of its time. The Soviet Republic became vastly superior to the Interventionists and White Guard in military art and methods of warfare.

World War II provided a great impetus to the development of methods of warfare.

*World War II,* which was prepared by world imperialism and initiated by its most militant and hostile wing—Nazi Germany in the West and militarist Japan in the East—involved sixty-one states, almost twice as many as World War I. Its military operations covered an area five times as great as that of World War I. The belligerents' armed forces numbered more than one hundred million men. Practically the whole of the economies of the belligerent states were devoted to military requirements.

World War II lasted six years. The armed combat, particularly on the Soviet-German front, was the most fierce and bloody in history.

The imperialists began to prepare for World War II long before they started it. Their preparations were along political, ideological, economic, and military lines.

The military preparations were particularly active. Germany, with the co-operation and direct support of the United States, England, and France, organized mass armies in spite of the restrictions imposed by the Treaty of Versailles. At the beginning of World War II, Nazi Germany had more than one hundred divisions completely equipped and manned, about 4,500 military aircraft, and powerful naval forces. Japan at this time also had about one hundred divisions and more than 2,600 planes. World War II was preceded by a whole series of local wars and military conflicts in which the fascist and militarist states trained their armed forces and tested the effectiveness of their military equipment.

Nazi German strategy was based on Schlieffen's and Seekt's concepts of a massive blow; on Ludendorff's theory of total war which envisaged not only the defeat of the enemy's armed forces but also the annihilation of the population, industry, transport, and cities; and on Fuller's and Guderian's theories of mechanized and tank warfare. All these ideas were incorporated in the Nazi theory of blitzkrieg or lightning war.

The aggressive imperialist states also developed their war plans in detail and in advance. The Nazi strategic plan at the outset of the war was to defeat Poland and occupy Denmark and Norway at the very beginning of the war, thus safeguarding Germany from the east. After that, the plan was to concentrate the main forces against the Anglo-French bloc, to capture France, Belgium, and Holland and to blockade the British forces, thus safeguarding Germany from the west. Then it was planned to attack the Soviet Union and to defeat it by the autumn of 1941, in order to clear the way for Germany's subsequent vast colonial expansion. After defeating the Soviet Union, Germany planned to turn her attention to capturing North Africa, the Near and Middle East, India, the remaining Western European countries, and the islands in the Atlantic, and finally to attack the United States. If these delusory plans were accomplished, Nazi Germany could completely dominate the world.

Nazi Germany intended to wage the war in stages. The first stage was the defeat of Poland in a single operation with a massed assault of ground and air force formations.

Using the favorable configuration of the border, the Nazi German High Command planned concentrated attacks on Warsaw from the southwest, northwest, and north. The main blow was struck from the southwest by the Tenth Army, which contained many tanks and motorized troops. Germany took only eighteen days to carry out this [part of the] plan.

After occupying Denmark and capturing Norway, Hitler prepared to attack France and England. The German Command's initial plan for war against France was based on the Schlieffen and Moltke plan used in World War I. The main attack was to be carried out by crossing northern Belgium and the south of Holland, thus outflanking the Maginot Line, so as to destroy the main forces of the allies in the north and then attack Paris. However, this plan was soon changed, and in February of 1940 a new version of the war plan was adopted called "Operation Sickle." [The plan] was developed on the basis of a proposal of

Manstein. According to this plan, the main blow was to be delivered by one army group across Luxembourg, the Ardennes, and northern France, to the shores of the Channel, in order to cut off the main allied forces from the south and destroy them in northern France and Belgium. Two other groups of armies would tie down the allied forces in northern Belgium and Holland, and along the Maginot Line. Then it was planned to strike deep into France. To achieve all this, the fascists took only forty-five days.

After France was defeated, Hitler began to prepare the invasion of the British Isles. Operation "Sea Lion" called for the landing of amphibious forces in England, and its occupation. The preparations for the troop landings were supposed to be completed on September 15, 1940. However, fear of growing Soviet strength compelled Hitler to review his timing. The rulers of Nazi Germany decided that they must first dispose of the Soviet Union, in order to conquer the world. Hitler decided to invade England after finishing the war with the Soviet Union so as not to weaken his forces and weapons [before challenging the latter].

The German imperialists considered war against the USSR decisive in their battle for world domination. Their military successes in the West had gone to their heads. Disregarding actual conditions, underestimating the power of a socialist country and its army, the German High Command planned to defeat the main formations of our troops in the border zones within one and a half to two months, then to paralyze the will of the Soviet people to resist, advance to the banks of the Volga by autumn of 1941, and bring the Soviet people to their knees. This, in essence, was Operation "Barbarossa."

According to this plan, the main strike was to be delivered north of the Polesye Region by two army groups, called "Center" and "North," in the general directions of Smolensk and Leningrad. Army Group "South" was to attack Kiev, south of Polesye. Then the German troops in the center would advance rapidly to Moscow, and toward the south to occupy the Don Basin.

In order to carry out this plan, 190 divisions, including 17 tank and 13 motorized infantry divisions, 3,410 tanks, and up to 5,000 aircraft were readied. The Army Group "Center" was the strongest, having 50 divisions, including 9 tank and 6 motorized. Italy, Finland, Romania, and Hungary joined Nazi Germany.

Militarist Japan's treacherous and predatory plans were no less grandiose. Japan's goal was to capture the British, Dutch, and American colonies, Southeast Asia, and the Pacific, and also to seize the eastern regions of the Soviet Union. The Japanese strategic plan provided for

the continuation of the war in China until the entire country was occupied, and then for the concentration of the powerful Kwantung Army
in Manchuria to attack the USSR when Germany's successes [created
a favorable opportunity]. [Japan planned] a surprise attack on a considerable portion of the American fleet in order to capture the Philippines, Thailand, Burma, Malaya, and Indonesia. Later Japan intended
to destroy or temporarily neutralize the American Pacific fleet, capture
Guam and Wake Island, invade the Aleutians, and occupy New Guinea
and the Solomon Islands. After accomplishing these missions, Japan
would shift to the strategic defensive in the Pacific and the South Seas
in order to direct her main forces against the USSR. All this was to
be accomplished between December 1941 and March 1943.

These were the strategic plans of the aggressive fascist bloc for
waging World War II. As the war demonstrated, these plans were
thoroughly adventuristic, since the fascist bloc had neither the forces
nor the means to accomplish them.

The rulers of the Nazi bloc relied primarily upon surprise attack
to stun the enemy and paralyze his will to resist, exploiting the at-
tacker's advantage to the utmost.

The level of weapons development on the eve of World War II,
and the possession by the Axis powers of large airborne and armored
forces, permitted them to achieve considerable success during the initial period of the war by surprise attacks against unprepared enemies.
The fascist countries had shifted to a war economy before their enemies,
to provide better technical equipment and essential material to their
armed forces.

Advance deployment of armed forces was particularly important in
this war. Nazi Germany deployed her armies in advance, and secretly.
At the moment of attack her troops were already fully prepared for
combat, deployed in appropriate strategic and operational positions,
and the main forces grouped along the main lines of attack. The same
applies to Japan. This gave the aggressive states considerable military
advantage at the start of the war.

The fascist bloc capitalized on the lack of unity in the camps of
their enemies, which made it possible to defeat them one by one: first
Poland and Norway, then France, Belgium, and Holland, then Yugo-
slavia and Greece. After the capture of the countries of Western Europe,
the USSR was attacked.

The strategic aim of the Anglo-French-American coalition was to
turn Germany and Japan against the USSR and to keep the bulk of
their own armed forces in reserve until the USSR, Germany, and Japan
were exhausted and would have to accept dictated conditions for the

postwar settlement of world problems. So convinced were the ruling circles of the [Western allies] that these aims could be accomplished, that they did not prepare seriously for war. It is sufficient to point out that when World War II started, France had only twenty-five divisions, and England and the United States six each, ready for combat.

Poland was also unprepared for war. She could only put thirty-three divisions and brigades against the Germans, and these were uniformly deployed near the German border. Poland did not succeed in mobilizing, creating reserves, or bringing her troops up to full readiness. All this facilitated the operations of the Nazi army.

In declaring war on Germany, Great Britain and France intended to sit it out behind the Maginot Line until Germany attacked the USSR, and they did everything to hasten this attack. Although, during the first three weeks, France mobilized 110 divisions and Great Britain an expeditionary corps of five divisions, these enormous forces remained inactive though opposed by only twenty-three German divisions.

The High Command of the Anglo-French bloc developed a passive strategy, called plan "D," according to which the allied armed forces would be committed to battle only after a German attack began.

If the Germans invaded Belgium, major forces would be sent into Belgium to defend it. The Ardennes was considered impassable for German mechanized troops, and therefore the area of the German main attack was weakly defended. The Anglo-French strategic plan "D" was essentially a plan of national treachery, since it proved catastrophic for a number of Western European states.

By May 1940, the Anglo-French bloc had 142 divisions, 3,000 tanks, most of which were dispersed among divisions [in the field], and more than 2,500 airplanes. When the German assault began, the Anglo-French military leaders, in accordance with plan "D," committed the main body of their troops to Belgium, playing right into the Germans' hands.

The unfavorable development of events for the Western Allies at the beginning of World War II compelled American and British ruling circles to replan the war. In the spring of 1941, the "Rainbow 5" plan was developed and was put into operation after the Japanese attack on Pearl Harbor. According to this plan, the main forces of the Anglo-American bloc were to be concentrated in the Atlantic and European theaters. Their immediate missions were to defend the territory of the Allied Powers, to reinforce United States domination in Latin America, and to deploy forces in the Atlantic for a subsequent attack on Germany and Italy; the timing of the latter, incidentally, was not determined. The air and naval forces had the mission of protecting naval communications and conducting air attacks on Germany and Italy.

In planning military operations in the Pacific, the American ruling circles expected Japan to use her "golden opportunity," the war of Nazi Germany against the USSR, to first attack the Soviet Union. This belief was encouraged when the Tojo fascist military clique came to power in Japan in October 1941. Tojo was known for his hostility toward the USSR. In case Japan attacked the American and British armed forces, a strategic defense was planned in order to hold Southeast Asia and the South Seas until the arrival of the American Pacific fleet. This fleet was first to be deployed in Hawaii, and then moved to the Philippines to join the British and Dutch fleets for subsequent joint operations. At the time of the Japanese attack, the Allies had 22 divisions, 1,300 planes, 11 minelayers [*sic,* apparently battleships are meant], 4 aircraft carriers with 280 planes, 35 cruisers, 100 destroyers and 86 submarines in the Pacific. These forces were dispersed over vast distances, their operations were unco-ordinated, and there was not even a unified command.

Thus the aggressive, carefully developed, purposeful fascist assault plans were opposed by the Western Allies' timid defensive war plans, which were very disorganized and did not provide the required forces and weapons. The hope that the fascist bloc would first attack the USSR did not materialize.

The gathering threat of a second world war had compelled the Soviet Union to take measures to prepare the country to repel aggression. The efforts of the Soviet people under the leadership of the Communist Party, and our prewar five-year plans, had created a powerful industrial base for manufacturing all types of armaments and military equipment in sufficient quantities during the war. During prewar years the Red Army had been reorganized, enlarged, and its military might considerably increased.

Serious mistakes were committed, as we have already noted, in preparing the country and Armed Forces to repel the fascist aggressor. The mass production of new military equipment, especially tanks, planes, and antitank and antiaircraft weapons was not accomplished in time; thus the fascist army initially was considerably superior in equipment to the Red Army. The Red Army had no combat experience and no trained command staff (especially at the operational and strategic levels) which to a certain extent was due to the repression that characterized the Stalin cult of personality. Troop training was not always suited to the combat methods used at the beginning of World

War II. Also the reorganization of the Soviet Armed Forces was dragged out.

In 1941 the Soviet Union excluded the possibility of a surprise fascist attack, at least in the immediate future. It was assumed that whether war was declared or arose from an aggressor's attack, the initial military operations would be conducted by limited covering forces for a finite period (about fifteen to twenty days); this would permit the manning of defenses, the deployment of the main forces, and their commitment to battle. Consequently, plans were made to cover and defend the western borders using [only] the forces in the frontier military districts. These forces, in the event of a German attack, were to repel the attack and cover the mobilization and deployment of the Armed Forces. With this aim, the border military districts uniformly deployed covering troops near the frontier to defend a front averaging as much as 50 kilometers [30 miles] per division. But even this [kind of] defense was not ready by the start of the war. Only individual subdivisions and units of the first echelon divisions were available to cover the border. The remaining units of these divisions were far to the rear. In addition to the covering troops, the border districts had units and subdivisions 300 to 600 kilometers [180–360 miles] behind the frontier. None of these troops had means of transportation for a rapid move to the borders. Moreover, the main forces were concentrated south of Polesye, while the fascist troops made their main attack north of Polesye. The operational war plan to deal with German aggression had not been worked out.

All this gave Nazi Germany tremendous advantages, which seriously influenced the course of combat during the initial period of the war.

One of the reasons why the Soviet Union was not properly prepared to repel aggression was Stalin's incorrect evaluation of the military and political situation and the mistakes produced by the cult of personality. This explains to a considerable extent the failure in good time of the Commissariat of Defense and the Red Army General Staff to alert the Armed Forces, to execute their strategic deployment, and to have the forces of the border districts take up defensive positions, according to a far-from-complete cover plan.

The aggressive states used essentially the same methods to carry out surprise attacks against a number of countries.

Nazi Germany unleashed war against the USSR by massive surprise air strikes against our airfields, PVO, towns and villages, railroad stations, river crossings, area of troop deployment and control points to a depth of 300 to 400 kilometers [180–240 miles]. This surprise attack, with combined arms, of unprecedented force caused enormous damage to our aircraft and Ground Forces, overwhelmed our weak PVO and disorganized movement along railroads and highways near the border.

Because the Soviet armed forces were unprepared to repel a surprise attack, the fascist troops hardly encountered serious resistance in their path. The enemy succeeded in seizing the strategic initiative at the very outset of the war and won air supremacy. The rapid penetration of German troops deep into our territory greatly hindered the mobilization and deployment of [Soviet] units and subdivisions, particularly in the border regions of Lithuania, Byelorussia, and the Ukraine. It also disrupted our economy in these regions.

From the very beginning, the Great Patriotic War confronted the Soviet Armed Forces with extremely complex and responsible tasks: to halt the enemy, decimate the fascist assault formations, seize the strategic initiative from the enemy, and protect the country's vital centers and regions. It was necessary to deploy the Armed Forces, commit them to battle, evacuate industrial enterprises and materials from threatened regions, and develop the necessary military production to foil the Nazi plans for a blitzkrieg, and create the conditions for a basic change in the course of the war.

A long and bloody struggle was needed to accomplish these tasks. Only at the end of 1941 was the enemy halted, in the Battle of Moscow. His planned blitzkrieg was foiled and conditions were created for the Red Army to pass to the counteroffensive. This constituted the initial period in the Great Patriotic War.

The successful counteroffensive before Moscow and the defeat of the Germans in the main western strategic area meant that the German plan had miscarried, that the myth of the invincible German Army had been exploded, and that the strategic initiative had passed into the hands of the Red Army.

On the whole, however, the outcome of the initial period of the war was generally unfavorable to us. Our failures at the beginning of the Great Patriotic War were mainly due to a number of temporary German advantages over the USSR: Nazi Germany had a more powerful material and technical base and was ahead of the USSR in placing its economy on a military footing; the enemy armed forces were better equipped militarily and had the necessary combat experience; Germany selected a favorable time to attack the USSR, when almost all of Europe was under the heel of fascism; Hitler could employ his main forces against the USSR at a time when the Soviet Union was alone; and finally, Germany used the advantage of surprise attack.

There were also purely military reasons, like the incomplete strategic deployment of our Armed Forces at the beginning of the war, their inadequate readiness at the moment of the surprise attack, and a certain backwardness in the Soviet military art, especially in the conduct of military operations in the initial period of war. These [shortcomings] produced passivity, the scattering of forces, and the formation of a continuous front [*sic*]. There were also inadequacies in the organization of strategic and operational control.

At the beginning of World War II, the Anglo-American bloc suffered serious losses in the Pacific. This was the result of the sudden Japanese attack, the unpreparedness of the Anglo-American bloc for war, and the passive defensive strategy employed by this bloc at the beginning of the war with Japan.

Japan followed Germany's example when she initiated war in the Pacific by a surprise attack. Japan selected an advantageous moment to deliver a surprise attack on the American naval base at Pearl Harbor. This one blow seriously weakened American forces in the Pacific. At the same time and in the same manner Japan attacked the Philippines and Hong Kong, invaded Thailand and the Malay Peninsula, and captured a number of American bases in the Pacific.

In spite of Japan's initial successes in World War II, her plans for a rapid victory were thwarted. She did not succeed in destroying the Anglo-American forces and compelling the United States to capitulate. The war became protracted and Japanese air and naval forces suffered great losses. The Japanese aggressors encountered unexpectedly stubborn resistance from the populations of occupied countries in Southeast Asia. They encountered particularly great difficulties in China, where there was increasing resistance from the Chinese people, under the leadership of the Chinese Communist Party.

In spite of the fact that the war involved most of the states of the world and the military operations were conducted over a tremendous area, the Soviet-German front was the principal and decisive front of World War II. It was on this front that the outcome of the entire war was decided. The Soviet-German front differed basically from all the other fronts of World War II. From the moment that Nazi Germany attacked the USSR until the moment that Germany capitulated, there was no pause in the fierce and bloody combat on the Soviet-German front. On the other fronts the military operations were of a limited and passive nature. The war shifted conclusively in favor of the anti-fascist coalition after the Red Army destroyed the fascist troops at the Battles of Stalingrad and Kursk. Germany's major and most battleworthy ground and air forces were annihilated on the Soviet-German front. This determined the victory of the anti-Nazi coalition in World War

II. In the concluding stages of the war, the Red Army defeated the Kwantung Army, the elite of the Japanese armed forces, which definitely speeded the end of World War II.

Here we cannot ignore the lies of bourgeois falsifiers of history who advanced the theory of so-called "turning points" in order to minimize the role of the Soviet Union and its Armed Forces in the defeat of the fascist army. In the face of historical fact, they attempt to prove that secondary military operations in Africa and Southern Italy, and at Midway in the Pacific, were the so-called "turning points" in World War II. The falsifiers of history misrepresent these secondary events as decisive battles in World War II. Churchill, Montgomery, Fuller, and others attempt to prove that the Battle of El Alamein and the landing of American troops in Morocco and Algeria changed the entire course of the war. Some wrongheaded bourgeois historians go even further and attempt to establish a direct relationship between the Soviet counteroffensive at Stalingrad and the British and American military operations in North Africa. In order to understand how unfounded and slanderous these assertions are, we need only point out that in the Battle of El Alamein the British were opposed by only twelve Italian and German divisions, whereas at Stalingrad our troops defeated about fifty enemy divisions.

For a long time Britain and the United States conducted a defensive war, concentrating their forces along secondary fronts which were often inactive, and stubbornly refused to open a second front in Europe. When it became quite clear to the entire world that the Soviet Union and its Armed Forces could deal unaided with Nazi Germany, American and British imperialists were forced to open a second front in Europe.

The real reason for opening a second front in this situation was not to hasten the surrender of Germany, but to grab more territory in Europe and prevent the establishment of rule of the people in European countries.

The second front had only secondary significance in the war, although its role is greatly exaggerated in the West. This is evident if only from the fact that there were 191 German divisions on the Soviet front at this time (not including the divisions of Germany's satellites), whereas the British and American troops in Western Europe faced only 60 German divisions, which were of low military caliber and at only 70 to 75 per cent of strength.

Hence the basis for evaluating the methods of warfare in World War II is the Soviet-German front, which was the main front of the war. In general outline, these methods were the following.

In the principal theaters of World War II, the belligerents deployed their armed forces, which consisted primarily of ground forces and air forces, along borders or along the front. This created a zone saturated with troops, intended in the final analysis to protect the country's economic regions and political centers, and to ensure the continuance of vital functions without which the war could not be conducted. In order to seize the enemy's [vital] centers and regions, whose loss would eliminate further resistance, it was necessary to defeat the enemy ground and air forces. Therefore, the salient feature of armed combat throughout the entire war was the mutual destruction of the armed forces of the contestants in ground theaters that comprised relatively shallow front areas of a few hundred kilometers [in depth].

The military operations of the armed forces can be reduced to two basic types of operation: strategic offense and strategic defense. The ground forces played the decisive role in strategic attack and defense; the other branches, including the air force and the navy, were used to support the ground forces.

The strategic offensive was the basic type of military operation and was employed to penetrate the enemy front, defeat his main forces, and seize his defense lines, [internal] regions, and administrative centers. In order to accomplish a breakthrough, enormous masses of artillery, aircraft, tanks, and infantry were concentrated in narrow sectors. The advance of the troops was preceded by powerful artillery and air preparation, although for a considerably shorter period than in World War I (one to two hours). Then the infantry divisions with tanks attacked with continuous artillery support (either successive fire concentrations or a rolling barrage) and low level air support. After the tactical defense had been breached, powerful formations of tank forces were committed to battle to develop the offensive in great depth. Large-scale offensive operations were extensively used to split, encircle, and annihilate operational and strategic enemy formations. In the past war, the Soviet strategic offense became highly developed; it was able to overwhelm the German strategic defense.

Strategic defense also played an important role in the past war. Its purpose was to hold the main lines of defense, prevent enemy forces from reaching the country's vital centers and regions, wear down the enemy forces, and create the conditions for a shift to the strategic offensive. The defense was more actively conducted than in World War I. The Red Army made extensive use of artillery and air counter-preparations, counterattacks and counterblows which often grew into a counteroffensive and finally into a general offensive.

During the first period of the Great Patriotic War, the Red Army primarily conducted a strategic defense. During this period, the Soviet defense was weaker than the German offense. At the end of 1942, however, the Soviet defense began to overcome the German offense. In 1943, our strategic defense withstood a powerful blow from the fascist army in the Kursk salient. From this point to the end of the war, the Germans were never able to overcome our defenses either on a strategic or even on an operational scale.

Consequently, the experience gained by the Soviet Armed Forces in carrying out strategic offense and defense considerably enriched military science in general and contributed to its development.

The offensive of the American and British armies against the weakened fascist German troops in Western Europe introduced nothing essentially new to the military art. The same can be said of their defense.

In general, we can say that offense prevailed over defense in World War II, in contrast to World War I where penetration of defenses was basically unsuccessful. The use of huge masses of tanks and large air forces played a decisive role; tanks and airplanes overcame defense and gave the war a mobile character.

Air forces became strategic in their significance in World War II. The main aerial forces were concentrated for air battles and support of ground forces on the decisive fronts in the past war. For this purpose, the belligerents had numerous short-range bombers, attack planes, and fighters at their disposal. The battle for air superiority became very important.

In addition to air forces intended for joint operations with ground forces and naval forces, long-range strategic aircraft appeared during World War II and were employed to execute the plans of the strategic commands. The United States and Great Britain had especially strong strategic air forces. Strategic air forces were used beyond the boundaries of ground theaters. Their operations aimed at the deep rear of the enemy, his economy, transport, population, and governmental system, and were intended to undermine the enemy's military and economic potential, disorganize his home front, and demoralize the population.

Conclusive results could not be expected from such operations, however, since at that time means of destruction powerful enough to ensure complete disorganization of the enemy's homeland were not available. Even in the initial period of World War II it was quite convincingly demonstrated that the strategic aims of war could not be executed solely by the use of strategic aircraft. Consequently such operations never attained great importance in the war between Germany and the USSR, and long-range aircraft did not undergo any significant development in the USSR.

The United States and Britain viewed the matter somewhat differently. These two countries adopted the theory of aerial warfare advocated by the Italian General Douhet. For a long time Britain's and America's entire active operations against Germany consisted of bombing cities and industrial targets. Germany also delivered massive aerial attacks on Great Britain and other Western European states. All the large cities of Western Europe were bombed. Germany suffered especially severe damage from these bombings. The American and British press proclaimed that Germany would be "bombed out" of the war by the use of aircraft.

The operations of American and British strategic air force, however, were not a decisive factor in the victory over Germany. Even the Americans say this. President Kennedy's present military adviser, General Taylor, has written: "During World War II, strategic bombing did not have a decisive influence on the destruction of Nazi German military industry. It contributed to the final victory, but was not the decisive factor." *

Professor Brodie is even more specific on this point: "It is necessary to indicate clearly that during World War II, the bombing of cities was unsuccessful." †

Although the German economy was severely damaged, it was able to support a prolonged and stubborn campaign in the military theaters. The American Crowley-Clayton Commission established the fact that Germany's entire machine-building industry at the end of the war had greater productive capacity than at the start of the war. Ten to fifteen government plants out of every hundred were out of commission; the blast furnaces and coking ovens were undamaged. According to American data, the aviation industry suffered the most. Nevertheless the production of military aircraft in Germany steadily increased right up to 1945. For example, in November 1943, 953 combat planes were manufactured, in April 1944, 1,224 planes, and in the following July, 1,855 airplanes.

Another aim of the American-British air strikes was not accomplished, i.e., the demoralization of the German people. True, the German people suffered relatively high losses from air attacks, but their ability to resist was not crushed by these attacks but by the operations of Soviet troops in Germany.

---

* M. Taylor, *Nenadezhnaia strategiia* [*Unreliable Strategy*], Voenizdat, Moscow, 1961, p. 42.

† B. Brodie, *Strategiia v vek raketnogo oruzhiia* [*Strategy in the Missile Age*], Voenizdat, Moscow, 1961, p. 149.

During World War II several countries accelerated work on the creation of an atomic bomb. It is understandable that if atomic bombs had been available, the results of the air attacks would have been quite different. The United States did not have an atomic bomb until 1945, when Germany had already been defeated and World War II was drawing to a close. Nevertheless, the ruling American circles decided to deliver an atomic attack against Japan, not for strategic reasons but for political ones.

The American militarists did this in such a way that the nuclear blow would kill the maximum number of people. The four Japanese cities selected for nuclear strikes were spared [ordinary] air raids after April 1945 and only individual aircraft occasionally flew over them. Consequently the Japanese stopped sounding the air raid warning. The populations of these cities became unconcerned. As a result of the nuclear strike on Hiroshima, 200,000 persons died; in Nagasaki, 120,000. This shows that American imperialism is capable of the most monstrous crimes in order to achieve its ends.

The development of strategic aviation during World War II and the creation of the atomic bomb and of the first long-range missiles pointed to the possibility that weapons could act directly against the economy, governmental system, and population deep within the enemy country. This provided the basis for a new type of military operation, in addition to offense and defense in the war theaters.

The need to protect the country's population, economy, and communications from air raids deep within its territory had already become critically important during World War II. This task was assigned to air defense, which also had become strategically significant. PVO forces and weapons such as antiaircraft artillery, fighters, and radar equipment, as well as methods of air defense, were developed extensively during the last war. Great Britain was compelled to develop not only air defense, but also antimissile defense; this was effective against the V-1 winged missile but powerless against the V-2 ballistic missile.

Thus, even in World War II, PVO forces became necessary to protect the country's rear areas from enemy missile and air strikes.

Naval operations were also conducted during the last war, as well as military operations in ground theaters and deep air strikes against the belligerents. In the war between Germany and the USSR, naval operations were conducted on a relatively small scale, and mainly in joint operations with ground troops. In the Atlantic and the Pacific, naval operations were conducted on a larger scale. In the Atlantic, these operations were primarily conducted to keep communication lines open, whereas in the Pacific they were mainly clashes between rather large formations of American and Japanese naval and air forces, and relatively small forces of ground troops.

During the initial part of World War II, the belligerents attempted to use large surface fleets (battleships and cruisers) to conduct naval operations, using the close-range fire which was typical of past wars. However, the use of air forces and submarines demonstrated that cruisers and battleships had lost their former advantage. They were replaced by aircraft carriers, which had a definite role to play even though highly vulnerable to both air and submarine attack. Naval battles became conflicts between carrier task forces. The struggle was waged primarily by aircraft whose purpose it was to destroy enemy submarine and surface fleets and air forces. Submarines were extensively used against combat and transport surface ships. Submarine packs were used as a mobile screen controlled by shore radio and directed against enemy ships and convoys. Close-range artillery battles between large surface vessels had become obsolete, although such battles did occur in World War II. Mine warfare in naval theaters and large-scale amphibious operations were widely used.

Naval operations were not of decisive importance for the outcome of World War II. For a long while the United States concentrated its main forces in a secondary theater, the Pacific. Here a fruitless and prolonged war took place for air and naval bases on islands and for the capture of many islands, most of them small.

The Anglo-American bloc acquired considerable experience in large-scale amphibious operations. However, the importance of such operations was decreased by the fact that the German and Japanese forces were completely inferior and offered little resistance. Each amphibious operation required lengthy preparation (six months for the landing in Sicily and fifteen months for the landing in northern France) and each operation was elaborately equipped.

In addition to these types of military operations, underground movements and extensive partisan warfare in the enemy rear played an important role in the victory over fascism in World War II. Partisan war in the enemy-occupied regions of the Soviet Union exerted a considerable influence on the course of the war. Partisan combat mainly took the form of paramilitary and reconnaissance operations; attacks by small units on enemy garrisons, important targets, and communications; battles between entire partisan units and enemy reserves; and finally, raids by large partisan formations deep in the enemy rear. The partisans disorganized the enemy rear and diverted much of the enemy's forces to themselves. Partisan combat and underground activities were a special and important type of military operation.

Thus, the basic forms of military operations in World War II were strategic offense and defense, carried out mainly by ground forces supported by air forces. Neither strategic air operations against the enemy rear, nor defense of the homeland from air attack, nor military operations in naval theaters were of decisive importance for the outcome of World War II, even though they were conducted on a large scale.

In order to achieve the final political, military, and strategic aims of the last war, several intermediate political and military strategic tasks had to be carried out. The execution of each of these took rather a long time and constituted a particular phase of the war.

The Great Patriotic War has been divided into four periods. The first period includes the interval between the Nazi German attack and the counteroffensive at Stalingrad in the autumn of 1942. Its main objective was the struggle for the initiative in the war. The second period represented a basic shift in the course of the Great Patriotic War and in World War II as a whole (autumn of 1942 to the end of 1943). The third period encompasses the events of 1944 and 1945: the expulsion of the fascist aggressors from Soviet territory, the transfer of military operations to enemy territory, and the final defeat of Nazi Germany's armed forces. The fourth period includes the attack of the Red Army in the Far East, ending with the capitulation of Japan.

Each period was characterized by certain military operations. In the first period, the Soviet troops carried out primarily strategic defense and withdrawal; in the second period, strategic defense and offense; in the third and fourth periods, continuous strategic offensives, which ensured the attainment of all the aims of the war.

World War II contributed to the further development of combat methods. This war clearly demonstrated the superiority of the Soviet military art and strategy over the adventuristic Nazi German strategy. The Red Army was able to create on a strategic scale an insurmountable defense that withstood the powerful blows of the fascist military machine; the Red Army was able to organize a strategic offense which crushed the German defense. The Soviet military art, which was the most advanced in the world, thus aided in attaining victory in World War II.

In World War II, the armed forces of the fascist bloc were utterly defeated, and the fascist regime in Germany and several other countries was destroyed. The anti-Nazi coalition of states was completely victorious. However, it was the Soviet Union and its Armed Forces which made the decisive contribution to victory over the fascist bloc in this war.

Having studied the development of combat methods in the most important wars of the nineteenth and twentieth centuries, we can draw the following conclusions.

Each war led to basically new and unique methods of combat. The new methods of warfare were based on accumulated historical experience. The [lessons of this] experience were perfected and refined to correspond to new weapons and the actual political conditions in which war broke out and was conducted.

The development of combat methods has continuously been accelerated, particularly in the twentieth century when capitalism entered the last stage of its development—imperialism. During this period, a basic upheaval has taken place in former methods of warfare. All attempts to start a new war by old methods have inevitably led to disastrous defeat.

The world wars of the imperialist era have drawn the majority of states and huge masses of people into their orbit.

The two past world wars have been clashes between two groups of imperialist states: one headed by Germany and the other by the United States and Great Britain. Even on the eve of World War II, the imperialists attempted to create a unified front against the USSR, but they failed.

During the age of imperialism, revolutionary and civil wars have often broken out against the rule of capitalism and toward the establishment of a new socialist system. The primary examples were the Civil Wars in the Soviet Union and the Chinese People's Republic, which ended with the conclusive victory of the Soviet and Chinese peoples. Wars of national liberation, very prevalent in colonial and dependent countries, have been aimed at achieving freedom from the imperialist yoke.

History has shown that aggressive states usually prepare for war carefully in advance, anticipate their enemies in deploying armed forces, and initiate war by a surprise attack. This took place in Napoleonic France, in Imperial and Nazi Germany, and in militarist Japan. These methods gave them definite advantages over the states they attacked. The aggressive states usually went on the offensive at the beginning, and often with success. The attacked states were usually not fully ready to repel an attack and were initially forced to take the defensive and wage a prolonged battle for the initiative. This was the position in which Britain, France, the United States, and the USSR found themselves at the start of World War II. The American imperialists avoided entering both world wars at their outset. They entered World

War I during its concluding stages. They were compelled to enter World War II somewhat earlier, though American troops only began to participate actively at the end of the war, when the enemy was already considerably weakened.

Wars in the imperialist era have become progressively larger, indeed worldwide in the full sense of the word, and have become increasingly intense and violent. In attempting to gain their predatory goals, the imperialist aggressors do not hesitate to commit any crime against mankind.

In the wars during the epoch of early capitalism, the struggle was conducted primarily between armed forces in military theaters. Later, the targets of military operations widened to include areas far in the rear, the population, the economy, and the system of government.

## War Plans of the Imperialists and Their Possible Methods for Initiating a New War

In the postwar period, the aggressive militarist world powers, in particular American, British, French, and West German imperialists, have entered into a criminal pact to prepare a new, third world war openly directed against the USSR and the other socialist countries. The driving force behind such aggression is American imperialism, the leader of the entire imperialist camp. American imperialism inspires and directs the aggressive bloc, which is a highly unified coalition of imperialists against the socialist camp. The imperialists have initiated an unprecedented arms race and the "Cold War," an intermediate and unstable condition between war and peace, a state of political hostility one step from armed combat. They continually inflame the international situation and have repeatedly brought the world to the brink of war.

In pursuing their aggressive policy of preparing a new war, the ruling circles of the imperialist states, especially the United States, do everything possible to oppose a peaceful disarmament solution and a decrease in international tension. They attempt to reinforce and expand aggressive military blocs, whip up war hysteria, and intensify reactionary policies within the imperialist states. The economic preparations for a new war are reflected in a continuous increase in the production of modern weapons, especially nuclear weapons and the means for delivering them; and also in the maintenance of various branches of industry at mobilization levels and in the preparation of all industry and transport for a rapid shift to a military footing and of theaters for military operations.

The military preparations have been actively pursued, and co-ordinated plans have been worked out and put into effect. The members of aggressive blocs, especially NATO, maintain large armed forces constantly ready for combat. Many of these are located near the borders of the socialist countries and surround the socialist countries with numerous military bases. Intensive and continuous training of the armed forces is accomplished by regular maneuvers and exercises of troops and their commanders, the conduct of periodic alerts, regular flights in the direction of the USSR, and the approach of aircraft carriers and missile-carrying submarines to the coasts of the socialist countries. Active reconnaissance is carried out continuously.

In the preparation of a new world war, the imperialist military ideologists are evolving every possible strategic concept [that might form] a basis for their plans.

The NATO countries have officially adopted the so-called sword and shield strategy, where American strategic air forces and nuclear weapons are the "sword," and the tactical air forces and ground troops of the European NATO countries furnish the "shield."

Judging from the numerous military exercises, it can be assumed that the military leadership of the imperialist bloc has developed a unified strategy, and possibly even a unified strategic plan for waging all-out nuclear war against the socialist countries.

Recently the West German militarists have been particularly active. The entire strategy of the Bonn militarists is to prepare for revenge, although this goes under the name of "defense." The General Staff of the Bundeswehr has worked out a program for revenge: to create the strongest army in Western Europe, to arm it with nuclear weapons and the latest military equipment, to transform Western Europe and part of Africa into a [rear zone of military and economic support], and to assume gradually the leadership of NATO. The ruling circles of the United States, Great Britain, and France are doing everything possible to encourage this program.

The press has published some information on the Bundeswehr's "DEKO-II" military plan, which provides for a blitzkrieg invasion of East Germany, Czechoslovakia, Poland, and Hungary. One group of armies is to strike from the south, in order to cut off East Germany from Czechoslovakia and Poland, and to capture East Germany within a few days. This [part of the plan] was worked out during the NATO "Sidestep" maneuvers in 1959. Another group of armies is to strike between Czechoslovakia and Austria in order to encircle Czechoslovakia, cut it off from Poland, and invade Hungary. The West German Navy is to strike from the north. These are the extremely dangerous plans of the West German militarists and revanchists.

The masters of the imperialist bloc are preparing to wage nuclear war on a world scale against the socialist countries by massive and surprise nuclear strikes. The terms "defense," "retaliatory blow," and "massive retaliation" are merely meant to conceal these preparations, which are all based on American superiority in nuclear weapons.

This strategy, however, arrived at an impasse at the end of the 1950's, when the ruling circles of the imperialist bloc had to acknowledge that their nuclear superiority was at an end.

Some military theorists see a way out of this situation in the use of outer space to achieve their military aims; allegedly this would create a balance of forces favorable to the imperialists. Other military theorists have advanced the idea of a "graduated strategy" or limited (local) war.

The real meaning of the "graduated strategy" is to give the United States the opportunity to use nuclear weapons without having the other side use them. The proponents of the "graduated strategy" believe that it would compensate for the inability of the American strategic air forces to attack Soviet strategic centers, and would enable them to cover up their plans for delivering nuclear weapons to the West German revanchists. [The purpose of these deliveries is to ensure] that someone else will take the initiative in starting war, since it has become very unpopular for the United States to do so. Whereas previously they raised the question of conducting local wars in Africa and the Near, Middle, and Far East, now they talk openly of local wars in Europe.

Under the guise of discussing local war, feverish preparations are being made for unlimited nuclear war against the socialist countries. Many telling facts indicate that the imperialists have not discarded the strategy of a surprise nuclear attack. It is true that the United States and its satellites have recently increased their allocations to conventional weapons, but at the same time they are accelerating the development of strategic missiles and are constructing missile bases at an accelerated rate. On June 6, 1961, American Under-Secretary of Defense Gilpatric stated: "We do not intend to decrease our nuclear forces, but we do intend to increase our conventional forces." [1] Many different military exercises and maneuvers, frequent alerts, and continuous patrols by strategic bombers carrying nuclear bombs and missiles, etc., are further evidence [of preparation for a surprise attack].

It follows that the American imperialists and the aggressive blocs they lead have in no way given up their plans for initiating an unlimited

---

[1] U.S. ED. NOTE—Gilpatric's actual words were: "Well, we are not going to, as I understand the present doctrine, reduce our nuclear capabilities. We are going to try to bring up our other capabilities so as to give ourselves more flexibility, more choice of responsiveness." Department of Defense, Press Conference Release, June 6, 1961, p. 11.

(total) nuclear war; on the contrary, in speeding up the nuclear and missile arms race, they have accelerated their preparations for initiating such a war.

Modern aggressive imperialist forces are studying the experience of Nazi Germany, militarist Japan, and other aggressive states that unleashed war in the past. The Nazi method of treacherous surprise attack has been incorporated in the official doctrine of the United States and its dependent imperialist states. Important military officials have mentioned this openly. The U.S. Secretary of the Air Force, Douglas, stated in 1959: "American strategy is based on a surprise attack with all available forces and means. The United States must be the first to make such an attack." [2]

The imperialists are not convinced that they would be able to achieve effective results in an open fight. Consequently they rely upon treachery, adventurism, and surprise attack with all possible modern weapons. They believe that a nuclear strike delivered by air forces and missiles can achieve incomparably greater results than those achieved at the beginning of the last war and can even accomplish the basic aims of war, i.e., forcing the Soviet Union and the other socialist countries into unconditional surrender.

However, as N. S. Khrushchev noted in his report to the fourth session of the Supreme Soviet of the USSR: "One can attack first; this requires more foolhardiness than sense, and we naturally take into account the fact that some of our potential opponents have inclinations in this direction. . . . But could an attacking opponent, even assuming for a moment that he succeeded in achieving surprise, put out of commission all the stockpiles of nuclear weapons and all the missile-launching equipment located in the territory of the power under attack? Certainly not. The state subject to surprise attack, if it is understood that we are talking about a state of sufficient size, would always have a chance to give the aggressor a proper rebuff. . . . Our country is vast in size, we can disperse our missile equipment and camouflage it well. We are creating a system which, if one of the instruments assigned to retaliate is put out of commission, will always be able to bring duplicate instruments into play and destroy the targets from reserve positions." [3]

In their aggressive plans, the imperialist bloc devotes considerable attention to the problems of the strategic deployment of the armed forces and their readiness to initiate war. The imperialists are attempting to repeat the methods used by aggressive states in past wars, par-

---

[2] U.S. ED. NOTE—It has not been possible to verify this statement.
[3] U.S. ED. NOTE—See Note A, p. 398.

ticularly those used by Nazi Germany in World War II. The masters
of the imperialist military blocs are making frenzied efforts, even in
peacetime, to bring the required armed forces to a state of complete
readiness in advance, and to deploy them in the proper formations, so
that at any convenient moment they could initiate war by surprise.

Imperialist military ideologists are ardent proponents of the theory
that it is impossible in modern war to mobilize and deploy the armed
forces and that, therefore, it is necessary at the beginning of the war
to have, in full fighting readiness, such armed forces as can execute
the main missions of the war in the shortest possible time.

For example, British Field Marshal Montgomery has written: "The
previous type of mobilization . . . is archaic under the conditions of
nuclear war. . . . We need a system which will give the desired results within several hours after radar warnings; the system should not
depend on vulnerable communication media. . . ." *

H. Kissinger is even more definite on this matter: "A general war
conducted with modern weapons will be decided by the operations of the
armed forces at the disposal of the opponents at the beginning of the war.
We can no longer count on a more or less prolonged period of time in
which to mobilize." †

This theory is very convenient for the imperialists. Consequently its
basic ideas have been put into force by the aggressive NATO bloc.
Already, large formations of strategic aircraft and missiles, naval forces,
air defense forces, and some ground troops have been set up and maintained at a high level of combat readiness. These formations are intended for a surprise attack; they are hardly meant for "defense" or
"a retaliatory strike."

What are the special features of the deployment and posture of
armed forces in the aggressive imperialist military bloc in the present
conditions?

Departing from the practice of past wars, the aggressive imperialist
states give priority, in preparing for a future war, to strategic weapons,
including nuclear weapons, strategic aircraft, intercontinental missiles,
intermediate-range missiles, carrier task forces, and missile-carrying
ships. These weapons are considered to be the main striking forces in
a future world nuclear war. At present, the Anglo-American bloc has
already created the essential instrumentalities and organization required
to initiate a new war.

As we noted in the preceding chapters, the United States and Britain

---

* *Journal of The Royal United Service Institution,* November 1958, p. 478.

† H. Kissinger, *Iadernoe oruzhie i vneshniaia politika* [*Nuclear Weapons and
Foreign Policy*], Izdatel'stvo Inostrannoi Literatury, Moscow, 1959, p. 150.

have built up large stocks of nuclear weapons and have established storage sites and bases in appropriate places for assembling these weapons. In addition, a certain amount of nuclear ammunition is always kept fully ready for immediate employment.

The American strategic air forces, which possess heavy and medium bombers, have been organized into air armies and divisions. The air armies are located in the United States and each army is intended to operate in particular areas. The Second and Eighth Air Armies are to deliver strikes on the socialist countries from the north, west, and southwest; the Fifteenth Air Army will strike from the northeast. To refuel the strategic bombers in the air, the United States has deployed tanker planes along the planned flight paths of the bombers. Numerous air bases have been prepared for American strategic aircraft, in the United States, England, Spain, North Africa, Greenland, and the Pacific.

American strategic aviation can deal blows from bases in the United States. However, there are not enough tankers to permit the employment of all the bombers from all these bases. Consequently, the plans are to move many medium bombers, in advance [of war], to bases in England, Spain, North Africa, and the Pacific under various pretexts (exercises, training flights, rotating units on duty in advance bases, etc.). The headquarters of the Sixteenth Air Army, permanently located in Spain, has been set up to direct strategic aircraft based in Spain and North Africa.

American and British strategic air forces are maintained at a high level of combat readiness. A certain number of crews are constantly on duty. Some of the heavy bombers are always on patrol, carrying nuclear bombs or missiles with nuclear warheads. Each crew is assigned a specific target for a nuclear strike on the USSR or some other socialist country. Control centers have been prepared and a system of rapid response to warning has been developed.

Thus, the strategic air force need not be specially deployed and mobilized for war. Essentially, it is now ready to deliver a surprise nuclear strike.

Although strategic bombers have lost much of their former combat value because of the development of antiaircraft weapons, all the same, they are still dangerous weapons. It must be remembered that the American strategic air force is aimed at our cities, industrial centers, and the regions where our armed forces are based and deployed; the mission of this strategic air force is to weaken socialist military strength, cripple our military and industrial potential, inflict massive losses on our population, and destroy its will to resist.

The American government is making feverish efforts to recover from its backwardness in missile weapons. The American press has published an extensive program for the development of missile formations armed with intercontinental and intermediate-range missiles. Considerable attention is being devoted to the location and technical equipment of launching pads. The launching pads are being set up primarily in mountainous, sparsely populated areas, and are being dispersed. Underground and semiunderground launchers are also under construction, and mobile railway launching platforms have been proposed.

The missile launching installations are maintained at a high level of combat readiness: the missiles are assembled, the fuel is ready, and nuclear warheads are stored in secret storage sites nearby; service personnel are on duty, a signaling system exists for the rapid preparation of missiles for launch, and each installation has a definite target to destroy. The strategic missiles are aimed at the same targets as the strategic bombers. The missile units are under the command of the strategic air force and are deployed in formations appropriate for the execution of the missions outlined in the plan for a future war.

The Anglo-American navy consists of seven attack carrier task forces, each including two or three attack carriers and other warships. They are all deployed in military theaters; three carrier units in the Atlantic, two in the Pacific, one in the Mediterranean, and one in the Indian Ocean. The Sixth Fleet in the Mediterranean and the Seventh Fleet in the Pacific are always in full combat readiness. The United States has just begun to organize the Fifth Fleet in the Indian Ocean. The remaining naval forces are also ready to proceed rapidly to these regions in order to conduct military operations. They can be deployed under the guise of good will tours, rotation of warships, exercises, and maneuvers. Large-scale maneuvers and exercises are particularly dangerous. At such times the naval forces of the United States, Great Britain, and other NATO members actually deploy in battle formation and approach the boundaries of the socialist countries.

The United States has planned and is carrying out a large-scale and intensive shipbuilding program, especially to procure missile-carrying nuclear submarines and attack aircraft carriers. Great Britain is also modernizing her warships, especially aircraft carriers. All NATO members are arming their navies with missiles.

The naval forces of the Anglo-American bloc have heavy attack aircraft, which can deliver nuclear strikes over a great distance using guided missiles and torpedoes carrying nuclear warheads. These are intended to deliver nuclear strikes on the most important coastal targets, to do battle with enemy naval forces, to protect maritime communications, to execute amphibious landings, and to blockade straits.

Thus the fleets and the strategic air forces of the Anglo-American military bloc need not be specially deployed and mobilized. They are maintained at a high level of combat readiness, and their final deployment in battle formation can be quickly accomplished.

In the European theater the imperialists are preparing large armed forces that are assigned the main role in a future world war. The main forces and weapons destined for use in this theater are under joint NATO command or, more properly, American military command.

The bosses of NATO plan gradually and secretly to prepare and deploy, in advance [of war], a first strategic echelon in the European theater of a size and complement that could execute the major strategic missions of the initial period of the war, and complete the mobilization of successive echelons in time.

Tactical aircraft, operational and tactical missiles, and nuclear artillery are the main striking forces in the military theaters. They are all capable of employing nuclear weapons. Nuclear ammunition for these weapons is being stockpiled in European states close to the boundaries of the socialist countries. The American press has noted that more than half of the tactical fighter aircraft are permanently based on foreign soil.

The forces being prepared for aggression in the European theater also include strong ground forces. These consist of West German motorized and tank divisions and the American Seventh Army, which is permanently stationed in West Germany.

The NATO leaders are well aware that these forces are inadequate for waging a large-scale war in Europe against the socialist countries, which are members of the Warsaw Pact. For this reason the groundwork is being laid for rapid mobilization and deployment of large forces in this theater.

The American imperialists do not expect to be able to carry out their mobilization while protected by their allies, as in previous world wars. General Clarke, former Commander of the U.S. Army, was quite specific about this: "We must have armed forces in the most important regions of the world in order to conduct military operations in those regions, and in other regions where troops can be rapidly transferred.

"We must have a base for the mobilization of armed forces in case of an all-out war. This requires reserves that are constantly ready for combat and appropriately equipped with modern weapons and materiel. We must create a flexible system of material and technical support for the troops in overseas theaters. . . . Finally, we must have strategic striking forces sufficient for rapid operations at any time and in any area." * 4

The European troops at the disposal of the NATO High Command are maintained at a high level of combat readiness. Two army groups have been created in Western Europe: the Northern Group under British command, and the Central Group under American command. There is also a southwestern army group (Italian troops), a southeastern group (Greek and Turkish troops), and a northern group of troops in the Scandinavian peninsula. Each theater has its own command and staff for the armed forces of the theater, for its army groups, and for its armies. The troops have designated areas for deployment, ostensibly defensive but actually offensive, and definite missions. In Western Europe, the major forces are deployed 50–120 kilometers [30–72 miles] from the western borders of East Germany; in the Balkans, they are directly at the borders of the socialist states.

In spite of the prevalent Western theory that it is impossible to conduct mobilization and deployment under present conditions, the preparation of the reserves has been accelerated, plans are being developed to carry out general mobilization of all the NATO countries, and comprehensive measures are being taken to ensure such mobilization. The imperialists wish to have all their armed forces in readiness, able to wage a large war without preliminary mobilization and deployment.

The United States also has, in addition to its fifteen existing divisions, a ready reserve of twenty-seven National Guard divisions, and ten infantry and thirteen training divisions in the Army Reserve, a total of more than one million men. These divisions, however, are by no means up to wartime strength in personnel or military equipment.

At the end of May 1961, President Kennedy asked to have ten reserve divisions completely manned and equipped; this is now being

---

* C. Clarke, "The Why of Strac," *Army*, No. 5, December 1958.

4 U.S. ED. NOTE—General Clarke's actual words were: "We need deployed forces in being in critical areas of the world to provide the Soviets with convincing evidence of our determination, to bolster the morale of our allies and to fight in place, or be redeployed rapidly if necessary. . . .

"We need a mobilization base sufficient to maintain a general war posture even while participating in limited wars. This places particular emphasis on the requirement for reserve component forces in a high state of training and properly equipped. We need a flexible logistic support system with overseas stockage to permit support of forces deployed anywhere. . . .

"Finally we need a strategic strike force sufficient to enable *rapid reaction* by use of *measured force* where and when required. This force must be able to accomplish assigned tasks with or without the use of atomic weapons." General Bruce C. Clarke, Commanding General, Continental Army Command, "The Why of Strac," *Army*, December 1958, p. 59.

implemented. Previously a considerable amount of time was necessary to mobilize reserve divisions. Now this time has been greatly reduced. At present three weeks are needed to mobilize two National Guard divisions, up to five weeks for four divisions and up to eight weeks for ten divisions. Thus, the number of combat-ready divisions can be doubled within two months.

In addition, a special strategic army corps has been set up (two airborne divisions, three infantry divisions, and one armored division). It can be rapidly flown to any point on the globe where armed conflict has broken out. General Clarke writes that:

> The main units of the strategic army corps are prepared to leave their permanent quarters within several hours after an alert has been sounded.

General Sink, Commander of the 101st Airborne Division, which is part of this corps, states that the division will be ready to fulfill "any task within two hours after the alert." *

The Americans often practice airlifts over great distances. For example, the 24th Infantry Division was airlifted from West Germany to the Near East by a special air transport group of 150 heavy and medium transport planes.

The other NATO countries, especially West Germany, France, and Great Britain, are also preparing large reserves for mobilization and deployment of ground troops. The deployment of large NATO ground forces is based upon the mobilization preparations of West Germany.

The mobilization plans of the aggressive imperialist powers are kept highly secret. The imperialists, having studied the [successful surprise] operations of the aggressive states during World War II, can hardly intend to carry out general mobilization at the beginning of the war. It can be expected that the present aggressors will make every effort possible to carry out their major mobilization measures in stages, and secretly, before the beginning of war and according to the severity of the situation. The military leaders of the NATO countries have accelerated the development of techniques for secret, rapid, final mobilization of auxiliary forces and for their transfer to military theaters before the beginning of hostilities.

Immediately before the war, the final measures of troop mobilization and deployment in military theaters will be carried out. These measures will be conducted under various guises, mainly as training drills for reservists, rotation of troops, and exercises and maneuvers. They will in-

---

* C. Clarke, "The Why of Strac" and F. Sink, "The What of Strac," *Army,* No. 5, December 1958.

volve the following: reinforcement of troops in border zones, creation of troop formations, bringing troops and headquarters to readiness, preparation of nuclear weapons for surprise attack, activation of reconnaissance, issuing supplies to the troops, establishment of special commands in military theaters, evacuation of civilians and valuable property, etc. The American General, M. Johnson, has indicated that the final measures may include "the moving of headquarters underground, the relocation of families of military personnel to the rear, bringing troops to the highest level of combat preparedness, the deployment of troops according to operational plans, the preparation of mine fields in the indicated regions. . . ." * 5

In 1958, in connection with preparations for aggression against Syria, the Turkish Army cancelled all leaves and called a halt to transfers of personnel to the reserves.

The forces and weapons prepared for operations in European military theaters have the task of delivering surprise nuclear strikes on troop formations of the socialist countries, particularly missile-launching sites and airfields, control points, communications, and important rear targets up to a depth of 1,000 kilometers [600 miles] from the borders. Immediately after the so-called nuclear offensive, the ground troops are to shift to a decisive offensive and complete the defeat of socialist troops deployed in military theaters. Then they are to invade the USSR, in order to exploit fully the aftermath of the strategic nuclear strikes, and to achieve unconditional surrender. There are also provisions for defensive operations, in case the nuclear attack does not achieve the desired results.

In addition to preparing their strategic air force, missiles, navies, troops, and weapons for the military theaters, the members of the imperialist bloc are also carrying out large-scale measures to ward off air and missile strikes. Intensive improvements in the air defense of the imperialist countries, especially America, England, and West Germany, have been organized and are being continued. The defense forces

---

* M. Johnson, "NATO—Shield or Sieve?" *U.S. News and World Report,* September 1959 [*sic*], p. 60.

5 U.S. ED. NOTE—General Johnson's actual words were: "But it appears to this observer that there is no real reason why NATO should expect an extended period of warning. For a shorter period of alert—despite such actions as moving headquarters into underground establishments, shuttling dependents to the rear, putting air and ground forces on more complete alert, moving troops to the field and putting mine fields into planned positions—it seems unlikely that NATO's outnumbered, somewhat scattered ready divisions could defend Europe for any considerable length of time unless the attacking force were chewed up by an atomic defense." Major General Max S. Johnson, U.S. Army, Ret., "NATO: Shield or Sieve?" *U.S. News and World Report,* November 16, 1959, p. 60.

and systems of all the NATO countries have already been deployed and are maintained in full fighting readiness. The American air defense system is particularly highly developed. It was originally developed as a defense against aircraft. However, the situation has now changed inasmuch as the Soviet Union possesses strategic missiles, against which air defense is useless.

At present the United States is intensifying work on developing an antimissile defense. A long-range detection and warning system, together with a system to identify targets and determine missile flight co-ordinates, is being constructed. New methods are being sought to detect missiles, including some infrared techniques and also passive methods for tracking missiles from the moment of launching. The development of active methods for combating missiles has been accelerated.

All these facts are convincing evidence that the aggressive imperialist bloc headed by the United States is making every effort secretly to prepare large armed forces in advance [of war], deploy them in the necessary strategic and operational formations, provide them with nuclear weapons and material supplies, and prepare them to initiate a world war or local war against the socialist countries at any time favorable to the imperialists. Simultaneously they prepare, mobilize, and complete the deployment of the armed forces, so as to increase the number of troops [ready to fight] during the course of the war.

Departing from the practice of past wars, the present deployment of the armed forces of the imperialist aggressors distributes troops and weapons not only along state boundaries, but also throughout the entire territories of the imperialist states and over wide expanses of ocean. Moreover, the main weapons of the future war, i.e., nuclear weapons, strategic air forces, and missiles, are deployed at great distances (even in far-off continents) from the lines where the ground forces clash.

The nature of the imperialist military preparations and the deployment of their armed forces are convincing evidence that the forces of world aggression are now preparing a surprise attack on the socialist countries, using all the forces and weapons at their disposal. The imperialists are preparing an offensive war involving the massive annihilation of populations, especially peaceful ones—a war of all-out destruction that will completely destroy entire countries and peoples. The numerous military bases surrounding the socialist countries are clearly intended for surprise attack. The maintenance of large forces of tactical aircraft, tactical missile troops armed with nuclear weapons, and ground troops close to the boundaries of socialist countries (in full readiness and appropriate formation) proves that these forces and weapons are being prepared for offensive war and for invasions deep into socialist territory. This is the real meaning of the aggressive imperialist states' military preparations. Accordingly, given present conditions, one cannot count on any period during the war (especially at the beginning) during which general mobilization and the deployment of the armed forces in strategic and operational formations could be conducted. Weapons development, the world balance of political and military forces, and the war preparations of aggressive imperialist blocs, openly directed against the Soviet Union and other socialist countries, urgently require that the socialist countries have such combat-ready armed forces as could deliver an immediate and devastating retaliatory strike and then rapidly develop active operations not only to curb the imperialist aggressor, but to defeat him completely.

Thus, the methods of strategic deployment of the armed forces in present-day conditions differ considerably from those of previous wars, including World War II.

The methods the imperialists may use to initiate a new world war depend on many factors. The imperialist aggressors calculate that the socialist countries, against which aggression will primarily be directed, will not be expecting war. The task of our military strategy is to foresee the possible ways in which the imperialists might initiate war, to warn the population and armed forces of the impending threat in good time, and [thereby] to exclude [the possibility of] anything unforeseen. To do this, one must carefully study and analyze the policies of the aggressive imperialist states, their war preparations, their military concepts, and how their armed forces are trained and readied, particularly how they conduct exercises and maneuvers.

How local wars are initiated is particularly important to study, since, in the past, aggressive states often used various types of local conflicts to test the validity of their plans and the preparedness of their armed forces.

We now have sufficient information to reach the following conclusions: The aggressive imperialist states will attempt to initiate a future world or local war without formal declaration, by means of surprise attack. This was the way the imperialists of Great Britain, France, and Israel operated in Egypt in 1956.

During the numerous NATO maneuvers and exercises a situation is usually created in which international tension gradually increases, and a war threat develops. Only then are military operations brought into the open. For example, during the preparations for aggression against Egypt, the foreign political activity of the imperialist states increased considerably.

However, exactly the reverse may occur. The imperialists may reduce tension in order to conceal preparations for a surprise attack as much as possible. For example, not long before the events in Egypt, British and French ruling circles agreed to renew negotiations with Egypt. These were scheduled for October 29, 1956; on the night of October 30, Israeli troops treacherously attacked Egypt. On October 31, the Anglo-French air force began to bomb Egyptian cities.

The Pentagon is preparing a surprise nuclear attack against the USSR and the other socialist countries.

Many authors in the capitalist West write openly about surprise nuclear attack. No attempt is made to hide the fact that the strikes will be delivered at places where the opponent's human and material resources are located.

The various ways in which nuclear war may be initiated are gamed in numerous exercises and maneuvers. During the first three days of war, continuous nuclear strikes are to be delivered over all of the opponent's territory, which presupposes the socialist countries. The first strike is to be delivered at night. Participating in this attack will be all the combat-ready strategic and tactical aircraft, all the strategic missiles, carrier-based assault planes, and missile-carrying nuclear submarines. Thousands of bombers, fighters, and reconnaissance planes can be sent aloft, and several hundred missiles with nuclear warheads may be launched. Strikes may be delivered on all the large cities, industrial centers, known missile-launching sites, airfields, naval bases, control points, troop formations, communications, etc.

In recent NATO exercises, the time for carrying out the first massive nuclear strikes has been reduced. Ground force formations are to move in immediately after the nuclear strike. The imperialists believe that such massive nuclear strikes will make it possible to overwhelm the enemy completely at the beginning of the war, and that the ground troops will only have to carry out the occupation. A number of authors in the American military press have expressed the opinion that the likelihood of subsequent military operations after such strikes depends to a considerable extent upon the effectiveness of the strikes.

The Western press also discusses whether the main targets of the first nuclear strikes should be nuclear complexes (missile launching sites, airfields, stockpiles of nuclear weapons, etc.), or political centers and economic targets. Some authors consider it necessary to deliver the most powerful strikes on large cities, industrial regions, and other military and economic targets where the peaceful population is concentrated. They argue thus because these targets do not require special prior reconnaissance as their location is known, and because a surprise nuclear strike against these targets could not but shake the morale of the entire population tremendously.

At the same time, some Western military theorists believe, and not without reason, that this way of initiating war is practically infeasible under present-day conditions. Liddell-Hart, for example, has stated that it is considerably more difficult now than in 1941 to deliver a surprise and completely crushing blow, since one cannot exclude an equally powerful retaliatory blow. In particular, he stated:

> The dream of complete neutralization of the enemy at the very beginning of the war has become even more preposterous since the creation of ballistic missiles which can be launched from any place on land, sea, or in the air.*

The ruling circles of the imperialist states, especially of the United States, recognize that, in conditions where the Soviet Union has superiority in strategic missiles, a surprise nuclear strike would be even more dangerous, since it would not obviate a crushing retaliatory missile-nuclear strike from the Soviet Union. Consequently the imperialists conduct an intensive search for other ways to initiate a new world war. To an increasing extent the imperialists count on inciting the West German revanchists and the Japanese militarists to [deal] the first blow, kindle the flame of a new war, and involve the socialist countries. Then, at a favorable moment, the United States will enter the war, in order to dictate not only to the opponent but also to its allies.

West Germany, whose state policy is revanchist, is assigned the principal role in unleashing a new war. For this reason, American, British, and French imperialists have permitted West Germany to create the strongest army in NATO and plan to provide it with nuclear weapons, thus encouraging to the utmost the revanchist aspirations of West German militarism.

History has demonstrated that the West German revanchists, encouraged by world imperialist forces, are ready for any adventures. At the end of 1944 [sic], the former commander of the German occupation forces in France, Otto von Stülpnagel, wrote in the newspaper, *Combat:*

> No defeat is final. A defeat is only a lesson that must be mastered while preparing for the next, more powerful strike. . . . Our defeat in this war should be considered only an unfortunate incident in the victorious advance of Germany toward conquest of the world. . . .[6]

---

* B. H. Liddell-Hart, *Deterrent or Defense: A Fresh Look at the West's Military Position,* London, 1960, p. 53.

[6] U.S. ED. NOTE—It has not been possible to verify this statement.

The present-day successors to Hitler in West Germany try to interpret the lessons of history in their own fashion, and again they are preparing a miltary attack against East Germany, Czechoslovakia, Poland, and the USSR.

It is not impossible that West Germany, either independently or with other NATO members, might initiate a local war in Europe by a surprise attack against East Germany. At the beginning of such a war nuclear weapons might not even be used. In this case, military operations might begin, for example, with massive blows by tactical aircraft and missile troops using conventional munitions against all of East Germany or another nearby socialist country, and with the invasion of large tank formations.

The imperialists might attempt to initiate a new world war using local conflicts in other parts of the world as well. Finally, a new world war might be brought about by their policy of preserving colonial rule and suppressing national liberation movements in colonies and dependent countries.

Under modern conditions, any local military conflict, if not nipped in the bud, can grow into a world war with unlimited use of nuclear weapons.

This is actually what the American imperialists are counting on. They are afraid to take the initiative in unleashing a nuclear war, since this would be disadvantageous from a political standpoint and extremely dangerous from the military standpoint. The whole point of their plans in this regard is to use nuclear weapons in the course of expanding local conflicts, particularly at critical moments, in order to alter the situation sharply in their favor. They expect to be able to limit the employment of nuclear weapons to the territory of their satellites and to defend their own territory, at least at the beginning of the war, from a crushing nuclear blow. This is the essence of their aggressive plans to initiate a new world war, using local wars and conflicts.

One cannot say that the ruling circles in the imperialist states dependent upon the United States do not understand the nature of these American imperialist plans. Blinded by their hatred of Communism and socialism, however, they could begin a new war at the dictation of American militarists without even considering that a future war would threaten the existence of their own countries. In 1958 a book by I. Branik, published in West Germany and entitled *German Trumps,* was warmly endorsed by Defense Minister Strauss. This book literally states the following:

> If a thermonuclear war begins, Germany, no matter what happens around her and no matter what the consequences, should do her duty.

She should fight again. . . . But would this war make any sense? Would not the death of mankind in radioactive mist negate all victories and everything in general? This we cannot know beforehand. Not only in a nuclear war, but in any war, the stakes are life or death.[7]

This kind of "resoluteness," exemplified by the West German revanchists, has spread to other participants in the aggressive blocs. The governments of Iran and Pakistan even agreed to the advance establishment by the Americans and British of zones of devastation in these countries. These zones included cities like Tabriz, Hamadan, Pahlevi, Kazvin, Shahrud, and Kuchan in Iran, and a number of cities in Pakistan.

Thus the American imperialists plan gradually to draw the whole world into a new world war by means of local wars. They would prefer to leave the initiative of firing the first shot to one of their more militant and aggressive satellites, especially the West German revanchists.

Does this mean that the American imperialists have given up their plans to initiate a new world war by a surprise nuclear attack on the USSR and other socialist countries, with the unlimited employment of all the forces and weapons at their disposal? No, it does not. It must be realized that their preparation for such a blow has gone too far, that too great financial and material resources have been expended [to permit a reversal of policy]. Moreover, it must be remembered that adventurism and recklessness have always been characteristic of imperialism. Blinded by their hatred of Communism, the imperialists may commit any crimes.

It should be taken into account that weapons developments have opened up greater opportunities for dealing surprise blows. Hitler required considerable time to concentrate and deploy large ground and air forces near our western borders, in order to deal a surprise blow to the Soviet Union. This deployment could not go unnoticed. Now, major imperialist forces and weapons which could be used for a surprise nuclear blow are already deployed and dispersed over vast areas and maintained at a high level of combat-readiness.

Therefore, in view of the level of capitalist morality, one must not underestimate the tremendous threat to peace posed by the new weapons of destruction in the hands of the imperialists.

Only the fear of a powerful retaliatory strike will stop the imperialists. Therefore the Soviet Union and all the socialist countries are compelled to have in readiness the necessary forces and weapons for instantaneous retaliation to aggression.

---

[7] U.S. ED. NOTE—It has not been possible to verify this quotation.

## U.S. ED. NOTE A: RECENT SOVIET CLAIMS ON THE PROTECTION OF MISSILE SITES

[In the same speech in which he mentioned the dispersal and camouflage of Soviet missile sites, Khrushchev also claimed: "We are locating our missiles in such a way as to ensure duplication and triplication."[8] This particular claim was not repeated in subsequent statements, but mention continued to be made of the dispersal and camouflage of Soviet missile installations. In his rebuttal of Secretary McNamara's Ann Arbor speech, Marshal Sokolovskii wrote: "It is a secret to no one that the territory of the Soviet Union allows us to locate and shelter our missiles, so as to make them invulnerable to enemy reconnaissance and to strategic means of attack."[9] For the word here rendered as "shelter," Marshal Sokolovskii employed the term *ukryt*. In Russian this can mean either to "shelter by concealment," or to "shelter by protection," or both. Since Sokolovskii talks about sheltering missiles from reconnaissance and from attack, one cannot be certain whether he is talking about camouflage or hardening or both. However, it is interesting that an article by Major General N. Talenskii, published a month later, made no reference to camouflage or concealment but emphasized hardening and mobility, and mentioned decoy sites for the first time. In arguing that a "considerable number" of Soviet missiles would escape destruction in an American first strike, Talenskii wrote:

> A large part, if not all the most important ones will be reliably protected and, consequently, to destroy them it will be necessary to have absolute accuracy, to hit a precise point located literally thousands of kilometers from the launch and aiming point. A part of the retaliatory means are mobile and it will be difficult to hit them at a particular place. Lastly, a substantial part of the attacking force will inevitably be diverted to striking decoy targets.[10]

## Methods for Conducting Modern Warfare

The appearance of powerful new weapons for armed combat, such as nuclear weapons and long-range strategic delivery vehicles, the unprecedented development of conventional weapons and military equipment, and changes in the political conditions in which a new war would break out—all these things indicate that modern war will be conducted by methods which differ basically from those of past wars. Consequently, any attempts to transfer the methods of warfare developed in

---

[8] *Pravda*, January 15, 1960.

[9] Marshal K. D. Sokolovskii, "A Suicidal Strategy," *Red Star*, July 19, 1962.

[10] Major General N. Talenskii, "Preventive War—Nuclear Suicide," *Mezdunarodnaia zhizn' (International Affairs)*, No. 9, 1962, p. 18.

World War II to modern conditions without change are very dangerous, inasmuch as they may impair the combat-readiness of the armed forces, and of the country as a whole, to repel aggression.

Every country has adherents of the old and battle-proven methods of combat. Moreover, there is an unfortunate tradition that the general staffs of many countries prepare to wage war with the methods of the previous one. The French military leaders have been particularly guilty of this. Many military specialists, on the theoretical as well as the practical side, are inclined to be conservative, as Engels pointed out. Although our socialist country does not even have a climate suitable for nourishing conservativism among its military leaders, nevertheless, it cannot be denied that we have among us people so burdened with past experience and so enamoured of it that they are unable to see what is new.

Our Party's Central Committee has defined the direction to be taken in the development not only of weapons but also of methods of waging war and of the military art. The XXth, XXIst, and XXIInd Congresses of the Communist Party of the Soviet Union and several of N. S. Khrushchev's speeches have disclosed the essentially political nature of modern warfare, have defined its character, and have pointed out how it should be waged. These directives are of basic importance in solving all problems connected with the protection of our Socialist Fatherland.

In determining how modern war is to be waged, we must first clarify the main aims of the armed forces' operations in war.

As we have already noted, the main objectives [of attacks] in earlier wars were ground force formations and air forces deployed in ground theaters along front lines or borders, and naval formations.

In modern war the opponent will also concentrate his ground troops and air forces along borders and front lines in ground theaters [and he will also concentrate] new weapons—missile troops—in ground theaters, and carrier attack forces and submarines striking forces in naval theaters, although not as closely deployed as in World War II. Before the political and military strategic aims of the war can be completely attained, therefore, these formations must be fought and defeated.

However, these forces will not be the sole or even the main object of military operations in a nuclear war. The decisive weapon in modern warfare is the strategic nuclear weapon. The long-range delivery vehicles for this weapon are located far from the front lines or the borders, at a great distance from the theaters of military operations. Unless these weapons are destroyed or neutralized, it is impossible to protect the country's vital centers from destruction, and one cannot count on successfully achieving the aim of the war even if the [enemy] troop formations deployed in the military theaters are destroyed. Since the Soviet Armed Forces have at their disposal powerful long-range weapons, i.e., strategic nuclear-armed missiles, it is possible to act directly against the opponent's strategic nuclear weapons, his economic base, and his system of governmental and military control. Any state, especially one with a small, densely populated area, can be eliminated from the war and even annihilated in a very short time without the invasion of its territory by ground troops.

Consequently, the main targets of military operations will be deep within enemy territory and behind the front lines. The focal points of the war will be deep within the belligerent countries, although fierce, large-scale combat will also be waged in military theaters near the front lines and borders.

The military and political aims of a world war can be achieved by annihilation of the enemy's strategic weapons, by destruction of his economic base and armed forces in military theaters (ground and naval forces), and by the seizure of his territory.

A local war might be another matter. Here, as formerly, the main events might develop in military theaters near the front, although even then the methods of armed combat would have changed considerably from those of the last war, since this war would be conducted with different weapons and the threat of a nuclear blow would constantly hang over the belligerents.

In determining how to wage modern war, it is not enough to clarify the main objective of armed combat. It is also essential to establish what kinds of military operation or what forms of strategic operation must be employed to attain the aims of the war, and what specific form these operations should take.

The types of strategic (or military) operations, the particular form they take in the course of the war, and the way in which they are combined and concerted constitute, in fact, the methods by which the war is waged. It can be said without exaggeration that working out modern methods of effective warfare depends primarily upon the correct selection of the types of strategic operations.

As we have noted, all the fighting in the last war could be reduced to two basic forms of strategic operation—strategic offense and strategic defense—in which ground forces played the main role. The other branches of the armed forces—the air force, navy, and in part the PVO—performed supporting functions. The main targets of armed combat were formations in military theaters. Rudimentary types of new strategic operations had already appeared in the last war: strategic air strikes deep within the enemy rear, aimed at cities and at the economy, and defense against such strikes. These operations had already passed beyond the limits of strategic offense and defense in military theaters. However, they had no decisive influence on the outcome of the war. Strategic offense and defense remained the basic types of strategic operations until the end of the war and thus established the basis for the conduct of the war. This can be explained in terms of the level of weapons development at that time.

Has the situation now changed? Can we assume that modern warfare will also be reduced to two types of strategic operation, strategic offense and defense in military theaters?

Some authors believe that the [old] situation remains essentially unchanged and that strategic offense and defense, as before, should be considered the basic types of strategic operations.* Strategic offense, they say, includes military operations on land, air, and sea, involving all branches of the armed forces. The aim of such an offensive is to penetrate enemy defenses, to open extensive breaches in his lines, and sometimes even to "chew up" his defenses and deliver strikes deep within his territory. The main role in strategic offense is ordinarily assigned to frontal offensive operations executed by ground troops. Operations by all other branches of the armed forces, including Strategic Missile Forces, the Navy, and even the National PVO, are carried out only to support the Ground Forces. The consequent practical recommendations [of this school of thought] are that the Strategic Missile Forces should deliver nuclear strikes deep within enemy territory in places where the Ground Forces are planning to operate, and should conduct so-called joint missile operations so as to pave the way for the front [army groups], as it were, with powerful nuclear strikes.

This concept of how to wage modern war is incorrect. It is the result of overvaluing the experience of the last war and mechanically applying it to modern conditions.

Tremendous advances have been achieved in weapons development since World War II. Nuclear and thermonuclear weapons with tremendous destructive power have appeared and strategic missiles with unlimited range have become the primary vehicles for the delivery of nuclear warheads to a target. A new branch has developed in our Armed Forces—the Strategic Missile Forces—and to it are assigned the primary missions of modern warfare, should an aggressor dare to disturb the peaceful construction of Communism in our country. The scope of warfare has expanded to include the entire territories of the states in

---

* Candidate of Military Science, Major General M. V. Smirnov, Colonel I. S. Baz', Colonel S. N. Kozlov, Colonel P. A. Sidorov, *O sovetskoi voennoi nauke* [*On Soviet Military Science*], Voenizdat, Moscow, 1960, pp. 245, 246, 282.

the opposing coalitions, and not simply military theaters as in the past.

The targets of modern warfare will be the enemy's strategic nuclear weapons, economy, system of governmental and military control, and, obviously, troops and naval forces in military theaters. Moreover, primary targets will be located beyond military theaters and deep within enemy territory. Powerful strategic means—the Strategic Missile Forces and to a certain extent the Long Range Air Force—have the mission of destroying enemy strategic weapons, disorganizing his country, and destroying major troop formations in ground theaters. This will be done by strikes with nuclear-armed missiles, in accordance with the plans of the Supreme High Command to attain victory over the enemy, [win] the armed conflict, and rapidly defeat the enemy states as a whole. The Strategic Missile Forces need not plan their attacks in relation to the activity of the Ground Forces. The Missile Forces are not a means of support for the Ground Forces; the Ground Forces have their own nuclear weapons (operational and tactical missile forces, and front-line aircraft) to secure their rapid advance.

The Ground Forces, in conjunction with front-line aircraft and naval forces in coastal regions, will exploit the blows of the Strategic Missile and Long Range Air Force against targets and enemy troop formations in military theaters, will complete the destruction of surviving enemy formations, will occupy enemy territory, and will defend their own territory.

Ground Forces activity on a strategic scale will be required to carry out these missions, but the nature of such operations has changed essentially since the last war. Today the Strategic Missile Forces, which are the main weapon of modern war, will not accommodate their operations to those of the Ground Forces, but vice versa. The Ground Forces should exploit missile strikes fully in order to execute their own missions rapidly.

One must also remember that the potential enemy will direct his strategic nuclear weapons primarily against large cities, the most important economic regions and targets, regions where missiles are based, the Long Range Air Force, naval forces, strategic reserves all over the socialist countries, and troop formations in military theaters.

The National PVO must support not only the Ground Forces, but the entire country against which the enemy's main nuclear strikes will be directed.

The Navy's operations, also, must not be tied to ground theaters, since naval forces are now primarily called upon to do battle on the oceans, often at a great distance from ground theaters.

In ground theaters, combat will be dominated by the offensive. But it will be carried on by the Ground Forces, together with their front-line air force, without direct support by other branches of the Armed Forces. Naturally, the Ground Forces will exploit the results of strategic missile and Long Range Air Force strikes against the major enemy formations. In this case the main mission of the Ground Forces will not be to break through the enemy defenses, but rather to "chew them up." The penetration of defense is no longer the central problem it was in past wars, especially in their initial periods. The defeat of surviving enemy troop formations in ground theaters during an offensive will be achieved primarily by destroying the enemy's nuclear weapons and his divisions with missile-nuclear strikes, and by vigorous tank operations and paratroop landings deep in the rear.

Strategic defense is sometimes understood to mean defensive operations by Ground Forces along an entire strategic front or in the most important strategic areas. Its aim is considered to be to defeat an enemy attack. In addition, even the Strategic Missile Forces are often declared to be a defensive instrument, while the National PVO is given the task of protecting the defending troops. In other words, defensive operations are [sometimes] expanded to include the main branches of the armed forces.

The adoption of the strategic defensive as a basic form of strategic operation in modern warfare means the adoption of a defensive strategy as a whole: in essence, the translation of the situation at the beginning of the Great Patriotic War into present-day conditions.

The imperialists are preparing an offensive war against our country, a war of total destruction and mass annihilation of the population with nuclear weapons. Consequently, they must be countered by the determined and active operations of our Armed Forces, and primarily by devastating strategic nuclear strikes. This is the only way to curb the imperialist aggressors, foil their criminal plans, and rapidly defeat them. Under present conditions, strategic defense and subsequent counteroffensive cannot guarantee that the aims of the war will be completely accomplished.

This does not mean that defensive operations, as a temporary necessity, will have no place in a future war. Our troops must study and master defense so as to master all forms of military operations. But here we are speaking of defense on an operational and tactical scale. As far as strategic defense and defensive strategy are concerned, they must unquestionably be discarded as extremely dangerous for the country.[11]

Consequently strategic operations in modern conditions must be ap-

---

[11] U.S. ED. NOTE—According to a Soviet military writer, "missile-nuclear blows have forced strategic defense to disappear from the arena of war." Lieutenant General N. Sbytov, "The Revolution in Military Affairs and Its Results," *Red Star,* February 15, 1963.

proached from a different direction, and new methods of warfare must accordingly be sought which will guarantee the rapid and decisive defeat of the aggressor.

The development of long-range weapons, and particularly the appearance of the Strategic Missile Forces, has created a fundamentally new type of strategic operation: missile strikes on targets throughout the whole of enemy territory. If the imperialists initiate war, strategic nuclear weapons will be directed against such enemy targets as the military-economic base, system of governmental and military control, and troop formations. This type of strategic operation is no longer limited to the confines of the former strategic offensive or defensive in which the Ground Forces played the leading role. Now the Strategic Missile Forces, and to a certain extent the Long Range Air Force, employing nuclear weapons will play the principal role, obviously, if we are forced to it.[12] However, it is difficult to classify the blows by Missile Forces as either offensive or defensive. The operations of the Missile Forces will always be of a decisive, rather than defensive, nature, no matter whether the troops are engaged in offense or defense on the ground front.

Missile strikes on targets throughout the whole of enemy territory, especially on his nuclear weapons, will create favorable conditions for the operation of other branches of the Armed Forces. At the same time, the Strategic Missile Forces and Long Range Air Force will strike strategic targets in military theaters as well, simultaneously destroying enemy troop formations, including reserves, bases for operational and tactical nuclear weapons, communications, the system of military command, etc.

Other types of strategic operation in modern warfare are military operations in ground theaters to complete the defeat of enemy troop formations, capture and occupy enemy territory, and prevent an invasion of the socialist countries. As formerly, this type of strategic operation will be very important in achieving the military and political aims of modern war.

The socialist countries have ground forces equipped with nuclear weapons, tanks, tactical air forces, and other new military equipment and armament. These troops have the necessary combat capability for decisive combat in ground theaters against a strong enemy. Their main mission is to exploit the results of nuclear blows by missile forces and air forces, to achieve the final defeat of enemy formations in military theaters, rapidly to occupy the territories of the countries in an enemy coalition, and to achieve a victorious end to the war on the continent.

The protection of our country from enemy nuclear strikes is an ex-

---

[12] U.S. ED. NOTE—The text could mean either that the opponent will force the Soviet Union to use missiles and air forces with nuclear weapons, or, more generally, force them to make war.

tremely important strategic operation, to be executed by the air defense and antimissile defense. Unless these operations are effectively executed, the successful conduct of modern warfare will be impossible, and the normal vital functioning of the country cannot be guaranteed. These operations are directed at repelling enemy air and missile blows, destroying his aircraft and missiles in flight, and preventing them from reaching the most important administrative and political centers, economic regions and targets, missile forces, air forces, naval forces, reserve mobilization areas, and other targets.

The territory of the country can only be successfully defended from enemy nuclear strikes by active National PVO operations. These operations go beyond the strategic defense of World War II, inasmuch as they are conducted all over the country and are directed against an air enemy, whereas strategic defense was [formerly] carried out in theaters of military operations as defined by the offensive fronts of the enemy.

Finally, military operations in naval theaters directed at the destruction of enemy naval formations, disruption of his maritime communications, and the protection of our own maritime communications and coasts from nuclear strikes from the sea are an independent type of strategic operation. This type of military operation will undoubtedly acquire much larger scope than in the Great Patriotic War. The equipping of the Soviet Navy with nuclear weapons, missile-carrying nuclear submarines, and long-range, missile-carrying aircraft provides considerable opportunity for successful combat over wide expanses of oceans and seas against a powerful enemy navy.

Thus, strategic military theory recognizes the following forms of strategic operations in a future war: nuclear strikes by missiles to destroy the enemy's military and economic potential, system of governmental and military control, strategic nuclear weapons, and major troop formations; military operations in ground theaters to complete the defeat of enemy forces; protection of the socialist countries and troop formations from enemy nuclear strikes; and military operations in naval theaters to destroy enemy naval forces.

Each of these forms of strategic operation will find application in a nuclear world war. In local wars some of these types of strategic operations may not find a place, or may be employed only on a limited scale. This [limitation] could apply, first of all, to military operations against targets in the far rear. In such wars military operations in ground and naval theaters may acquire decisive importance.

During a world war, the role of one or another type of strategic operation cannot remain unchanging. Depending on various conditions, each form of operation may become critical or secondary in importance.

The form of the strategic operation may vary. During the course of the war each type of strategic operation acquires a specific form and method of combat, depending on the aims, available weapons, space, and time. Operations are understood to mean organized combat by operational formations of various branches of the Armed Forces, executed according to a unified concept or plan to accomplish certain operational and strategic missions.

The first type of strategic operation is used in missile-nuclear strikes, and also in the operations of the Long Range Air Force. Military operations in ground theaters will be conducted as in previous wars, by Ground Force offensives and defensives. The National PVO (antiaircraft and antimissile) is to protect the country from enemy nuclear strikes. The Navy will conduct armed combat in naval theaters on the seas.

In tactics this takes the concrete form of combat by units and formations of the various branches of the Armed Forces and types of troops in order to accomplish specific tactical objectives.

World War I gave rise to the "operation" as a specific form of armed combat. Even before the beginning of the Great Patriotic War, Soviet military science had a well-developed theory of "operations," which played an important role in the successful conduct of the war. Numerous operations of different types took place on all scales and with various results during the Great Patriotic War. However, the main types of operation in the last war were offensives and defensives conducted by operational units of the Ground Forces in conjunction with or supported by units and formations of other branches of the Armed Forces. There was also a limited number of relatively independent air and naval operations in the last war.

The postwar period saw the rapid development of Long Range Air Forces, strategic missiles, antiaircraft missiles, and submarines. A new branch of the Armed Forces appeared—Strategic Missile Forces—and the importance of the National PVO increased considerably. The nature and methods of modern warfare changed. New types of strategic operations developed, causing changes in the theory and practice of operational art.

Each operation is conducted by particular forces, makes use of certain materiel, and takes place in a specific area and in a particular time. The operation is carefully planned and equipped to execute its task and carry out the intended action.

Military theory has made use of many decades of experience in developing an organized concept of operations as an independent entity. An operation is carried out by one operational formation or by groups of operational formations, such as armies (combined arms, tank, air armies of the PVO) or fronts, PVO districts, or fleets.

No form of strategic operation or operation by any branch of the Armed Forces is executed in isolation or independently. No operations by units or branches of the Armed Forces are independent in the strict sense of the word. A future war can only be conducted successfully if all strategic operations are strictly co-ordinated by a unified centralized command and single strategic plan, and are purposefully directed toward the execution of the general aims of the armed combat.

Let us make a more detailed examination of these types of strategic operation and of the basic combat operations of each branch of the Armed Forces, remembering, however, that there can be no independent military operations in a modern war.

*Nuclear strikes by strategic missiles* will be of decisive, primary importance to the outcome of a modern war. Massive nuclear blows on the enemy's strategic nuclear weapons, economy, and system of governmental control, and the concurrent defeat of his armed forces in military theaters will permit the attainment of the political aims of war much more rapidly than in previous wars.

In case of war, our Armed Forces will be obliged to employ this form of strategic operation. The aggressive imperialist bloc is preparing a war which will involve general destruction of cities, industrial regions and targets [in these regions], and communication networks, and mass annihilation by nuclear blows of the civilian population throughout the entire territory of the socialist countries. The major aim will be to destroy the economy and weapons of war, to disrupt the system of governmental control, and to demoralize the population, thus undermining its will and capacity to resist.

By using highly destructive weapons—nuclear weapons and other weapons of mass destruction—the imperialists will attempt to destroy the social system of the socialist countries even to the point of the complete annihilation of entire states of the socialist commonwealth. And they are not concealing their plans. For example, H. Kissinger wrote in his book, *Nuclear Weapons and Foreign Policy:*

> The notion that wars are won by destroying the enemy's industrial plant and undermining civilian morale has been as cardinal a tenet in British as in American strategic thought.*

For a long time the United States has had a special section in the Department of Defense to plan the targeting of the strategic nuclear weapons of attack. This section notes all important targets in the so-

---

* H. Kissinger, *Iadernoe oruzhie i vneshniaia politika* [*Nuclear Weapons and Foreign Policy*], Izdatel'stvo Inostrannoi Literatury, Moscow, 1959, p. 373 [English edition p. 275].

cialist countries intended for annihilation by nuclear strikes. The United States and other imperialist countries attempt to use strategic reconnaissance to provide continuous observation of these targets and to discover new ones. All the known targets have already been assigned to the crews of strategic, carrier, and tactical aircraft, and to the crews of missile bases and missile-carrying submarines. Missile launching pads and aircraft on the ground and in flight with nuclear bombs have been put on constant alert, and a system of signals, alerts, etc., has been developed.

That is why the Soviet Armed Forces and those of the other socialist states must prepare to deal massive strategic retaliatory strikes against the imperialist bloc's military and economic base, system of governmental and military control, and armed forces. Our strategy considers this the primary form of strategic operation, and assigns it the decisive role in accomplishing the aims of a future war which might be initiated by the imperialist aggressors.

Such blows can devastate the major regions of enemy states, where the economic war base of the imperialist coalition is located; where their strategic nuclear weapons (i.e., the strategic air forces, intercontinental and medium-range missiles), tactical bombers, and naval forces are based; and where the main stocks of nuclear munitions, war materiel, assembly areas for units and formations, major troop concentrations of the armed forces, strategic reserves, and principal centers of governmental and military control are located.

The basic aim of this form of military operation is to undermine the military capacity of the imperialist coalition by destroying its nuclear weapons, and to destroy its military and economic potential by destroying the economic war base and the governmental and military system of control. Strategic Missile Forces equipped with intercontinental and intermediate-range missiles carrying powerful thermonuclear and atomic warheads, and also the Long Range Air Force armed with missiles carrying nuclear warheads—hydrogen and atom bombs—are the main weapons to attain these goals.

These aims can be accomplished by nuclear strikes delivered by missiles and aircraft to selected targets. The most powerful strike may be the first, massive, missile-nuclear strike with which our Armed Forces retaliate against the operations of the imperialist aggressors who initiate a nuclear war.

Nuclear strikes by missile and aircraft can subject to destruction military bases (air, missile, and naval); industrial targets, primarily nuclear, aircraft, missile, power, and machine-building industry; communication networks, ports, control points, etc.

A primary target of the strikes will be strategic air bases. The bases of strategic air forces are quite vulnerable since the airfields occupy large areas and all of them are really quite well known.

Depriving strategic air forces of airfields is tantamount to making them incapable of combat.

Missile bases and launching pads are now also quite vulnerable. If in 1943 and the beginning of 1944 Great Britain succeeded in putting most of the German V-1 launching sites out of commission with aircraft using conventional bombs, the destruction of missile-launching sites by using missiles with nuclear warheads is now not such a difficult task.

Much has been said in the foreign press about nuclear submarines armed with Polaris missiles. The assertion has been made that these are the most invulnerable means for the use of missiles. Actually, these weapons are also vulnerable. Homing missiles launched by submarines and surface ships are an effective weapon against missile-carrying nuclear submarines.

Missile-carrying aircraft can also fight nuclear submarines by taking advantage of certain of their weak features, particularly the lengthy preparations required to launch missiles. In addition, strikes by the Missile Forces can destroy submarine bases.

Naturally, the task of annihilating the enemy's nuclear weapons must be realiably executed. It is particularly important to have a reliable reconnaissance beforehand of air bases, missile-launching sites, nuclear weapon stockpiles and supply bases, and locations of fuel stores and control points.

The destruction of the enemy's military-economic potential is one of the most important missions. The key to the execution of this mission is the need for a large number of nuclear weapons to attain decisive results in destroying the enemy economy. In addition, it is necessary to remember that the first massive nuclear missile strikes may not immediately influence the course of the war.

Inasmuch as the imperialists are preparing devastating nuclear strikes against the economic base of the socialist countries, the latter are compelled to answer in kind.

The military and economic base of the imperialist bloc is very sensitive to nuclear-missile strikes. Imperialism's main economic base for war is located in the United States. It is here that the basic production capacity of the imperialist camp is concentrated (i.e, the manufacture of nuclear weapons, missiles, aircraft, tanks, ships, armament, and other weapons) and the materiel base for military operations. The second economic war base of imperialism is located in West Germany, which has significant industrial capacity. Great Britain, and France to a certain extent, also has considerable industrial capacity. The major human resources of the imperialist bloc are concentrated in the European countries. The main petroleum base for the imperialist camp is in the Near and Middle East and in South America.

The imperialist economy has a number of vulnerable regions, a circumstance that should be taken into account in preparing retaliatory operations if the imperialists unleash nuclear war.

The vulnerable features of the imperialist bloc's economy include high industrial concentration in small areas, dependence upon imports, and the vulnerability of communications. The United States depends upon imports of atomic raw materials and of nonferrous and rare metals, and Great Britain depends upon the import of iron ore, petroleum, atomic raw materials, foodstuffs, nonferrous and rare metals, etc.

The economy of the socialist countries is in a more favorable position. It is more dispersed and does not have the density of industrial concentration characteristic of many imperialist countries. It is also less dependent upon imports.

Thus the unlimited nuclear war of total destruction and annihilation being prepared by the imperialists will undoubtedly be turned against them. To do this, it is essential to have the means for retaliation in constant readiness: Strategic Missile Forces, the Long Range Air Force, and nuclear weapons—and it is necessary to master effective techniques for delivering rapid and devastating nuclear blows to the enemy, if the socialist countries are compelled to do so.

*Military operations in ground theaters* will be of broad scope in a future world war, in spite of the use of long-range nuclear weapons. The final defeat of enemy troops, the capture of his territory, and the establishment of the appropriate order and the peaceful regulation of all postwar questions can only be achieved as a result of ground troop operations.

The imperialist bloc is preparing vast ground forces, tactical air forces, and tactical missiles to achieve its aggressive aims in military theaters. These forces can be deployed in offensive formations along the boundaries of the socialist countries to a depth of 1,000 kilometers [600 miles]; consequently they must be destroyed in case of war.

The main aim of the military operations in ground theaters is the decisive defeat of enemy formations, the capture of vitally important regions and targets, the occupation of enemy territory, and also the prevention of an invasion of the socialist countries by ground troops.

In a future world war, the basic weapons in ground theaters will be nuclear weapons, used primarily with operational and tactical missiles and front-line air forces (bombers, fighter bombers, and fighters). In addition, Strategic Missile Forces and the Long Range Air Force will deal nuclear blows to important targets in the zone of the advancing fronts. Airborne operations will be extensively used. As formerly, tank units and formations will be extensively employed on the battlefield. Motorized infantry also has not lost its combat value, although it will no longer be the Queen of Battle. Nuclear fire power will have the decisive role on the battlefield. The other weapons will exploit the results of nuclear strikes to defeat the enemy conclusively.

The primary targets of armed combat in military theaters will be enemy nuclear weapons. Unless these nuclear weapons are destroyed or neutralized, one cannot expect, nowadays, to conduct any military operations successfully, offensive or defensive, in military theaters. At the same time, the destruction of the enemy's tank, airborne, and motorized divisions also remains an important task.

A characteristic feature of military operations in future ground theaters will be the absence of linear deployment in continuous fronts. Military operations will develop simultaneously over large areas along the front, and in depth. To a certain extent, they will be characterized by isolated engagements.

Another important feature of armed combat in military theaters will be the great mobility of the military operations and the extensive use of vehicles, helicopters, and aircraft for troop maneuvers. Maneuver of fire and nuclear blows will also be of fundamental importance.

Finally, armed combat in the military theaters will be extremely violent and will involve mass destruction of troops, tremendous damage, and the formation of large zones with a high level of radioactive contamination.

The belligerents in the ground theaters will attempt to achieve their aims primarily by offensives. If even in the last war defense did not prove equal to offense, in a future war the offensive will be even stronger than the defensive. However, defense as a means of combat to oppose offense will not disappear from the scene, although the boundaries between offense and defense will not be as distinct as in previous wars.

*Offensive operations* will be the principal means of accomplishing the aims of combat in ground theaters. They will be conducted by armies with combined arms and by tank armies. Operational and tactical missile troops and front-line air forces equipped with nuclear munitions will be assigned the major role in executing combat missions. Tanks, motorized infantry, and airborne troops will also be used.

During the Great Patriotic War, the offensive as a rule was conducted against a prepared, positional type of defense whose strongest zone was the tactical [forward] zone, manned by infantry and infantry weapons, antitank guns, artillery, and mortars. The initial task was to penetrate the defensive front for which purpose large masses of troops—artillery, tank, and infantry—were concentrated on narrow sectors. Massed air strikes were also delivered. Into the breach thus created were introduced mobile formations consisting primarily of tank troops.

In a future world war, particularly at the start, the belligerents will attempt to achieve their aims in ground theaters primarily by offensives. Considering modern nuclear weapons and the great mobility of tanks, motorized infantry, and airborne troops, it is possible to foresee that offensive operations will be complexes of isolated battles and encounters that will often have the character of meeting engagements. It is also possible that even future offensives will be checked by the defenses. [Successful] defense will be based on firepower: atomic artillery, missiles, tactical aircraft using nuclear weapons, antitank weapons (guided antitank missiles), and antiaircraft missiles. Infantry and tank divisions will deploy the bulk of their forces to the rear, and will maintain only a covering force in the forward positions. The zone of defense may extend to a depth of 100 kilometers [60 miles]. Under such conditions, penetration of the defensive front will not be the complex problem that it was in the last war, but developing the offensive in depth will be very complicated where the attacking forces are subject to powerful counterstrikes from enemy forces and nuclear blows. The primary mission of the attacking troops will be the destruction of atomic artillery, missiles, and tactical aircraft throughout their zone of deployment. The areas where these are located are within the range of operational and tactical missiles and front-line aircraft, and they can be rapidly destroyed by nuclear strikes if they have been accurately detected beforehand. Airborne troops will land immediately after the nuclear strikes, and tank formations will begin a swift offensive, their task being to penetrate rapidly into the regions subjected to attack by the Strategic Missile Forces, in order to accomplish the final aims of the operations. Enemy infantry and tank divisions will be neutralized and destroyed by nuclear blows and by the rapid operations of tank and motorized troops. But it must be mentioned that the assault on the defense must be prepared even more carefully than in the last war, because of the greater difficulty in destroying the chief weapons of defense, i.e., nuclear weapons dispersed over large areas of the defense zone.

The question of the organization of troops for offense, the direction of the blows, the width of the zone of attack, the depth of the operation, and the tempo of the offensive will be solved differently [than in the past].

Assault formations will be assembled in the rear, at a considerable distance from the front lines (state borders). The main elements of the operational force composition will be formations of missile troops, and armies of tanks and combined arms. The tank armies will operate in the first echelon, in the principal areas. Their basic purpose is rapid and uninterrupted penetration to great depth, all the way to the final objective of the operation. Armies of combined arms also will develop offensives to complete the defeat of enemy troop formations.

Offensives will be purposefully executed in several directions in order to split opposing enemy formations and annihilate them piecemeal. The main forces of the attacking troops, however, should be concentrated in principal and decisive areas. The zone of maximum effort will now be determined by the areas where the main nuclear strikes have been delivered, and also by the directions of advance of the main forces.

The zones of attack of units and formations are being expanded. For example, the American leaders consider an infantry division capable of attacking along a 10–20 kilometer [6–12 mile] sector, and most effectively along a 12 kilometer sector; they consider a field army capable of attacking along a 100–160 kilometer [60–96 mile] sector. The offensives will be conducted in various directions with wide gaps between them. Enemy formations will be destroyed by nuclear strikes delivered by Missile Forces and air forces. The battlefields will be relatively empty. Troops will be widely dispersed and will have opportunities for extensive maneuever.

The offensive operations of a future war will be executed very rapidly. In their exercises and maneuvers, the NATO troops have developed an offensive at the rate of 60–70 kilometers [36–42 miles] per day. Our tank and motorized units must achieve higher rates of advance. In order to do this, it will be necessary to carry out a continuous battle with the enemy's nuclear weapons and deliver nuclear strikes on his centers of resistance (until the attacking troops reach the enemy) and on his counterattacking formations. The advancing troops must be continually supported by aircraft, technical and chemical weapons, etc.

The offensive should be carried out primarily by tanks, armored troop carriers, and helicopters. Attack on foot will seldom be employed. Fire and maneuver by mobile forces will now predominate on the battlefield. It will be essential to search for breaches and gaps in the enemy's combat formations, to deliver strikes on his flanks and rear, and to divide, surround, and rapidly destroy or capture [his formations].

When it is impossible to bypass enemy centers of resistance, they will be subjected to nuclear strikes or perhaps to concentrated rocket and artillery fire, or tank fire from defiladed positions.

Tactical and operational paratroop landings will be extensively employed during operations. Paratroop landings may be assigned the task of making rapid use of the effect of massive nuclear strikes, capturing regions where nuclear weapons are based, important targets, river crossings, build-up areas, mountain passes, and defiles, and destroying strategic targets that cannot be put out of commission by other means. Helicopters may be used primarily for carrying out tactical paratroop landings. As far as operational landings are concerned, transport aircraft can be employed. In order to make large paratroop landings in great depth, it is necessary to neutralize the enemy PVO weapons by electronic countermeasures and by air and missile strikes.

A very complex problem of modern warfare is the traversal of highly radioactive zones. The potential enemy is preparing to create such barriers by surface nuclear explosions in areas where troops are on the offensive. Radioactive contamination from one's own nuclear strikes is also inevitable. The troops should bypass highly radioactive zones. If it is not possible to bypass these zones, they must be crossed in tanks and closed vehicles with the necessary shielding, or by helicopter and airplane. It is possible that particular regions can only be crossed by troops after the level of radiation has declined, and then with the observance of antinuclear and antichemical protective measures.

The troops will inevitably suffer losses from enemy nuclear strikes during an operation. It is possible that entire subdivisions, units, and even formations will be put out of commission. However, this should not affect the speed at which operations develop.

The high combat potential of our Armed Forces, their weapons and military equipment, especially missiles and tanks, and the mobility of tank and motorized infantry units are all a reliable basis for the successful execution of offensives with decisive aims in a future war.

*Defensive operations* are also possible in a future war. One must not assume that the war will consist entirely of offensive operations. During certain periods and in particular areas, and possibly theaters, the situation may demand a temporary shift to defense. Consequently, our Armed Forces should completely master the methods of executing these operations. The refusal of Soviet military strategy to acknowledge strategic defense and defensive war in general must not extend to operational or tactical defense. Such defense obviously is still important. It will inevitably appear, during the course of the war, as a means for disrupting the offensives of superior enemy forces. Current operational defense still has a number of strong points, such as the possibility of making more effective use of fire, favorable terrain, artificial obstacles, etc. In addition, it should be noted that the organization of defense and the methods of its conduct are undergoing considerable changes.

In modern warfare, defense in ground theaters may be used to gain time, to economize forces, to consolidate successes, and in a number of cases even to repel an attack by superior enemy forces. Nevertheless this type of military operation is forced on one. It is to be resorted to only when the situation cannot be changed in our favor by an offensive.

During the Great Patriotic War, defense was organized along a continuous front and included a number of positions and zones running parallel to the front lines. The main forces of the defending troops were deployed within a tactical [forward] zone. In the main sectors there were established a high troop density, artillery, and antitank weapons, as well as antitank and anti-infantry obstacles. Trenches and communication trenches were the basic fortification features of the positions and zones. In a future war such a defense will not be reliable; it will not be able to withstand attack. The attacking troops can easily create huge gaps in such a defense by nuclear strikes.

Defense under present-day conditions is based on the use of missile and nuclear weapons, and the maneuver of ground force formations. There is no need for continuous defense positions and zones, with dense deployment of troops and equipment. The troops will hold separate positions which are the most important (key) regions and positions in the principal zones, and will be dispersed both along the front and, particularly, in depth. The gaps between such regions will be covered by missile troop fire, air operations, and obstacles. The major formations of the defending troops will be located to the rear of the defense [area] and not near the front lines as formerly.

Defense should be primarily antinuclear, i.e., should provide maximum protection of personnel and equipment from destruction by nuclear strikes. It is essential, therefore, in the areas where troops and equipment are located, to provide shelters (foxholes, trenches, and more resistant structures) equipped for antinuclear defense.

Defense should be provided against both missiles and aircraft. To do this, the defending troop formations, the firing positions of the missile troops, airfields, control points, and rear targets should be reliably protected by antiaircraft and antimissile defense weapons.

Finally, a most important requirement of defense under modern conditions is its ability to withstand massive tank attacks, i.e., there should be an antitank defense. For this it is essential to use antitank weapons, especially guided antitank missiles for destroying enemy tanks. The great effectiveness of the new antitank weapons provides a considerable number of opportunities to frustrate enemy tank attacks.

The successful conduct of defensive operations can be assured by

decisive operations to undermine or greatly weaken the enemy's prepared offensives as much as possible. Nuclear strikes are necessary for
this, as well as air strikes with conventional ammunition to destroy the
enemy while he is deploying his forces and occupying his initial positions. At the moment the enemy is ready for attack, it is highly expedient
to strike his main forces and weapons with massive missile-nuclear and
air blows, to strike his airfields for tactical aircraft, his missile-launching
sites, the firing positions of his atomic artillery, his tank and infantry
divisions, and his control points. Modern weapons of destruction permit
decisive results to be attained by means of counterpreparations, up to
and including the complete break-up of the prepared offensive.

An attack by enemy troops can be repelled by destroying them with
the firing weapons of the defending troops, and also by decisive counterattacks against units and formations. Enemy airborne units and also
formations that are driving wedges into the defenses should be destroyed
by weapon strikes, counterattacks, and counterblows by troops located
in the rear. From this point of view, the methods of waging defensive
battle approach those of the offense.

The American press often states that it is inexpedient to conduct a
determined defense of areas and defense lines. Instead, delaying operations and mobile defense are proposed.

The Soviet military art takes the view that defense under current conditions should be based on a combination of determined defense of the
most important regions and [defense] lines, together with operations
by mobile troops. During the defensive engagements it is essential to
prevent the enemy forces from invading the socialist countries, to defeat
the enemy, and to prepare the conditions for carrying military operations deep into enemy territory.

During the course of the war, the situation in individual sectors may
be that forces can be saved from destruction only at the cost of relin-
quishing territory they have conquered, i.e., by temporary *withdrawal*.
Troops may be forced to withdraw because of an unsuccessful defensive
engagement or because of an unsupported offensive carried out by individual formations. Withdrawal will sometimes be deliberate, so that
the troops can gain a more advantageous position for subsequent operations.

Withdrawal has always been neglected in all armies. History teaches
that armed forces that have not mastered the organized withdrawal cannot be considered ready for war, since such troops are very often defeated. In the past the Russian Army suffered most of its losses precisely during withdrawals. V. I. Lenin thought that

he who has learned to attack, and not to retreat under certain difficult conditions, thus adapting to them . . . will lose the war. Wars begun and concluded by a continuing victorious offensive either have never occurred or have been exceptions.*

In all cases, withdrawal should only be carried out under the orders of the senior command, in an orderly fashion and without panic. The crucial point in withdrawal is to leave the battle and to disengage the main forces from the enemy suddenly and under cover of a strong rear guard. In some cases this will require a counterattack along a broad front, and possibly even the delivery of nuclear strikes.

Withdrawal can either be carried out while offering organized resistance on successive lines or by unopposed retrograde movement to the final line [of resistance]. During the course of the withdrawal it is essential to take measures for the rapid defeat of air-dropped enemy troop formations and of groups of enemy troops that break through [on a line] parallel to [that of] the retreating troops, and also to destroy his nuclear weapons.

*Protection of the country's rear areas and formations of armed forces from nuclear strikes by the enemy* has, as its aims, to preserve the vital activity of the state, to secure the uninterrupted functioning of the economy and transportation, and to safeguard the combat potential of the Armed Forces. These aims will be achieved primarily by destroying the enemy's nuclear weapons where they are based. However, there is no guarantee that significant aircraft and missile forces can be destroyed at their bases, especially at the outset of a war, if the enemy attacks by surprise. Therefore the necessary forces and weapons must be available to destroy large numbers of enemy aircraft and missiles in flight in order to prevent nuclear strikes against the country's most important targets. This can be done by conducting military operations to defend the country from enemy air and missile attack.

Reliable protection must be provided to the major administrative and political centers, the most important industrial targets and regions, strategic materiel reserves, highway and communication centers, governmental and military control points, strategic missile-launching sites, airfields for long-range and transport aircraft, naval bases, mobilization and training centers for reserves, troops, etc. The protection of these targets from enemy nuclear strikes also has another highly important aim: the prevention of massive losses among the civilian population.

The National PVO, as well as the civil defense forces, is basic in

---

* V. I. Lenin, *Sochineniia* [*Works*], Vol. 33, p. 74.

protecting the interior of the country and the formations of its armed forces from enemy nuclear strikes. They have the task of creating an insurmountable defense system for the entire country, except for the frontal zone, as well as taking measures for the rapid elimination of the results of enemy nuclear strikes. Such a system should be prepared in advance, even in peacetime, and should be kept at a high level of combat-readiness. Antiaircraft and antimissile defense of the frontal zones will be carried out by Troop PVO in conjunction with the National PVO.

The country's antiaircraft system was set up to intercept in good time and to destroy enemy aircraft, air-breathing missiles, and air-to-surface missiles in flight. This system consists of the following: electronic equipment to detect aerial targets and guide air defense weapons to them; antiaircraft missiles and fighters to intercept and destroy aerial targets on the approaches to state borders or on the distant approaches to protected regions and targets; antiaircraft missiles and fighter interceptors to destroy aerial targets that have penetrated the direct approaches to protected regions and targets.

The PVO should be concentrated in the principal areas so as to cover the most important regions and targets. Uniform coverage of the entire country cannot guarantee reliable defense against nuclear strikes; it will only lead to the scattering of the PVO forces and equipment, which would facilitate enemy penetration of our PVO system.

It is essential to keep in mind that the enemy will use the most diverse methods for delivering air strikes to the socialist countries: converging attack from many directions; breaking through the PVO on a narrow or wide sector in several directions; aircraft flights at extremely high and low altitudes; active and passive radar countermeasures; and decoy operations. Only an active and flexible antiaircraft defense will be effective against all these forms of enemy air operations. Modern antiaircraft weapons—antiaircraft missiles, fighters, and electronic equipment—will ensure the complete frustration of enemy air and air-breathing missile strikes and the destruction of the main body of aircraft and air-breathing missiles on the approaches to the protected regions and targets. Successful defense depends upon skillful use of all these forces and weapons, and upon their combat potential.

World War II demonstrated that combat against aircraft and air-breathing missiles could only be carried out successfully by the combined use of all antiaircraft forces and weapons. In Great Britain, for example, the defense against the German V-1 missile included a radar and visual detection system, an outer defense line where fighters operated, a second line of defense covered by antiaircraft artillery, and a third line using barrage balloons. Antiaircraft defense has made great strides since then. Modern antiaircraft missiles, fighter interceptors, and new types of radar have become powerful weapons against aircraft and air-breathing missiles.

The destruction of ballistic missiles in flight is a more complex problem. During World War II, Great Britain was unsuccessful in attempting to destroy German V-2 ballistic missiles. Efforts to create an antimissile missile (project "TAMPER") proved unsuccessful since the technology of that time did not permit the solution of that complex task. In our country, Soviet science and technology have successfully solved the problem of destroying missiles in flight. Thus, there is a realistic possibility of creating an insurmountable antimissile defense.

The country's antimissile defense system should obviously be capable of early detection of missiles by radar (ground and airborne) or by other automatic instruments (on earth satellites), which will ensure the detection of missiles during their initial trajectories (at the moment of launching or during the power phase of flight); determination of missile trajectories; timely warning; and guidance of defense weapons. It should possess antimissile batteries and electronic-countermeasure weapons, which will deflect missiles from their intended targets, or possibly detonate warheads in flight.

It is interesting to note that the problem of antimissile defense in the West is still far from a final solution. The United States has developed the Nike-Zeus and Wizard systems, which use nuclear warheads that require a direct hit on the missile by the antimissile missile. The foreign press has mentioned the possibility of throwing up a screen of fine metal fragments in the flight path of ballistic missiles, by detonating conventional warheads carried by antimissile missiles. The use of a stream of high-speed neutrons to detonate the nuclear warheads of missiles is under consideration, and also the use of electromagnetic energy to destroy the missile warhead in the descent phase of the trajectory or to deflect the missile from its target.

The interior of the country and formations of the Armed Forces will be protected from enemy nuclear strikes by the antiaircraft (antimissile) operations of the National PVO. The first air defense operations at the start of the war, to break up the surprise enemy air strikes completely, will be particularly important for the successful conduct of war.

The most common ways of conducting air defense operations may be the following: electronic detection of the attacking enemy aircraft and missiles; active and passive interference with aerial targets; distant fighter interception of aircraft and air-breathing missiles on the approaches to frontiers; destruction of aircraft before they are close enough to launch missiles; destruction of enemy aircraft and missiles by long-range antiaircraft missiles in co-operation with fighters, on the approaches to the most important regions and targets; concentration of fighter interceptors to intercept and destroy the main body of aircraft and missiles in the flight approaches to the strike targets; complete destruction of penetrating aircraft and missiles at all altitudes by antiaircraft missiles, fighters, and antimissile missiles on the approaches to protected targets; pursuit and complete destruction of departing enemy planes by fighter aircraft.

The successful execution of air defense operations will depend upon the activity and the maneuvering of all antiaircraft and antimissile defense weapons, and their rapid concentration in the principal areas against the main enemy formations of attacking aircraft and missiles.

However, it should be remembered that no matter how effective an antiaircraft and antimissile defense system may be, it is essential to have prepared civil defense forces to eliminate rapidly the aftermath of nuclear attack, evacuate people from regions subjected to nuclear attack, organize emergency medical aid, extinguish fires, re-establish order, and carry out other urgent measures. Special civil defense groups should be prepared to carry out these tasks. Moreover, the entire population should be prepared to act in the conditions created by an enemy nuclear attack.

*Military operations in naval theaters* in a future war will take place on a large scale, although these operations will hardly be decisive for the outcome of the war.

During the Great Patriotic War, our Navy was primarily confined to limited military operations in closed seas—the Baltic and Black Seas. The operations in northern and far eastern seas also were of limited scope. Naval operations were basically intended to support the Ground Forces in coastal operations and to protect maritime communications, especially in the north.

A future world war may confront the fleet with more responsible tasks. The world's oceans may prove to be military theaters.

The main aim of the fleet operations in naval theaters is to defeat the enemy navy and to sever his maritime communications. In addition, the need may arise for missions to deliver missile-nuclear strikes on coastal targets, joint operations with units of the ground forces, naval transport, and protection of one's own naval communications. The specific form of naval combat operations will consist in operations on the high seas. Nuclear submarines and naval aircraft armed with missiles will permit decisive naval operations against powerful enemy navies.

One of the most important tasks of our navy, from the first minutes of the war, will be to destroy enemy carrier attack forces. The enemy will attempt to deploy these units in the most imporant theaters near socialist countries in order to deliver surprise nuclear strikes on the most important coastal targets (naval bases, airfields, and missile sites), and possibly on targets much further inland. For example, in the NATO "Autumn—60" exercise, a carrier-based striking unit deployed in the Norwegian Sea hypothetically delivered two hundred nuclear strikes on targets on our coasts and deep within our territory. Moreover, most of these nuclear strikes were made within twenty-one hours. This type of strike presents a serious danger if the navy is not able to break it up and destroy the attack carrier forces. This task can only be executed by a navy with a high level of combat-readiness, deployed in advance, and capable of making skillful use of the weak points of the enemy's attack carrier forces.

Attack carrier formations, whose mission is to deliver strikes, are meant to be deployed in limited areas, accompanied by large concentrations of surface ships. Attack carriers located in the center of these forces represent major and very vulnerable targets for nuclear strikes with missiles or torpedoes. The attack carriers are protected by anti-submarine surface ships and aircraft. Radar picket forces will be located on the perimeter of the area. The radar picket forces need only be penetrated or neutralized to make the carriers and other units of the force defenseless against missile strikes from submarines and naval aircraft. It is essential to attempt to destroy the attack carriers before they reach aircraft launch positions, to destroy their screening forces, replenishment groups, and the carrier bases. It should be noted that these formations are quite vulnerable during passage, when refueling, and when maneuvering to launch and recover aircraft.

Missile-carrying nuclear submarines are an effective weapon for combating aircraft carriers and other surface vessels. Earlier models of submarines destroyed enemy vessels primarily by direct torpedo hits below the waterline at close quarters and barely submerged. Consequently the destruction of these submarines was easily accomplished. Nuclear submarines armed with guided missiles have become a formidable weapon against surface ships. These submarines have considerable capacity for independent action, travel rapidly under water, and can deliver missile strikes at great distances even while submerged. Thus the nuclear submarine, which is highly mobile and less vulnerable, can successfully combat attack aircraft carriers and other surface vessels.

Attack carrier units can also be successfully combated by long-range naval aircraft. These planes have air-to-ship missiles with nuclear warheads and can deliver strikes without coming within the firing range of a carrier force's antiaircraft defense.

Coastal missile installations can also be used to destroy enemy naval forces.

The socialist countries can be protected from nuclear strikes delivered from the sea by the concentration and effective use of all these forces and weapons against the main attack carrier forces of the enemy in the principal theaters.

Combat against enemy submarines, especially missile-carrying nuclear submarines, is an important naval task.

The aggressive plans of the Anglo-American bloc attach considerable importance to the use of nuclear submarines for delivering missile strikes to targets deep within the socialist countries. At the beginning of the war, missile-carrying submarines can be deployed in launching positions up to 1,800 kilometers [1,100 miles] from the coast, especially in the Arctic Ocean, the northern seas, the northeastern Atlantic, and the western Pacific. The other submarines are intended to combat our naval forces and disrupt communications.

Submarines will become the main striking force at sea, not only in our Navy but also in the navies of the Anglo-American bloc. The nuclear submarine is a formidable underwater vessel. Consequently, armed combat in naval theaters may take the form of underwater operations.

Submarines can be successfully combated by hunter-killer submarines armed with missiles and torpedoes, and by airplanes, missile-armed antisubmarine hydrofoil surface vessels, destroyers, high-speed patrol boats, and helicopters. Successful combat requires a reliable system of reconnaissance, which will ensure advance detection of enemy submarines, particularly those carrying missiles, the exact determination of the co-ordinates of their location, and the guidance of active weapons against them. All the antisubmarine forces must be highly co-ordinated. This will make it possible to frustrate enemy submarine missile strikes and to protect the naval forces and communications from submarine attack.

Also included among the main naval tasks of war are the disruption of enemy ocean and sea shipping, and the disorganization of his communications. It should be noted that up to three-fourths of the potential enemy's entire material and human resources are on the other side of the ocean. According to the calculations of some military theorists, in the event of war, 80 to a 100 large transports would arrive daily in European ports, and 1,500 to 2,000 ships would concurrently be en route, not to mention escort vessels. The enemy will take the most varied measures to safeguard his communication lines: he will create "giant convoys" requiring fewer protecting forces, and will make extensive use of "patrolled zones" where transports can proceed without escort. He will use high-speed liners individually (without escort), cargo ships, minesweepers, underwater transports, etc.

Operations against enemy communications should be conducted on a large scale from the very outset of the war. This can be accomplished by the delivery of strikes by the Strategic Missile Forces and nuclear submarines against naval bases, ports, canals, narrow straits, and ship-building and ship repairing yards, and also by the destruction of convoys and transports at sea by submarines and aircraft. The flexible use of nuclear submarines, which can provide a maximum concentration of forces against enemy communications within a short period, will be most important in the destruction of the enemy's maritime communications. Diesel-electric submarines will obviously still be used against lines of communication. They will be used, as in the last war, to form moving barriers and to undertake co-ordinated operations or free search.

Although joint operations with the Ground Forces will not be a primary naval task, considerable forces will still be required for this. In conjunction with the Ground Forces, the navy can annihilate enemy naval landing forces at loading points, at sea, and upon their debarkation. The fleet itself will be assigned the mission of executing naval landing operations on enemy shores and of controlling straits and major water obstacles in the path of the Ground Forces. The navy will combat the enemy's naval forces, especially his aircraft and missiles, and thus protect Ground Force formations against strikes from the sea. It is possible that the naval forces may be involved in delivering strikes on enemy troop formations and nuclear weapons near the coast. Missile-carrying submarines, aircraft, and coastal launching installations can successfully execute this mission.

Mine warfare, as formerly, will find extensive use in modern warfare. Mines will be used to defend coasts, blockade enemy bases, ports, and straits, disrupt naval communications, and for other purposes.

In modern warfare the combat conditions of our naval operations will differ radically from those of the Great Patriotic War. Our fleets will cross wide expanses of ocean and will be opposed by a strong and experienced naval opponent. The American and British commands assign great importance to combat with our naval forces, especially our submarines. Consequently, strikes are to be delivered on naval bases and large antisubmarine forces are being created. The American naval forces have prepared seven antisubmarine groups equipped with large antisubmarine aircraft carriers. Four of these are intended for operations in the Pacific Ocean and three for the Atlantic. All this must be taken into account in preparing to repel possible aggression.

These are the basic forms of strategic operation applicable to modern world war, and their specific means of employment in strategic operational art and tactics.

The victorious conduct of modern warfare is possible only with the co-ordinated use of all forms of strategic operation, and with the purposeful conduct of operations and combat by a carefully centralized, unambiguous, and flexible leadership of the Armed Forces. In order to defeat a strong and treacherous opponent like the aggressive bloc of imperialist states, highly active and decisive military operations are vital. Only by such operations can the enemy be completely defeated.

## Problems of Using Outer Space for Military Purposes

The conduct of war on the ground, in the air, and on the sea with modern weapons, for which the aggressive imperialist forces are feverishly preparing, was reviewed above. However, the imperialists do not stop here. They are also planning to use the most important scientific achievements in the conquest of space for their aggressive military aims, and they have allocated huge financial resources to this purpose. As far back as 1958, a special agency, the Advanced Research Projects Agency (ARPA), was created in the United States Department of Defense. It directs projects aimed at mastering space for military purposes. Somewhat later the National Aeronautics and Space Agency (NASA) was created. It is also concerned with the use of space for military purposes. A network of ground stations is being built to track all artificial earth satellites.

These questions have been extensively and openly discussed in the American press, where it has been plainly stated that "outer space is the strategic theater of tomorrow." There are discussions of specific methods for using outer space and space devices for military purposes, and much attention is devoted to the plans of the American government and military establishment in this area. Moreover, some American military theorists do not even conceal their masters' plans to master space in order to regain lost military superiority over the USSR.

American militaristic circles see their way to world supremacy through the mastery of outer space. President Kennedy has stated in this connection: "Control of space will be decided in the next decade and the nation which controls space can control the earth." *

The United States is currently conducting large-scale scientific studies for the conquest of space, and is launching a large number of earth satellites and other space vehicles with supposedly scientific purposes. But all these "scientific studies" and launchings of space vehicles are

_____

* *Missiles and Rockets,* October 24, 1960 [p. 13].

really only a screen to cover up far-reaching military plans that are not, incidentally, concealed by the American press.

The United States uses its space vehicles primarily for reconnaissance and espionage, and has already established reconnaissance by earth satellites on a practical basis. In 1960, the American magazine *Missiles and Rockets* published a program for the creation of several types of artificial satellites for military purposes, including Discoverer, Mercury, Midas, Samos, and Tiros.

The Midas project provides for the creation of a reconnaissance satellite for infra-red detection of ballistic missile launchings. The United States Air Force intends to launch several of these satellites into polar orbits for continuous monitoring of Soviet missile launchings. Project Samos provides for the launching of reconnaissance satellites with powerful television and aerial photographic equipment to photograph and transmit to earth pictures of various targets. This espionage satellite has been called U-3, after the U-2 reconnaissance plane. Project Tiros provides for the launching of meteorological reconnaissance satellites.

In 1960, eleven reconnaissance satellites were launched, of which only six went into orbit. The United States has succeeded in recovering instrument capsules from reconnaissance satellites. Although this program of space reconnaissance has often been interrupted, the size of the financial investment in it has continued to increase.

Reconnaissance satellites are intended to determine and verify the co-ordinates of military industrial targets, launching sites for intercontinental missiles, military bases, airfields, and other targets in the socialist countries, and to map the earth's surface and to plot weather.

Moreover, since reconnaissance satellites moving in definite orbits can be destroyed, maneuverable manned space vehicles with various reconnaissance devices are planned. Such a vehicle, to make a reconnaissance of important areas, should descend to an altitude of about 130 kilometers [78 miles].

Considerable attention has been devoted to navigational satellites. In 1960, TRANSIT-I B was launched to an altitude of 800 kilometers [480 miles] in an almost circular orbit. In the same year, the THOR-ABLE-STAD missile was launched with two TRANSIT-II A navigational satellites to facilitate aerial and naval navigation, especially of submarines, and to compile navigational charts, study the shape of the earth, etc.

Communication satellites are considered highly important. In 1958, the United States launched the SCORE satellite which can receive signals from the earth, record them on tape, and transmit them back to the earth, as well as relay telecasts. The ECHO satellite with its parabolic antenna is used for communication between the United States and France. There are also plans to launch satellites for electronic countermeasures.

Satellites for reconnaissance, navigation, communications, and electronic countermeasures only comprise a part and not the major part of the American program to exploit space for military purposes. The main part of this program is the creation of an aerospace plane, or other maneuverable space vehicle, to carry nuclear warheads. The American press has published information on the preparation of the following space systems: a bombardment satellite equipped with space-to-earth missiles; piloted space bombers (Dyna-Soar); piloted bombers (SR-79 821) for operations at great heights; and an orbital bombardment system (Boss) for the destruction of ground targets. These vehicles are to be launched into orbit when war threatens, in order to deliver nuclear blows on targets in socialist countries at a command from earth. Whereas reconnaissance, navigational, communication, and electronic-countermeasure satellites are discussed at great length and in much detail in the open American press, the work on space vehicles intended for delivery of nuclear strikes is kept highly secret.[13]

Finally, a considerable part of the American military space program is devoted to the creation of antisatellite weapons to destroy space vehicles. The American press reports that work is being carried out at the present time on satellites which will carry antimissile (antisatellite) missiles and jamming devices that will be launched into a polar orbit at an altitude of 500–700 kilometers [300–420 miles], and whose period of rotation around the earth will be 94–98 minutes. These satellites will be employed, at a command from the ground, to destroy satellites and other space vehicles as well as intercontinental ballistic missiles. Work on antimissile missiles and other types of antispace weapons is being accelerated.

All this shows that the American imperialists intend to make direct use of space to carry out their aggressive plans against the socialist countries.

The USSR has achieved impressive success in the mastery of space. The Soviet Union was the first to put a satellite into orbit around the earth; a Soviet spaceship circumnavigated the moon and photographed its far side; and Soviet space vehicles have penetrated into the infinite

---

[13] U.S. ED. NOTE—An updated discussion of the U.S. space program, including other alleged bombardment space systems, was published in 1963. See Major General B. Teplinsky, "Pentagon's Space Programme," *International Affairs,* No. 1, 1963, pp. 56–62.

depths of the universe. Major Gagarin, in the "Vostok I" spaceship, was the first in the world to fly around the earth. Then Major Titov, in the "Vostok II" spaceship, flew around the earth more than seventeen times. This is convincing proof of tremendous Soviet achievements in science, in technology, and in the whole economy. It also proves the great advantages of the world's most advanced social system, socialist society.

Our achievements in space research serve peace, scientific progress, and the benefit of all mankind on our planet. Soviet space flights are an expression of the unstinting efforts of the entire Soviet people to achieve lasting peace on earth.

However, the Soviet Union cannot disregard the fact that American imperialists subordinate space research to military purposes and that they plan to use space to accomplish their aggressive purpose—a surprise nuclear attack on the Soviet Union and the other socialist countries.

Consequently, Soviet military strategy acknowledges the need to study the use of space and space vehicles to reinforce the defense of the socialist countries. The need to ensure the security of our Motherland, the interests of the whole socialist commonwealth, and the desirability of preserving peace on earth demand this [Soviet military study of space]. It would be a mistake to allow the imperialist camp to gain any superiority in this area. The imperialists must be opposed with more effective weapons and methods of using space for defense. Only in this way can they be forced to refrain from the use of space for a destructive devastating war.[14]

A modern world war, if the imperialists succeed in initiating it, will be nuclear, and will be the most destructive war in the history of mankind. The methods of conducting such a war will differ basically from those of past wars, including World War II.

In the victorious conduct of such a war it will be of the utmost importance to have retaliatory military operations to destroy strategic nuclear attack weapons, destroy the military economic base, disrupt the system of governmental and military control, and defeat the troops of the aggressive bloc of imperialist states. These aims can be achieved by massive nuclear strikes of the Strategic Missile Troops and the Long Range Air Forces against the most important countries of the enemy coalition, against the regions and targets which form the basis for the enemy's military and economic power, and against his troop formations.

In spite of the use of strategic nuclear weapons, military operations

---

[14] U.S. ED. NOTE—See Note B, pp. 429–430.

in ground theaters, as formerly, will be important to the achievement of victory. In local wars, these military operations may play a decisive role in defeating the enemy.

The main purpose of military operations in ground theaters will be to defeat enemy troop formations deployed in the theater, the annihilation of operational and tactical nuclear weapons, the capture of vitally important enemy territory, and the prevention of an invasion of the socialist countries. These tasks will be carried out mainly by the Ground Forces in conjunction with tactical aircraft employing nuclear weapons. The Ground Forces should make the fullest possible use of the results of massive strategic nuclear strikes in order to achieve the final defeat of enemy troops in the most important theaters.

Military operations to protect the interior of the country and our Armed Forces from the aggressors' nuclear strikes will be extensive in a modern war. The aim of these operations will be to ensure the vital functioning of the socialist states and their economies, the combat potential of our Armed Forces, and the protection of the population. These aims can be achieved by the determined action of the country's antiaircraft and antimissile defense, whose purpose it is to frustrate enemy air and missile strikes, and by the complete annihilation of the attacking air forces and missiles beyond the limits of the defended regions and targets.

Military operations in naval theaters will also be very important for the successful conduct of war. The basic aim of these operations will be to defeat enemy naval forces, particularly attack carrier forces, to annihilate missile-carrying nuclear submarines, and to disrupt enemy naval communications. These tasks will be carried out by the Navy, the main role being assigned to underwater forces and missile-carrying naval aircraft equipped with nuclear weapons. In contrast to the practice of previous wars, our fleet will have to develop active military operations over wide expanses of oceans and seas, and against a strong naval enemy.

The successful conduct of modern war is possible by co-ordination of all military operations and strictly centralized control of all Socialist Armed Forces. All operations should be conducted according to a unified plan by the Supreme High Command. The aggressor can be decisively defeated by active military operations both at the front and deep within the country.

The search for the most effective methods for waging future warfare and the mastery of these methods, as well as the constant readiness of the Armed Forces of the socialist countries, will guarantee victory over the aggressor in a modern war.

## U.S. NOTE B: CURRENT INDICATIONS OF SOVIET MILITARY USE OF SPACE

[While the U.S. space program has been frequently discussed in Soviet literature, relatively little is published about possible Soviet interest in the military use of space. It is therefore interesting to note that in 1962 one of the Soviet authors of this book, who also prepared the book for the press, Colonel V. V. Larionov, published two important articles on this subject.

In his first article, Larionov cited the Soviet "global" missile as an example of superior Soviet missile technology and stated that "the precision of the calculations was demonstrated by the flights of the spaceships Vostok I and Vostok II." [15] He went on to assert explicitly that Soviet space technology was superior to that of the United States: "A level of scientific-technical progress which is higher than in the United States permits the Soviet Union confidently to retain its lead in the conquest of space for scientific aims."

In his second article, Larionov was more explicit concerning Soviet interest in the military use of space:

> The Soviet Union, which is resolutely opposed to the utilization of outer space for military purposes, cannot ignore all these preparations of the American imperialists and is forced to adopt corresponding measures in order to safeguard its security against an attack through outer space. It is no secret that the technical basis for the launching of earth satellites and spaceships is the ballistic missile and its guidance system. Such complex, perfected technical equipment, which is many times superior to [the products of] American technology, is in the possession of the Soviet Union. [16]

Larionov stated that the Soviet Union should study military operations in space and asserted that Soviet technological advances had increased the possibilities of solving the relevant technical problems. The article concluded with the statement:

> The Soviet reader must clearly realize that the unbridled speed of scientific-technical progress demands continuous attention to the study of the newest achievements in the field of military-technical equipment and military theory. Therefore, even though today one cannot yet speak of a complete conquest of outer space as a new and fully-mastered sphere of military operations, one must clearly see the prospects that are opening in the field of military-technical equipment

---

[15] Lieutenant Colonel V. Larionov, "Missiles and Strategy," *Red Star*, March 18, 1962.

[16] Larionov, "Outer Space and Strategy," *Red Star*, March 21, 1962.

and military strategy [in relation to] those aggressive plans hatched by the ruling circles of the leading imperialist states.

Another article, by Major General I. Baryshev, published in September 1962, discussed the Soviet "global" missile and American efforts to develop a space system to destroy it.[17] The author referred to Khrushchev's earlier claims that "our missiles can, so to speak, hit a fly in outer space," and pointed out that the Soviet manned space flights demonstrate "what sort of technology and what sort of people our Soviet state has, and that our people have everything necessary to cut short any aggression."

In a speech on February 22, 1963, Malinovskii indicated great Soviet interest in antisatellite or outer space defense. Speaking of Soviet air defense, he declared that it now comprised "not only anti-air but also antimissile defense forces," and that these forces were "assigned the extremely important role of combating an aggressor's modern means of nuclear attack and his attempts to reconnoiter our country from the air and from space." [18]

In another speech, the Chief of the Soviet Strategic Missile Forces, Marshal Biriuzov, hinted at a possible Soviet development of a bombardment satellite. He declared in a broadcast interview that "the successes in the development of Soviet arms and their high quality, reliability, and precision are witnessed also by the rockets used in the exploration of the cosmos. It has now become possible, at a command from the earth, to launch rockets from a satellite, and this at any desirable time, at any point in the satellite trajectory." [19]

It may be appropriate to note that in the past Soviet expressions of interest in new weapon systems that later passed over into claims of successful development and deployment have usually reflected genuine Soviet activity, although actual progress often has lagged behind claims.]

[17] Major General I. Baryshev, "What Is Anti-Space Defense?" *Red Star*, September 2, 1962.

[18] *Pravda*, February 23, 1963.

[19] Foreign Broadcast Information Service (FBIS), *USSR and Eastern Europe*, February 25, 1963, p. CC-24; *Los Angeles Times*, February 22, 1963.

# ★ 7

# Preparation of a Country To Repel Aggression

As shown by the preceding chapters on the nature and methods of waging modern war, victory in war is quite unthinkable without thorough and timely preparation of the country and the armed forces.

In preparing the country and the armed forces for war, each state draws upon its economy, science, technology, and the fruits of its civilization, and also takes into account the forces and capabilities of its potential enemy, about whom information is constantly kept up to date.

Systematic preparation of a country for war should assure the capability to repel an aggressor at any moment and to deal him a shattering nuclear retaliatory blow with the object of seizing the strategic initiative. It should also assure the attainment of victory in the shortest possible time; the capability, if need be, to wage war over a protracted period; the ability to "stand up" under massive nuclear assault by the enemy, with minimum losses; and the maintenance of a high level of morale and will-to-win among the population.

Preparation of a country for war is accomplished along three main lines, by preparing the armed forces, the national economy, and the population—taking into account at the same time the development of the means of warfare and changes in the international situation.

Under contemporary conditions, a country's war preparations are influenced by the following factors:

First, the availability of missiles and nuclear weapons of megaton yields, which reduce outlays on military preparations in peacetime since they permit the possibility of considerable cutbacks in production of all other types of armament without lowering the firepower of the armed forces.

Second, as a result of nuclear blows, the technical and material basis for waging a long war can be shattered at the very outset, particularly with respect to nuclear weapons production.

Third, one cannot disregard the psychological shock to the homeland population, which will suffer huge immediate losses in a very brief time span—something which has never happened in previous wars.

Therefore, under present-day conditions, each state strives to prepare itself for war in such a way as to achieve victory in the shortest possible time. In practice, this means that in making preparations for war, special attention is given to employment of the newest strategic weapons.

This, in turn, provides the prerequisites for successful waging of a protracted war, because a country which is prepared to strike powerful nuclear blows with the latest strategic weapons and has sufficient industrial resources and domestic sources of raw materials at its disposal can always produce simpler, conventional types of weapons during an extended conflict.

After these general remarks, let us consider the separate aspects of preparing a country for war.

## Preparation of the Armed Forces

The peacetime preparation of the armed forces takes on decisive significance under contemporary conditions. The character of their preparation, which is conditioned by the political and economic situation, by scientific, technical, and industrial progress, and by new methods and means of warfare, has changed greatly even in comparison with the recent past—the period of World War II and the Great Patriotic War.

Preparation of the armed forces today involves determining their composition and organization for peacetime and for waging war, providing for their mobilization, and ensuring their attainment of a high level of combat readiness. It also involves the continuous development of various branches of the armed forces in accordance with their roles and missions, making certain that they are materially and technically equipped to conduct military operations, preparing the country and the theaters of military operations, and organizing and carrying out strategic intelligence activities.

*Mobilization and Combat Preparation of the Armed Forces.* The various governments determine what the peacetime strength and composition of their armed forces should be. In view of the threat of surprise attack by an enemy using modern means of mass destruction and the attendant difficulties this poses for the completion of mobilization, it would seem advisable to have peacetime forces set up on such a basis as to achieve the main objectives of the initial period of a war without additional mobilization.

However, to maintain armed forces on such a basis is not within the economic capability of any, even the strongest, state. Therefore, in peacetime in even the most powerful states, sufficient forces are maintained capable of dealing a nuclear blow in good time, repelling a surprise air attack, and actively conducting land and naval operations, while speedily augmenting the power of the first blows by bringing into action additional mobilized units. At the present time, it is considered that existing peacetime forces must be capable, from the very first hours of the war, of seizing the strategic initiative and ensuring the attainment of the most immediate strategic objectives.

One provides for a peacetime military establishment of such a size by maintaining in a state of constant readiness strategic forces and weapons of the amount and composition required for attainment of war aims, a nation-wide air defense system, and a certain portion of the other branches of the armed forces: ground troops, naval forces, air forces, and civil defense rescue and rehabilitation troops.[1] The strength of these numerically larger branches of the armed forces is, as a rule, increased at the outbreak of war by mobilization. Moreover, some of the ground force units and formations designated to conduct initial operations and stationed in the border districts (and some of the submarines in the naval forces) are maintained in peacetime at a strength adequate to permit the execution of the main tasks of the initial period of the war. Another portion of these forces has a short mobilization period, enabling them to participate in the initial operations; and finally, a certain portion is kept at reduced strength in peacetime.

In contrast to the covering forces of previous wars, the combat-ready part of the ground forces must in modern conditions be numerically much stronger to be capable of executing its assignments.

Consequently, peacetime forces under present-day conditions differ considerably with regard to function and composition from those on hand prior to previous world wars. Now they not only play the role of a "shield" covering the deployment of the country's main forces, but in essence they themselves form a part of the main forces which are augmented at the outset of war.

---

[1] U.S. ED. NOTE—Civil Defense Troops are to be distinguished from the regular civilian civil defense units organized throughout the USSR. However, in a war, the latter may be militarized and included in the Civil Defense Troops.

Determination of the wartime make-up of the armed forces is a very important task of the political and military leadership, since all the mobilization measures carried out in the country depend on it.

As commonly understood, mobilization or mobilization-deployment of the armed forces means their conversion from a peacetime to a wartime footing in accordance with a war plan.

In practice, mobilization consists either of filling out existing military units with combat-trained personnel and equipment or forming new units of various sizes. The command cadres for new formations usually are drawn from existing units.

It is very difficult to forecast in peacetime the exact dimensions of the forces that may be needed throughout a war, because at the very beginning of a war the massive reciprocal use of nuclear weapons can fundamentally alter the situation.

Therefore, in light of the situation which happens to prevail at the time, and while mobilization is still under way according to plans developed beforehand, new formations may be created for subsequent expansion of the armed forces. A significant part of these formations, however, can be brought together through administrative arrangements, taking into account existing manpower and material resources.

With regard to methods and means used, the mobilization of armed forces today can be general or partial, open or concealed.

General mobilization is declared by governmental decree and is carried out openly. In previous wars, up to and including the first world war, it generally began during a period when the international political situation was strained, and prior to the beginning of military operations.

In the case of World War II and the Great Patriotic War, mobilization in some belligerent countries, including the USSR, was carried out mainly during the war, rather than before.

Under contemporary conditions, there is little likelihood of general mobilization starting prior to the opening of military operations, since it cannot go on without the enemy taking notice.

Partial mobilization in the past was carried out simultaneously or in succession only in certain military districts closest to the probable theater of operations. Partial mobilization was sometimes effected in a concealed fashion by mobilizing only certain units under the guise of various types of tests, assembly for training [exercises], maneuvers, and so on.

Concealed mobilization is also possible under present-day conditions, but it will be carried out somewhat differently from before. As relations between the contending sides become increasingly strained, they will gradually bring up to full combat readiness part of the forces earmarked for tasks in the initial period of the war. It must be kept in mind, however, that with present-day means of strategic intelligence, widespread mobilization measures, even though concealed, cannot remain undetected. Therefore, all the major countries of present-day coalitions strive to keep their armed forces in a state of maximum and constant readiness.

The system of bringing the armed forces up to prescribed strength in peacetime and during mobilization is an important factor affecting their level of preparation. A system of territorial build-up of troops during mobilization is considered the most acceptable. Under the conditions of nuclear war this system considerably speeds up the process of putting one's troops on a war footing. As for a peacetime army, its principal mission of promptly repelling an aggressor and preparing trained reserves for war can only be fulfilled on the basis of cadre formations.

The manpower resources for bringing the armed forces up to strength during mobilization are customarily kept in reserve and are carried on the military roster. The roster lists all persons of appropriate age groups subject to military service, both with and without military training. Some of those liable for military service are "deferred" by enterprises and institutions of the economy and are not called up during mobilization.

Keeping account of the number of men eligible for military service, especially of trained men, is one of the bases on which mobilization rests.

Personnel annually mustered out of the peacetime army provide the main source of replenishment for the trained reserve. However, no peacetime army anywhere, as a rule, ever fully absorbs a scheduled age class [for military service] in its entirety. Therefore, there always remains a certain percentage of persons in the reserve who have not undergone training in the regular forces.

These persons are prepared for the military by means of a network of civilian training institutions which turn out various types of specialists useful to the armed forces: mechanics, radio and telegraph operators, drivers, and so on. Trained personnel without military service, but with a civilian specialty which can be used by the armed forces, are enrolled in the reserve. In addition, persons not conscripted by the army receive partial training in specially organized sessions at military training centers.

It is generally known that the shorter the period of military service, the greater the number of men with military service discharged into the reserve each year. However, the quality of training and, consequently, the combat readiness of those released are correspondingly reduced.

At the same time, one must note that conditions nowadays open up possibilities for more rapid preparation and training of enlisted and noncommissioned personnel since almost all of the mechanical devices found in the Armed Forces are akin to those used in the civilian economy. Further, such skilled personnel as operators and mechanics of diesel, gasoline, and electric engines, specialists in radio and electronics, in optics, and other fields are the same in principle both in the military establishment and in civilian production.

The availability of a sufficient number of officers of all specialities also plays an important role in the creation of a trained military reserve.

The number of officers released from the Armed Forces annually and retained on the military roster is usually quite small in comparison with mobilization requirements. Therefore, a reserve of younger officers is created in peacetime mainly from the ranks of noncommissioned officers, especially those with secondary and higher education who go into the reserve each year. The reserve of younger officers with technical specialities is also replenished by graduates of special civilian institutions of higher education who have not had any actual service in the military establishment.

During mobilization, the network of intermediate military training institutions is usually expanded, with an intensified program designed mainly to turn out junior officers. Higher command levels are filled by promotion of officers in service, since combat and other service experience is usually more valuable than accelerated training in refresher courses.

The mobilization build-up of existing peacetime units and especially the formation of new units have special features in each branch of the Armed Forces. Thus, mobilization has little effect by and large upon the composition and organization of the Strategic Missile Forces and the National PVO.

The Air Forces operate from the outset of war with the same force composition as in peacetime and also form anew [viz., after being attacked] combat and especially transport units and airfield service units.

Mobilization in the Navy is carried out by fully stocking ships in commission with supplies and removing from them surplus materiel and personnel in training; by reactivating reserve ships; by converting certain vessels of the civilian fleet into warships and auxiliary craft; and by organizing base facilities for the fleet. For the latter purpose, the facilities of civilian ports and shipyards are used.

The most extensive mobilization takes place in the Ground Forces and the civil defense troops.

In addition to the availability of trained manpower, the formation of new units of various sizes in the remaining branches of the Armed Forces depends also on the length of time required for receipt of weapons and war material from industry in the course of the war, since stockpiling these materials in peacetime is not expedient because of rapid obsolescence.

It should be noted that formation of certain specialized units (repair, auto-transport, hydro-meteorological, hospitals, and so on) can be accomplished directly by civilian ministries and departments.

The great losses which may result from enemy nuclear strikes, together with inevitable, large-scale disruption of the whole transport and communications system, demand that present-day mobilization be simplified, dispersed, and carried out at maximum speed. Only thus will mobilization forces be able to take part in operations during the initial period of the war.

Mobilization can be simplified by carrying it out according to the territorial method, by not attempting to transport mobilized troops, armaments, and materiel to mobilization or forming-up centers (so-called mobilization transit movements), and by simplifying the system of assigning conscripts to units.

By dispersed mobilization is meant organizing mobilization in such a fashion that a single troop unit is formed at each center. The fullest possible autonomy of mobilization centers (military commissariats) should be achieved, enabling them to form units independently.

The inevitable large-scale disruption of the transport and communications system will not permit us under present-day conditions to use the rigidly centralized method of mobilization employed in previous wars. Therefore, each troop unit must be completely mobilized locally.

In wartime it will be impossible, of course, to dispense with certain movements of specialists from one region to another. But these movements under present-day conditions must be reduced to a minimum. A depot complex with a full inventory of necessary items should be set up at mobilization centers. During the last war, the equipment for outfitting units often had to be brought from dozens of depots located hundreds and even thousands of kilometers from the mobilization centers. Such a situation will be intolerable in a future war since it does not fit present-day time limits on carrying out mobilization.

The system of assigning trained conscripts to military units can be simplified by more widespread substitution of one specialty for another (related) specialty. The employment of a large percentage of so-called untrained personnel to flesh out military units will permit us to dispense with bringing in specialists from afar and will increase the autonomy of the mobilization centers.

Large and small units intended to replace combat losses occupy a very important place among the new formations created during mobilization.

The scope and importance of troop replacement during a war can be illustrated by the case of the German army in World War II. In 1942, it received an average of 250,000–300,000 men per month as replacements. In 1943, as a result of inaccurate estimates of the country's capabilities to provide the army with systematic personnel replenishment, the replacement rate in the German army fell off to 150,000 per month. At the same time, thanks to strict and centralized planning in the USSR, the replacement rate did not drop during the entire war.

In modern warfare, the problem of replacing manpower losses will become particularly acute from the very first hours of the war. In previous wars losses were made good mainly by forming, during mobilization, reserve and training units which received accelerated training. Troops were sent to the front from these reserve contingents as replacement companies, batteries, or battalions. Another way of providing replacements was the "casual replacement" method, that is, sending to the troop units a certain number of more or less trained men.

Because of the likelihood of great losses from weapons of mass destruction and the possible liquidation of entire small units and even large formations, it will hardly be expedient in modern warfare to limit ourselves merely to creating reserve and training units, and sending to the front replacement subunits. The predominant way of restoring losses apparently will now be to form fully trained and integrated large formations or separate units which are ready to step into battle upon arrival at the front.

No matter how mobilization may be carried out, however, it must, as previously, be planned in detail beforehand, during peacetime.

The disruption of peacetime mobilization plans and calculations by a nuclear attack will obviously call for administrative control over mobilization, so that plans can be changed and corrected in accordance with the prevailing situation. Therefore, mobilization plans developed in peacetime must be flexible and adaptable to carrying out mobilization by various methods: open or concealed, general or partial. Only if each mobilization center possesses maximum autonomy in forming the units for which it is responsible can all of these requirements be met.

The proper allotment of manpower resources for forming mobilization units and for replacing casualties is one of the most important tasks of mobilization planning. The planning agencies must take into strict account the possible manpower requirements for the entire war, and they must see to it that all eligible men in the young age classes are not called up during the initial mobilization. A portion of them must be kept for replenishing the army during the course of the war itself.

The General Staff sets the time needed to execute a unified mobilization plan and furnishes basic planning data to military districts, troops, and mobilization centers after the government has decided upon the level of mobilization of the Armed Forces to be attained and the quota of national resources which may be drawn upon.

The abundance and diversity of data with which both the General Staff and local registration and mobilization agencies must cope are such that electronic computers are required. These are linked together in a unified system into which the General Staff is tied. The computers ensure the necessary speed and accuracy in mobilization planning. In particular, their use makes it easier to determine which locations are the most suitable for raising new formations when mobilizing on the territorial system. [This determination among] locations depends on the quantity and quality (special skills) of available manpower resources.

Under conditions where missiles and nuclear weapons are used, both belligerents will be subjected to attacks in the very first hours of the war, and it can be assumed that both will find themselves in approximately the same circumstances as regards techniques of carrying out mobilization and moving troops to the theater of military operations. It follows, therefore, that the side which manages to penetrate more deeply into enemy territory in the very first days of the war will naturally acquire an opportunity to exploit the results of its nuclear attacks more effectively and to disrupt the enemy's mobilization. This is particularly important with regard to the European theaters of operation with their relatively shallow operational depth.[2]

The most important aspect of preparing the Armed Forces for war is by their direct training in methods of conducting military operations, including operational, combat, and political training. In addition to keeping the armed forces at a high level of combat readiness, the basic aim of these types of training are to impart [mastery] of the principal means of warfare and to teach methods of conducting a battle, an operation, and armed conflict as a whole. Another is to develop and test new methods of conducting military operations and the workability of plans and calculations for wartime. Still another is to indoctrinate the troops

---

[2] U.S. ED. NOTE—The USSR is apparently not included in this reference to the European theater of operations.

politically and militarily. It must be noted that the system of training troops under modern conditions involves a great increase in the importance of technical training, and in particular, of the interchangeable character of crews and teams servicing machines, instruments, and assemblies.

Troop training should be organized and carried out in such a way that the theory and practice of military art are at all times developed on a mutually supporting basis along with perfecting the means and methods of warfare. From this viewpoint, it is of great importance to formulate generalizations based on experience gained in operational, combat, and political training. This furthers the development of the theory of military art. In order to prevent one-sided conclusions from being drawn, it is necessary in the process of operational and combat training to study the enemy carefully and to follow changes in his views on the conduct of military operations.

The theory of military art and the practice of training troops serve as the basis for development of all sorts of official manuals, regulations, and instructions, which in sum reflect the military doctrine of the state. The timely preparation of such documents, their revision in accordance with developments in the means of warfare, and their thorough study by the troops constitute one of the most important aspects of the preparation of the Armed Forces.

The development of the Armed Forces in peacetime is planned for definite periods—tied to over-all plans of the national economy, new scientific achievements in weapons and military technology, and the nature of the international situation. Long-range plans for development of the armed forces, approved by the government, determine the quantitative and qualitative development of the means of warfare, the organizational structure of the armed forces, methods of employing them in war, the creation of reserves of armament, military equipment and other material means, and the preparation of trained military manpower and command cadres. Depending on specific conditions, the long-range plans may also include other, additional items.

*Preparation for Material and Technical Support of the Armed Forces.* No matter how perfect the armament, organization, training, and combat readiness of the Armed Forces may be, they will not be able to carry out the missions assigned to them if their material and technical support for conducting military operations is not organized and thoroughly prepared in peacetime.

The character of the initial period of a modern war makes it imperative that the material means needed for the first operations not only be prepared in peacetime but that they be dispersed in accordance with the requirements of antiatomic defense. Moreover, the necessary reserves of materiel should be assembled in the interior of the country at points of troop mobilization. Provision should also be made for reserves to replace losses.

Materiel reserves of the Armed Forces are divided into categories according to their intended use. These are emergency and mobilization stocks, strategic and state reserves.

Emergency stocks are stored directly by small and large peacetime units, in quantities that ensure the units of meeting their mobilization deployment schedules (if provided for) and, most important, of conducting military operations for a specified period of time.

Mobilization stocks are intended for replacement of materiel expenditures and losses during operations in the initial period of the war. The quality and distribution of mobilization stocks depend on the probable requirements of the Armed Forces for fighting this phase of the war.

By strategic materiel reserves, one means that part of the state reserves which is put at the disposal of the high command. All remaining stocks constitute state reserves.

The size of strategic and state reserves is determined on the basis of requirements for uninterrupted supply of the Armed Forces until industrial mobilization brings production up to programmed war levels. This took about three months in the case of the Great Patriotic War, while for industries evacuated to the interior, six to nine months were required.

The enormous scale of materiel expenditures to meet the needs of the Armed Forces was demonstrated in both previous world wars. It suffices to recall that the Russian army in World War I expended about one million tons of various kinds of ammunition. During the Great Patriotic War the expenditure of ammunition by the Soviet Armed Forces came to about eight million tons. The consumption of fuels and lubricants increased even more sharply. Whereas the Russian army used only some tens of thousands of tons of fuels and lubricants in World War I, during the Great Patriotic War consumption amounted to more than thirteen million tons. Thus, in previous world wars, along with a steep over-all increase in materiel expenditures, one notes a trend toward more rapid increase in requirements for fuels and lubricants.

Under contemporary conditions, owing to the complete motorization and mechanization of the Armed Forces and the continuously increasing level of their technical equipment, the importance of fuels and lubricants for support of combat operations has grown even more. Some idea of the demand for these materials in the Armed Forces is given by the quantities required to conduct a single frontal offensive. An approximate calculation shows that such an operation requires about 300,000 tons of fuel and lubricants. One of the large fleets alone can consume up to 150,000 tons of fuel in an operation. In this connection, one must note the ever-increasing requirement for special types of missile fuels. On the whole, fuels and lubricants may account for more than 50 per cent of the total weight of material required by the Armed Forces.

The requirement of the Armed Forces for technical equipment of all types also has increased sharply. According to rough calculations, this requirement has grown by a factor of 2–2.5 in comparison with that during the Great Patriotic War.

At the same time, owing to the enormous firepower of missiles and nuclear weapons, there has been a noticeable decrease in the amount of conventional ammunition required by the Armed Forces. While during the Great Patriotic War the weight of ammunition was about two-thirds that of fuel and lubricants, today, according to rough calculations, it will scarcely exceed one-half.[3]

Materiel requirements of the Armed Forces can be determined more or less accurately only for the first operations in the initial period of the war and for the supply of troops deployed or newly formed according to the mobilization plan. While all other calculations are quite tentative, they are used as a basis for developing the plan for material and technical support of the Armed Forces. Upon this plan in turn are based levels of peacetime production for military purposes and a plan for industrial mobilization at the start of war. All calculations of requirements are made with allowance for probable heavy losses of materiel even before it reaches the hands of troops. The extent of such losses will undoubtedly be much greater than in the last war.

Timely delivery to the troops of necessary supplies from depots set up in peacetime plays an important role in the logistic support of the Armed Forces. In previous wars the railways were the principal means of transport, both from the interior of the country and in the theater of operations. Under present-day conditions, even if railways are in centers of destruction, restoration of trackage is possible by utilizing industrial methods for repair and by advance stockpiling of roadbed and bridge components. However, this can only be done at a rate

[3] U.S. ED. NOTE—This indicates a great reliance of the Ground and Tactical Forces on the use of nuclear weapons.

not greater than 40–50 kilometers [24–30 miles] per day, while reconstruction of bridges cannot be accomplished at a rate greater than 120–150 meters [360–450 feet] per day.

In theaters of operations, railways today cannot fully ensure the delivery of materiel to the troops. Therefore, motor transport will play a decisive role. Along with motor transport, pipelines are taking on an ever-increasing importance. For an offensive operation, a single present-day front alone requires the daily delivery from depots to troops of as much as 25,000 tons of fuel and lubricants. More than 10,000 five-ton tank trucks would be required to deliver this amount of fuel over a distance of 300 kilometers [180 miles]. This is not only uneconomical but also unreliable. In order to deliver fuel and lubricants throughout the entire depth of a modern frontal operation, the number of trucks required would be many times greater. The problem of supplying troops on the offensive with fuels and lubricants from main underground pipelines and dumps situated in the theater of operations can be solved only by using field pipelines. These are laid down behind the advancing troops, and extend also to airfields and naval bases.

In the future, transport aircraft of types not dependent on airfields may provide a very effective and mobile means of delivering supplies. For the time being, the role of aircraft in supply operations is limited because of inadequate payload capacity, requirements for complicated airfield installations, and the need for escort during flight. Military transport aviation evidently will be employed primarily for dropping (or landing) of airborne forces and delivery of missiles and fuels to the missile forces.

Water transport will play a substantial role in delivery of supplies to the troops when river systems without a large number of locks can be used (locks can be destroyed by the enemy).

Under contemporary conditions, it is absolutely necessary to use all forms of transport in combination. This will make it possible, if the need arises, to switch the flow of supplies from one type of transport to another.

Provisions for medical support of the Armed Forces under conditions of missile and nuclear warfare will be an important aspect of the overall system of material and technical support. The number of people requiring medical aid will be immeasurably greater than in past wars, so that a different approach to the organization of medical services in the Armed Forces will be needed. In previous wars, the handling of casualties consisted mainly in the evacuation of the majority of sick and wounded to the relatively quiet rear of the army, the front, or even into the zone of the interior. This required a large amount of specially-equipped transport of various kinds. For treatment of the sick and wounded, dozens of hospitals with all necessary equipment were set up in the armies, fronts (and fleets).

In a modern war there will obviously be no "quiet" areas where medical treatment can be given. Hence, it will hardly be possible or suitable to undertake a large-scale evacuation of nuclear casualties to the zone of the interior. The main problem will be to move casualties from zones of radioactive contamination and to organize on-the-spot medical assistance outside the immediate areas in which combat formations are located. In this connection, the organization of medical services must be directed largely toward forming mobile detachments of medical personnel (doctors, nurses, and administrators), equipped with medical supplies, instruments, and some hospital furnishings. These detachments must be capable of setting up a "hospital" at any spot, using household articles (beds, linen, and so on) donated by the local population or confiscated from it. Thanks to such measures, the medical detachments can be relieved of their cumbersome equipment to a considerable extent.

The same principle should govern the organization of the so-called technical support troops. Combat equipment put out of commission should be collected and salvaged rather than sent to the rear. The task of collecting it should not be assigned to the troops but to repair agencies of the front, which move into the places where they are needed for this purpose.

Repair agencies of the front must also base their operations to a considerable extent on utilization of local repair facilities (factories and workshops). The repair of military equipment by troops themselves should be limited to replacement of parts or complete assemblies. Supplies of parts and assemblies for this purpose are prepared in peacetime.

Preparation of the rear support establishment is an important part of the process of readying the Armed Forces.

The rear establishment of the Armed Forces takes in many units, enterprises, depots, and other institutions designed to furnish all-round materiel and technical support of the troops for their conduct of combat operations. In peacetime, only the rear support elements of various units earmarked for action in the initial period of the war are kept at full strength. The majority of the rear elements of armies, fronts, and fleets are deployed or formed during mobilization.

*Preparation of the country to serve as a theater of military operations* is another aspect of readying the nation and the Armed Forces for war. This has the object of creating optimum conditions for employment of all branches of the Armed Forces. It should be observed that such preparation prior to earlier world wars was carried out mainly in border regions, and for the most part involved construction of fortifications for the covering forces and the development of the railway network. Construction of airfields was also carried out in the border zone prior to World War II.

Under contemporary conditions, the territory of the entire country, not just the border regions, will be given over to launch sites of the missile forces, airfields, and troop positions of the National PVO, airfields for long-range and other types of air forces and airborne troops, as well as troops and various [civil defense] means designated to deal with the aftermath of enemy nuclear attacks. Now the entire territory of the country will be subject to enemy nuclear strikes and, in this sense, will become a military theater. Therefore it will be necessary to make the appropriate preparations throughout the entire country and not just in its border zones.

At the same time, the concept of ground and naval (ocean) theaters of military operations will remain valid for regions where direct engagements between ground, sea, and air forces are prepared and conducted. These theaters include the territories (and bodies of water) of foreign countries and part of our own. The preparation of theaters of military operations will be as important as before, since, first of all, the enormous scope of a future war will require skillful organization of combat under the most diverse military and geographical conditions; second, the preparations of each theater will be distinguished by particular features resulting from the operations planned for the theater during the initial period of war (the preparation of communication systems, pipelines, depots, etc.).

The preparation of the entire territory of the country as well as the theaters of military operations involves an extensive series of measures, partly executed by the Armed Forces themselves and partly by civilian ministries and departments within the framework of the state's overall plans.

The measures carried out by the Armed Forces are directed toward preparing the operations of all branches of the Armed Forces as a whole, as well as of each branch of the Armed Forces.

Preparing the theaters of military operations for the Ground Forces by fortification and other engineering measures, an important type of preparation in the past, has lost its former significance.

The peacetime development of a railway network in theaters of operations has also lost its former significance since railways no longer serve as the main type of transportation for the operation of ground forces.

A network of airfields is being prepared in advance for the use of the Air Force. In view of the fact that airfields will be the targets of the very first nuclear strikes, their number must considerably exceed the needs of the Air Force assigned to operate in a given theater of military operation.

Dispersion of naval bases (including navigational and radar bases, coastal missile-launching sites, and minelaying operations in certain zones, etc.) will be very important in the preparation of naval theaters of operation.

*Strategic intelligence* organized by the Armed Forces during peacetime is also a very important aspect of the preparations for war, not only for the armed forces but for the country in general. Strategic intelligence makes possible more rational war preparations by providing information on the potential enemy's plans and capabilities, makes possible a certain gain in time for preparatory measures before an enemy assault, and also aids in making proper decisions in the conduct of operations from the very outset of hostilities.

It is almost impossible to completely conceal preparations for sudden attack from current strategic intelligence, with its high level of technical development, since there are definite indicators which, if studied and compared, will provide information on the likelihood of attack. Consequently, well-organized strategic intelligence can ensure for a government and high command the possibility of carrying out some precautionary measures of a political and military nature.

Strategic intelligence, both in peace and war, provides political, military, economic, scientific, and technical data on the states which are potential enemies; it also studies their military capabilities.

Soviet intelligence differs basically from the intelligence of capitalist countries with respect to its class nature as well as to the content of its assignments and how they are carried out.

Intelligence [activities] by imperialist states are not confined simply to collecting the above data. It is also assigned tasks of organizing political pressure on domestic and foreign policy, particularly in small countries. For this purpose, the intelligence agencies of capitalist countries either exploit or organize internal political dissension and dissension among nationalities [and races in a particular state], conspiracies, and political assassinations. They blackmail and bribe statesmen, party leaders, prominent scientists, newspaper publishers and editors. Moreover, they rely on the most reactionary bourgeois, nationalistic and other antidemocratic elements and groups. Such missions and techniques are alien to Soviet intelligence.

Current strategic intelligence by capitalist countries takes the following forms: political intelligence carried out by the ministries of foreign affairs, economic intelligence carried out by agencies in charge of foreign trade relations, and military intelligence organized and carried out by armed forces. All these forms of intelligence are closely related and co-ordinated. Sometimes they are even organized in a single agency subordinate to the head of state (for example, the Central Intelligence Agency in the United States).

Military strategic intelligence, which occupies an important place in the general system of strategic intelligence, is part of the state's over-all intelligence service. It is not confined to the study of narrow military questions but also includes military-political and military-economic questions, thus co-operating with political and economic intelligence.

The basic missions of military strategic intelligence are the procurement of data on the military-political plans and the mobilization measures of [other] countries; the assessment of their military, political, and economic potential; the discovery and comprehensive study of the composition and organization of the Armed Forces in theaters of military operations; the study of the potential enemy's military science; the discovery of the planned nature of enemy military operations during the initial period of the war; the procurement of data on the development and improvement of military equipment and weapons; the procurement of information and the study of data on theaters of military operations and their facilities, and the study of the state of political morale in the army and population.

These assignments by no means completely exhaust the full range of intelligence activities, but give only a general picture of the basic directions of intelligence activity.

The main forces and means of capitalist military strategic intelligence are intelligence by [secret] agent networks, the legal foreign intelligence agencies, radio and electronic intelligence, aerial and naval reconnaissance, and finally, the information analysis service which studies and processes the open sources of foreign states.

Intelligence gathered by networks of agents is the principal means of military strategic intelligence, which permits the discovery of the most closely held secrets of the plans and intentions of the potential opponents. Such intelligence operates continuously, in peace and war, deep within the enemy homeland, as well as in border zones.

The legal foreign agencies sanctioned by international law consist of the military, naval, and air force attachés and heads of military missions with their official organizations. The basic methods of operation used by the military attachés' offices of capitalist countries consist of personal observation, official visits to military units and institutions, exercises and maneuvers, parades and military ceremonies, as well as trips through the country, and also the study of the press. It should be noted that the military attachés of a number of capitalist countries also usually engage in the illegal organization of networks of intelligence agents, and of acts of terror and subversion.

Radio and electronic intelligence is one of the most important means for gaining intelligence data. It operates continuously, secretly, and almost independently of the season, hour, or weather.

The widespread use of electronic equipment in the armed forces enables radio and electronic intelligence to establish the location of ground, air, and naval forces, and the radio communications employed by them, and to obtain the most diverse data, which are electronically transmitted in open or coded form.

Air strategic reconnaissance is of great importance for obtaining information, primarily in wartime, since aircraft flights over foreign states in peacetime are ordinarily limited to existing international [air] corridors. The imperialist states, violating every international right and law, often use aircraft for reconnaissance in peacetime also. However, these attempts have been definitely and successfully stopped, a clear example of which was the ignominious end of the American U-2 adventure in May of 1960.

Naval intelligence procures information on naval forces and also on theaters of naval operations. It uses the same methods and means as military strategic intelligence to carry out its assignments, i.e., intelligence by networks of secret agents, the legal foreign agencies, radio intelligence, aerial reconnaissance, and in addition, by naval forces, particularly submarine forces.

The information analysis service uses all the legal sources, like the press and periodicals, radio and television broadcasts, motion picture films of the country under study, etc.

The painstaking and systematic study of all legal [open] information, its methodical processing and comparison with data obtained from illegal sources can supply intelligence agencies with very important and precise information concerning all questions of preparations for war in peacetime. This branch of intelligence is no less important than the others.

The intelligence of imperialist states, above all that of the United States and Great Britain, uses every means possible to discover our state and military secrets; sparing no forces nor means for this purpose. Consequently, our counterintelligence agencies are carrying on a continuous struggle against capitalist intelligence, relying on the broad support of the entire people, who display the greatest vigilance; our counterintelligence employs all the latest technical achievements as well as their own methods of operation.

## Preparation of the National Economy

The *preparation of industry* to operate in wartime conditions constitutes the most important part of the entire preparation of the country's economy. As was noted earlier, the volume of military production sharply increases with the start of military operations. As an illustration, it is sufficient to recall that in World War II, from 1939 to 1945, the United States produced 296,000 airplanes, 86,000 tanks, and 363,000 guns and mortars; from 1941 to 1945, the USSR produced about 150,-000 airplanes, about 110,000 tanks, and about 900,000 guns and mortars.

Increased production of armaments and military equipment naturally requires the corresponding provision of industry with power and strategic raw materials. New military weapons (missiles, supersonic planes, etc.) require especially stable alloys; many nonferrous and rare metals are required for military production, as well as a fully developed machine- and instrument-building industry.

According to rough calculations, approximately 250,000 tons of aluminum are necessary to produce 40,000 fighter aircraft weighing an average of 10 tons each. In order to produce this much aluminum, it is necessary to mine and process about 800,000 tons of bauxite, which requires the expenditure of 4 billion kilowatt hours of electricity, i.e., more than the annual production of a powerful station like the Lenin Volga Hydroelectric Power Station.

It must be kept in mind that the requirements of the troops in World War II cannot serve as comparable data for calculating the requirements for materiel in a future war. While the number of actual weapons in use at any one time in the theaters of military operations may be somewhat less than in the last war, the [absolute] magnitude of the losses will be immeasurably greater. Thus, in the Great Patriotic War, the average monthly irretrievable losses of aircraft amounted to about 21 per cent of the aircraft at the front, whereas the losses of tanks and artillery were 19 per cent and 9 per cent, respectively. According to calculations made by NATO specialists concerning their own troops, under current conditions the losses of aircraft during the very first two weeks of war may range from 60 per cent to 85 per cent, whereas the losses of ground troops may amount from 30 per cent to 40 per cent. Thus it is quite likely that the losses of weapons and military equipment will be about six to eight times as great as in the past war.

It is also possible that a future war might not require anything more than the reserves of armament and military equipment which had been stockpiled in advance. However, it would be dangerous to rely on this possibility, and industry must therefore be prepared during peacetime to make up for heavy losses in the armed forces.

A most important duty of the strategic leadership in preparing the national economy and, especially, industry for war is the accurate calculation of the material requirements of the Armed Forces during the initial period of the war.

On the basis of calculations of possible losses of military equipment in theaters of military operations, appropriate lists of requirements are usually drawn up, which, after receiving governmental approval, enable peacetime industry to create the necessary production potential to satisfy them.

Under current conditions it is difficult to rely upon large-scale development of new military production after the onset of war, as was done in the past. Therefore, the necessary reserves for at least the initial period of the war are stockpiled during peacetime, and the appropriate production potential and power sources are being prepared so that they can be rapidly switched at the onset of war to wartime military production. Some specific defense enterprises are provided with reserve production capacity. In the United States, for example, this reserve amounts to approximately 50 per cent of the currently operating enterprises.

Measures are examined beforehand in peacetime to bring the mobilization of industry speedily to its final stage [i.e., when war threatens or begins]. In this connection, it is most important to standardize the design of military and commercial equipment, since a company adapted to the mass production of a particular product will require a considerable interval of time to switch over to the production of a different product.

One of the most important conditions for the rapid mobilization of industry is the standardization of items supplied to the armed forces. Numerous different models should be replaced by one or several models suitable for rapid mass production.

Under current conditions there is extensive co-operation between industrial enterprises where one type of production depends on many others. Some factories supply parts or semifinished products, others supply instruments and assemblies, and still others are engaged in assembly, etc. Automation and mechanization of production, and mass as well as serial production are now based on dividing the parts [of the manufactured item] and work specialization.

In a planned economy, co-operative production is organized by economic regions, thus reducing the transport of individual parts, assemblies, semifinished products, and fuel. This accelerates production and industrial mobilization and assures a steady flow of supplies to the armed forces in case of war.

One of the most important aspects of the industrial preparations for war is ensuring the viability of industry, particularly heavy and defense industry. In previous wars this problem was solved rather simply by the appropriate geographical distribution of important industrial installations deep in the country, beyond the reach of attacking enemy aircraft and ground forces in case of a successful assault. Now, no geographical distribution of industrial installations will guarantee their protection from missile strikes, and therefore their survivability must be secured through compulsory dispersion, duplication of production, and antinuclear defense measures.

One must especially stress the need for the dispersal of industrial power sources under present conditions.

In discussing the dispersal of industry, it must be kept in mind that historically many industrial installations were established and located at a time when no one thought of nuclear attack. Therefore, we are now speaking primarily of the proper distribution of newly built installations and the partial and gradual dispersion of existing ones.[4]

From the viewpoint of antinuclear defense, it is preferred to place particularly important industrial enterprises underground in spaces prepared in advance for this purpose. During the last war, the Germans planned to construct approximately 9 million square meters [96,875,000 square feet] of underground space to shelter industry. However, by the end of the war they succeeded in only building 1.5 million square meters [16,144,500 square feet]. Naturally, under current conditions the preparation of underground facilities must be carried out on a particularly extensive scale. As far back as 1956, the United States had located and had listed approximately 400 million square feet of underground space for this purpose, mainly mines, suited to military facilities.

The need for increasing the viability of new industrial enterprises above ground is being taken into account. The most valuable equipment is being placed in very strongly constructed premises under concrete

---

[4] U.S. ED. NOTE—Soviet city planners and civil defense authorities have shown considerable interest in urban and industrial dispersal. Soviet publications have stressed the desirability of locating factories at considerable distance from each other and from urban residential areas, as well as building new factories far removed from the borders of the Soviet Union. See, for example, L. Gouré, *Civil Defense in the Soviet Union,* University of California Press, Berkeley and Los Angeles, 1962, pp. 62–70. On several occasions Khrushchev has pointed out that Soviet industry is more dispersed, and consequently allegedly less vulnerable, than U.S. industry. See, for example, "Khrushchev's Interview with Henry Shapiro," *Pravda,* November 19, 1957.

cover, and materials and equipment for rapid restoration of damage are prepared in advance. Naturally, it is beyond the means of any, even the most powerful state, to shelter a considerable portion of the industrial facilities underground. Therefore, such shelters are provided only for the most important installations; for the rest only hardened underground control points are built.[5]

Particular attention should be given to the evacuation of industrial enterprises to the interior of the country at the beginning of war or when war threatens. This measure played an important role in previous wars, especially in the Great Patriotic War. In missile and nuclear warfare, the importance of evacuation will change fundamentally.

If the threat of war should become real, it is obvious that only a very small and most important part of the industrial enterprises could be evacuated, primarily from the regions and places where the enemy's first nuclear strikes are most likely to take place and where extensive destruction is unavoidable.

As for other centers located in the interior of the country and in the border regions, any preliminary evacuation of industrial enterprises from these centers would produce additional difficulties, disorganize production, and complicate mobilization measures. Moreover, the evacuated industries would be as subject to enemy strikes at the new sites as at the old.

Usually, plans to mobilize the economy provide for the evacuation of industry in close co-ordination with the mobilization plans of the Armed Forces.

In summarizing what has been said on the preparations of industry for war, it must be emphasized once more that in the event of war, in addition to meeting the requirements of the Armed Forces, industry must satisfy the needs of the country's entire population. Thus, industries not engaged in military production should be ready to produce some new goods or even in some cases to change completely to a different type of production when industry is mobilized.

The speed at which all industry mobilizes depends largely upon how thoroughly, in peacetime, the enterprises have mastered the technology of production according to the military program—by filling experimental orders—and upon the provision of industrial enterprises with raw materials, semifinished products, and skilled and unskilled labor.

---

[5] U.S. ED. NOTE—The reference to hardening of industrial installations is most unusual in Soviet literature. The statement appears to imply that some Soviet industrial facilities and industrial administrative control centers are being hardened.

*The preparation of agriculture,* which supplies the entire country with food and raw materials, is also a most important task in preparing the economy for war. Ordinarily the conditions of agricultural production change appreciably with the onset of war because a considerable portion of the labor force and the machines engaged in agriculture are drawn into the Armed Forces.

Under current conditions, the portion of agricultural production which formerly contributed to army supplies can now be replaced by the appropriate synthetics (for example, leather, wool, all types of fiber, etc.). However, this in no way diminishes the importance of agriculture as the supplier for the main sectors of production, since the production of synthetics may suffer from nuclear blows at the outset of the war to a much greater extent than agriculture.

The following are the main requirements for the peacetime preparation of agriculture. First, it must be developed to a level where it can ensure the creation of considerable food and raw material reserves in case of war. Second, it must be so organized that the mobilization of the Armed Forces will be facilitated. And finally, from the very beginning of war, agriculture must maintain a scale of production that ensures the current needs of the population and the Armed Forces for food and the needs of industry for raw materials.

The socialist system of agriculture, in which the great bulk of agricultural produce is concentrated in the hands of the state, assures the necessary reserves in case of war. The advantage of the socialist system in this respect was quite clearly manifested during the Great Patriotic War, when our collectivized agriculture was able to withstand extremely great stress.

Now, the possibilities of creating the necessary reserves have increased immeasurably. Within a short period of time (1954–1956), 36 million hectares of virgin land in the eastern regions of the country were brought under cultivation (all the tilled acreage of Great Britain, France, and West Germany together amounts to 32–33 million hectares), and there has been an eightfold increase in the acreage devoted to corn during the period from 1954–1960, and a postwar increase from 28 million horsepower to 125 million, in the power available to agriculture —these powerful instruments for developing agriculture are at the disposal of the socialist state.

Agriculture in the USSR is systematically improving the yields of grain and industrial crops and the productivity of animal husbandry. This is accomplished by extending the tilled acreage through cultivation of virgin and fallow land, as well as thorough extensive irrigation and land reclamation, more mechanization and electrification, by improvements in tilling the soil, seed selection, by using more chemical fertilizer and intertillage, by the creation of an adequate fodder base and the introduction of scientific methods of animal husbandry and care.

The development of agriculture is closely connected with the state of machine, building, chemical, and food processing industries. In peacetime these industrial facilities are readied so that, from the beginning of the war, they can compensate for the decrease in the number of machines and workers engaged in agriculture resulting from mobilization.

As a rule, the creation of reserves of agricultural produce requires the construction of a sufficient number of storehouses, under central and local governmental control, located close to consumers and processing centers in order to reduce the volume of freight at the beginning of the war.

It must be remembered that the conditions of modern warfare demand that foodstuffs not be stored in large cities.

Industrial packaging of food in small units is highly important in protecting food supplies from contamination. The packaging materials must be impermeable and must enable the food to be stored in warehouses which are not hermetically sealed. From this point of view, the development of high nutrition concentrates and preserves is particularly important from the onset of the war, especially for supplying the Armed Forces.

Mobilization of the Armed Forces can be accelerated by introducing into agriculture the standard machines and equipment used by troops, such as trucks, farm tractors, prime movers, gasoline tank trucks, automotive repair detachments, road equipment, containers [probably tank trucks], etc. Thus small newly organized units and formations will be able to obtain equipment and materials at the places where they are organized.

The *preparation of transport* in peacetime for wartime operation is extremely important. The transportation system, as in peacetime, will have to serve industrial operations and the functioning of the whole economy. In addition, the transportation system has the task of delivering [newly] mobilized troops and supplies of all kinds to the Armed Forces, from the country's interior to the frontal regions. The troops are a very large materiel consumer, thereby causing large-scale redirection of freight traffic.

In peacetime, the transportation system is being developed by new construction and the improvement of railways and highways, waterways, pipelines, and airlines, the improvement of the technical and economic properties of all forms of transport operations, and by measures to increase its survivability to enemy nuclear strikes and to ensure rapid restoration after destruction.

In order to prepare for wartime transportation requirements, transport reserves are created in rolling stock and fuel on railways, waterways, and airfields; in equipment for restoring highways, bridges, communication lines, wharves, and airfields; and reserve equipment for railway cars, ships, and military air transport. Cadres of specialists are also trained for repair and rehabilitation.

Rail transport is the most important of all in the national economy. However, its share in peacetime transportation is decreasing regularly with the growth of other forms of transport facilities, especially trucks and pipelines. Thus, in 1940, the various types of transportation existed in the following ratios: rail, 85.1 per cent; sea and river transport, 12.3 per cent; pipeline, 0.79 per cent; truck, 1.8 per cent; and air, 0.01 per cent. The seven year plan anticipates the following transport ratios in 1965: rail, 71.3 per cent; sea and river transport, 15.6 per cent; pipeline, 6.8 per cent; truck, 6.2 per cent; and air, 0.07 per cent.

As is evident, railway transport in the future will still be basic in the national economy. But as was previously noted, under present conditions, truck transport, pipelines, and aircraft will have the dominant role in military theaters. However, in the interior of the country, it will obviously be necessary to use all forms of transport because none of them can independently ensure the entire requirements of the economy and the Armed Forces.

Railways are used more efficiently in the USSR than in the capitalist countries. For example, although the USSR has less than half the railway mileage of the United States, Soviet railways transport 25 per cent more freight than American railways, because of high efficiency in the use of rolling stock and better traffic organization. By 1965, the freight turnover on our railways will be twice that of the United States, though the ratio of railway transport in the national economy will diminish as a whole.

The role of railways in supplying the Armed Forces will remain very great even with the increase in truck transport, since the delivery of freight from the interior of the country to the military theaters will primarily have to be carried out by rail. For example, during the Great Patriotic War an average of almost 10 per cent of the nation's operating stock of railway cars was required daily for the transport of military freight; and in certain periods, it increased to 23 per cent. There are no reasons to assume that the Armed Forces' requirements for railway transportation will decrease under present conditions. The increase in the role of truck transport for carrying freight to military theaters is not due merely to its efficiency and economy but also to the fact that railways are more vulnerable to nuclear attack and are more difficult to re-establish in operation.

In preparing railway transport for war, it should be kept in mind that a denser railway network can always survive better, since it permits bypassing destroyed areas. Moreover, greater survivability is achieved by creating reserves of railway capacity and by taking measures to ensure the rapid reconstruction of railway lines.

Reserve railway capacity is created not only by increasing the stock of cars and locomotives (steam engines, diesel engines, and electric engines) but also by other measures. Thus, for example, the acceleration of loading and unloading procedures by widespread mechanization is very important, as is also the introduction of containers and standard-size packages, etc., which will cut down wasted space in railway cars and increase their turnover. Another method of increasing the efficiency of rail transport is to increase the weight of the trains and their speed.

Distant bypasses around railway junctions and tunnels are constructed in order to increase the survivability of railways in the most critical areas, especially those leading to military theaters.

When nuclear weapons are used, railways will obviously be subject to destruction, primarily in the regions of bridges, tunnels, and other elaborate constructions which are difficult to restore. Cadres of specialists will be required to repair the damage with the necessary parts and special cranes to restore the structures. Provision must also be made to use railways of different gauges, to prepare wide bypasses into adjoining territories, to prepare transshipment areas, and to create rolling stock reserves in those areas.

The preparation of water transport for war is also very important, since armies, freight, and even naval forces may be transported along internal waterways, not only within the country, but also in allied and enemy countries.

Water transport will be prepared by constructing new ships of high speed and shallow draught (in particular, with underwater fins), the development of wharves and river ports, particularly by providing cranes, and the development of the approaches to ports, and also by the improvement of all the technical and economic properties of this form of transport.

The adaptation of floating facilities for rivers, especially barges, for laying temporary floating railway and automobile bridges and for ferrying is quite important.

The development of motor vehicle transport will not only be important for the Armed Forces in military theaters but also to meet the needs of the economy if railway movement in the interior of the country is disrupted. Motor vehicle transport is less vulnerable than railway transport and, moreover, is not affected by the seasons, which frequently limit the potentialities of water transport.

The increase in motor vehicle transport inevitably calls for the development of highways and facilities for servicing motor vehicles during heavy traffic. Consequently, refueling and repair centers, technical aid centers, etc., will have to be constructed. Thus, it is quite important to develop intercity motor vehicle transport during peacetime.

The improvement of the motor vehicles themselves during peacetime is also important. Even now, all the new motor vehicles have greater fuel capacity, more roadability, mechanical viability, and economy than those of the Great Patriotic War. Their load capacity and roadability are being improved and self-loading and unloading devices are also being developed.

Under present conditions, pipelines for transporting liquid fuel are becoming increasingly important because of their great economy and low vulnerability to nuclear explosions. Whereas, in 1955, our pipelines carried about 14 billion ton/kilometers of liquid fuel, in 1965, it is planned to pump about 200 billion ton/kilometers. In case of war, pipelines can play a major role in transporting petroleum and petroleum products to potential military theaters and to main industrial regions.

The importance of air transport will increase with the production of high-load capacity helicopters, not requiring well-equipped airfields.

The extensive development of different types of equipment to ensure rapid transfer of loads from one type of transport to another is extremely important in the peacetime preparation of all forms of transport for war.

*The preparation of communications* not only includes securing the control of the Armed Forces when war breaks out, but also control of the country as a whole, and particularly of its economy.

To do this, one must create in peacetime reliable control points capable of operating normally during an enemy attack with weapons of mass destruction and capable of ensuring reliable communication between these control points.

The creation of reliable control points involves their proper locations and equipment and the preparation of duplicate facilities provided with modern communication equipment.

Reliable communications to assure the direction of the country as a whole during wartime cannot be considered apart from the peacetime system of communications. Peacetime and wartime communications must be developed on the principle of systematic continuity.

Multichannel radio, radio relay, and underground cable lines should be a basic means of communication in preparing for an enemy nuclear attack. Above ground communication lines passing through major population centers and communication centers must include underground cable bypasses at these points and alternate communication centers.

Important communication centers should be constructed underground and protected from nuclear explosions. These centers should be distributed in a communications network which will allow bypassing in case any of the centers are put out of commission. It is very important to create reserve mobile radio centers to support needed areas.

## Preparation of the Population

The peacetime preparation of the population for war is carried out in three basic directions. These are, first, the political preparation of the morale of the people; second, the preparation of the population to protect itself from weapons of mass destruction and to deal with the aftermath of such an attack, usually called civil defense preparation; and third, the military preparation of the population. These three types of preparation are interrelated and supplementary to one another.

*The political preparation of the morale of the people* is of decisive importance in present-day conditions, since the use of weapons of mass destruction in war imposes exceptionally high and unprecedented demands on the political morale of the population.

The political preparation of morale of the Soviet people for war consists primarily in inculcating in them the spirit of Soviet patriotism, love of the Motherland and the Communist Party, and in instilling in them the readiness to bear any of the hardships of war in the name of victory.

The Soviet people are indoctrinated with the idea of defending their Fatherland and the achievements of the socialist revolution, and with the conviction that the socialist is superior to the capitalist system, and faith in the [possibility of] building the communist society.

In struggling for the peaceful coexistence of the two opposing systems —socialist and capitalist—the Communist Party of the Soviet Union wages an unremitting struggle against bourgeois ideology and morality, against opportunist tendencies in the workers' and communist movements, and against revisionism as the chief danger threatening the unity of the workers' movement. To relinquish or slacken our ideological struggle would be to capitulate to bourgeois ideology and morality, and would increase the danger of war.

Therefore, one of the tasks in indoctrinating the population is to clearly expose the reactionary essence of American policy and its propaganda, which attempts to present "the American way of life" in rosy hues, to pretend that there is a "people's capitalism" that is peaceable and humane, to draw a veil over the aggressive nature of its politics, and to present the preparations for initiating war as a defensive measure.

It is extremely important to convince the people of the justice of the aims which the Soviet Union and the entire socialist camp will pursue in war. The people must be deeply convinced of the unshakable unity of the socialist countries, the wise leadership of the communist and workers' parties, and the economic power of the Soviet Union.

The people must be imbued with a belief in the might of our Armed Forces and with love for them, as well as with faith in the firmness of the comradeship-in-arms of the armed forces of the socialist states.

Socialist internationalism and respect for the peoples of capitalist countries should not weaken our burning hate of the imperialists, whose aim is to destroy by war the achievements of socialism and to enslave the peoples of the socialist countries. Hatred of the enemy should arouse the desire to destroy the armed forces and military-industrial potential of the aggressor and achieve complete victory in a just war.

The political preparation of the morale of the people for war is directed by the Communist Party and the Soviet Government, and is executed by every governmental and public organization in the country, and by the whole system of education and public information. For this purpose all of the instruments of propaganda and agitation are used (the periodical press, science, literature, motion picture films, the theater, etc.).

As the result of socialist transformations and the extensive indoctrination carried out by the Communist Party and the Soviet Government, a new Soviet man is developing in our country, an active builder of Communism, a fervent patriot of the Motherland, and an ardent champion of the new life, ready to make any sacrifices in the name of freedom and independence of his country, and capable of overcoming any difficulties on the way to victory. This new man, possessing a high level of morale and technical training, will be a decisive factor in our victory in case of war.

*Preparation for the defense of the population against weapons of mass destruction* has the following basic features: warning the population in advance of imminent danger, its partial evacuation, building shelters, providing individual means of protection, water, and foodstuffs, the proper instruction of the population, and the creation of a service to maintain order and prevent the outbreak of panic.[6]

---

[6] U.S. ED. NOTE—It is not clear whether reference is made to the existing Soviet Civil Defense Service for Maintaining Public Order and Safety or to a special new organization for this purpose. See Gouré, *op. cit.*, pp. 23, 28, 30.

It is extremely important to warn the population in time of the danger of an attack, since this enables it to take measures to decrease the losses from an enemy attack. Warning should be centralized, comprehensive, and based on extensive use of radios, and particularly of radio broadcasting stations.

Since the military command of the PVO has the most complete picture of the air situation and, consequently, of the threat of an attack to an area of particular importance, it is also obliged to warn the appropriate civil defense agencies which in turn should warn the population.

In warning the population, it is quite important not only to warn it of the threat of attack from the air, but in particular cases also to inform it of enemy nuclear strikes which have already occurred. It is necessary to remember that the explosion of a bomb or missile in any region may, depending upon the direction of the wind, cause dangerous radioactive contamination of a large area. Therefore, for timely warning of the danger of radioactive contamination, it is essential to have a special system of air and surface reconnaissance, using all the data of the meteorological services.

Great importance is now attached to the prior and thoroughly planned evacuation of the population from large cities and border zones during the period when war threatens or during the first days of war.

Because of the inevitable contamination of food and water from an enemy nuclear or bacteriological attack, it is extremely important to prevent such contamination in order to protect the population.[7]

It should be said that water pipes in cities are usually vulnerable to destruction and are not readily adapted to filtering the water of radioactive particles and harmful bacteria. Therefore, with the threat of nuclear attack comes the problem of re-establishing and decontaminating the destroyed water system, which requires extensive decontamination equipment and supplies.

It is very important to teach the population the rules of conduct during an enemy air attack, particularly the simplest medical first aid and self-aid measures.

The effectiveness of the aid to a stricken population will depend to a great extent on how well the necessary order is maintained and panic of the population avoided, since uncontrolled streams of refugees can disrupt the deployment and mobilization of the Armed Forces. The maintenance of order should be entrusted to the militia or, when neces-

---

[7] U.S. ED. NOTE—Soviet civil defense publications and instructions pay a great deal of attention to measures designed to protect food, water, and fodder as well as farm animals from the effects of nuclear, chemical, and bacteriological weapons. Gouré, *op. cit.*, pp. 125 127, 137–138.

sary, to the troops. They should organize and control the movement of all kinds of transport.

All sections of the service for maintaining order and regulating traffic should learn very thoroughly in peacetime what they have to do in case of enemy attack, and they should proceed to carry out their duties without additional orders or commands. To assist the militia and the troops, brigades to maintain order could be organized at plants and offices.

In the maintenance of order it is very important to establish a regimen of operations for all industrial plants, institutions, and transport.

*The military preparation of the population* under present conditions is extremely important, and not only to replenish the Armed Forces during war. A militarily trained population can be enlisted in organized combat against saboteurs and spies, and also against small enemy air and naval landings to carry out sabotage and destruction. Moreover, the population in potential military theaters must be ready for determined partisan operations against individual enemy formations invading our territory.

Consequently, the population should understand as much as possible about modern infantry weapons, antitank weapons, and other military equipment. It should be given some information about the enemy's possible methods of operation so that none of these operations are unexpected and cause confusion.

Whatever measures agencies carry out in the military training of the population for war, an important function will naturally be to teach individuals to protect themselves against the weapons of mass destruction, and to help the injured.

## Civil Defense

The threat of the use of weapons of mass destruction in modern warfare against areas deep in the homeland as well as against troops on battlefields has produced a new form of strategic protection of the state's vital functions, generally known as civil defense. Consequently, all countries have recently devoted considerable attention to the preparation and organization of civil defense. The United States and Britain, for example, have created special civil defense administrations headed by government officials. These administrations directly supervise numerous practice atomic alerts, prepare a large system of antinuclear shelters, and are in charge of the military training of the population.

Civil defense is of particular strategic importance because its effective organization and functioning are a requirement not only for the defense of the home front to a great extent, but also makes possible the mobilization of the armed forces during the initial period of the war.

The basic tasks of civil defense are to assure the necessary conditions for the normal activity of all the country's agencies of leadership during the war, and to assure the effective functioning of the economy. This is achieved by the maximum protection of the population against weapons of mass destruction, extensive aid of all kinds to the victims, and the rapid clean-up of the aftermath of enemy nuclear strikes.

The tasks enumerated above are closely related, and the execution of one considerably aids the solution of the others. But civil defense may employ various methods in solving the problems confronting it. Some civil defense measures are executed by governmental decrees on a national scale, for example, partial evacuation of the population, measures to secure the country's communications and control, the creation of special civil defense troops, etc. Other measures are carried out by decrees of specialized ministries and departments, but again throughout the state. And finally, the execution of a third group of measures is decentralized in cities, industrial plants, and institutions.

Thus, civil defense represents the sum of very diverse measures, whose execution, in different degrees, is the duty of all Party, Soviet, and economic agencies. All the civil defense measures are so interrelated that they cannot be separated from over-all problems in the organization of the direction of the country and its economy.

The civil defense system in the USSR is based on a principle of strictly centralized direction. It is led by the all-union Headquarters for the civil defense of the country. There are, moreover, republic, provincial, and municipal headquarters composed of representatives of different departments. To them are subordinated the following special services: medical, food supply, transport, warning, communication, and others. The staffs organize their own centers of command.

Such organization of civil defense, however, in the event of war, does not relieve the ministries, departments, services, and organizations of the responsibility for ensuring the operation of enterprises and institutions according to a plan, or of the responsibility to ensure that the needs of the population are met and comprehensive facilities provided.

In view of the enormous potential destruction and losses from enemy thermonuclear attacks, a large number of special civil defense formations must be organized to deal with the aftermath of an enemy attack to the homeland. These may be rescue and rehabilitation detachments, medical aid detachments, truck convoys, etc. These detachments should be equipped to travel considerable distances under their own power; i.e., they must have their own vehicles.

In order for the civil defense troops to carry out their missions, it is necessary to station them at a proper distance from large cities and industrial targets.

If the enemy succeeds in carrying out a nuclear, chemical, or bacteriological attack, all civil defense forces with the resources at their disposal will direct their efforts to giving medical aid to the population, extinguishing fires, organizing rescue work and clearing away debris, removing the injured from the zones of destruction, and evacuating the healthy population from zones of radioactive contamination, as well as maintaining order.

The enormous scale of organizing aid of this sort, particularly medical aid, to the population must be kept in mind. Moreover, it should be remembered that in the majority of cases, aid must be rendered from the outside, i.e., by forces and resources from places which have escaped nuclear blows, since the civil defense agencies and the resources in the stricken points will suffer great losses.

In order to render timely medical aid, it is important that all physicians, regardless of their specialization, receive peacetime training in the pathology of the effects of nuclear, chemical, and bateriological weapons. This obviously applies to nurses also.

In order to render aid in case of an enemy bacteriological attack, it is very important to develop in peacetime a procedure for the rapid diagnosis of contagious diseases, and also to determine the regimen of operations for the enterprises, factories, and transport, to organize a system to isolate infected individuals, and to determine the quarantine system.

In summary of the above it should be emphasized once again that in organizing civil defense, centralization, decentralization, and energetic preparation of all measures are very important. It must also be noted that the extent of the civil defense measures executed should be constantly increased.

## U.S. ED. NOTE A: RECENT DEVELOPMENTS IN THE SOVIET CIVIL DEFENSE PROGRAM

[As was pointed out in the Analytical Introduction, the Soviet Union has been actively engaged for many years in developing a civil defense capability. Despite occasional deprecation of Western civil defense efforts by Khrushchev and other Soviet officials, the Soviet civil defense effort has been publicly endorsed by many prominent Soviet military leaders, who view it as an integral part of the Soviet defense posture.

The Soviet civil defense program consists of a large variety of measures, including urban and industrial dispersal, organization of a large civil defense corps, shelter construction, compulsory training of the population, evacuation, and preparation to deal with and recover from the effects of a nuclear, chemical, and bacteriological attack. The Soviet civil defense organization operates under centralized control and is divided into specialized formations and units located at all administrative levels, from the national, republic, and district levels down to cities, villages, factories, and even large public and apartment buildings. It is assisted by military civil defense units. Khrushchev has claimed that the Soviet civil defense organization comprises at least twenty-two million persons.

Construction of various types of shelters to provide protection against the effects of nuclear, chemical, and bacteriological weapons was begun in the early 1950's and appears to have been fairly extensive.[8]

Compulsory training of the population was instituted in 1955 and by 1962 comprised four consecutive training courses totaling 64 hours of instruction, including extensive practical work and exercises. Despite various shortcomings it was reported in 1962 that the "major part of the adult population" had been exposed to some training.[9] Evacuation procedures for the urban population were instituted in 1958. Public training in these procedures was incorporated in the fourth civil defense training course, which was put into effect in 1960.[10]

As noted in the Analytical Introduction, there is some evidence of an internal debate in late 1961 or early 1962, in the wake of Soviet tests of very high-yield nuclear weapons, on the value of the Soviet civil defense program. The acting head of the Soviet Civil Defense Organization, Colonel-General O. Tolstikov, reported in an article: "The development of new super-powerful weapons of mass destruction has given rise among some comrades to mistaken views on the problem of protecting the population, to a skeptical attitude towards the possibility of solving this problem. They are especially doubtful about the engineering-technical [shelter] measures."[11] Tolstikov rejected this criticism and stressed that civil defense was "one of the most important

---

[8] See, for example, Seymour Topping, "A Shelter System in Soviet Hinted," *New York Times,* March 23, 1962.

[9] "Report by the Chairman of the Central Committee of DOSAAF, Comrade D. D. Leliushenko," *Pravda,* May 22, 1962.

[10] For a detailed description of the Soviet Civil Defense Program up to 1962, see Gouré, *op. cit., passim.*

[11] Colonel-General O. Tolstikov, "An Undertaking of Great Importance to the State," *Voennye znaniia (Military Knowledge),* No. 2, 1962, p. 22.

defense activities of the state" and that it was "an inseparable part of the defensive strength of our Motherland."

The controversy was resolved by the time of the meeting in May 1962 ot the All-Union Congress of DOSAAF, the organization charged with the civil defense training of the population.[12] Not only was this congress given special prominence by the attendance of Malinovskii and the chiefs of the armed services, but continued civil defense preparations were given an unusual endorsement in a resolution of the Central Committee of the CPSU. The resolution stated that DOSAAF "must continue" among other activities to "train the population in ways and means of defense against modern means of mass destruction."[13] In a speech to the congress, the chairman of the Central Committee of DOSAAF, General of the Army Leliushenko, stressed the great significance of civil defense "in view of the present international situation,"[14] and the Chief of the Ground Forces and Deputy Minister of Defense, Marshal Chuikov, declared civil defense to be "one of the main elements in the general defense preparation of the country."[15] Subsequently, Chuikov's views were repeated in an article by Lieutenant-General L. Vinogradov, who stated that civil defense measures "will have in truth an enormous significance for the attainment of victory."[16]

As a consequence of the decision of the May DOSAAF Congress to accelerate and expand civil defense training of the population, it was announced on September 30, 1962, that because "the majority of the citizens have familiarized themselves with the effects of such [nuclear chemical, and bacteriological] weapons, and with collective [shelters] and individual means of protection,"[17] a new 19-hour training course would be instituted for the population. The new course was to deal with people's behavior in contaminated areas, comprehensive first aid, evacuation, use of shelters, and various post-attack problems. Current Soviet press reports indicate that the Soviet authorities are making a considerable effort to further develop and improve the Soviet civil defense capability.[18]]

[12] L. Gouré, *The Resolution of the Soviet Controversy over Civil Defense,* The RAND Corporation, RM-3223-PR, June 1962.

[13] *Pravda,* May 23, 1962.

[14] *Pravda,* May 22, 1962.

[15] *Sovetskii patriot (Soviet Patriot),* May 26, 1962.

[16] Lieutenant-General L. Vinogradov, "The 30th Anniversary of Civil Defense," *Sovetskii patriot (Soviet Patriot),* October 7, 1962.

[17] *Sovetskii patriot (Soviet Patriot),* September 30, 1962.

[18] See, for example, the "Second Plenum of the Central Committee of DOSAAF," *Sovetskii patriot (Soviet Patriot),* December 23, 1962.

## ★ 8

# Command of the Armed Forces

### The System of the High Command and Methods of Strategic Command of the Armed Forces in the Most Important Capitalist States during World War II and at Present

Command of the armed forces encompasses the activities of the organs of strategic command in the preparation and conduct of war. The basic problems in this area, taking into account the political aims and character of the war, are to determine the military-strategic aims of the entire war, and its particular stages; to direct the processes of the preparation, mobilization, and strategic deployment of the armed forces; to organize military operations and their comprehensive support.

As the past war demonstrated, the armed forces are properly led in modern warfare only if there is a comprehensive assessment of the political, economic, and military conditions under which the war is prepared and conducted, if the enemy's opportunities and [probable] operations are realistically evaluated, and if the efforts of the entire country and the Armed Forces are mobilized to achieve victory over the enemy. Consequently, the leadership of armed forces should be able to evaluate not only the situation and its possibilities, but also to change it in its own favor. It should be able on a scientific basis to foresee the development of events over a considerable period of time, and to make decisions in good time and execute them resolutely.

The organization and the methods of command of the armed forces have developed differently and are variously organized in different states. However, common to all states is the desire to co-ordinate, as completely as possible, the system and organization with the nature of warfare and to ensure unified political, economic, and military leadership.

In World War II, Hitler completely usurped the direction of Nazi Germany and her armed forces. As Supreme Commander and Chancellor, and after December 1941, as Commander in Chief of the Army, all civil ministries and the higher organs of military command were directly subordinate to him. The higher command agencies included the Supreme Command or High Command of the Wehrmacht (OKW) and the Armed Forces command staff which formally was part of Supreme Headquarters but actually was directly subordinate to Hitler. The Army High Command (OKH) and also the Commander in Chief of the Air Force and the Navy with their staffs were also subordinate to him. The commanders of the army groups at the front were subordinate to the Commander in Chief of the Ground Forces and to Supreme Headquarters.

In general, the system of higher military command, based on duplication and overlapping control, caused serious frictions and could only furnish adequate control as long as military operations were conducted in a situation favorable to Nazi Germany. However, when its armed forces encountered stubborn resistance and, subsequently, blows of growing force from the Red Army, Hitler's command system could not effectively direct the country and the armed forces.

The bloc of Fascist states could not solve the problems of coalition leadership either. During the war this leadership amounted, in essence, to direct military and political dictation to her allies by Nazi Germany. Hitler's numerous negotiations with Mussolini, Horthy, and other leaders of the Axis countries were irregular and unsystematic. Hitler usually made all the decisions himself. Daily diplomatic contact between the Axis countries through ambassadors and military attachés was also poor. Each of Hitler's allies pursued definite aims in the war, and did not wish to include the other in its own plan of operations. The contradictions inherent in blocs of capitalist countries were thus evinced.

In Great Britain, the highest command agency for the country and armed forces was the War Cabinet, which included the Prime Minister (who was Minister of Defense), a lord who was secretary of the council, the Secretary of State for Foreign Affairs, the Chancellor of the Exchequer, the Minister of Labor and National Conscription, the Secretary of State for Home Affairs, the Minister of Supply, and other ministers.

However, in practice it was the Prime Minister who exercised command at the highest level, through staffs of the War Cabinet. Three groups of committees were created to handle questions arising during the course of the war: defense problems; questions relating to the Civil Department, which had jurisdiction over civil defense of the metropolitan area and general economic problems; and committees responsible for the Services and Supply Departments.

The military committee included the Committee of Defense (operational group and supply group), the Joint Staffs' Committees, the Committees of the Chiefs of the Home Front, the Committee of Military Supply, the Joint Planning Staff, and the Joint Intelligence Staff.

The Chiefs of Staff Committee had the most important role in this group; the members of this committee were the Chief of the Imperial General Staff (Chairman), the Directors of Plans for the Admiralty, War Office and Air Ministry, and the Chief of Staff of Combined Operations Headquarters.

In essence, this committee was the principal organ of leadership on a large number of military matters, which were decided at its conferences, co-opting interested persons from other committees; the War Cabinet retained its position as the highest organ only from a jurisdictional point of view, and actually was responsible only for the conduct of foreign policy and for the country's economic condition. The functions of the Chiefs of Staff Committee were supported by the work of the Joint Intelligence Staff, which included the Chiefs of Intelligence of the War Office, Air Ministry, and Admiralty, by the work of the Joint Planning Staff, which consisted of the Directors of Plans for the War Office, Admiralty, and Air Ministry, and also by other staffs.

The Prime Minister who, as noted, also acted as Minister of Defense, commanded the armed forces through several channels. Thus, for example, he personally met with the Chiefs of Staff, participated at conferences of the committees of the Chiefs of Staff, or gave them written instructions; in other cases, he maintained direct contact with the Joint Planning Staff and other committees; sometimes he even corresponded directly with commanders in various military theaters.

In the United States of America, the President was at the head of the armed forces and was, himself, the Commander in Chief. The President commanded the armed forces through his own personal staff, created in wartime, through the Joint Chiefs of Staff, and through the Department of the Army and Department of the Navy.

The President's personal staff aided him, as the Commander in Chief, in the work of commanding all the armed forces during the war.

The tasks of the Joint Chiefs of Staff were: to secure co-ordination of the army and naval forces, co-ordinate the general development and employment of armed forces, to discuss and present to the President for approval the strategic plans for the conduct of the war, and to issue directives to the commanders in the various military theaters. In addition, the committee was responsible for over-all planning of all types of military orders to industry and for the utilization of strategic raw materials in accordance with general strategic policy.

The Joint Chiefs of Staff included the Chief of Staff under the President (Chairman), the Chief of Staff of the Army, the Chief of Staff of the Navy, and the Commander of the Army Air Force.

The President directed the work of the Chiefs of Staff through the chief of his own personal staff, who presided at conferences of the Committee and informed it of the President's directives. Sometimes the President personally intervened in the decisions of the Committee.

The President, as head of the Executive Branch of the United States, and the Commander in Chief of the Armed Forces, was also the chief of all agencies regulating the war economy. An Office of Emergency Management was created in 1940 to handle emergency measures; this office was part of the Executive Office of the President and was directly subordinate to him. It consisted of various bureaus and civilian agencies through which the War Department issued military orders. The Secretary of War, his Deputy, and other representatives of the army participated in directing the office. The war economic agencies were similarly related to agencies of the Department of the Navy.

Thus, the President of the United States, like the British Prime Minister, depended on a rather complex system of various agencies investing them with appropriate powers to solve all problems concerned with war in general.

Coalition leadership of the Anglo-American forces during World War II was executed in the following manner: The Combined Chiefs of Staff of American and British armed forces, with headquarters in Washington, were created in the spring of 1942 to co-ordinate the operations of the armed forces of the two countries.

The Combined Chiefs of Staff were subordinate to the President of the United States and the Prime Minister of Great Britain.

The tasks of the Combined Chiefs of Staff were to develop and carry out strategic plans under the direction of the heads of state of the United States and Great Britain, to determine the military requirements necessary for the execution of these plans, and to distribute military supplies, as well as fill shipping requirements.

To carry out this responsibility, the Combined Chiefs of Staff held regular conferences [in Washington] which the Chiefs of the British Staff could not always attend. They were replaced by the chiefs of the missions [in Washington] of each branch of the armed forces, who [together] made up the Combined Mission Committee of the British Chiefs of Staff. The Chief of the British Mission was a full and equal member of the Combined Committee of the Chiefs of Staff, and participated at all its meetings even when the Chiefs of Staff of all branches of the British armed forces were present.

During the war, the Combined Committee of the Chiefs of Staff met on an average of once a week to solve current problems of strategic planning.

The strategic war plans for the future were approved at conferences of the American and British heads of state, in which the members of the Combined Committee of the Chiefs of Staff and also political advisers participated.

The Combined Committee of the Chiefs of Staff was given the power of strategic command in all military theaters where British and American forces were located. It was directly responsible for the development and execution of operational plans on the European continent and in the Mediterranean.

The British Committee of the Chiefs of Staff directed the execution of the Allied plans in Southeast Asia and in the Middle East. The Atlantic Ocean was divided into a British and an American zone of military operation, and the commander of each naval force was responsible for the operations in his zone. Command of the Pacific operation was completely assigned to the Joint Chiefs of Staff of the American armed forces.

In military theaters where all three branches of the Allied Armed Forces were operating, command was exercised by a supreme commander or commander in chief, to whom was assigned the responsibility of using the combined forces to achieve the general Allied aims, and who was subordinate to the Combined Chiefs of Staff. Actually, in most cases he followed the political and strategic outlook of his own government, which led to friction and differences of opinion. The post of deputy was created to iron out these differences. If the supreme commander or commander in chief was an American, then his deputy was British, and vice versa.

This was how strategic command was organized in the coalition scale, and this was the method of organizing the higher agencies of joint command, the development of coalition strategy, the co-ordination of efforts of the Allied Armies, and also the command of operations in military theaters.

However, these agencies could not always successfully solve the problems confronting them, because of conflicts in the Allies' foreign policies. The conflicts led to a situation in which the strategic decisions of one ally would not be accepted by the others if they found such decisions to vie with their interests. For example, the American plan proposed in August 1942, for military operations against the Axis countries in Western Europe in 1943, called for an invasion of Europe which was categorically rejected by the British, who insisted on an Anglo-American landing in North Africa at the end of 1942. It was also at British insistence that the main Allied forces were directed to secondary theaters of operation in 1943. As is known, the opening of the Second Front in Europe was repeatedly postponed. This permitted the Axis countries, particularly Nazi Germany, to concentrate their main forces in the principal theater of military operations, the Soviet-German front.

There was also lack of agreement within the Allied agencies commanding in the military theaters. The functioning of these agencies of strategic command was seriously hampered by conflicts due to the differences in political and military aims of the Allied countries in each theater, and also by the endeavor of each Allied country to gain a dominant position to achieve more easily its own aims in that area. An example was the Supreme Command in Europe.

Thus, in spite of the fact that the Casablanca Conference in January 1943 decided to assign a British general as the Supreme Commander of Allied Forces in Europe, this post was occupied by an American general. The British government yielded in this matter only after the Americans agreed to open the Second Front in 1944 rather than in 1943, as had been planned previously. However, the British government acknowledged the authority of the Supreme Commander only in the organization of joint operations and over-all leadership, which did not extend to the level of operational questions.

The Supreme Commander of the Allied Forces in Europe was directly subordinate to the Combined Chiefs of Staff in Washington, and maintained contact with the American and British Committees of the Chiefs of Staff. The Headquarters of the Supreme Commander dealt with the most diverse problems, from command of troops to diplomacy and policy. In composition it was quite mixed and cumbersome, containing in addition to military specialists, various political and economic advisers, each with his own opinion on international and political questions. This greatly complicated the work of the Supreme Commander and required that he spend considerable time reconciling plans, making compromises, and smoothing over countless differences of opinion.

As is generally known, the Soviet Union was also a member of the anti-Nazi coalition in World War II. However, the ruling circles in the United States and Great Britain, pursuing their own selfish interests in the war, sought the maximum weakening of the Soviet Union. During the war they delayed in every possible way the fulfillment of the alliance obligations they had accepted, and intentionally prolonged the war by not concentrating their efforts on the main tasks.

But our former Allies, in the conduct of a war against a common enemy, had to concert as a political and military policy with the Soviet Union. Agreements were reached at periodic conferences of the Soviet, American, and British heads of state, with the participation of representatives of the armed forces (the Moscow, Tehran, and Yalta Conferences); by regular correspondence between the heads of state; by dispatching responsible representatives to the Allied countries; and through diplomatic channels.

As we already noted, soon after the end of World War II, the American and British imperialists began to create various aggressive military blocs directed against the Soviet Union and other socialist countries, as well as organizations for the command of these blocs. What these organs of higher military command in the imperialist coalitions represent can be examined in the military and political system of command of the North Atlantic bloc. Its highest political command organ is the NATO Council, which includes ministers of foreign affairs, defense, and finance; if necessary, even the heads of state of the member countries may participate in the work of the Council.

NATO Council sessions are held two or three times a year to discuss general problems, to work out a unified political course and strategy, to determine the total NATO military budget and the particular military budget of each country, to direct the build-up and organization of armed forces, and to handle other problems.

A permanent council directs NATO activity between sessions. It consists of permanent representatives of the NATO countries, at the ambassadorial level, to whom are assigned the appropriate powers to solve current problems.

The highest military agency is the Military Committee, which solves questions of military and strategic planning, the organization and training of armed forces, and other problems. It is staffed by representatives of the Joint Staff of the Chiefs of Staff of the United States and Great Britain and by Chiefs of the General Staffs of other countries in the bloc. The executive agency of the Standing Group consists of permanent representatives from the Committees of the Chiefs of Staff of the United States and Great Britain and from the General Staff of National Defense of France. The permanent group of the military committee actually commands the armed forces of the bloc.

Direct military command of the combined NATO forces is executed by the Supreme Commands for Europe and the Atlantic, by the Channel

Committee, and by the Canada-United States Regional Planning Group.

The chief of these commands is the Supreme Allied Command Europe, which is in charge of the major troop contingents, and naval units and aircraft assigned by the NATO countries.

An American general occupies the post of Supreme Commander of the combined NATO Armed Forces in Europe, and his deputies are representatives of the armed forces of Britain and France. The staff of the Supreme Allied Command consists of representatives of countries in the bloc. A military representative of the United States also heads the staff.

The territory covered by the European Command is divided into the North European, Central European, South European, and Mediterranean theaters of operation. The commanders of the armed forces in these theaters are directly subordinate to the Supreme Commander of all the NATO Armed Forces. Certain armed forces are at the disposal of these commanders in chief, and are combined into army groups, field armies, tactical air commands, air armies, and naval units. Command of strategic air forces, missiles, attack carrier forces, missile-carrying submarines, and nuclear weapons is in the control of the United States and, to some extent, Great Britain.

The Supreme Command of the Atlantic is next in importance. The supreme commander of the combined British and American forces in this theater is also an American admiral. Only one command in the English Channel, which includes air and naval forces placed at NATO's disposal by Britain, France, Belgium, and Holland, is headed by a British military representative.

It is apparent from the entire organization of the NATO military and political command that even during peacetime, the Americans have attained complete supremacy in this major military body and have converted it into their obedient instrument. However, ruling circles in Great Britain, France, and particularly West Germany, have been very persistent in seizing leading posts in NATO. The very same internal conflicts characteristic of earlier coalitions of imperialist states can be discerned in the struggle for NATO posts of leadership.

This is the organization of the political and military command agencies in NATO, which is the most important coalition of imperialist states.

The present organization and functions of higher political and military commands of the armed forces of the most important capitalist states, the United States, Great Britain, France, and West Germany, are generally as described below.

In the United States, the political and supreme military power is vested in the President, who is also Commander in Chief of the Armed

Forces. The President has considerable power to solve military matters. In wartime, his rights are even further extended and the influence of Congress diminishes. The National Security Council, which is subordinate to the President, is the highest agency for the preparation and conduct of war. This council includes the President (Chairman), the Vice President, the Secretary of State, the Secretary of Defense, the Secretary of the Treasury, the Director of Emergency Planning, and the head of the Bureau of the Budget.

The Committee of the Chiefs of Staff and its working agency, the Joint Staff, are technically the President's consulting and working organs for developing and executing strategic plans, but in fact they are the highest wartime strategic commands of the armed forces.

During peacetime, the Secretary of Defense commands all the branches of the armed forces, and he is directly subordinate to the President, as are the Secretary of the Air Force, the Secretary of the Navy, and the Secretary of the Army. The Secretary of Defense is responsible for planning mobilization and strategy, for the organization and utilization of all branches of the armed forces, and for the direction of scientific research work.

The Joint Staff is responsible for developing mobilization and strategic plans, supervising their execution and for operational control of the joint command of the armed forces of the United States in Alaska, the Atlantic and Pacific Oceans, the Caribbean, the European Zone, the air defense of the continental United States, and also special strategic air and naval commands of American forces in the Eastern Atlantic and Mediterranean.

In Great Britain, the Cabinet under the chairmanship of the Prime Minister is in charge of the country's preparations for war, and the wartime command of the country and armed forces.

The Defense Committee, which is subordinate to the Cabinet, determines the general directions in the organization of British armed forces, has direct command over these forces, and also determines the measures to be taken to prepare the country for war. It also is supposed to co-ordinate the activity of all the ministries and departments in organizing the armed forces and preparing them for war. The Committee includes the Prime Minister (Chairman), the Minister of Defense, the Secretary of State for Home Affairs, the Secretary of State for Foreign Affairs, the Defense Minister, the Air Minister, the First Lord of the Admiralty, the Minister of the Exchequer, and other ministers.

The Ministry of Defense, which is subordinate to the Defense Committee, is concerned with the organization of all branches of the armed forces as a whole and each separately, and with military research projects and war production.

The Committee of the Chiefs of Staff is the agency for operational and strategic command of the British armed forces. In peacetime, this committee works out strategic plans that are presented for consideration and approval by the Defense Committee. In wartime, it is called on to issue specific orders in the name of the Defense Committee to Commanders in Chief in various military theaters.

In France, all military power is concentrated in the hands of the President, who is the Supreme Commander of the Armed Forces and also Chairman of the High Council of Defense and of the General Staff of National Defense. The General Staff of National Defense and the Ministry of the Armed Forces are subordinate to the President and Prime Minister.

The Supreme Council of National Defense, as an advisory agency, expresses its opinion on problems confronting the President, the Prime Minister, and other cabinet members. It consists of the Prime Minister, ministers, the Chiefs of the General Staff of National Defense, and inspectors and representatives of other agencies of the armed forces.

The Committee of National Defense solves, on a lesser scale, all problems pertaining to preparing the country for war and to organizing the armed forces. The Committee includes the Prime Minister, the Chief of the General Staff of National Defense, the Minister of the Armed Forces, and representatives of branches of the armed forces.

The General Staff of National Defense develops the plans for war and deploys the armed forces according to the general strategy, determines the trends in further development of the armed forces, observes the military and political situation and informs the President, Prime Minister, and the interested ministers. It also devotes its attention to progress made by the several ministries in mobilizing economic and other resources for military needs.

The Ministry of the Armed Forces is responsible for the actual enactment of measures taken in organizing the armed forces, preparing them for combat, and putting mobilization into effect.

It is essentially the Nazi system of higher military command that has been re-established in West Germany. The Federal Chancellor is the Commander in Chief of the West German Armed Forces during wartime. The Defense Council is his advisory agency. The council includes the Federal Chancellor (Chairman), the Vice-Chancellor and the Minister on Nuclear Matters (Deputy Chairman), and the Ministers of Defense, Foreign Affairs, Internal Affairs, Finance, and Economics.

The Defense Council is called on to develop and make fundamental decisions on all important questions involving the organization of the country's armed forces. It presents proposals to the Cabinet of Ministers for co-ordination of the activities of the higher civil and military departments in the areas of military organization and mobilization.

The Ministry of Defense is the highest agency of command for the armed forces. It consists of the Chief of Staff of the Armed Forces (actually the General Staff), and its subordinate Chiefs of Staff for the ground, air and naval forces, territorial forces, medical troop administration, and a number of departments. The armed forces' main agency of operational command is the Chief of Staff of the Armed Forces (Bundeswehr). It develops the general plans for organizing and employing the armed forces, co-ordinates the activity of the Chiefs of Staff, deals with questions concerning West Germany's participation in imperialist blocs, and directs various militarized organizations in the country.

It is evident from the above that in wartime governmental and military leadership is highly centralized in the most important imperialist states, and that all power is concentrated in the hands of the President or Prime Minister, who is given unlimited authority. The higher government agencies under the President have primarily advisory or consultative functions. Such a system of higher government and military command can easily be used by the most militant imperialist circles to initiate war without the consent of parliaments, and in spite of public opinion.

## The Structure and Function of the Higher Command Agencies of the Soviet Armed Forces during the Civil War, in Peacetime, and in the Great Patriotic War

*The Origin and Organization of the Agencies of Military Command during the Civil War.* The command agencies of the Soviet Union Armed Forces were created together with the new army, an army of workers and peasants, when the economy had practically collapsed, when the masses were incredibly weary of the imperialist war, when counter-revolutionary revolts broke out, [when the Western powers conducted] a military intervention, and when the old army was being demobilized. During the demobilization of the army and navy, the old apparatus of military control fell apart and a new one was created.

These radical changes took place from the very first days of the socialist revolution. On October 26 (November 8), 1917 [new calendar], a decree of the IInd All-Russian Congress of Soviets created the Committee for Military and Naval Affairs. It was given the direction of the military and naval ministries. At the time this committee was created, a special decree of the Congress of Soviets instructed all armies to create provisional revolutionary committees whose responsibility would be to preserve the revolutionary order and the stability of the front.

In December of the same year, the Committee for Military and Naval Affairs was transformed into a Collegium of People's Commissars for Military Affairs. The Collegium of the People's Commissariat for Military Affairs gradually built up an apparatus [where direction was centralized]. Many administrations and departments of the former war ministry were abolished as the old army demobilized, and those administrations and departments that were used in organizing the Red Army were radically changed.

The Soviet of People's Commissars published a decree on January 15 (28), 1918, creating the Workers' and Peasants' Red Army directed and led by the Soviet of People's Commissars, itself, whose head was Lenin.

Direct command and direction of the army was concentrated in the People's Commissariat for Military Affairs and its subordinate agency, the All-Russian Collegium for Organization of the Red Army.

The All-Russian Collegium was responsible for co-ordinating the activities of local organizations who were mobilizing the army, for keeping track of newly formed units, for training and provision of the army with armaments and supplies, for developing new regulations, and for compiling military plans and solving various operational tasks and questions of troop deployment.

The All-Russian Collegium, however, was not able to develop rapidly a sufficiently powerful apparatus to organize a Red Army for all of Russia. Therefore, the enormous task of organizing the Red Army was placed upon the Soviets of Workers, Soldier and Peasant Deputies.

In accordance with the instructions of the All-Russian Collegium, the creation and direction of the Red Army was entrusted locally to the Territorial, Provincial, and Regional Soviets [i.e., Councils], and in the army, to army and corps committees.

All local detachments of the Red Army were created by decree of the Regional Soviets, in co-ordination with the local Soviets, and were completely directed and supplied by them. Military departments were created under each Soviet, from small rural districts to provincial districts, and military staffs for organizing the Red Army were created under the army and corps committees. The military departments of the Soviets included representatives of the Soviets and military staffs. The military staff consisted of representatives of army and corps soldiers' committees.

This system of army command, created on a voluntary basis, was from the very outset the best suited to the existing situation, in which it was extremely important not only to finish with the old army and its apparatus, but also to keep the front from disintegrating completely, to unite the toiling masses—including the soldiers of the old army—into the Communist Party, and to inspire them to defend the conquests of October. This was why such extensive powers for building up the Red Army were granted to the Soviets, as the mass organization of the working classes.

This system of army command was necessary because there were almost no experienced military leaders to aid the young Soviet Republic in organizing its army. The command staff in the army was elected. The relations between the servicemen were regulated by general meetings of soldiers and elective organizations. Naturally, it was not possible to observe fully the principle of consistent centralization in leading and commanding the army. Some local Soviets reserved Red Army detachments for the needs of their countries, districts, and provinces, and only placed them at the disposal of the higher agencies after repeated demands.

The Naval Forces were originally led by the Naval Collegium elected from the delegates of the IInd All-Russian Congress of Soviets. Later, in November 1917, the Supreme Naval Collegium was formed, which directed the work of the Naval Department. In February 1918, the People's Commissariat for Naval Affairs was established. The Supreme Naval Board was renamed the Collegium of the People's Commissariat for Naval Affairs.

The Air Force was originally directed by the Bureau of Commissars, created in October 1917. In December of the same year, the All-Russian Air Force Collegium was established, which was responsible for the creation of aircraft and aeronautical units, their administration, and for the assembly and maintenance of aircraft equipment, and also the selection of a cadre.

At the beginning of March 1918, the Supreme Military Soviet consisting of three persons, a military commander and two political commissars, was created by decree of the Soviet of People's Commissars for the command of all military operations.

At first, the most important function of the Supreme Military Soviet was the organization of operational units or so-called detachments of screening forces along the boundary lines established by the Treaty of Brest-Litovsk, which separated the Soviet Republic from the regions occupied by the German aggressors. Later, the staff and tasks of the Supreme Military Soviet were considerably expanded.

After April 1918, the staff of the Supreme Military Soviet included the People's Commissars on Military and Naval Affairs, a member of the Collegium of the People's Commissariat for Military Affairs, and also military and naval specialists. The People's Commissar on Military and Naval Affairs was Chairman of the Soviet. The Supreme Military Soviet executed the functions of the Armed Forces Supreme Command and was directly subordinate to the Soviet of People's Commissars.

In May 1918, the All-Russian Collegium for the Organization of the Red Army, and several other agencies, were replaced by the All-Russian Main Headquarters, which included the Directorate for the Organization of the Army, the Directorate of Operations, the Directorate of Military Communications, and the Directorate of the army command personnel [officers]. During the same month, the All-Russian Air Force Collegium was replaced by the Main Directorate of the Worker and Peasants Red Fleet. The supply agencies were also reorganized.

The functions of the All-Russian Supreme Headquarters and the central supply administrations were combined with that of the Collegium of the People's Commissariat for Military Affairs. The All-Russian Supreme Headquarters and each of the directorates of the military departments were headed by Soviets composed of a director and two military commissars.

The selection of command personnel was also regularized. The election [of officers] was abolished by decree of the All-Union Central Executive Committee on April 22, 1918. The command personnel, from commanders of individual units on up, were appointed by the People's Commissariat for Military Affairs with the approval of the Supreme Military Soviet.

The organization of troops and the agencies directing them was perfected to repel the counter-revolutionaries and foreign interventionists, who were developing active military operations in the north, on the eastern front, in the Tsaritsyn region, and in the North Caucasus during spring and summer of 1918.

In June of 1918, all the separate detachments of Soviet troops operating against the interventionists and the White Guards in the Volga region, the Urals, and in Siberia were placed under the unified command of the Eastern Front, headed by that Front's Revolutionary Military Soviet. All detachments were combined into regular military units and formations. Five armies, for example, were thus created on that front. There organs directing the troops defending Tsaritsyn and operating in the North Caucasus were basically reorganized. The Military

Soviet of the North Caucasian Military District was created during the
second half of June. The Southern Screening Force was created in
August to guard against violations of the demarcation line by the Germans occupying the Ukraine and to combat the counter-revolutionary
formations of General Krasnov; the Northeastern Screening Force was
created to combat the interventionists and White Guard in the north.
These screening forces were also under the command of revolutionary
military Soviets.

However, it was already evident in August 1918 that the command
of the fronts and screening forces was not unified. Thus, the Supreme
Military Soviet, occupied with the screening forces, lost sight of other
fronts, especially the eastern front. Operations against the Czechoslovaks
in the east and against the White Guard in the southeast were directed
by the operations department of the Moscow District Military Commissariat. The operational command also tried to carry out operational
control of the All-Russian Supreme Headquarters. The areas of responsibility of these agencies were not defined. This confused the command
structure of the troops and weakened the defense of the republic. Urgent
measures were needed to eliminate these shortcomings and to create a
unified central command for the Red Army's combat operations.

On September 2, 1918, the All-Union Central Executive Committee
issued a special decree declaring that the country was a military camp
and establishing the Revolutionary Military Soviet of the [Russian]
Republic as the highest directing agency of the Red Army. As the direction of the army command was centralized in the hands of the Revolutionary Military Soviet of the Republic, the Supreme Military Soviet
was abolished. The Revolutionary Military Soviet was also entrusted
with the functions and rights of the Collegium of the People's Commissariat for Military Affairs, whose members became part of the staff
of the Revolutionary Military Soviet. The People's Commissar for Military and Naval Affairs was the Chairman of the Revolutionary Military Soviet of the Republic.

When the Revolutionary Military Soviet of the Republic was created,
the post of Commander in Chief of all the Armed Forces was also established, to command all ground and naval forces of the army in the field.
The post of Commander of Naval Forces was created under the Commander in Chief, for operational command of the fleets and flotillas.
The Naval Staff was formed at the same time.

A Field Headquarters of the Revolutionary Military Soviet of the
Republic was created to command the military operations of the army
in the field, and a Field Aircraft and Aeronautical Command was

created for the Field Headquarters of the Revolutionary Military Soviet of the Republic, to command air operations.

Along with the Field Headquarters, the All-Russian High Command was retained to execute all orders of the Revolutionary Military Soviet of the Republic concerning the defense of the country, recruitment, deployment and combat preparation of the army, creation of new formations, and regulation of military life.

The Revolutionary Military Soviet of the Republic, like all other departments and institutions, received its orders from the Communist Party's Central Committee. The Central Committee of the Party published a special decree in December of 1918 "On the Policy of the Military Department," indicating that "The policy of the military department, as well as all other departments and institutions, is strictly based on the general directives issued by the Party through the agency of its Central Committee, and is under its direct supervision." *

The Revolutionary Military Soviet of the Republic was a collegial agency of command and was the only agency possessing complete military power. The Commander in Chief could independently solve operational-strategic problems within the directives of the higher agencies of the Communist Party and the Soviet government. However, the Commander in Chief was still accountable to the Revolutionary Military Soviet of the Republic, of which he was a member. All orders of the Commander in Chief had to be countersigned by one of the members of the Revolutionary Military Soviet, without which they were not valid.

The command of the troops at the front was based on this same collegial principle, whose organization continued unchanged.

The Revolutionary Military Soviets of the Northern, Southern, and Caspian-Caucasian fronts created during the autumn and winter of 1918, included a commander, who was a military specialist, and two military commissars. The Revolutionary Military Soviets of the armies were similar. All orders issued by the commanders of the front had to be countersigned by one of the members of the Revolutionary Military Soviet.

The armed intervention of international imperialism against the Soviet Republic demanded the most effective unification of the activities of all the agencies of the Soviet government under the command of a single agency subordinating its activity to the defense of the country. For this purpose the All-Union Central Executive Committee issued a decree in November 1918, establishing the Soviet of Workers and

* *KPSS o Vooruzhennykh Silakh Sovetskogo Soiuza [The CPSU on the Armed Forces of the Soviet Union],* Gospolitizdat, Moscow, 1958, p. 402.

Peasants Defense under the chairmanship of Lenin. This higher agency of command for the country and armed forces was able to achieve more complete and efficient mobilization of all the country's resources and efforts for the successful defeat of internal and external counter-revolutions, and also for the unification of political, economic, and military leadership.

The Defense Soviet was the highest agency for directing the country's defense. It had full command of combat on the fronts, and of all activities of the People's Commissariats and departments for mobilizing all industrial and transport resources behind the fighting lines. The most important areas of activity for the Defense Soviet were provision of foodstuffs, mobilization of transport, industry, fuel resources, and the organization of military supply. The Defense Soviet directed the entire military economy of the Republic. It constantly supervised the activities of the Revolutionary Military Soviets other military agencies.

The Defense Soviet carried out its entire work through its members, who directed the most important departments of the country and bore the responsibility of executing the Defense Soviet's resolutions concerning their own departments. The Defense Soviet did not possess its own apparatus, and depended in all its activities upon the apparatus of the Soviet of People's Commissars and the appropriate departments. Special commissions were created to execute the most important defense tasks of the Republic, and the Defense Soviet sent plenipotentiaries to solve urgent problems on a local level.

Thus, by the end of 1918 an orderly system of central command for the Armed Forces had been organized from top to bottom; it was based on the collegial principle in conjunction with the personal responsibility of each commander.

The most essential feature in this system of command was the complete influence and dominance of the Communist Party in all organs and agencies of the Armed Forces' command. The most striking demonstration of the undivided influence and leading role of the Communist Party was that all the most important questions of military policy, organization and strategic employment of the Armed Forces were solved only by directives of the Central Committee of the Party. This direct influence and command by the Communist Party throughout the entire complex army organization, from top to bottom, was achieved through military commissars and political agencies who relied on the party cells in their activities.

The Central Committee of the Party and the Soviet government constantly analyzed the military situation, determined which front was the most important at each stage of the war, and developed strategic plans for defeating the enemy, at the same time as they concerned themselves with organizing the activity of the rear areas to supply the front.

The command system of the Armed Forces, created in the autumn of 1918, was retained throughout the Civil War with only some changes.

The most important of these changes was the transformation of the Soviet of Workers and Peasants Defense into the Soviet of Labor and Defense. The occasion was the pause in the Civil War after the defeat of the Second Entente Campaign. Some armies were transformed into labor armies to restore the national economy. The Soviet of Workers and Peasants Defense began to expand its economic functions and was transformed by the Soviet of People's Commissars' decree of April 16, 1920, into a special commission under the Soviet of People's Commissars and named the Soviet of Labor and Defense (STO).

The tasks of the Soviet of Labor and Defense were to co-ordinate and strengthen the activities of all people's commissariats and departments in economic construction and the defense of the country.

*Agencies of Military Command during the Period of Peaceful Construction after the Civil War.* After the Civil War ended, changes were made in the agencies of military command throughout the entire period of peaceful construction; these were brought about by changes in the economic, political, and cultural development of the country, the structure of the Armed Forces, and views of the nature of a future war.

A special decree of the People's Commissariat for Military and Naval Affairs of the USSR was published in November 1923, outlining the tasks and functions of the military department and defining more precisely the structure of the central agencies of military administration.

According to this decree, the People's Commissariat for Military and Naval Affairs was responsible for developing and executing the plans and measures for ground and naval defense of the USSR; the organization of Ground and Naval Armed Forces, including territorial troops and their command; the maintenance of the Armed Forces in constant readiness; the direction of the agencies of local military and naval administration; the formation, manning, and training of units of the Workers' and Peasants' Red Army; the political education of the servicemen; provision of the army and navy with all foodstuffs and materiel; registration and conscription of the population for military service; training of command cadres, and the solution of many other problems.

General orders from the People's Commissar or his deputy to the entire People's Commissariat for Military and Naval Affairs were issued as orders of the Revolutionary Military Soviet of the USSR, which was the Collegium of the People's Commissariat for Military and Naval Affairs.

In addition to the People's Commissar for Military and Naval Affairs, who was Chairman of the Revolutionary Military Soviet, the latter included the Deputy of the People's Commissar (who was the Deputy Chairman), the Commander in Chief of all the Armed Forces, and members appointed by the Soviet of People's Commissars of the USSR.

The Commander in Chief of the Armed Forces was the chief of all ground and naval forces. He was independent in all operational-strategic questions within the limits of the authority granted him by the higher agencies. These directives were received through the People's Commissar for Military and Naval Affairs or through the Revolutionary Military Soviet of the USSR.

The Headquarters of the Workers' and Peasants' Red Army was concerned with the solution of problems involving the defense of the country, recruiting, deployment and combat preparation of troops, equipment, conditions of military life, mobilization of the Armed Forces and military registration of the population, and many other problems.

A decree of the central command agencies gave legislative sanction to the organization and functions of the central agencies of command, which were actually exercising these functions by the concluding stages of the Civil War. However, some of them lost their importance during peacetime, and others had to alter their functions and methods of operation.

For example, the post of Commander in Chief was no longer necessary, since this function was very indefinite in peacetime and duplicated the work of other agencies. There was also a need to reorganize the Headquarters of the Workers' and Peasants' Red Army, which could not adequately execute the tasks assigned to it because it was concerned with problems of the defense of the state as a whole as well as with organization of the army's combat training and the daily regimen of the troops.

All this demanded the reorganization of administrative agencies, which was accomplished under the initiative and direction of the Communist Party during the military reforms of 1924–1925.

The post of Commander in Chief was eliminated during the reorganization of the control agencies, and the Red Army Headquarters was put in order.

The main functions of preparing the country and Armed Forces for war were concentrated in the Headquarters of the Workers' and Peasants' Red Army. It directed the general preparation of all branches of the Armed Forces: the army, navy, and air forces. All agencies performing these functions to some extent in other directorates, such as the Directorate of the Naval Forces and the Directorate of the Air Forces, were transferred to the Headquarters of the Workers' and Peasants' Red Army, and the agencies not directly concerned with performing these functions were eliminated from the Headquarters.

Control of military training and inspection, recruitment of army personnel, equipment and troop service, and also the daily regimen of the army was concentrated in the Main Directorate of the Workers' and Peasants' Red Army. The Supply Directorate of the Workers' and Peasants' Red Army had the task of supplying all except special types of provisions to the Armed Forces. The directorates of the Naval and Air Forces retained only the organization of special services for the personnel of these branches of the Armed Forces, their combat and special [technical] training, and the provision of special supplies. Thus the structure of the central agencies was considerably simplified, their functions were more clearly defined, and the number of departments, directorates, and personnel in the apparatus was reduced.

Because of the continued strengthening of the Armed Forces, the increase in their technical equipment resulting from the industrialization of the country, and the development of air forces, the Navy and armored troops required further improvement in the organs of military command.

In June 1934, a decree of the Central Executive Committee of the USSR abolished the Revolutionary Military Soviet of the USSR, and the People's Commissariat for Military and Naval Affairs was changed to the People's Commissariat of Defense of the USSR. The Commissariat of Defense was assigned the command of all branches of the Armed Forces, special troops, and also local agencies of military control (military commissariats). New administrations also had to be created, for example, the country's Air Defense Directorate and Armored Troop Directorate.

The Soviet of People's Commissars of the USSR, in connection with the increased importance of the Headquarters of the Workers' and Peasants' Red Army as the main agency of the People's Commissariat of Defense, issued a decree in September 1935, renaming it the General Headquarters.

The General Headquarters was charged with the development of plans for the operational-strategic employment of all branches of the Armed Forces to defend the country, their provisioning, the preparation of military theaters, mobilization and deployment, the drafting of orders to industry, the creation of reserve mobilization supplies, and numerous other measures related to increasing the country's defense capabilities as a whole.

To further defend the Soviet Union's sea frontiers, the Central Executive Committee and the Soviet of People's Commissars of the USSR adopted a resolution on December 30, 1937 to create the People's Commissariat of the Navy, which was to develop the plans for organizing, arming and manning the Naval Forces, to direct their combat and political training, to organize the PVO in the country's naval theaters, and to prepare cadres and develop naval regulations.

Military Soviets composed of a commander and two members of the Military Soviet were set up in the military districts, fleets, and army by decree of the Central Executive Committee and the Soviets of People's Commissars of the USSR on May 10, 1937. The military soviets of the districts had complete responsibility for constant maintenance of the combat and mobilization readiness of the troops located in the district's territory.

The Main Military Soviet of the Red Army and the Main Military Soviet of the Navy were created in 1938. The military soviets studied the basic problems of organizing the army and navy and preparing them for war.

Thus, for example, the expanded conference of the Main Military Soviet of the Red Army, held by decree of the Central Committee of the All-Union Communist Party (Bolshevik) in April 1940, discussed the lessons of the war with Finland. These discussions resulted in the decree "Concerning measures to be taken for military training and organization of the troops of the Red Army on the basis of the experience of the war in Finland and military experience of recent years." This decree introduced important changes in the nature and methods of training, directing, and organizing the troops. Many administrations of the People's Commissariat for Defense were reorganized; some, including the country's air defense directorate, were changed to main directorates. On the eve of the war the Directorate for Airborne Troops began to be organized.

The Main Military Soviet also recommended the removal of obsolete types of military equipment and the development of new types of weapons, especially aircraft, armored equipment, and communication facilities. The People's Commissariat for Defense and other people's commissariats carried out the resolutions of the Main Military Soviet.

However, everything had not yet been accomplished by the beginning of the Great Patriotic War. For example, the High Command had not been created in good time. There were serious gaps in the organization of communications between the General Headquarters and the fronts. It was considered inexpedient to have the communications unit of the Revolutionary Military High Command provide communication with the front. This communication was to be provided during wartime by the communication lines and centers of the People's Commissariat of Communications. These and other inadequacies made additional measures necessary to improve the military command agencies during the war.

*Agencies of Military Command during the Great Patriotic War.* From the first days of the Great Patriotic War, the Central Committee of the Party and the Soviet government took a number of measures to convert the country into a unified war camp. Military tasks henceforth predominated over all others. The activity of all state agencies shifted to a war footing to render all-out aid to the front. The whole rear area of the country was at the service of the defense. The entire activity of the Communist Party and all state agencies was imbued with a spirit of iron discipline and very strict centralization.

A state of war was declared in the European part of the country by decree of the Presidium of the Supreme Soviet of the USSR on June 22, 1941. On the next day, the Central Committee of the Communist Party and the Soviet government issued a resolution creating a Stavka under the chairmanship of the People's Commissar of Defense, to command the combat operations of the Red Army and Navy.

On June 30, 1941, a joint resolution of the Central Committee of the Party, the Supreme Soviet, and the Soviet of the People's Commissars of the USSR created the State Defense Committee under the chairmanship of J. I. Stalin, who, by acquiring complete state power, unified the military, political, and economic leadership of the country. This act enabled the country's forces to be mobilized rapidly for repelling the enemy.

The State Defense Committee was organized along the lines of the Soviet of Workers' and Peasants' Defense during the Civil War. Like that Soviet, the State Defense Committee was the highest agency of command for the country and Armed Forces. The State Defense Committee made full use of the positive experience of the Soviet of Workers' and Peasants' Defense. To shift the economy to a war footing, plenipotentiaries of the State Defense Committee, People's Commissars, their deputies, and the directors of main committees were sent into the country's rear areas. They performed enormous tasks in mobilizing all the forces of the Soviet nation to repel the enemy and guarantee his defeat.

The State Defense Committee made possible more effective co-ordination of the activity of the Soviet of People's Commissars, All-Union and Union Republic People's Commissariats, as well as all local agencies of Soviet authority, in accordance with the general directives of the Party's Central Committee. Systematic and comprehensive use was made of the country's economic, patriotic, political, and military potential to achieve victory. Duplication of effort among some agencies that had been concerned with problems of defense before the war was also eliminated.

Possessing complete state and military power, the State Defense Committee rapidly and thoroughly mobilized all the nation's forces to create a well-co-ordinated, rapidly expanding military economy. In the very first days of war, industry, transportation, agriculture, and military production were rapidly reorganized. New people's commissariats, directorates, committees and Soviets, and all-union people's commissariats for the production of tanks, munitions, guns, and mortars were created. There were also formed main directorates to organize military industry and materiel reserves, committees to register and distribute labor forces, an evacuation council, and other agencies.

A considerable part of the work of the State Defense Committee consisted in solving problems concerning redistributing manpower in the economy, training qualified labor forces, getting cadres for the most important branches of industry and, particularly important during the entire war, raising the necessary contingents for the Armed Forces.

The State Defense Committee devoted special attention to instilling all Soviet people with an awareness of the extremely great danger menacing our Motherland, with the need to discard peacetime attitudes and to devote full attention to the solution of military problems, to maintain a high patriotic spirit among all the Soviet people, to increase the productivity of labor in all branches of the economy, and also to maintain a burning hatred of the enemy.

Fulfilling the tasks assigned to them by the State Defense Committee, the Soviet people rapidly achieved decisive success in the mass production of arms such as airplanes, tanks, antitank weapons, antiaircraft and heavy artillery, in the production of munitions, uniforms, foodstuffs, and in their delivery to the fronts in time.

The State Defense Committee attached exceptional importance to the development of military equipment.

In this area, the State Defense Committee proceeded from the dialectical proposition that the constant development of weapons produces important changes in the conduct of combat. Therefore, the State Defense Committee and the Supreme High Command, while studying the enemy's capabilities, continually concerned themselves with the design, production, and introduction of the newest weapons into the Armed Forces, with the search for the latest methods of warfare, and with the study of the appropriate organization of each branch of the Armed Forces for the conduct of the struggle.

During the war the organization of the direction of the strategy of the Armed Forces was improved and the most effective methods of its implementation were sought.

As we have noted, the Stavka was in command of the strategy of the Armed Forces from the outset of the war. However, the first weeks of the war demonstrated that, because of the rapidly changing strategic situation and the frequent disruption of communications between the General Headquarters and the operating fronts and armies, the Stavka could not cope with the problems of direct command of the troops. Consequently, the high commands of the northwest, west, and southwest areas were created by a resolution of the State Defense Committee on July 10, 1941. Each of these high commands co-ordinated the operation of several fronts for the accomplishment of a general strategic mission in a specific area.

This decision of the State Defense Committee changed the Stavka of the High Command into the Stavka of the Supreme High Command under the direction of the Chairman of the State Committee of Defense, who was appointed by the People's Commissar of Defense, and in August it was placed under the direction of the Supreme Commander of the Armed Forces of the Soviet Union. Then the Stavka of the Supreme Command was renamed the Stavka of the Supreme High Command. The group consisted of certain members of the Politburo of the Party's Central Committee, the Chief of the General Headquarters, and individual higher command personnel.

During the entire Great Patriotic War, the Stavka was the highest agency of strategic command for the Armed Forces. It was a collegial agency. All the most important decisions were made after the Stavka discussed them with the front commands, the commanders in chief of the branches of the Armed Forces, the service commanders, as well as with other individuals concerned.

The high commands of the various areas created in July 1941 became unnecessary as the front became stabilized and as the operations of the fronts' headquarters improved, so that eventually these high commands were abolished. The Stavka exercised anew direct command of all active fronts and individual armies.

However, it should be noted that during the concluding stages of the war, the High Command of troops in the Far East was created to lead the Armed Forces in the war against Japan, and the fronts, navy, and air forces were directly under this command. The reason was the remoteness of this military theater and its limited strategic importance. The Stavka communicated directly with the Commander in Chief of the Far Eastern troops and the commanders of the fronts and the navy, and supervised the course of operations. The High Command was given complete authority and had the forces, reserves, and all weapons necessary to successfully execute its missions.

Therefore, the main system of command, which proved its effectiveness during the war, was the Stavka-Front system, that is, the direct command of the fronts by the Stavka. The Stavka assigned missions to the fronts, made their supply its concern, and supervised the execution of their tasks. This made it possible for the Stavka to follow the development of military operations continuously, to reinforce the front units with its reserves in proper time, re-establish co-ordination of the front units in case it was disrupted, redirect the main forces of the fronts or of a front, and assign additional or new missions.

When the Stavka was created, there was a reorganization of the People's Commissariat of Defense of the USSR, as a result of which each of its organs had specific functions, thus assuring more effective command and provision of the Armed Forces.

There was also a reorganization of the General Headquarters, a most important agency of the People's Commissariat of Defense, which had become the main working agency of the Stavka. The General Headquarters was assigned to develop plans for strategic operations, to provide for their full execution, to verify the fulfillment of their orders, to develop the organization of the Armed Forces, to supervise the formation and re-establishment of units, to organize operational and strategic shifts of personnel, and to deal with many other questions bearing on the direction and co-ordination of the combat activity of all branches of the Armed Forces on the numerous fronts. The General Headquarters was also required to study and draw conclusions from the experience of the war.

During the reorganization of the People's Commissariat of Defense, the Main Directorate for Activating [New Units] (UPRAFORM) was created. It was responsible for guiding and controlling the activation of reserves (except the Air Forces, the artillery, and the Armored Tank and Mechanized Troops), training of replacements, and the command of reserve and training units. Activation of air, artillery, and tank troop units was carried out by the appropriate directorates in the apparatus of the commanders in chief of the branches of the Armed Forces and the commanders of services.

When the UPRAFORM was created, the useful experience of the All-Russian Main Headquarters in dealing with new formations during the Civil War was taken into account. The UPRAFORM, which essentially provided trained formations for the Stavka to use on the fronts during the Great Patriotic War, relieved the General Headquarters of the extremely complicated functions of activating and training reserves, commanding interior military districts, etc., so that it could concentrate all its attention on the command of the active fronts.

The post of Chief of the Rear Areas of the Red Army was established directly under the Stavka to co-ordinate the operation of the Armed Forces rear. A Central Headquarters of the partisan movement was also created under the Stavka.

The fronts, which were organized at the beginning of the war from border military districts, were the operational-strategic units of the Armed Forces. As in the Civil War, military Soviets commanded the fronts. They were also collegial organs commanding all the troops subordinate to them. As in the Civil War, they were assigned all the functions of the state authority in the areas of defense, maintaining order and state security in localities designated by order of the Presidium of the Supreme Soviet to be on a war footing. The commands at the fronts were agencies for the developing, planning, preparation and all-round support of operations.

Thus, the experience gained during the Civil War helped in the creation of the organs of military leadership and in their activity during the Great Patriotic War, although this was not simply a repetition of the past.

Thus, the magnificent achievements of the Soviet people in the construction of socialism contributed to the successful operation of the State Defense Committee. The Soviet Union was transformed from an underdeveloped agricultural country into a strong industrial power with a strong rear area and with a monolithic multinational Soviet population. In all its operations the State Defense Committee depended on the superiority of the economic system, which permitted the rapid concentration of all the material and morale resources of the Soviet Union for the victorious conduct and conclusion of the war.

In its operations, the Stavka did not simply duplicate past experience. Like the Revolutionary Military Soviet of the Republic in the Civil War, the Stavka was a collegial agency of military command. However, it differed fundamentally from the Revolutionary Military Soviet in organization. As noted previously, the Chairman of the Revolutionary Military Soviet was the People's Commissar for Military and Naval

Affairs, and the Commander in Chief was a member of the Revolutionary Military Soviet. Their decisions were controlled by the Revolutionary Military Soviet.

The organization of the Stavka was completely different during the Great Patriotic War. The combination of the posts of leader of the Party, head of the government, Chairman of the State Defense Committee, Chairman of the Stavka, People's Commissar of Defense, and the Supreme Commander provided the most unified political, economic, and military direction to the Armed Forces.

This type of organization for the Stavka meant further centralization of leadership and the merger of the general leadership of the country with the strategic leadership of the Armed Forces. In this new centralization of political, economic, and military command, the unity of policy and strategy found its most perfect expression, as did the influence on strategy of the economy, whose importance had increased immeasurably during modern war.

*Methods of Strategic Leadership of the Great Patriotic War.* As was pointed out, the Stavka was the collegial organ of the strategic command of the Armed Forces. The most important strategic decisions were adopted on the basis of its discussions.

The Stavka's decisions were transmitted to the commanders of the front troops, fleets, and flotillas as directives from the Supreme High Command. The directives usually indicated the aim of the operation, the forces to be employed in its execution, the area for concentrating the main forces (the main blow), when the plan of operations was to be presented to the Stavka, and the time the operation was to be ready or a procedure for transmitting information that it had started. When carrying out the directives of the Headquarters, the front obtained specific instructions from the Stavka, the commanders of branches of the Armed Forces and service chiefs.

The Supreme Commander personally issued the most important instructions to the commanders of the front troops by summoning them to the Stavka or by sending representatives of the Stavka to the fronts. Specific missions were accomplished by brief instructions sent by the chief of the General Headquarters in the name of the Supreme Commander.

The same procedure was used when the Stavka required reports on the conduct of operations from the military Soviets of the fronts. The front commands frequently presented such reports on their own initiative. The Stavka used these to co-ordinate the operations of the fronts and branches of the Armed Forces and then sent directives to the fronts. Thus, the right to make final decisions in such cases remained with the Stavka. Operational plans worked out by the military soviets of the fronts in executing the Stavka's directives were also subject to confirmation by the Stavka.

This system of assigning missions to the fronts, together with the rigid centralization of strategic command by the Stavka, made it possible for the commanders of the front troops to exercise considerable initiative.

The same practice was also used when the Stavka issued orders directly to armies, bypassing the fronts. This was not a regular practice, and was used only in exceptional cases when the situation demanded rapid action and did not permit delay. Moreover, the Stavka immediately informed the commander of the front troops of the orders it had issued.

As offensive operations developed along the entire Soviet-German front, and when the large-scale operational and strategic aims of the Supreme High Command's plans were accomplished by the co-ordinated, simultaneous operations of several fronts, it became necessary to bring the strategic command closer to the troops to aid the fronts in preparing operations, to co-ordinate their activity, and to supervise the execution of the assigned missions.

For this purpose representatives of the Stavka were sent to the fronts. The working staff consisted of operational groups that included representatives of the General Headquarters, commanders of troop arms, and chiefs of the rear areas and of other central agencies of military administration.

The representatives of the Stavka aided the front commands in carrying out the plans of the Supreme High Command and in making decisions concerning the role and location of one or another front in the conduct of an operation. These representatives also solved problems of operational strategic co-ordination on the spot. However, there were also basic shortcomings in the activity of the Stavka's representatives, mainly where the representatives of the Stavka substituted for the front troop commanders, constricted the initiative of the latter, and reinforced and supplied one front at the expense of other fronts.

The Stavka required different methods of front command primarily because of the difficulties involved in conducting armed combat over a vast area and keeping track of the situations in various areas. Moreover, the Stavka was compelled to aid the commanders of the fronts in commanding the troops.

Consequently, during the Great Patriotic War, the methods of command of the Armed Forces were not constant but varied according to the conditions of battle and according to the experience and skill in the art of command acquired by the commanders of the fronts.

As is generally known, operational units and operational and tactical troop formations of our allies, Poland, Czechoslovakia, Romania, Bulgaria, and Hungary, fought on the Soviet-German front along with Soviet troops, and the troops of the Mongolian People's Revolutionary Army participated in the defeat of Japanese troops in Manchuria. These units were incorporated into Soviet existing front formation, by agreement with the governments of the states that furnished them, and executed their assigned missions under the operational command of the commanders of the fronts. To achieve unity of operation when carrying out operational and strategic missions by joint forces, the Soviet and allied commanders exchanged representatives.

This proved to be a proper method of commanding troops of allied states during the Great Patriotic War.

In summary, it must be emphasized in particular that strict centralization of strategic command of the Armed Forces by the Stavka and flexible leadership responsive to changing situations ensured the successful conduct of a victorious war and the complete attainment of its aims.

## Possible Agencies of Command of the Soviet Union's Armed Forces in Modern Conditions

The positive experience gained in commanding the country and Armed Forces during the Great Patriotic War is relevant to present conditions. However, it is essential to take into account the fundamental changes that have occurred in the nature of war and in how it breaks out and is fought; these changes are caused by the development of completely new weapons and other factors.

The principles of the unity of leadership of the conduct of the armed struggle in its political, economic, and military aspects, and the centralization of the direction of the Armed Forces, [modified] by an intelligent combination of collegial and personal responsibility of the [military] leaders, have been developed in our country and their validity confirmed in practice. These principles are obviously quite applicable to present conditions.

The whole country and the Armed Forces will be led in wartime by the Central Committee of the Communist Party of the Soviet Union, possibly with the organization of a higher agency of command for the country and Armed Forces. To this higher agency of command may be delegated the same powers the State Defense Committee held during the Great Patriotic War; its presiding officer may be the First Secretary of the Central Committee of the Communist Party of the Soviet Union and head of the government to whom the functions of Supreme Commander in Chief of all the Armed Forces may be assigned.

The concentration of the leadership of the country and its Armed Forces within a single higher political agency of governmental control, as in the past war, is an essential condition for the victorious conduct of war in case the imperialist aggressors initiate it. Only an organic relationship between the leadership and the Armed Forces can assure the most effective employment of the national scientific and technical attainments, and the full mobilization of material and political resources and their correct employment to attain victory.

Such is the general outline of the agencies of military and political command for the country and Armed Forces in a modern war.

However, the division of the world into two opposing socio-economic systems means that a future war will be a coalition war. Consequently, this poses the problem of command on a coalition scale.

To successfully repel an attack and completely break up the aggressive plans of the imperialists, it is obviously essential to unify the political, economic, and military forces of all the socialist countries, to organize mutual support and to mobilize all their economic, human, and military resources, to establish a single military, political, and strategic plan for the entire war and for its particular stages, and to achieve complete unity in the leadership of the combined armed forces.

The highest political agency for co-ordinating all the efforts of the socialist countries during war may be the Political Advisory Committee created according to the Warsaw Pact.

The higher military command may operate by co-ordinating the activity of the higher military agencies of the Allied countries who are commanding in various military theaters.

Operational units including armed forces of different socialist countries can be created to conduct joint operations in military theaters. The command of these units can be assigned to the Supreme High Command of the Soviet Armed Forces, with representation of the Supreme High Commands of the Allied countries. In some military theaters, the operational units of the Allied countries will be under their own supreme high command. In such cases, these units can be commanded according to joint concepts and plans of operation, and by close co-ordination of troop operations through representatives of these countries.

## The Role of the Military Commander in Directing Armed Forces

Marxism-Leninism, which has revealed the role of the people in creating history, and the role of the political organization in leading the masses, vigorously refutes the attempts of bourgeois ideologists to explain all the events of a war by the actions of individuals.

By idealizing individuals, imperialist ideology attempts to instill a feeling of obedience in the masses, to make them believe their fate depends on the actions of these individuals, to undermine the faith of the masses in their own strength, to distract them from the solution of urgent problems of the class struggle, and to prepare obedient tools for war. The true meaning of various military events is distorted and every possible effort is made to mislead the broad masses or to conceal from them the true reasons for war, military defeats, and failure.

This was particularly evident in the bankruptcy of the command of the former Nazi German Army. As long as the Nazi army was successful, particularly in wars against economically and militarily weak countries, all bourgeois theorists extolled Hitler in every possible way, emphasizing in particular his qualities as an outstanding political and military leader. However, after the Nazi war machine had been shattered by the Soviet Army, and especially now, when the Bonn revanchists have again set their course on initiating a third world war, western military theorists, particularly in West Germany, claim that all the defeats in the war were the direct result of Hitler's personal qualities, his incompetence in military affairs, his unwillingness to follow the advice of the army commanders, etc.

Such assertions are nonscientific, since they do not put the role of the individual in the context of the development of the social and political system, the nature of the war, and the conditions under which it is waged, and do not take into account the factors influencing the course and outcome of the war.

Criticism of subjective and idealistic views from a scientific point of view, however, does not minimize the actual role of the leaders, including those of military commanders. In evaluating the role of the people as the makers of history, Marxism-Leninism does not deny the importance of the individual, but gives a scientific basis for the correct understanding of the activity of a leader. In any social organization where collective action is in the forefront, authority and subordination are necessary. Unqualified denial of authority in general, and in military affairs in particular, means disorganization, dispersion of strength, and undermined discipline.

The history of human society provides no examples of a class asserting its authority without leaders capable of organizing and directing the movement. There are also no examples of armies lacking definite organization, and led by inexperienced military leaders, successfully waging war against an army led by an experienced military leader. However, the will of the military commander and his activities are not absolute [in determining the course of events].

In executing his role he does not act apart from the masses, nor do the military personnel oppose his authority, but he acts in inseparable harmony with them.

Contrary to the assertions of bourgeois ideologists, the history of past wars convincingly demonstrates that a military leader can lead an army successfully only if the war aims, operations, and the views of the leaders are comprehensible to the people. For example, Napoleon could only appear as an outstanding general within the specific context of the French Revolution. His armies were victorious mainly because they pursued the goals of a new class. Napoleon's armies differed radically from feudal armies, being the armies of emancipated bourgeoisie and peasants. Their new strategy, tactics and organization, in the words of Friedrich Engels, was "a military expression of this emancipation."

The leaders of the Soviet Armed Forces are representatives of the Communist Party and the Soviet government who carry out Party policy expressing the basic interests of the entire Soviet people. This is why the bond between the command cadres of our army and the people is inseparable and why the people trust and respect them so much. This is what distinguishes Soviet leaders from the military leaders of the armies of capitalist countries. A military leader of the Soviet Armed Forces enjoys the confidence and support of his subordinates, not only because he is chief, but primarily because he represents his people, who trust him to indoctrinate, train, and lead Soviet soldiers into battle, and protect the Motherland with weapon in hand from any imperialist encroachments.

In accordance with the tasks assigned by the Communist Party for strengthening the defensive power of the socialist states, the leaders of the Soviet Armed Forces directly guide the organization and development of the Armed Forces, including their provision with modern military equipment and arms—above all with nuclear and missile weapons—and organize the indoctrination and training of the Armed Forces' personnel.

The Soviet Armed Forces have achieved great success in carrying out these missions during recent years: the personnel have completely mastered the techniques of modern warfare and can use them competently to solve various problems. The quality of the operational, combat, and political training has improved, and the level of combat readiness of the army and navy has sharply increased. Our military command has played a substantial role in achieving these successes.

Modern warfare, which aims at conclusive results, given the increasing scope, and the dynamism of military operations, makes extremely high demands on military leaders. The present-day military leader must not only have an excellent knowledge of how war is waged, but also a profound understanding of the laws of social development, the objective laws governing modern warfare, and the ability to command troops according to these laws and with a careful assessment and utilization of the country's economic potential. In carrying out his plans, the military leader of today depends more than ever on the materiel requisites for waging war provided by the economy of the country. The effectiveness of military plans and the correct selection of methods and forms of warfare and operations depend greatly on the ability of the military leader to take sober and thorough account of the actual opportunities for conducting war, and to use them skillfully.

These requirements can really be fulfilled only in a socialist system, which provides unlimited support to the army by the people. A military leader of the Soviet Armed Forces has opportunities in commanding his troops that no military leader of a capitalist state has ever had or now has. These opportunities derive from the superiority of our social system, which is distinguished by continuous and systematic development of all branches of the socialist economy, and by the political unity of the Soviet people with the Communist Party, and the Soviet government.

Generals and officers of the Soviet Armed Forces are not mechanical executors of the plans and will of their seniors. While understanding that an order is law, they execute it with deep awareness [of its purpose]. The initiative and creative command of the generals and officers of our army was one of the most important reasons for the successful accomplishment of the strategic and operational plans during the Great Patriotic War. This remarkable quality of our military leaders has been steadfastly developed by the Communist Party. The Communist Party and Soviet government have always highly valued and supported military commanders who exhibited bold and intelligent initiative.

However, it would be incorrect to suppose that the capitalist generals and officers do not have the necessary qualities, or that they are untalented, and that this to a certain extent predetermines that their plans will be adventuristic and their tactics incompetent. The capitalist armies are by no means lacking in capable officers and generals, but for the most part they are from the privileged class, are intimately associated with the bourgeoisie, and therefore are faithful servants of capitalist monopolies, active agents of their aggressive policies, and represent a military caste separated from the people. This naturally determines their ideology and views, which are alien to the masses and limit their potential as military leaders.

The strength and greatness of our command cadres lie in the fact that in executing the policy of the Communist Party, they subordinate their entire activity to the noble aim of defending the achievements of the great October Socialist Revolution, and that they are supported by the initiative of the personnel of the Soviet Armed Forces and by the entire people. Closeness to the army masses helps our commanding cadres to improve and develop the military art, draw the necessary theoretical conclusions, and make correct generalizations.

The command and political cadres of the Soviet Armed Forces, which have been reared by the Communist Party, proved during the Great Patriotic War that they are capable of successfully and responsibly solving problems of any complexity. Our military leaders, who have been raised on the ideas of Marxism-Leninism, have thoroughly mastered the advanced Soviet military art and have imparted the necessary qualities to the Soviet troops, skillfully combining courage with the art of commanding troops on the battlefield.

The success of the Soviet Supreme High Command in carrying out bold and extensive strategic plans during the Great Patriotic War was the result of the creative efforts of many generals and officers, the heroism of the Soviet soldiers on the battlefields, and the toilers in the rear areas. As the war demonstrated, the operational and strategic missions were not planned and carried out by individuals, but were the result of collective creativity. Centralized command of the troops does not exclude, but rather presupposes, the use of collective creativity. Consequently, the successful execution of operational and strategic plans during the Great Patriotic War was not only the result of the activity of the Stavka, but also of the commands of the fronts, armies, units, and their headquarters.

The Communist Party always has been and is particularly concerned with problems of training and educating military cadres on all levels During the years that the Soviet Armed Forces have been in existence, the Communist Party has trained and promoted many talented officers and generals.

The military leaders of the highest rank, just as all command and political personnel in the Soviet Armed Forces, possess high morale and combat qualities. Utterly devoted to their people, the socialist Motherland, and the Communist Party, they are capable of commanding troops in battle under the most complex conditions of missile and nuclear war.

At the present stage, great and responsible tasks confront the command cadres of our Armed Forces. The increased power of the army and navy, because of the introduction of nuclear and missile weapons, makes new demands on the training of command personnel and all others. The military command will be required to possess exceptional skill in performing their functions, flexibility in control of troops, creative and competent solution of problems arising from rapidly and radically changing situations, and also the ability to foresee how military operations will develop.

In training the personnel of the Armed Forces, the main task of the commanders is to teach them to operate effectively in the conditions of nuclear and missile warfare.

The successful execution of these missions will guarantee the further increase in the combat capability of the Armed Forces and their preparedness to frustrate the aggressive plans of the imperialist states.

## Agencies of the Communist Party in the Armed Forces and the Principles of Party and Political Work

*The leadership of the Communist Party is the main source of the might of the Soviet Armed Forces.* The leadership of the Communist Party of the Soviet Union is the main source of the might of the Soviet Armed Forces and the basis of their ideological training, organizational make-up, and all-round preparedness.

Soon after the victory of the great October Socialist Revolution, the Central Committee of the Party under the direction of Lenin began the great task of creating an army for the world's first state of workers and peasants. In doing this, the Communist Party had to proceed along new, unknown paths, because our Party had no ready theoretical concepts or practical experience to follow. The Communist Party and its leader, V. I. Lenin, worked out the theoretical concepts of the tasks of the Armed Forces in the socialist state and defined the principles for organizing the Red Army. It was necessary to create a new military organization appropriate to the aims of the socialist revolution, to the tasks of protecting the Soviet state, and capable of solving the problems of defense. It was also necessary to work out the principles of armed defense for the young socialist state.

A profound and thorough exposé of these concepts is to be found in V. I. Lenin's numerous addresses and works, in the resolutions of the Congresses, the decrees of the Central Committee of our Party, and also in the resolutions of the government pertaining to the defense of the Soviet state.

The ability of the leadership of the Communist Party and its Leninist Central Committee to rouse, mobilize, and organize the working class and the enormous mass of working peasants to do battle with the enemies of the revolution was a decisive factor in the victories of the Red Army in the Civil War. The Central Committee headed by Lenin directed the entire struggle to repel the armed assaults on the Soviet Republic. All questions of the conduct of the war, deployment of forces, supply, armaments, and operational and strategic planning were decided by the Central Committee of the Party. The Communists entered the army in response to the call of the Central Committee of the Party. During the Civil War, 300,000 Communists fought in the ranks of the Red Army, or 65 per cent of the entire Party, which attests to the exceptionally important role of the Party in the leadership of the army. Everywhere—in the rear, on the front, and in the underground in enemy-occupied territory—the Bolshevist Party together with the people led a gigantic battle ending in the victory of the Red Army in the Civil War.

After the end of the Civil War, the Central Committee of the Party devoted its entire attention to transforming the Red Army into an advanced, highly equipped and trained army, responsive to the defense needs of the socialist state and the requirements of the conduct of war. The main directions to be taken in the development of the Soviet Armed Forces were defined in the decree of the Central Committee of the Party on July 15, 1929, "On the state of defense of the USSR." The Communist Party's main tasks at this period were to re-equip the forces and to create the necessary military and technical base for the defense of the Soviet Union. At the same time, the Central Committee of the Party approached the task of creating a sufficiently powerful Air Force and Navy and further enlarging the technical arms. This decree of the Central Committee outlined the course to be taken in providing the Soviet Armed Forces with technical equipment. The Communist Party followed this course during all the subsequent years.

As a result of the energetic activity of the Central Committee of the Party, which mobilized the working class and engineering, technical and scientific personnel for development and production of military equipment, the Soviet Armed Forces obtained various types of armament and military equipment during the prewar Five Year Plans.

Throughout the entire history of the Armed Forces, the Central Committee of the Party demonstrated particular concern for the training of command and political cadres. The decrees of the Party's Central Committee and the Soviet government placed the main emphasis on improving the ideological and political education of the command cadres, raising the level of their military and technical training, reinforcing unity of command, increasing the unity of the command and political personnel, studying and correctly employing trained cadres, preparing reserves of officers, etc. One of the Party's most important measures in preparing command and political cadres was the creation of a network of military schools. By decree of the Party Central Committee and the Soviet government, six military academies were opened in 1932 (mechanization and motorization, artillery, engineer, chemical, electrical engineering, and transport). The number of students increased considerably, and the network of military schools was expanded, primarily in the technical areas.

Because of the increased demand for military cadres during the second Five Year Plan the Central Committee of the Party again expanded the network of military schools, creating the Military-Economic Academy and the Academy of the General Staff. The Academy of the General Staff was assigned the training of higher command cadres for the Armed Forces. In addition to the creation of military academies, the network of military schools was extended.

The efforts of the Party Central Committee in the training of cadres yielded remarkable results. Every year the Armed Forces were reinforced by highly qualified command and political cadres.

As the result of all this work performed by the Communist Party and the efforts of the Soviet people in the successful execution of the plans for socialist construction, the Soviet Armed Forces became a modern and well-prepared force possessing a well-trained command cadre.

The surprise attack by Nazi Germany confronted the USSR with a very severe test. The first months of the war were especially difficult when the Red Army, under the blows of superior enemy forces, was compelled to retreat deep into the country.

The Communist Party inspired and organized the Soviet people and its armed forces against the predatory Nazis. It directed all efforts to organize the armed defense of the Socialist Motherland and determined resistance to the fascist aggressors and their defeat.

As in the Civil War, the Central Committee of the Party directed the entire organization of the defense of the socialist state. The Party's Central Committee overcame enormous difficulties in mobilizing the forces of the Party, the people, and all the resources of the Soviet state to achieve victory over the aggressor.

The Communist Party exhibited its leadership in the most diverse areas of the country's economic and military activity, in the Armed Forces (primarily in the activity of the Party's political agencies and Komsomol organizations), and also in the personal example of the Communists. The Communists called into the army were sent to the most difficult and dangerous sectors of the front, where there was a need for bold and courageous individuals who could organize the masses and set a personal example for the soldiers in the execution of any mission.

A resolution of the Central Committee of the Communist Party of the Soviet Union sent approximately 48,000 leading Party, Soviet, trade union, and Komsomol workers to reinforce the Armed Forces within the first months of the war. Almost one-third of the members and candidates of the Party Central Committee were on the fronts during the Great Patriotic War. Prominent Party and Soviet government figures were assigned command functions in the Armed Forces.

Hundreds of thousands of Communists, those mobilized and volunteers, were sent to the front. Almost all the Party organizations in regions near the front joined the ranks of the army. At the end of 1941, there were approximately 1,300,000 Communists in the Red Army. In 1942, the Armed Forces contained more than two million Communists, or 54.3 per cent, and by the end of the war, about 3.4 million, or 60 per cent of the entire Party. The Lenin Komsomol became the Party's fighting assistant. During the very first days of the war, 900,000 Komsomol members poured into the ranks of the army.

The Communist Party roused and rallied behind itself the entire Soviet people in the struggle against the predatory Nazi Germans, deployed and strengthened the Soviet Armed Forces, and organized the activity of the country's rear areas to supply the front with everything necessary. Thus, the most important prerequisites for victory over Nazi Germany and its satellites were fulfilled.

During the very first days of the war, the Central Committee of the Party performed an enormous task of organization in shifting the country's economy to a war footing. This was complex and difficult. The work was complex because it was carried out during major military setbacks, the withdrawal of our troops deep into the country, the evacuation of industry from the country's western regions to the east, and when skilled labor was in very short supply. It was necessary to develop industry and military production within a very short time, in new and sometimes in completely uninhabited regions.

Because of the measures adopted by the Party, the tasks of shifting the country's economy to a military footing and organizing military production in facilities evacuated to the east were successfully executed. During the second half of 1942, the re-equipment of the Red Army with modern military equipment was completed.

The Central Committee of the Party daily dealt with the questions of developing new weapons, equipment, and munitions. Some of the new weapons and equipment developed by Soviet designers and mass produced were tactically and technically superior to the arms of the Fascist army.

As a result of the organizational work of the Central Committee of the Party, the Armed Forces were continuously reinforced with fresh forces and military equipment. Our army was converted into a cadre army; it acquired the necessary combat experience and learned to use all the rules of the military art to defeat the enemy.

During the postwar period, the Communist Party and its Central Committee have been in direct command of the Armed Forces and have been constantly concerned with their further development. All the most important problems of the organization and military and political training of the Armed Forces are discussed at the Presidium of the Central Committee and the Council of Ministers of the USSR. Recognizing that, as long as imperialism exists, the danger of the initiation of aggressive wars will continue, the Communist Party considers the protection of the Socialist Fatherland, the strengthening of the defense of the USSR, and the might of the Soviet Armed Forces to be the sacred duty of the Party and the entire Soviet people, and also as the most important function of the socialist state.

The Party does everything necessary to provide the Armed Forces with the most modern weapons—atomic and thermonuclear weapons, missiles of all ranges, and all forms of military equipment and weapons —to ensure that the Armed Forces are an efficient and well-co-ordinated organism, are highly organized and disciplined, and are exemplary in executing the tasks assigned to them by the Party, government, and people, and are constantly ready to deal a devastating blow to imperialist aggressors and to defeat an enemy who dares encroach on the Soviet Motherland. Unity of command is a most important principle in the organization of the Soviet Armed Forces.

The Party is constantly concerned with strengthening the unity of command in the Soviet Armed Forces and devotes special attention to training command, political, and technical army and navy cadres devoted to Communism and recruited from the best representatives of the Soviet people. Emphasizing the important role of command personnel in strengthening the Armed Forces, the Central Committee of the Communist Party of the Soviet Union, the Council of Ministers, and the Presidium of the Supreme Soviet of the USSR stated in an appeal to the Soviet troops on the 40th Anniversary of the Great October Socialist Revolution: ". . . Our greatest wealth is the remarkable military cadres who are boundlessly devoted to the Motherland, Communist Party, and Soviet government, who are courageous and manly, who know the newest combat equipment and can use it skillfully under the most complex conditions of modern warfare." *

*Party and Political Agencies in the Armed Forces and Their Working Principles.* The leading Party agencies of the Communist Party involved in party and political work in the Armed Forces are political agencies whose activities are entirely guided by the Program and Rules of the Communist Party of the Soviet Union, the decrees of the Party Congresses, its Central Committee, and the Soviet government.

Political agencies were established in the Armed Forces during the first days of the organization of a mass regular army. During the entire existence of the Soviet Armed Forces, the Communist Party has continued to manifest unremitting concern for the improvement and strengthening of political agencies and army party organizations, because it considers party and political work to be one of the most important areas of activity in the Soviet Armed Forces, and the party and political agencies are considered to be inseparable components of the Soviet Armed Forces' organizational structure.

The army and navy's party and political apparatus were created and perfected with the growth of the Armed Forces. The duty of the political agencies and party organizations is to instill qualities of high political morale in the Red Army soldier and commanders.

The party and political work in the army and navy were first directed by the All-Russian Bureau of Military Commissars, and then by the Political Department created under the Revolutionary Military Soviet of the Republic to replace the All-Russian Bureau, by resolution of the VIIIth Party Congress in March 1919. In May of that year, the Political Department was changed to the Political Directorate of the Revolutionary Military Soviet (PUR). The PUR had at its head a member of the Party Central Committee who also had the rights of a member of the Revolutionary Military Soviet of the Republic. This emphasized the strict party character, high purpose, and responsibility of the Red Army's higher political agency and placed its activities directly under the Party Central Committee.

The creation of the Political Directorate was extremely important in guiding the organization of military forces, the activity of the Red Army's political agencies and party organizations, and raising the level of party and political work among the troops.

Inasmuch as they were agencies of the Communist Party in the army,

---

* *KPSS o Vooruzhennykh Silakh Sovetskogo Soiuza* [*The CPSU on the Armed Forces of the Soviet Union*], Gospolitizdat, Moscow, 1958, p. 402.

and the direct executors of its policies, the political agencies played an important role in the victorious outcome of the Civil War.

In evaluating the role of the army's political agencies during the Civil War, M. V. Frunze stated: "The Russian Communist Party was indisputably the organizer of our victories. This was made possible by the creation of a network of political agencies encompassing the army from top to bottom and welding it together by a single outlook and state of mind. Therefore, the honor of organizing victory belongs to our political agencies." *

In addition to creating political agencies, the Party took measures to further strengthen the army's party organizations, improve their leadership, reinforce their role and influence on the masses of Red Army soldiers, and work out firm principles for co-ordinating the political agencies and party organizations with the commanders. These problems were solved concurrently with the tasks of developing command cadres from workers, peasants, and intelligentsia who were militarily best prepared and loyal to the Party, and concurrently with the strengthening of unity of command.

The enormous and fruitful work performed by the Communist Party in strengthening the organization of the Armed Forces, improving their equipment and in training command cadres dedicated to communism, together with the results of the socialist transformations in our country and the indoctrination of the Soviet people, enabled the Central Committee of the Party to establish unity of command in the Armed Forces.[1] This was one of the most important problems in the development of the military organization.

The commanders were made completely responsible for all aspects of the military and political life of the troops. This practice contributed to further strengthening all party and political work. Thousands of commanders began to participate in the direct organization of party and political work, which became more intimately related to the troops' daily assignments.

The commanders with undivided authority were able to direct skillfully the work of the party organization, relied on them daily, and successfully executed the task of further increasing troop combat readiness and improving the training of the personnel.

---

* M. V. Frunze, *Izbrannye proizvedeniia* [*Selected Works*], Vol. II, Voenizdat, Moscow, 1957, pp. 121–122.

[1] U.S. ED. NOTE—Unity of command (*edinonachalie*) is the Soviet term for the complete authority of the military commander on military questions. Establishing the precise areas of responsibility of purely military and political officers has always been a problem in the Soviet Armed Forces. As the following pages show this problem has not yet been fully resolved.

The Communist Party is constantly concerned with the strengthening of unity of command in the Armed Forces. Present-day conditions and the nature of a future missile and nuclear war require firm and continuous control of the troops, courage, initiative, and independence of the commanders of all ranks. They must be prepared to assume complete responsibility for the accomplishment of their missions and for the unquestioning execution of orders by subordinates. This is possible only with unity of command.

While strengthening unity of command and considering it to be one of the most important principles in the organization of the Soviet Armed Forces, the Party continues to devote unremitting attention to increasing its own organizational and administrative influence on the entire activity and life of the Armed Forces, not only through commanders with individual authority and military Soviets, but also through political agencies, and party organizations.

The Central Committee of the Party directs the party and political work in the Armed Forces through the Main Political Directorate of the Soviet Army and Navy, which functions as a department of the Central Committee of the Communist Party of the Soviet Union. Under the Main Political Directorate there is a party commission, whose staff is approved by the Central Committee of the Communist Party of the Soviet Union.

The party and political work in military districts, troop formations, and fleets is directed by the corresponding political directorates. It is directed by political departments in the armies, flotillas, corps, divisions, and brigades. Under all the political agencies there are party commissions that are elected at the appropriate party conferences.

The Minister of Defense and the Chief of the Main Political Directorate (because of the special character of the Armed Forces), rather than have them elected, appoint all the political agencies up to and including the political departments of large units according to the organization established by the Central Committee of CPSU.

Party committees elected at party conferences direct the party and political work in central directorates of the Ministry of Defense, in military schools, in scientific research institutions, as well as in the headquarters of military districts, troop formations, PVO districts, military establishments, and some other institutions.

The creation of party committees has increased the activity of Communists in solving vitally important problems, has expanded the bond between party committees and all Communists, has increased the responsibility of party organizations as a whole, and has further improved the entire system of party and political work in directorates, institutions, and schools.

During their existence, the Soviet Armed Forces' political agencies have traveled a glorious path. Although they have undergone organizational changes, their aims and tasks remain unchanged. They played a great role in the achievement of historical victories by our Armed Forces over numerous imperialist aggressors, and have successfully executed their tasks of strengthening the Armed Forces during the present time.

The most important work of the political agencies and party organizations of the Armed Forces is the daily, unremitting establishment of the Communist Party's undivided influence in all aspects of Armed Force life and activity; insuring the unity of military training and political education, its continuity and purposefulness; the combination of collegial [military] leadership and high personal responsibility of leaders to the Party in the work entrusted to them; criticism and self-criticism; and a close relationship of the party and political agencies with the broad masses of Communists and nonparty members.

The Communist Party's influence on all aspects of Armed Force life and activity is the fundamental working principle of the political agencies and party organizations. This principle follows from the very essence of party and political work, from the Leninist concept that the military organization of our country cannot be considered separate and apart from the construction of the communist society.

This concept is clearly reflected in the new Program of the Communist Party. The program points out that the military organization is based fundamentally on the leadership of the Armed Forces by the Communist Party, and on strengthening the role and influence of party organizations in the army and navy.

Thus, the party and political work carried out by the Party in the Armed Forces is an inseparable part of the varied activity of the Communist Party. The practical party and political tasks stem from the Party's general struggle for the triumph of Marxist-Leninist teachings, for strengthening the security of our Socialist Motherland and the entire socialist camp, and for the victory of the forces of peace over the forces of aggression. Party and political work serves as a major instrument in creating political consciousness and high moral qualities in the Soviet soldier—selfless devotion to the Party and government, manliness and courage, initiative, steadfastness, a high degree of discipline and performance, and the ability to withstand the rigors of army life.

In their entire activity the command, political agencies, and party organizations must rally the personnel of the Armed Forces around the Communist Party, its Leninist Central Committee and the Soviet government, and must instill in the troops a spirit of high personal responsibility to the Party and the state in guarding the freedom and independence of the Soviet people and the state interests of our Motherland. The entire system of party and political work must be directed toward firm and consistent execution in the Armed Forces of the policies of the Communist Party.

Accordingly, the organization of party and political work in the Armed Forces is based on resolutions of the Central Committee of the Communist Party of the Soviet Union and the Soviet government, orders and directives of the Minister of Defense and the Chief of the Main Political Directorate of the Soviet Army and Navy. The practical activity of commanders and chiefs of political agencies and party organizations is directed by the "Regulations of the political agencies of the Soviet Army and Navy," and by instructions approved by the Central Committee of the Communist Party of the Soviet Union. The content of the party and political work in each specific case is determined by the tasks confronting the troops.

As organizer, leader, and inspirer of the Soviet Armed Forces, the Party strictly prohibits any violation of this principle and firmly condemns attempts to minimize the importance and role of party and political work. This is evident in the resolution of the October Plenum of the Central Committee of the Communist Party of the Soviet Union in 1957, "On the improvement of Party and political work in the Soviet Army and Navy."

The October Plenum of the Central Committee of the Communist Party of the Soviet Union occupies a particular place in the life of the Soviet Armed Forces. The decisions of this Plenum are important in that they re-established the Leninist principle of command of the Armed Forces, decisively improved the conditions in the army and navy, aided in promoting solidarity of the forces and increased unification of the activities of command and political cadres, and created the conditions for improving party and political work.

As a result of the measures taken by the Central Committee of the Party, the party organizations were ideologically and organizationally strengthened, and there was a noticeable increase in their activity and militancy in solving all the most important problems.

The decisions of the Plenum aided the unification of the efforts of commanders, political agencies, and party organizations in their activity to further reinforce the unity and organic relation between military education and political training.

The most important principles of party and political work are the continuity, unity, and purposefulness of military education, and political training. The honoring of this principle is a most important obligation of commanders with undivided authority, political agencies, and party organizations. It will ensure to the maximum extent the further increase in the combat potential of the Armed Forces and their constant readiness to frustrate the aggressive plans of the imperialists.

In emphasizing the importance of these tasks, N. S. Khrushchev stated at the reception of graduates of military academies in November 1957: "The further increase in the combat potential of the army and navy is the general task of all Communists, commanders and political workers. This great state task can only be fulfilled if there is friendly and co-operative work between commanders and political workers to improve the education and the training of the soldiers and the combat readiness of the troops, and only if there is further improvement of unity of command and the improvement of party and political work in the army and navy." *

The collective solution of problems in party and political work is of great significance.

It permits a more comprehensive and complete solution of vitally important questions, makes it possible to overcome the excesses of administration in the solution of problems of party and political work in the leadership of lower political agencies, and in party organizations, and prevents errors connected with excessive administration. This presupposes close communication between the leader of the political agency and his working apparatus, between the secretary of the party committee and the members of the bureau and party committee, the collective determination of ways and means to solve urgent problems of political and party work, the discussion of plans and results of work, etc.

However, the collective decision of problems of party and political work by no means diminishes the personal responsibility of the leaders of political agencies and party organizations for the quality of the work in all areas of the life and activity of the troops. Each leader bears personal responsibility to the chief (commander) of higher political and party organizations for the political condition and morale as well as military discipline of the personnel, for combat training, and for the quality of the party and political work as a whole.

Combination of collective decisions with personal responsibility ensures a high sense of ideals and principles in the activity of political agencies and party organizations, that is, a Bolshevist intolerance for the smallest deviations from Marxism-Leninism, for any distortions whatever of the party policies and directives, and for any other shortcomings. A high sense of ideals and principles is the primary directing

---

* *Pravda,* November 26, 1957.

factor in the activity of the political agencies; in solving all questions, they place the interests of the Party and state foremost.

Such direction in the activity of the political agencies is inconceivable without honest criticism and self-criticism.

The Communist Party has always viewed criticism and self-criticism as a powerful means to strengthen its ranks and has never been afraid to openly acknowledge its mistakes. V. I. Lenin stated: "The Party of the revolutionary proletariat is sufficiently strong to criticize itself openly, to acknowledge its mistakes clearly and call a spade a spade." * He also noted that "by analyzing yesterday's errors, we thus will learn to avoid the errors of today and tomorrow." †

V. I. Lenin demanded the extensive development of criticism and self-criticism in all areas of our life and activity, including the army. He devoted particular attention to the daily aspect of "life in the factory, village, and regiment, where everything is being built anew, and where there is a demand for increasing attention, publicity, social criticism, and extirpation of the bad, and appeals to learn from what is good." ‡

The new Program of the Communist Party of the Soviet Union again emphasizes the importance of criticism and self-criticism as indispensable conditions for the ideological and organizational strength of the Party itself, the unity and solidarity of the Party ranks, the comprehensive development of democracy within the Party, and the corresponding activation of all the Party's forces to strengthen the bond with the masses. During the construction of communism, the Party poses the task of maximum development of criticism and self-criticism as a tested working method and a way to detect and correct errors and inadequacies, and for the proper education of cadres.

By virtue of the special organization of the Soviet Armed Forces, only the orders and directives of commanders are not subject to criticism. All other aspects of troop life and activity should be subjected to healthy party criticism and to self-criticism. Fundamental criticism and self-criticism makes it possible to reveal to a maximum the deficiencies in the education and training of troops, military discipline, and activities of political agencies, and it aids commanders with undivided authority to take advance measures to eliminate these inadequacies.

The close relationship of political agencies and party organizations with the masses will make it possible to grasp all aspects of combat and political preparation of the troops, to reveal and eliminate inadequacies, and, most important of all, to reveal their causes. Consequently, daily

---

* V. I. Lenin, *Sochineniia* [*Works*], Vol. 21, p. 150.
† V. I. Lenin, *Sochineniia* [*Works*], Vol. 26, p. 32.
‡ V. I. Lenin, *Sochineniia* [*Works*], Vol. 28, p. 80.

communication with the masses is a most important principle for their work.

In general, educational training and purposeful leadership are unthinkable if no close communication exists with the people. The inevitable results will be ignorance of the real state of affairs, disorganization and drifting, blind action and tardy measures to rectify inadequacies as well as other blunders and failures.

Daily close contact between political agencies and the masses is accomplished by various methods; conferences, meetings of the most active members, general meetings, periodic reports of the Party agencies to Communists, personal communication between the leaders and rank-and-file Communists, through periodicals, radio, television, etc. This relationship is enhanced by Party and Komsomol organizations, Party and non-Party activists, and the army and navy social organization.

However, no matter how this connection is established, its content remains the same—strengthening the party influence in all aspects of troop life and activity, and improvement of the forms and methods of party and political work to further increase the might and constant combat readiness of the Armed Forces.

The comprehensive political and organizational activity of the Communist Party of the Soviet Union and the extensive development of party and political work in the army and navy were some of the most decisive factors in the historical victories of the Soviet Armed Forces during the Great Patriotic War, and also ensure their high combat readiness under modern conditions. The political agencies and Party organizations play an important role in all these successes. Their painstaking and constant efforts in the midst of the army masses have helped to consolidate the Armed Forces, which now are the most powerful in the entire world.

The political agencies and Party organizations should consciously scrutinize all aspects of troop life and activity, continuously carry out political and organizational work among the personnel, and campaign for exemplary behavior among communist and Komsomol members in the execution of their military duties. They must reinforce unity of command, elevate the authority and role of commanders as organizers of battles and operations, and develop and improve their command capabilities—their will, exactingness, initiative, and executive abilities; they must also develop a spirit of conscious obedience and respect for commanders among the personnel, and train them to aspire to manifest creative initiative in executing military missions, which will thus ensure the further increase in the power of the Armed Forces of the Soviet Union and their preparedness to repel any imperialist sallies.

# Conclusion

A ny truly scientific theory reflects the objective laws governing the various phenomena of social life. Soviet military theory, which is just such a theory, reflects the laws of war as an armed struggle in the name of the interests of the most progressive social class—the proletariat. Consequently, in this work the study of the various aspects of war could not be in the nature of an objective investigation. Although war, as a two-sided process of struggle, has a number of objective features, the authors as representatives of the Soviet Armed Forces naturally could not consider these features from the position of an outside observer, but always started with the Marxist-Leninist concepts of the essential nature of war in the modern epoch, its causes, and how it starts.

According to Marxist-Leninist dialectics, objective evaluation of the various phenomena of social development means that the investigator cannot be neutral, but is always the representative and proponent of the ideology of his class.

Lenin stated: "For the first time in the history of the world struggle, the army contains elements which do not carry the banners of a despised regime, but who are guided by the idea of the struggle for liberation of the exploited." * Only a firm conviction in the triumph of these ideas permits the correct evaluation of so complex a phenomenon of social life as war, and permits the most valid definition of the content and tasks of military strategy.

---

* V. I. Lenin, *Sochineniia* [*Works*], Vol. 26, p. 421.

In the study of any branch of military knowledge, including military strategy, the subject of the investigation is of great importance. War, military operations on a strategic scale, and armed forces as the main instrument of war have always been the subjects studied in military strategy. In investigating them, military strategy not only studies the experience of past wars and the general principles and rules formulated from them, but also predicts the character of the war of the future. This is the essence of military strategy.

Consequently, in addition to considering general and theoretical questions of military strategy related to its content and place in the general system of military knowledge, in addition to the laws governing the armed conflicts, and in addition to the determination of the main categories of strategy, etc., this book devotes considerable attention to modern warfare, its nature, and how it breaks out and is waged. In the majority of cases all these questions were considered in conjunction with the potential enemy's views on future warfare.

The military and historical experience of the past has been used in writing this book. However, the authors have not attempted to give a comprehensive picture of all past wars and the development of military strategy during various epochs, inasmuch as history for the sake of history is of little value. The experience of past wars was only used to demonstrate various propositions and also to confirm new laws and phenomena of armed combat whose origin could be traced to past wars.

What conclusions can be drawn from this work as a whole?

As was demonstrated, the development of military strategy is based upon the experience gained from wars and military operations on a strategic scale, from directing warfare and armed forces in the preparation and conduct of armed combat. This experience has proved to be a source for understanding the phenomena of war and has led to the formation of strategic views which gradually were organized into a definite system.

Each newly arising social and economic system made its contribution to the development of military strategy and determined its features. Moreover, the main factor determining the nature of military strategy has always been the material state of society and the economy of one or another state.

With the appearance and development of the capitalist system of production, military strategy came to depend heavily upon the economy. There was an enormous increase in productive forces; the militaristic aspirations of the capitalist states increased, and mankind entered the epoch of imperialist wars.

This produced an aggressive capitalist ruling class policy which guided the development of military strategy. The aggressive tendencies of world capitalism were especially striking after the victory of the Great October Socialist Revolution in Russia and the appearance of the world's first socialist state. In modern times, when the aggressors have at their disposal powerful new weapons, these tendencies have become an enormous danger to peace. Force is becoming the chief weapon and instrument for the attainment of major aims in the policies of the modern imperialist states. Thus, in spite of the bourgeois ideologists, the Leninist proposition that war is a continuation of the politics of classes and states, especially by violence, not only remains true at the present time but has been even more strikingly confirmed.

The class essence of bourgeois military strategy lies in the fact that it serves the reactionary aim of preparing war to destroy the most progressive social system—socialism—and to prevent the inevitable development of mankind along the road to communism.

Soviet strategy is superior to the military strategy of the imperialist states because it serves the most advanced social system and defends the achievements of the workers of the entire world.

The class nature of Soviet military strategy is defined by Soviet military doctrine, that is, the views that the socialist state adopts on war, its attitude toward war, the nature and methods of conducting war, the organization of its Armed Forces, and the preparation of the country for war. Soviet military doctrine views war as the inevitable product of imperialism and believes that war will disappear totally only with the destruction of imperialism. At the same time, the Communist Party has concluded that war is not fatally inevitable during the modern epoch, when political and economic opportunities have been created to prevent world war, even if imperialism continues in parts of the world. These opportunities are due primarily to the military might of the socialist camp, which has now become an insuperable obstacle to the initiation of a new world war by the imperialist madmen.

The imperialist states are preparing a new world war, employing to this end all the best achievements of science and technology and all the means that modern capitalist industry can produce.

The theory of Soviet military strategy is also based on the achievements of socialist industry and on the development of Soviet science and technology, which is the most advanced in the world.

However, although from the technical point of view the capitalist and socialist armies have many common features, and although bourgeois military strategy also has much in common with Soviet military strategy, nevertheless the class political aims of the capitalist and socialist armies differ fundamentally.

The military strategy of the imperialist states, serving the interests of the bourgeoisie, is directed toward the preparation of *war* as a means for solving international problems. Soviet military strategy prepares *for war* in order to defend the conquests of the workers and to defeat the aggressor.

Moreover, Soviet military strategy proceeds on this assumption about the nature of a future war, and the most likely methods for its initiation and conduct.

The nature of war in the current epoch is determined by economic, political, geographical, and purely military factors. Such great changes have taken place in these factors since the last world war, that a future war can by no means be compared with World War II.

In addition to the vast political changes which have taken place in the world since then, and the unparalleled increase in productive forces, the modern epoch is characterized by the appearance and development of unprecedented weapons, particularly missiles and nuclear weapons.

Consequently, a future world war will primarily be a missile and nuclear war. The enormous destructive powers of the new weapons, the unlimited spatial scope of war, and the inevitable involvement of the majority of the earth's population in the sphere of destruction means that a new world war, if the imperialists start it, will inflict incalculable deprivation and suffering on mankind. It is difficult even to imagine the magnitude of the destruction and the human losses in such a war.

The initial period of the future war will be of critical importance. In this period both sides will endeavor to achieve maximum results, applying the greatest possible efforts. Consequently, the most important factor determining the duration of the war will not be the time during which the war is conducted, but the effectiveness of the efforts made at its very beginning. Thus, the duration and intensity of the war must be measured by two standards, as it were: the duration of the war as a whole and the effectiveness of employment of forces and resources within a definite interval of time.

The more effectively a state uses the weapons and forces accumulated before the war, the greater the results it can achieve at the very beginning of the war and the more rapidly victory can be achieved. At the same time, each state must obviously take into account the possibility of a protracted war, for which it is necessary to prepare potential forces.

The character of modern war as a war in which great masses of troops participate is quite consistent with the foregoing. Consequently, there is an intensive build-up and development of armed forces in all highly developed countries of the world. This development is mainly determined by the economic potential of the countries, and their capacity to produce nuclear weapons and highly efficient, complex military equipment.

The probable nature and methods of waging a future war have had a strong influence on the development of armed forces. Consequently, the directions of their development, organizational structure, and equipment are selected to conform to the requirements of a modern war.

The morale and political preparation of armed forces have acquired considerable importance in the conduct of modern warfare. The socio-political nature and class character of the armed forces of the socialist and capitalist states determine the different directions they take in educating and training personnel, and in their principles of organizing and recruiting armies.

The capitalist armies are obedient tools in the hands of the monopolistic bourgeoisie and serve reactionary and inhumane aims. Predatory and grasping aims are alien to the Soviet Armed Forces. Their entire training is based on principles of preservation of peace, assertion of equal rights, and respect for the independence and sovereignty of all countries and peoples.

Moreover, it is impossible to ignore the fact that the capitalist and socialist armies are technically equipped in much the same fashion, since their weapons and technological development are subject to the same general, objective laws.

In establishing the principles for the conduct of war, the authors have depended upon historical trends in the development of weapons, taking into consideration the modification of weapons by various political, economic, and geographic factors. Wars during the epoch of imperialism were primarily used as examples.

The forms and techniques of modern warfare are in many respects determined by the most likely techniques that will be used by the imperialists in initiating a future war, and by their military plans and preparations.

The techniques of conducting war in general represent an aggregation of the forms of military operations: nuclear and missile strikes for the simultaneous destruction of enemy military and economic potential, the destruction of strategic nuclear weapons, and the disorganization of military and governmental control; military operations to defend the country and armed forces from enemy nuclear strikes by missiles and aircraft; military operations in ground theaters; military operations in naval theaters; and probable types of military operations in space.

Because the imperialist aggressors have devoted considerable attention during recent years to studying the possibilities of military operations in space and through space, Soviet military strategy must also study the possibilities opening up in this sphere of military operations.

Determination of the nature of war, the directions of the organization and development of armed forces, and the techniques for conducting a future missile and nuclear war make it possible to discover the basic directions to be taken in the preparation for war. The preparation of the country for war consists of preparing the economy, the armed forces, and the population. Under modern conditions, questions of advance organization of civil defense are highly important; these are assigned a special section in Chapter VII, although they also comprise one of the aspects of preparing the population.

Leadership in the war and of the armed forces is the function of higher military-political leadership, which differs in different countries depending on the governmental and social system and the traditions created over centuries. However, the functions of these agencies indeed have much in common. The system by which leadership of the country and the armed forces is organized changes continuously under the influence and impact of external and internal conditions in the state. It is difficult to say now exactly how this system will be organized in a future war. Consequently, the authors have depended basically upon the experience gained in leading armed forces in past wars.

Recognizing that military affairs do not stand still but constantly develop under the influence of various conditions, the authors have attempted as much as possible to anticipate and outline some prospects in the development of the various branches of military strategy.

At the same time, it is important to recognize that the propositions expressed in this work depend on the appraisal of the political and economic conditions of today. Consequently, they must not be considered invariable and eternal. Only a creative approach based on Marxist-Leninist dialectics will enable the Soviet command cadres to correctly understand and employ the various conclusions and recommendations of this work.

MILITARY STRATEGY
Moscow, Voenizdat, 460 pp.

Editor Colonel B. N. Morozov
Cover by artist N. A. Vasil'ev
Technical editor E. K. Konovalova
Proofreader E. L. Kazhdan

Submitted for composition 12.3.62
Approved for printing 24.5.62
G-82252
Format 60 x 90 1/16—28 3/4 printer's sheet
28.75 usl. printed sheet = 28.555 uch. published sheet
Publication No. 5/4326     Number of copies printed 20,000     Order No. 117
BZV No. 6-62

Printing Plant No. 2 of the Military Publishing House
of the Ministry of Defense of the USSR.
Leningrad, D-65, Dvortsovaia Pl. 10
Price 1 ruble 60 kopeks

ВОЕННАЯ СТРАТЕГИЯ
М., Воениздат, 460 с.

Редактор полковник *Морозов Б. Н.*
Переплет художника *Васильева Н. А.*
Технический редактор *Коновалова Е. К.*
Корректор *Каждан Е. Л.*

Сдано в набор 12.3.62 г.
Подписано к печати 24.5.62 г.
Г-82252
Формат бумаги 60×90 1/16 — 28 3/4 печ. л. —
28,75 усл. печ. л. = 28,555 уч.-изд. л.
Изд. № 5/4326     Тираж 20000     Зак. № 117
БЗВ № 6—62 г.

2-я типография Военного издательства
Министерства обороны СССР
Ленинград, Д-65, Дворцовая пл., 10
*Цена 1 руб. 60 коп.*

# Glossary

DIRECTION [*napravlenie*]—In Russian is used to describe an active area or sector of the front, rather than a direction of movement as "the direction of the main effort," "offensive operations in several directions" or "concentration of troops in the main direction." In this translation the term "area" has been used wherever appropriate.

FRONT [*front*]—In its most frequent use the term refers to a military organization equivalent to the Army Group in American terminology, as in "Northwestern Front." However, it may also be used to refer to the front lines in general.

FRONTLINE AIR FORCE [*frontavaia aviiatsiia*]—Tactical air force attached to and operating along the front. In this translation the terms "frontline air force" and "tactical air force" have both been used.

GREAT PATRIOTIC WAR [*Velikaia Otechestvennaia Voina*]—Also called the "Great Fatherland War." The Soviet term is used to refer to Soviet participation in the Second World War in the period 1941–1945. Soviet authors on occasion use the term "World War II" to describe the 1939–1941 period when Germany was fighting only the Western powers and the Soviet Union was neutral. Thus Soviet writers often talk of "World War II and the Great Patriotic War."

MAIN BLOW [*glavnyi udar*]—The major concentration of forces and efforts in an offensive operation.

MISSILE-NUCLEAR [*raketo-iadernoe*]—When used to characterize war, as in "missile-nuclear war," the term is defined in Soviet literature as meaning: "that the principal means of armed combat, the main means of destroying the enemy will be nuclear weapons, while the basic means of delivering them to target will be missiles." When the term is applied to weapons, as in "missile-nuclear" weapons, it usually means missiles with nuclear warheads. In this translation the term "missile" is used to describe missiles with nuclear warheads, except when the nuclear character of the weapons is stressed, in which case "missile and nuclear" is employed.

NATIONAL PVO [*protivovozhdushnaia oborona strany*]—The Air Defense Command and forces charged with the protection of the Soviet Union from air, missile, and space attacks. These forces are equivalent to the U.S. Continental Air Defense Command and are distinct from the air defense troops used for the protection of the combat forces.

OPERATIONAL ART [*operativnoe iskustvo*]—In contrast to American usage which distinguishes between strategy and tactics, Soviet military science is divided into three components: strategy, "operational art," and tactics. Soviet preference is for a narrower use of the term "strategy," than is usual in the United States. The Soviet concept of "operational art" falls within the category of topics covered by the American term "strategy" and is somewhat similar to the old concept of "grand tactics." Thus according to the Soviet definition, "operational art" deals with the planning, organization, command, and control of operations by army groups or armies. "Tactics" refers to operations by subordinate units such as corps, divisions, and smaller units. In this translation, the Russian term "operational" will be retained where appropriate since there is no English equivalent for it.

OPERATIONAL MISSILE [*operativnaia raketa*]—The distinction between strategic, operational, and tactical missiles, is uniquely Soviet. The distinction is based both on the character of the missile and on command and control over them. Strategic missiles are under the control of the Strategic Missile Forces which are directly subordinated to the Soviet High Command, and include intercontinental as well as medium and intermediate-range ballistic missiles. Operational missile troops are subordinated to army group and army commands and will in most instances have tactical missiles.

OPERATIONAL REAR [*operativnyi tyl*]—The area behind the front lines under the control of the commanders of army groups and armies.

PVO [*protivovozdushnaia oborona*]—Russian abbreviation for air defense forces, which include antiaircraft troops and fighter aircraft units. They are also charged with antimissile and antisatellite defense. The term "PVO" is retained in this translation.

REAR [*tyl*]—The Russian term refers not only to the area immediately behind the front lines, but, depending on the context, is also used to describe the entire territory of a country, or zone of interior. Sometimes the term "deep rear" is used to refer to the area of a country more remote from the battle zone. In the present translation *tyl* will be rendered either as "the rear" or as "homeland."

STAVKA—The General or Supreme Headquarters of the Soviet Supreme High Command.

STRATEGIC FRONT [*strategicheskii front*]—Soviet term used to describe the front lines where a breakthrough can achieve strategic results, i.e., results affecting or determining the course of the war. The term may be used to refer to a major sector of the front lines or to the battle front as a whole.

STRATEGIC REAR [*strategicheskii tyl*]—Soviet term used to describe the rear area behind the strategic front where the support units and facilities required for strategic operations are located. The term may also be used to describe a major portion of the country employed in supplying and servicing the front.

# Appendix I

CRITIQUE OF SOVIET MILITARY STRATEGY
by General of the Army P. Kurochkin,
*Red Star,* September 22, 1962

Soviet military scientific thought has always paid a great deal of attention to questions of military theory. In the last few years a number of major works have been published on the theory of combat and operations. For a long time, however, no such works have been published on the highest level of the military art—strategy. The last major work devoted to problems of military strategy in general, A. Svechin's *Strategy,* was published as far back as 1926.

That is why publication of the book, *Soviet Military Strategy,* written by an authors' collective under the leadership of Marshal of the Soviet Union V. D. Sokolovskii, is a very welcome event. This substantial, valuable work of scientific research not only fills a known gap in our military-theoretical literature, it also represents a remarkable contribution to the development of the theory of the military art.

The work is composed of eight chapters. They review in detail all the major problems of strategy. Stressing the class nature of bourgeois and Soviet military strategy, the authors outline the interrelation between military strategy, politics, economics, and the morale-political factor, and reveal the essential nature of military doctrine and how it dominates military strategy. The book reviews, in detail, the essentially reactionary nature of the military strategy of the contemporary imperialist states—aimed at a third world war that they are preparing. The authors outline the path along which Soviet military strategy will develop.

A large part of the book is devoted to a profound, substantial analysis of the concrete questions that come under the heading of military strategy: the character of contemporary war, the organization of the armed forces, how war is waged, the preparations of the country for repelling aggression, and the leadership of armed forces.

On the whole the organization of the book can be termed successful. The book's contents also deserve attention. It establishes a whole series of new conclusions and propositions as they apply to the conditions of contemporary missile and nuclear war.

The historic XXIInd CPSU Congress made an outstanding contribution to the theory of Marxism-Leninism and to one of its components— the Marxist-Leninist teaching on war and the army. The CPSU Program and the CPSU statutes, the reports, and the concluding speech of N. S. Khrushchev profoundly illuminate many aspects of our party activities aimed at strengthening the defense capacity of the Soviet state and protecting the socialist countries against imperialist aggression. The well-known decision of the fourth session of the USSR Supreme Soviet of the fifth convocation marked another development of Soviet military theory. The basic tenets of Soviet military doctrine as formulated in the materials of the XXIInd CPSU Congress and the fourth session of the USSR Supreme Soviet were the basis for the work reviewed here.

Using these propositions as a basis, the authors analyze the military strategy of the imperialist states with great force and conviction and expose the aggressive nature of imperialism, primarily that of American imperialism, stressing the consolidation under the latter's aegis of all imperialist forces against the Soviet Union and other socialist countries.

The mightiest military power of the capitalist world—the United States—exerts political and military pressure on its partners in military blocs and leads them along the path of preparing aggression against the socialist countries. It constantly expands its military potential and rearms its forces with the newest weapons and equipment. Its calculations are based on the preparation of mighty and technically well-equipped armed forces ready for a surprise attack. Such an imperialist strategy can at any moment lead to a war with the most modern weapons.

In contrast to imperialist strategy, which is thoroughly reactionary and aggressive in spirit and content, Soviet military strategy, as the authors emphasize, serves the most advanced and progressive social regime. Its efforts are not directed at preparations to attack anyone, but at protecting our country and other socialist countries against imperialist aggression. Hence, working out means to reliably repel a surprise nuclear attack by an aggressor is the main problem of Soviet military strategy.

Basing themselves on a firm historical foundation, the authors explain in detail how strategic views on the character and methods of armed struggle have changed in the Soviet Army, and how the art of strategic leadership has been perfected. They show how the Communist Party and its Central Committee led the way in determining the political goals of the strategy and leadership of the Armed Forces. The book states that in the Civil War and the Great Fatherland War the party Central Committee was the battle staff and the true organizer and inspirer of the Soviet people in the struggle against the interventionists. The Central Committee reviewed all major questions of the organization and strengthening of the Armed Forces, their strategic war plans, the establishment and distribution of reserves, the appointment of commanders, etc.

The historical approach to the analysis of strategic questions undoubtedly facilitates the understanding of the present state of the theory of Soviet military strategy. At the same time one would like to point out that, in our opinion, the authors should have dealt more extensively with [the views of those] people who took a direct part in the working out of strategic theory, strategic planning and leadership, and that the authors should have given more emphasis to the continuity of the best traditions of the Russian National Military School.

The foundation of Soviet military theory and the inexhaustible source of its development is the enormous legacy of V. I. Lenin's works on strategic leadership in the Civil War and the foreign military intervention, and the wellspring of Lenin's military-theoretical views.

Prominent military functionaries of our party and state like M. V. Frunze, B. M. Shaposhnikov, and M. N. Tukhachevskii made a tremendous contribution to the theory of strategy. The well-known military theoreticians A. A. Svechin, A. A. Neznamov, V. K. Triandafillov, and E. A. Shilovskii also exerted a definite influence on the development of military and strategic thought in the Soviet Army. S. N. Krasil'nikov and others are doing important work on this problem.

In developing the questions of Soviet military strategy, the authors of the book should, without fail, have approached these people. The work would have been richer and it would have promoted the correction of the conditions existing in the period of the cult of personality when all that was new and advanced in military theory was ascribed to Stalin alone.

The book devoted considerable space to a Marxist-Leninist analysis of the nature of modern war and to the influence of modern weapons on war.

"One of the important tenets of Soviet military doctrine," stress the authors, "is that a world war, if the imperialists initiate it, will inevitably assume the character of a nuclear war with missiles, i.e., a war in which the nuclear weapon will be the chief instrument of destruction and missiles the basic vehicle for their delivery to target."

As is known, the character of the armed struggle is influenced not only by the means with which it is waged, but also the social nature of the war. The new world war, if the imperialists initiate it, will be characterized by the participation of two opposing worldwide social systems—the capitalist and the socialist systems. This very fact will determine the resolve and ferocity with which the war is fought.

The problem of the duration of a future war is of great importance for understanding its character. On the basis of their investigation, the authors conclude that in a future war, one must make plans for victory over the aggressor in the shortest possible time. In this connection, as the USSR Minister of Defense Marshal of the Soviet Union R. Ia. Malinovskii pointed out, the initial period of the war will be of decisive importance for the outcome of the whole.

The recommendations of the authors for the organization of the armed forces are undoubtedly of scientific interest. They stress that the basic means for speedily defeating whole countries and putting them out of the war are missiles and nuclear weapons. It is these weapons that determine, at present, the main tendencies in the organization of the armed forces and the means by which a future war will be waged. "The firepower," says the book, "of all branches of armed forces is now based on nuclear weapons." The main task, now, in organizing and developing forces, both in peace and war, is to be superior to the enemy in nuclear weapons and the techniques of their employment."

These conclusions correctly reflect the basic tendencies in the organization of armed forces in modern conditions. We think only that in this chapter the authors should have more fully developed the relationship between different forces and services as well as the basic principles of their organizational structure and buildup.

One cannot agree fully with the authors' judgments on strategic maneuver. The book points out that "strategic maneuver in missile and nuclear warfare can be described as the shifting of the [main] effort from one strategic direction or target to another, mainly by the fire-maneuver of nuclear weapons." The authors recognize maneuver of forces and materiel only within the theater of battle and mainly on the operational scale. In addition they omit the obvious truth that not a single grouping of troops can be formed according to the war plan either before the war begins or in its course without the maneuver of forces and materiel. Strategic transfer of forces and materiel to theaters of operations to replenish or replace particular groupings also cannot be excluded. Naturally the country preparing for war will deploy its forces and materiel so as to initiate operations with the groupings in-being. But even these groupings cannot be formed without preliminary maneuver on a strategic and operational scale. And if we take into account that as a result of the first nuclear blows groupings of forces may be considerably weakened, or that the first strategic echelon in the theaters of military operations may suffer heavy losses, then the necessity for strategic maneuver of forces and materiel will become obvious— a point that the authors of this work do not mention for some reason.

Importance is given in the book to examining how war on a strategic scale is conducted. A new classification of types of strategic operations is given. The authors believe that all strategic operations by the armed forces in a future war will be reduced to the following: "Nuclear strikes by missiles to destroy the enemy's military and economic potential, system of governmental and military control, strategic nuclear weapons, and major troop formations; military operations in ground theaters to complete the defeat of enemy forces; protection of the socialist countries and troop formations from enemy nuclear strikes; and military operations in naval theaters to destroy enemy naval forces."

The concrete recommendations by the authors on how a missile and nuclear war is to be conducted are of great scientific interest and deserve diligent attention. It must be noted, however, that the authors, having justifiably concentrated their main attention on the strategic missile forces, have neither assigned sufficient weight to, nor analyzed deeply enough, the role and methods of operations of other types of armed forces, particularly of the ground forces.

In the chapter dealing with opinions on the methods of warfare, the authors also examine such important questions as the use of space for military purposes. They adduce a number of facts showing that American imperialists have embarked on the path of using space directly to execute their aggressive plans directed against the socialist countries. The American press openly says that "outer space is the strategic theater of tomorrow."

The Soviet people are occupied in the peaceful conquest of space. As is known, the flights of our cosmonauts Iu. Gagarin, G. Titov, A. Nikolaev, and P. Popovich, which have amazed the whole world, did not pursue any military aims. But it is quite obvious that if the imperialists continue to search for ways of using outer space for military purposes, then the interests of ensuring the security of the Soviet state will require definite measures by our side as well. In this connection the authors draw attention to the fact that Soviet military strategic thought should consider the problem of using space for forestalling the aggressive aims of the imperialists.

The reader will find Chapter VII on "Preparation of a Country To Repel Aggression" an interesting one. This chapter considers the main problems in such preparation, giving a general picture of the character of the measures taken by our country for strengthening its defense capacity. The authors draw a number of important practical conclusions. They correctly observe in particular that "in contrast to the covering forces of previous wars, the combat-ready part of the ground forces must in modern conditions be numerically much stronger to be capable of executing its assignments." (Page 433.) In our opinion their recommendations are also important on simplifying mobilization, on utilizing motor transport and VTOL transport aviation for moving troops and materiel, on constructing industrial enterprises of military importance, on organizing civil defense, and on other things.

In the last chapter of the book the authors, using considerable historical material, show how the capitalist states framed and pursued their military strategy in World War II. They discussed the basis of present-day leadership of the armed forces, evaluating its good and bad aspects.

The structure and functions of the higher organs of leadership of the Soviet Armed Forces during the Civil War, in the period of peace, and during the Great Patriotic War are examined in detail. From this examination, the conclusion is drawn that "the principles of the unity of leadership of the conduct of the armed struggle in its political, economic and military aspects, and the centralization of the direction of the Armed Forces, [modified] by an intelligent combination of collegial and personal responsibility of [military] leaders, have been developed in our country and their validity confirmed in practice. These principles are obviously quite applicable in modern conditions." The book outlines in general the possible organs of leadership of the Armed Forces of the Soviet Union in conditions of a modern war.

In the concluding chapter, the authors examine briefly the questions of the leadership by the Communist Party of the Soviet Armed Forces and the principles of party-political work. Unfortunately, these important problems are examined very cursorily and superficially. Certain confused formulations are made which in fact distort the question of the role of the party organizations in the Soviet Army. It appears that the authors of this chapter have not thought enough about the tenet of the new statute of the CPSU which states that "the party organizations of the Soviet army assure the execution of the party policy in the armed forces. . . ." [Ellipsis in original.]

There is no possibility in the framework of a newspaper article to examine all the numerous, important questions raised in the book *Soviet Military Strategy*. As indicated above, we cannot share completely the authors' opinions on a number of these questions. These problems deserve a special discussion. But on the whole I would like to stress once again that a necessary and valuable military-technical work has been published, both in content and significance. The general Soviet reading public will undoubtedly find much in this book that is interesting and new. The work will undoubtedly be profitable to all generals and officers of the Soviet Army and will be an important handbook in their military-theoretical training.

# Appendix II

Western Military Works
Available in Russian Translation
in the Soviet Union

M ajor Western military works available to Soviet readers are
listed below.

Boucher, Jean N. L., *L'arme blindée dans la guerre,* Payot, 1953, 272 pp. (Soviet edition, 1956).

Bradley, Omar Nelson, *Soldier's Story,* Holt, New York, 1951, 618 pp. (Soviet edition, 1957).

Brodie, Bernard, *Strategy in the Missile Age,* Princeton University Press, Princeton, N. J., 1959, 423 pp. (Soviet edition, 1961, 10,000 copies).

Brophy, Arnold, *Air Force,* Gilbert Press, New York, 1956, 362 pp. (Soviet edition, 1957).

Butler, J. R. M., *Grand Strategy* (History of the Second World War), Vol. II, United Kingdom Military History Series, HMSO, London, 1957 (Soviet edition, abbreviated, 1959).

Copeland, Norman, *Psychology and the Soldier,* Military Service Publishing Co., Harrisburg, Pa., 1951 (Soviet edition, 1958).

Dixon, Cecil A., and Otto Heilbrunn, *Communist Guerrilla Warfare,* Praeger, New York, 1954, 229 pp. (Soviet edition, abbreviated, 1957).

Ehrman, J., *Grand Strategy* (History of the Second World War), Vols.

V and VI, United Kingdom Military History Series, HMSO, London, 1956, 1957 (Soviet edition, 1958).

Fane, Francis D., and Don Moore, *Naked Warriors,* Appleton-Century-Crofts, New York, 1956, 308 pp. (Soviet edition, abbreviated, 1958).

Fuller, John Fred. Ch., *Second World War, 1939–1945,* Duell, Sloan and Pearce, New York, 1949, 17–431 pp. (Soviet edition, 1956).

Gallois, Pierre, *Stratégie de l'âge nucléaire,* Calmann-Levy, 1960, 238 pp. (Soviet edition, abbreviated, 1962, 8,000 copies).

Gavin, James M., *Airborne Warfare,* Infantry Journal Press, 1947, 186 pp. (Soviet edition, 1957).

Gibrin, Charles, *Atomique secours,* Charles-Lavauzelle, 1953, 180 pp. (Soviet edition, 1957).

Hampe, Erich, *Im Spannungsfeld der Luftmächte,* Maximilian Verlag, Köln, 1956, 76 pp. (Soviet edition, 1958).

Jacquot, Pierre Elie, *La Stratégie périphérique devant la bombe atomique,* Gallimard, 1954, 230 pp. (Soviet edition, 1956).

————, *Essai de stratégie occidentale,* Gallimard, 1953, 202 pp. (Soviet edition, 1955).

Kingston-McCloughry, Edgar J., *Direction of War,* Praeger, New York, 1955, 261 pp. (Soviet edition, 1957).

————, *Global Strategy,* Praeger, New York, 1957, 270 pp. (Soviet edition, 1959).

Knorr, Klaus E., *War Potential of Nations,* Princeton University Press, Princeton, N. J., 1956, 310 pp. (Soviet edition, 1960).

Krueger, Walter, *From Down Under to Nippon,* Combat Forces Press, Washington, D. C., 1953, 393 pp. (Soviet edition, 1958).

Lee, Asher, *Air Power,* Duckworth, London, 1955, 200 pp. (Soviet edition, 1959).

Liddell-Hart, Basil H., *Strategy: The Indirect Approach,* Praeger, New York, 1954, 420 pp. (Soviet edition, 1957).

Linebarger, Paul M. A., *Psychological Warfare,* Combat Forces Press, Washington, D. C., 1955, 318 pp. (Soviet edition, 1962, 5,500 copies).

Lockwood, Charles A., and H. C. Adamson, *Hellcats of the Sea,* Greenberg, New York, 1955, 335 pp. (Soviet edition, 1958).

Matloff, Maurice, and E. M. Snell, *United States Army in World War II: The War Department: Strategic Planning in Coalition Warfare, 1941–1942,* Department of the Army, Washington, D. C., 1953, 454 pp. (Soviet edition, 1955).

Mellenthin, Friedrich W. von, *Panzer Battles, 1939–1945,* University of Oklahoma Press, Norman, Okla., 1956, 371 pp. (Soviet edition, abbreviated, 1957).

Middledorf, Eike, *Taktik im Russlandfeldzug,* Mittler und Sohn, Darmstadt, 1956, 239 pp. (Soviet edition, 1960).

Miksche, Ferdinand O., *Atomic Weapons and Armies,* Praeger, New York, 1955, 222 pp. (Soviet edition, abbreviated, 1956).

Montross, Lynn, *Cavalry of the Sky,* Harper, New York, 1954, 270 pp. (Soviet edition, 1956).

Morison, Samuel Eliot, *History of United States Naval Operations in World War II,* Vols. I–X, Little, Brown, Boston, Mass., 1947–1956 (Soviet edition, abbreviated, Vol. I, 1956, Vol. II, 1959).

Morse, Philip McCord, and G. E. Kimball, *Methods of Operations Research,* Massachusetts Institute of Technology, Cambridge, 1951, 158 pp. (Soviet edition, 1956).

Mueller-Hillebrand, Burkhart, *Das Heer 1933–1945,* Vols. I and II, Mittler und Sohn, Frankfurt-am-Main, 1954, 1956 (Soviet edition, Vol. I, 1956, Vol. II, 1958).

Multop, Charles, and W. G. Barrett, *Infantry Unit Leader's Guide,* Military Service Publishing Co., Harrisburg, Pa., 1954, 186 pp. (Soviet edition, 1956).

Osgood, Robert E., *Limited War,* University of Chicago Press, Chicago, Ill., 1957, 315 pp. (Soviet edition, 1960).

Pogue, Forrest C., *The Supreme Command,* Office of the Chief of Military History, Washington, D. C., 1954, 607 pp. (Soviet edition, abbreviated, 1959).

Rathbun, Frank F., *Rifle Squad and Platoon in Defense,* Military Service Publishing Co., Harrisburg, Pa., 1955, 104 pp. (Soviet edition, 1957).

Ridgeway, Matthew B., *Soldier Memoirs,* as told to Harold H. Martin, Harper, New York, 1956, 371 pp. (Soviet edition, 1958).

Rigg, Robert B., *Realistic Combat Training and How To Conduct It,* Military Service Publishing Co., Harrisburg, Pa., 1955, 239 pp. (Soviet edition, 1956).

Roscoe, Theodore, *United States Submarine Operations in World War II,* U. S. Naval Institute, Annapolis, Md., 1949, 577 pp. (Soviet edition, abbreviated, 1957).

Rosebury, Theodore, *Peace or Pestilence,* McGraw-Hill, New York, 1949, 218 pp. (Soviet edition, abbreviated, 1959).

Ruge, Friedrich, *Der Seekrieg 1939–1945,* K. F. Koehler, Stuttgart, 1954, 320 pp. (Soviet edition, 1957).

Sherman, Frederick C., *Combat Command,* Dutton, New York, 1950, 427 pp. (Soviet edition, abbreviated, 1956).

Smith, Dale, *U. S. Military Doctrine,* Duell, Sloan and Pearce, New York, 1955, 256 pp. (Soviet edition, 1956).

Taylor, Maxwell D., *The Uncertain Trumpet,* Harper, New York, 1959, 203 pp. (Soviet edition, 1961, 10,000 copies).

Townsend, Elias C., *Risks: The Key to Combat Intelligence,* Military Service Publishing Co., Harrisburg, Pa., 1955, 82 pp. (Soviet edition, 1957).

U. S. Strategic Bombing Survey, *The Campaigns of the Pacific War,* U. S. Government Printing Office, Washington, D. C., 1946, 395 pp. (Soviet edition, 1956).

Worley, Marvin L. J., *Digest of New Developments in Army Weapons, Tactics, Organization and Equipment,* Military Service Publishing Co., Harrisburg, Pa., 1958, 261 pp. (Soviet edition, 1959).

# Index

## A SELECTED LIST OF OTHER RAND BOOKS

Baum, Warren C. *The French Economy and the State*. Princeton, N.J.: Princeton University Press, 1958.

Bergson, Abram. *The Real National Income of Soviet Russia since 1928*. Cambridge, Mass.: Harvard University Press, 1961.

Brodie, Bernard. *Strategy in the Missile Age*. Princeton, N.J.: Princeton University Press, 1959.

Buchheim, Robert W., and the Staff of The RAND Corporation. *Space Handbook: Astronautics and Its Applications*. New York: Random House, Inc., 1959.

Davison, W. Phillips. *The Berlin Blockade: A Study in Cold War Politics*. Princeton, N.J.: Princeton University Press, 1958.

Dinerstein, H. S. *War and the Soviet Union: Nuclear Weapons and the Revolution in Soviet Military and Political Thinking*. New York: Frederick A. Praeger Inc., 1959.

Dinerstein, H. S. and Leon Gouré. *Two Studies in Soviet Controls: Communism and the Russian Peasant; Moscow in Crisis*. Glencoe, Ill.: The Free Press, 1955.

Fainsod, Merle. *Smolensk under Soviet Rule*. Cambridge, Mass.: Harvard University Press, 1958.

Garthoff, Raymond L. *Soviet Military Doctrine*. Glencoe, Ill.: The Free Press, 1953.

George, Alexander L. *Propaganda Analysis: A Study of Inferences Made from Nazi Propaganda in World War II*. Evanston, Ill.: Row, Peterson and Company, 1959.

Goldhamer, Herbert, and Andrew W. Marshall. *Psychosis and Civilization*. Glencoe, Ill.: The Free Press, 1953.

Gouré, Leon. *The Siege of Leningrad, 1941–1943*. Stanford, Calif.: Stanford University Press, 1962.

Hitch, Charles J., and Roland McKean. *The Economics of Defense in the Nuclear Age*. Cambridge, Mass.: Harvard University Press, 1960.

Hsieh, Alice L. *Communist China's Strategy in the Nuclear Era*. Englewood Cliffs, N.J.: Prentice-Hall, Inc., 1962.

Johnson, John J. (ed.). *The Role of the Military in Underdeveloped Countries*. Princeton, N.J.: Princeton University Press, 1962.

Johnstone, William C. *Burma's Foreign Policy: A Study in Neutralism*. Cambridge, Mass.: Harvard University Press, 1963.

Kecskemeti, Paul. *Strategic Surrender: The Politics of Victory and Defeat*. Stanford, Calif.: Stanford University Press, 1958.

Kecskemeti, Paul. *The Unexpected Revolution: Social Forces in the Hungarian Uprising*. Stanford, Calif.: Stanford University Press, 1961.

Leites, Nathan. *On the Game of Politics in France*. Stanford, Calif.: Stanford University Press, 1959.

Leites, Nathan. *The Operational Code of the Politburo*. New York: McGraw-Hill Book Company, Inc., 1951.

Leites, Nathan. *A Study of Bolshevism*. Glencoe, Ill.: The Free Press, 1953.

Leites, Nathan, and Elsa Bernaut. *Ritual of Liquidation: The Case of the Moscow Trials*. Glencoe, Ill.: The Free Press, 1954.

Mead, Margaret. *Soviet Attitudes toward Authority: An Interdisciplinary Approach to Problems of Soviet Character*. New York: McGraw-Hill Book Company, Inc., 1951.

Melnik, Constantin, and Nathan Leites. *The House without Windows: France Selects a President*. Evanston, Ill.: Row, Peterson and Company, 1958.

Moorsteen, Richard. *Prices and Production of Machinery in the Soviet Union, 1928–1958*. Cambridge, Mass.: Harvard University Press, 1962.

Rush, Myron. *The Rise of Khrushchev*. Washington, D.C.: Public Affairs Press, 1958.

Selznick, Philip. *The Organizational Weapon: A Study of Bolshevik Strategy and Tactics*. New York: McGraw-Hill Book Company, Inc., 1952.

Smith, Bruce Lannes, and Chitra M. Smith. *International Communication and Political Opinion: A Guide to the Literature*. Princeton, N.J.: Princeton University Press, 1956.

Speier, Hans. *Divided Berlin: The Anatomy of Soviet Political Blackmail*. New York: Frederick A. Praeger Inc., 1961.

Speier, Hans. *German Rearmament and Atomic War: The Views of German Military and Political Leaders*. Evanston, Ill.: Row, Peterson and Company, 1957.

Speier, Hans, and W. Phillips Davison (eds.). *West German Leadership and Foreign Policy*. Evanston, Ill.: Row, Peterson and Company, 1957.

Tanham, G. K. *Communist Revolutionary Warfare: The Viet Minh in Indochina*. New York: Frederick A. Praeger Inc., 1961.

Trager, Frank N. (ed.). *Marxism in Southeast Asia: A Study of Four Countries*. Stanford, Calif.: Stanford University Press, 1959.

Whiting, Allen S. *China Crosses the Yalu: The Decision To Enter the Korean War*. New York: The Macmillan Company, 1960.

Wolf, Charles, Jr. *Foreign Aid: Theory and Practice in Southern Asia*. Princeton, N.J.: Princeton University Press, 1960.